Budget Support as More Effective Aid?

Budget Support as More Effective Aid?

Recent Experiences and Emerging Lessons

Edited by
Stefan Koeberle
Zoran Stavreski
Jan Walliser

THE WORLD BANK
Washington, D.C.

1818 H Street NW
Washington DC 20433
Telephone: 202-473-1000
Internet: www.worldbank.org
E-mail: feedback@worldbank.org

1 2 3 4 5 10 09 08 07 06

Rights and Permissions

ISBN-10: 0-8213-6463-4
ISBN-13: 978-0-8213-6463-5
eISBN-10: 0-8213-6464-2
eISBN-13: 978-0-8213-6464-2
DOI: 10.1596/978-0-8213-6463-5

Cover photos (from top right): © World Bank/Curt Carnemark, World Bank/Eric Miller, World Bank/Curt Carnemark, © iStockphoto.com/Wang Sanjun

Library of Congress Cataloging-in-Publication data has been applied for.

Contents

BOXES

FIGURES

TABLES

Foreword

Since the Monterrey Consensus of 2002 highlighted the mutual accountability of all development partners, more effective partnerships have emerged, along with broader agreement on the agenda on what needs to be done to make development more effective. Better policies and institutional frameworks in developing countries, notable advances in the leadership exercised by aid-partner countries, stronger performance-based allocation mechanisms for aid, a more purposive focus on results, and increased harmonization and alignment have all helped to strengthen donors' commitment to raise the level of development aid.

Against this backdrop, attention has increasingly focused on the question of resource mobilization to achieve the Millennium Development Goals (MDGs). To make aid more effective in reaching these global goals, recipient countries will need to implement sound social and economic policies, articulate clear development frameworks and goals, and bolster their governance and institutional capacities. The international community and multilateral agencies are being asked to scale up their aid, commensurate with countries' socioeconomic goals and constraints. This calls not only for substantially larger resource flows but also for more effective aid modalities.

Mechanisms for providing aid should allow larger resource flows and a greater performance orientation to be phased in as country policies and capacities improve. Among other things, donors need to find ways to support public expenditures in countries whose progress toward the MDGs is held back by difficulties in meeting recurrent costs, such as the salaries of teachers and health workers, and operating and maintenance expenditures, such as for water schemes. Such expenditures typically form the bulk of a country's financing requirements and are essential for delivering critical services.

As countries improve their public expenditure management and fiduciary arrangements, the provision of recurrent financing through budget support for government policy and expenditure programs has emerged as an important aid instrument. Compared to traditional modes of aid delivery, budget support underlines greater country ownership, higher spending on services that countries prioritize in their own budgets, more predictable support for sustained policy and institutional reforms, and scaled-up efforts to reduce poverty. To the extent that it reduces the typical transaction costs of project fragmentation, encourages donor harmonization, and strengthens a sensible prioritization of public spending, budget support can enhance the development impact of aid as well as enhance accountability for delivering better services to poor people. In countries with strong ownership and a good track record, this aid modality can provide flexible and sustained medium-term support for complex institutional and policy reforms, improve the predictability of aid flows, and increase the results focus of government activities.

While the development community has broadly embraced budget support as a promising vehicle for delivering effective aid, this form of aid poses many challenges: the perceived fiduciary risk, tensions between predictability and uneven country performance, the practical intricacies of effective donor coordination, and the need for close alignment with country programs.

This volume brings together some initial practical lessons of the experience with budget support, drawing on the contributions of practitioners, academics, and government officials from around the world. Its aim is less to provide definite answers than to contribute to the understanding of a promising aid modality. Clearly, this is the beginning of the debate, and we are all looking forward to learning more over the coming years.

James Adams
Vice President and Head of Network
Operations Policy and Country Services
World Bank

Editors' Preface

Is development aid more effective if it is provided directly to a recipient country's budget? What exactly is budget support, and why has it emerged as a promising financing modality? Can it deliver on its potential for reducing transaction costs, ensuring predictable financing, increasing country ownership, and strengthening domestic accountability?

While it may be too early for definite answers to some of these questions, this volume aims to provide a first comprehensive overview of the emerging experience with budget support. It presents a variety of views and approaches by a broad range of development practitioners from recipient country governments, international financial institutions, academia, and donor agencies. Most of the contributions to the volume were discussed at a Practitioners' Forum on budget support that took place in May 2005 in Cape Town, South Africa. Other valuable inputs for the volume were the conclusions from a May 2005 workshop conducted by the Budget Support Working Group of the Strategic Partnership with Africa (SPA). Although there are many areas of emerging consensus among the authors, we do not try to reconcile the different perspectives or advocate a particular point of view. The aim is rather to contribute to the ongoing debate on the effectiveness of development aid by clarifying key concepts, identifying implementation issues, and highlighting specific country experiences with budget support as an aid modality.

The volume is structured as follows:

- Part I provides an introductory overview of the concept of budget support and key issues, including fiduciary aspects.
- Part II summarizes recent evaluations of budget support by the World Bank, the European Commission, OECD-DAC, USAID, and the Overseas Development Institute.
- Part III discusses how budget support can be aligned with country programs, including by reconciling the provision of performance-oriented financial support with a country's poverty reduction strategies and budget management.
- Part IV focuses on the predictability of budget support, reviewing experience to date and the possibility for improvement.
- Part V takes up the issue of donor coordination and conditionality in the use of budget support, including conceptual problems and emerging lessons on good practice.

- Part VI presents country experiences with budget support in Uganda, Mozambique, Afghanistan, and South Asia.
- Part VII brings together a range of perspectives on budget support by different international financial institutions, development agencies, and bilateral donors, including the IMF, the United Kingdom, Germany, Norway, Japan, and the Netherlands.
- Part VIII conveys the main messages from the Practitioners' Forum on Budget Support, summarizing the general discussion and participants' concluding remarks.

The editors wish to thank the participants at the Practitioners' Forum on Budget Support, the South African government for hosting the forum, and Minister Lynn Brown of Western Cape province for providing a warm welcome to participants on behalf of the government. The contributors to this volume deserve a particular note of thanks for their discipline in meeting deadlines and patience in redrafting.

Rachel Weaving provided valuable editorial support. Book design, editing, production, and printing were coordinated by Stephen McGroarty, Rick Ludwick, and Nora Ridolfi of the World Bank's Office of the Publisher. A valuable contribution was also made by Gero Verheyen during the Practitioners' Forum and the technical preparation of the manuscript. The editorial team was assisted by Pansy Chintha and Philomene Koya.

The contributions to this volume reflect the views of the authors and do not necessarily represent the views of their institutions with which they are affiliated.

Stefan Koeberle
Zoran Stavreski
Jan Walliser
World Bank, March 2006

List of Contributors and Discussants

Abrar, Suleiman	Lecturer Department of Economics University of Sheffield
Adams, James	Vice President and Head of Network Operations Policy and Country Services World Bank
Alonso, Rosa	Senior Public Sector Specialist East Asia Region World Bank
Amin, Nick	Head of Profession for Economics Department for International Development United Kingdom
Arakawa, Hiroto	Director General Development Assistance Department Japan Bank for International Cooperation
Atingi-Ego, Michael	Executive Director Research Bank of Uganda
Basu, Anupam	Deputy Director African Department International Monetary Fund
Binkert, Gregor	Lead Specialist Africa Region Front Office World Bank
Booth, David	Research Fellow/Group Coordinator Overseas Development Institute London

Brouwer, Maarten	Director Quality and Effectiveness Department Netherlands Ministry of Foreign Affairs
Celasun, Oya	Economist Research Department International Monetary Fund
Christiansen, Karin	Research Fellow Overseas Development Institute London
Devarajan, Shantayanan	Chief Economist South Asia Region World Bank
	Development Information Services
Eifert, Benn	Junior Professional Associate Development Economics Vice Presidency World Bank
European Commission	Directorate General for Development
Factora, John M.	Operations Officer Operations Policy and Country Services World Bank
Gelb, Alan	Director Development Economics Vice President World Bank
Ghosh, Atish	Division Chief Policy Development and Review Department International Monetary Fund
Gunning, Jan Willem	Professor Free University Amsterdam and Tinbergen Institute
Hammond, Mike A.	Head of Evaluation Department UK Department for International Development and Chair of the Steering Group for Joint Evaluation of General Budget Support, OECD-DAC
Hervio, Gilles	Unit Head Directorate General for Development European Commission

Hoven, Ingrid-Gabriela	Deputy Director General Ministry for Economic Cooperation and Development Germany
Judge, Lindsay	Consultant Poverty Reduction and Economic Management World Bank
Kasekende, Louis	Deputy Governor Bank of Uganda Uganda
Klugman, Jeni	Lead Economist Africa Region World Bank
Koeberle, Stefan	Director Latin America and the Caribbean Region World Bank
Lawson, Andrew	Research Fellow Overseas Development Institute London
Manning, Richard	Chairman Development Assistance Committee Organisation for Economic Co-operation and Development
Morrissey, Oliver	Professor School of Economics, University of Nottingham, and Director, Centre for Research on Economic Development and International Trade
Mosley, Paul	Professor Department of Economics University of Sheffield
Msuya, Meleki	Daima Associates Dar es Salaam
NORAD	Norwegian Agency for Development Cooperation
Osei, Akoto	Deputy Minister Ministry of Finance and Economic Planning Ghana

Plant, Mark	Senior Adviser Policy Development and Review Department International Monetary Fund
de Renzio, Paolo	Research Fellow Overseas Development Institute London
Shah, Shekhar	Economic Adviser South Asia Region World Bank
Shahrani, Wahidullah	Deputy Minister Ministry of Finance Afghanistan
Shand, David	Consultant Operations Policy and Country Services World Bank
Stavreski, Zoran	Senior Economist Operations Policy and Country Services World Bank
Sulemane, Jose	National Director for Research and Policy Analysis Ministry of Planning and Development Mozambique
Walliser, Jan	Senior Economist Operations Policy and Country Services World Bank
Wangwe, Samuel	Daima Associates Dar es Salaam
Williamson, Tim	Research Associate Overseas Development Institute London
Wolgin, Jerome Morris	Secretariat of the Strategic Partnership with Africa World Bank
Zongo, Tertius	Ambassador of Burkina Faso to the United States

List of Abbreviations and Acronyms

ACP	Africa, Caribbean, and Pacific
ADB	Asian Development Bank
AFD	Agence Française de Développement
AFR	Africa
ALCID	World Bank Adjustment Lending Conditionality Implementation Database
APERL	Andhra Pradesh Economic Reform Loans
APR	Annual Progress Report
BOU	Bank of Uganda
BSWG	Budget Support Working Group
CABS	Common Approach to Budget Support
CAS	Country Assistance Strategy
CDF	Comprehensive Development Framework
CFAA	Country Financial Accountability Assessment
CFF	Compensatory Financing Facility
CIDA	Canadian International Development Agency
CPAR	Country Procurement Assessment Report
CPIA	Country Policy and Institutional Assessment
CPRGS	Comprehensive Poverty Reduction and Growth Strategy
CSO	Civil Society Organization
CY	Calendar Year
DANIDA	Danish International Development Agency
DAC	Development Assistance Committee
DfID	Department for International Development
DPL	Development Policy Lending/Loan
DRC	Democratic Republic of Congo
DSC	Development Support Credit
EAP	East Asia and Pacific
EC	European Commission
ECA	Europe and Central Asia
ESAF	Enhanced Structural Adjustment Facility

EU	European Union
FMIS	Financial Management Information System
FY	Fiscal Year
GAE	Group on Aid Effectiveness
GBS	General Budget Support
GDP	Gross Domestic Product
GoJ	Government of Japan
GOU	Government of Uganda
HIPC	Heavily Indebted Poor Countries
IBRD	International Bank for Reconstruction and Development
IDA	International Development Association
IFEM	Inter-bank Foreign Exchange Market
IFF	International Financing Facility
IMF	International Monetary Fund
IPSAS	International Public Sector Accounting Standards
JBIC	Japan Bank for International Cooperation
JICA	Japan International Cooperation Agency
JPPR	Joint Portfolio Performance Review
JSA	Joint Staff Assessment
JSAN	Joint Staff Advisory Note
KERL	Karnataka Economic Reform Loans
KfW	Kreditanstalt für Wiederaufbau
LCB	Local Competitive Bidding
LCR	Latin America and Caribbean
LDP	Letter of Development Policy
LIC	Low-income Country
MCA	Millennium Challenge Account
MDGs	Millennium Development Goals
M&E	Monitoring and Evaluation
MFP	Ministry of Finance and Planning
MOU	Memorandum of Understanding
MTEF	Medium-term Expenditure Framework
NAO	National Audit Office
NGO	Nongovernmental Organization
NEER	Nominal Effective Exchange Rate
NEPAD	New Partnership for Africa's Development
NORAD	Norwegian Agency for Development Cooperation
OD	Operational Directive
ODA	Official Development Assistance
ODI	Overseas Development Institute
OECD	Organization for Economic Co-operation and Development
OED	Operations Evaluation Department
OP	Operational Policy
PAF	Performance Assessment Framework
PBA	Program-based Approach

PEAP	Poverty Eradication Action Plan
PEFA	Public Expenditure and Financial Accountability
PER	Public Expenditure Review
PETS	Public Expenditure Tracking Survey
PFC	Provincial Finance Commission
PFM	Public Financial Management
PFMRP	Public Financial Management Reform Program
PPER	Participatory Public Expenditure Review
PRBS	Poverty Reduction Budget Support
PRGF	Poverty Reduction and Growth Facility
PRS	Poverty Reduction Strategy
PRSC	Poverty Reduction Support Credit
PRSP	Poverty Reduction Strategy Paper
PSC	Private Sector Credit
REER	Real Effective Exchange Rate
RER	Real Exchange Rate
ROSC	Review of Standards and Codes
SAR	South Asia Region
SPA	Strategic Partnership with Africa
SWAp	Sector-wide Approach
SIDA	Swedish International Development Cooperation Agency
TA	Technical Assistance
TB	Treasury Bills
TSP	Transition Support Program
UK	United Kingdom
UNDP	United Nations Development Program
USAID	United States Agency for International Development
WAEMU	West African Monetary and Economic Union

PART I
Introduction

1

Budget Support: Concept and Issues

STEFAN KOEBERLE AND ZORAN STAVRESKI
World Bank

Budget support has become an increasingly important mode of development assistance, receiving growing attention from bilateral donors and international financial institutions in the context of a partnership-based approach to aid. This form of aid promises benefits for both donors and recipient countries: increased scope for scaling up development assistance, reducing transaction costs, strengthening country ownership, and achieving greater development effectiveness than traditional modes of aid delivery. Yet the concept of budget support itself is still emerging and subject to different interpretations, and skeptical observers question its impact and fiduciary soundness and the incentives it provides.

This chapter reviews the objectives and potential advantages and risks of budget support and outlines some key issues in its design and implementation. Section A provides a brief perspective on the context and trends that have led to the emergence of this form of aid. Section B gives an overview of definitions and key characteristics and explores the rationale for budget support. Section C outlines key factors to consider when assessing whether or not to provide budget support. Section D highlights issues in design and implementation, and Section E concludes and summarizes.

A. Context for the Emergence of Budget Support

The preferred choice of aid modalities and the appropriate mix of approaches have evolved over time, and typically depend on the partner country's needs and priorities, the consensus on policies and capacity for implementation, and specific donor objectives and constraints. Several recent trends in the international aid architecture have increased the emphasis on budget support:

- *Shift away from traditional project support.* The effectiveness of traditional project financing in many countries has been questioned by donors that were concerned with parallel systems outside the government's budget framework, low disbursement rates, and limited impact. Increasingly, donors are moving away from supporting specific projects toward more strategic medium-term assistance and exploring budget support as a mode of aid delivery.

- *Shift from traditional ex ante conditionality to a partnership-based approach.* Disillusion with traditional conditionality has given way to an emphasis on the need to strengthen the mutual accountability between donors, and recipients achieve greater predictability of funding, harmonize donor support, and reduce transaction costs for recipient countries. International financial institutions and multilateral donors, in particular, are embracing innovations such as programmatic lending and variable tranching.[1]
- *Greater emphasis on country ownership, systems, and capacity.* The 1990s brought a realization that local ownership and partnership around country-owned development programs are prerequisites for achieving sustainable results.[2] By departing from a narrow project intervention that is often based on physical impacts in a geographically confined area, the budget support approach recognizes the critical importance and benefits of countrywide and sectorwide development perspectives that are based on country-specific policy programs and institutions. In particular, the country's own budget process has been increasingly emphasized as the central institutional framework for exercising choices on where resources should be channeled and for holding governments accountable (see, for instance, World Bank 2001b).
- *Shift from short-term to medium-term reforms.* Reflecting the experience and changing needs of recipient countries, development assistance in the 1990s began giving more attention to sustained structural and social policy programs, as well as capacity building and institutional reforms. Although supporting short-term policy measures remains appropriate in some cases, most developing countries have moved beyond first-generation reforms, and there are now far fewer economies with economic distortions than in the early 1980s. Most policy-based aid programs now take a medium-term perspective, supporting complex policy and institutional reforms that are critical to sustainable development.[3]
- *Recognition of the disruptive role of volatile and unpredictable aid.* Poorly delivered and unpredictable aid can disrupt program implementation and development spending in aid-dependent countries. Past aid flows tended to be particularly prone to sudden surges and withdrawals of funds—in response to perceived progress or backsliding in reform efforts—and in turn the fluctuations in funding tended to exacerbate weaknesses in macroeconomic management. A study by OECD-DAC (2005a) identified "uncoordinated donor practices" and "delays in disbursements" as two of the five most burdensome donor practices. Recognizing this problem, donors called for the creation of new aid mechanisms aimed at reducing aid volatility. The United Kingdom proposed the International Financing Facility (IFF), a plan to increase aid flows to help achieve the Millennium Development Goals, stating that the IFF would provide, "for the first time, a predictable and stable flow of a critical mass of aid" (DFID and HM Treasury 2003). The Development Committee of the World Bank and IMF called in 2004 for the provision of "predictable and timely financial assistance to countries committed to sound policies."
- *Greater selectivity in favor of good performers.* The research on aid effectiveness suggests that aid can achieve results in good policy environments, but that aid does

not work in countries that are pursuing inappropriate policies or are not committed to development (World Bank 1998). In response, donors now typically allocate more aid to countries with stronger performance (see, for instance, World Bank 2003b). Budget support in particular is seen as a financing instrument suitable for countries with strong ownership, commitment, and sufficient capacity to allocate resources effectively and in accordance with their development priorities.

- *Enhanced focus on results.* In the past, policy-based lending and other forms of development assistance focused on policy *actions* and did not always pay enough attention to intended *outcomes* (see, for instance, World Bank 2001a and OED 2003). Today, a sharper focus on achieving and measuring development results has promoted better monitoring and evaluation of development programs. In particular, the Millennium Development Goals have provided an impetus for greater aid effectiveness with a strengthened focus on measuring and delivering results.
- *Scaling up.* Recent years have seen growing recognition that the Millennium Development Goals can only be reached if donor countries provide more adequate and predictable resource flows, and if recipient countries demonstrate an effective use of available resources through measurable progress (World Bank 2005u, World Bank and IMF 2005). There is now a prospect of a very substantial increase in official development assistance over the coming five years. A range of commitments have been made for additional financing, including at the G8 Gleneagles summit in 2005, which called for a doubling of aid to Africa. Budget support for countries that perform well may offer one of the more promising ways to help ensure effective use of the promised additions to aid.

B. Definitions, Key Characteristics, and Rationale for Budget Support

Donor organizations use a range of definitions for budget support. In current usage, budget support typically refers to predictable, usually annual, aid flows that are disbursed in response to a low-income country's progress in implementing a national poverty reduction strategy (PRS).

For the purpose of this paper, we define budget support as financial assistance that supports a medium-term program and is provided directly to a recipient country's budget on a regular basis, using the country's own financial management systems and budget procedures. The qualitative monitoring of this financing process and its outcomes is a fundamental aspect of this approach (Box 1.1).

Aid provided as budget support is linked to sector or national policies rather than to specific project activities or budget line items. This reflects the potential of budget support to address key cross-cutting issues such as public sector reform, public financial management, or improvements in governance. Budget support typically aims to promote pro-poor growth through encouraging fiscal and macroeconomic stability and more efficient allocation of public funds.

While multilateral donors have long provided balance-of-payments support in the form of policy-based lending, budget support is a relatively recent introduction. Most

BOX 1.1 Definitions

Policy-based lending: Provision of untied donor resources directly through the government's budget, using the government's own financial management, procurement, auditing, and implementation processes and systems, and based on a set of policy or institutional reforms fulfilled either ex ante (conditionality), if designed as a multitranche operation, or ex post (prior actions), if designed as a single-tranche operation.

Development policy lending (DPL): The World Bank's term for policy-based lending, DPL replaced *adjustment lending* as the Bank's financing instrument to provide quick-disbursing resources to client governments.

Poverty reduction support credit (PRSC): A programmatic approach to DPL in low-income countries that is tied to the country's medium-term PRS and typically consists of a series of three or four single-tranche operations (see, for instance, World Bank 2005e and Chapter 3).

Program-based approaches (PBAs): A general term that refers to coordinated donor support for a comprehensive program or a specific sector/thematic strategy (for example, in education or environment) that is country-derived and relies on a single budget framework and domestic processes. PBAs include budget support and SWAps.

Budget support: Donor instruments (including the PRSC) that support the implementation of a country's medium-term poverty reduction strategy and consist of regular (annual) disbursements of untied resources to the budget. Budget support is typically based on an agreed set of performance indicators in the form of institutional or policy reform measures or outcome indicators.

Sectorwide approach (SWAp): An approach that involves financing of a specific sector through various financing modalities, including budget support and investment financing.

often, it supports country poverty reduction strategies that span multiple sectors. Particularly in the context of aid-dependent African countries, budget support is aligned with the PRS's annual cycle of performance review and with domestic planning and budget processes.

The World Bank formally recognized the notion of budget support only recently, with its introduction of development policy lending, although it had used this approach informally for a number of years (World Bank 2004e). The Bank's budget support is best typified by the poverty reduction support credits (PRSCs) that it provides to well-performing low-income countries with credible poverty reduction strategies (World Bank 2005e; also see Chapter 3 of this volume).[4]

Donor Definitions

Bilateral donors use their own array of definitions, aligned around the premise that budget support is a subset of program aid (program-based approaches):

- The OECD definition outlined in recent DAC guidelines defines budget support "as a method of financing a partner country's budget through a transfer of resources from an external financing agency to the partner government's national treasury. The funds thus transferred are managed in accordance with the recipient's budgetary procedures" (OECD-DAC 2005a).

- CIDA (2004) defines budget support as "program support that is provided directly to host-country institutions to be spent as part of their budgets using their own financial management systems."
- A policy paper by the UK Department for International Development (DFID 2004d) refers to poverty reduction budget support (PRBS) as a form of financial aid provided (1) in support of a government program typically focusing on growth, poverty reduction, fiscal adjustment, and strengthening institutions, especially budgetary processes; and (2) directly to a partner government's central exchequer, to spend using its own financial management, procurement, and accountability systems.

Common to all these definitions is the notion of direct financial support to a country's budget, which provides flexible funding for country-led poverty reduction efforts. Typically, this involves augmenting the share of freely available resources without earmarking. A more restrictive form of financing is the sector budget support provided by some donor agencies that want to earmark funding to specific types of expenditures (Box 1.2).

Characteristics

Key characteristics of budget support include the following:

- channeling of donor funds to a partner country using its own allocation, procurement, and accounting systems;
- support for a recipient country's own development programs, typically focusing on growth, poverty reduction, fiscal adjustment, and the strengthening of institutions, particularly the budgetary processes;
- policy content, performance assessment, and an accountability framework that focus on policy measures and benchmarks related to overall budget and policy priorities, as set out in the country's own poverty reduction strategy and medium-term expenditure framework;
- provision at regular intervals, ideally in alignment with the country's annual budget cycle; and
- agreement on general budget priorities and expenditures, so that in principle there is no need to earmark funds for specific items.

Budget support is provided in foreign exchange, which is placed with the central bank to be converted into local currency and credited to the central government account at the central bank. A government can use these funds to reduce or repay debts, as well as to augment budget spending. Its choices will depend on the overall macroeconomic and fiscal situation and the agreement on development priorities between the partner country and the donor.

Accountability for the use of budget support is generally based on audited accounts of budget revenues and expenditures, although some donors may ask for accounting

BOX 1.2 Sector Budget Support

Several bilateral donors distinguish between two types of nonproject aid that they refer to as *direct budget support*:

- *General budget support*—defined as a general contribution to the overall budget (sometimes referred to as *macro support)*,
- *Sector budget support*—defined as financial aid earmarked to a discrete sector (with any conditionality relating to these sectors).

Sector budget support, thus defined, is usually related to a broad area, such as education and health, or a subsector, such as primary health care financing. The dialogue focuses on sector-specific concerns rather than on overall budget priorities. Sector program assistance supports the implementation of reforms and other actions needed to overcome sector-based development constraints. Additional sector reporting may supplement standard government accounting, although the disbursement is usually based upon government procedures.

To some extent, sector budget support could be considered as an intermediate category between budget support and SWAps, as it combines use of government systems with "real" earmarking of funds to specific sector(s). (However, sector budget support can involve the pooling of funds through a SWAp to finance state expenditures in priority development sectors.) The use of "real" earmarking is one of the features distinguishing sector budget support from general budget support.

- *Real* earmarking relates to situations where spending on agreed budget lines needs to precede the release of tranches.
- *Virtual* earmarking is used where the control over the use of provided funds is exercised ex post. Funds are provided to the budget, and the use of resources is then justified against agreed budget lines.

Most of the expectations associated with budget support relate to general budget support that is not earmarked and made freely available to recipient countries. By contrast, financial aid that is earmarked to a specific sector can be an effective tool to reflect donor preferences, but may not necessarily capture the essential features and promises of a general direct contribution to the budget. It is this broader definition of budget support without earmarking that is referred to in this paper.

against specific budget expenditures. If there are weaknesses in public financial management, additional fiduciary arrangements and accountability mechanisms may be warranted in order to address these issues. There may be an understanding between donors and the government that funds may be directed to certain sectors, but there is typically no formal limitation on where they may actually be spent. A transparent budget can help provide assurances that adequate funds will be allocated to expenditures associated with poverty reduction, and thus limit the calls for earmarking often voiced by donors that are concerned over misappropriation of funds or excessive public spending in areas not related to development.

Expectations

Underlying the shift to increased budget support is the hope that this mode of financing will make aid more effective by:

- strengthening country ownership and ensuring the sustainability of reforms;
- reducing transaction costs for the government by avoiding parallel project and reporting arrangements;
- increasing the predictability of funding;
- addressing cross-cutting government-wide policy, expenditure, and institutional priorities that cannot be tackled with stand-alone and sector projects;
- promoting government accountability, both internal (to parliament and taxpayers) and external (to donors);
- improving the efficiency and transparency of budget spending, reducing the fragmentation of public expenditure management, and integrating recurrent and capital expenditures;
- buttressing the recipient country's own budget process and public financial management; and
- encouraging a greater orientation to medium-term results by focusing on national development objectives rather than on donor-driven priorities, operational issues, or activities with limited scope and effect.

Concerns

At the same time, in the public debate on this aid modality, concerns are frequently raised that budget support may:

- raise fiduciary risk in countries with weak financial management systems;
- increase the volatility of aid flows in cases where country performance is poor;
- increase transaction costs in the short term, particularly for donors;
- provide limited scope for hands-on sector dialogue and capacity building in sectoral agencies;
- reduce the incentives for line ministries to make progress in their respective areas to meet specific conditions for the release of donor funds that will augment the general budget but will not necessarily provide additional funding for their sector; and
- strain the capacity of the ministry of finance as the main interlocutor and coordinator of cross-cutting development priorities.

Specific country experiences over the coming years will provide more evidence for assessing the benefits and risks of budget support. Already, though, several evaluations have been done and several are in progress (Box 1.3). While it may be too early to draw definite conclusions, the following sections draw on current knowledge to present a number of key issues and emerging lessons.

C. When Is Budget Support Appropriate?

Budget support is not the right approach for all countries at all times; each case requires a specific judgment on the appropriate choice of instruments by donors and partner countries.

BOX 1.3 Recent and Ongoing Evaluations of Budget Support

- *Harmonizing Donor Practices for Effective Aid Delivery, Volume 2: Budget Support, Sector-wide Approaches, and Capacity Development in Public Financial Management* focuses on good practices in providing budget support and support to SWAps. It particularly acknowledges the special relevance of public financial management issues for both aid modalities (OECD-DAC 2005a).
- *A Stocktaking of Poverty Reduction Support Credits* takes stock of the World Bank's experience with PRSCs and highlights lessons learned, key issues, emerging practices, and recommendations. With very few countries having completed their first series of PRSC operations, the general thrust of the paper is on design and implementation issues. The paper does not attempt to assess development impact, although it highlights preliminary medium-term outcomes from the more mature PRSC programs (World Bank 2005e; see also Chapter 3 of this volume).
- *European Commission Budget Support: An Innovative Approach to Conditionality* deals essentially with general budget support in Africa, Caribbean, and Pacific countries. It describes the rationale and mechanism for the EC approach to budget support based on annual fixed and variable tranches. It also analyzes the experience to date, including issues of scope, program design, and implementation (EC 2005; see also Chapter 4 of this volume).
- *Evaluation Framework for General Budget Support,* commissioned on behalf of the OECD-DAC Evaluation Network, presents an evaluation framework intended to guide the conduct of joint evaluation work on general budget support (GBS) at the country level. It is intended as a practical tool that can be used to assess whether GBS is a relevant, efficient, effective, and sustainable mechanism for poverty reduction (Lawson and Booth 2004; see also Chapter 5 of this volume).
- *Survey of the Alignment of Budget Support and Balance of Payments Support with National PRS Processes* describes the current status of efforts to align the delivery of budget support and balance of payments support with national policymaking processes, budget cycles, and systems for reviewing progress. Secondary objectives are to promote policy dialogue on this subject, disseminate good practices, and identify countries where follow-up activities by the SPA might yield benefits (SPA 2005).
- *General Budget Support: Key Findings of Five USAID Studies* briefly describes program assistance, including GBS, in Mozambique, Malawi, Nicaragua, Tanzania, and Timor-Leste and summarizes key findings, which focus on the relationship of GBS to: (1) host country ownership of its development program; (2) budget allocation and performance assessment; (3) donor coordination and harmonization; (4) transaction costs; (5) management capacity; (6) fiduciary risk; and (7) progress towards democratic and development goals. (USAID 2005b; see also Chapter 6 of this volume.)
- *Joint Evaluation of General Budget Support to Tanzania 1995-2004.* This report to the Government of Tanzania and to the Poverty Reduction Budget Support (PRBS) Development Partners evaluates the efficiency and effectiveness of budget support, as an aid modality, over 1995 to 2004 and assesses its contribution to the processes of growth and poverty reduction (Daima Associates and Overseas Development Institute 2005; see also Chapter 7 of this volume).

Choice of Instruments

The choice of an appropriate aid modality depends on the country characteristics and development objectives, along the lines of the decision tree in Figure 1.1. A considered judgment typically involves a variety of factors, including the extent of agreement on policies and budget priorities at the country level, and the institutional capacity of the recipient country to implement the policy program and account for the use of resources. Decision makers also need to carefully assess risks, which can include the potential adverse impact for recipient countries of the fiscal adjustments that will be needed if budget support is suddenly reduced in case of inadequate performance. For donors, the risks include fiduciary and political concerns.

FIGURE 1.1 Decision Tree for Choosing Aid Instruments

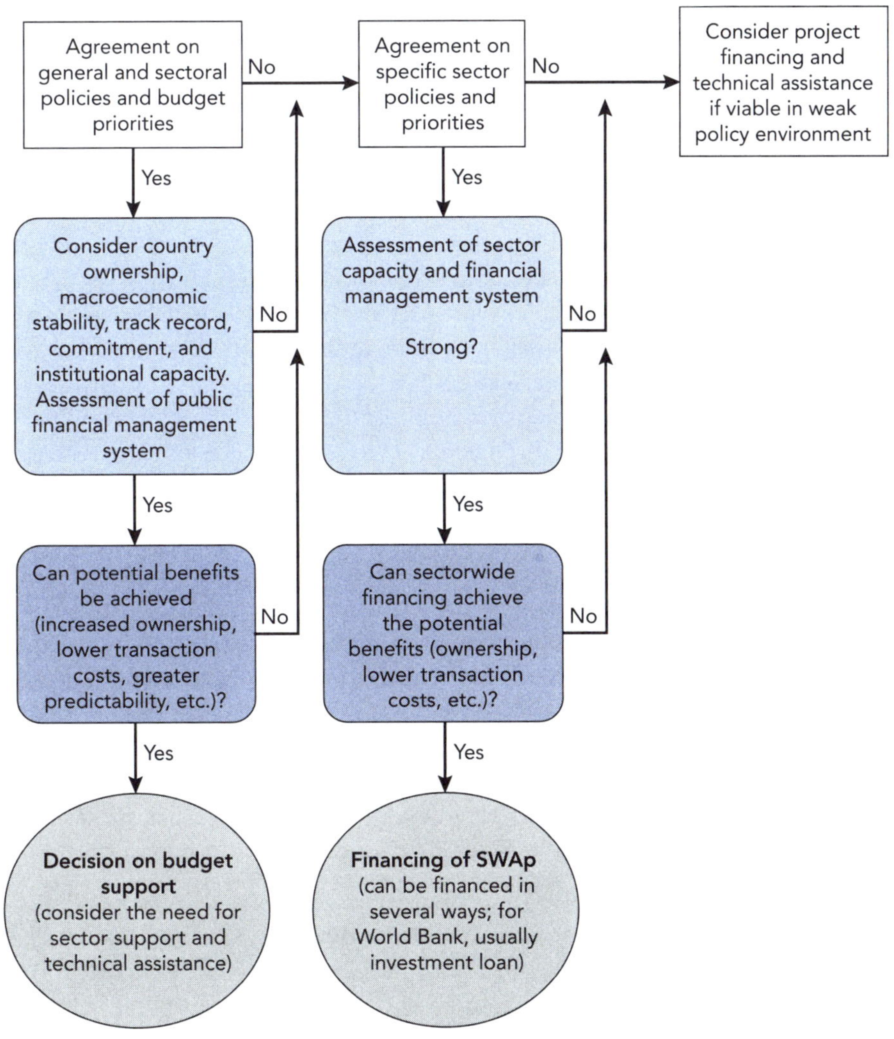

Country realities often call for a phased, incremental approach to the choice of aid instruments, which emphasizes capacity development, trust building, and the progressive adoption of new mechanisms such as budget support (Pavigniani 2001). Such choices can be made along a spectrum of interventions depending on the degree of control and scope for policy change appropriate for the specific country circumstances (Figures 1.1 and 1.2):

- *Budget support.* The emerging consensus among donors is that budget support is an approach better suited to countries with a good track record and a reasonably sound policy and institutional framework, including transparent budget management and adequate financial management arrangements. For such countries, it may be appropriate for budget support to be the main aid instrument, accompanied by complementary technical assistance and project financing as needed.

- *Sectorwide approaches (SWAps).* In some country situations, budget support cannot be considered appropriate, particularly where the potential benefits are outweighed by perceived risks. For example, budget support may not be appropriate if there is no adequate public financial management system in place, if the country has not developed a viable poverty reduction strategy, or if donors cannot find sufficient common ground with a recipient country's general policies and budget priorities. In this case, a greater degree of control may be required and financial support at a sector level could be considered through a sectorwide approach (SWAp).[5] Using this approach may help a country build appropriate implementation arrangements with which it can establish a track record of reform and growing confidence to facilitate an eventual transition to general budget support. This said, SWAps require a clearly articulated sectoral strategy and agreement on sectoral priorities. Similarly, a decision whether to provide SWAps should be based on a careful assessment of the sector's institutional capacity to implement the expenditure program and to achieve the program objectives. While supporting a sectoral expenditure program through a SWAp can help accounting for the use of resources, it will not necessarily reduce overall fiduciary risks, given the fungibility of aid resources.

- *Investment projects.* Where a policy consensus between donors and recipient government cannot be achieved at reasonable costs or within a realistic time frame, traditional investment projects may have an important role.[6] In the context of a weak policy environment and lack of consensus on overall expenditure priorities, stand-alone projects with a narrower focus may have the advantage of allowing greater oversight of the use of aid funds. Individual projects may be effective in promoting detailed implementation changes within a confined area even when the overall policy dialogue on the country's development strategy is uncertain, but are less suitable for scaling up and achieving policy changes than budget support.

- *Pilot projects.* If profound differences of opinion between government and donors make the implementation of traditional projects difficult, technical assistance, analytical and advisory work, or limited pilot projects may be helpful in establishing common ground, creating demonstration effects, and encouraging domestic debate on policy options. However, such interventions may not always be possible or advisable in countries experiencing deteriorating governance or a prolonged crisis (World Bank 2005l).

Considerations in Choosing Budget Support

Once the choice of instruments has been made, key considerations in determining whether the conditions for budget support are appropriate include country ownership and accountability, selectivity and preconditions, macroeconomic issues, and fiduciary risk.

Country Ownership and Accountability

As is widely recognized, sustainable reform requires deep and broad country ownership, because successful policy implementation ultimately depends on strong political commitment. In countries where such commitment does not exist, budget support could not effectively support a program of policy actions and reforms.[7]

Compared to other aid modalities, budget support creates a framework more conducive to strengthening country ownership, for a number of reasons:

- *Integration of external assistance into the national budget.* Providing a larger share of aid through budget support increases the share of aid funds that are included in the national budget process and makes donors less prone to micromanage individual programs. At the same time, donors are more likely to engage with recipient governments in a policy dialogue on the overall budget process.[8]

FIGURE 1.2 Spectrum of Instruments

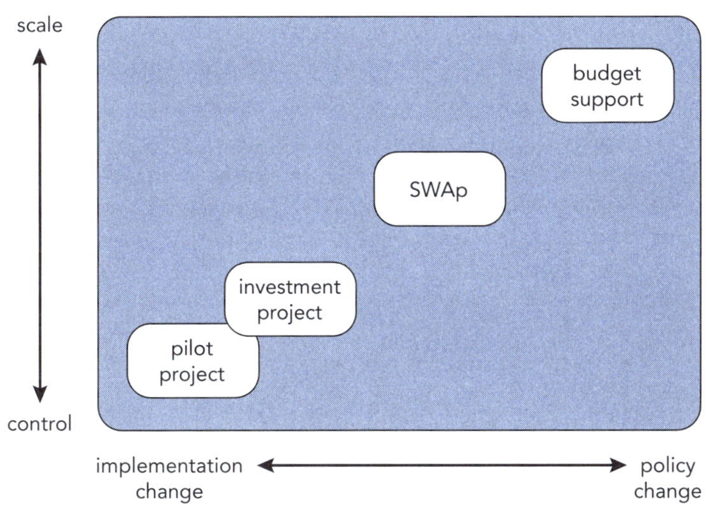

Source: Developed from Alain Locussol and Ato Brown, "Getting Results: The Water Sector and PRSC in Uganda." Presentation.

- *Better management of public expenditures*, as a centerpiece of budget support programs. Providing aid as budget support allows a government more flexibility in executing the budget, as it can use the funds to finance both recurrent and capital expenditures.
- *Reinforcing accountability relationships within recipient governments*. Budget support has the potential to strengthen intragovernmental accountability by providing line ministries an incentive to work with the finance ministry to determine priorities and allocate funds instead of competing for donor funding. Rather than being accountable to individual donors that are funding their projects, line ministries are accountable to the ministry of finance. On the other hand, budget support arrangements could also weaken the incentives of line ministries to work toward the overall program results expected for the release of funds, since the overall results are considered to be the responsibility of the finance ministry rather than the sector ministries.
- *Budget support provides more discipline in the budget process* by reducing fragmentation and limiting the access of line ministries and other government agencies to extra-budgetary financing. It also can be expected to strengthen the government's capacity to design and implement programs and poverty reduction strategies.[9]

Donors and recipient governments can further strengthen local ownership by (1) focusing on national development policies and priorities, rather than donor priorities; (2) encouraging a broad national debate and ensuring that the program of policy actions is endorsed by a broad spectrum of stakeholders—or at least has the acquiescence of vested interests; (3) aligning conditionality to reflect development priorities identified in the PRSP and medium-term expenditure framework; and (4) avoiding restricting the use of the funds once the country has met the agreed conditions.

Selectivity and Preconditions

As noted above, the literature on aid effectiveness stresses the importance of a good policy environment for effective aid (World Bank 1998). This is consistent with the emerging lesson that budget support is most appropriate for countries with a good track record, strong ownership of the reform program, and a reasonably sound policy and institutional framework, as well as commitment and sufficient capacity to allocate resources effectively and in accordance with development priorities.

Donor decisions to provide budget support should generally be based on a positive assessment that a number of critical preconditions for its effectiveness are in place, including:

- an agreement with the recipient country on policies and budget priorities,
- demonstrated commitment and capacity to implement a viable medium-term reform program,
- a clear strategy for prioritizing pro-poor expenditures,
- a transparent budget, and
- commitment to strengthen the public financial management system.

Most major budget support donors implicitly or explicitly consider such criteria in making their decisions.

- The World Bank is typically selective in providing budget support, tending to provide PRSCs to better performers. According to a recent stocktaking (World Bank 2005e and Chapter 3 of this volume), this is evident in the relatively high rankings of PRSC countries based on the country policy and institutional assessment index (CPIA)[10]; all but one PRSC country fall in the top three quintiles of this rating, with most falling in the top two.
- The Strategic Framework for IDA's Assistance to Africa reinforces this focus on selectivity, suggesting that larger resource flows could be provided to support programs through national budget and planning processes if recipient countries had improved capacity and demonstrated a strong track record (World Bank 2003b).
- The European Commission's approach under the Cotonou Partnership Agreement involves granting direct budgetary assistance in support of macroeconomic or sectoral reforms if: (1) public expenditure management is sufficiently transparent, accountable, and effective; (2) well-defined macroeconomic or sectoral policies, established by the country itself and agreed to by its main donors, are in place; and (3) public procurement is open and transparent (European Commission 2000).
- The DFID's essential preconditions for engaging in budget support are an agreement on the policy framework and on revenue and expenditure priorities, and a government track record of implementing stated policies. Eligibility is then based on the government's planned budget priorities to support poverty reduction; its commitment to making administrative, technical, and financial systems robust and reliable; and the relative benefits of budget support compared with other financing instruments (DFID 2004d).

Macroeconomic Issues

A country's macroeconomic situation is an important consideration in determining the suitability of budget support. A stable macroeconomic environment provides a solid framework for efficient use of resources and helps maximize the effectiveness of budget support. Donors' financing decisions typically consider the adequacy of the country's macroeconomic policy framework.[11]

The volume and timing of the payments involved in budget support can affect the predictability of budgetary resources and the relative cost of funding budget deficits. In addition, these transactions may have monetary and foreign exchange rate implications, depending on the timing of exchange conversion and on the potential use of monetary policy instruments for sterilizing the liquidity effects.

Fiduciary Risk

Budget support allows donors little if any influence on individual spending categories once resources are transferred, so a thorough ex ante assessment of the government's capacity to use resources effectively is of critical importance.

Low-income countries with the greatest need for budget support also tend to have inadequate financial management systems, suffering from serious weaknesses in budget formulation and execution, financial reporting, procurement, and oversight systems. Most also have only weak links between agreed policies, budget planning, and budget execution. Providing budget support to these countries raises legitimate fiduciary concerns that scarce aid resources may be misappropriated or wasted. At the same time, however, budget support has been used effectively even in fragile countries with extremely weak fiduciary systems—such as Timor-Leste and Afghanistan—where clear expenditure priorities and a strong government commitment to addressing institutional weaknesses reduced the risk to an acceptable level relative to expected benefits (World Bank 2005l).

Budget support should help to strengthen partner countries' public financial management systems, including their transparency and accountability. Improvements in financial management are both a precondition for and a goal of this aid modality.[12] In countries with weak public financial management systems, additional measures may need to accompany budget support. These could be in the form of conditionality, earmarking, or additional accountability requirements. Support may be linked to technical assistance to address specific weaknesses in fiduciary arrangements.

One of the complicating factors is the use of different assessment tools by various donors, which implies a risk of divergent and uncoordinated policy actions. To strengthen recipients' and donors' ability to diagnose public expenditure, procurement, and financial accountability systems, to develop capacity-building actions, and to standardize assessment tools, the World Bank and the EC introduced the Public Expenditure and Financial Accountability (PEFA) program in 2001.[13]

Adequate risk management and mitigation measures can reduce fiduciary risk to some extent. Donors and governments have sought to address weaknesses in financial management mainly by focusing on institutional approaches and actions for treating fiduciary risks. These include (1) enhancing governments' ability to track public expenditures; (2) strengthening internal and external audit mechanisms; (3) supporting capacity building; (4) undertaking additional safeguard measures; and (5) clearly agreeing on actions to be taken in case of nonperformance. The main challenges appear to be the implementation and enforcement of measures and regulation in the area of public financial management.

D. Key Issues in Design and Implementation

Experience highlights certain issues that have major implications for the success or failure of budget support programs.

Design

Key issues to take into account in designing budget support programs include the tensions among predictability and performance, outcome orientation, and institutional capacity.

Predictability, Performance, and Moral Hazard

Achieving greater predictability of funding is a key objective when considering budget support.[14] Predictability is even more important in the case of budget support than in other aid modalities, since the funds provided may finance recurrent budget expenditures. Partner countries need clear, reliable, and timely information on estimated amounts, the timing of disbursements, and the conditions for release of funds. Predictability also implies synchronizing disbursements with the government's budget cycle, timing resource flows as much as possible to coincide with when the government needs them most—typically at the beginning of the fiscal year. Predictability enables the recipient government to incorporate the funds in the early stage of the budget process and encourages the timely involvement of line ministries in the internal policy dialogue on the priorities and budget allocations. Predictability also enables more efficient strategic planning and the maintenance of adequate links between development priorities and budget expenditures, as set out in the medium-term expenditure framework.

By providing medium-term assistance based on agreement about policies and budget priorities, budget support can potentially help make aid flows more predictable. But since budget support is a flexible form of assistance, the disbursement process may also be more volatile: funds can easily be held up if circumstances change, or can be quickly withdrawn in case of nonperformance. Volatility of resource flows is of special concern in countries where overall performance is less than adequate—particularly those that are highly aid dependent—and in those aid-dependent countries in which budget support comprises a large share of aid. Unexpected shortfalls in these countries will require ad hoc mid-year adjustments, making cash flow more difficult to manage and the budget process less credible. Ultimately, it could undermine the achievement of poverty reduction objectives.

Requests for more predictable donor funding should be met only in the context of a partnership-based approach that provides accountability for country performance, keeping in mind the risk that budget support can be viewed as an entitlement irrespective of country performance or financing needs. Brautigam (2000) and Moore (1998) have found that high levels of aid tend to dampen the incentives for governments to remain accountable to their citizens and to further develop their own revenue sources.

Donors' approaches vary. Over the past few years, the World Bank's policy-based lending has mainly followed a programmatic approach to assessing a country's overall progress, based on flexible expected prior actions (or "triggers") (Koeberle 2005). This approach allows for a graduated response to variable country performance, potentially combining variations in the amount, recalibration of the program, or delay of the operation (World Bank 2005j). Some donors have promoted a more rules-based approach that aims at greater predictability and less subjectivity, using a fixed tranche that is based on a minimum level of conditionality (for example, continued macroeconomic stability, improved monitoring and evaluation systems) and a variable, performance-oriented tranche that is linked to specific actions or indicators. Different design options have emerged, including the outcome-based conditionality favored by the European Commission for their budget support (European Commission 2005 and Hauck, Hasse, and Koppensteiner 2005).

In a few countries that receive budget support, commitments and disbursements seems to be more volatile for budget support funds than for other aid modalities, particularly in the initial stages. The reasons may include complicated internal donor procedures, nonalignment of the budget cycles of donors and recipients, obscure disbursement conditions, complex fiduciary requirements, politically motivated commitments, weak alignment of the budget process with the PRSP, or poorly defined policy reforms (some practical experiences in the interaction between the PRSP process and the budget in five countries—Bolivia, Burkina Faso, Cambodia, Tanzania, and Vietnam—are elaborated in Chapter 9 of this volume).

Achieving greater clarity and predictability of funding presents significant challenges to both donors and partner governments (see, for example, the analysis of the predictability of budget aid in eight African countries presented in Chapter 11).

For donors, this effort usually requires: (1) announcing multi-annual commitments in advance; (2) disbursing funds as early as possible in the partner country's budget process and fiscal year; (3) better donor coordination and exchange of information about the likely timing and conditions of disbursement; and (4) an attempt to minimize in-year suspension of committed funds, to avoid disrupting development expenditures.[15] Donors should transparently announce any coordinated responses to perceived shortfalls in country performance early enough for the country to take them into account in its budget preparation. Ideally reductions in budget support in response to poor performance should be graduated to avoid sudden unexpected disruptions in resource flows.[16] To some extent, the typical alignment problems can be addressed through the introduction of a common performance assessment framework (PAF): donors use the PAF performance benchmarks and targets in making their commitments and deciding on disbursements.[17] However, funding may remain hard to predict when some donors reserve the right to disburse against their own assessments of progress, while others seek to reach a consensus on assessing the partner government's progress against PAF actions during the annual review.

Partner countries can help to make funding easier to predict by better aligning their budget priorities with the medium-term policy programs and PRS objectives, by preparing contingent spending plans that indicate how additional resources would be spent or shortfalls adjusted, and by disciplined implementation of agreed policy actions.[18]

Outcome Orientation

Budget support is conducive to a results-based approach. Its effectiveness needs to be measured in terms of budget outputs (more predictable budget financing, more efficient public spending, stronger budget process, stronger intragovernment relations and accountability), and outcomes (enhanced capacity for poverty reduction, environment conducive to private sector development and growth, better delivery of public services) relative to government policy objectives.

While donors and governments generally recognize the virtues of a results-based approach, its implementation faces significant challenges. Lack of adequate data and practical difficulties in measuring outcomes pose tensions between governments and donors, but also among donors themselves. Some donors advocate a formal outcome-based approach to calibrate disbursements.[19] While outcome and impact indicators are useful to monitor progress toward development objectives, governments are often wary of using outcome and impact targets as conditions of disbursement, particularly when they are held accountable for outcomes that are subject to exogenous shocks or outside their control (World Bank 2005e; also see Chapter 13 of this volume). Moreover, quantifiable outcome indicators are often not available on a timely basis and may be easier to obtain for the social sectors (such as health and education) than for institutional processes such as governance and public financial management (World Bank 2005f).

While poverty reduction remains the ultimate objective of budget support, the links are indirect and necessarily long term. Budget support can facilitate modifications toward poverty-oriented public policy and expenditure shifts in favor of targeted services, but the effects are likely to be uncertain, and little is known about the ultimate results chains to poverty reduction over the long term. The challenge therefore is to avoid undue expectations and fixation on distant goals while focusing on realistic contributions of budget support that are typically likely to be slow and incremental.

Institutional Capacity[20]

Capacity constraints are typical in aid-dependent countries that are candidates for budget support. Experience underlines the importance of institutional development and capacity building for ensuring the sustainability of policy reforms in these countries (World Bank 2005f).

Budget support arrangements, and in particular the institutionalized policy dialogue between recipient countries and donors that is associated with budget support, provide an opportunity for identifying major bottlenecks and designing measures for reducing capacity constraints. Budget support relies on the recipient's capacity, which is strengthened when resources are managed more effectively. By using a country's own procedures and addressing cross-cutting issues of governance, budget support may improve the effectiveness of the government systems as a whole. Increased aid delivery through budget support and reduced off-budget project financing create incentives for line ministries to comply with budget procedures and directives, contributing to a more structured approach to policy development.

None of these benefits can be taken for granted, however. The ability of government systems to shoulder numerous responsibilities delegated from projects should not be overestimated. The increased use of budget support adds to the burden on the ministry of finance for coordination of a broader range of reform efforts and development priorities. Donor capacity can be an issue, too, as budget support requires different analytical skills from project financing, as well as the ability to engage in a substantive policy dialogue. Budget support can provide a solid framework for addressing institutional weaknesses, but it requires sustained efforts to strengthen both donor and government capacity for formulating and implementing policy programs.

Implementation

Key issues in implementing budget support include the quality of the policy dialogue between donors and aid recipients, transaction costs, and donor coordination.

Policy Dialogue and Conditionality

The shift to budget support has major implications for the way donors engage in the policy dialogue with partner countries:

- Development partners focus more on ex ante issues, most notably discussing budget priorities, sector allocations, and balance between major budget categories, with less concern for ex post control over the use of funds.
- The policy dialogue focuses more on national budget priorities than on specific expenditures and procedures. This approach recognizes that with fungible financial assistance, the policy dialogue is more effective if concentrated on programs and allocations of budget resources to priority sectors for poverty reduction (such as education, health, agriculture, water, roads).

Budget support brings a new dimension to the partnership-based approach by shifting the emphasis from traditional conditionality to a more long-term mutual accountability framework. Drawing on the lessons learned during the past two decades, "conditionality" is now seen to be somewhat of a misnomer (Koeberle 2005). Budget support has supported the notion of a partnership with a mutual commitment to support medium-term policy and institutional changes, in which the country formulates and implements its own development strategy, and donors provide advice and financial support—with associated frameworks for measuring results—as appropriate with policy-based loans and grants. Good practice suggests that is advisable to agree upfront on a coordinated accountability framework that is tailored to country circumstances and involves only a few measures that are critical for achieving results. While significant challenges remain, the evidence shows encouraging progress in embedding this approach to conditionality in recent policy-based operations (World Bank 2005p).

Many donors consider the opportunity for an open dialogue on broad policy reforms and general budget priorities to be one of the most important elements of budget support arrangements. Smaller bilateral donors, in particular, value the opportunity to contribute effectively to the dialogue on government policies. The policy dialogue between donors and partner country has to be informed by well-targeted analytical work and needs to discuss constructively and candidly what budget support can and cannot achieve. The changing relationship and increased focus on policy dialogue are reflected in recent organizational and strategic changes, including a greater in-country presence of many donors (Gill and Pugatch 2005).

Another important aspect is the quality of dialogue. Capacity constraints on the side of both partner countries and donors mean that procedural issues sometimes prevail over policy issues at the expense of the depth of the dialogue. Enhancing the quality of the dialogue and engaging in relevant policy issues in adequate depth requires a substantial investment in analytical work, continuous engagement, and adequate skills on the part of both donors and government senior policymakers (Besley and Zagha 2005). These needs suggest the value of a clear division of labor among donors in line with their comparative advantage and sectoral expertise. Efforts to strengthen capacity and better understand the complexities of budget support as an aid modality may also be more effective when they involve oversight institutions, such as parliaments and civil society organizations. A balanced and well-informed dialogue between the legislative and the executive branches of government requires adequate access to resources and knowledge for decision makers to exercise their roles properly (Corre 2004).

Notwithstanding the central role of the policy dialogue for budget support, it is typically overshadowed by domestic political factors. Even in aid-dependent countries where budget support and the related conditionality have become an important and regular mode of aid delivery for years, its influence on processes of public sector reform, institutional development, and expenditure prioritization is often modest (for example, Lawson and others [2005] for Tanzania). Domestic policy considerations tend to dominate the choices made by policymakers, even at the risk of creating tensions with the donor community—as shown by increased funding for the military in Uganda in 2004 or the repression of political opposition in Ethiopia in 2005.

Budget support can promote governance and facilitate a process of political change that shifts the balance of power among domestic stakeholders—but it cannot substitute for institutions of domestic accountability. The provision of funds to a partner country's treasury should provide an incentive to strengthen both internal and external accountability. Finance ministries should demand that sector ministries deliver sustainable development results, line ministries have an interest in receiving adequate funds on a regular basis, supreme audit authorities monitor the proper use of public funds, and parliaments can hold governments accountable for delivering on their promises. Ultimately, however, the quality of this process is dominated by domestic political dynamics that can either support or block whatever modest contributions may be made by the policy dialogue underpinning budget support.

Transaction Costs

Reduction of transaction costs is one of the key objectives of providing budget support. Compared to other aid modalities, the expectation is that budget support reduces the need for separate audits, project management, or implementation planning. Moreover, there should be associated improvements in donor coordination and harmonization.

In practice, however, experience shows that costs are likely to be reduced only over the medium term, as the various processes associated with providing budget support gradually improve. In the short term, costs could even be higher, reflecting the start-up costs and coordination requirements of establishing new modes of interaction between governments and donors. The type of policy dialogue supporting effective budget support requires specific skills and inputs at the central and sector levels, which typically generate significant transaction costs in the initial period.

Transaction costs by their nature are very difficult to measure. Four characteristics of transactions are typically thought to influence them: frequency, complexity, uncertainty, and specificity (Doan and Lestrange 1998). One of the rare studies that has attempted to gather quantitative information on transaction costs (Brown and others 2000) developed surveys and carried out interviews on several indicators: (1) number of projects, (2) number of reports, (3) number of meetings, (4) number of steering committees, and (5) total time civil servants spent on aid administration versus policymaking; the authors found that measuring these indicators and gathering quantitative data appeared to be difficult and costly.

The evidence to date suggests that there is still a long way to go to fully reap the promise of reduced transaction costs through budget support arrangements. Recipient governments in the SPA review (SPA 2005) point to insufficient progress in harmonization and alignment across the board as a determining factor. Similar skepticism has been expressed by Killick (2004), who suggests that the rhetoric on lower transaction costs is not sufficiently evidence based. Lawson and others (2005) find that in Tanzania the lack of evidence of reductions in transaction costs arises substantially from the fact that budget support arrangements have been additional to continuing large numbers of donor projects in the public sector and the parallel rise in the importance of common-basket funding.

Donor Coordination

Donor coordination has become a critical aspect of budget support, especially where the latter comprises a large share of donor flows. Better donor coordination, and simplification and harmonization of donor requirements, can contribute to local ownership, reducing transaction costs and enhancing the overall effectiveness of development assistance. Efforts to improve donor coordination are of course not new, but their effectiveness under different aid modalities was often limited by differences in donor procedures and the lack of a common framework.

The institutionalized policy dialogue within budget support arrangements provides a promising framework for better donor coordination and harmonization of policies, procedures, and practices. Considerable benefits could also be expected from better alignment of donor budget support with the poverty reduction strategy process and country priorities. Reviews of budget support to poverty reduction strategies in Benin, Burkina Faso, Mozambique, Malawi, Tanzania, and Uganda point to significant progress on donor coordination and harmonization in these countries (Evans and Coyle 2002).

Achieving better coordination and harmonization in countries that receive budget support still faces significant challenges. In the first place, as noted above, more effective donor alignment requires deeper analytical skills and implies greater management responsibilities for donors, both in headquarters and in the country. The challenges are greater in those countries in which there is no critical number of donors in favor of budget support, or where the authorities lack the capacity or will to take a leadership role. Donors may disagree on how to determine whether a recipient country has adequate capacity to effectively manage resources provided as budget support. Donor coordination is also hampered by different approaches to measuring fiduciary risks and the degree to which donors scrutinize budget and disbursement allocations. Despite common efforts at greater harmonization, donors still tend to add issues of their own to the agenda. In some African countries, up to 10 different donor missions were dispatched to assess the public finance management system (SPA 2005).

No single approach to donor coordination is suitable for all countries and conditions, since the right choice depends on the local context and institutional capacity. However, emerging good practice suggests the framework for coordination: (1) the recipient country aligns its PRS implementation with its own budget cycle; (2) donors align their budget support programs with the priorities set out in the PRS; (3) donors coordinate their programs in order to achieve consistency in setting benchmarks and to harmonize the procedures and documentation required; and (4) donors aim to synchronize their missions (World Bank 2005k). The Paris Declaration on Aid Effectiveness pointed to the need to implement common arrangements for financing, disbursements, monitoring and evaluation, and the reduction of duplicative missions and diagnostic reviews (High-Level Forum 2005).

E. Summary and Conclusions

Budget support has become increasingly important in the context of a partnership-based approach to development assistance. Donors and recipient countries alike have expressed an interest in exploring an aid modality that promises greater country ownership, reduced transaction costs, scaling up of poverty reduction, and potentially greater development effectiveness than traditional modes of aid delivery.

Budget support is defined as financial assistance provided directly to a partner country's budget on a regular basis, using the country's own financial management systems and budget procedures. In current usage, the term "budget support" typically refers to predictable, annual, medium-term resource flows, based on progress in achieving the goals of the government's poverty reduction strategy.

The rationale for an increasing emphasis on budget support has been provided by recent trends in the international aid architecture: greater selectivity in favor of well-performing countries, a stronger focus on cross-cutting economy-wide development programs with a greater impact than a fragmented project approach, greater emphasis on country ownership, a shift from short-term reforms to complex medium-term institutional and policy changes, a replacement of traditional ex ante conditionality with a programmatic partnership-based approach based on mutual accountability, a recognition of the need for greater predictability of development aid, and an enhanced focus on results.

Compared to other aid modalities, budget support promises a more effective scaling up of funds aimed at poverty reduction in countries with strong ownership and a sound institutional and policy framework. Budget support offers scope for providing funds in a more predictable and sustainable manner, coordinating external financing with the country's budget cycle, addressing cross-cutting issues and constraints on development, ensuring a more efficient use of resources, and enhancing institutional capacity. To the extent that budget support helps to simplify disbursement procedures and reporting requirements, it further facilitates the scaling up of development aid.

Budget support involves the channeling of donor funds to a partner country using its own budget system, in support of the country's own development programs linked to national or sector policies. The value added of budget support consists in the combination of an increase in the volume of discretionary funding that can be used for development purposes with a policy dialogue linked to the effective implementation of the recipient's broader development strategy. In principle, there is no need to earmark funds for specific budget expenditures. However, if there are weaknesses in public financial management, additional accountability arrangements may be warranted.

The qualitative monitoring of progress toward development outcomes is a key aspect of budget support. Conditionality focuses on policy measures and expenditure allocations that relate to overall development priorities, as set out in the PRS and medium-term expenditure framework.

An appropriate mix of instruments is needed to ensure the greatest effectiveness of development assistance. The choice of lending instruments depends on the extent of agreement about policies and budget priorities, and on the recipient country's institutional capacity to implement the reform program and account for its use of resources.

Key considerations in determining whether the conditions for budget support are appropriate include:

- *Country ownership and accountability.* Budget support encourages ownership by increasing the overall share of funds that are included in a national budget process, using a country's own system. It reinforces accountability relationships within recipient governments and potentially strengthens governments' capacity to design and implement programs.

- *Selectivity and preconditions for effectiveness.* Selectivity is critical to effective budget support. This form of aid is most appropriate for countries with a good track record, strong ownership of the reform program, a reasonably sound policy and institutional framework, and commitment and sufficient capacity to allocate resources effectively.

- *Macroeconomic issues.* A stable macroeconomic environment provides a solid framework for efficient use of resources and helps to maximize the effectiveness of budget support.

- *Fiduciary risk.* Budget support can help address fiduciary risk by strengthening public financial management systems. Where governments are not committed to addressing fiduciary weaknesses over time, budget support may not be appropriate. Financial support in a form of sectorwide approach or stand-alone projects may be more appropriate in this case.

Key issues in designing and implementing a budget support program include:

- *Policy dialogue.* The opportunity for an open dialogue on broad policy reforms and general budget priorities is a key element of budget support arrangements. Enhancing the quality of the dialogue and covering relevant policy issues requires continuous engagement and adequate skills from donors and recipient governments.

- *Tensions between predictability and performance.* Budget support may provide a more predictable flow of medium-term aid funds. However, the disbursement process can also be more prone to volatility.
- *Results orientation.* Budget support should be built around a country-specific accountability framework that allows for transparent regular reviews of progress toward tangible development results.
- *Institutional capacity.* By using the country's own procedures, budget support helps strengthen institutional capacity. However, it may also entail additional strains on the capacity of ministries of finance. Donor capacity can also be an issue, as budget support requires specific analytical and other skills.
- *Transaction costs.* The use of established government systems, instead of the parallel reporting and accounting systems traditionally associated with project-based aid, should result in reduced transaction costs. However, experience shows that costs are likely to be reduced only over the medium term and could even rise in the short term.
- *Donor coordination.* The institutionalized policy dialogue embedded in budget support provides a promising framework for improved donor coordination and harmonization. Challenges for the harmonization agenda include questions on how to determine the adequacy of a recipient country's financial management systems, how to scrutinize budget and disbursement procedures, and how to respond to uneven country performance.

Endnotes

1. For an overview of changes in the approach to conditionality in the European Commission, IMF, and World Bank respectively, see IMF (2005b), European Commission (2005), World Bank (2005p), and Koeberle and Walliser in Chapter 13 of this volume.
2. This vision has been articulated in various documents and policy statements, as summarized in the 2003 multipartner evaluation of the World Bank's Comprehensive Development Framework (OED 2003).
3. For instance, privatization and trade reform now account for only a small share of World Bank conditionality, which is increasingly supporting medium-term strengthening of public financial management.
4. For an overview of the evolution of the Poverty Reduction Strategy approach, see World Bank and IMF (2005).
5. See for example, the Report of the Commission for Africa (2005), which suggests that while the best way to deliver support is to put aid into government budgets and let governments prioritize the spending of it, "this will only work where a government has a clear development strategy in place and where the budget system is open and transparent. Where this is not the case, a sectorwide approach to a particular area such as education or health may be more appropriate" (p. 28).

6. The Report of the Commission for Africa (2005) argues that "where governance is too poor for donors to have confidence in sector-wide approaches aid may best be paid into specific projects run by aid agencies or other non-governmental organizations." Similarly, the Strategic Framework for Investment in Africa (SFIA) notes that IDA remains committed to traditional interventions where they are most appropriate.
7. Country ownership is an elusive concept that is difficult to assess. A number of indicators could be used for assessing government commitment and ownership: the extent of national policy debate; the track record in confronting difficult policy choices; the degree of endorsement by the central and line ministries, civil society, parliaments, and so on. One of the more robust indicators for ownership and reform readiness is a country's track record. See World Bank (2001a).
8. Provision of budget support may allow donors to influence discussion of certain issues over which they might have had little if any influence without providing budget support. However, this is not in itself a negative feature.
9. Support for local ownership in this context is not just a matter of enabling control over the reform agenda for the recipient country. It implies commitment that is shared among a broad number of participants, including civil society, parliaments, and so forth.
10. The CPIA is an aggregate of performance ratings on public sector management, economic management, and social and economic policies. The CPIA ratings for the year prior to the calendar year of PRSC approval were used (for example, for projects approved in CY 2004, scores for CPIA 2003) since the ratings are usually finalized by the end of the year and become the operational ratings for the next calendar year.
11. Bilateral donors often based their assessment on the status of the recipient country's Poverty Reduction and Growth Facility arrangement with the IMF.
12. See Shand in Chapter 2 in this volume.
13. In the meantime, the initiative has evolved into a partnership among the World Bank, the EC, the IMF, the United Kingdom and the SPA. The PEFA Performance Measurement Framework is available at www.pefa.org.
14. The multipartner evaluation of the CDF recommends that donors provide "predictable and reliable financing with transparent, multi-year financing indicators, based on clear country performance criteria" (OED 2003, p. xviii).
15. As a result of these measures, evidence suggests that in recent years, budget support to countries such as Tanzania has become more predictable and less variable than project aid. See World Bank (2003d).
16. See good practice principles in World Bank (2005p) and Chapter 13 of this volume.
17. Again, see good practice principles in World Bank (2005p) and Chapter 13 of this volume.
18. See, for instance, Booth, Christiansen, and de Renzio in Chapter 10 of this volume.
19. The EC disbursement model specifies that a portion of the budget support is disbursed against an overall assessment and another portion against progress on a set of specific indicators. See EC (2005) and Chapter 4 in this volume.
20. Institutional capacity in this paper encompasses the institutional framework (laws, regulations, policies), the professional knowledge of government employees, and the organizational structure of the relevant institutions.

2

Managing Fiduciary Issues in Budget Support Operations

DAVID SHAND
World Bank

Fiduciary issues have been viewed as a key factor in budget support operations,[1] but fiduciary risk in particular has been little articulated.[2] This paper surveys and analyzes approaches to fiduciary issues and by doing so seeks to demystify the concept of fiduciary risk. Having a clear understanding of fiduciary risk should assist in the dialogue between donors and development partners on budget support operations. Donor institutions' country teams in particular may find this useful.[3]

Some donors see budget support as inherently more risky than traditional project-level support. This is because of the poor quality of many partner countries' systems for public financial management (PFM), through which donor assistance flows, and also because, by definition, it is not possible to track the end use to which the funds are put. Major donors of budget support now normally take the view that the best assurance that their funds are well managed is the existence of sound PFM in the partner country. According to this view, the key issue in analyzing fiduciary risk is the quality of a country's PFM systems, including for procurement. Sound PFM is crucial for poverty reduction, permitting a partner country to develop, implement, and report on a budget that is comprehensive, realistic, well prioritized (in terms of poverty reduction) and has a medium-term focus. PFM issues have become a key aspect of the policy dialogue between donors and partner countries, which also emphasizes the need for government ownership of and commitment to PFM reforms.

To guide their decisions on budget support, donors put strong emphasis on finding out about the quality of partner countries' PFM systems, and in the past few years, several have undertaken extensive diagnostic assessments of these systems.[4] The approach of the UK Department for International Development, in particular, stresses the need for full documentation of the grounds on which budget support decisions have been made, to serve as a basis for accountability to taxpayers. Some donors have taken the view that fiduciary risk needs to be set out in an explicit statement on areas of risk and/or the overall level of risk, which in some cases is expressed in narrative terms or even quantified.

This paper suggests there is a need to avoid overcomplicating fiduciary issues, in particular in the development of explicit risk statements or assessments. Though no financial assistance from donors to partner countries can be risk free, the risks need to be compared with benefits, both in absolute terms and comparatively for each aid modality. Donors should also be realistic about how quickly the level of fiduciary risk can be lowered by improved PFM and procurement systems, since experience suggests that such institutional and systems reforms only produce results in the medium to long term.

Section A defines fiduciary risk, distinguishing it from other common types of risk in development assistance, and emphasizes its relationship with the quality of a country's systems for public financial management and procurement. Section B reviews issues in fiduciary risk, focusing on procurement, corruption, and the flow of funds, and explains approaches for evaluating risks in these areas. Section C examines how donors use information on the quality of PFM in decisions about budget support. Section D looks at donors' approaches to measuring fiduciary risk, and also reports on a proposed comprehensive framework for measuring a country's PFM performance. Section E reviews strategies for managing and mitigating fiduciary risk over the short and long terms. Section F concludes with some tentative findings that show budget support has improved financial management.

Fiduciary risk has been seen as a donor issue. Yet partner governments too have an interest in reliable information on how budget funds are used, so that they can be accountable to their own taxpayers. The challenge therefore is to develop this commonality of interest into a country-led concern with sound PFM that is supported by donors and includes dialogue based on mutual objectives and trust.[5]

A. Fiduciary and Developmental Objectives: Two Sides of the Same Coin

The general view appears to be that PFM development and fiduciary issues are two sides of the same coin and cannot usefully be separated.[6] The same knowledge base about the operation of the PFM system is used for both purposes. For example, the World Bank's guidelines for country financial accountability assessments (CFAAs) (World Bank 2003c) explicitly state that these assessments, in identifying weaknesses in PFM systems, have both a developmental and a fiduciary objective. Donors and partner countries have an interest in both. Their challenge is to work collaboratively to meet both developmental and fiduciary needs within a framework led by the partner country.

What Is Meant by Fiduciary Risk?

The literature and donor country statements on fiduciary risk vary in their definitions, but generally include all or some of the following:

- The risk that donor funds may not reach the budget, being diverted beforehand for unknown or unauthorized purposes. This concern with the flow of funds through the partner country's central bank to the ministry of finance and thus the budget is an explicit aspect of the approach to fiduciary risk taken by the World Bank and previously the European Commission.

- The funds reach the budget but there is no reliable and timely reporting on overall budget execution. Thus donors do not know how (or perhaps even whether) their funds (as part of the budget) have been spent. Poor fiscal reporting is a major PFM deficiency in many countries.[7]
- The funds reach the budget but are misspent, because the budget is not adequately implemented[8]and/or the budget is not sufficiently pro-poor (does not achieve value for money), and/or budget funds (including donor assistance) are used for inappropriate, unauthorized, unknown, or corrupt purposes.

A well-functioning PFM system will reduce the risk of such occurrences.

Other Risk Concepts and Their Relationship with Fiduciary Risk

Fiduciary risk is regarded as separate from *sovereign financial risk*, which is the risk that donor assistance provided in the form of a loan will not be repaid. Sovereign financial risk is a lending risk, but it is assessed differently, through fiscal sustainability analysis and other tools, and is also managed differently.

Another risk identified in all modalities of assistance is *development risk*: the risk that the assistance will not achieve its development objectives of economic growth and poverty reduction. Development risk is a wider concept than fiduciary risk and it is assessed through a broader results-measurement approach than is used for fiduciary risk. In the sense that poor PFM systems will increase development risk, fiduciary risk can be seen as a component of development risk. The definition of fiduciary risk used by the UK Department for International Development, specifically the component "whether the expenditure is likely to achieve value for money" (that is, whether it will reduce poverty), is partly a development risk issue.

Reputational risk arises in all modalities of financial support. This is the risk of perceptions, real or otherwise, of poor management of funds, including corruption. Reputational risk is often perceived as a donor issue, resulting in political costs to donors that may affect their ability to continue budget support, but it is also relevant to partner country governments in their accountability to their own citizens for the management of public finances. Reputational risk thus imposes costs or limitations both on donors and partner countries. Mitigating this type of risk is often the reason for some of the risk mitigation strategies that are required by donors of budget support.

Practical Approaches to Fiduciary Issues in Budget Support

Donors' approaches to assessing fiduciary risks are based on the quality of the PFM and procurement systems, along with appropriate anticorruption diagnostics. There are now generally accepted templates for good PFM and procurement systems, and systematic performance measurement frameworks are being developed to assist in measuring the quality of both these systems.[9]

We now review the approaches to fiduciary issues in budget support of the two donors that provide the most detailed documentation of their approaches: the World Bank and the UK Department for International Development (DFID). Other donors that have documented their approaches include the European Commission, Denmark, and Sweden (Broback and Sjolander 2002; European Commission 2003b; DANIDA 2003).

World Bank

The World Bank's approach to budget support requires an ex ante assessment of the partner country's PFM and public procurement systems. The information for this assessment may come from a variety of sources. The Bank's CFAAs have been a prime source of information. Others are the Bank's public expenditure reviews (PERs) and country procurement assessment reports (CPARs), along with the International Monetary Fund's *Report on Observance of Standards and Codes—Fiscal Transparency Module*, and the joint Bank-IMF expenditure tracking assessments for heavily indebted poor countries (HIPCs). In some cases, diagnostic information from other donors is also used. Bank reviews of these sources shape decisions about individual budget support amounts, tranching, program content, conditionality, and risk mitigation measures.

The Bank has not sought to develop an overall concept of fiduciary risk; its explicit approach to fiduciary risk covers only the financial management risk. The Bank has two prime fiduciary concerns in budget support: that the funds reach the country's budget and that they are appropriately managed as part of the budget resources (World Bank 2004f, 2004g).

The Bank's CFAA guidelines (World Bank 2003c) provide an indicative list of relevant public financial management issues to be examined, while acknowledging that the relative importance of individual issues may depend on the individual country. These guidelines discuss financial management risk as the probability that the PFM system will not provide appropriate management of all public funds. Key factors contributing to this risk are thus PFM systems issues, including the risk that the budget is not implemented as passed, that there are significant off-budget activities, that insufficient information is available on budget implementation, and that the financial control rules are not enforced. Under the CFAA guidelines, the financial risk assessment should draw from an analysis of the overall quality of the PFM system.

The CFAA guidelines discuss financial management risk as one component of overall fiduciary risk, the other components being:

- Procurement risk, which is calculated from an analysis of the public procurement system: the country procurement assessment report (CPAR). The Bank's CPAR procedures (World Bank 2002a) provide for discussion of various risk elements, as discussed further in Section C.

- The risk of misuse of Bank funds through official corruption, which is to be assessed from anticorruption diagnostics carried out by the World Bank and others.

The CFAA approach to fiduciary risk does not include an assessment of whether the expenditure is likely to be appropriately managed, in the sense of achieving value for money or focusing on poverty reduction. While this is an important issue in all the Bank's budget support operations, it is not perceived as a "fiduciary" issue. Instead, it is analyzed through the Bank's PERs and other diagnostic work, and included as appropriate among the policy issues addressed in each budget support operation.

The question of the appropriate management of expenditures is, however, included in the expenditure tracking assessments used for HIPCs (IMF and World Bank 2005). These assessments, carried out jointly by the World Bank and IMF, are a diagnostic tool that provides the ability to track through the PFM system the intended additional pro-poor spending arising from the debt relief granted to HIPCs. To analyze the PFM system, the HIPC assessments use 16 benchmarks, including a measure of whether the budget is pro-poor in its focus.

United Kingdom (DFID)

DFID's approach (DFID 2004b) defines fiduciary risk as the risk that funds:

- are not used for intended purposes;
- do not achieve value for money (economy, efficiency, and effectiveness); and
- are not properly accounted for.

Fiduciary risk is perceived as the measure of uncertainty as to whether the three fiduciary requirements listed above are actually met, and as the combination of both likelihood and impact.

The risk is required to be explicitly discussed, and it must be outweighed by the perceived benefits if the budget support is to proceed. DFID's guidelines indicate that high fiduciary risk does not necessarily preclude the provision of budget support, but that fiduciary risk must be thoroughly evaluated and clearly presented. Deficiencies identified in the PFM system call for a judgment: What impact will individual deficiencies have on the overall quality of the PFM system?

The DFID definition of fiduciary risk is wider than that of the World Bank, specifically in the second aspect listed above. While DFID's PFM assessment is not a direct or substantive assessment of whether value for money (meaning pro-poorness) of expenditures (and revenues) is achieved, DFID's 12 good practice principles and related 15 PFM benchmarks include the extent to which the budget supports pro-poor strategies.[10] Thus the DFID approach analyzes the operation of the PFM system in terms of its pro-poor focus, asking whether the PFM *system* provides for an adequate focus on poverty reduction. However, it does not involve any substantive analysis of the pro-poorness of budget expenditures.

B. Issues in Fiduciary Risk

Procurement

The functioning of the public procurement system is obviously important in all the possible components of fiduciary risk discussed above, given that in many partner countries a high proportion of budget expenditures flows through the public procurement system. In this sense the procurement system is an integral part of the PFM system. But in practice procurement operates as a professional activity somewhat separate from the rest of the PFM system. Different professional groups within donor countries and donor institutions manage the diagnostic or analytical work on country procurement systems, including developmental work to improve country procurement systems. Likewise in international work on donor and country harmonization and alignment, PFM and procurement issues tend to be covered by separate working groups.[11]

The World Bank has a separate diagnostic tool for public procurement systems: the CPAR (World Bank 2002a). A CPAR is designed to provide a comprehensive analysis of a country's public procurement system; assess institutional, organizational, and other risks associated with procurement; develop a prioritized plan for institutional improvements; assess the competitiveness and performance of the country's private sector in its involvement in public procurement; and gauge the adequacy of commercial practices related to public procurement. Past CPARs have mainly focused on assessing the acceptability of country public procurement systems for use in Bank-financed investment projects, and their discussion of risk is still largely couched in terms of such projects. However, the usefulness of procurement assessments in decision making about budget support operations is now also recognized, from both a developmental and a fiduciary perspective.

The World Bank's CPAR procedures (World Bank 2002a) discuss fiduciary risk issues in some detail. A central feature of the CPAR is the evaluation of different risks associated with the country's procurement system. The risks to be managed are:

- loss of economy and efficiency in procurement (recall that this is outside the scope of fiduciary risk, as defined in the CFAA guidelines);
- exclusion of certain eligible bidders from competing for bids;
- unfair and inequitable treatment of suppliers and contractors; and
- lack of integrity, fairness, and public confidence in the procurement system.

The CPAR procedures require a risk assessment that indicates whether the procurement risks are high, medium, or low, but they do not advise on how to assess the level of risk. Most CPARs lack an explicit discussion of procurement risks in relation to budget support operations.

Other diagnostic work by donors on PFM covers procurement issues. DFID's Guidelines (DFID 2004b) include a good practice principle on procurement: this states that procurement is carried out in line with principles of value for money, covering two benchmarks on procurement issues, that feed into its overall risk assessment. The HIPC tracking indicators have recently been expanded to include a benchmark on effective procurement—which is described as promoting competition, transparency, and value for money in procurement—but, as previously mentioned, the judgment on procurement quality is not part of an explicit risk assessment. The PFM performance measurement framework now being finalized by the Public Expenditure Working Group of the World Bank, IMF, and the Public Expenditure and Financial Accountability (PEFA) program incorporates a measure of the performance of the procurement system. In addition, the World Bank has been developing more detailed indicators to evaluate a country's public procurement system, as part of a move to pilot the increased use of country systems in the investment operations the Bank finances.

Thus procurement issues are identified as part of the information base to be used in assessing fiduciary risk, but no methodology has yet been developed for explicitly assessing fiduciary risk.

Corruption

Clearly, if official corruption is present it will affect the functioning of the PFM and procurement systems, whether through diversion of funds or in some other way, and will affect the level of fiduciary risk. Both the World Bank's CFAA guidelines and the DFID guidance mention the need to use anticorruption diagnostic information in decisions on budget support operations. The CFAA guidelines mention focusing on those aspects of the PFM system that may be most likely to facilitate corruption—for example, nontransparent off-budget accounts or a failure to observe internal controls. DFID requires an explicit statement on corruption information as part of the information base for decisions on budget support operations, although it does not require any explicit corruption risk rating.

The World Bank's revised CPAR procedures also address corruption issues by requiring a review of transparency and accountability in the procurement system. Issues examined include the existence or otherwise of a code of ethics for government employees, adequacy of procedures for reporting bribes, adequacy of access to administrative review and appeal, and other measures and initiatives to curb or control corruption, including legislation.

Flow of Funds

Under budget support arrangements, foreign exchange is provided by the donor to the partner country's central bank, and is generally converted into local currency and credited to a government account that forms part of budget funds and is held at the central bank. The ultimate use of the foreign exchange cannot be traced, given the fungibility of the country's foreign exchange reserves.

The risk that donor funds for budget support might not reach the budget is discussed extensively in World Bank good practice guidance on development policy lending (World Bank 2004f). The Bank does not seek to assess the appropriateness of the use of the foreign exchange.[12] Rather its approach is to review—based on the IMF safeguards assessments of central banks (where available)—the control environment within which the country manages the foreign exchange.

Where the review indicates potential weaknesses, or where information is inadequate, the Bank can use several risk mitigation strategies. These include deposit of the Bank's loan proceeds into a dedicated account at the central bank that is used exclusively for this operation, with the possibility also of an audit of the dedicated account. The purpose is to ensure that the amount has been correctly transferred to a government account that forms part of the budget and/or to ensure that payments from such an account were (or were not) made for specified purposes.

C. Using PFM Diagnostic Information

Different donors will tolerate different amounts of fiduciary risk in order to undertake budget support. Some may wish to set minimum PFM and procurement standards. Others may prefer to focus on a trajectory of change for commitment to and achievement of improvements in PFM and procurement systems. But it now seems generally agreed that all should draw from the same information base on the partner country's PFM system, which should be developed collaboratively between donors with the country's participation and ownership to the greatest extent possible.[13]

The World Bank has articulated its general approach to the use of PFM diagnostic information as follows (World Bank 2004f):

- No minimum PFM standard has been established as a precondition for budget support.
- Budget support may be provided in a country with weak PFM where there is government commitment to an adequate PFM reform plan and there is reasonable evidence that improvements are occurring in a timely manner.
- Thus improved PFM may be an outcome of, rather than a precondition for, budget support.

The diagnostic information feeds into Bank decisions about the size of individual budget support operations, tranching, program content, conditionality, and risk mitigation measures. Other donors might also address these issues, in which case the Bank need not duplicate the effort.

Recommendations that may arise from the risk assessment might include the following for a proposed budget support operation:

- integrating more fully into the operation actions to deal with known PFM weaknesses;
- where adequate information on the operation of the PFM system is not yet available, delaying the operation until adequate information is available;
- reducing the size of the operation;

- having a programmatic operation, to "ratchet up" any PFM conditions at each successive stage; and
- not proceeding with the operation.

A further possible decision is at what point to withdraw budget support because of increased fiduciary concerns. This raises the question of the design of conditionality. It seems generally agreed that the relevant conditions should be clear and the circumstances under which budget support might be withdrawn should be transparent and understood by all parties. For example, the UK National Audit Office has suggested that DFID should develop criteria for this and early warning indicators (National Audit Office [NAO] 2002).

D. Measuring and Calibrating Fiduciary Risk

The generally accepted view is that assessing fiduciary risk necessarily involves judgment rather than finely calibrated risk measurements, and that the judgment is country specific. Different approaches are in use.

The World Bank's CFAA guidelines (World Bank 2003c) call for risk to be assessed on a four-part scale: low, medium, significant, and high. They suggest that the overall assessment should focus on a few key factors and should be a relatively brief summary of the reasons underlying it. Detailed guidance on using the scale is not provided, and a recent review by the Bank (World Bank 2004h) found considerable variations in approach. Of the 31 CFAAs or equivalent that were reviewed for this paper, financial management risk was assessed as high in 13 countries, significant in 8, moderate in 3, and low in only 1. Six of the CFAAs contained no explicit risk assessment.

DFID's guidelines (DFID 2004b, paras. 58–63) provide for an overall risk rating using a three-part scale: low risk, where there are no significant weaknesses in compliance; medium risk, where there are some significant weaknesses; and high risk, where there is substantial failure to comply. The scale is applied "on a conservative basis" to each of 15 PFM benchmarks. Because of its perceived complexity, the rating process is not perceived as an exact science. Like the CFAA guidelines, those of DFID set no explicit criteria for the use of the rating scale. To supplement the formal risk assessment, a "trajectory of change" (indicating whether the situation is improving or not) is noted for each benchmark, along with a statement on risks of corruption and information on PFM and procurement reform plans and improvements. Thus for decisions on financial assistance, DFID supplements its formal risk assessment with a judgment on country commitment to PFM reform.

The HIPC expenditure tracking assessment, while not a formal fiduciary risk assessment, uses 16 benchmarks, as noted earlier, to rate countries' PFM systems on a three-part scale: those needing little upgrading (meeting at least 11 of the 16 benchmarks); needing some upgrading (meeting 8 to 10 of the benchmarks); and needing substantial upgrading (meeting 7 or fewer of the benchmarks) (IMF and World Bank 2005). A donor wishing to set a minimum standard of eligibility for budget support might consider using a standard based on a country's performance in meeting some or all of these 16 benchmarks.

A Comprehensive Performance Measurement Framework

Recent work by the Public Expenditure Working Group (comprising PEFA, the World Bank, and the IMF) has focused on developing a comprehensive PFM performance measurement framework that is consistent with the overall move to a greater results focus in development operations and a harmonized approach broadly acceptable to all donors and partner countries (World Bank 2005t). Building on the HIPC indicators, the working group has developed some 28 indicators, including on procurement. The indicators have been tested in a number of countries for clarity of definition and discussed at a workshop organized by PEFA for country officials in Africa. In general, they have been well accepted as relevant and useful.

The working group proposed a system of calibration for each indicator. However, there is as yet no clear consensus on the calibration and "scoring" mechanism that might be applied to such indicators. In particular, discussions are still in progress on how or whether to use an overall summary measure to represent the quality of the PFM system, and on whether the assessment should be a narrative or numerical or otherwise quantitative one.

If numbers are attached to individual indicators there may be a tendency to add them up, with or without some explicit weighting of each indicator, and to play a complex but ultimately subjective numbers game, possibly encouraging a minimum PFM standards approach. Some countries, particularly middle-income countries with access to private capital markets, express concern that the PFM performance measurement framework would become a de facto rating system, with comparisons being made among the "scores" of individual countries. These countries stress the need to recognize differences in country circumstances that would affect the relative importance of individual indicators and the necessarily subjective nature of some of the judgments. But the risks of possible misuse (or perhaps overuse) of such performance information are lessened if the framework focuses as intended on whether a country's PFM system is improving over time.

There also appear to be some concerns about possible complexity and over-engineering of the performance measurement framework, and whether the situation conveyed is sufficiently dynamic, recognizing the change trajectory rather than absolute positions.

Focusing on Key Areas of Potential Risk

Given the principle that the best fiduciary assurance comes from a well-performing PFM system, an overall measure of the quality of the PFM system is clearly closely linked with the overall fiduciary risk assessment. However, it differs from the risk assessment, not only because it excludes the funds flow component of fiduciary risk but also because it may not focus explicitly on key areas of fiduciary risk, which may vary among countries.

Recognizing this, the DFID guidance refers to the need to identify key or priority areas of risk. For example, if a substantial proportion of a country's budget spending relates to the civil service payroll, or to public procurement, greater attention should be paid to the payroll and public procurement systems. DFID also identifies large transfers to state-owned enterprises, significant decentralization of resources to subnational governments, and major sources of revenue such as oil revenues, as potential high-risk areas needing more detailed attention. The Bank's CFAA guidelines, for their part, highlight extrabudgetary funds with little or no transparency concerning their operations as another potential key area of risk, which is likely to differ significantly between countries.

E. Strategies to Manage and Mitigate Fiduciary Risk

Actions by the partner country (reflecting mutual accountability) are important in mitigating fiduciary risk. The key medium- to long-term strategy to mitigate fiduciary risk is to work with the country to have it lead a comprehensive agenda for PFM and procurement reform, with donors providing coordinated technical assistance as necessary. This is the development side of the PFM coin. Meanwhile, certain donors use shorter-term measures to mitigate fiduciary risk. In this section we deal with each in turn, before looking at the European Community's audit-based approach.

PFM Improvement Plans: the Longer-Term View

There is now a considerable body of experience with partner country PFM and procurement reform action plans, not all of which is good. Problems include an overloaded reform agenda, with too many separate action plans and too many individual components; reforms that outstrip the country's capacity; donor competition rather than collaboration on technical assistance; and lack of country ownership. Many of these experiences have been distilled into recently issued good practice notes on PFM and procurement capacity development (OECD-DAC 2004a, 2004d, 2005b). Experience also suggests that PFM improvement requires time, and that different components need appropriate sequencing.

A study commissioned by PEFA (Brooks 2003) reviews practices across 17 multilateral and bilateral agencies and outlines a "platform" approach to a PFM reform program to address the perceived problem of diverse and uncoordinated and unrealistic donor reform plans and requirements, some of which may originate from donor conditions for providing financial assistance. The study suggests identifying various platforms of key requirements on which subsequent reforms may build, in effect providing the building block for a sequenced reform program.

DFID (2004b) discusses in some detail the need for a credible program to improve PFM and recommends that its components should:

- be government led, realistic, and achievable;
- contain a comprehensive, effectively sequenced framework;

- be relevant and sustainable;
- focus on developing local capacity;
- build demand for change; and
- include specific performance indicators.

To this list could be added the need to assess real government ownership. This may be reflected by:

- a good track record in implementing reforms, particularly in areas that might be particularly difficult either technically or politically;
- reform proposals initiated by the government;
- publicly stated political support for reforms; and
- government leadership in coordinating the technical assistance of a range of donors.

Audit and Other Shorter-Term Approaches

The PEFA study (Brooks 2003) identifies 60 to 70 different shorter-term approaches to mitigating fiduciary risk that have been adopted by a range of donors. Some are reflected in the conditions for budget support, and some are suggested or required by donors' national audit institutions.

One such approach is to "deem" or earmark budget support to particular purposes. For example, under a previous DFID approach, budget support funds were linked to certain budget line items, so as to protect these items—for example, civil service salaries, other designated "pro-poor" expenditures, or repayment of debt. In some cases DFID required an audit by an external party to verify that the relevant expenditures had been incurred. A variant of this approach involves the creation of separate poverty funds within the budget into which donor assistance is paid. But while this expedient may be important to sustaining political support for budget support and reducing reputational risk, its real impact is limited, particularly because budget resources are fungible. Indeed, the 2003 PEFA study suggests that such short-term safeguards are often fragmented and ineffective in providing substantive fiduciary assurance; while recognizing the fiduciary concerns of donors it suggests that these concerns cannot be solved immediately and that implicit acceptance of a degree of risk is necessary.

Another of the shorter-term approaches is to adopt a "negative list" concept, under which budget support funds are somehow divorced from perceived non-"pro-poor" budgetary expenditures such as those on internal security or defense. The World Bank maintains such a "negative list" in its new policy for development policy lending (DPL). Although clearly the fungibility of budget resources makes it problematic to implement, such a list can help mitigate reputational risk. A review of the operation of the negative list by the Bank indicated that "it has been very difficult to track the use of adjustment loan proceeds beyond the initial receipt of funds."[14] The Bank's new DPL policy does not address the inherent contradiction between a negative list and fungibility, but it has removed the previous option of an attestation of non-expenditure on ineligible items in any audit of the deposit account.

A third approach is to undertake public expenditure tracking surveys (PETS), which analyze the extent to which budgeted funds actually reach the intended point of local service delivery as opposed to being properly or improperly diverted. Evidence suggests a dramatic improvement in the rate of budget execution at the local level when the budget allocations for local service delivery units are made public. PETS also have other objectives, such as improving service delivery arrangements.

Some donors of budget support require countries to implement specific controls or new legislation, either to meet specific concerns of individual donors and capacity enhancement requirements or to address a specific deficiency of concern to the particular donor. Both these types of requirements may contribute to the problem of uncoordinated and unrealistic PFM improvement plans.

In principle, another way to mitigate fiduciary risk is to require timely audited aggregate financial statements (focusing on budget execution) from the partner country as a condition of budget support. This is a way to address the risk component of not knowing how the budget support was spent. But in practice, as mentioned above, few partner countries are yet able to provide such statements. And a 2000 proposal that such a requirement be part of World Bank policy for budget support was rejected by the Bank's board of directors, apparently because it was perceived as unnecessarily intrusive.

Donors increasingly recognize the need to move away from short-term and fragmented approaches to focus on longer-term developmental objectives through government-led reform PFM programs. Yet there is still a pattern of fragmented and partial measures, with little coordination among donors and even within individual donor organizations, and this may undermine the development of realistically sequenced PFM reform programs (Brooks 2003).

The European Commission Approach

The EC has previously required ex post audits of its budget support operations, although the focus is now changing. These audits, carried out by a firm contracted by the EC, assessed the country's PFM system. They focused on the legality and regularity of expenditures in terms of the agreement between the EC and the country concerned. In the cases of "targeted" budget support, which sought to protect social expenditures, EC funds were paid into a separate account with the EC and the country authorities as dual signatories. Audits reviewed the extent to which the EC funds were managed in accordance with the country's budget rules and procedures. To the extent that the funds covered in the audit sample were not spent in accordance with the agreement or managed in accordance with the country's own systems, the assistance would have to be repaid, or at least treated as an advance against subsequent assistance.

This system often involved significant transaction costs and delays. The EC has now moved to place greater emphasis on ex ante assessments of the overall PFM system, working in collaboration with other donors (European Commission 2003b); for example, it has been a major participant in the PEFA program. The assessment of the PFM system is intended to be complemented by a compliance test, to provide evidence of the functioning of the country's PFM system and in some cases the quality of public expenditures.

The Influence of Donor Oversight Institutions

It appears to be generally accepted that fiduciary issues should be clearly explained to and discussed with donor legislatures and external audit institutions, in order to develop and maintain political support for budget support.[15]

Because of the perceived riskiness of budget support, the European Parliament and the EU Court of Auditors appear to have taken a strong interest in the EC's budget support operations, as indicated by a number of special reports (for example, European Commission 2001) and to have influenced the EC's approach to fiduciary issues, outlined above. In some cases it appears that special audits have been undertaken at the request of parliaments.[16]

F. Is Budget Support Improving PFM?

The first question to be asked here is whether PFM systems are improving in partner countries. Answering this question is difficult, and attributing any improvements to budget support operations is even more difficult. The discussion below therefore represents a tentative approach to this issue.

Is PFM Improving in Partner Countries?

The most systematic review of improvements in PFM across a range of countries appears to be the updates on the assessments and implementation of action plans under the HIPC expenditure-tracking exercise. The most recent review, of changes since March 2002 across 24 HIPC, shows a mixed picture of performance across countries and indicators, but with some improvement overall (IMF and World Bank 2005). The average number of benchmarks met per country rose slightly, though substantial improvement is still required. Budget reporting showed the largest improvement, but performance under budget formulation and execution was more limited or marginal. The same review also indicates progress since 2002 in implementing countries' action plans for improving PFM. Well-targeted action plans, with partner country commitment and coordinated donor systems, appear to be effective in improving PFM performance. Procurement systems in HIPCs were found to be weak, with no country meeting the new procurement benchmark. Because this was a new indicator, there were no prior years' ratings against which to judge performance.

The HIPC indicators have also been applied in a number of non-HIPC, but no follow-up reviews have been done in these cases to indicate whether improvements are occurring.

The World Bank's annual country policy and institutional assessment (CPIA) exercise measures the quality of budgetary and financial management as one of 20 components in an overall assessment that is used in determining the allocation of funds under IDA. CPIA preliminary assessments for 2004, which cover more than 130 client countries, indicate improvement in 40 countries, deterioration in 14, and no change in the rest. While the final assessments are likely to be somewhat lower, overall there is an indication of progress on PFM.

The Declaration from the Paris High-Level Forum on Harmonization, Alignment, Results, and Mutual Accountability commits the donor and partner country community to the use of a series of indicators of progress, which include "increases in the number of partner countries that have procurement and public financial management systems that either (a) adhere to broadly accepted good practices or (b) have a reform program in place to achieve these" (High-Level Forum 2005, p. 9).

The Impact of Budget Support Operations

Improvements in PFM and procurement systems are sought through the use of conditions and benchmarks in budget support operations and associated capacity development activities. Recent reviews of such World Bank conditionality (for example, Koeberle 2003), feeding into the new policy on budget support, have suggested that:

- conditionality cannot substitute for country ownership;
- conditionality needs to be used more selectively and tailored to country circumstances; and
- a move to ex post rather than ex ante conditionality is desirable (reflecting greater reliance on programmatic operations).

These comments apply also to PFM and procurement conditions and benchmarks. The World Bank's guidelines on the design of budget support operations (World Bank 2004i) suggest:

- Select a limited number of conditions and triggers (which should be within the government's control).
- Be more liberal in the use of milestones that indicate the progress of the operation but do not constitute legally binding conditions.
- As the program progresses, make benchmarks more outcome-focused and modify them appropriately.

Overall in the Bank's budget support operations, PFM- and procurement-related conditions and benchmarks accounted for some 14 percent of total conditions and benchmarks over the period 2001 to 2005, ranging from 17 percent in 2004 to 10 percent in 2005.

Budget support through the Bank's poverty reduction support credits (PRSCs) is appropriate for separate review because of the programmatic nature of these credits, involving the phasing of reforms over a period of years as part of a medium-term reform program. Programmatic PFM-related benchmarks have covered a range of issues, including budget preparation, budget execution, accounting and reporting, auditing, and external oversight. PFM-related conditions include legal conditions of effectiveness, prior actions, conditions for presentation of the proposed operation to the Bank's board, and conditions for release of tranches. PFM-related conditions and policy actions were 19 percent of all conditions in FY01–04 PRSCs, and their share rose continuously during the period. (PFM-related conditions were 9 percent of all conditions in FY01, rising to 21 percent in FY04.) As well as conditions, PRSCs included policy actions that are not legally binding but were included in the policy matrix to describe the government's program. Of the 937 policy actions in these PRSCs, 182 were related to PFM and 41 to procurement.

Some of these conditions and benchmarks have been legal or regulatory; they include the passing of laws or regulations. Others have been more institutional, such as improvements in information systems, the introduction of medium-term expenditure frameworks, and new budget classifications. It is now generally thought that (like many other conditions and benchmarks on PFM and procurement) they have been oriented too much to process and not enough to results. However, it can be argued that process measures are appropriate at earlier stages of operations, and that measures of results should be factored into the later stages when results should be expected to emerge.

While it is still premature to judge how much poverty reduction support credits are contributing to improvements in PFM and procurement systems, some tentative observations can be made for those countries that have had several phases of PRSCs. The HIPC expenditure-tracking assessment indicates the following changes for countries having multiyear PRSCs (Table 2.1).

Improvements through PRSCs are also reflected in countries' performance on the conditions that have been legally required to be met at each phase of the PRSC. These conditions have focused mainly on process issues such as passing legislation, completing reports, or publishing data. Desirably such conditions are based on a clear assessment of what key PFM performance improvements will result from them in the medium term, but this may not always have been the case. PRSC conditions have put heavy emphasis on budget preparation issues, and to a lesser extent on accounting, reporting, and audit issues, and arguably insufficient emphasis on budget execution.

TABLE 2.1 Progress in Meeting PFM and Procurement Benchmarks

Total benchmarks met	2001	2004
Burkina Faso	8	9
Ethiopia	6	7
Ghana	1	7
Tanzania	8	11
Uganda	9	8

Note: Assessments done in 2001 used 15 benchmarks and those done in 2004 used 16.
Source: World Bank HIPC expenditure-tracking assessments, as reported in 2002 and 2005.

Endnotes

1. Budget support operations include sector budget support and budget support to subnational governments, where this support is intended to be managed through the recipient country's own systems for public financial management and procurement.
2. For example, there is no explicit discussion of fiduciary issues in the 2003 *Evaluation of General Budget Support, Evaluation Framework*, Overseas Development Institute, February 2002, prepared for a group of donors.
3. For example, both the United Kingdom and the Netherlands stress the importance of their operational staff understanding PFM issues. The DFID has a program for training of staff through "How-to Notes" (so far produced on Direct Budget Support and Supreme Audit Institutions), and the Netherlands has a PFM Support Program to train embassy staff in PFM issues. In its 2004 review of issues in PFM assessment and reform (Allen, Schiavo-Campo, and Garrity 2004), PEFA recommended that governments and donors should agree on how to define fiduciary risk, and that the role of assessments in evaluating fiduciary risk and contributing to long-term development goals should be clarified. PEFA is a partnership between the World Bank, the EC, the DFID, the Swiss State Secretariat for Economic Affairs, the French Ministry of Foreign Affairs, the Royal Norwegian Ministry of Foreign Affairs, the IMF, and the Strategic Partnership with Africa. See www.pefa.org.
4. See Allen, Schiavo-Campo, and Garrity (2004) and OECD (2003) for a description of this range of work.
5. The Declaration from the Paris High-Level Forum on Harmonization, Alignment, Results, and Mutual Accountability includes a commitment by partner countries to take the lead in the reform of PFM and procurement systems (High-level Forum 2005).
6. Allen and others (2004) suggested that consideration should be given to splitting the development (improving PFM systems) and fiduciary (assessing the quality of PFM systems to determine the likelihood that funds will be appropriately managed, as input to decisions on budget support operations) aspects of PFM assessments into separate processes and reports, while recognizing that they are both looking at the same issues. It now appears that donors have not accepted this approach.
7. The 2004 HIPC expenditure-tracking assessment indicated that only 28 percent of countries were able to produce audited financial statements within 12 months of the end of the fiscal year. However, this was the major area of PFM improvement revealed by this assessment—up from 18 percent in the previous assessment (2002). It can be noted that an International Public Sector Accounting Standard on Disclosure Requirements for Recipients of External Assistance is currently under development by the International Public Sector Accounting Standards Board, at the request of the donor community.
8. This covers the situation where donors are required to ensure that their funds are "used for the purposes for which they were intended," such as applies under the World Bank's Articles. The formal budget is thus perceived as representing "intended purposes."
9. The activities of the Public Expenditure Working Group (World Bank, PEFA, and IMF) and the OECD-DAC Procurement Roundtable are of particular note here.
10. These principles and benchmarks are to be used pending agreement between donors and partner countries on a common set of PFM performance indicators. See Section D.
11. This is well illustrated by the separate OECD-DAC Joint Venture on Public Financial Management and the OECD-DAC Procurement Roundtable.
12. This is perceived as an IMF issue.

13. See OECD-DAC (2003) and Allen and others (2004). Both these documents discuss the need for donor collaboration to reduce the number of separate PFM diagnostics, both to improve the quality of diagnostic work and to reduce transaction costs to donors and partner countries.
14. The discussion continues: "One option would be to recognize this reality and simply eliminate the requirement for a negative list. This may however expose the Bank to reputational risks. . . . The preferred option is therefore to retain the borrower's undertaking in the legal agreement that it will not use adjustment loan proceeds to finance items on the negative list. This option should however be based on a clear understanding of the limits in monitoring and enforcing such a requirement. Basically such an undertaking would serve as a self-implementing 'code of conduct'. . ." (World Bank [2004e], p. 29).
15. The PEFA review refers to short-term measures, some of which have been suggested or required by donor national audit institutions.
16. For example, the UK National Audit Office (NAO) has closely reviewed DFID's approach to fiduciary risk management in budget support. Its special report on this issue (NAO 2002) commends DFID for the publication of its March 2003 paper, "Managing Fiduciary Risk when Providing Direct Budget Support," and indicates the NAO's willingness to contribute to DFID's work in developing its approach to mitigating fiduciary risk.

PART II
Recent Evaluations of Budget Support

3

Poverty Reduction Support Credits (PRSCs): A Stocktaking

JOHN M. FACTORA
World Bank

The World Bank introduced poverty reduction support credits (PRSCs) in May 2001 as one of IDA's main vehicles to support low-income countries in implementing their poverty reduction strategy papers (PRSPs). The PRSC is a programmatic approach to development policy lending (DPL) in low-income countries; it typically consists of three or four annual, single-tranche operations, phased to support the government's medium-term development objectives. It embodies the Bank's contribution to the emerging use of budget support, which is commonly understood to mean the provision of financial assistance directly to a partner country's budget on a regular basis, using the country's own financial management systems and budget procedures.

The PRSC's overarching goal of bolstering the PRSP approach, and particularly of reinforcing the country ownership embedded in the initiative, was intended to be achieved through several mutually reinforcing objectives:

- *Operationalize and implement PRSPs* to help implement a medium-term program that builds upon and draws from the PRSP's priorities and objectives.
- *Improve resource predictability* through medium-term annual commitments that are disbursed in line with domestic planning, budgeting, and review processes.
- *Harmonize aid* to provide a framework for countries' coordination with development partners, particularly with the International Monetary Fund (IMF), through its Poverty Reduction and Growth Facility (PRGF), and other budget support donors.

From FY01 to FY05, the World Bank's Executive Board approved 38 PRSCs to 22 countries, committing approximately US$3.3 billion to support PRSP implementation (Table 3.1). About 60 percent of PRSC operations and commitments, and half of all PRSC countries, have been in Sub-Saharan Africa. Within IDA's development policy lending, the share of PRSCs has grown steadily and by FY05, PRSCs accounted for nearly 53 percent of the operations and 61 percent of the commitments. For IDA as a whole, however, investment lending is still the dominant financing instrument, making up about 80 percent of total IDA operations and nearly 75 percent of total IDA commitments.

TABLE 3.1 PRSC Countries and Commitments, FY01–05

($ million)

Region	Country	PRSC 1	PRSC 2	PRSC 3	PRSC 4	PRSC 5	Total	% Total
AFR	Benin	20	30				50	2
	Burkina Faso	45	35	50	60	60	250	8
	Cape Verde	15					15	0.5
	Ethiopia	120	130				250	8
	Ghana	125	125				250	8
	Madagascar	125					125	4
	Mozambique	60					60	2
	Rwanda	65					65	2
	Senegal	30					30	1
	Tanzania	132	150				282	9
	Uganda	150	150	150	150		600	18
	AFR total	887	620	200	210	60	1,977	61
EAP	Lao PDR	10					10	0.3
	Vietnam	250	100	100	100		550	17
	EAP total	260	100	100	100		560	17
ECA	Albania	20	18	10			48	1
	Armenia	20					20	1
	Azerbaijan	20					20	1
	ECA total	60	18	10			88	3
LAC	Guyana	12					12	0.4
	Honduras	59					59	2
	Nicaragua	70					70	2
	LAC total	141					141	4
SAR	Nepal	70					70	2
	Pakistan	300					300	9
	Sri Lanka	125					125	4
	SAR total	495					495	15
	Grand total	**1,843**	**738**	**310**	**310**	**60**	**3,261**	**100**

Source: World Bank SAP Business Warehouse.

Note: AFR = Africa; EAP = East Asia and the Pacific; ECA = Europe and Central Asia; LAC = Latin America and the Caribbean; SAR = Southeast Asia.

The World Bank recently reviewed the experience with PRSC implementation. Although only a few years have elapsed since the PRSC was introduced, the review was done at a critical juncture in the PRSP initiative and the Bank's support to it. Several countries that have completed their first-generation PRSP and associated PRSC series are now taking stock of implementation experience to guide their next medium-term strategy. The Bank is also looking to initiate PRSC programs in countries new to the PRSP, and lessons learned from the past four years are expected to help shape these programs. Moreover, while budget support has become a prominent means of delivering development assistance, there are some reservations within the donor community about its efficacy and ability to achieve medium- and long-term development goals.

Operational lessons will continue to evolve as the Bank gains more experience. This paper outlines the main findings of the review. It gauges the extent to which the PRSC has made progress in achieving its objectives and original expectations, and highlights emerging trends, lessons learned, operational challenges, and evolving good practice. Section A discusses the extent to which PRSCs have helped to operationalize and implement PRSPs. Section B looks at the alignment of PRSCs with the priorities reflected in countries' poverty reduction strategies (PRSs). Section C looks at their record in fostering donor harmonization and resource predictability, and Section D concludes.

A. Operationalizing the PRSP

PRSPs are comprehensive documents that attempt to diagnose constraints on, and outline strategies for, sustainable growth and poverty alleviation. They provide the central framework for government and donor partnerships in low-income countries, but they often have major weaknesses that make their implementation difficult: for example, they may not develop sector and thematic strategies sufficiently, they may lack an operational blueprint for implementation, or they may not be well linked to underlying analytical work, budget priorities, and broader objectives (World Bank and IMF 2003). Nearly 67 percent of joint staff assessments (JSAs)/joint staff advisory notes (JSANs) for PRSC countries note the need for greater elaboration of underlying strategies; 72 percent for costing and financing scenarios; and 85 percent for greater specificity, prioritization, and sequencing of time-bound actions. Since the PRSP process is dynamic it allows changes to be made to improve the operational framework of the strategy. PRSCs have proven to be an integral part of this process, focusing the policy dialogue to address these shortcomings and, in effect, making PRSPs more fully operational.

Elaborating Strategies

Gathering sector programs and strategies under one strategic framework allows stakeholders to understand the multidimensional constraints on development. For many capacity-constrained countries, formulating these strategies is a challenging task. While some PRSPs build upon strong sectorwide approaches, particularly in education and health, strategies for other areas have been more uneven and require greater elaboration (OED 2004a). The Bank provides technical support and analysis to help countries strengthen their sector and thematic strategies. The policy dialogue associated with the PRSC has also helped, by introducing specific benchmarks and measures in the policy matrix that help focus government attention.

In many cases, the aim is to accelerate a sector's readiness for program lending. For example, in Ethiopia, policy dialogue leading up to the PRSC focused on making progress on the government's rural development and private sector development strategies. The PRSC also helped to accelerate a sectorwide program in rural water supply in Madagascar, a public sector reform strategy in Ghana, a rural development strategy in Mozambique, a water and sanitation strategy in Nicaragua, and a health sector development plan in Burkina Faso. Bank analytical and diagnostic work in public financial management (PFM) has underpinned the reform agendas in this area for all PRSC countries, providing specific recommendations to address key issues.

Policy Matrices as Performance Frameworks

PRSPs have been charged with multiple expectations that have resulted in tensions and challenges for governments and donors alike. On the one hand, they are expected to be comprehensive documents that provide an over-arching framework for development. On the other hand, they are expected to be operationally relevant, with specific implementation plans and links to budgets. Few of them provide the level of operational detail that specifies how objectives are to be achieved through policy actions. Where an implementation plan or program matrix is included, it normally takes the form of a long list of actions across a wide range of areas, leaving the intended focus of the strategy unclear. The PRSPs often fail to prioritize, sequence, and establish a timeline of actions that are vital to achieving medium-term objectives. These problems often limit the operational usefulness of the PRSP to both national authorities and development partners (World Bank 2003a, p. 42).

The Bank and other donors have used several approaches to help make PRSPs more operational. The most common is to develop an annualized medium-term operational plan that contains specific policy measures[1] negotiated with government by donors and based on, but independent from, the PRSP itself. In Nicaragua, Uganda, and Vietnam, the PRSC policy matrix acts as the implementation plan for several budget support donors. In Cape Verde, Ethiopia, Ghana, Mozambique, Tanzania, and many other African countries, this matrix is identical to or is a subset of the common donor matrix (often referred to as the performance assessment framework, or PAF), which itself draws upon the PRSP and its objectives. The European Union and several bilateral donors, while including policy measures in PFM, generally focus on output and outcome indicators. Their experience has been similar to the Bank's: key indicators and annual targets are typically negotiated with governments, given their absence from many PRSPs.

While these approaches have the clear advantage of filling the PRSP's operational gaps and clarifying criteria for budget support disbursement, they have also prompted discussion over country ownership, conditionality, and mutual accountability. In several countries, differing donor approaches to budget support have also resulted in challenges to donor harmonization.

The PRSC policy matrix summarizes the programmatic alignment with the PRSP. It sets out key indicative reform measures in an annual, flexible, medium-term framework that is sequenced with the PRSP and linked to measurable outcomes. While policy matrices are not formally required, they have emerged as a broad reference framework and a management tool for the government and its development partners. The design of the policy matrix provides stakeholders with a transparent understanding of the scope, logical sequence, and expected results of the government's measures, and allows them to keep track of progress made (World Bank 2004b). The matrix presents the set of:

- binding measures upon which disbursement decisions are made;
- other measures, or indicative benchmarks, that are not binding but comprise key components of the policy agenda;
- triggers, or expected actions, that determine whether enough progress has been made to warrant the continuation of the program; and
- outcome indicators over the entire PRSC period.

The components of the program are typically organized by broad policy area, with measures presented in a way that shows a logical sequence of reform from year one to year three. However, the policy matrix is not designed to be static. It is an integral part of a step-by-step, flexible process that takes account of changes in the reform program.

The natural starting point for designing the policy matrix is the PRSP itself. A recent survey conducted by the Strategic Partnership with Africa (SPA 2005) indicates that while very few binding measures in budget support programs for Africa are drawn directly from the PRSP, most come partly from the PRSP and partly from other government documents. Typically, the designers of the matrix—the government, the Bank, and other donors—need to make hard choices in prioritizing, refining, elaborating on, and adding to the policy actions contained in the PRSP, based on policy dialogue and underlying analytical and diagnostic work. The policy dialogue with the government is critical in gauging what is realistic in terms of timing, sequencing, and government commitment, given capacity constraints, lessons learned, political considerations, and available analytical work. The ideal product should be a single policy framework that builds on the PRSP, is developed by government with donor support, and promotes domestic accountability.

Typically, the policy and institutional measures in a PRSC program are drawn from, or elaborate on, a subset of the PRSP. They derive from a negotiated process with government, based on a shared understanding of the actions needed to achieve the country's development objectives. In countries where the PRSC is part of a harmonized multidonor framework, negotiations on policy measures are typically done multilaterally. In most cases, shared understanding has translated into strong government ownership. However, several governments and some donors view these measures as excessively intrusive, perceiving them as negotiated more like traditional conditionality, and not reflective of government views on the proper pace, timing, or priorities of the reform program.

Twenty years of adjustment lending conditionality have shown that country ownership plays a critical role in sustainable reform implementation (World Bank 2001a). In light of this experience, the Bank has moved away from ex ante conditionality to support reform measures that the government is committed to (Koeberle 2003; World Bank 2004b). In PRSCs specifically, the Bank envisaged that focusing on actions already implemented—that is, using ex post conditionality—would provide a pragmatic way to balance, and ultimately reconcile, the tension between country ownership and donors' need for due diligence and results. In practice, however, the distinction between ex ante and ex post conditions may not always be clear, especially for subsequent PRSC operations where future policy measures are identified as "triggers" for future support. World Bank teams acknowledge that the tension between country ownership on the one hand and due diligence and results on the other is inherent in any policy dialogue. The challenge for the Bank is to build an honest and transparent relationship that keeps this tension in check, and that leads to a mutually agreed program of reforms that is technically sound, within the capacity of the government, results oriented, and consistent with PRSP objectives while reinforcing accountability toward domestic stakeholders.

For the Bank and other donors, lessons learned include the need to distinguish between policy reforms that are feasible early on and those that should be undertaken later. A balance needs to be struck between signaling the need for better progress and rewarding continued government commitment and the implementation of good policies. In Ethiopia, for example, progress on private sector development is expected to be slow, given the tradition of mistrust between the private sector and the government, and the role of the Bank should be to support a more open dialogue between the government and the private sector with a strong and flexible partnership, a wide range of analytical work, continued in-depth policy dialogue, and strong monitoring of reforms. (World Bank 2004c).

Experience with the preparation of policy matrices has been generally positive. The more advanced PRSC programs show that strong country ownership can derive from a negotiated process. In the PRSC stocktaking in Uganda and Burkina Faso, the governments clearly claimed the reform measures in the PRSC program as reflective of their own priorities. In a budget support workshop, an official from the Ugandan Treasury noted that the term "conditionality" should not be used, in light of the government's commitment to the PRSC's reform measures.[2] Several other African government representatives have expressed similar views in other forums. Vietnam's government has expressed appreciation of the need to underpin the policy dialogue with a medium-term framework of specific policy actions. Newer PRSCs also provide good practice examples. In Pakistan, the preparation of the PRSC policy matrix encouraged a dialogue among various parts of the government and with nongovernmental stakeholders that helped define priority actions and expected outcomes.

Donor-negotiated processes and instruments are always a second-best option in operationalizing the PRSP. In Ethiopia and Mozambique, where the governments have taken a more assertive role in leading the process of deriving priority measures from their PRSP policy matrices, and the Bank and other donors play more of a consultative role, the result is a much more prioritized set of actions directly linked to the PRSP, which all budget support donors use as a joint framework to draw disbursement triggers and to assess performance. In Mozambique, this process entailed the establishment of 19 working groups to develop specialized matrices in five key areas of the PRSP. Representatives of the government and a lead donor jointly chaired each working group. In Ethiopia, the government created four interministerial working groups to develop matrices for each of the four main themes contained in the PRSP. While these processes have required substantial amounts of time and resources, they are an integral part of the PRSP—a fact that helps to reinforce strong domestic accountability.[3]

Though not perfect, these examples of country-driven processes for defining conditionality show the path ahead for other budget support arrangements. The second generation of PRSPs provides ample opportunities for governments to build upon lessons learned and to take into account emerging good practices. Donors should recognize the importance of the PRSP as a tool for domestic accountability. Governments, too, should reinforce this by feeding back into the PRSP—and therefore to domestic constituents, including parliament—the reform measures they have agreed with donors. In Nicaragua, the second PRSP will amalgamate the first PRSP and the PRSC policy matrix and will draw on progress reports, local development plans developed by regional and departmental development councils, and sector plans developed by new sector working groups (ODI 2004). Similarly, in both Burkina Faso and Tanzania, the second PRSP is expected to provide both the overarching framework and a specific implementation plan, building on the processes and instruments from the first PRSP, and replacing the negotiated policy matrices (the PAF, in the case of Tanzania) with matrices derived by the government from the PRSP. Albania has a similar process under way to bolster country ownership of the reform measures supported by the second generation of PRSCs.

Improving Strategic Budgeting

In addition to elaborating strategies and specifying priority reform measures, governments can make the PRSP more operationally relevant by linking it to other country processes. Most notably, reform measures should be costed, and PRSPs should be strongly linked to the annual budget allocation and execution, as well as to a medium-term expenditure framework (MTEF) that relates likely expenditures with the resources projected to be available. Such links serve as a budgetary reality check for policymakers, encouraging them to prioritize and rationalize the PRSP's broad array of strategies, programs, and reform measures.

Costing and budget linkages remain weak in many countries. These weaknesses stem from a variety of causes, ranging from institutional (different institutional arrangements for PRSPs and MTEFs) to external (unpredictable resource flows) (World Bank and IMF 2004). According to a progress report on the Comprehensive Development Framework, only six PRSP countries are using MTEFs to prioritize the content of their PRSPs and link them to the budget. Four of these countries—Nepal, Rwanda, Tanzania, and Uganda—are implementing PRSCs. Nearly 40 percent of countries using the Comprehensive Development Framework are taking action to ground PRSP priorities in the budget and the MTEF, while about 35 percent are in the planning stages of developing MTEFs. Another 10 percent of countries have taken little or no action in this area (World Bank 2005q). All of the MTEFs are at very different stages of development and institutionalization, and the support provided by PRSCs has also varied considerably from country to country.

Almost all PRSCs monitor resource use—through either policy dialogue or explicit measures in the matrix—to ensure consistency with PRSP priorities, maintain fiscal discipline, and enhance allocative and operational efficiency. Many also support the development and institutionalization of the MTEF for improved medium-term strategic planning. In some countries that are at the pilot stages of developing the MTEF, such as Armenia, or the planning stages, such as Senegal, the PRSC supports these processes through complementary budget reforms, such as on budget classification and reporting, and decentralized execution in line ministries. In Nicaragua, when the MTEF was in the planning stages, the PRSC explicitly sought to accelerate this process by including measures in the policy matrix to establish and prepare MTEFs. In countries such as Mozambique that have already established MTEFs, PRSCs have helped to institutionalize these frameworks by including measures to ensure that budgets are based on and consistent with PRSPs and drawn from the MTEF. In Burkina Faso, the adoption of the MTEF was complemented by PRSC support for training sessions on program budgeting for budget officers in several line ministries. In countries where the links between the PRSP and budget processes are more advanced, and priority sectoral programs are reflected in budget allocation decisions and their costs are integrated into the MTEFs, the PRSP is at the front end of the budget process.

While notable progress has been made, in some cases rapidly and with very positive results, such as in Rwanda and Albania, challenges remain. Albania failed to meet its expenditure objectives in education and health, due to fiscal realignment and weak budget preparation and sector strategies in the line ministries. In Vietnam, the preparation of annual budgets is shaped by the government's five-year Socioeconomic Development Plan, which is the overarching development strategy to which the PRSP and sectoral development plans provide operational support. In Burkina Faso, the impact of the MTEF was limited by the readjustment of budgetary ceilings following resource shortfalls, and by the lack of integration between the ongoing program-budgeting exercise and the MTEF. The resulting weaknesses in the health ministry's program budget meant that the health budget could not maintain its share of the national budget.

Lessons from a study by ODI (2003) point to the need to:

- put the basics of budget management in place, preferably before adopting the MTEF;
- use a single central agency to coordinate spending as well as to oversee PRSP implementation—this greatly strengthens the budget links to PRSP priorities; and
- establish strong sector working groups that coordinate strategic approaches to budgeting—this helps to cement links among policy, planning, and budgeting at the sector level.

Monitoring and Evaluating PRSP Results

The PRSP has underlined the importance of strong monitoring and evaluation (M&E) frameworks to keep track of development outcomes and to assess progress toward development targets. Such a framework has several elements: a manageable set of defined and measurable indicators, the availability and reliability of data, and the institutional arrangements to coordinate and use data for effective policy making. The

JSAs/JSANs of all PRSC countries almost always note the need for greater attention to M&E frameworks to support PRSP implementation, in terms of more coordinated institutional arrangements, and improving the measurability, specificity, and policy-outcome linkages of indicators. PRSCs have helped address these shortcomings. While the coverage of M&E systems varies from country to country, there are some good examples where M&E forms a central part of the program and which show the path for other PRSC programs.

According to the CDF progress report (World Bank 2005q), Uganda, Tanzania, and Mozambique have well-developed national systems that are linked to the systems within line ministries and produce reports for domestic and external stakeholders. Their intermediate indicators are manageable in number and relatively easy to monitor. In other countries, M&E systems are a work in progress. In countries such as Ghana and Senegal, the PRSC policy dialogue has been used to track and maintain the momentum of reforms to collect timely data, to address resource and personnel constraints, and to clarify institutional arrangements within government. In other countries, such as Burkina Faso, Cape Verde, Honduras, Pakistan, Rwanda, and Vietnam, the PRSC includes explicit actions in the matrix to speed up the implementation of reforms to improve M&E systems. The Bank has also provided technical support to complement several PRSCs through trust funds that improve statistical capacity and PRSP implementation, as well as targeted capacity-building operations.

A few PRSCs have placed M&E at the front and center of the reform program, signaling the importance of M&E as an integral part of the poverty reduction strategy. In Albania and Tanzania, where the PRSC programs are relatively small and narrowly focused on cross-cutting public sector reforms, the Bank has worked with development partners to support the whole of the government's M&E agenda through the PRSC and other budget support programs, much as sectorwide programs in education have been folded entirely into other PRSCs. Work on M&E in Albania has focused on improving the availability and reliability of data, as well as on institutionalizing the M&E functions across line agencies. However, ministries still have varying capacity to define and monitor indicators and to analyze data to make a meaningful input into policy making. In Tanzania, which has a sound framework in place, the PRSC is addressing the capacity constraints of core M&E entities, the linkages and coordination among sectors, and the coordination between central and local governments. Tanzania's PRSCs have included a broad range of policy initiatives, financing, and activities: the development of a M&E strategy for the PRSP; budget allocation to fund and staff the statistical institute; identification of PRSP objectives, indicators, baseline, and targets; carrying out household survey programs; producing PRSP annual progress reports; and strengthening and sustaining the capacity of pertinent agencies. Tanzania now needs to further define and sharpen outcomes and related indicators and clarify links between outcomes and sector strategies, and between outcomes and budget allocations. The M&E framework in Tanzania is made even more critical with the introduction of greater results orientation in the second PRSP for 2005–10, which is organized around key outcomes in three clusters.

PRSPs that have weak M&E frameworks do not provide a ready source of targets and indicators for the PRSC, and the indicators that they do provide tend to vary widely in scope and quality (Hicks 2004). Hence many PRSCs—as well as multidonor budget support programs—include indicators in their M&E frameworks that are agreed with government and consistent with PRSP strategies but are separate from the PRSP itself. The EU's experience reveals the difficulty in relying solely on the PRSP for outcome indicators against which to disburse (European Commission 2005). Even among PRSCs that do not strictly draw indicators and targets from the PRSP, the choice and formulation of indicators varies in quality. In some cases, it is difficult to gauge how specific policy actions correspond to stated outcomes; in other cases, indicators are not easily measurable; and in other cases, output indicators are used in place of outcomes (World Bank 2004b; Hicks and Bassing 2004). These kinds of problems undermine clarity and predictability.

However, notable progress has been made in building good results frameworks in PRSCs. Reflecting progress in PRSPs, recent PRSC programs have tended to outline a clearer results framework in the program document, working with government counterparts to better link specific measures to output and outcome indicators, setting quantitative targets, and providing baseline data. There is a growing emphasis on providing support for M&E, ensuring not only the availability and quality of data, but also the demand for and management of their use.

Outcome-based conditions have been used pragmatically when appropriate. Initial PRSCs typically provide indicators and targets related to policy actions, although in some cases indicators are given without targets, particularly where future performance is uncertain or no goal has been agreed with the government. As PRSC programs evolve, outcome and impact indicators and targets receive increasing emphasis, particularly in the social sectors. Areas that are concerned with institutional changes (such as governance and PFM) are less amenable to quantifiable outcome indicators than to process indicators. In some cases, particularly where outcomes and impact are less affected by exogenous factors, results chains are clear, and indicators are available, it may be possible to move to a greater reliance on outcome and impact indicators as conditions and triggers. But governments are rightly wary of using outcome and impact targets for this purpose, particularly when they are held accountable for outcomes outside their control (see Morrissey in Chapter 16 of this volume). Most PRSCs remain conditional on inputs and outputs, and there are good reasons to remain pragmatic in the use of outcome-based conditionality.

B. PRSP Alignment: Content and Coverage

The breadth of policy areas typically covered by PRSPs attests to the complex and multidimensional nature of poverty. PRSCs, as one of the Bank's primary means of supporting the policy reform agenda, are expected to encompass the entirety of PRSP policy reforms while making the most strategic use of limited staff time and resources. These conflicting expectations lead to trade-offs in sectoral and thematic coverage, and in the modality of support provided. In making these trade-offs, the Bank must consider a number of critical factors, as well as addressing internal Bank incentives for working across sectors. Not surprisingly, first-generation PRSCs have tended to focus mostly on systems and processes that underpin PRSP implementation (notably public financial management) as well as on well-established sectorwide programs.

General Trends

On average, PRSCs cover seven thematic/cross-cutting areas and eight sectors—about twice as many sectors and themes as typically supported by other policy-based lending (Figure 3.1). Compared to other DPL operations, PRSCs address more systematically the cross-cutting constraints affecting various sectors. For example, all PRSCs have sought to improve core public sector functions, especially the coherence of government programs, policies, and budgets, as well as the quality of and access to propoor service delivery through public expenditure management. The PRSC is an effective instrument to support these efforts because it works directly through the government's planning and budget processes to support reforms that enhance the effectiveness of public sector institutions and systems. This cross-cutting approach has built upon and reinforced the coordination and collaboration among different government ministries and agencies that underpin the PRSP process.

Beyond cross-cutting issues, PRSCs have also addressed in-depth sectoral reforms. Some PRSCs, notably in Uganda and Benin, address the broader sector policy dialogue by subsuming entire sectorwide approaches (SWAps). Others focus on specific sectoral issues while the broader sectoral dialogue is advanced through other operations. The education and health sectors are typical examples of the former, because these sectors are more suited to SWAp frameworks.

PRSCs have come to be associated with bringing more of a social sector orientation to Bank DPL. About 95 percent of PRSCs support reforms in the health sector, while 86 percent address issues in education and agriculture. Among other DPL operations, by contrast, only 53 percent address health, 42 percent education, and 23 percent agriculture. Roughly 48 percent of PRSC operations address water and sanitation issues, more than double the proportion for other DPL operations (Figure 3.2).

While PRSCs tend to be much more multisectoral than other DPL, they have tended to support institutional reforms to strengthen public sector governance (Figure 3.3). More than 45 percent of all PRSC binding measures entail public sector reforms, of which upward of 64 percent specifically address weaknesses in PFM. The share of measures targeting financial management is very similar to that of the EC's variable tranche (EC 2005). The remaining share of binding measures is more or less evenly distributed among other sectors and themes. PRSCs have a smaller share of binding measures (12 percent) that support financial and private sector reforms, compared to other DPL operations (27 percent). These trends are also broadly similar, with some minor differences: among PRSCs, the share of indicative benchmarks increases in environment and natural resource management, and social protection and development. The reverse is true for private sector development.

As a PRSC program progresses, its sectoral and thematic coverage typically broadens (for example, Burkina Faso's PRSC program grew from four sectors to seven, Vietnam's from five to eight, and Uganda's from six to eight). Within sectors and thematic areas, too, the scope tends to broaden. The Benin PRSC's public sector

FIGURE 3.1 Sectoral and Thematic Content among PRSCs

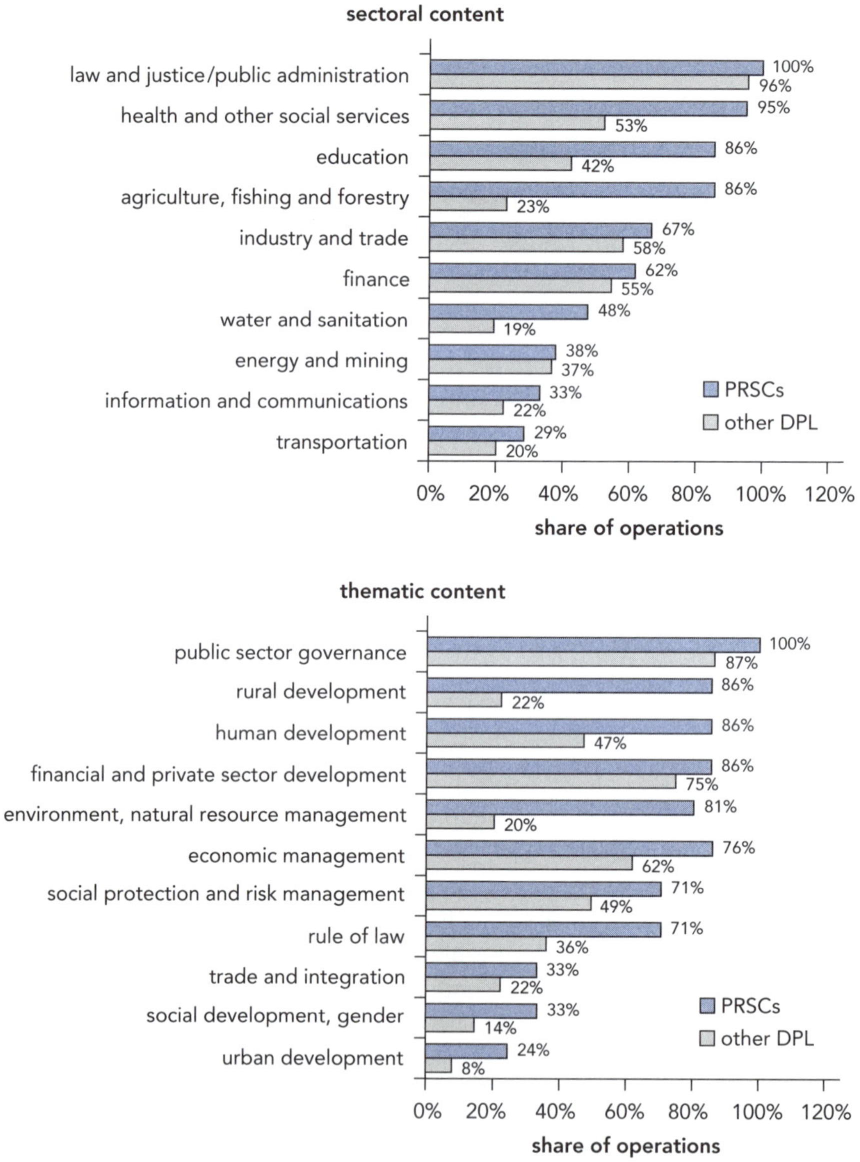

Source: ALCID database.

agenda initially addressed public expenditure management and corruption, but the second operation will also encompass internal audit and control, procurement, civil service reform, decentralization, and public communication; the approach taken to widen the scope of this PRSC is largely country specific. In Vietnam, the PRSC reform agenda moved beyond structural reforms in trade, investment climate, and public expenditure management to other cross-cutting issues of governance, land administration, and access to information. PRSCs in many countries begin with cross-cutting issues and

FIGURE 3.2 Sectoral Distribution of Binding Measures in PRSCs (top) and Other DPL Operations (bottom)

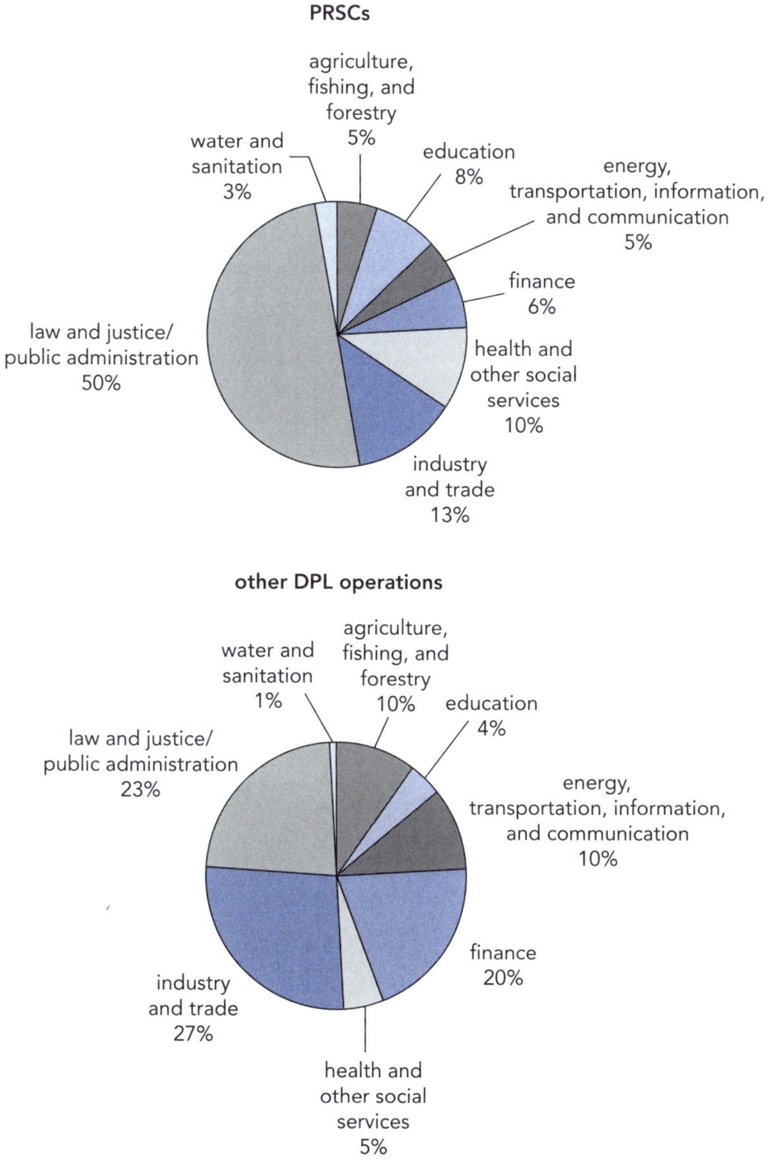

Source: ALCID database.

move to address sectoral issues in depth. Among the more comprehensive PRSCs, specific criteria were used to determine a sector's "readiness" (as discussed further below), with the breadth of coverage reflecting the Bank's and the government's capacity to manage the transition away from project-based aid.

Over time, given a solid track record of reform implementation, the policy dialogue and support to specific sectors have reverted to what has become known as

FIGURE 3.3 Thematic Distribution of Binding Measures in PRSCs (top) and Other DPL Operations (bottom)

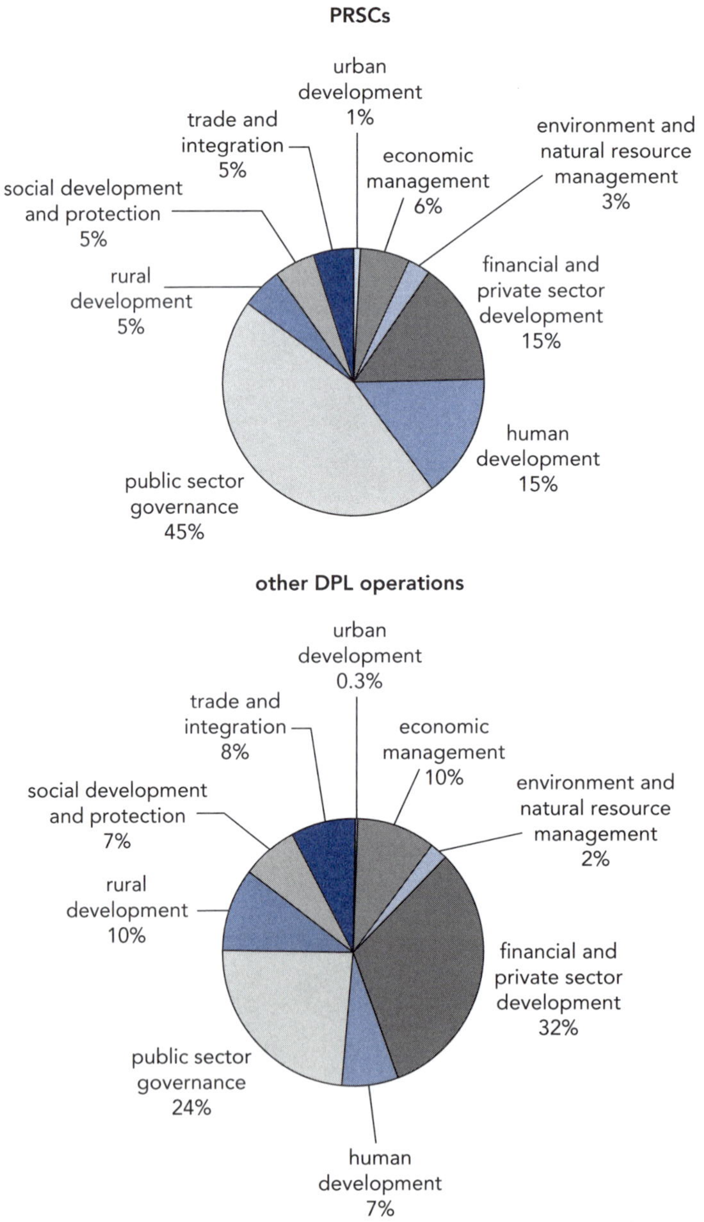

Note: For operations approved through end-February 2005.
Source: ALCID database.

"maintenance mode," which refers to the steady implementation of well-advanced sector programs (World Bank 2003b). In Uganda and elsewhere, this has implied that while sectoral policy dialogue in education continues through annual reviews that monitor the progress of overall reform implementation and outcomes, the sector or thematic area would not be subject to specific binding actions but rather to broadly based indicators of performance. For example, measures supporting education reform made up 15 percent of the total measures in Uganda's PRSC 1. That share dropped to 2 percent of all measures in PRSC 4 (Table 3.2).

Some PRSCs have incorporated existing sectorwide approaches, which then have typically been placed in "maintenance mode" at the outset of the PRSC program. This entails no binding actions for the sector, but rather general evidence of "satisfactory progress in implementation." Such is the case for the mature sectors in Uganda (education, health, and water), Madagascar (education, health), and Benin (forestry, environment). The pace of reforms in a given sector or thematic area ultimately determines how quickly a maintenance mode can take shape. In Burkina Faso, given the difficult transition in the health sector from project to program support, the share of policy measures remained constant throughout the program, reflecting the need to maintain a level of engagement to ensure continued reform implementation. Similarly, given the critical and complex nature of the public sector reform agenda, particularly in public financial and expenditure management, a consistent share of policy measures reflects the need to ensure incremental progress.

Public Financial Management

Despite the breadth of coverage in PRSCs, most programs have managed to maintain a core emphasis, stemming from the Heavily Indebted Poor Countries (HIPC) Initiative, on increased poverty-focused expenditures and expanded service delivery. This has, in turn, typically been accompanied by a strengthened drive to improve PFM. While it is still too early to determine the long-term poverty impact of PRSCs, preliminary results in a number of key areas in several countries with well-established PRSCs attest that the PRSC is contributing significantly to the implementation of poverty reduction programs.

TABLE 3.2 Evolution of Sectoral Content of PRSC Binding and Nonbinding Measures

(percent)

Sector group	Burkina Faso				Uganda			
	PRSC 1	PRSC 2	PRSC 3	PRSC 4	PRSC 1	PRSC 2	PRSC 3	PRSC 4
Agriculture, fishing, forestry	29	13	8	7		8	10	9
Education	11	13	14	7	15	2	3	2
Energy and mining			3	3				
Information and communications			3	2				
Transportation					3	2	3	2
Water and sanitation			8	12	32	18	16	2
Finance		13		2	3	3	1	2
Health and other social services	21	13	17	20	32	5	3	8
Industry and trade				3			3	2
Law and justice/public admin.	39	50	47	45	15	64	61	74
Total	**100**	**100**	**100**	**100**	**100**	**100**	**100**	**100**

Source: ALCID database.

The Bank recognizes the critical role that a transparent and efficient public expenditure framework plays in delivering more and better services to the poor. More broadly, PFM is a key government responsibility that contributes to improved overall public administration. Modernizing PFM typically entails improving controls, planning and execution procedures, transparency, and accountability. Given the large donor resource flows to many low-income countries, modernizing PFM is a legitimate interest for donors, and particularly for those providing budget support, because it is critical to reducing fiduciary risks. For PRSCs, PFM is a core component of the reform agenda. This is manifest in the significant analytical and diagnostic work undertaken in PFM, the policy dialogue that centers on PFM issues, and the relatively high concentration of PRSC measures that support the modernization of PFM systems.

All PRSCs have been underpinned by ex ante fiduciary assessments of the country's PFM and expenditure systems. The country financial accountability assessment (CFAA), country procurement assessment report (CPAR), and public expenditure review (PER) typically focus on aspects such as the comprehensiveness and transparency of the budget, systems that facilitate budget implementation and monitoring, fiscal transparency (reliable information on fiscal results and position), and financial accountability for the use of public resources. The purpose of the assessments is to identify deficiencies, assess the level of fiduciary risk, and identify additional steps needed to secure acceptable fiduciary arrangements. PFM-related measures with PRSCs have covered a range of issues, including budget preparation and execution, accounting and reporting, audit and oversight, and diagnostic studies. Many of the reforms are legal or regulatory, such as enactment of laws on fiscal responsibility, financial administration, procurement, and internal audit. Other measures are more institutional and include the introduction of MTEFs and information systems, legislative oversight functions, and new budget classifications.

Given that the PRSC cycle is short, the institutional reforms supported tend to have relatively limited scope. Support for changes in PFM has been common: PRSCs have supported policy actions related to legislation in PFM, such as the enactment of a budget law, fiscal responsibility act, financial administration act, and procurement decree. PRSC program documents discuss the enactment of such legislation, but not enough attention is always paid to implementation and to how such reforms would improve PFM. The other issues often addressed are the introduction of MTEFs and integrated financial management information systems, and strengthening internal audit, external audit, legislative oversight functions, and new budget classifications. In many cases, PFM conditions have been process oriented, reflecting difficulties in establishing measurable indicators in this area (Table 3.3). However, some of the process-oriented indicators have measurable intermediate outcomes. For example, the Sri Lanka PRSC provided 12 intermediate monitorable and measurable indicators, which should be viewed as good practice examples.

Because only a few countries have progressed to subsequent PRSC operations, it is still premature to judge the extent to which PRSCs are contributing to improvements in basic PFM infrastructure. In Uganda, the 2004 CFAA noted that fiduciary risks were still high, despite improvements, because not all of the risks had yet been

TABLE 3.3 Share of Public Financial Management Conditions in PRSCs

(percent)

	FY01	FY02	FY03	FY04	Avg.
Budget preparation	13	40	50	42	40
Budget execution	25	0	14	12	13
Accounting/reporting	25	0	14	38	26
Audit and oversight	25	60	14	8	17
Diagnostic studies	13	0	7	0	4
Total	**100**	**100**	**100**	**100**	**100**

Source: "Financial Management Issues in PRSCs, FY01-04," November 2004.

properly addressed. In Vietnam, progress has been made but public resource management was found to fall significantly short of international best practices; in particular, the government still lacked a rigorous and transparent MTEF. The latest tracking assessment for the HIPC Initiative concluded that Burkina Faso has a solid PFM system: in 2001, the system met 8 of 16 benchmarks, and in 2004, it met 9. At the start of the Tanzania PRSC program, the country had met 8 of the 16 benchmarks, according to the 2001 HIPC assessment, making the country one of the top performers in Africa. Tanzania currently meets 11 benchmarks.

Selectivity and Sequencing of Coverage

The multisectoral approach of the PRSC has raised some questions that reflect tensions and competing expectations. PRSCs are meant to anchor the Bank's policy dialogue across a broad range of areas, and so there has been pressure for the PRSC to mirror the breadth of policy areas contained in the PRSP. At the same time, a PRSC's coverage cannot be too comprehensive without becoming overloaded.

These competing expectations have shown themselves in different ways. Concerns have arisen within the Bank, for example, that rural development and growth agendas have not received enough attention (World Bank 2005r). Similarly, guidelines are being drafted to further advance water and sanitation coverage in PRSCs (World Bank forthcoming). At the same time, discussion has surfaced about the feasibility of having multiple PRSCs in a country, each addressing the policy dialogue of different sectors and themes. In countries including Albania, Pakistan, Honduras, and Tanzania, the PRSC is running concurrently with other policy-based operations. In determining the scope and coverage of the PRSC, teams must assess the intersectoral and intrasectoral trade-offs in the PRSC, the specific type of support to be provided to the sector (policy dialogue, financing, maintenance) and a host of other considerations that shape the priorities for overall growth and poverty reduction. In this regard, country-specific solutions will have to be defined as part of the country assistance strategy process without expecting to achieve uniform treatment across all sector and thematic areas of the PRSP.

In deciding which sectors and themes to support, how to support them, and when to sequence them into the PRSC, the Bank considers a number of factors. In many

African countries, the consolidated approach that incorporates many sectoral programs and investments under the PRSC responds to governments' call for less fragmentation and greater ownership of development assistance. Outside Africa, the preference has often been to maintain sectoral financing through SWAps in order to guarantee a certain level of funding and technical support. More broadly, the PRSC's heavy emphasis on improving and expanding pro-poor service delivery reflects the priorities of most PRSPs.

Among the African PRSC programs that are consolidating the lending portfolio under the PRSC, the question of sectoral readiness is of paramount concern. For donors, budget support implies a loss of control over program implementation and earmarked financing. The experience with the health sector in Burkina Faso, described above, illustrates the need to ensure a calculated transition to budget support. In Uganda, the Bank has established strict criteria for sectors adopting the PRSC framework: the quality of the sector strategy, an existing sectoral MTEF, a strong M&E framework, strong coordination with the central ministries, and overall administrative capacity of the line ministry. In Rwanda, the approach has been to include the energy and water sectors in the first PRSC, with the intent to prepare these two sectors for fuller engagement in subsequent operations. To make informed decisions on which reforms to support, PRSCs must also be underpinned by sufficient analytical work. In Uganda's water and sanitation sector there was no previous sectorwide approach, but the Bank had undertaken extensive analytical work on the needed policy and institutional reforms, and this created the basis for a strong program supported by the PRSC. One explanation for the apparent weak coverage of growth and rural development among PRSCs is the lack of coherent strategies in these two areas in the PRSPs.

The content of the PRSC must accord with the Bank's Articles of Agreement, which prohibit the Bank's direct involvement in political concerns. This issue has been brought up in the context of efforts by several bilateral donors to attach political governance conditions and human rights concerns to joint budget support programs.

The PRSC must also reflect the Bank's comparative advantage in the country, and in almost all cases, the areas targeted by the PRSC are those where the Bank has had significant experience. The exceptions include Cape Verde, where the Bank had very little previous experience in health sector investments but the PRSC was seen as an opportunity for the Bank to engage in policy dialogue on the health system, particularly on insurance mechanisms and other financial framework issues. In Senegal, the areas of justice and labor had been relatively neglected by donors but are priority areas for the PRSC, given their significant associated externalities for the country's growth and equity agenda. Comparative advantage also extends to the PRSC itself and the value added it offers as a high-profile instrument. In Ghana, for example, local stakeholders broadly view the PRSC as the centerpiece in policy dialogue, supporting key issues in growth, service delivery, and governance. The selection of issues and their elevation to the center of government is likely to increase the chances of progress on decisions, with maximum buy-in from important segments of the society.

The Bank tries to avoid duplication with other donors and, as much as possible, to harmonize budget support programs. In Albania, the decision to keep the PRSC relatively small reflected the emphasis of the country assistance strategy on infrastructure financing—necessary because of the vacuum left by the EU's shift away from this critical area. In Tanzania, donor harmonization resulted in the PRSC focusing narrowly on cross-cutting issues, an arrangement that had been put in place by the existing budget support donor group. With the government drafting Tanzania's next PRSP, the Bank and other donors are discussing the possibility of extending the coverage of the joint budget support programs to include social and other sectors.

Some interventions are better supported by well-targeted project financing than by PRSCs. They include large multiyear infrastructure-type projects, which require upfront commitments, multiyear contracts, and international procurement. Similarly, capacity building entails specific activities linked to a defined budget and is more suited to project financing. This also applies to interventions such as microfinance and community-driven development approaches, which address issues at the local or grassroots levels.

C. Harmonization and Predictability

The PRSP represents an opportunity to enhance aid effectiveness. A key element of the new development architecture is the concept of mutual accountability: Governments undertake a wide range of policy and institutional reforms that are critical to improving development outcomes and achieving national objectives for poverty reduction, and in return, donors support government leadership of the development process by reducing aid fragmentation and associated transaction costs, and improving aid predictability. In heavily aid-dependent countries with multiple budget support programs, the emerging aid architecture will support harmonized donor budget support programs and processes that are aligned with the government's annual PRSP process and budget and planning cycles, and that provide timely and predictable resource flows. The harmonization and alignment agenda is ambitious and challenging. Full effectiveness is still hampered by different approaches and requirements on the part of donors and governments, the weak links between the PRSP and domestic processes, and the fact that practice is still emerging and subject to change. While experience suggests the Bank is generally moving in the right direction, expectations on the speed and size of the shift to the new aid architecture must be properly managed.

Donor Coordination and Harmonization

Over the past few years, the political momentum for harmonization and alignment has grown. At the March 2005 High-Level Forum on Aid Effectiveness in Paris, donors strengthened their commitments to coordination and harmonization made in Rome and Monterrey.[4] The Bank has been a leader in the aid coordination and harmonization agenda at both the corporate and country levels, and the PRSC has provided an effective vehicle to coordinate and harmonize with other budget support donors.

Coordination and Harmonization Modalities

Operational experience during the past five years has produced various models of how the PRSC facilitates Bank coordination and harmonization with other donors: for example, traditional coordination and sharing of analytical work, donor cofinancing, and harmonization of budget support programs. Each approach reflects different country circumstances, the role of the government, and the nature, timing, and role of the PRSC in the country. In some countries, the PRSC provides the framework for harmonization; in others, coordination and harmonization evolve through successive operations. In any given country, the Bank engages in various types of coordination and harmonization activities with budget support donors and donors focused on project financing. In Benin, for example, the Bank provides budget support jointly with the EC and other donors while working closely with non-budget-support donors, such as the US Agency for International Development (USAID), to elaborate on the private sector development strategy, and the UN Development Programme (UNDP), to support the PRSP M&E system.

In certain PRSC countries where there are few donors, or where budget support plays a relatively minor role in donor assistance, the Bank and other donors coordinate in traditional ways, ensuring adequate exchange of information and identifying areas of comparative advantage to avoid overlap and reduce the likelihood of leaving critical gaps. For example, in Albania, whose relations with the European Union are leading to closer alignment with EC legislation, the PRSC has been kept small in relation to both overall donor flows and the Bank's lending portfolio. Donor coordination on the PRSC has included joint work with the UK Department for International Development (DFID) on the PRSP policy M&E, and with UNDP on the Millennium Development Goals. In Pakistan, the Bank undertook several joint analyses with the Asian Development Bank (ADB) and DFID. The Pakistani government considers the PRSP and PRSC to be good instruments for increased coordination on policy dialogue and program support. DFID has expressed interest in disbursing budget support against PRSC actions, and the United States has laid out its aid objectives in a document that was prepared in consultation with the Bank and includes many of the PRSC's areas of focus.[5]

Development partners view the PRSC as an effective vehicle for supporting the policy dialogue on the objectives and programs of country PRSPs. In Vietnam, development partners helped to finance the PRSC, disbursing commitments against policy measures in the PRSC policy matrix. The governments of Denmark, the Netherlands, Sweden, and the United Kingdom provided close to US$75 million in parallel financing for the first two PRSCs, and in Vietnam's PRSC 3, they are likely to be joined by the ADB, Canada, the EC, and Japan. Many of these development partners have also played important roles in the policy dialogue and the preparation and design of the PRSC and, together with others, have provided technical assistance grants to support the PRSC. They have divided the task of engagement in tripartite meetings with the Bank and the government among themselves according to their comparative strengths.[6] The German aid agency KfW has provided parallel financing to PRSCs in Armenia, Nicaragua, and several African countries, disbursing its funds against the Bank's assessment of the fulfillment of prior actions and conditions.

In many PRSC programs, including all those in Africa, harmonization around budget support is a key element in the PRSP process and a key objective of the Bank's engagement. Broadly speaking, harmonization entails a concerted effort by budget support donors and the government to reduce the transaction costs of aid delivery by supporting a single broad comprehensive reform program based on the PRSP and by engaging in a consistent policy dialogue. Key characteristics typically include formal, signed memoranda of understanding that lay out the rules for providing budget support, including the joint assessment of country performance and disbursement against a common PAF, multiyear donor commitments, joint donor missions, and streamlined reporting requirements (World Bank 2005s). Such frameworks also aim to facilitate early commitments of aid, the integration of these commitments into the budget formulation process, the front-loading of disbursements within the fiscal year to enhance the predictability of aid flows, and setting out the obligations of countries and their partners in the PRSP process. It is still too early to judge the effectiveness of such arrangements. However, the start-up costs of establishing joint monitoring frameworks have been considerable, and the process often time consuming.[7] In Ethiopia and Mozambique, for example, the process of agreeing on a common set of indicators and monitoring modalities took well over a year (World Bank 2004d).

Approaches to Harmonization

The Paris Declaration on Aid Effectiveness emphasized the need to implement common donor arrangements for financing, disbursements, and M&E, and to reduce duplicative missions and diagnostic reviews.[8] As more donors provide aid in the form of budget support, key principles and good practices on harmonization have begun to emerge, and while harmonization approaches differ from country to country, donors generally strive to stay within the spirit of these principles and practices.

It is the government that should drive efforts to harmonize budget support, spelling out the "rules of the game" in keeping with the PRSP's country-driven approach. Many country teams have suggested that multidonor budget support initiatives are helping governments take leadership of overall development assistance coordination. This requires the establishment of clear mechanisms for coordination and usually the assignment of a lead agency. In Ghana, Pakistan, Rwanda, Tanzania, Uganda, and Vietnam, a central ministry is responsible for strategy formulation, budget preparation, and external assistance coordination, and Honduras is consolidating its mechanisms for coordinating development assistance.

Genuine country leadership in coordinating donor assistance is often hampered by capacity and institutional constraints. In Nicaragua, coordination between the Bank and the Inter-American Development Bank has been a challenge, partly because the IDB's counterpart is the Ministry of Foreign Affairs, while that of the Bank is the Ministry of Finance. In Cape Verde, the Ministry of Foreign Affairs takes responsibility for government relations with bilateral donors, while the Ministry of Planning and Finance oversees relations with multilateral donors. Nevertheless, the harmonization process in these countries has moved forward through a partnership framework with the government (Table 3.4).

Where governments have taken an active role in aid harmonization, they have also taken an active role in developing their respective partnership framework agreements, which stipulate the separate accountabilities of government and budget support donors.

Good practices suggest that the PAF should be country driven and used by all budget support donors (OECD-DAC 2005a). Most PAFs reflect an ongoing policy dialogue, and they derive to varying degrees from processes negotiated between donors and governments. In Ethiopia, the government led an iterative process of identifying a subset of indicators from its own PRSP policy matrix to establish a common framework for all budget support programs, including the PRSC. In Nicaragua, Uganda, and Vietnam, the PRSC policy matrix serves as the common framework for several budget support donors who disburse their commitments when the Bank's board

TABLE 3.4 Harmonized Budget Support in PRSC Countries

	Belgium	Canada	Denmark	EC	Finland	France	Germany	Ireland	Italy	Japan	Netherlands	Norway	Portugal	Sweden	Switzerland	UK	Regional bank
Albania																	
Armenia																	
Benin			X	X							X				X		X
Burkina Faso	X		X	X		X					X			X	X		X
Cape Verde				X							X						X
Ethiopia		X		X			X	X						X		X	X
Ghana		X	X	X			X				X				X	X	X
Guyana																	
Honduras																	
Madagascar																	
Mozambique	X		X	X	X	X	X	X	X		X	X	X	X	X	X	
Nepal																	
Nicaragua				X	X		X				X	X		X	X	X	
Pakistan				X												X	X
Rwanda	X			X			X				X			X			
Senegal																	
Sri Lanka																	
Tanzania		X	X	X	X			X		X	X	X		X	X	X	
Uganda				X			X	X			X	X		X		X	X
Vietnam		X	X	X						X	X			X		X	X

Note: The table shows joint budget support programs where donors are cofinancing the PRSC or are using a common PAF; data are based on program documents of the most recent PRSCs approved as of April 2005.

approves the PRSC.[9] In other countries, the PAF was developed before PRSC approval. In Tanzania, when the Bank joined the existing framework, changes to the PAF were made to accommodate the PRSC, such as broadening the coverage to include rural development and environment efforts. In Burkina Faso, there were difficulties at first in integrating the PRSC into the existing memoranda of understanding of bilateral donors, which foresaw only disbursement against outcome indicators, and in Ghana, the first PRSC proceeded without a PAF in place. These initial difficulties were eventually overcome, and in most countries with multiple budget support programs, donors have moved toward a common PAF.

A certain level of agreement among budget support donors on key issues is needed to ensure proper harmonization. Agreement on a common PAF, for example, typically defines a joint budget support group. However, donor groups differ from one another as to the flexibility individual donors have to determine specific benchmarks. For example, while the Bank bases disbursement decisions on the achievement of specific actions, the EC bases its decision on the achievement of outcome targets. In Ghana, Uganda, and Vietnam, donors must reach the same judgment on performance, based on a common set of indicators in the PAF. In Tanzania, individual donors make separate assessments of how the common assessment of progress translates into financing decisions. The latter practice conforms to an emerging view among budget support donors that allowing staggered or multitranche approaches by different donors may limit "herd behavior" (which can lead to disruptive fluctuations in aid flows). The practice allows donors to disburse a set commitment amount against different triggers, so that satisfactory progress in one policy area can be rewarded independently of progress in other areas. In this view, allowing different donors to respond to performance in different ways spreads risks for the recipient country. On the other hand, it weakens any signaling function and prevents the reductions in transaction costs that can be expected from a coordinated donor response.

Development partners often express reservations about the Bank's role within budget support groups and its willingness to engage in harmonization efforts. Most development partners respect the Bank's technical capacity, understanding of complex developmental issues, and ability to take a lead in many areas of the policy dialogue. But the Bank is often viewed as the oversized member of the budget support group, with unmatched influence within the group and disproportionate access to government. Although the PRSC has increased the opportunities for joint work within the donor community,[10] donors still express concern that the Bank proceeds on its own when it wants to. The size of PRSC teams can often be overwhelming during missions, when important meetings, discussions, and decision making are compressed into a narrow time frame. The scope of these missions may complicate the task of ensuring that all donors are well informed of changing schedules and agendas, and that they reach consensus on key issues before negotiating with the government. Despite the Bank's strong decentralization efforts over the past years, in several countries, donors encourage an even stronger field presence of senior sectoral staff who can engage in continuous dialogue with partners and with government and thus reduce the need for large missions.

Risks and Challenges in Harmonization

While harmonization can enhance aid effectiveness, current harmonization approaches raise some notable risks and challenges:

- *Volatility.* Aid volatility rises substantially as more donor resources are provided through budget support. In some countries, budget support receipts have varied greatly from year to year. Malawi offers a worrying example of unsatisfactory performance resulting in a total disruption of budget support flows. As already noted, the risk of volatility rises if all donors use the same disbursement indicators and respond in the same way to performance and underperformance.
- *Size of PAF/number of indicators.* While the PAF is a useful guidepost and management tool for the government's reform program, care must be taken to limit the size of the PAF matrix. Donors must judge how significant an individual indicator is to the overall success of a program. Allowing donors to choose disbursement indicators within the PAF may lead to a net increase in conditionality for the government.
- *Weight of donor influence.* Budget support groups range in size from 3 donors in Cape Verde to 17 in Mozambique. Harmonization has raised various issues in relation to how groups should be managed and decisions made. Should small providers of budget support have an equal say in decision making with large providers? What should be the influence of donors with limited technical expertise in any given policy area, or of non-budget-support donors whose programs may be affected by the decisions of budget support groups? In Tanzania, it has been suggested that thresholds could be set at US$50 million in annual commitments, or 70 percent of the donor's total assistance (ODI 2004). Such an approach can reduce transaction costs, but it risks deterring some donors, particularly small ones and those that are not "like-minded," from continuing their venture into budget support.
- *Donor collusion.* To avoid increased donor dominance through coordination, governments may prefer to maintain bilateral relations alongside those they have with the joint donor group. In this regard, the harmonization process has evoked some contradictory reactions from governments. On the one hand, they welcome that harmonized donors speak with "one voice"; on the other, they are weary of donors "ganging up" on difficult or sensitive issues, as in Pakistan. In Ethiopia, the government reluctantly agreed to accept bilateral donors as parties in the budget support policy dialogue after the World Bank insisted on a harmonized approach to budget support. Some governments have requested clear rules of the game. Without such rules, although governments prefer budget support as a modality for financing PRSPs and lowering transaction costs, they may be willing to forgo those benefits if they perceive harmonization as donor collusion.

Improving Predictability

Improving the predictability of resource flows is an explicit goal of many PRSCs and of budget support programs in general. Predictability is of particular concern in aid-dependent countries, where budget support represents a large share of public spending. The concern is of both a short- and medium-term nature, because (a) more donors are channeling aid through budget support, and the reliability of commitments and the timing of disbursements are critical for budget execution, and (b) the PRSP process has underlined the need for governments to improve their medium-term budgeting and planning and reduce resource volatility so they can carry out the country's development program.

Increasingly, the donor community is framing the challenge of resource predictability in the long-term context of achieving the Millennium Development Goals, in line with the Monterrey Consensus. The following discussion seeks to assess the extent to which PRSCs are improving resource predictability. It looks at how the programmatic design of the PRSC helps to reconcile the need for predictability with strong country performance, and provides suggestions on how to enhance predictability through improved transparency and better alignment with domestic planning and budgeting processes and timetables, including the PRSP annual progress reports.

Programmatic Alignment with the PRSP

The programmatic approach of the PRSC reflects an evolution in the design of policy-based lending. Adjustment lending operations in the 1980s and 1990s were typically multitranche operations with a short-term horizon, and based on ex ante conditionality that often proved insufficiently responsive to changing circumstances. Traditional conditionality was viewed as insufficiently tailored to specific country circumstances, overlooking important considerations of political economy, government capacity, and commitment. As a result, governments often were unable or unwilling to implement policy conditionality, leading to a "tap on, tap off" pattern of disbursement and high volatility in resource flows.[11] Sometimes, donors waived unmet conditions and proceeded with disbursement, undermining the implementation of reforms (World Bank 2001a). The PRSC was designed to reflect country priorities and to be flexible, with a step-by-step, medium-term approach based on completed (as opposed to promised) actions. These design features help reconcile the tension between the need to stabilize public expenditures through resource predictability and the need to show that the policy environment allows for effective use of aid resources.

PRSCs are designed on the basis of a medium-term program of support. Ideally, the country assistance strategy (CAS) overlaps with the PRSP time frame and sets out the three or four annual PRSC operations within that time frame. The CAS assigns an indicative commitment amount for each operation in the program, providing an envelope of budget support for the PRSP program and a critical input to the government's MTEF. There are no formal mechanisms to provide a rolling commitment scenario,[12] because the CAS does not indicate commitments beyond the time frame it covers. In the context of the government's and the IMF's annual medium-term macroeconomic and fiscal projections exercise, the Bank's informal indications about multiyear financing commitments are naturally subject to the country performance allocation and available IDA resources. Over time, it may be useful to consider formalizing commitment projections on a rolling basis, to be in line with the programmatic design of the PRSC and the need to enhance governments' medium-term budget planning.

Another key element of the programmatic design is the use of triggers to assess country performance and to serve as the basis for disbursement decisions. While each PRSC is based on prior actions, triggers allow the Bank to judge whether enough progress has been made to move to the next operation. Triggers help shape the preparation of the subsequent PRSC, and they typically form the basis of its required prior actions. However, triggers allow considerable flexibility: the prior actions required by the subsequent PRSC need not be identical to the triggers; they can be adapted to changing circumstances or made clearer, more specific, or more measurable. The flexibility comes not from defining vague or easily met triggers, or from allowing continued financing despite poor performance, but rather from identifying key reform measures that the government is committed to, and then measuring progress against them, using reasoned judgments to allow for disciplined adaptation.

The PRSC's programmatic approach allows for a graduated response in the case of uneven country performance:

- *Proceeding with full amount.* Where overall progress is judged to be adequate even if certain triggers have not been fully met as expected—perhaps because delays in some areas were offset by advances in others—the prior actions required can be adapted and the next operation can proceed with a full amount. Experience to date is that 95 percent of the triggers are met by the time the program document is completed. In cases where actual implementation has deviated from expectations, the Bank has responded in a graduated manner—it has determined that substantial progress in other areas shows continued government commitment and justifies moving toward the next operation. Many of the unmet triggers have been simply delayed, rather than reflecting a lack of government commitment.

- *Postponing operations.* Where triggers have not been met, because of backtracking or failure to implement, the Bank has given serious consideration to delaying the operation. In Tanzania, the government preferred to postpone the subsequent operation by about two months to fully implement all prior actions that, for technical reasons, had taken somewhat longer than originally anticipated. The postponement was made in response to the Bank's offer to continue the program as scheduled but with a reduction in the commitment amount. Delays caused by inadequate performance have marked the PRSC programs in Nepal and Sri Lanka.[13]

- *Reducing commitment amounts.* Graduated modulation of PRSC commitments avoids the inflexible "tap on, tap off" pattern of disbursement in traditional policy-based lending. For Ethiopia's PRSC 1, the original commitment was somewhat lower than was intended prior to board approval, given the lack of progress in one key policy area.

- *Interrupting programs.* PRSC programs have been suspended in a few cases where progress in improving the policy environment was inadequate to justify moving to the next operation. Guyana is the only country where the PRSC program has been disrupted. A deadlocked parliament, political and ethnic tensions, and institutional weaknesses have made it difficult for the government to implement triggers for PRSC 2 in a timely fashion. The implementation completion report for the first operation suggests that the original schedule of one PRSC per year was too optimistic.[14] Eventually, the country team decided to discontinue the PRSC as a series of annual policy loans and to prepare a new set of policy-based operations that are more widely spaced, taking into account lessons learned and country circumstances.

The Record on Predictability

PRSCs have helped to improve the predictability of resource flows in PRSC countries, as reflected in (1) the extent to which the Bank has delivered on its medium-term commitments outlined at the outset of the PRSC program; (2) the regularity and volume of PRSC disbursements; and (3) the regularity of PRSC approvals.[15] The seven countries that have moved to subsequent PRSC operations have seen improved predictability on all counts. Table 3.5 compares commitments to actual disbursements for countries that have moved past their second PRSC. The data show a strong correlation between commitments made at the start of the program and disbursement upon board approval.

In countries with PRSCs, flows from policy-based operations were disbursed much more regularly and predictably than before the PRSC program. This is particularly evident for Albania, Burkina Faso, and Vietnam, which used policy-based lending sporadically in the past. Another trend in disbursement shows an increase in the volume of DPL, even in countries where the PRSC is a small share of the country's total portfolio. The sample is still relatively small and the time period relatively short, but the trends so far are promising: they fulfill the expectation that the PRSC's programmatic annual cycle helps to reduce volatility and improve the regularity of annual aid flows for countries making consistent progress in reform implementation.

TABLE 3.5 Commitments and Actual Disbursements

($ million)

Country	Original commitment (OC)				Disbursement (D)				D/OC
	PRSC 1	PRSC 2	PRSC 3	PRSC 4	PRSC 1	PRSC 2	PRSC 3	PRSC 4	(%)
Albania	20	10	10		20	18	10		120
Burkina Faso	45	35	40	60	45	35	50	60	106
Ethiopia	150	150			120	130			83
Ghana	125	125			125	125			100
Tanzania	150	150			132	150			94
Uganda	150	150	150	150	150	150	150	150	100
Vietnam	250	100	100		250	100	100		100

Note: Original commitments are based on figures provided in the program document for PRSC 1 or the CAS.
Source: World Bank SAP Business Warehouse.

Aggregate disbursements (DPL plus investment) have increased sharply in most PRSC countries (see Figure 3.4). The finding parallels the assessment by the World Bank's Operations Evaluation Department that, in general, PRSPs have provided a basis for higher, more stable flows (OED 2004a). This trend, however, depends on the structure of the country portfolio. In Vietnam, while PRSCs provide a more predictable flow of quick-disbursing resources, the higher aggregate disbursement levels are driven by new investment projects.

PRSCs have been broadly successful in maintaining an annual cycle of operations, and the annual cycle has proven beneficial in several respects. As long as performance is judged sufficiently satisfactory, the government can expect resource flows to be more regular and predictable. Among the seven PRSC programs that have moved past the first operation since FY01, the average lag time between board approvals was about a year (379 days).[16] In contrast, during the same period, the average lag time between tranche disbursements of multitranche policy-based lending was 14 months (441 days). More than 26 percent of these multitranche operations also required waivers or tranche restructuring. While actual lag times vary and are influenced by a number of factors, the annual cycle provides greater focus and emphasis on regularity, and some limit on the amount of time that both donors and governments have to make decisions and take action.

Design Options to Further Improve Predictability

Although the Bank's PRSC disbursements have been quite predictable, the Bank can exercise significant discretion in modulating disbursements of subsequent PRSCs as a response to underperformance. Similarly, an element of discretion is introduced in some PRSC programs when triggers are vaguely defined (for example, as "satisfactory progress with implementation"). While some flexibility is advantageous, undue discretion carries the risk of uncertainty. Transparent decision rules and clearly specified triggers can help set out clear expectations for donors and recipients and clarify their mutual accountability.

The Bank and other donors of budget support have introduced a range of innovations that address the concerns over excessive discretion. In some PRSC countries, they have incorporated a more formal response to underperformance. In Benin, for example, each of the three core sectors accounts for one-third of the total commitment, so that if implementation were off track in one sector, commitments would be reduced accordingly; however, the definition of "satisfactory implementation" is not clearly articulated. The Vietnam program uses a more specific approach: attainment of all triggers is considered a strong indication that Vietnam is ready to move to high-case lending, as established in the CAS; progress on most triggers and no backtracking on any of them leads in principle to the preparation of the next PRSC operation in base-case lending, while backtracking could lead to delaying the next operation—which in practice is equivalent to moving to the low case in the CAS.

All but three PRSC operations have been single-tranche annual operations: the first PRSC operations in Vietnam and Nicaragua were two-tranche operations, a design choice that reflected pragmatic considerations such as IDA allocations and

FIGURE 3.4 Increased Predictability and Volume of Bank Disbursements to PRSC Countries ($million)

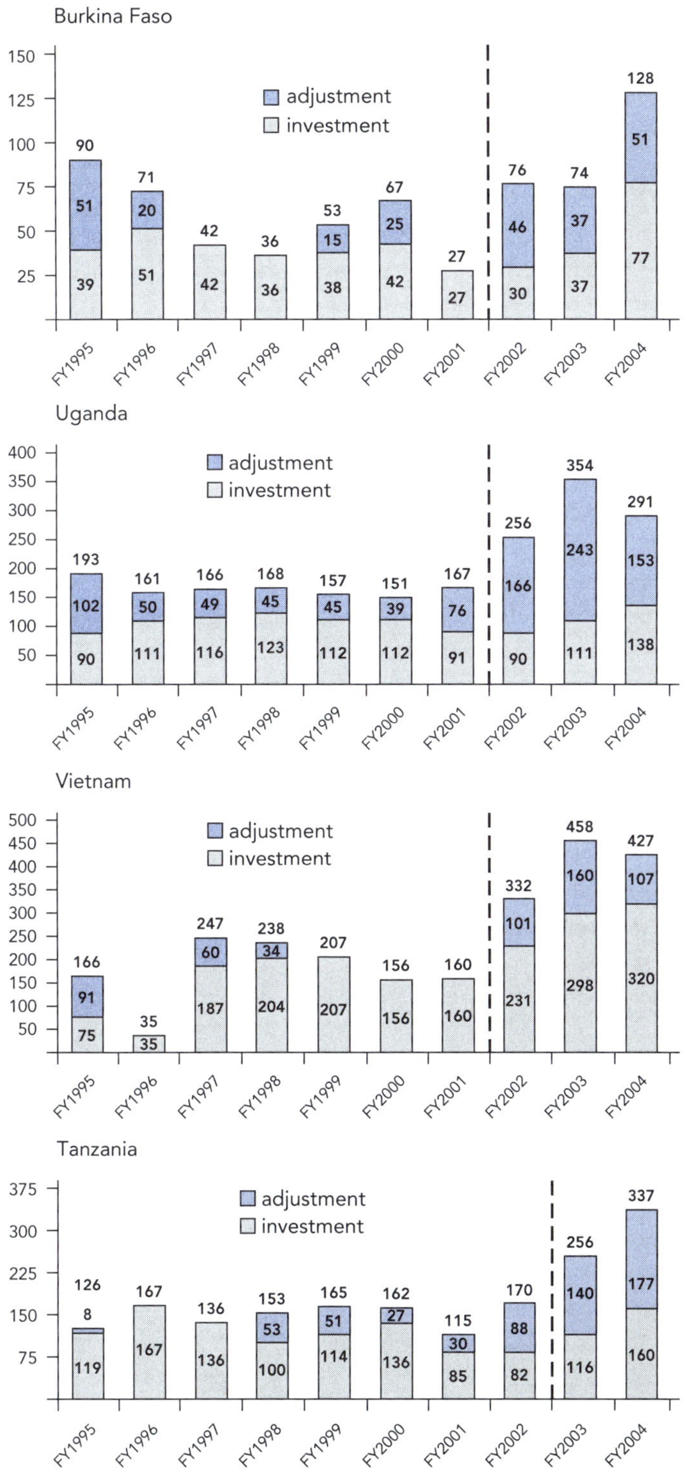

parliamentary approval, rather than the need for greater transparency or predictability. The Uganda PRSC 2 had a floating tranche whose conditions were particularly sensitive but were satisfied by effectiveness; thus it was disbursed along with the main tranche.

Given the PRSC's country selectivity, an argument has been made to move toward longer-term predictable commitments through an aid allocation model similar to IDA's (Foster 2005). This approach proposes that commitment levels be determined by an assessment of public expenditure needs and broad country performance ratings, such as the Bank's country policy and institutional assessment. Under these circumstances there would be less need for detailed conditionality at the operational level or for any specific actions or indicators that may be binding—as long as there is sufficient ownership and the country broadly pursues its overall development program. In fact, some donors have argued in favor of moving away from explicit conditionality on specific policy areas and confining conditionality to fiduciary concerns and overall adequate budget management. For Bank-supported programs, such a clear distinction between policy and fiduciary conditionality may not be appropriate: typically PRSCs address fiduciary issues as part of the development program. But for countries that are performing well and have benefited from more mature multiyear PRSC programs, the concept of a broader assessment of overall performance, based on fewer and perhaps less detailed progress indicators at the operational level, would be a natural evolution of emerging good practice lessons.

The EC and several bilateral donors have incorporated a graduated approach that combines fixed and variable tranches. Under this approach, the fixed tranche is designed to provide a relatively predictable base flow of budget support. Disbursement of the fixed tranche is broadly linked to input, output, or outcome indicators that are fundamental to program success and are very likely to be met, such as sound macroeconomic management (for which judgment is based on the IMF's assessment). The variable tranche is explicitly linked to performance. It may be linked mechanically to performance against specific indicators, whether formulated as specific measures, outputs, or in the case of EC aid, on outcomes; and it may be disbursed partially.

The Bank's regional strategy for Africa encourages experimentation with approaches such as variable tranching (World Bank 2003b). However, some caution is warranted in exploring this approach in the World Bank context. In the first place, variable tranching would reintroduce the traditional ex ante conditionality of multiple tranching that must be specified and met without flexibility. Because the programmatic approach is based on a series of annual operations, variable tranching in PRSCs would imply tranches that are explicitly tied to deadlines and precise measures rather than leaving the freedom to modulate, postpone, or withhold lending based on a new performance assessment. Under the Bank's operational policy, even a fixed tranche would still be conditional on an adequate macroeconomic policy framework and overall satisfactory implementation. Moreover, the difference in the size of the fixed and variable tranches would need to be significant to create incentives for governments to perform; otherwise, a large fixed tranche with minimal conditions might be viewed as an entitlement.

Timing of Disbursements and Alignment with Country Processes

Beyond design options, another way to make the PRSC more predictable is to strengthen the alignment of the PRSC cycle (preparation, approval, and disbursement) with the country's planning, review, and budget calendar and processes. While PRSCs have generally succeeded in providing stable annual disbursements, the aim of improving alignment with country processes is to ultimately disburse at, or close to, the beginning of the fiscal year, thus providing the government the maximum level of confidence and certainty it needs to execute the annual budget and begin program implementation.[17] To achieve such alignment, donors must time their assessments of country performance in a way that allows them to confirm commitment amounts when the government is setting the resource ceilings for budget formulation. This entails proper sequencing of several processes: sectoral and cross-sectoral program reviews, macroeconomic assessments, budget preparation, donor confirmation of commitments, donor disbursement, and budget reporting. Delays in any one process could disrupt sequencing.

An emerging consensus is that the PRSP annual progress report (APR) should play a central role in this process. The OED evaluation suggests that APRs have played a constructive role in reporting on progress and in adjusting strategies. This role could be strengthened, however, by more closely linking these reports with the budget and other domestic processes and ensuring that their timing is country driven (OED 2004a). Essentially, the PRSP APR allows governments to link planning, budgeting, and sectoral and thematic reviews while meeting donor reporting requirements. To implement this scenario, the APR must look forward as well as back: it needs to review the past year's progress across a range of sectoral and cross-cutting areas, and also inform current policy choices and articulate the government's priorities and budget needs for the next year. Such a comprehensive review would necessarily be linked to sectoral program reviews, PERs, macroeconomic assessments, and budget projections for the current and upcoming years. In this regard, the APR could contain the input, output, and outcome indicators on which donors and governments have agreed for assessing country performance. Such a comprehensive review would provide donors with the basis for making firm commitments of support for well-costed programs that are drawn from the PRSP (IMF 2004).

To achieve this alignment, the government must obviously first ensure strong links between the annual PRSP process and the budget and planning cycles. These links are still not well developed, and many governments have expressed uncertainty over the value and the intended purpose of the APR, often viewing it merely as an added burden.[18] The SPA survey referred to earlier (SPA 2005) revealed that among 15 countries currently receiving budget support, only Rwanda had complete alignment between the APR and the budget cycle and six countries had partial alignment; in most countries, the APR was still a pilot exercise or a limited progress report with shortcomings. It is important to note that, just like the PRSP itself, the APR should be seen as an instrument of domestic accountability. It should primarily serve domestic purposes and hence each country will determine for itself how it will carry out its annual reporting and how it wishes to use the APR. Guidance has been perhaps purposely vague specifically to give countries flexibility to determine the content of the reviews

(IMF and World Bank 2003). However, as a result of these weaknesses, many donors also remain uncertain about the operational usefulness of the information contained in the APR.[19]

While the role of the APR is clearly the responsibility of the government, donors may provide assistance to facilitate domestic PRSP alignment. The Bank's engagement through the PRSC could help remedy some of the weaknesses in PRSPs. This is particularly so in countries where the Bank and other budget support donors have coordinated their programs behind the policy priorities of the PRSP and where a substantial part of dialogue with the government has focused on improving links among policy, budget, and results monitoring and reporting. Good examples include:

- In Ethiopia, improved alignment with domestic processes was instrumental in the government's effort to design a single M&E system covering the PRSP, the PRSC, and other budget support programs.
- In Mozambique, budget support donors have encouraged the use of an existing annual progress report to Parliament as the main instrument for assessing PRSP implementation and as the basis for an annual joint donor-government assessment of budget support. The move places considerable importance on improving the quality and coverage of the report to Parliament.
- In Albania, one of the main components of the PRSC is to improve PRSP M&E through a variety of actions, such as establishing a baseline for regional distribution of health facilities and sufficiently staffing and funding the Institute of Statistics.
- Efforts to strengthen PRSP monitoring have gone farthest in Tanzania, where the PRSC focuses mainly on institutionalizing the M&E of PRSP targets.

Aligning domestic processes and calendars has implications for when to assess whether prior actions have been met. Although the aim of disbursing at the beginning of the fiscal year is important for many countries, PRSC disbursements often come later as a result of insufficient alignment with the budget cycle. To align PRSCs more closely with the budget cycle, PRSC teams have proposed to modify PRSC timetables to align with the budget cycle. In Burkina Faso, the Bank accelerated the preparation and approval of PRSC 4 to follow the previous operation after only ten months. The aim is to eventually catch up with the government's fiscal calendar, with PRSCs approved and disbursed in April-May. In Mozambique, the PRSC currently disburses halfway through the year, and the plan is to approve three PRSCs within six months of each other in order to align with the joint review and to disburse at the beginning of the calendar year. By contrast, for PRSC countries such as Ethiopia, Tanzania, and Uganda, the timing of resource flows is less important than the early confirmation of disbursement.

D. Conclusions

The PRSC has emerged as a robust and effective lending instrument that has been successfully introduced in almost all developing regions and broadly delivered on its promises. It is an appropriately flexible approach that is most suited to countries with strong commitment and sufficient capacity to undertake a medium-term reform program.

Although results vary from country to country, the PRSC has reinforced country ownership by (1) building upon the objectives, priorities, and measures set out in the government's PRSP with strong analytical foundations and sustained policy dialogue; (2) providing more predictable medium-term budget resources based on reform implementation and accompanied by increased attention to core public sector functions; (3) aligning with the annual PRSP process to better streamline donor performance reviews, assess implementation challenges, and determine future direction; and (4) reducing transaction costs by providing a framework for donor harmonization around budget support.

Certain features of the PRSC have emerged as strong points, in particular its combination of flexibility and predictability in responding to uncertainty and uneven performance, and its reliance on analytical and diagnostic work. As PRSC programs mature and are extended to more countries, emerging issues include the challenge of achieving closer donor harmonization and alignment with country processes and building a strong results framework to link implementation with development outcomes.

Endnotes

1. Policy measures in the PRSC include all policy and institutional reforms laid out in the policy matrix. However, a distinction is made between conditions (on which disbursements are contingent) and nonbinding measures or indicative benchmarks. Given the single-tranche, programmatic approach of the PRSC, conditionality essentially consists of "prior actions," which must be met prior to Board approval. For the purpose of this paper, conditionality or prior actions will be referred to only as conditions.
2. SPA, Budget Support Workshop, Kigali, Rwanda, June 2004.
3. In both Ethiopia and Mozambique, the initiatives are still evolving, and experience suggests a need to further clarify the role of the policy matrix and the process for deriving them. Certain line ministries apparently wanted to be more closely consulted on specific measures in the government matrix. Identifying reform measures may also benefit from greater consultation and participation by parliament and other key stakeholders, such as the private sector, in the case of Ethiopia.
4. www.aidharmonisation.com.
5. "Program Document for Pakistan PRSC 1" (28268-PK), World Bank, Washington, DC, August 2004.
6. See Table 7 of the "Program Document for Vietnam *PRSC 3*" (28916-VN) for a detailed description of the areas of involvement of each cofinancier.
7. One donor field-staff member noted the need to "harmonize harmonization," given the number of surveys and studies undertaken to track progress on country-level harmonization.
8. Paris Declaration on Aid Effectiveness: Ownership, Harmonization, Alignment, Results and Mutual Accountability, High-Level Forum, March 2005; www.aidharmonization.org.
9. In Uganda, these donors include the DFID, Ireland Aid, KfW, and the Netherlands. Several other donors, including the EU, DANIDA, Norway, and Sida, remain closely associated with the process but disburse against a separate set of indicators.
10. In Tanzania, donors point to the Bank's proactive role in involving donors in the PER process, and in Ethiopia, to the Bank's insistence with government that other donors be included in the policy dialogue.

11. While there is also considerable unpredictability in investment or project lending, it does not directly affect government planning and budgeting because disbursements typically reflect physical implementation and not recurrent expenditure. Volatile project disbursement therefore does not necessarily imply a funding gap that needs to be filled. See Foster (2005).
12. Thus a PRSC approved and disbursed in FY05 indicates the budget support envelope for FY06–08, and the next PRSC in FY06 updates the envelope for FY07–09.
13. The Sri Lanka PRSC program may be modified to reflect the revised PRSP currently being drafted by the new government.
14. The implementation completion report for Guyana PRSC 1 nevertheless rated the operation "satisfactory."
15. One other indicator of predictability is the synchronization of disbursement with the government's budget cycle, in the sense that resource flows should be timed as much as possible to when the government needs them most, typically at the beginning of the fiscal year.
16. The data do not include the time lag between Vietnam PRSC 1 and PRSC 2, because the former was a two-tranche operation, with the second tranche disbursed 200 days before the Board approval of the next operation. Moreover, actual lag time varies, from 10 months between Burkina Faso's PRSC 3 and PRSC 4 to nearly 16 months between Albania's second and third PRSCs.
17. The importance of the timing of disbursements varies among countries. The governments of Ethiopia Tanzania, and Uganda, for example, have noted that the firmness of the commitment is more important than the timing.
18. SPA, Budget Support Workshop, Kigali, Rwanda, June 2004.
19. SPA, Budget Support Workshop, Kigali, Rwanda, June 2004.

4

European Commission Budget Support: An Innovative Approach to Conditionality

DIRECTORATE GENERAL FOR DEVELOPMENT
European Commission

The European Commission (EC) has developed an innovative approach to budget support, drawing on lessons from previous balance of payments support for structural adjustment, international research on conditionality, and notably the Strategic Partnership with Africa (SPA) joint pilot of new approaches to budget support in Burkina Faso. The EC recently conducted a review of experience with this approach between 1999 and mid-2004. This paper outlines the main findings of the review.

A. The EC Approach: How Does it Work?

The conditionality framework in EC budget support programs is based on annual fixed and variable tranches, both subject to a minimum of general conditions related to macroeconomic stability (usually linked with an IMF judgment), progress with public financial management (PFM), and the existence of a poverty reduction strategy (PRS) (in low-income countries usually a poverty reduction strategy paper [PRSP]). Fixed tranches are released in "all or nothing" form provided that the general conditions are met. Variable tranches provide a greater or lesser amount depending on the extent to which targets are attained for a number of indicators, mainly pertaining to results and service delivery in social sectors, budget allocations and execution in social sectors, and PFM (Figure 4.1).

The EC's Poverty Reduction Budget Support (PRBS) is normally provided in the form of general budget support directly to the central treasury account.

The indicators used to determine the amount of the variable tranche to be disbursed need to be measured annually and capable of reasonable annual variation—probably in response to government action. Thus the kinds of results in question are not medium-term or long-term impacts such as literacy rates or life expectancy, but indicators, linked to the Millennium Development Goals or powerful proxies for them, at the level of annual service delivery outcomes (Box 4.1).

The full report on which this paper is based can be found at http://www.spa-psa.org/resources/2005/EC_GBS_VT_Review.pdf.

FIGURE 4.1 Typical Elements of Each Year's Operation in a Fixed + Variable Tranche Program

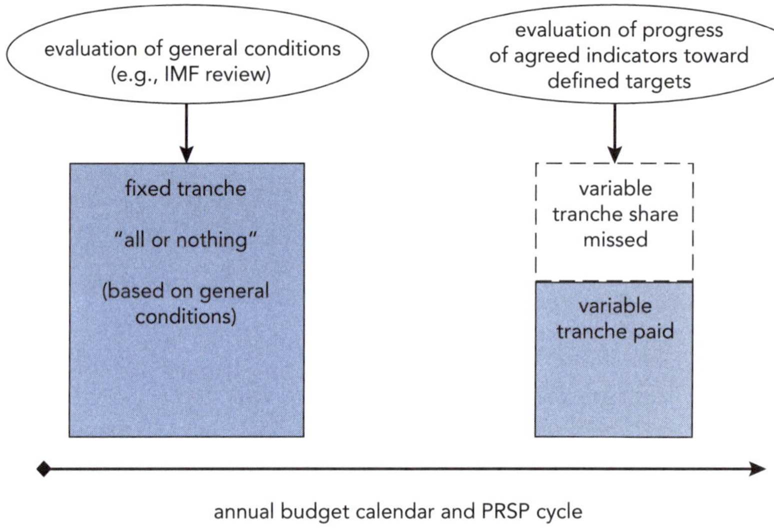

The maximum value of a variable tranche is defined in advance. In principle indicators should be drawn from the PRSP or other national—usually sectoral—strategy. Once indicators are chosen, targets are agreed for each year. Ideally these too are drawn from the PRSP or other national strategy, though in some cases (for example where this sets targets only for the medium term, such as the end of the PRSP period) annual target values have to be set specifically for the EC's PRBS variable tranche.

Once the data are available, actual outturns can be compared with target and baseline values. A range of options for scoring were tested in early programs, but in July 2003 the EC decided on a model of best practice: outcomes are scored 1 when the target is met; 0.5 when there is progress from the baseline but the target is not achieved; and 0 when there is no significant progress or actual regression. The weighted

BOX 4.1 What Does "Results" Mean?

Indicators used in variable tranches are usually at the level of the effectiveness, coverage, or uptake of public service delivery related directly to poverty reduction. A typical example would be primary school enrollment. This is classified as "outcome" in the EC "input-output-outcome-impact" typology: whereas the amount spent on primary education would be classified as an "input," the number of primary teachers trained would be an "output," and literacy rates would be an "impact."

Indicators are selected for their relevance to measuring progress toward poverty reduction, and are mostly chosen from, or close to, indicators used for the Millennium Development Goals. Some, however, deal directly with the coverage of key public services such as primary-level health care that are not among the globally agreed definitions of dimensions of poverty, but are accepted as strong proxies for its health aspects.

TABLE 4.1 Calculation of a Variable Tranche—Amount to Be Disbursed

	Baseline	Target	Actual	Score
Gross primary education, year 1 admission rate *(%)*	40.3	45	45.6	1
Gross primary education, year 1 admission rate for girls *(%)*	34.7	38	39.2	1
Gross enrollment rate for primary education *(%)*	43.4	48	45.8	0.5
Girls' gross enrollment rate for primary education *(%)*	37.2	40	39.0	0.5
Primary education dropout rate *(%)*	16.6	16	15.2	1
Total education				**4/5**
Vaccination coverage *(%)*	85	90	90.3	1
Births attended by qualified personnel	38.8	41	35.5	0
Use of curative services: consultations per capita	0.28	0.3	0.334	1
Total health				**2/3**
Total poverty reduction				**6/8**

Note: Because the total score is 6/8 = 0.75, the actual disbursement would be 75 percent of the tranche's maximum amount.

total score (which will be between 0 and 1) determines the share of the tranche disbursed.

A stylized worked example (Table 4.1) shows how this is done (the figures are taken from actual examples from more than one country). Note that in this case, only indicative titles of indicators have been given to illustrate the calculation methodology: in a real-world case, more specific concrete definitions would have been agreed, together with calculation methodologies and data sources, and the analytical report from the government would have assessed the reasons underlying the results as well as detailing their calculation. This example does not include any examples of PFM indicators, but the process of calculation would be exactly analogous.

In process terms, the EC seeks to work within joint donor groups wherever possible. These are usually organized around the national budget calendar, to which the commission has been encouraging countries to align their PRSP processes. If this is done so that a review of the past year's performance (for example, a PRSP annual report) takes place soon after mid-year, and if partner governments request it, it should be possible for the value of the variable tranche to be calculated in time to contribute to budget planning for the subsequent year, and for the payment to be made at the start of that budget year. This would allow the budget to be planned on the basis of a known level of EC PRBS, avoiding any in-year variability as a result of the variable tranche mechanism.

B. The EC Approach: What Is the Rationale?

The rationale for PRBS is based on expectations of its developmental value, both from budget support in general and from the results-based variable tranche approach. For budget support in general, the EC's expectations are to:

- support macroeconomic stability and growth, and provide additional resources for public expenditure of benefit to poor people;

- bring donor resources within national planning and accounting systems (especially the budget);
- enhance coherence in planning and resource allocation;
- give greater scope for local parliamentary scrutiny;
- give a stake in improving public financial management—for the whole budget; and
- reduce transaction costs, including by working jointly with other donors.

While these are all familiar to budget support donors, there are further expectations for the results-based variable tranche approach:

To encourage a focus on results. Traditional policy conditionality failed to look at what was actually happening in the lives of poor people. The commission's approach seeks to shift the focus of donor effort away from actions that donors wish to see taken and toward the results of government actions on the ground in terms of reducing poverty. Linking funding explicitly to the results actually delivered provides an incentive for all stakeholders to take results seriously and give priority to reducing poverty.

The linkage of funding to outcomes is a means, not an end. The results-based approach does not seek to calibrate EC funding exactly to the real achievements of a country in improving social sector outcomes. Rather, the goal is to encourage evidence-based policy making and ensure that resources make the maximum possible impact on poverty. This has implications for the role of donors.

By using indicators of service delivery/poverty reduction results, to protect the political space for governments to determine policy. Using indicators of results (vaccination coverage, primary enrollment) instead of policy conditions protects governments' ownership of the policy process. Instead of donors telling governments what they must do, using outcome indicators allows the commission to agree with government what results are expected and leave government the political space to decide how to reach them.

In addition to the research-based consensus on the importance of ownership, the use of outcome indicators also draws on two further insights. The first is that a modicum of humility is needed in view of the varied track record of donor policy prescriptions in the past. Indeed, donor advice on matters such as user fees has sometimes been sadly wrong. Countries' situations and capacities vary widely, and donors may not have as deep an understanding of the feasibility and acceptability of policies as would be desirable.

The second is that, when stated intentions may not reflect true national priorities (as revealed, for example, when a law is passed but not applied), and levels of policy effort are not directly observable, results-based conditionality provides the most appropriate set of incentives for a government to achieve the stated goals of poverty reduction.

In practice, results-based variable tranche operations have not suffered from the problem of credibility that has undermined much traditional policy conditionality. Whereas it has been common for waivers to be granted in policy-conditional "all or nothing" operations, no waivers have been granted for variable tranche indicators in PRBS operations (apart from for reasons of lack of clarity of definition and so forth).

To streamline conditionality. In addition to variable tranches, the commission also usually provides annual fixed tranches. These are increasingly subject to only the general conditions—usually those essential for determining the eligibility of a country for budget support.

To allow a graduated response to partial performance. Traditional conditionality has been "all or nothing": either conditions are met, and the funds are released in full, or they are not, and no funds are provided. In practice, few countries fully meet the letter and the spirit of all conditions on time, hence waivers or less formal relaxations of the interpretation of conditionalities have become common. This has reduced the credibility of conditionality, but has not sufficed to avoid the volatility created by "on-off" support.

In contrast, the variable tranche approach responds to partial performance with partial disbursement. The amount provided reflects the extent to which targets are met. This steers a middle course between the loss of credibility arising from waivers (suggesting that donors do not really stand behind their rhetoric about the issues for which waivers are granted) and the drastic fiscal impact of sudden suspension of support.

To promote domestic accountability. Bringing donor funds under government control also makes it possible to see the big picture—the totality of what is achieved. Because PRBS uses results indicators, this helps to focus attention on what is actually delivered, not just on where money is spent. Domestically, this makes it possible for citizens, through parliament, to hold government accountable for the results of its choices in policies and resource use.

Taken together with the increased scope for parliamentary scrutiny intrinsic to budget support, this should help to improve governance and promote evidence-based accountability. It will however only be fully effective if governments are ready to allow greater public scrutiny of their relations with the EC—requiring a significant shift in culture for both organizations.

To stimulate demand for quality data on poverty. The need for high-quality data for the variable tranche, together with enhanced domestic accountability, should create a demand for higher-quality data on results. Indeed, this impact on data quality is in itself one of the important expected gains from the PRBS results-based approach. When data on results are publicly available, it may be hoped that domestic interest in them will increase. When funding is attached to their achievement, there is increased interest in high-quality data being available—which is the essential condition for sustainable improvements in data quality. However, there is also a greater risk of deliberate distortion of results, which needs to be managed carefully.

C. EC Approach: What Does the Review of Experience to Date Show?

The recent review covers 34 programs in 20 African, Caribbean, and Pacific countries to end-July 2004. These programs will eventually consist of 100 fixed and 44 variable tranches, totaling €1,951 million. The review covers 20 variable tranches disbursed to date, of a maximum total of €252 million, and 33 fixed tranches totaling €591 million.

On average, fixed tranches make up 65 percent of commitments in programs with both fixed and variable tranches.[1] Fixed tranches have on average three general and one specific condition per tranche.

Variable tranches have on average around 15 indicators, with about 4 to 5 each in health and education. Though in principle indicators and targets should be drawn from the PRSP, in practice this has proved difficult, though alignment is improving. On average, PFM and budget indicators account for 45 percent of the value of variable tranches, with education averaging 22 percent and health 25 percent.

On average, 71 percent of a variable tranche is disbursed (the range being from 65 percent to 85 percent). Thus the difference between most and least successful countries is around 20 percent of the variable tranche, or about 8 percent of the total program—relatively limited variability (and relatively modest incentives). However, performance within sectors varies much more than the total.

There has been no need for waivers, despite the possibility of excluding indicators from the calculation if they are affected by exogenous shocks. However, it is disappointing that only half of countries used their variable tranche reports to analyze the reasons for failure to meet targets, and fewer drew concrete policy conclusions. It is also disappointing that few reports have been shared, and then only with other donors, not with parliamentarians or civil society.

Overall, experience with the approach has broadened. Since the 2003 guidelines reviewed the wide range of early pilots, the scoring methodology has stabilized and

FIGURE 4.2 Average Number of Conditions

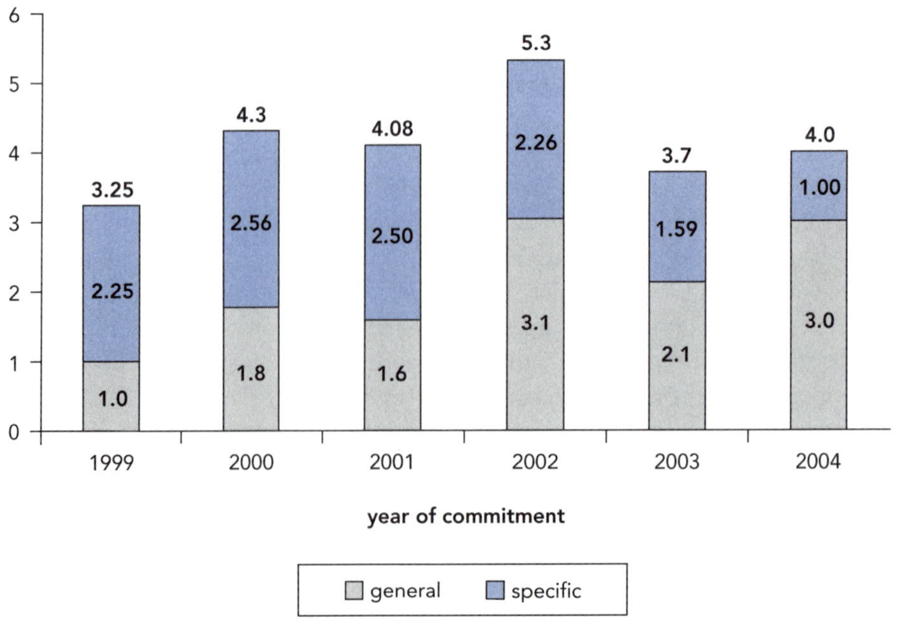

FIGURE 4.3 Average Composition of a Variable Tranche

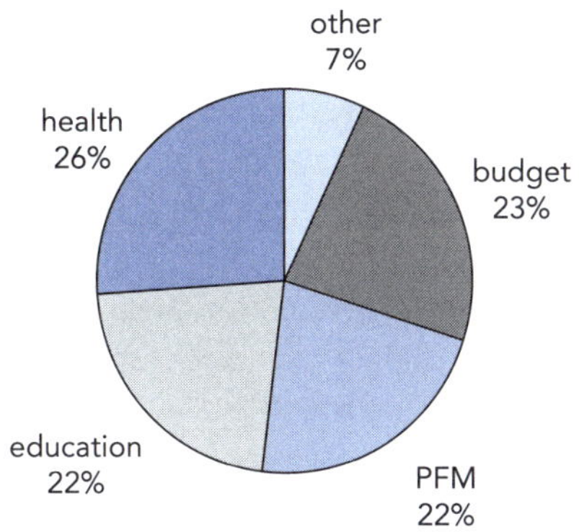

FIGURE 4.4 Average Yearly Disbursement Rate

(percent disbursed)

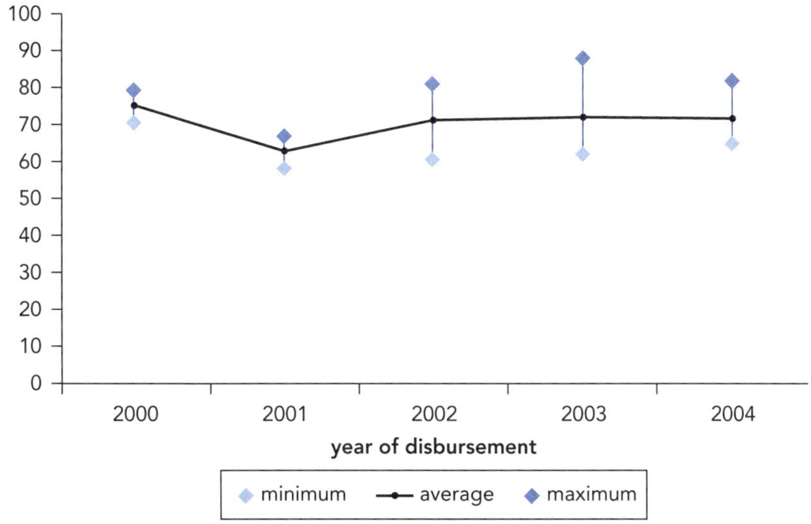

almost all programs now have annual results-based variable tranches. The proportion of funding linked to results has risen slightly over time, though it remains around one-third of the total—broadly in line with evolving policy. Within this, the difference between the disbursements in high-performing and less successful countries is fairly small, so the incentive effect is real but limited.

The number of conditions remains small, and specific conditionality has been streamlined. The variable tranches have indeed provided a graduated response to partial performance. The use of results indicators rather than policy conditions in social sectors has provided greater transparency in the judgment of performance, with less subjective elements in the assessment of compliance.

PRBS funds are indeed integrated into national budget systems. Disappointingly, there is little evidence yet of the use of PRBS results indicators in domestic political discourse or parliamentary scrutiny. However, there has been an increase in the weight of PFM and budget-related indicators in variable tranches. Together with the move to universal use of PFM conditions, this indicates that PFM is receiving greater attention, as intended.

There are signs that the alignment of PRBS indicators with PRSPs is improving. When variable tranche results and budget indicators are drawn from the PRS process, and their annual analysis forms part of the PRS annual review, as is increasingly the case, this approach does not add transaction costs for government but rather aims at ensuring that the dialogue around the PRS implementation takes the analysis of the results achieved as a departure point.

BOX 4.2 Frequently Asked Questions about the Commission's Approach to Budget Support

Does delay between taking actions and seeing results vitiate the approach?

In general, the kinds of indicators chosen can respond relatively swiftly to actions. PFM indicators usually move relatively fast in response to government decisions. Results in poverty reduction, too, can be quite fast moving: vaccination coverage rates can vary greatly from year to year, as can enrollment rates. It is true that some indicators—such as completion rates—vary more slowly, but even here, they may well be appropriate, with targets in later years becoming more ambitious to reflect actions taken in early years.

It is true that initially some indicators would reward past policy actions that shape present trends. However, because in general the commission has been supporting PRBS recipients for many years—often with previous budget support operations—this also reflects past assistance and dialogue.

Are there examples of this approach leading a government to focus on results and/or to change its policies when results are poor?

In one country, several education and health indicators missed their targets. The government's analysis of reasons suggested that there were demand weaknesses in education and restricted physical access to basic health services. As a result, the next annual implementation plan for the country's PRS included commitments to revise the primary education curriculum and broaden the network of rural health centers.

In several countries, poor results led to intensive reflection within government and intensive dialogue with donors. In one country, for example, failure to increase health center use led to an extensive revision of the health sector strategy.

Which are the most common indicators?

The most common indicators relate to budget allocation and execution rates in health and education and results in these two sectors: vaccination coverage, rate of assisted deliveries, use of basic health services, primary school enrollment and completion rates, and the gender gap in education.

Broadly, these findings confirm that the approach has made progress toward most of the key expectations held for it, though considerable further progress is possible. It is appropriate to persist with the basic approach.

Six areas for further work are identified:

- definition and revision of targets;
- PFM indicators in variable tranches;
- enhanced domestic accountability and the broader use of variable tranche reports;
- quality of data and support for statistical systems;
- choice of indicators when national strategies lack key aspects; and
- wider acceptance of the approach, which so far has been used only by the EC.

A number of frequently asked questions, and elements of the discussion they provoke, are explored at the end of the full report. A few are extracted in Box 4.2.

Endnotes

1. There are also a (declining) number of fixed-tranche-only operations, usually in response to shocks or conflict.

5

A Framework for Evaluating General Budget Support

MIKE A. HAMMOND
UK Department for International Development, and
Chair of Steering Group for Joint Evaluation of General Budget Support, OECD-DAC

General budget support (GBS) has increased in importance both financially and politically in recent years. This aid instrument provides financial assistance as a contribution to a government's overall budget, with conditionality focused on improving public financial management and the effectiveness of the budget.[1]

Now is an opportune time for a comprehensive evaluation of GBS. Few evaluations have been done to provide an overall picture of its results, relevance, efficiency, and effectiveness in different local contexts. Meanwhile, donors' shift to GBS has increased the attention given to key issues of development cooperation such as ownership, partnership, transaction costs, coordination, and alignment.

This paper reports on a framework for evaluating GBS that is being applied in a joint evaluation by the Development Assistance Committee of the Organisation for Economic Co-operation and Development (OECD), managed by the UK Department for International Development (DFID) on behalf of the joint partnership. The evaluation is assessing to what extent, and in what country contexts, GBS is relevant, efficient, and effective for achieving sustainable impacts on poverty reduction and growth. The evaluation is designed to yield lessons for future programs while also documenting the joint accountability of donors at the individual country level. Section A reviews the evolving goals of budget support and the current expectations of GBS as an aid instrument; Section B outlines the purpose, subject, and scope of the evaluation. Section C presents the evaluation framework, and Section D outlines the plans for implementing the evaluation.

A. Evolving Goals of Budget Support

Financial program aid—that is, budget support and balance of payments support—became widely used in the 1980s and early 1990s, mainly in relation to structural adjustment programs. Throughout this period, donors gradually shifted away from balance of payments support toward budget support.

Since the mid-1990s, the approach and underlying principles of budget support have changed. There is now widespread recognition that traditional forms of conditionality have been less effective than expected, that domestic political considerations are the prime factor in determining economic and political reform, and that development needs should be addressed jointly by donors and recipients (Koeberle and others 2005). Rather than using conditionality as a "stick," donors have come to view conditionality as a set of milestones to be agreed between themselves and the partner government. Meanwhile, the advent of poverty reduction strategy papers (PRSPs) has shifted the focus of aid toward objectives and strategies that are owned by the partner country, implying that GBS should be partnership based and should support country ownership. Acceptance that macroeconomic reform programs should center on the fight against poverty has increased the focus of budget support on pro-poor spending and, in particular, on protecting spending in social sectors. There is also widespread agreement within the aid community on the need to prioritize institution building (strengthening democratic accountability and transparency) and sound management of public finances, including macroeconomic stability.

A GBS program now normally comprises four elements: (1) the funds, which in most cases are disbursed in tranches linked to the fulfillment of objectives; (2) the policy dialogue; (3) the conditions attached to the support; and (4) technical assistance and/or capacity building activities, which are often linked to public financial/expenditure management.

Increasingly, GBS is seen as an alternative to more traditional project-based development cooperation. This follows from the broadened awareness of the problems of traditional development cooperation: high transaction costs, unpredictable funding, donor-driven priorities leading to inefficient public spending; and parallel off-budget systems that undermine the effectiveness of government systems and accountability.

Hence a long list of expectations of GBS as an aid instrument has developed. GBS is expected to focus on and support:

- better coordination and harmonization among donors, and alignment with partner country systems (including budget systems and results systems) and policies;
- lower transaction costs;
- higher allocative efficiency of public expenditures as (1) aid resources are increasingly on budget and spending is better prioritized against priority (poverty reduction strategy) targets, (2) the policy dialogue focuses on overall budget allocations rather than particular expenditure items, and (3) aid is delivered with lower transaction costs and more predictably;
- greater predictability of funding (to avoid earlier "stop-go" problems of program aid);
- more effective state and public administration as GBS is aligned with and uses government systems for resource allocation and financial management; and
- improved domestic accountability through increased focus on the government's own accountability channels.

These expectations, priorities, and objectives, further disaggregated, are reflected in the evaluation framework.

B. Purpose, Subject, and Scope of the Evaluation

The evaluation is explicitly designed as a cooperative effort of multiple agencies, and as such it is more concerned with the overall roles, processes, and results of GBS than with the specific results of a particular country's or agency's funds. The cooperative approach makes sense because GBS itself is partnership based and the financial support is "pooled," making it difficult if not impossible to distinguish that of one donor from that of another. Thus the evaluation focuses on the achievement of high-level development objectives that are influenced by the collaborative efforts of several actors.

Purpose

The evaluation is expected to identify evidence, best practices, lessons, and recommendations regarding to what extent, how, why, and when (in what contexts) GBS has reached and/or could reach its objectives and fulfill the expectations. The evaluation results should serve as useful inputs for (1) implementation of future GBS operations; (2) possible changes in policy, approach, and/or methods; and (3) decisions on when/where GBS is the appropriate and relevant instrument. The evaluation should also contribute to further development of the evaluation framework and to general guidelines for evaluating GBS.

The evaluation recognizes both the policy and operational interests of the donor agencies and the partner countries. Its primary audiences are donor agencies engaged in GBS, or planning to initiate GBS programs, and the governments in the case study countries. The results will probably also be of interest to a wider audience including governmental and civil society partners in both partner and donor countries.

Subject

The subject of the evaluation is GBS. As defined for the purpose of the evaluation, program aid can be divided into food aid and financial program aid. Financial program aid includes both budget support and balance of payments support, such as debt relief and import support. Budget support in turn can be divided into sector budget support and GBS (Figure 5.1).

All types of budget support include a lump-sum transfer of foreign exchange; differences then arise on the extent of earmarking and on the levels and focus of the associated policy dialogue and conditionality. GBS is direct, meaning that the currency provided generates an amount of local currency of equivalent value, but without any requirements regarding the justification of the use of the foreign exchange in the form of import documentation, because free convertibility of the domestic currency is permitted. GBS funds are in principle not earmarked, in the sense that the funds may be virtually accounted for against certain sectors, but there are no formal limitations on where funds may actually be spent.[2]

FIGURE 5.1 Program Aid

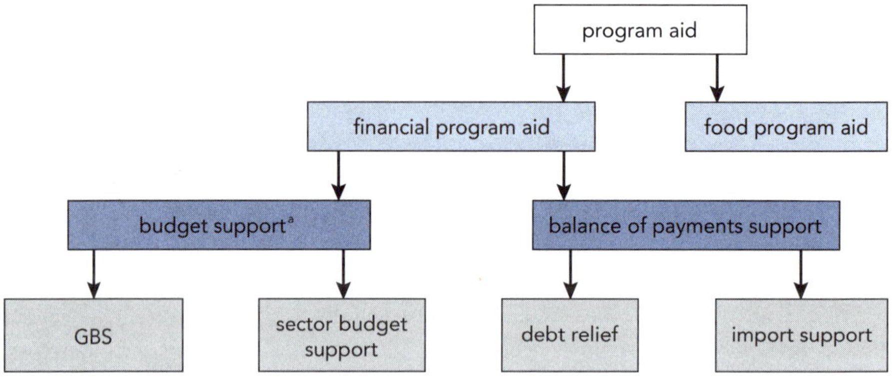

Note: a. Indirect budget support is provided through import programs or food aid, that is, it is provided in kind or in the form of a currency facility and requires the justification of the use of the foreign exchange through import documents and a countervalue fund in local currency.

The precise nature and definition of GBS may differ among donors, among partner countries, and over time.[3] An inventory of program aid commissioned by the Policy and Operation Evaluations Department of the Netherlands Ministry of Foreign Affairs (2003) found a lack of internationally agreed definitions on the different types of program aid, including GBS, and noted that reliable data on program aid are difficult to obtain. Hence the evaluation team is using a pragmatic approach in the inception phase, analyzing and discussing the types of GBS[4] provided by the different bilateral donors and the international financial institutions to the case study countries and the implications of the identified differences for the focus, approach, and methodology of the evaluation.

Though not the subject of the evaluation, other types of program aid such as food aid, balance of payments support (import support and debt relief), and sector budget support often interact with GBS and support the same objectives. Hence, to understand and learn about GBS and to make a correct assessment of its effectiveness and efficiency, the evaluation is considering other types of aid (bilateral and multilateral), and in particular other forms of financial program aid, in the context of GBS.

Though it will not seek to identify the specific contributions of different agencies, the evaluation is assessing the effectiveness of different approaches to GBS, such as the use of conditionality (ex ante and/or ex post), the use of indicators (process and/or results), the use of technical assistance (purpose and extent), the type of policy dialogue (focus and channels), the existence and use of coordination and harmonization forums, models for delivering/tranching funds, and exit strategies.

Scope

The evaluation covers the implementation and results of GBS during the period 1994–2004. Case studies will be conducted in partner countries, including Burkina Faso,

Malawi, Nicaragua, Rwanda, Uganda, Vietnam, and Mozambique, to illustrate different experiences of GBS in different country contexts.

C. The Evaluation Framework

The five-level evaluation framework developed for the study constitutes a structure for undertaking country-level evaluations of GBS operations. It builds on prior work and insights, including a literature review funded by the Swedish International Development Cooperation Agency (Sida) that summarizes existing findings, lessons, and recommendations in relation to the different levels of the framework. The framework also reflects extensive discussions at a workshop hosted by the DFID's Evaluation Department under the aegis of the Development Assistance Committee Network on Development Evaluation[5], and a subsequent workshop[6] hosted by the Ministry of Finance, Planning, and Economic Development of Uganda, where preliminary testing of the framework had been undertaken.

The five levels of the framework track the cause and effect links and the time dimension of the effects (Figure 5.2 and Figure 5.4):

1. *inputs* by GBS donors;
2. *immediate effects:* changed relationship between external assistance and national budget/policy processes;
3. *outputs:* positive changes in the financing and institutional framework for public spending and public policy;
4. *outcomes:* government capacity to reduce poverty enhanced; and
5. *impacts:* poverty reduced.

The framework is more general and broader in scope than the focus of the major evaluation and therefore requires further elaboration for use in specific country case studies.

The Levels of the Evaluation Framework

Levels 1 and 2 describe and analyze the inputs and immediate effects of the GBS programs: disbursement of funds, use and content of dialogue, application of conditionality and indicators (ex post/ex ante, results/process), focus and use of technical assistance (TA), and alignment and harmonization. To be able to assess the effectiveness of the different approaches to GBS, it is equally important to describe and analyze the GBS policies of the major donors, including the objectives linked to the inputs and exit strategies.

The effects and impacts of the different approaches to GBS on poverty reduction are being evaluated as far as possible, given the limits of the evaluation and that GBS has been in place only for a limited period in some of the case study countries.

FIGURE 5.2 The Evaluation Framework: A Simplified Version

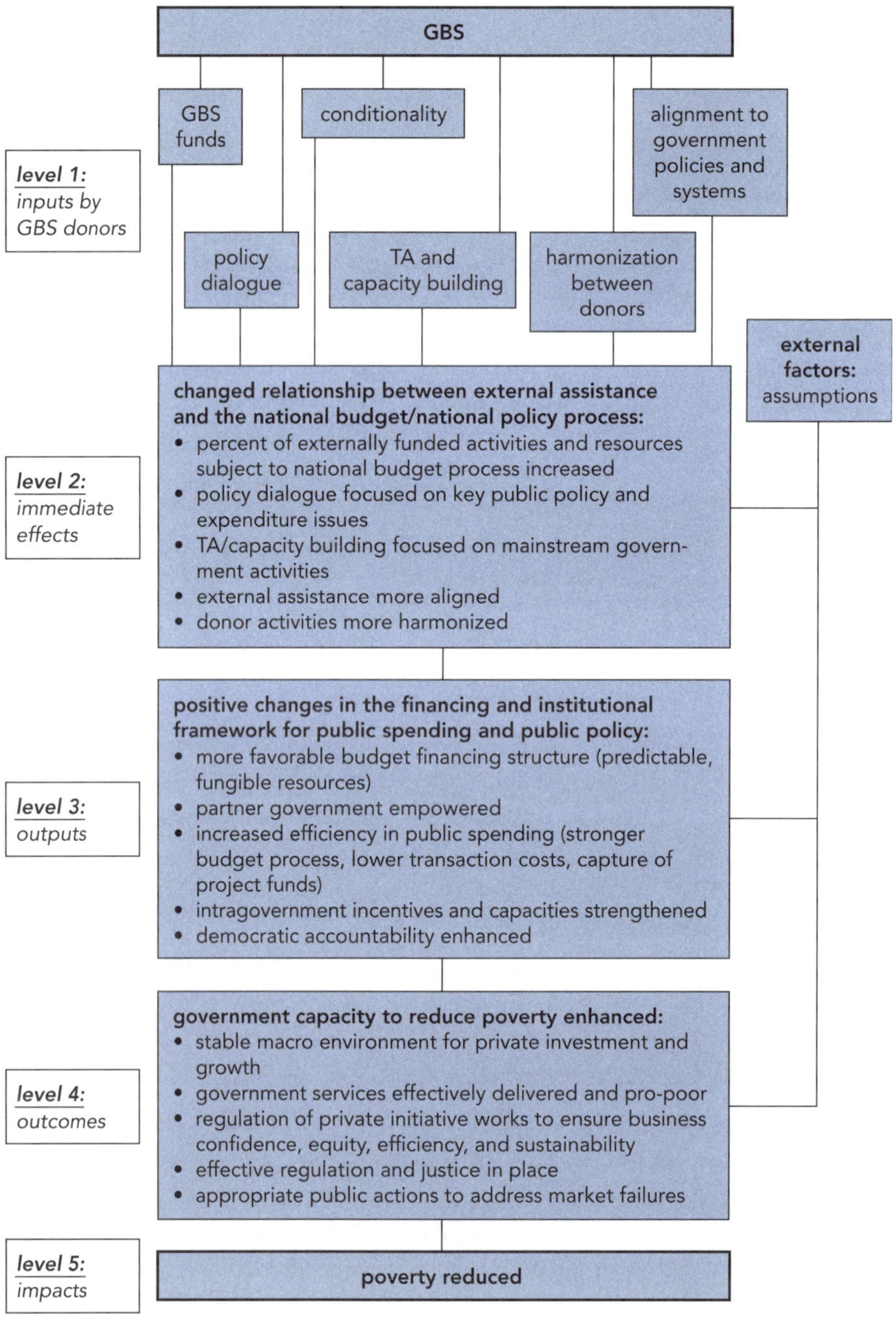

The effects up to level 3 are assumed to be short- or medium-term effects, and it is reasonable to expect attributable effects of GBS at these levels during the evaluated period.

The evaluation is also assessing the longer-term changes at levels 4 and 5, attributing to the GBS inputs where possible and discussing plausible links to the GBS inputs where not. It will discuss potential future effects on these levels given the findings at levels 1 to 3. The assessment of the changes at levels 4 and 5 will capture the issues specified in the framework—for example, the effects on public service delivery, the investment and business environment, and the role of the state.

The evaluation will try to capture the full chain of effects (input-output-outcome-impact) to be able to make a judgment on (1) the current effects and impacts of GBS, (2) the potential future effects and impacts of GBS, and (3) the importance of factors in the country context to the observed changes. This understanding is also very important in order to be able to assess the sustainability of the effects and impacts of GBS.

Though the main focus is on the intended effects of GBS, to ensure maximum learning, the evaluation is also assessing the intended and unintended (positive and negative) effects and impacts of GBS at all levels of the framework.

Institutional and Macroeconomic Effects

The evaluation covers both the institutional and macroeconomic effects of GBS. It seeks to capture the institutional effects at central and local levels of government in terms of (1) changes in allocative and operational efficiency of public expenditures, (2) effects on democratic accountability, and (3) the effects on public financial (expenditure and revenue) management. As regards the macroeconomic effects, it is assessing (1) the financial effects, including budget allocation and execution (sector allocation, pro-poor spending, discretionary spending, recurrent/investment spending) as well as domestic revenue and deficit effects;[7] (2) the impact on the balance of payments, including import level, capital account, and foreign exchange reserves; and (3) the possible effects on macroeconomic indicators (level and variability), such as the inflation rate, the real exchange rate, and the real interest rate.

Specific attention will be given to assessing how GBS has supported the PRSP process and the implementation of the PRSP.

Expectations of GBS as an Instrument

The evaluation is assessing the process and institutional effects of GBS against the expectations of GBS as an aid instrument, specifically regarding the predictability of funding, the transaction costs (types and levels), partnership and ownership, and donor coordination, harmonization, and alignment.

Donor coordination and harmonization and alignment of donor processes with national budget and planning processes (including the production and implementation of poverty reduction strategies) are key issues in GBS programs to support partnership and country ownership and decrease transaction costs (see the first two levels of the evaluation framework). The evaluation is assessing the progress in coordination, harmonization, and alignment, and analyzing the role of key actors (bilateral donors, international financial institutions, government) in the policy dialogue, in particular in relation to the principles of partnership and country ownership.[8]

Relevance and Cross-Cutting Issues

The evaluation includes an assessment of the relevance of GBS, particularly in relation to the country context (priorities, needs, and demands) and in relation to the objectives and problems addressed.[9] It is also addressing the cross-cutting issues of gender equality, environment, democracy, human rights, and HIV/AIDS.

Attribution and Causality

The evaluation emphasizes lesson learning. In analyzing the reasons and determining factors behind the observed changes and developments, the evaluators will give special attention to:

- the country context—including important changes and developments in the country, other types of aid present (bilateral and multilateral), quality of institutions, budgetary system, level of development, and exchange rate system, as well as the regional and global context—for example, trends in international trade and oil prices;[10]
- the different inputs of GBS—funds, dialogue, TA, conditions (which program inputs were the most important factors to the identified changes?);
- the different donors' approaches to GBS; and
- the development of GBS over the evaluated period.

D. Implementing the Evaluation

This is primarily a formative evaluation that requires a combination of several evaluation strategies and approaches, including a mix of qualitative and quantitative methods, to ensure its rigor and independence. Interviews with a broad range of actors, including donor and partner country representatives, constitute an important part of the approach.

The main elements of the evaluation are (1) a comprehensive inception phase; (2) seven country evaluations, including extensive field work resulting in seven country reports; and (3) a synthesis phase resulting in a final report, including global lessons and recommendations to donors and partner governments at both operational and policy levels (Figure 5.3).

To ensure broad participation in the conceptualization, oversight, and management of the evaluation, the commissioning organizations have constituted a steering group

FIGURE 5.3 Main Elements of the Evaluation

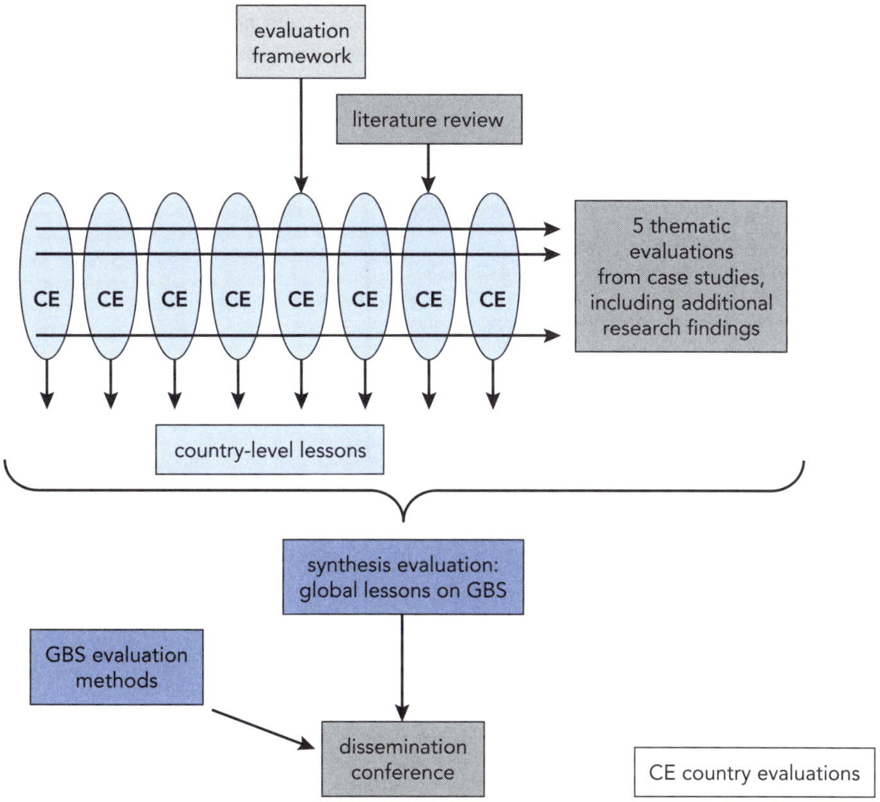

and a management group. The steering group includes representatives of the participating organizations and of the invited partner countries[11] and is chaired by the Evaluation Department of DFID. The management group comprises the Evaluation Department of DFID, the Evaluation Unit of EuropeAid at the European Commission, and the Department of Evaluation and Internal Audit at Sida. Country reference groups have also been established in the case study countries. The options for arranging these groups have been discussed and agreed with the partner country representatives. Broad participation was sought, including from civil society. Where possible, existing groups are being used.[12]

It is envisaged that the evaluation will be completed by January 2006. An international conference is planned for early 2006 to disseminate the findings and discuss the lessons and recommendations and their implementation. The Swiss government is carrying out a study on learning from experience with performance assessment frameworks (PAFs) and will issue its report in time for consideration along with the main study at the dissemination conference.

FIGURE 5.4 The Evaluation Framework

	cause and effect links	*assumptions (and risks)*
Level 1: inputs by GBS donors	1. GBS funds paid into national budget	
	2. policy dialogue linked to the budget funds	
	3. conditionality linked to budget funds	
	4. TA/capacity building linked to the budget funds	
	5. efforts to align donor's aid with national goals and systems	
	6. efforts to harmonize donor's aid with that of other donors	
Level 2: immediate effects on the relationship between external assistance and national budget/ national policy	1. proportion of external funds that is subject to national budget process is increased	other donors do not take offsetting action by moving funds off-budget
	2. policy dialogue in the country is focused on key public policy and public expenditure issues and processes	national authorities welcome this reorientation of dialogue
	3. TA/capacity building in the country is focused on key public policy and public expenditure issues and processes	national authorities are willing to accept and able to absorb increased TA or capacity building in this area
	4. aid in the country is more aligned with national goals and systems (especially, policy dialogue/conditionality is based on national objectives and plans)	other donors are willing and able to align with national goals and systems national plans are sufficiently robust to be a basis for dialogue/conditionality
	5. donor activities in the country are more harmonized (especially in respect of consistency in setting benchmarks reporting requirements and synchronizing missions)	other donors are willing and able to harmonize their procedures

FIGURE 5.4 ***(continued)***

	cause and effect links	*assumptions (and risks)*	
Level 3: outputs **improved financing and institutional framework for public spending/ public policy**	1. more favorable budget financing structure: • more predictable funding flows • higher level of fungible resources, which can be used flexibly • incidence of liquidity shortfalls reduced, hence less use of central bank overdrafts and less accumulation of arrears • cost of funding budget deficit reduced	GBS inputs not undermined or offset by high level of earmarking of other budget support donors disburse on terms that provide predictability to the partner government partner government does not take actions that compel interruptions in disbursement partner government has adequate reserve to cushion minor unplanned variations cash management by ministry of finance allows predictability of funding to line ministries/local government, encouraging them to plan.	
	2. partner government is empowered to: • use the budget to bring public sector programs into line with government goals (including poverty reduction) • align PRSP processes with government systems and cycles • promote alignment and harmonization by donors	political competition in the country is moving away from use of state resources for patronage toward a focus on results political leaders are prepared to take on political costs of new thinking centered on public expenditure management	Note: *model of GBS "club" suggests conditions for predictability:* • partners do not enter into GBS unless they both share key objectives and understand each other's constraints • **exit (non-disbursement) is limited by loyalty to this "club"** • effective consultation mechanisms are in place; the voice that this affords compensates for limitations on exit (see DFID, [2004])
	3. efficiency of public expenditure is enhanced: • by a more effective budget process (results-oriented, transparent, participatory, with effective execution and audit) • by reductions in certain types of transaction costs to partner government • by improvements in allocative efficiency from increased capture of project funds in budget • with efficiency gains in public service delivery in particular	government is committed to budget reform, and this has been internalized in the civil service transaction costs are large, with previous aid modalities there were significant inefficiencies in previous allocations	

FIGURE 5.4 ***(continued)***

	cause and effect links	*assumptions (and risks)*
Level 3: outputs *(continued)*	4. intragovernment incentives and capacities are strengthened: • official reporting lines are more respected (vertical through government to cabinet, not horizontal to donors) • public service performance incentives are strengthened so that policies are made and implemented, audit and procurement systems work, and corruption is reduced • brain-drain effects of parallel project management structures (permanent "poaching" + temporary de facto employment of key staff) are reduced	official reporting lines are still recognized in public service government applies pay and performance assessment policies that that contribute to incentives the political balance in the country is shifting toward punishing official corruption other donors do not increase parallel project management structures
	5. democratic accountability is enhanced: • greater role of parliament in monitoring budget results • accountability through domestic institutions for donor-financed spending is enhanced • conditions for all-round democratization are thereby improved, including the trust of people in their government and hence their level of expectations	constitutional and political conditions exist for parliament to increase its role there are domestic constituencies and pressures for higher standards of accountability
	↓	
Level 4: outcomes **enhanced influence of government on the proximate determinants of poverty reduction**	1. macroeconomic environment is favorable to private investment and growth: • inflation controlled • realistic exchange rate attained • fiscal deficit and level of domestic borrowing sustainable and not crowding out private investment	there is political commitment to macro stability and pro-poor spending reform macro conditionalities and recommended reform sequences are well chosen and executed Central bank sterilizes inflows so as to avoid negative effects on incentives to firms and households via exchange and interest rates

FIGURE 5.4 ***(continued)***

	cause and effect links	*assumptions (and risks)*
Level 4: outcomes *(continued)*	2. public services effectively delivered and pro-poor: • service delivery targets met for key pro-poor services • evidence of increased use of services by poor (including poor women)	key service delivery targets can be established, agreed, and monitored pro-poor services can be effectively prioritized service personnel are responsive to better and more pro-poor funding and management access of poor to services can be positively influenced by better targeting
	3. regulation of private initiative works to ensure business confidence, equity, efficiency, and sustainability; • policies on corruption, property rights resolutely pursued • market-friendly institutions developed	legitimacy of state is sufficient for regulatory role of public sector to be accepted confidence is not powerfully weakened by factors outside national control, e.g., regional instability
	4. more effective and accountable government improves administration of justice and respect for human rights, as well as general confidence of people in government	threats to national security do not become so acute that justice and rights are unable to share in general improvements in accountability and capacity
	5. sector policies include public actions to address major market failures, including those arising from gender inequalities	sector authorities do not confuse intervention to correct market failures with state interventions that prevent markets developing
Level 5: impacts **empowerment and poverty reduction in all its dimensions**	1. poverty is reduced (in all dimensions)	private agents accumulate assets, and/or total factor productivity increases, leading to faster economic growth the pattern of growth is pro-poor and/or effective redistributive mechanisms are in place the growth is environmentally sustainable the incidence of insecurity, injustice, and abuse of human rights is reduced
	2. poor people are empowered and socially included	ethnic factors that justify exclusion are reducing gender factors that restrain productivity and welfare of women and children are reducing

Endnotes

1. Budget support is channeled directly to partner governments using their own allocation, procurement, and accounting systems, and is not linked to specific project activities.
2. In practice, it might be difficult to distinguish between unearmarked, virtual, and real earmarked GBS, hence the application of a pragmatic approach to the fieldwork.
3. This explains the significant difficulties with data on GBS as found by Lanser (2004).
4. To include ODA grants and concessional loans as appropriate.
5. Evaluating General Budget Support, Glasgow, March 3–4, 2003.
6. Kampala, May 28, 2003.
7. Asking, for example, does GBS replace domestic revenue, increase expenditures, and/or decrease the deficit? Is GBS used for debt repayment, and could it in turn decrease debt service expenditures in the future?
8. The survey of alignment of budget support with poverty reduction strategy processes conducted by the SPA working group on budget support is an important reference.
9. Relevance: "The extent to which the objectives of a development intervention are consistent with beneficiaries' requirements, country needs, global priorities, and partners' and donors' policies." See definitions in Figure 5.4.
10. When assessing the importance of the context, it is particularly important to take into account the alternative aid instruments available for transferring resources and the long-term objective of poverty reduction.
11. Members of the steering group as of April 2005 are the governments of Burkina Faso, Malawi, Mozambique, Nicaragua, Rwanda, Uganda, Vietnam, Australia, Belgium, Canada (CIDA), Denmark, France, Germany (BMZ), Ireland, Japan (JBIC, MoFA), the Netherlands, New Zealand, Norway, Portugal, Spain, Sweden (Sida), Switzerland (SECO), United Kingdom (DFID), and USA (USAID). Also participating are the European Commission, Inter-American Development Bank (IADB), IMF, OECD-DAC, and the World Bank.
12. To ensure broader learning and knowledge generation, the DAC Network on Development Evaluation is establishing a "learning platform" for this and other evaluations of program aid.

6

General Budget Support: Key Findings of Five USAID Studies

Development Information Services

The aid instrument known as general budget support (GBS) is increasingly being used by donors, who argue that it gives host governments ownership of the development process by encouraging them to assume a more active role. When governments and donors work together to identify development priorities, development programs are likely to be more efficiently managed and sustainable. The policy dialogue encourages harmonization as donors work in concert to achieve common objectives. However, for GBS to be effective, it is critical that the recipient government be capable of responsibly managing donor funds and implementing development programs effectively, within a policy and institutional framework that is conducive to growth.

Donors who select GBS as an aid instrument are aware of its advantages. USAID has acknowledged in its white paper on foreign aid that these advantages include fostering important development principles, such as "increased ownership, partnership, and participation in country assistance strategies" and "improved donor coordination and harmonization" (USAID 2004b).[1] In this analysis, program assistance is most appropriate to promote transformational development in countries that are reasonably stable and have been assessed as top or good performers.

GBS is not appropriate for all activities, for example, if the host government does not have sufficient capacity to manage programs and funds. In such cases, project support may be used to strengthen capacity, either ex ante or in tandem with GBS. Other assistance instruments may also be more appropriate when donors do not agree on a coordinated approach to address sector issues. Other instruments may also be indicated when there is a need to strengthen democratic accountability, including support to parliaments, citizen oversight groups, and the media.

During 2003–04, USAID funded five studies to examine how well program assistance and GBS are working in Mozambique, Malawi, Nicaragua, Tanzania, and

---

This paper was first published by USAID as PPC Evaluation Paper 7 in October 2005 and is reproduced by permission. Anne Beasley, David Colin, Jeff Malick, Andrew Melnyk, Maxine Pitter-Lunn, Diane Ray, and Robert Burke of Development Information Services, and Brian Frantz and Joe Lieberson of USAID all contributed to this paper.
The views and interpretations expressed in this report are those of the authors and not necessarily those of the US Agency for International Development.

Timor-Leste.[2] The studies did not assess the impact of GBS and program assistance, but analyzed conditions that may contribute to their effectiveness. The countries studied all have poverty reduction strategy papers (PRSPs) or national development plans that define their poverty alleviation objectives.[3] This synthesis describes some key findings, reviews definitions of GBS, and summarizes discussions of issues such as ownership, budget allocation, performance assessment, donor coordination and harmonization, management capacity, fiduciary risk, and progress toward democratic and development goals.

The definition of GBS used in the studies was accepted in 2003 by donors participating in planning workshops for the Joint Donor Evaluation of General Budget Support and endorsed by the DAC Network on Development Evaluation.[4] Participating donors represented a range of bilateral and multilateral agencies, including USAID. The Terms of Reference for Joint Donor Evaluation (DFID 2004c) define GBS as a type of program assistance that can take the form of food or financial program aid. Financial program aid is subdivided into budget support (sometimes referred to as direct budget support) and balance of payments support, such as debt relief and import support.[5] Participating donors define budget support as a type of resource transfer in which funds are channeled directly to recipient governments. The recipient uses its own procurement and accounting systems, and the funds are not linked to projects. Budget support entails "a lump sum transfer of foreign exchange, but there may be differences on the extent of earmarking and on levels and focus of the policy dialogue and conditionality" (DFID 2004c, p. 3) (Figure 6.1).

There are two types of budget support: GBS and sector budget support. GBS contributes to the overall budget of a country; it tends to move away from requiring specific conditions to be met prior to disbursement. Instead, GBS moves toward using assessments of performance for a past period to determine future disbursements. Funds are not specifically earmarked.

Sector budget support is a resource transfer to support activities in an area with a common theme, such as health or education. But sector budget support should not be confused with the sectorwide approach (SWAp). Whereas sector budget support is a financing instrument, a SWAp is a coordinated strategy in which donors and host governments agree on a single sectorwide policy and expenditure program.[6] A SWAp is not an aid delivery instrument, though it may be supported with different financing instruments.

A. Issues Analyzed

Host-Country Ownership

Host-country ownership refers to the leadership role a recipient country takes in initiating and moving forward its development program. It includes the government's commitment to key reforms and the building of civil society agreement around priorities.[7] Host-country ownership also strongly implies alignment of donor policies and priorities with those of the national government. Processes that strengthen ownership

FIGURE 6.1 Joint Donor Categorization of Program Assistance

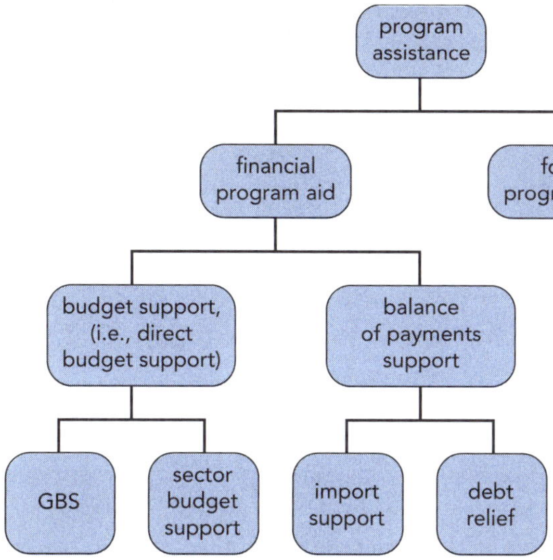

include the ongoing policy dialogue with donors, led by ministries of finance, and evolving internal accountability relationships within recipient governments.

Under GBS, donors channel funds through host-government systems for allocating, monitoring, and managing financial resources. This encourages long-term commitment to development objectives and helps the government institutionalize its own development management. Commitment to sound policies is critical to the effectiveness of GBS.

Governments may revise policies or take political risks to achieve poverty objectives. For example, the government of Mozambique agreed to revise its primary education curriculum and broaden its network of rural health centers after education and health targets were missed. Donors viewed this willingness to change as evidence of the government's commitment to its poverty reduction plan (EC 2005, p. 50). Another example was provided by the Bolaños government in Nicaragua, which committed in 2003 to reducing spending and increasing productive activities to accelerate GDP growth in line with its national development strategy.[8] Conversely, in Malawi, the government was not able to stay on track with IMF programs; thus, in March 2004, GBS disbursements were suspended (Lieberson, Ray, and Frantz 2004, pp. 1, 19–21).[9]

Policy Dialogue

An important input to the GBS process is policy dialogue between recipient governments and donors that assesses past performance and sets future targets. Ministries of finance normally lead policy discussions, and this process strengthens their commitment to the development agenda. Reviews focus on progress on indicators in a performance assessment framework, an action matrix, or a medium-term budget expenditure framework. The studies recommend that these discussions include measures aimed at improving the enabling environment for private sector business, economic growth, and social service delivery.[10] This has not always occurred.

Donors in all the countries studied consider participation in policy dialogue one of the most important aspects of the GBS process because it enables them to coordinate on and influence policy. Participation is especially important for smaller donors because it allows them to increase the impact of their limited resources (Frantz 2004). Several donors in Timor-Leste commented that working toward common objectives fostered collaboration. They also said that including items on the action matrix was the most effective way to influence government policy (Malick, Beasley, and Melnyk 2005, p. 16).

Participation of non-GBS donors in the policy dialogue varies by country. In Tanzania, Timor-Leste, and Nicaragua, all donors participate in the dialogue, although with some restrictions. In Tanzania, meetings where targets are negotiated are closed to non-GBS donors. The Budget Support Group that negotiates with the Government of Nicaragua includes both GBS donors and those who provide technical assistance to the government. In Mozambique, USAID, a non-GBS donor, is an observer, as opposed to a full participant in budget and policy negotiation (Lieberson, Ray, and Lunn 2004, p. 9).

The quality of the dialogue may be compromised when the government does not fully participate or when important issues are omitted. For example, lack of senior government participation in Tanzania led some donors to conclude that the government might view the process as more technical than policy-oriented (Frantz 2004). The country study questions whether the government would be willing to seriously discuss non-poverty-reduction priority expenditures or have its internal processes scrutinized.

One caveat noted is that host-country ownership may be compromised when ministries of finance have capacity constraints and donors are closely aligned on policy issues.[11] The study team concluded that rigorous biannual reviews with donors might have caused the Government of Timor-Leste to have a perception of diminished sovereignty.

Internal Accountability

Internal accountability refers to interactions of government ministries with each other during the budget process. Three studies (Nicaragua, Mozambique, Tanzania) indicate that line ministries vie with each other for scarce resources and justify their requests to central ministries (Nilsson 2004, p. 30). Over the long term, this process strengthens internal coordination and management within the recipient government, but it may cause tension between ministries over the short term.

Under projectized aid, line ministries often negotiate directly with donors for funds. Weaker ministries may need to be institutionally strengthened so that they can effectively carry out these negotiations. Within the Government of Nicaragua, donors universally acknowledge that health and education are the strongest ministries. These ministries have been strengthened since the mid-1990s by donor resources used for projects in these sectors. Frequently, the ministries negotiated directly with donors, bypassing the Ministry of Finance and the Presidential Secretariat for Strategy and Coordination, which normally play lead roles in planning and budgeting. Under GBS, the responsibility for budget allocation is expected to return to these two central ministries, a healthy process that is expected to strengthen the government's management of its development (Burke and others 2005, p. 10).

Budget Allocation, Performance Assessment, and Disbursements

Unlike project funds, GBS funds are not earmarked, and their use is determined through the budget allocation process. This results in on-budget donor funding and contributes to strengthening poverty reduction strategies (PRSs) and tracking expenditures. GBS also entails compromises from donors and the host government as they negotiate priorities.

Funds on Budget

GBS proponents maintain that there is less opportunity for access to extrabudgetary finance when donor funds are channeled through the central government budget. Nevertheless, there is greater budgetary discipline in some of the countries studied than in others. In Tanzania, GBS has become the predominant aid delivery mode.[12] In Timor-Leste, highly centralized budget and payments systems have contributed to on-budget finance. On the other hand, in Mozambique and Malawi, many donor projects have been off budget,[13] and significant expenditures have been excluded from the recurrent budget.[14]

Performance Targets versus Conditionality and Predictability

GBS donors are attempting to use performance targets to guide disbursements, as opposed to ex ante conditionality. Much of the current literature on aid effectiveness concludes that basing disbursements on policy reforms is not very productive unless recipient governments are committed to such reforms over the long term.[15] Accordingly, GBS donors hold reviews with the government to discuss progress and outcomes on mutually agreed targets in an assessment framework or action matrix. The "new" GBS focuses on shared objectives for public sector reform and reducing poverty (University of Birmingham 2005; DFID/FCO/HMT 2005). Performance is usually assessed on indicators related to both poverty alleviation and macroeconomic stability.[16] A stable macroeconomic environment is necessary for growth, so staying on track with IMF programs is important.

Another approach is to divide budget support funding into tranches linked to different criteria.[17] This is what bilateral GBS donors have done in Nicaragua.[18] In Malawi, GBS disbursements have been delayed because of poor fiscal management, notably large government deficits.[19] In Tanzania, a number of indicators in the assessment framework are based on the development of laws, strategy documents, plans, and reports rather than poverty alleviation results (Frantz 2004, p. 5). Assessing the impact of programs spent on poverty alleviation implies additional costs, because instruments such as surveys must be up and running to measure results.

Timor-Leste differs from the other countries studied because it is a new, post-conflict, and fragile country.[20] Early milestones stressed building new institutions, establishing a legislative and regulatory framework, and strengthening management of core government functions. Some early targets were intentionally ambitious and could not be achieved. Discussions thus focused on progress rather than achievement of goals, and disbursements could occur when progress was deemed satisfactory (Malick, Beasley, and Melnyk 2005, p. 17).[21] Less ambitious and more achievable indicators were set in Timor-Leste's third Transition Support Program (TSP) at the urging of the World Bank and other donors.

Poor fiscal policy can cause delays in GBS disbursements. When donor funds provide a large portion of a government's recurrent budget, predictable disbursements are critical to the government's ability to plan, function, and provide services to constituents.[22] The studies find that some GBS donors have adopted practices that contribute to more predictable disbursements:

- Assessments of past performance affect disbursements for future periods rather than the current budget cycle, improving predictability.
- Disbursements are coordinated with the budget cycle of the recipient government.

Donor Coordination and Harmonization

A premise of GBS is that donors will work with host governments to achieve development goals that correspond to the recipients' priorities. Donors working together harmonize their activities and aid management procedures, including their reporting requirements, conditionality, disbursement mechanisms, and provision of technical assistance.[23]

Donor Coordination

The studies find that GBS is typically participatory: donor groups and host governments engage in discussions on development objectives, set targets, and review progress. When the groups are aligned, their impact on development objectives is significant. This is often cited as a principal advantage of GBS. Nevertheless, close alignment of donors may inadvertently compromise ownership of a host government's program, especially when donor funding constitutes a large portion of the government's budget.[24]

In the African countries reviewed, donors formed groups that facilitate coordination. In Tanzania, the group refers to itself as the Poverty Reduction Budget Support Donors; in Mozambique, it is the G-11,[25] in Malawi, the group is called Common Approach to Budget Support (CABS). In these countries, donors are aligned on most issues and work with host governments to set priorities on the assessment framework. Coordination issues may arise when donors do not agree on all issues or when the host government's agenda is not aligned with that of the donors. For example, donor alignment in Mozambique is not completely harmonized on issues such as fiduciary risk and corruption. In Malawi, the government's failure to meet fiscal targets caused a coordination problem between donors and the IMF. The IMF had to make some optimistic assumptions to show that the country was moving ahead on indicators to which CABS disbursements were tied. This created a stalemate: progress could not be made without the disbursements, and disbursements could not occur until targets were met.

Donors may coordinate by participating in SWAps, which are discussed in the Mozambique, Malawi, and Nicaragua studies. An underlying assumption of a SWAp is that donors and the host government agree on a sector strategy. Collaboration enhances donor coordination and encourages ministry leadership of donor activities. For example, when a number of donors in Mozambique and the Ministry of Agriculture adopted a common strategy to support raising incomes in rural areas, they collaborated by participating in Pro-Agri, a SWAp. USAID uses various instruments, including program assistance, to support Pro-Agri.

In Nicaragua, however, donors and the government have not been able to agree on overall strategies in the agricultural sector. Some European donors and the UNDP favor the development of smallholder agriculture, whereas the government and other donors (including USAID) prefer to assist large-scale producers with more commercial and export potential. These differences impede the development of a common strategic sector approach.

Donor Harmonization

GBS advocates maintain that the process of implementing the aid mechanism will lead to harmonization as donors adopt common procedures for disbursements and reporting requirements. The studies find that although progress has been made, harmonization is not complete. Donors in four of the five countries—Mozambique, Malawi, Nicaragua, and Tanzania—continue to use individual criteria laid out in bilateral agreements to guide disbursement decisions.[26] Timor-Leste is somewhat distinct: funds are disbursed by the World Bank rather than by individual donors.

Transaction Costs

Transaction costs refer to staff requirements such as time and personnel, as well as financial outlays required to design, manage, and evaluate activities.[27] Early supporters of GBS argued that harmonization of procedures and reduced numbers of projects would lower costs for both donors and the recipient government. Few studies have focused exclusively on this issue, but the evidence is that GBS may initially cause donor transaction costs to rise. Harmonizing procedures and processes may take longer than envisioned and require significant additional effort (Nilsson 2004, p. 43). For donors, transaction costs are expected to fall once common systems are in place and capacity is built up. But demands on staff time increase when donors manage project portfolios concurrently with the design of new programs, including GBS. Senior members of donor agencies often find their increased responsibilities include negotiating with the host government. Measuring the impact of budget support assistance on poverty alleviation may also increase costs.

When a multilateral organization takes a lead role in administering GBS, donor transaction costs may fall. This is the case in Timor-Leste, where the World Bank has primary responsibilities for administering funds and assessing progress in the country's TSP.[28] TSP donors participate in and review missions and meetings organized for the World Bank, and they receive reports that summarize findings.

As GBS is implemented, there is likely to be heavy involvement of finance and other central ministries that take a lead role in organizing the policy dialogue, allocating budgets, and monitoring and evaluating activities carried out with donor funding.[29] Government negotiators need to be knowledgeable and trained in macroeconomic analysis and have the ability to address complex issues. In Nicaragua, some responsibilities have shifted from line ministries (which had previously negotiated with donors) to the Ministry of Finance, although project management responsibilities under GBS will increase for line ministries. In Timor-Leste, the Ministry of Planning and Finance takes the lead in preparing for and organizing meetings for intensive review missions led by the World Bank.

Management and Technical Capacity

Ongoing discussions focus on the required level of management capacity in GBS-recipient countries and how this capacity can be effectively provided. Management capacity refers to the ability of the government to plan and administer its own development program as well as handle funds responsibly.[30] Disparities in capacity may exist between different ministries, within the same ministry, and between central and local levels of government. The need to strengthen management and technical capacity is recognized as an issue in all country studies.

Donors realize that technical assistance must be a component when they provide GBS to countries where there is weak management capacity (Nilsson 2004, p. 23). A particular concern for donors is the capacity of the host government to transparently manage its finances and track funds. Donors are moving to the position that capacity building can be concurrently carried out as funds are disbursed.[31] Technical assistance to build capacity is provided (often through projects) by donors.

Capacity to Manage Financial Resources

Host-country capacity to manage financial resources is critical because the GBS mechanism uses a country's own financial and procurement systems. It is important that processes are adequate to allocate funds, execute the budget, and generate timely financial reports. An integrated financial management system is a key element that facilitates linking expenditures to budgets. With the exception of Timor-Leste, technical assistance is being used to install these integrated systems in the countries studied:[32]

- In Mozambique, a new integrated financial management system is user friendly; it is designed to be operated by relatively untrained staff, and training is planned so that users can train additional users.

- In Tanzania, the installation and use of an integrated financial management system is progressing slowly, especially in offices with capacity constraints (such as the National Audit Office and local government agencies).
- In Nicaragua, much of the World Bank conditionality focuses on successfully implementing an integrated financial system.
- In Malawi, an integrated system was first introduced in 1996, but the World Bank was still trying to install it in 2004, which led to the conclusion that the government was not strongly committed to using the system.

Capacity Constraints in Ministries and Local Governments

GBS requires central ministries to play significant roles in budget formulation and implementation, negotiating with donors and overseeing policy reforms. However, adequate management capacity was found only at the highest ministerial levels in Nicaragua, Mozambique, and Timor-Leste. In Mozambique and Malawi, the strongest planning and budgeting capabilities are in ministries of finance. The Tanzania study noted that delivery of GBS is expected to strengthen the capacity of the Ministry of Finance to plan, budget, and negotiate.

Lack of ministerial capacity to implement projects was identified as an issue in the Nicaragua and Timor-Leste studies. In Timor-Leste, expatriate advisers occupy critical positions in a number of ministries, including the Ministry of Planning and Finance,[33] and management capacity and institutional strengthening have been ongoing since independence in 2002.[34] A recent TSP review mission identified capacity building as a high-risk area, and a program is being designed to strengthen skills in budget allocation, execution, and macroeconomic forecasting (Malick, Beasley, and Melnyk 2005, p. 42). Once significant oil revenues come on stream, the government of Timor-Leste plans to phase out the TSP and opt for projects. Though the government believes that project assistance can address their capacity constraints at the micro level through joint planning and implementation, the study team believes that project assistance is insufficient to address the capacity constraints that exist throughout the government (Malick, Beasley, and Melnyk 2005, p. 28).

In Nicaragua, some line ministries have more capacity than the Technical Secretariat of the President. This is the central ministry responsible for public investment planning and budgeting, where staff need training in basic budgeting skills. The country study concludes that management weaknesses are more serious constraints than technical weaknesses because technical experts (consultants) can be hired to provide specific expertise (Burke and others 2005, p. 14). Limited managerial capacity to implement projects was identified as the greatest single obstacle to rapid transfer of donor resources to GBS.

All studies found that capacity tends to be weakest at local government levels. The Tanzania study indicates that only about 25 percent of local government agencies have adequate capacity to manage funds (Frantz 2004). In Mozambique, low management capacity in line ministries coupled with low capacity in the provinces result in long delays before allocated resources reach the local levels where service delivery takes place.[35] In Malawi, similar constraints and insufficient local staff result in delays in resource transfers and service delivery, but the World Bank is encouraged by a high level of commitment to improving financial management at lower levels of government (Lieberson, Ray, and Frantz 2004, p. 23).

Fiduciary Risk

Fiduciary risk is defined in World Bank documents as "the possibility that actual expenditures will diverge from authorized expenditures, whether because of misappropriation or misallocation" (Allen, Schiavo-Campo, and Garrity 2004, p. 10). However, GBS donors add a third dimension that incorporates concepts of economy, efficiency, and effectiveness: funds "do not achieve value for money" (University of Birmingham 2005, annex F 154; DFID 2004). Corruption—defined as the "abuse of entrusted authority for private gain" (USAID 2004)—is not synonymous with fiduciary risk but is usually addressed as a corollary to it.

The studies assessed fiduciary risk as high in Mozambique, Tanzania, and Malawi, low in Timor-Leste, and significantly decreased in Nicaragua under the Bolaños administration. In part, the high rates in Malawi and Mozambique were caused by budgets that were not comprehensive and only weakly linked to policy. In Mozambique, line ministry budgets were not directly linked to the PRSP, and line items may not have reflected PRSP needs. In Malawi, neither parastatal funding nor normal ministry utility costs were included in the recurrent budget; ministries were expected to cover these items with supplementary budget requests later in the fiscal year (Lieberson, Ray, and Frantz 2004, p. 22). Donors noted that the Government of Malawi's effort to fully fund pro-poor expenditures was a "significant achievement," but the number of budgeted pro-poor expenditures increased, as did the number of "special activities."

Though budget allocation in Tanzania is fairly consistent with PRSP priorities, the government spent more on priority sectors than it received in official development assistance in FY 2003, when the budget increased. Proportions allocated to priority sectors did not increase faster than expenditures for nonpriority items.[36] Another issue for donors was that a key pro-poor ministry—health—was also one of the worst in accounting for funds and supplies and monitoring results. This unresolved issue could have an impact on the value for money dimension that many GBS donors include in their definition of fiduciary risk.

The system of public expenditure in Timor-Leste is sound and fiduciary risk is low. This is due to a highly centralized system of internal controls, World Bank oversight, and a significant number of expatriate personnel in key positions in the Ministry of Finance and line ministries. However, there are two potentially weak areas in the system of checks and controls: the Banking and Payment Authority reports to the Ministry of Planning and Finance (absence of check on payments), and the auditor reports directly to the prime minister (affecting perceptions of the integrity of independent findings) (Malick, Beasley, and Melnyk 2005, p. 23).

Systems Designed to Decrease Fiduciary Risk

Donors have different levels of tolerance for fiduciary risk. Risk can be reduced when a sound budget process is governed by a clear set of rules, allocations are linked to

PRSP policies, and expenditures follow allocations and are spent on services or programs related to poverty alleviation. Other factors are transparent procurement systems, timely and accurate financial reporting to track expenditures, and regular internal and external audits as controls.[37] If satisfactory systems are not in place, GBS donors join in a partnership with the host government to monitor and improve financial management, transparency, and accountability.

The ability to track public expenditures is facilitated by integrated financial systems. GBS donors widely use the public expenditure review (PER), the country financial accountability assessment, and the country procurement assessment, designed by the World Bank to strengthen the budget process, financial accounting, and controls and procurement.

The PER has become a forum where these and other issues are resolved. In Tanzania, the World Bank, Ministry of Finance, other government representatives, donors, UN agencies, academic institutions, and civil society all participate in preparing the PER agenda. This reduces fiduciary risk. However, several Public Expenditure Tracking Surveys suggest that a significant proportion of resources are not reaching local schools and hospitals in Tanzania. This lack of transparency is probably attributable to both low capacity and outright corruption (Frantz 2004, p. 11–12).

Budget Execution

When budget and procurement processes are highly centralized, fiduciary risk may be reduced. But bottlenecks in these processes also slow down budget execution, thereby delaying local-level activities identified for funding. Weak budget execution was identified as an issue in Mozambique, Malawi, and Timor-Leste. In Mozambique, this resulted from poor accounting, partial reporting, and weak cash management, which contributed to major delays in transferring funds from the Ministry of Planning and Finance to line ministries, and then on to provincial and district activities (Lieberson, Ray, and Lunn 2004, p. 19).

In Timor-Leste, highly centralized controls and little delegation of authority contribute to poor budget execution. The problem lies with an insufficient number of local staff trained to carry out rigorous procedures associated with procurement and payments. Only a few key officials have approval authority, and this holds up procurement and spending. To overcome these problems, the government established a budget execution committee to monitor expenditures and drafted legislation to delegate procurement and financial authority to line ministries. A UNDP pilot project to provide block grants to districts is also being initiated (Malick, Beasley, and Melnyk 2005, p. 23–24).

Corruption

Governments with weak financial systems offer more opportunities for abusing authority, and less transparent financial and reporting systems contribute to an environment conducive to corruption. Unsatisfactory or untimely financial reports make it difficult to discern whether resources have been stolen or simply not adequately tracked. In the five countries studied, procurement weaknesses along with the capacity to track expenditures to the service-delivery level can contribute to corrupt practices.

GBS donors work together to address these issues and discuss anticorruption measures and civil service reform with host governments. Donors in Malawi use the share of investigations brought to court by the Anti-Corruption Bureau as an indicator of progress (Lieberson, Ray, and Franz 2004, p. 20). In Nicaragua, the World Bank's performance assessment includes indicators linked to transparency in procurement (Burke and others 2005, p. 21–22).

Some donors argue that there are fewer opportunities for diversion when funds are channeled and tracked through projects. GBS proponents counter that funds are fungible: those used for a specific project or activity can free up funds for less transparent uses (Allen, Schiavo-Campo, and Garrity 2004, p. xi).[38] GBS donors work with recipient governments to improve financial management because they believe that improved systems will result in less overall corruption. Donors interviewed for the Tanzania study do not believe that the increased use of GBS has been associated with more corruption. However, corruption may become more apparent as financial systems are strengthened, regardless of whether more funds are actually diverted (Nilsson 2004, p. 31).

Progress toward Democratic and Development Goals

Governance is key to achieving development objectives[39] and includes supporting parliamentary oversight, private sector NGOs, and media and civil society. NGOs and think tanks can encourage transparency and responsiveness by conducting public surveys and making the results easily available. Investigative reporting by strong media can discourage corruption. Project assistance, rather than GBS, may be more appropriate for strengthening these institution-building activities (Lieberson, Ray, and Frantz 2004, p. 13).

B. Conclusions

The selection of development approaches and instruments—such as project and non-project assistance (including GBS)—should be based on country contexts. The five case studies give country-based examples of the uses and limitations of GBS. They do not evaluate the impact of GBS on poverty alleviation. Instead, they focus on perceived benefits within specific conditions and time frames, adding examples and explanations relating to whether or why the benefits have been achieved, as well as the following issues:

- *Host-country ownership.* Ownership of development programs has been strengthened through the policy dialogue and improved accountability. The discussion includes progress on indicators, many of which are drawn directly from PRSPs or their equivalents. Other indicators relate to fiscal and macroeconomic achievements and sound financial management practices. A government's internal accountability is improved as line ministries justify policies and activities to each other and to their ministry of finance, rather than negotiating directly with donors for funds.

However, when donors are closely aligned on policies, the host government may feel pressure to adhere to donor priorities, and this may compromise ownership somewhat.

- *Budget allocation, performance assessment, and disbursement predictability.* A benefit of GBS is that more donor funds tend to be "on budget" because ministries have less access to other sources of funding. This has been the case in Tanzania, where a high proportion of official donor funding is channeled through GBS. However, bilateral donors in some countries may continue to negotiate off-budget projects and other arrangements with favored ministries. Using performance targets, as opposed to ex ante conditionality, tends to increase predictability of donor funding, because assessments usually have an impact on disbursements in future—rather than current—periods. Aligning donor disbursements with the budget cycle of recipient governments also contributes to predictability.
- *Donor coordination and harmonization.* GBS and coordinated SWAps assume that differences in donor policy, philosophy, and approach are reconciled. The studies conclude that this is usually, but not always, the case: donors may not share an approach,[40] or they may have different concerns that feed into their individual criteria for disbursement. In most countries studied, harmonization of donor procedures, policies, and reporting is taking longer than anticipated and has not yet been completed.
- *Transaction costs.* For both donors and host governments, staff time required to design, manage, and evaluate activities initially increased. When donor portfolios include projects, additional time is dedicated to designing GBS programs and participating in policy dialogue. The same is true for host-government staff, especially in their ministries of finance. Many donors, however, are optimistic that these costs will drop once programs are running and policies and procedures are more harmonized.
- *Management and technical capacity.* Weak management and technical capacity are noted in all country studies. In Mozambique and Malawi, capacity in ministries of finance exceeds that in line ministries. However, Nicaraguan line ministries, favored in the past by donors, have stronger capacity than central ministries. Weaknesses in local government capacity impede service delivery in Tanzania and Malawi. The assumption is that the process of delivering GBS will in itself build capacity because it is "learning by doing." Nevertheless, capacity building (including the provision of expatriate advisers) may be also be offered concurrently through other aid mechanisms. To increase financial management capacity, integrated financial management systems are being installed and personnel are being trained.
- *Fiduciary risk.* The possibility that funds will be used for unauthorized expenditures is important to GBS donors, who use the host government's financial and procurement systems. Donors have different tolerance levels for fiduciary risk, which may influence their decisions to use GBS. Instruments such as the public expenditure review, developed by the World Bank, are commonly used to assess the budget process and financial risk. Fiduciary risk is often linked to low capacity, so donors work in

partnership with host governments to strengthen financial management. When financial systems are highly centralized, poor budget execution may result, delaying procurement and spending. Weak procurement systems and poor expenditure tracking are conducive to corruption. Some donors believe that these issues can be addressed during the policy dialogue and that corruption does not increase with GBS.

- *Progress toward democratic and development goals:* GBS, which channels funds through the executive branch of the central government (usually the ministry of finance), may not be the most appropriate assistance instrument for strengthening parliament, civil society, the media, or NGOs. These entities have important roles in democracy, because they contribute to good governance and the ability of citizens to hold their government accountable for providing services and contributing to poverty alleviation and development. Assistance mechanisms, such as projects, that complement GBS may be appropriate for supporting these activities.

The studies find that the following contribute most to the effectiveness of GBS:

- strong host-government commitment to sound poverty reduction and fiscal and democratic policies;
- agreement by donors and host governments on common approaches to development objectives;
- sufficient host-government capacity to manage development programs or, if not sufficient, capacity-building mechanisms provided by donors, either as projects or as a component of GBS;
- low fiduciary risk.

Endnotes

1. USAID's White Paper, *US Foreign Aid: Meeting the Challenges of the Twenty-first Century,* is intended to stimulate discussion of major policy issues surrounding development and foreign aid. It is not a statement of official US Government policy.
2. MALAWI: "General Budget Support and Sector Program Assistance", Malawi Country Case Study Evaluation Working Paper 19, by Joseph Lieberson, Diane Ray, and Brian Frantz (PN-ADA-999). "What Conditions Favor the Success of General Budget Support and Sector Program Assistance?" Malawi Country Case Study Evaluation Brief 12, by Joseph Lieberson, Diane Ray, and Brian Frantz (PN-ADA-356). MOZAMBIQUE: "General Budget Support: An Alternative Assistance Approach", Mozambique Country Case Study Evaluation Working Paper 19, by Joseph Lieberson, Diane Ray, and Maxine Lunn (PN-ACW-878). "What Conditions Favor the Success of General Budget Support?" Mozambique Country Case Study, Evaluation Brief 11, by Joseph Lieberson (PN-ACU-999). NICARAGUA: "General Budget Support in Nicaragua: A Case Study of an Alternative Assistance Approach", PPC Evaluation Paper 6, by Robert V. Burke, David Colin, Aldén J. Jirón Z., and Lissette González (PN-ADD-631). TANZANIA: "General Budget Support in Tanzania: A Snapshot of Its Effectiveness", by Brian Frantz (PN-ADA-029). TIMOR-LESTE: "Program Assistance: The Democratic Republic of Timor-Leste Country Case Study." by Jeff Malick, Anne Beasley, Andrew Melnyk, and Shinichi Mizuta. The Mozambique, Malawi, Nicaragua, and Timor-Leste studies were commissioned by USAID's Bureau

for Policy and Program Coordination. The Tanzania study was prepared by USAID's Bureau for Africa to inform the development of the USAID-Tanzania Country Strategic Plan for 2005–14.

3. Two of the countries studied, Mozambique and Nicaragua, were ranked as eligible for Millennium Challenge Account (MCA) funding, while three—Malawi, Timor-Leste, and Tanzania—were ranked as MCA threshold countries. Timor-Leste had the status of a post-conflict or fragile state in 2002, when budget support began through the Transition Support Program (USAID 2004b, p. 19).
4. The definition was developed by Lawson and Booth (2004) for this evaluation and drew on a schematic developed by White (1999).
5. USAID divides foreign assistance into two broad categories: project assistance and program assistance. Program assistance, also referred to as nonproject assistance, "provides a generalized resource transfer, in the form of foreign exchange or commodities, to the recipient government (USAID 2005a). USAID identifies two types of program assistance (1) sector program assistance and (2) balance of payments and budget support.
6. A program-based approach is "a way of engaging in development cooperation based on the principle of coordinated support for a locally owned program of development, such as a national poverty reduction strategy, a sector program, a thematic program, or the program of a specific organization" (Lavergne 2003).
7. See Johnson and Wasty (1993) and annex F in the final inception report (University of Birmingham 2005) for discussions of ownership that focus on these issues.
8. The government agreed to continue to meet social targets. Although donors had some reservations about this policy, they approved it and encouraged the government to revise its PRSP to recognize its new strategy (Burke and others 2005, p. 4).
9. With the election of a reform-minded government in mid-2004, performance has improved, and Malawi is now an MCA-threshold country.
10. See Harvey (2002) for a provocative discussion of the situation in Mozambique.
11. See Fozzard (2002) for a discussion of the role of the Ministry of Finance in Mozambique and Odén and Tinnes (2003) for a similar discussion on Tanzania.
12. In Tanzania in FY 2002, the share of assistance provided as program support was 58 percent, up from 32 percent in FY 1999 (Frantz 2004, p. 1).
13. The proportion of total funding provided through program assistance and GBS was not available in the Mozambique study, although it ranged from 0 to 75 percent as proportions of individual donor aid packages.
14. In Malawi, extrabudgetary requests were a standard part of the budget process (Lieberson, Ray, and Frantz 2004, p. 22).
15. Interesting discussions that support this argument include Dijkstra (1999, p. 1), Dollar and Pritchett (1998), Nilsson (2004, p. 47), and DFID-FCO-HMT (2005).
16. Donors may also develop their own additional, specific assessment criteria.
17. The European Commission (EC) disburses by fixed tranches, linked to performance on IMF programs and macroeconomic performance, as well as variable tranches, linked to the achievement of indicators related to PRSPs and poverty alleviation indicators (EC 2005).
18. Poverty alleviation indicators are related to social services and private sector development (Burke and others 2004, p. 18).
19. As a result, donors suspended disbursements, which resulted in government deficits financed with domestic debt. This drove interest rates up and impinged on the government's implementation of its poverty reduction program.
20. Timor-Leste became an independent country in May 2002.

21. In Tanzania and Nicaragua, individual donors determine the size of disbursements, based on their perception of progress made by the recipient governments toward achieving targets (Frantz 2004, p. 4; Burke and others 2005, p. 18).
22. The Tanzania study (Frantz 2004: 16) suggests that budget support has been less variable than project support, although no political events have occurred to test this suggestion. However, in Uganda, Ireland delayed disbursements of GBS when a defense issue came up that could not be resolved.
23. Nilsson (2004) presents definitions and findings from the literature.
24. These are conclusions of USAID studies in Nicaragua and Mozambique. Nilsson (2004) found similar situations in Mozambique and Tanzania.
25. The G-11 are the 11 countries providing GBS; this name is expected to change to the G-14 to reflect the enlarged membership.
26. In Tanzania, the universe of indicators that trigger disbursements are set out in a framework developed by the government and donors.
27. Killick (2004) examines the argument that program aid is associated with lower transaction costs than project aid. He classifies costs as *administrative tying*, which occurs when the recipient government loses national ownership as a result of tying aid to a large number of projects or procures imported goods and services. He also classifies costs as *fiscal* when fiscal discipline erodes in the recipient country as a result of a large number of off-budget projects being negotiated between line ministries and donors.
28. The World Bank charges a flat 2 percent administrative fee from donors' contributions. Many donors perceive that this is lower than what they would expend administering the program themselves.
29. This was a finding in Tanzania, Mozambique, Nicaragua, and Timor-Leste.
30. The development of a PRS or national development plan by the recipient government is an indication of these skills.
31. The DFID, for example, stated in its Mozambique Country Assistance Plan, "We recognize the weaknesses which exist in planning and budgeting, in expenditure management, and in the responsiveness of government to civil society; but these weaknesses can only be addressed if donors work within the system" (DFID 2002, p. 17).
32. In Timor-Leste, a computerized system was installed, presumably before the TSP, and used to track funds.
33. In September 2004, 58 critical posts were filled by expatriate advisers under the UN Mission to East Timor, of which 19 were in the Ministry of Planning and Finance (Malick, Beasley, and Melnyk 2005, p. 42).
34. In Timor-Leste, capacity was devastated when 28,000 high- and mid-level Indonesian civil servants fled after independence.
35. The study team found that fewer than 3 percent of personnel in provinces and districts had university degrees.
36. This became an issue in the 2003 budget review (Frantz 2004, p. 8).
37. These principles are laid out in the DFID policy paper on managing fiduciary risk when providing direct budget support (DFID 2004b). DFID plans to publish a policy paper related to procurement systems.
38. The argument is also presented in the Nicaragua study (Burke and others 2005, p. 5).
39. Kaufman (2003, p. 17) provides evidence that improving rule of law and controlling corruption lead to a fourfold increase in per capita income, significant literacy gains, and reduced child mortality.
40. For a discussion on different approaches to productive sectors in Nicaragua, see Burke and others (2005, p. 10).

7

Does General Budget Support Work? Evidence from Tanzania

ANDREW LAWSON, DAVID BOOTH, MELEKI MSUYA, SAMUEL WANGWE, AND TIM WILLIAMSON
Overseas Development Institute
and DAIMA Associates

Direct financial support to a country's budget is a long-established form of aid—as old as development assistance itself. But the last five years have witnessed an important development—the rapid growth of budget support operations informed by a new and distinctive aid philosophy emphasizing flexible funding for country-led poverty reduction efforts.

How important is "new" budget support, or general budget support (GBS)? Category problems make this difficult to quantify using OECD-DAC aid statistics. But in a number of countries in Africa, it already accounts for 20–40 percent of the government budget. Several major donors have indicated a firm intention to scale up their aid programs relying primarily on GBS. Recipient governments are increasingly expressing a preference for this modality.

Is this is a good use of aid funds? Is GBS the most effective way of contributing to poverty reduction in the South? This paper describes the results of the first major joint evaluation of country experience with GBS, carried out in Tanzania in 2004. It was commissioned jointly by the Government of Tanzania and the 14 external financing agencies currently providing GBS.

A. How Can We Judge Success?

Evaluations have to make assumptions about the intentions, and "theories of change," that underlie the programs being investigated. Success is judged by whether the intentions have been realized and whether the results have been brought about in the expected ways.

Some budget support programs have quite limited objectives (for example, facilitating a narrow set of public sector reforms). Others are meant to support poverty reduction in a country without an explicit concept of how this is to be achieved. However,

This paper was originally published by the Overseas Development Institute, London, in July 2005, and is reproduced by permission. The full report on which this summary is based may be downloaded from www.mof.go.tz or www.tzdac.or.tz/budgetsupport.

donor policy thinking is increasingly informed by more fully developed ideas about why GBS is to be preferred over other ways of supporting poverty reduction.

The Tanzania evaluation was the first to make use of an "evaluation framework" that articulates these stronger claims that are now made about GBS as an aid modality. The framework is summarized in Figure 7.1.

Figure 7.1 shows the way GBS is supposed to contribute to the final objective of poverty reduction. The framework can be used to investigate the effects of programs with limited objectives. But its main value is in detailing the intermediate changes in institutions and systems that are seen as important in "new" GBS theory. These changes are seen as the crucial mechanisms by which poverty outcomes and impacts will be improved over a period of time.

Figure 7.1 is a simplified version of the evaluation framework used in the Tanzania study. It concentrates on describing the chain of beneficial effects claimed for GBS. The counterfactual is what would have happened if equivalent resources had been delivered by other means. Factors external to the GBS program, such as the direction of change in the country's political system, are recognized as important. In its more complete version, the framework includes a fuller treatment of "risks and assumptions"—that is, the conditions under which the model is expected to work.

B. The Tanzanian Context

The evaluation covers 1995–2004. This period corresponds roughly to the two terms of President Benjamin Mkapa, who was the winning candidate of dominant party CCM in Tanzania's first multiparty elections in 1995. Helped by the kind of policies Mkapa has pursued, this has been a period of general improvement in the aid relationship. The scene was set more specifically by the ground-breaking Helleiner Report, an independent study that was highly critical of both government and donors. Helleiner suggested the need for a fresh approach, including stronger government leadership of development efforts. An important feature of the Mkapa period has been the emergence of a strong and capable Ministry of Finance. Major improvements in public financial management took place during the first half of the evaluation period.

GBS has been provided in its present form (poverty reduction budget support) since financial year 2000–01. The number of development partners (donors) involved in the arrangement has steadily expanded since the signing of the first memorandum of understanding in October 2001. In FY 2004–05, some US$400 million was expected to be disbursed by 14 development partners. When added to HIPC debt relief, this represents more than 20 percent of Tanzania's total budgeted expenditure.

C. Findings

The findings cover each of the five levels of the evaluation framework. They tell us whether there is evidence of the expected changes occurring, whether the changes seem to be attributable to GBS or other processes linked to GBS, and what other factors have been important in making changes happen.

FIGURE 7.1 Simplified Logical Framework

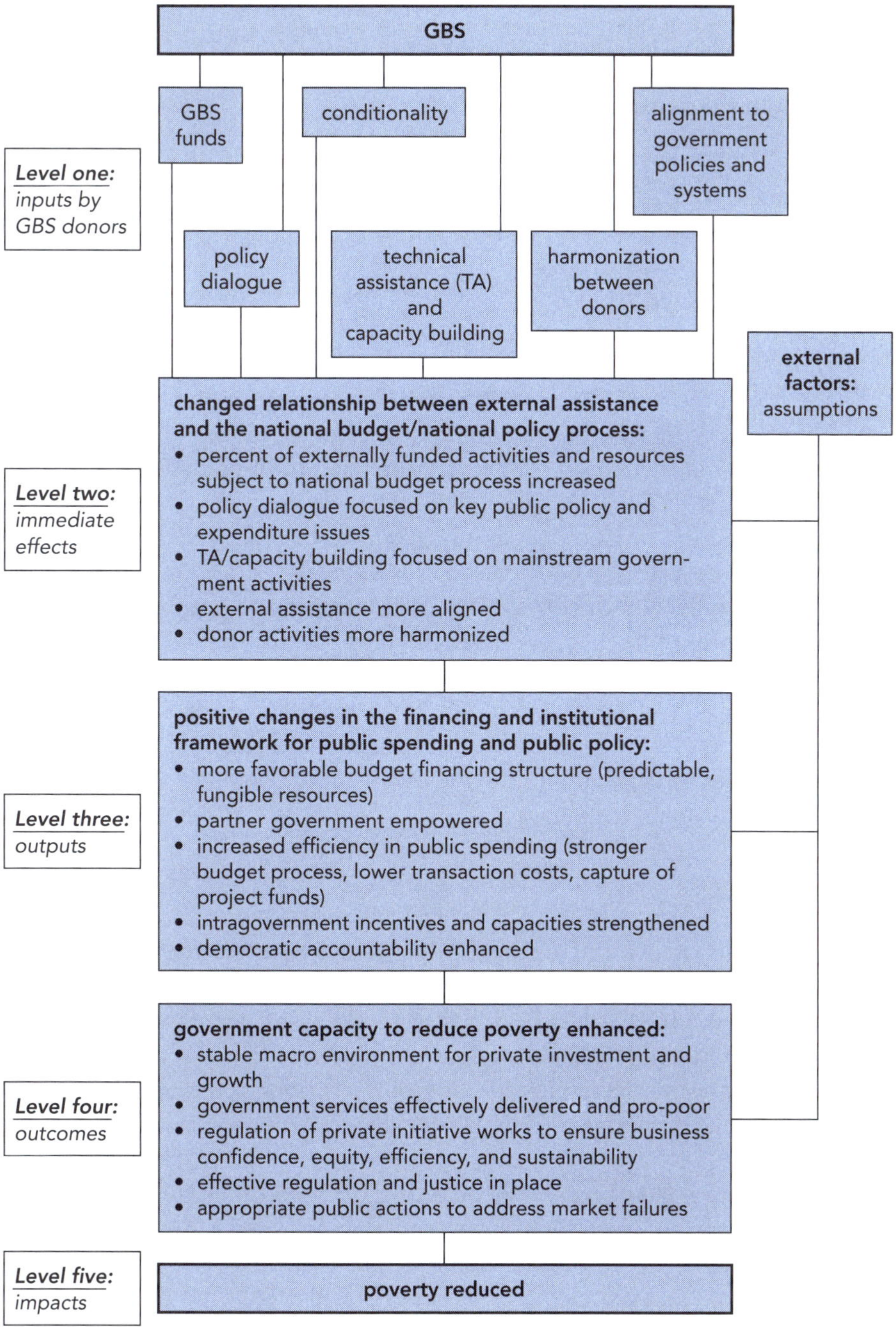

The Input Level

At the input level, evaluation findings that are of particular interest relate to:

- changes in the overall scale of aid and GBS;
- the management of the GBS package; and
- whether GBS partners share the assumptions of the framework.

The Scale of Aid

The most striking change in aid to Tanzania in recent years is not the rise in budget support, but the increase in the overall scale of assistance. As shown in Figure 7.2, aid is now at an unprecedented level, more than double its real value in the early 1990s. After declining in the mid-1990s, "program aid" (now corresponding to GBS plus HIPC debt relief) is once again more than 50 percent of all aid. The proportion of GBS alone is around 36 percent. However, total aid is substantially greater than it ever was in the past.

This means that the situation is not one in which the GBS modality of assistance is dominant. The government distinguishes three modalities: GBS, common baskets, and projects. Considered sector by sector, only education and health show a decisive shift away from project funding, and this reflects in part the increasing popularity of common-basket funding. Since 2000–01, common baskets have accounted for an increasing proportion of nonprogram aid flows, accounting for about a third by 2002–03. Other sectors, such as agriculture, are still characterized by the incentive structures typically associated with high levels of project funding, not those generated by funding through the budget.

Management of the Package

All six inputs associated with GBS were found to be present in the Tanzanian case, not just the element of unearmarked budget finance. Since 2001–02 poverty reduction budget support (PRBS) has been linked to a unified performance assessment framework (PAF), which is the main basis for both policy dialogue and conditionality. Dialogue focuses on the implementation of the actions and measures agreed by the government and its partners for inclusion in the PAF. Progress is reviewed twice a year.

TA and capacity building have been provided for many of the core administrative and policy processes on which PRBS is focused. In most cases, this has been through project arrangements separate from GBS, but the PRBS dialogue has increasingly influenced the focus and volume of such support.

PRBS monitoring and disbursement processes are to a large extent harmonized across the 14 donors and aligned with the budget cycle and the national priorities in the poverty reduction strategy (PRS). Some departures from alignment and harmonization were necessary, but care has been devoted to minimizing the resulting distortions and transaction costs.

FIGURE 7.2 The Changing Composition of Aid

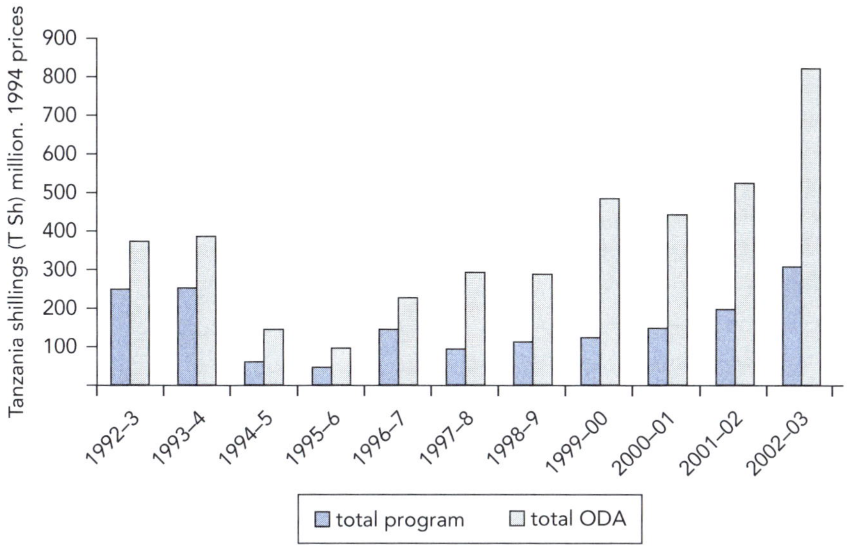

There is ongoing debate about the suitability of the management and disbursement arrangements for the GBS program. Much of this centers on the PAF, and three issues:

- The PRBS dialogue around the PAF is additional to the structures for government-donor dialogue that were established previously (including public expenditure review and sector review processes). There is a need for streamlining of the various structures and processes if increased transaction costs for government are to be avoided.
- The dialogue is strongly focused on a relationship with senior officials in the Ministry of Finance. Overall, the degree of access to senior government officials is considered very good. However, there are no regular channels for dialogue between the PRBS development partners and the Minister of Finance or other cabinet members.
- The way the PAF rolls together dialogue and conditionality is unsatisfactory. Conditionality for the disbursement of GBS funds has three elements: (1) the assessment of satisfactory overall progress in implementation, on which all PRBS disbursements are conditioned, (2) the assessment of the prior actions that must precede the renewal of the poverty reduction support credit (PRSC) agreement by the World Bank, and (3) the assessment of performance against the public financial management and service delivery indicators agreed for the European Commission's variable tranches. The fact that there are three types of conditionality in the PAF introduces a degree of complexity.

A more consistent criticism is that the processes of dialogue and conditionality are completely interwoven. This has two negative effects: (1) it crowds out the space for a dispassionate and noncommittal sharing of views between government and donor representatives, and (2) it undermines country policy ownership, because it creates the impression that conditionality has no boundaries.

Program Intent

The evaluation framework presents a hypothetical model for the use of GBS. The shift to GBS is seen as generating a more favorable budget financing framework (with more predictable, more discretionary resources), subjecting external funds to greater domestic accountability, and shifting incentives in favor of the improvement of national policies and systems. The evaluation investigated the degree to which the actual objectives of the government and donors in Tanzania correspond to this model.

On the Tanzanian side, there is a strong general aspiration to bringing external assistance under the control of government. However, this is not yet accompanied by an equally forceful view on the relative roles of budget support and projects.

There are comparable ambiguities on the donor side. The Partnership Framework—signed by all 14 development partners—aims to promote harmonization of performance benchmarks, linking of disbursements to preagreed targets, reduction of transaction costs, and increased predictability of donor flows. All of these objectives are closely consistent with the framework. However, there are two important points of difference:

- Most of the donors providing budget support do not appear to believe that its beneficial institutional effects are dependent upon a reduction in the number of external projects within the public sector.
- Most donors continue to believe strongly in the "policy leverage" afforded by GBS. In contrast, the evaluation framework envisages policy dialogue primarily in terms of monitoring the government's commitment to its stated policies. It sees stronger domestic accountability as being the primary driver of improved results and GBS as a way of facilitating this process.

Level Two: Immediate Effects

The evaluation found the immediate effects of the GBS program to be more or less as expected. That is:

- As a greater proportion of aid as well as a larger absolute amount, GBS has dramatically increased the proportion of external funds subject to the national budget process.
- GBS has helped to focus dialogue on strategic issues of economic management, and in the process made some significant contributions to the design of policy.
- GBS has helped to focus TA and capacity building on core public policy and public expenditure processes.
- GBS has made a major contribution to alignment and harmonization. The PRBS management arrangements are considered an outstanding example of efforts to max-

imize alignment to the PRS and the budget cycle while harmonizing procedures across donors.

Level Three: GBS Outputs

The evaluation's findings at this level are of interest under all five headings suggested by the framework:

- provision of a more favorable budget financing structure,
- empowerment of the government to pursue its policies,
- efficiency of public spending,
- the effect on internal government incentives and capacities, and
- effect on democratic accountability.

Budget Structure

The expansion of the Tanzanian budget over the past decade has been dramatic. Equally remarkable is the proportion of the funding recorded in the budget over which the government has discretion. This is indicated by Figure 7.3.

The background to this is a simultaneous expansion of donor inflows and domestic revenues since 1996. In real terms, domestic revenues increased 89 percent in the decade between 1993–94 and 2003–04, while over the same period donor inflows

FIGURE 7.3 Increasing Discretionary Funding in the Budget

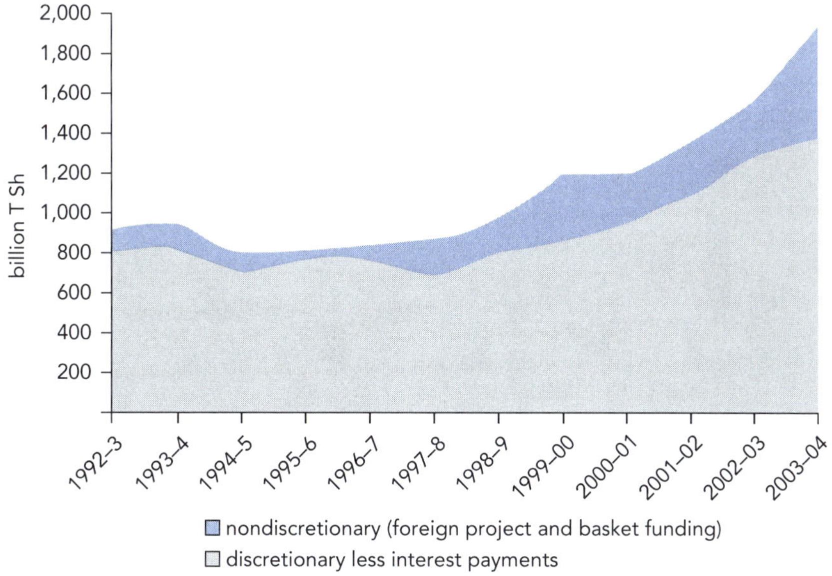

Source: Ministry of Finance.

increased by 70 percent. That is, the increase in domestic revenue has outperformed that of aid. This reflects a combination of GDP growth and a strong performance by the Tanzania Revenue Authority.

The strong recovery in overall government revenues has substantially reduced the costs of budget funding. Interest payments have fallen in relative terms from 20 percent to 5 percent of budgeted expenditures, and have also fallen in absolute terms. In addition, accumulated arrears have been cleared. The volume of funds available to be used flexibly has increased significantly.

The record on predictability was initially poor, but there are strong signs of improvement. Between 2000–01 and 2001–02, budget support was the most unpredictable of all of the major government revenue sources, being on average 19 percent below budgeted levels (Figure 7.4). However, data for 2002–03 and reports for 2003–04 and the start of 2004–05 suggest higher levels of predictability in budget support.

The improvements in Tanzania's fiscal position must be attributed first and foremost to political leadership. Improvements in the capacity of key institutions enabled the changes to take place. Alongside the role of the Tanzania Revenue Authority, capacity improvements within the Policy Analysis Department and the Accountant General's Department of the Ministry of Finance were significant. Donor TA and capacity building facilitated these improvements, but did not cause them.

Empowerment to Pursue Policies

Increased availability of discretionary resources has permitted a range of politically important budgetary actions that would not otherwise have been feasible. In addition to reducing domestic debt and arrears, the government was able to double per capita spending on PRSP priority sectors between 1998–99 and 2002–03 and protect

FIGURE 7.4 Budgets versus Receipts, by Revenue Source

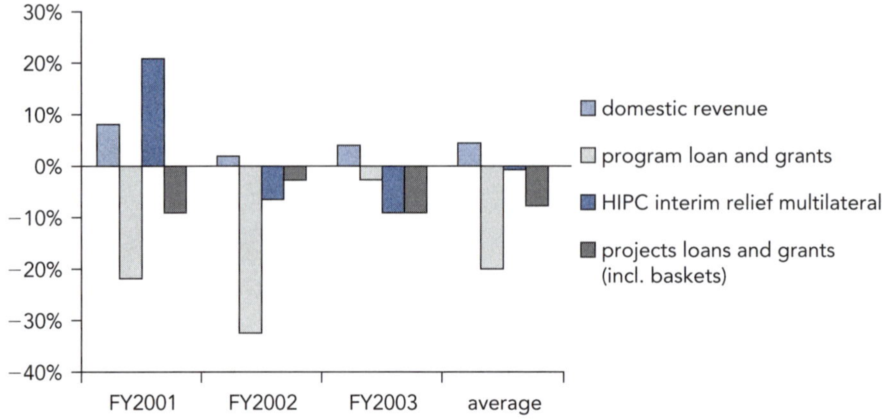

Source: Ministry of Finance.

FIGURE 7.5 Real per Capita Spending on Priority Sectors

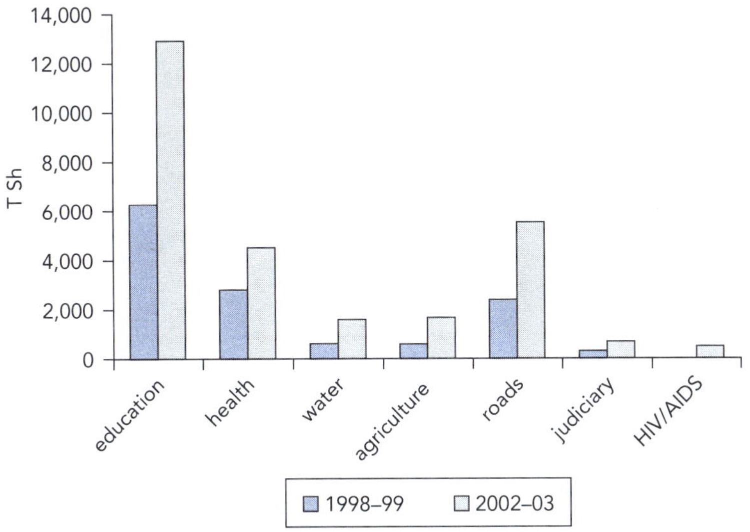

budget disbursements to those sectors (Figure 7.5). This has permitted a major expansion in education and health service provision.

PRSP priority sectors have not received consistently high budgetary priority. Over the five year period 1998–99 to 2003–04, there was a shift in budgetary shares first toward and then away from the priority sectors identified in Tanzania's first PRSP (PRS1). There has been a constant shift toward economic services, which until 2004–05 appears to have been the implicit priority of government (Figure 7.6).

The evaluation suggests the following interpretation. Initially, the PRS process may have helped the government to establish a formalized set of strategic objectives. GBS funds and dialogue then facilitated a reallocation of budgeted expenditure toward those priorities, defined in sectoral and subsectoral terms. But as time passed and priorities evolved, the gap between the priorities expressed in PRS1 and the government's actual priorities widened.

This was not simply a matter of weak commitment to the objectives of the PRS. Rather, the use of the "priority sectors" concept as a mechanism for judging the effectiveness of resource allocations proved overly simplistic—failing to distinguish the specific outputs and outcomes that were most important within the priority sectors, and giving no attention to questions of feasibility and absorptive capacity. The new approach adopted by PRS2, with "cluster strategies" linked to PRS outcomes in place of sectoral priorities, is in principle a more promising approach, although weak political engagement with the PRS remains a limiting factor.

Efficiency of Spending

GBS has been part of a process leading to a major expansion in levels of social service delivery (Figure 7.7). However, it is not clear that it has yet contributed to any

FIGURE 7.6 Sector Shares for Priority and Nonpriority Sectors

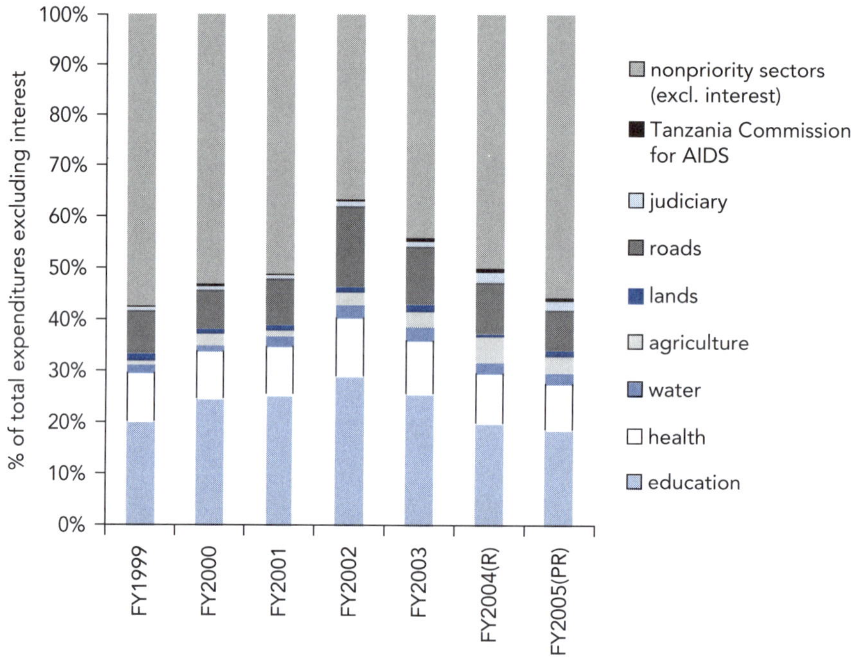

Source: Ministry of Finance.

improvement in the efficiency of public expenditure. Other than sectoral reallocations, there have been few shifts in the pattern of expenditure. This tends to confirm the impression that key constraints on service delivery have not been addressed.

The lack of efficiency improvements needs to be seen in perspective. Realizing efficiency gains along with a rapid expansion in service volumes has proven difficult even in the United Kingdom, with substantially greater management capacity. On the other hand, the scope for increasing the efficiency of public expenditure in Tanzania is probably large, and some of the issues to be confronted have been known for many years. Some signs of headway in tackling them might have been expected at this stage.

There are other worrying signs. The recurrent budget for administration has expanded in relative terms while the share of the budget going to local authorities has remained the same. In some sectors, most notably education, there has been a large increase in administrative overheads. There are also significant deviations between approved budget allocations and actual expenditures across and within spending agencies.

The evaluation was unable to reach firm conclusions on the reduction of transaction costs as a result of GBS. The distribution of transaction costs has certainly changed. They have fallen in some areas, but increased in others. There is certainly a higher administrative burden on the Ministry of Finance, although this reflects the Ministry's deeper involvement in reform processes as well as more extensive dialogue with donors. There is no clear evidence that transaction costs in line ministries have fallen.

FIGURE 7.7 Expanding Service Delivery in Health and Education

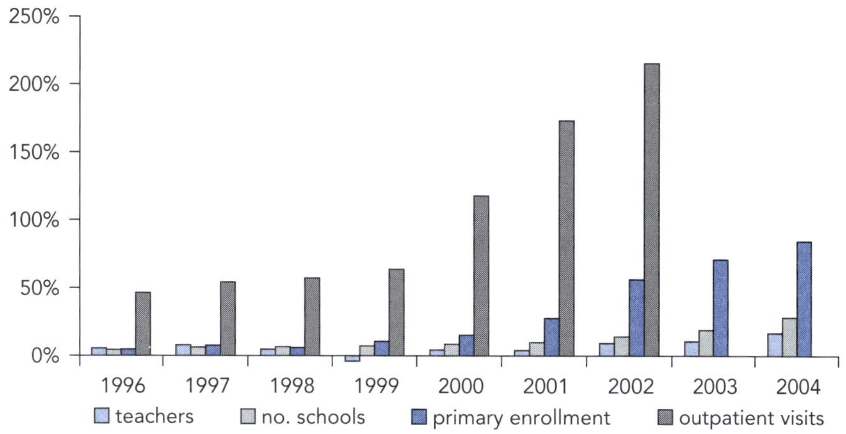

Source: Ministry of Health, Ministry of Education, base year 1995

Why has GBS not been associated with a significant improvement in efficiency? One reason is the scale of the donor funding that is not fully subject to the budget process. With as much as 80 percent of development spending still funded by donor projects, there is limited scope for using the budget to improve allocative efficiency.

Another relevant factor is the weakness of the "challenge function" within the country's budget process. Within the executive branch, neither the Ministry of Finance nor the Cabinet has exercised a strong pressure on the quality of line ministries' budget bids. More broadly, the lack of critical scrutiny of budget proposals and budget execution reports by Parliament means that there have been few political incentives to improve the efficiency of public spending.

Ultimately, this has to do with the character of the executive-legislature relationship and Cabinet government in Tanzania. However, there are also problems in the design of the budget process that might be easier to remedy.

The way the budget is presented does not foster a reorientation of ministers, parliamentarians, or managers toward results. The activity-based costing used in the medium-term expenditure framework appears technocratic. There has been little mention of results in the budget guidelines, which set out the government's medium-term spending strategy. The budget timetable is not Parliament friendly. Finally, the annual public expenditure review, an open process led by the Ministry of Finance, has helped improve budget analysis. But it has yet to have a substantial impact on resource allocation, because it has no institutionalized link to the budget process.

Intragovernment Incentives and Capacities

By using government systems, GBS is expected to enhance the functioning of the public sector. The hope is that it will reverse the erosion of institutional incentives and capacities caused by the previous combination of projects and highly conditional program aid. However, the evaluation found only limited changes in this regard.

There have been major efforts to strengthen public expenditure management systems and capacity, and these have been quite successful. The most impressive achievement has been the upgrading of financial control, accounting, and reporting. However, outside the immediate sphere of public financial management, change is hard to detect. At the central level, there appears to be little strengthening of performance incentives. The public sector reform and local government reform programs are achieving their immediate objectives as programs. But the reforms do not appear to have delivered systemic changes in incentives for service improvement.

This can be put down to a combination of factors. The most important is a lack of consistent political drive behind the public sector and local government reforms, with an undue focus on the programs rather than their wider purposes. The lack of challenge in the budget process and the continuing domination of project funding in the development budget reinforce this effect.

Democratic Accountability

In principle, putting aid funds through the budget should make them subject to more effective domestic control. However, there is little evidence of Parliament's scrutiny of public finances improving significantly since the expansion of discretionary funding in the budget. Some technical assistance has been provided to parliamentary committees to help to address this problem. But this is unlikely to have a significant impact in the absence of a concerted effort to improve the presentation of the budget, and until the political role of parliament is enhanced.

From an admittedly low base, the capacity of Tanzanian NGOs to engage in debate on policy questions in forums such as the public expenditure review has increased remarkably. Doubts remain over the depth of this capacity and the potential of NGOs to challenge decisions over resource allocation.

In summary, the evaluation did not find clear evidence of improving accountability to domestic stakeholders. This confirms the assumption of the evaluation framework that, if domestic political change is not generating improvements in accountability, a GBS program cannot create it.

Level Four: Outcomes

The evaluation framework directs attention to five groups of outcomes that may be considered critical to reaching poverty reduction objectives. The evaluation records the changes observed and discusses which changes can plausibly be considered results of the budget support program. In many cases, both data gaps and time lags prevent firm conclusions.

A Macroeconomic Environment Conducive to Growth

The most significant success story of the last decade is the improvement in the macroeconomic position. From a situation in the mid-1990s of stagnating growth, double-digit inflation, and unsustainable foreign and domestic borrowing, GDP growth has now averaged just under 6 percent per year for the last three years, inflation is below

5 percent, and borrowing has been reduced to comfortably sustainable levels. This has had important effects on the overall business environment. Foreign direct investment has now reached an annual average inflow equivalent to 3 percent of GDP.

There remain concerns, however, about the pattern of growth. Agriculture's performance has improved in the last five years (average 4.4 percent per year) and is showing signs of increasing resilience to external shocks. However, it has failed to keep pace with the improvements in other sectors, most notably mining and formal services. There are also reasons to think that the improvement in agriculture's aggregate performance is unevenly spread, regionally and by crop type. So there is an urgent need to accelerate improvements to agricultural marketing, agricultural credit, and rural transport.

The restoration of macroeconomic stability has been the result of strong political support for tight expenditure control and strict monetary policy. GBS funds permitted sharp increases in social spending while maintaining prudent borrowing. In the absence of such resources, it would have been difficult to meet the expanding recurrent cost commitments without a significantly higher level of deficit financing.

Has GBS had any unintended negative macroeconomic effects? The evaluation considered two potential problems: Dutch disease effects and problems of monetary sterilization.

A Dutch disease effect occurs where aid sharply increases the availability of foreign exchange, leading to an appreciation in the real exchange rate. This reduces the income of the export sector, forcing its relative contraction. Recent IMF analysis suggests any effects of this sort have been small. Other factors—such as fluctuations in imports due to mining and other investments—have been more significant disruptions than changing aid flows.

It does remain relevant to ask whether the benefits of aid are likely to be greater than the costs to the tradable goods sector. A priori, the real exchange rate would have been more favorable to exporters in the absence of aid. But in Tanzania, where public goods provision and public infrastructure capital are almost certainly below their optimal levels, it seems unlikely that these costs would exceed the potential benefits. In any case, structural impediments to exports are almost certainly of greater significance.

The monetary sterilization problem is potentially more significant. To avoid inflation, GBS foreign exchange inflows to finance public expenditure have to be sterilized by means that can have negative side effects. The central bank has to either sell foreign exchange reserves to the domestic market (which further appreciates the nominal exchange rate) or sell treasury bills (bonds) to the domestic market (which drives up interest rates). The evaluation looked at the data between 2001 and 2004. There was no evidence of unintended negative macroeconomic consequences on a scale that would outweigh the positive macroeconomic effects of GBS.

Quality and Targeting of Services

The period of 2000 to 2004 witnessed a very significant expansion in the scale of services within education, health, and road maintenance. This is an important achievement. However, it has proven difficult to expand services while maintaining quality. In primary education, pupil-teacher ratios have risen to alarming levels as a result of the difficulties in ensuring that teacher recruitment (and distribution to rural areas) keeps pace with enrollments. In the health sector, difficulties in placing personnel in rural areas have also been common, and there are reports of poor discipline and absenteeism. There would also appear to be demand problems, particularly among the poor, whose use of government health services remains substantially lower than might be desired.

Regulation and Business Environment

The investment climate for the private sector has been improving as a direct result of government policy changes, which have been a major subject in an expanding public-private sector policy dialogue. The prospects for significant poverty reduction have improved as a result of these changes. Limitations include the fact that many of the most significant changes are extremely recent, and others take the form of commitments to act in the future. Many of the key changes correspond to both presidential policy commitments and prior actions identified in the PAF.

Justice and Human Rights

There has been some recent progress in improving justice and human rights protection in the context of a legal reform program. However, these reforms are recent and have been rather slow. Their impacts will be felt largely in the future. The current state of human rights and administration of justice is still a matter of great concern.

Public Action to Address Market Failures

Some of the most critical needs under this heading relate to agriculture and agricultural trade. In agricultural policy, there has been less consistency and less action than on the business climate as a whole, despite donor promptings in the PAF reviews. The government has found it hard to find its way to correcting key market failures, such as those affecting agricultural marketing and input supply, while remaining true to its liberal economic policy stance.

It would not be reasonable to attribute this to limitations of the budget support approach. The budget process is not yet a powerful driver of policy improvement. Yet it has hardly been tested in relation to agriculture, because the principal sector donors and government stakeholders still prefer project or common-basket modalities.

Outcomes and GBS

Overall, the record on outcomes is very mixed, and progress has been recent. The prospects in the longer run may be better, if current policy trends—particularly in addressing the structural impediments to balanced growth—are continued. In this respect, it might be argued that the period of analysis is the wrong one. Current policy and spending actions facilitated by the PRBS and promoted by debates around the PAF may be more reasonably expected to contribute to improved outcomes in a future period.

Level Five: Poverty Impacts

The link to poverty reduction is indirect and long term. Lack of data means that we really do not know what has happened to poverty in Tanzania in recent years. The upcoming 2006 Household Budget Survey will provide an important new set of data.

Data from the 1990 and 2001 Household Budget Surveys suggest that the incidence of income poverty did not fall significantly between the early 1990s and 2001. It was only in Dar es Salaam that there was statistically significant reduction, from 28 to 18 percent. Per capita GDP fell in the early 1990s—largely because of poor macroeconomic management—whereas recent years have seen quite high rates of growth. It is therefore quite likely that poverty first increased and then declined, resulting in only a small net decline over the whole period.

The relatively better performance of Dar es Salaam compared to the rest of the country is probably explained largely by the sectoral unevenness of growth highlighted previously. It is in agriculture and closely related activities that most of the poor gain their living.

There are reasons for being soberly realistic about what is likely to have been happening to human development indicators, too. Again, the most recent data are not recent enough to suit the evaluation's purposes. Preliminary Demographic and Health Survey results suggest recent improvements in infant and child mortality. However, it is quite probable that the overall picture of health conditions in the country remains dismal.

In brief, what we know about the impact trends suggests that Tanzania is not yet on a path of definite and sustained improvement.

D. Overall Conclusions

The GBS evaluation used a more rigorous set of benchmarks of success than any hitherto applied to individual aid operations in Tanzania. It was not content to ask whether immediate effects and outputs were produced efficiently. It also asked how far GBS has been able to enhance the capacity of government to influence the determinants of poverty and whether there is evidence of poverty levels falling as a consequence. This sets quite a demanding standard.

Tanzania has realized a number of major achievements in the past 10 years. They include:

- continuously good macroeconomic management, with low inflation and solid GDP growth;
- consistent improvements in the quality of public financial management;
- the stabilization of the domestic debt position, the clearing of domestic arrears, and substantial increases in expenditure within the PRS priority sectors; and
- the initiation of important reforms to improve the business environment and promote investment.

Fundamentally, progress has been driven by internal political commitment to change in these areas. But it would have been considerably more difficult if there had not been donor budget funding, together with the associated dialogue and other inputs—or if such funding had been channeled through other aid modalities.

In some crucial outcome areas, GBS is not yet successfully facilitating changes. There are important reform initiatives in local government, the public sector, and the legal sector where clear-cut results have yet to be achieved. The policy constraints on agricultural growth remain to be properly addressed. While access to social services has improved, the poor still predominantly fail to use government services, and in large part this is due to shortfalls in efficiency and in quality.

Poor service delivery outcomes can be traced back to weaknesses at the output level. The efficiency of public expenditure is low, intragovernment incentives remain weak, and the democratic pressure that might drive improvements is substantially absent. In the evaluators' opinion, without further policy and institutional changes, major improvements in poverty and human development indicators are likely to stay out of reach. It is equally clear that internal changes would be assisted by a continued reduction in the number of aid projects and programs within the public sector.

GBS in Tanzania has not had all the effects indicated by the evaluation framework. Yet many of these, especially at the outcome and impact levels, depend strongly on underlying political and institutional factors that no aid modality can expect to influence over the medium term. The question to ask is whether the important positive changes that have been witnessed could have been enabled so effectively by alternative aid modalities. The Tanzania evaluation suggests not. GBS was a crucial facilitating factor in these changes (Box 7.1).

E. Learning from Tanzania

In some important respects, generalizing from Tanzania's 1995–2004 experience might generate an excessively optimistic perspective. In retrospect, it is clear that the country was favored during this period by several factors that seem likely to improve the chances of GBS working in the way that its advocates expect. A stable political regime, high-level political support for structural reforms, and a strengthened and capable finance ministry are among the conditions that were present in Tanzania, but are absent in a good many other countries in the region.

On the other hand, in very many ways the evaluation has highlighted issues that Tanzania shares with other countries throughout the region. The most obvious are the high level of both financial and institutional aid dependency and the shortage of sustained political support for the more difficult reforms. The limited capacity of even a substantially empowered Ministry of Finance to enforce changes in the incentive structures of line ministries and local governments is a typical problem. Above all, the continued dominance of projects and other modes of aid delivery that bypass the national budget process offsets any advantages that Tanzania might otherwise possess as a test case of the benefits of budget support.

BOX 7.1 Summary of Findings—GBS in Tanzania

- In Tanzania, GBS is provided by 14 donors and, together with relief under the HIPC facility, contributes 20 percent of public expenditure. Despite this, however, GBS is not yet a dominant aid modality.
- The immediate effects of the GBS program have been strongly positive, but its role has been to facilitate a nationally driven reform process; domestic revenues have grown even faster than aid.
- GBS has been associated with a large growth in government discretionary spending and a major expansion in health and education services. However, there are few signs of improved efficiency of public spending or of long-term obstacles to service quality being addressed; the "challenge function" in the budget process remains weak, mainly for political but also for more technical reasons; the expected improvements in intragovernment incentives and democratic accountability are not yet apparent; and the scope for change in these respects has been limited by the fact that 80 percent of development spending is still funded by donor projects.
- Outcomes have improved remarkably in respect of macroeconomic stability, investment and growth, while the negative macroeconomic effects of increased aid flows appear manageable.
- Outcome improvements are otherwise rather mixed, with large questions about service quality and significant legal changes that are too recent to have yielded results.
- Poverty impacts are uncertain for the last half-decade, the most relevant period, because there has been no household survey since 2001.
- The unevenness of growth and service delivery improvements give reasons for caution about future poverty trends.
- In summary, GBS in Tanzania has not had all the positive effects expected of it, some of which are necessarily long term. But the gains that have been made are important and would not have been so effectively facilitated by any other aid modality.

With this in mind, Tanzania suggests several wider lessons regarding GBS as a modality:

- Domestic political considerations have a dominant influence. The Tanzanian experience is a useful reminder that budget funding and the related dialogue, conditions, and TA are never likely to have more than a modest influence on processes of public sector reform and institutional development.

- Increasing the volume of discretionary funding that can be used for development purposes is the main contribution of GBS. Given the importance of this aspect, it is vital to give close attention to the sustainability, predictability, and timeliness of the financial flows.

- GBS can contribute to reduced transaction costs. In Tanzania, the lack of evidence of transaction cost reductions arises substantially from the fact that the GBS arrangements have been additional to continuing large numbers of donor projects in the public sector and the parallel rise in the importance of common-basket funding.

- The reinforcement of democratic accountability is not automatic. At most, GBS can facilitate a process of internal, politically driven change in which domestic actors assume new roles. It is domestic political change that is the prime mover, and without it the immediate effect may be limited to a more constructive donor-government dialogue.

- The link to poverty reduction is indirect and necessarily long term. The intermediate changes needed are well established in theory but hard to realize in practice. GBS can facilitate such changes, most obviously by funding an expansion in the volume of targeted services. But key problems will only be solved by domestic shifts of a necessarily slow and incremental kind.

8

General Budget Support and Public Financial Management Reform: Emerging Lessons from Tanzania and Uganda

TIM WILLIAMSON
Overseas Development Institute

As international donors have increased the amount of aid channeled as general budget support (GBS), so has attention shifted toward the role played by recipient countries' public financial management (PFM) systems in ensuring that better public sector outcomes are achieved.

This paper considers the effects of the shift toward GBS on PFM outcomes and reforms in Tanzania and Uganda—two countries where donors have decisively increased the amount of aid they provide in the form of GBS in absolute and relative terms over the last decade. Section A looks at the role that budget support could theoretically play in strengthening budgetary systems, as posited in the OECD-DAC evaluation framework for general budget support (Lawson and Booth 2004), and Sections B–D examine whether this theory holds in practice, by comparing the cases of Uganda and Tanzania. Section E draws conclusions and lessons from this comparison.

The paper draws from the author's involvement in the recent joint evaluations of budget support in Tanzania and Uganda; however, the reflections here are the author's own and should not be considered as results of the formal evaluations.[1]

A. The Hypothesis

How might GBS improve PFM systems? The OECD-DAC evaluation framework examines the effect of a generic package of inputs associated with GBS—funds, dialogue, conditionality, technical assistance (TA), capacity building, harmonization, and alignment—on government policies and systems, public sector outcomes, and ultimately on poverty reduction.

An important subset of hypotheses in the evaluation framework sets out how budget support funding and associated inputs might affect PFM systems and the outcomes of those systems (Figure 8.1).

This paper is based on a presentation made at the Center for Aid and Public Expenditure's Conference on Budgets and Accountability held at the Overseas Development Institute, London, in October 2005.

FIGURE 8.1 The Hypothesis—How GBS Might Affect Public Financial Management Outcomes

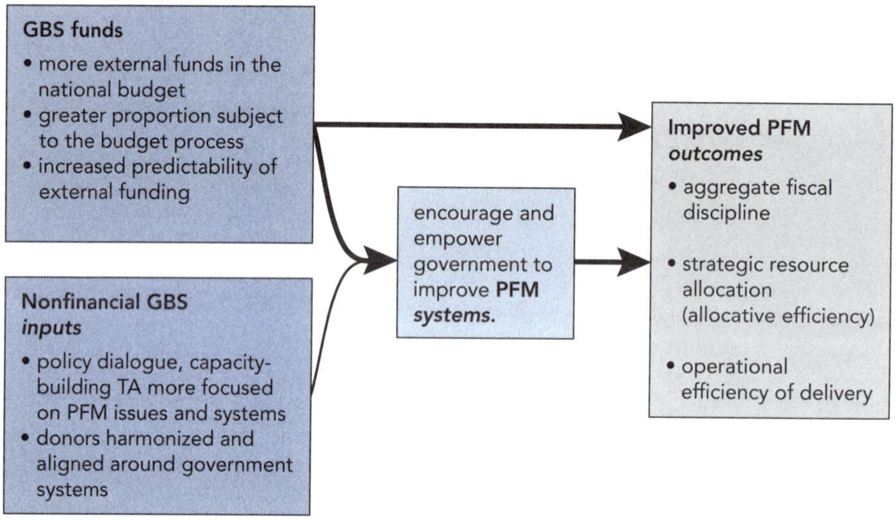

Note: The figure shows a subset of the potential effects of GBS in the evaluation framework.

The first set of effects posited by the evaluation framework relates directly to GBS *funds*. By definition, as GBS is channeled through the national budget, it is subject to the government's budgetary systems. It is also a source of flexible budgetary funding and is potentially more predictable than project support. If GBS funds indeed provide flexible and predictable funding through the budget, budget support can then help improve PFM outcomes *directly*. The maintenance of aggregate fiscal discipline should be made easier by the availability of flexible, predictable foreign exchange and on-budget funding. The evaluation framework assumes that supporting the recipient's budget is likely to be more efficient than other forms of aid, such as project support with its associated inflexibility, multiplicity of systems, and transaction costs. This assumption means that strategic resource allocation and operational efficiency should be directly improved by a relative and absolute shift toward GBS, because the government is able to allocate funds in a flexible way toward its objectives and through a system that delivers greater operational efficiency. The framework also envisages *indirect effects* of budget support funding, by enabling the recipient government to make its own resource allocation decisions, and by strengthening the roles of the ministry of finance, parliament, and the executive in the budgetary process. In addition, increasing reliance on government systems should make it easier to improve those systems.

The second set of presumed effects of GBS on PFM outcomes comes from *nonfinancial* inputs associated with GBS—such as policy dialogue, capacity building, and TA—provided these are focused on key PFM systems and processes rather than on individual projects and their constituent parallel systems. The new approach to conditionality in the context of PFM reform takes the view that conditionality relating to PFM should be agreed by governments and based on government-owned PFM reform programs, rather than being imposed by donors. Because this approach allows greater local ownership, it should in turn increase the likelihood that government reforms will be successfully implemented. In addition, if donors are increasingly harmonized with each other and simultaneously aligned with government PFM systems, this should mean that those government systems become relatively more important to government stakeholders than donor-specific processes.

In summary, the evaluation framework envisages that GBS provides a complementary set of inputs that together should speed the pace of improvements in PFM systems, contributing directly and indirectly to better PFM outcomes.

B. Direct Effects of GBS Funding in Tanzania and Uganda on PFM Outcomes

We now examine the direct impact of GBS funding (excluding nonfinancial GBS inputs) on PFM outcomes in Tanzania and Uganda. It is important first to compare the relative levels of GBS funds in those countries (Figure 8.2).

Both Uganda and Tanzania have seen very similar rapid shifts in the composition of aid, from project support to budget support. In both countries, program aid (largely budget support) made up about 30 percent of aid in the late 1990s, but by 2003, its share had risen to more than 50 percent. The rise largely reflected increases in budget support, but also savings from debt relief under the Heavily Indebted Poor Countries Initiative.

The first major difference between Uganda and Tanzania is the level of aid dependence, and more specifically the size of aid relative to public spending. In Uganda, aid has supplied about half of public spending for the last five or six years, which means that budget support has gone up from funding 15 percent to 30 percent of the budget. In Tanzania, a less aid-dependent country, budget support had only reached 18 percent of the budget by 2003, while aid actually declined as a proportion of public expenditure.

The second major difference between the two countries is Uganda's use of notional earmarking of GBS in the late 1990s; much of GBS was notionally earmarked as additional allocations to programs within the Poverty Action Fund, which represents the part of the budget devoted to priority poverty-reducing expenditures. None of Tanzania's GBS has been earmarked. Due to concerns over the ballooning deficit, since 2002, the government of Uganda no longer warrants that increases in notionally earmarked budget support will result in additional allocations, but instead commits to maintaining allocations to Poverty Action Fund programs as a share of the total budget.

What were the direct effects of the absolute and relative increases in GBS funding on PFM outcomes in Tanzania and Uganda, and what differences are observed?

The first effect was that GBS funding made aggregate fiscal discipline easier to maintain (Figure 8.3). Attaining and sustaining fiscal discipline requires political and

FIGURE 8.2 Tanzania and Uganda: Program Aid as a Proportion of Aid and Public Expenditure

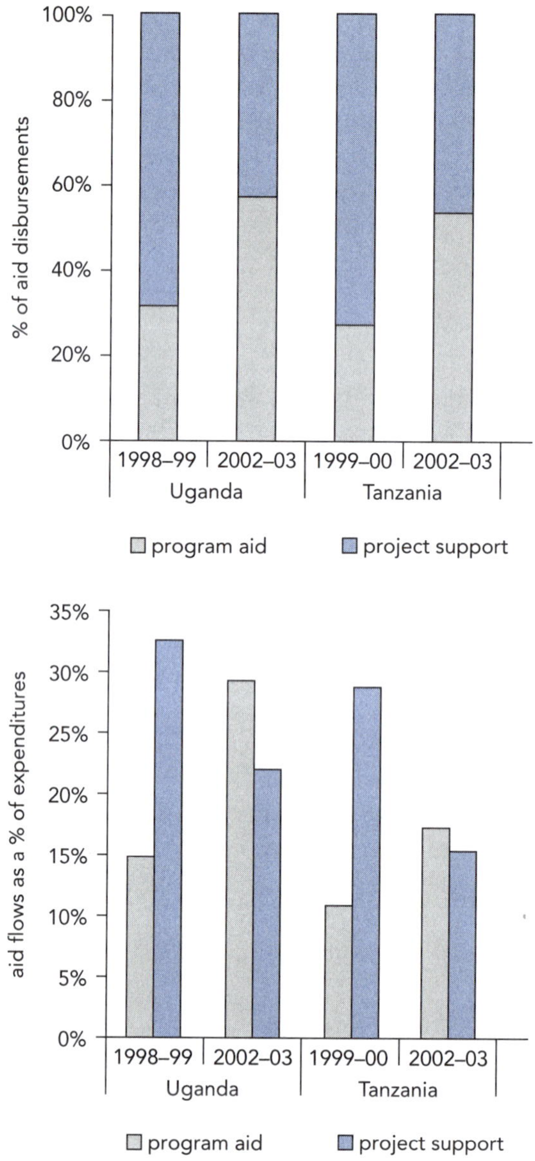

Source: Tanzanian and Ugandan Ministries of Finance.

institutional commitment, and both countries had established aggregate fiscal discipline before the move to GBS. GBS funding made fiscal discipline easier by providing the fiscal space to clear arrears and, in the case of Tanzania, to reduce the burden of domestic debt. In principle, GBS also makes macroeconomic management easier, in that it provides a long-term predictable source of budgetary funding and foreign

FIGURE 8.3 Tanzania and Uganda: Trends in PFM Outcomes

What?	Uganda	Tanzania
Aggregate fiscal discipline	Established in the early 1990s and maintained	Established in the mid/late 1990s and maintained
Strategic resource allocation	Rapid relative and absolute rise in spending on social service delivery (Poverty Action Fund)	Rapid relative, and absolute rise, then relative but not absolute fall in pro-poor spending
Operational efficiency of delivery	Clear improvements in efficiency of noninterest spending, but rise in interest costs	Little change in efficiency of allocations signals problems in delivery not being addressed

exchange. In both Tanzania and Uganda, however, flows of budget support have proved very volatile. Although their short-term predictability has markedly improved, these flows have not been more predictable than project financing in aggregate. In Uganda, the Ministry of Finance now discounts budget support pledges as well as project support, and it budgets on the assumption that it will receive only 90 percent of the aggregate commitments for budget support. It manages short-term volatility through its increased stock of foreign reserves. Despite this, the knowledge that budget support is going to arrive at some time during the budget cycle facilitates macroeconomic management.

Second, the experience of Uganda and Tanzania shows that an absolute increase and relative shift to GBS can directly improve strategic resource allocation. In Uganda, 30 percent—and in Tanzania, 23 percent—of the real increases in public expenditures since 1998–99 can be attributed to increases in program aid (Figure 8.4). In both countries, GBS funding enabled the government to allocate and spend significantly more on PRSP priorities in absolute and relative terms. In Uganda, the notional earmarking of budget support to the Poverty Action Fund was not initially a barrier to increases in allocative efficiency, because it accelerated the shift of expenditure allocations toward PRSP priorities, but more recently the commitment to maintain the size of the fund has led to increased rigidities in the budget Meanwhile, Tanzania has been able to reduce the proportion of funding allocated to original poverty-reducing programs to cater for other emerging priorities.

In Uganda, evidence suggests that public expenditures as a whole have become more efficient: the share of public administration in the budget is falling, and a slight increase can be seen in the share of on-budget sector funding that is channeled to service providers in central and local government (Figure 8.5). Such improvements were not seen in Tanzania, reflecting that country's weaker budget formulation process. The gains in efficiency observed in Uganda have, however, been undermined by increases in domestic interest payments caused directly by the higher domestic borrowing that was undertaken to sterilize the increasing foreign exchange inflows from aid,[2] and there are increasing concerns about the level of corruption.

Also, in Uganda, there is concrete evidence that the shift away from donor-financed projects to budget support has helped to lower transaction costs and reduce reliance

FIGURE 8.4 Tanzania and Uganda: Improved Strategic Resource Allocation—Pro-poor Public Expenditures

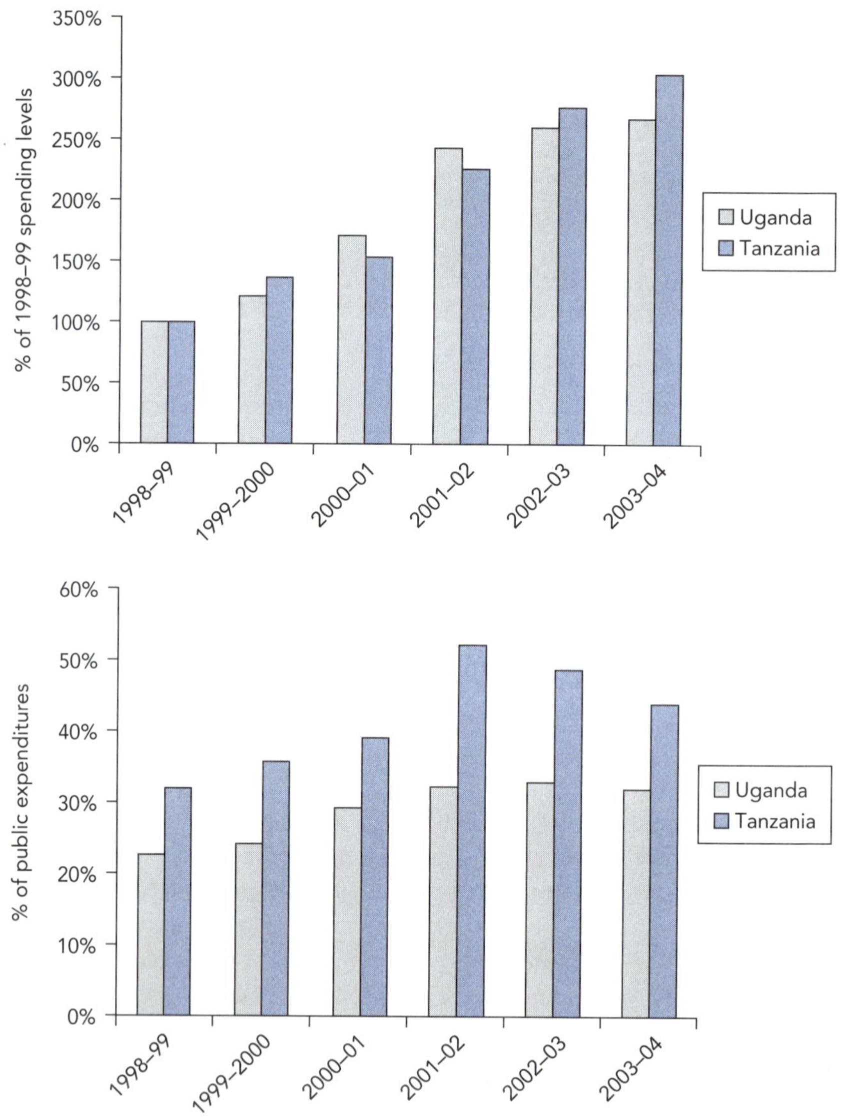

Note: Tanzania's definition of pro-poor expenditures is far broader than Uganda's (entire sectors rather than priority subsectors).
Source: Tanzanian and Ugandan Ministry of Finance data.

on parallel systems, increasing the efficiency of the development budget. The World Bank disburses 50 percent more per dollar spent on administering poverty reduction support credits than traditional projects (Miovic 2005), and administrative overheads appear to be lower in government-financed development projects than in donor financed ones.[3] Though comparable evidence is not available for Tanzania, it is reasonable to infer that budget support has similar benefits relative to project support.

FIGURE 8.5 Uganda: Increasing Efficiency of Public Spending

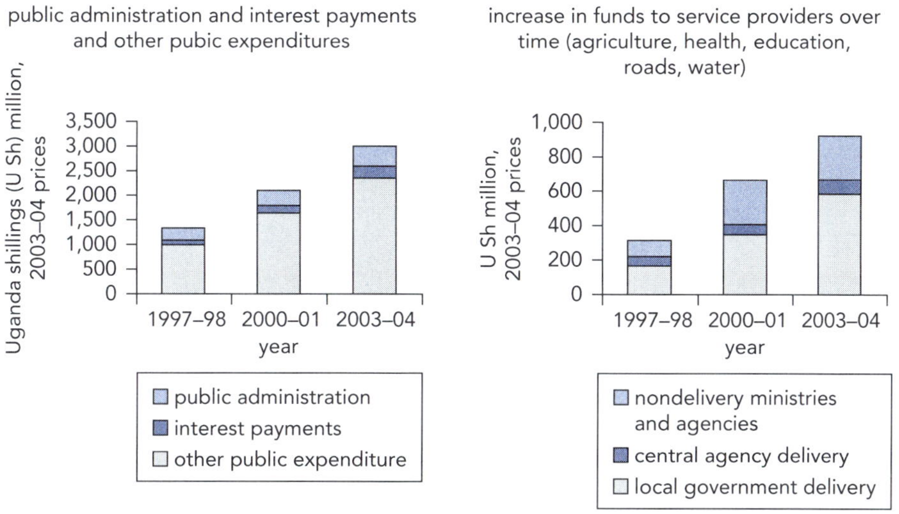

Government of Uganda expenditures, excluding donor projects

Source: Lister and others (2005).

However, in Tanzania, the development budget remains more than 80 percent funded by donor projects, compared with only 65 percent in Uganda (2003).

Both countries thus show evidence that the recipient's budget is likely to be more efficient with budget support than with other forms of aid. Greater direct improvements in efficiency took place in Uganda, partly because in Uganda, budget support supplies a much larger share of public spending than in Tanzania, but also because Uganda had a more effective budget formulation process.

Given these observations, it is important to note that although PFM *outcomes* may have improved as a direct result of GBS funds, PFM *systems* have not, and any changes in these systems necessarily take effect over the longer term. For example, in Tanzania, the Ministry of Finance played a weak challenge role in the budget formulation process, so that little improvement took place in the operational efficiency of budget expenditures over the evaluation period. This meant that budget allocations in Tanzania from the outset were less likely to improve efficiency than in Uganda, where a stronger challenge function was observed early on.[4] In contrast, the accounting function is weaker in Uganda than in Tanzania, where far more attention has been given to strengthening that aspect of PFM systems. In Uganda, the relative weakness of the accounting function means that the budget is less likely to be delivered as planned than it is in Tanzania.

In both Tanzania and Uganda, the shift toward GBS has increased the focus of sector institutions on the budget process (although there remains a strong incentive to approach individual donors for project funding). This increased focus on the budget process in turn has strengthened the positions of the ministry of finance and parliament, which have greater discretionary funding at their disposal as a result of GBS. Therefore, although GBS funding does not cause improvements in PFM systems, an absolute and relative rise in GBS funding increases the potential impact of improvements in PFM systems on PFM outcomes. This happens because if more discretionary funding is available to the government to channel through the budget, and government institutions pay greater attention to the budget, then PFM outcomes will improve correspondingly more than if the same quantity of funding were channeled outside the budget.

C. Major Factors behind Improvements in PFM Systems

We now consider the track record of improvements in PFM systems in Tanzania and Uganda, and the role of GBS in improving those systems. There are common areas of improvement in both countries, but also key differences (Figure 8.6).

Both Tanzania and Uganda have improved their macroeconomic and consequently their overall fiscal management, but much of this improvement preceded the move toward budget support. Tanzania made early progress in strengthening the accounting function starting in the late 1990s, unlike Uganda, which did not embark on upgrading the accounting function before 2001 and has made slow progress. Uganda made early progress in budget formulation with the introduction of the medium-term expenditure framework in 1997, but improvements in budget formulation processes have been slower to gain pace in Tanzania. Both countries are improving the timeliness of audits, but the external scrutiny of their public expenditures remains weak. In Uganda, the pace of improvement in PFM systems has slowed, but there is little objective evidence of deterioration in PFM systems.

In Uganda, the key factors behind the successes of PFM reforms were the strong technical leadership in the Ministry of Finance, combined with support for that lead-

FIGURE 8.6 Trends in PFM Systems in Uganda and Tanzania

What?	Tanzania	Uganda
Budget formation process	Progress has been slow—technocratic medium-term expenditure framework and limited budget challenge	Strong budget challenge early on, with increases in political involvement, but little recent technical progress and increasingly routine
Budget execution and accounting	Strong—successful accounting reforms, effective controls, and functioning integrated financial management system	Little focus early on—recent emphasis on PFM law, accounting function, and integrated financial management system
External scrutiny	More timely audit but weak parlimentary scrutiny	More timely audit, but parlimentary scrutiny weaker than interest in budgeting

Note: See IMF and World Bank (2004) and World Bank (2004j) for further details.

ership from the president. This crucial political support helped the Ministry of Finance to push macroeconomic and budgetary reforms. Similarly in Tanzania, high-level political support for PFM was evidently important in supporting accounting reforms, where strong technical leadership was also ensured.

In both countries, the role of GBS in upgrading PFM systems was secondary to these factors, but significant. It is attractive to believe that GBS can *cause* improvements in PFM systems, but GBS only supports and facilitates these improvements; political support and technical leadership are more important. In this context, it is evident that GBS funds have a greater impact than nonfinancial inputs associated with GBS, because they increase the relative importance of PFM systems and attract capacity toward those systems. The latter effects have been stronger in Uganda than in Tanzania, but the effects of policy dialogue, conditionality, TA, and capacity building on PFM systems have been significant in both cases. In fact, the nonfinancial aspects of GBS have been instrumental in improving the effectiveness of politically supported cross-cutting PFM reform, and to these inputs we now turn.

D. The Role of Nonfinancial GBS Inputs in Improving PFM Systems

Policy dialogue, conditionality, TA, and capacity building clearly focus on government systems and processes in both Tanzania and Uganda, as envisaged in the evaluation framework.

Dialogue and participation in the domestic budgetary process, combined with due process conditions relating to adherence to that process, have helped maintain the Ugandan, and improve the Tanzanian, government's adherence to their public expenditure cycles and ensure the continued openness of those cycles. Uganda's open and consultative budget process, established before the move to budget support, and Tanzania's open public expenditure reviews, which have become increasingly important forums in the budget process, have helped to ensure transparent and open budget debates. Similarly, budget reporting has become more disciplined.

This transparency, and the increase in information in the budget process, in turn present the opportunity to strengthen one of the basic rationales for budget support domestic accountability systems, although domestic constituents have yet to take full advantage of this.

Though one of the key reasons for budget support is to reinforce domestic accountability systems, donors can inadvertently undermine domestic accountability if they dominate the dialogue and its agenda. For example, in Tanzania, there is a trend for policy documents to be prepared in English rather than Kiswahili, and in 2005 in Uganda, donors' objections to the content of the 2005 budget gained a higher profile in the press than those of parliament, even though both sets of objections were similar.

Policy dialogue and conditionality associated with unearmarked GBS have been useful in addressing reform issues in cross-cutting areas such as PFM. Performance assessment frameworks and PRSC matrices played an initial role of increasing the coherence of PFM reform, simply by requiring the policy actions and activities relating to PFM to be discussed in a single document for the first time, instead of as part of separate donor-funded projects. Conditions and dialogue play a positive role by exerting managerial pressure on institutions to undertake policy actions and thereby maintain the pace of reform. For example, if the production of timely audit reports is a policy action in the performance assessment framework, and the disbursement of GBS funds hinges on this action, an auditor general may be more likely to ensure that audit reports are produced on time. However, this leverage only works where progress is possible at a technical level, and it does not work at political levels. For example, actions in controlling public administration expenditures, which include state house expenditures, have had less effect in Uganda than actions that are purely technical.

Herein lies a major problem: policy dialogue and conditions have not been applied strategically, either by development partners or recipient governments. Although performance assessment frameworks and the dialogue around these have served to increase coherence, they provide no substitute for a strategic, government-led PFM reform process. Those taking part in the dialogue have not been very good at predicting where progress is likely, and thus in focusing the dialogue on those areas and supporting strategic PFM reform. For example, it may not be expedient to tackle corruption head on by targeting high-profile cases, as development partners in Uganda seem to be demanding; a better approach would be to tackle it indirectly through improving accountability processes. In addition, dialogue on PFM reforms themselves tends to be conducted largely between donors and the ministry of finance, and not in as open and consultative manner as dialogue on other reforms, such as those in sectors. This feature may undermine the wider ownership of the PFM reforms being discussed. For example, the fact that the Ugandan Budget Act in 2000 was developed outside the dialogue by Parliament illustrates a case where specific interests were not taken into account (although this is also a positive indicator that Parliament was taking more interest in the budget process).

In many cases, the dialogue can get hijacked by big issues, such as defense expenditure and corruption in Uganda or presidential jets in Tanzania, rather than focusing on the nature and effectiveness of PFM systems themselves. Though admittedly of symbolic importance, these big issues have tended to dominate the policy dialogue at the expense of more systemic issues, such as improving the overall efficiency and effectiveness of expenditure systems or reinforcing democratic accountability processes.

In both Tanzania and Uganda, donor staff are replaced every two years or so, and this undermines the quality of the dialogue: the participants on the donor side are likely to have a limited understanding of the systems under discussion, let alone the most strategic ways of addressing the issues. Institutional memory among donors is also very limited. This undermines the incentive for recipient governments, where staff turnover is far less common, to engage in the dialogue. This is particularly apparent in Uganda, where the Ministry of Finance is now markedly less enthusiastic in entering into the dialogue with donors than it was when GBS began.

In several anecdotal examples, TA in policy formulation and institutional capacity building has helped to support PFM reform and improvements in PFM systems. Although TA and capacity building are rarely an explicit part of GBS, they are often strongly linked to it. If TA and capacity building are oriented toward reforms that feature in the policy dialogue, then their effectiveness is likely to be improved. For example, efforts to computerize the accounting system in Uganda failed in the 1990s, but today, when supported by policy dialogue and conditionality in the context of GBS, institutional support for the introduction of an integrated financial management system in Uganda is proving more effective.

Nonfinancial GBS inputs are more effective when they are combined with funds, but there are few examples of these complementarities being exploited. In Uganda, there has been a large relative and absolute increase in funds channeled to local government, but this shift has not been accompanied by an increase in TA or capacity-building efforts. (In Tanzania, more coordinated institutional support has been provided to local governments, but without corresponding shifts in resources to local governments.)

In summary, TA and capacity building with respect to PFM remain fragmented and poorly coordinated in both countries, and their potential effectiveness is not being maximized. Performance assessment frameworks are inadequate for targeting and coordinating TA and capacity building, and again are no substitute for strategic PFM reform programs.

E. Conclusions and Their Implications

The hypotheses in the evaluation framework appear to hold, and GBS funds when combined with nonfinancial GBS inputs have proved effective in supporting recipient governments' efforts to strengthen PFM systems and improve PFM outcomes.

GBS funds themselves can directly improve PFM outcomes. In such circumstances, both the scale of aid relative to public expenditure and the need for a decisive change in the mix of aid instruments, toward GBS and away from project support, are important.

To maximize the effect of GBS on PFM outcomes requires accompanying reforms in PFM. GBS funds per se do not improve PFM systems, but they do empower recipient governments to improve those systems. The most important factors behind the success of PFM reforms are political and institutional. To succeed, PFM reforms need political and technical interests to coincide, or—where they do not coincide—coalitions of interests to be built. At the technical level, reforms require a consensus among the ministry of finance, line ministries, and development partners. Political support, either implicit or explicit, is also necessary. This does not mean that political leaders need to talk about PFM reform, but they do need to allow the space for successful reform to take place.

Nonfinancial GBS inputs contribute significantly to PFM reforms and can help improve the quality and maintain the pace of reforms. However, the contribution of dialogue, conditionality, TA, and capacity building has not been strategic or systematic in either Tanzania or Uganda. More coherent, sequenced, and strategic PFM reform programs are needed to provide the framework for and support dialogue, conditionality, TA, and capacity building.

What do these conclusions imply for those involved in PFM reform programs and managing GBS?

Clearly, the provision of GBS funds needs to be linked to a package of nonfinancial GBS inputs that support a program of strategic and targeted PFM reform. This requires attention to three key issues.

First, those involved in the dialogue need to understand and take into account the political economy of PFM reform. Understanding needs to be developed of where political support and opposition lie, and of the likely winners and losers from reforms. With such an understanding, it will become easier to predict where progress is likely to be feasible and concentrate the policy dialogue on these areas. Where political support is lacking for reforms that are deemed crucial for improving PFM systems, there is a need to think about how to develop mechanisms for building such support—or at least for achieving political engagement.

Second, the potential complementarity of GBS inputs needs to be actively exploited if the impact of GBS on PFM outcomes is to be maximized. It is important to identify where GBS funds have effects and make these areas the focus of reform, and consequently the focus of dialogue, conditions, TA, and capacity building.

Third, effective budget formulation processes, and in particular budget challenge, need support. If there is limited progress in this area, as has been the case in Tanzania, and the budget process does not deliver strategic and operationally efficient resource allocation, the ultimate impact of strengthening other elements of PFM systems on PFM outcomes will be limited.

Taking these factors into account would enable the development of more strategic and better sequenced PFM reform programs, which would be more likely to address the weaknesses in PFM systems and yield the best PFM outcomes and the most effective GBS. This would also necessitate a change in the way development partners engage in the dialogue; they will need to develop a deeper, more consistent understanding of recipients' systems and link the provision of TA and capacity building to strategic reform.

Endnotes

1. The Uganda evaluation was part of the ongoing OECD-DAC seven-country evaluation, and used an enhanced version of the evaluation framework developed by the University of Birmingham, which is leading the evaluation. The Tanzania evaluation, which was carried out in 2004 as a stand-alone exercise, used the original OECD-DAC framework.
2. The increased need for sterilization is a result of an increased volume of aid, not of general budget support per se (although it can be argued that GBS facilitated a rapid expansion in aid) and the chosen composition of public expenditure (in particular, the propensity to spend on wages and domestic goods and services rather than imports). The increase in domestic borrowing is a result of Uganda's chosen sterilization strategy. See also Atingi-Ego in Chapter 17 of this volume.

3. For example, between 1999 and 2004, the government of Uganda spent only 2 percent of its project funding on consultancy services, compared to the 14 percent spent by donors in their projects. Much consultancy spending in donor-financed projects tends to be used in project administration, or project-specific issues, rather than policy/systems-focused TA.
4. However, the budget process is becoming increasingly routine in Uganda, and the challenge role played by the Ministry of Finance appears to be weakening.

PART III
Aligning Budget Support with Country Programs

9

PRSPs and Budgets: A Synthesis of Five Case Studies

ROSA ALONSO, LINDSAY JUDGE, AND JENI KLUGMAN
World Bank

Public finance management and the poverty reduction strategy paper (PRSP) process can reinforce each other. Public sector reforms and reforms aimed at improving the pro-poor focus of public spending have often suffered from unsupportive political and institutional environments, which the reforms have failed to address. The absence of champions and processes to foster the proposed reforms has often led to weak implementation and poor sustainability. The PRSP process, with its focus on data and information for evidence-based policy making, open and participatory policy-making processes, poverty results, and country-led donor coordination, alignment, and harmonization, has the potential to significantly improve the pro-poor focus and general accountability of budgeting processes. Also, by taking a "process" or "repeated-game" approach to reform with a focus on changing incentives, it has a greater chance of succeeding, especially in unsupportive political environments, than the "single-game" approach taken in public sector reform projects.[1]

The reverse is also true. The PRSP process requires its key principles and objectives to be sustained through the implementation phase via budgetary processes. Unless budget processes themselves use, produce, and publicize good data, become more open to representatives of the interests of the poor within and outside government, and lead to more pro-poor resource allocation and service delivery, and unless donors adjust their policies to long-term, reliable support to country-driven priorities established in PRSPs, the latter cannot be successfully implemented. PRSP processes and public finance management (PFM) hence need each other.

This paper synthesizes the findings from a series of case studies on the interaction between the PRSP process and the budget.[2] The studies, on Bolivia, Burkina Faso, Cambodia, Tanzania, and Vietnam, assess the extent to which PFM and budget allocations reflect the principles and content of the PRSP and hence provide insights into progress in poverty reduction strategy (PRS) implementation. The studies also shed light on whether the PRSP process itself had fostered more accountable, efficient, and pro-poor budget processes and allocations as of 2003.

The cases confront a number of methodological challenges. First, in some countries and sectors, lack of appropriate data constrained the extent to which the some of the research questions could be answered. Second, since the PRSP remains a relatively recent innovation in all the countries studied, many of our findings are preliminary and require additional confirmation over time. Third, any assessment of the value added by the PRSP approach needs to acknowledge the initial conditions in-country—both to avoid ascribing successes to the PRSP that predate its existence and to temper expectations about what the approach can deliver in a relatively short time. To address this last challenge, the case studies explicitly acknowledge the pre-existing situation in-country and try to assess the value added of the PRSP process.

The five countries studied have a number of common features. They all have a stable macroeconomic situation, minimum public expenditure management "basics" in place, and a good pre-existing basis for donor coordination. Except for Vietnam, they are relatively small, have a majority of the population in poverty, a strong partnership between a technocratic government team and the donor community, an active civil society and a weak parliament, and they face severe budget constraints and a high degree of aid dependence (though with important differences from country to country). In Burkina Faso, for example, fears about rising indebtedness have led to IMF-imposed caps on borrowing; Cambodia has an exceptionally low tax-to-GDP ratio; and Bolivia has run large budget deficits in recent years and faced political and social upheaval as it attempted to address them. Finally, and perhaps most important, all five countries share a high-level political commitment to addressing poverty, although they vary in the extent to which this commitment permeates their government agencies.

The five countries also display many distinctive features. Bolivia and Cambodia, for example, both suffer from high degrees of political fragmentation, which in Bolivia has shown itself as civil unrest on a number of recent occasions. Burkina Faso, Tanzania, and Vietnam, on the other hand, benefit from more stable political systems and an inherited commitment to pro-poor policies from socialist governments. Tanzania and Bolivia both have a recent track record of participatory processes, compared with Burkina Faso, Cambodia, and Vietnam, whose policy-making systems were relatively closed before the advent of the PRSP process. Likewise, Bolivia, Tanzania, and to a lesser extent Vietnam have a history of reform of public expenditure management dating back to the 1990s, although arguably the gains from these reforms have been much greater in Tanzania.

Finally, there are obvious temporal differences: Tanzania and Burkina Faso both completed their first PRSP in 2000 and have already finalized their second strategies. Vietnam and Bolivia produced their PRSPs in 2001, though, in Bolivia, a change of government and political disruption has slowed implementation to date. Cambodia completed its strategy only in late 2002.

The paper has six parts. Section A looks at the production and availability of data and whether data have usefully informed budget processes in our sample countries. Section B considers budget formulation processes and assesses whether the PRSP process has helped to make them more open and participatory, either within or outside government. Section C looks at accounting for expenditures and results, and reviews the roles played by different actors in enhancing accountability. Section D provides an overview of actual budget allocations and the extent to which expenditures have become more aligned with PRSP priorities. Section E reviews the role of donor coordination and alignment with PRSP priorities as well as the predictability and variability of aid flows. Section F draws overall conclusions.

A. Data Production, Availability, and Use

The case studies analyze the extent to which the demands of the PRSP process for the production of good data are leading to the availability of more timely, more disaggregated, better-quality data on poverty and social indicators to support the budgeting process. They also examine whether the PRSP-led focus on country ownership, sectorwide approaches, and general budget support is helping to improve the availability and dissemination of fiscal data within government and to parliaments, donors, and civil society. The orientation of the PRSP process to the achievement of poverty outcomes can also provide an added incentive for results-based, or at least results-oriented, budgeting. The case studies thus also aim to ascertain to which extent this added incentive is enhancing the results orientation of budgeting processes.

Data Production

The production of relevant, readable, and timely data has an important bearing on the policy-making process, as well as on government accountability for policy implementation.

Greater Coverage and Disaggregation of Poverty and Fiscal Data

Generally, the case studies show a PRSP-supported increase in the coverage and disaggregation of poverty and fiscal data and poverty analysis. In Tanzania, for example, the PRSP process has contributed to improvements in data on development expenditure, and ongoing efforts will greatly improve the ability to consistently identify and track PRS priority sector expenditures in the budget. In Tanzania and Burkina Faso, the PRSP process has also added impetus to the elaboration and use of disaggregated poverty data—for instance, through the establishment of gender-disaggregated targets in education and health. In both Tanzania and Vietnam, recent and reliable poverty data are publicly available and used to elaborate high-quality studies. The improved data coverage makes it easier to monitor progress in PRS implementation and, more generally, in the evolution of the quality of public spending.

In all five countries, the PRSP process has underscored the problems caused by the unavailability of adequate expenditure classifications for policy analysis, monitoring, and evaluation. Monitoring in particular is rendered difficult by the incompleteness of the functional and program classification of budgets and the lack of systematic and consistent identification of PRSP expenditures.

All the countries studied organized their budget information using multiple classifications, but generally each retained only one classification for widespread use by all agencies throughout the budget process. Bolivia and Cambodia, for example, use line-item classifications for most budget functions; Burkina Faso employs administrative categories as well as a program budget, but uses only the former for budget execution and monitoring purposes. Using one simple classification by all government agencies has some clear advantages in terms of simplicity and control, but also has shortcomings. In particular, it does not allow a country to match spending allocations with expenditure priorities at the budget execution stage beyond the very broad level of sector headings.

All countries in the study seem to have recognized the weaknesses of such an approach, but only Tanzania is successfully using other classifications, including economic, programmatic, and functional formats as well as disaggregating spending by geographic region and gender.[3] Tanzania's successful introduction and use of these classifications was probably made possible by its longer history of PFM reforms, strong focus on poverty reduction by both the Ministry of Finance and the PRSP unit, and pressure from the donor community and civil society. In other contexts, including Bolivia and Burkina Faso, donors have encouraged the production of budget classifications that generate information more amenable to policy analysis, but these classifications do not yet seem to be fully used by either government or donors to execute or monitor budgets.[4] It is important to acknowledge that the development and use of new information formats takes time, and the Tanzanian example seems to imply that sustained production and dissemination of these classifications in conducive policy environments has good prospects for success in the medium term.

Moreover, there is some evidence of the successful use of programmatic classifications in our sample. In Cambodia, for example, programmatic categories are used for expenditures under the Priority Action Program, and in Bolivia, there is some evidence of their effective use in the context of sectorwide approaches in health and education. Similarly, Burkina Faso's first full-fledged programmatic budget with a medium-term horizon has been developed in the context of an education sector program. The development of such "islands of excellence" has been noted in other country studies, and usually occurs in the context of programs that give a degree of financing predictability within a longer-term time frame (Roberts 2003). Clearly, with the right conditions and support, countries that have traditionally organized their budgets by line items can generate information in more useful formats, although experience from Cambodia (and, to a lesser extent, Burkina Faso) shows the danger that this can lead to the development of parallel budget systems that do not tackle the core problems of the PFM system.

Data Requirements for PRS Monitoring

The need to monitor budget execution for PRS monitoring purposes has also emphasized the importance of comprehensive budget data

The PRSP process seems to be leading to clear improvements in the integration of external assistance into regular budgetary processes and budgets. Outside the area of budget support, however, the degree of progress in capturing aid in budgets has very much depended on government leadership and the capacity of external financing units in ministries of finance. In Tanzania, great strides have been made in integrating donor financing into the budget—because of a move toward budget support and because of better recording of in-kind and direct project support into government accounts. This progress chiefly reflects the role played by the external assistance unit of the Ministry of Finance, which led efforts to harmonize donor reporting requirements and developed a comprehensive database of donor finance in FY2002 (subsequently used to establish the resource envelope for the FY2004 budget). In Cambodia, by contrast, no one agency has responsibility for coordinating donor inputs and, consequently, much external finance goes untracked. In some other countries, even when external aid is recorded, the recording is often done in formats that are incompatible with the rest of the budget. In Burkina Faso, for example, few donors distinguish capital from current expenditures, and many provide funding directly to the local level, circumventing all systems designed to capture comprehensive information on spending patterns.

Similarly, information on budget execution at the local level is without exception poor and is usually captured, if at all, by weak systems that suffer from significant time lags. As a result, a large percentage of expenditures remains essentially untracked, especially in highly decentralized fiscal contexts such as Bolivia's. Tanzania is making efforts to tackle this problem, publishing local government expenditures on a quarterly basis, although to date only at an aggregate level.[5] A further difficulty noted in some cases is that a significant amount of spending is off budget and is never reported at any point in the budget cycle. In Vietnam, for example, budget analysis is hampered by lack of comprehensive reporting and, in particular, the exclusion of the significant quasi-fiscal activities of state-owned enterprises and extrabudgetary funds.

Data Availability

The focus of the PRSP process on evidence-based transparent and participatory policy making and on budget support as the preferred aid modality requires broad availability of information for all stakeholders. Our case studies provide some evidence that the PRSP process is indeed contributing to improving the availability and dissemination of strategy, poverty, and fiscal data within government as well as to parliaments, donors, and civil society. There is no doubt that the introduction of the PRSP in the five case-study countries has heightened the interest in collecting poverty data and social indicators and, to a lesser extent, carrying out benefit incidence analysis and program impact evaluations. At the same time, the PRSP process is also highlighting the important remaining obstacles in this area. In particular, for information to be usable, it needs to be available in formats that are readable and facilitate analysis, allowing connections to be traced among inputs, outputs, and results. Less progress has been made in this regard, but pressure is mounting, especially from civil society and the donor community.

Information on Government's Strategic Priorities

The PRSP process seems to have improved the extent to which government strategies and policies are made available and actively disseminated to the public. This is true even in countries such as Tanzania, where much information was already made public before the start of the PRSP process.[6] In all the countries studied, the PRSP process has been accompanied by an extensive dissemination campaign by both government and civil society organizations. In Vietnam, the PRSP—the Comprehensive Poverty Reduction and Growth Strategy (CPRGS)—was widely disseminated, including in summary form to local government, communities, and civil society as well as through radio and television. Similarly, in Burkina Faso, the PRSP process has fostered debate about the country's development strategy and has created an expectation that the PRSP should be linked to sector strategies and budgets. The stakeholders most engaged in this debate in Burkina Faso, however, are donors and, to a lesser extent, government ministries, civil society, and the private sector, with the National Assembly still playing a rather marginal role.

The amount of budget information that is currently available publicly varies considerably among the five countries. In Tanzania, much budget information is disclosed as part of the participatory public expenditure review (PPER) process, with this exercise providing a forum for stakeholders to discuss the available data as well as express their need for additional types of information. In Burkina Faso, public availability of budget data is more limited; in particular, although budget documents are published in the official gazette and posted on the Ministry of Finance's Website, difficulty in obtaining budget data was identified as a problem in the country fiduciary accountability assessment (CFAA) and the Review of Standards and Codes (ROSC) and was confirmed by our interviews with members of the donor community and civil society.

In Cambodia and Bolivia, the readability of data is a problem because Web interfaces provide the public with access to budget information but in formats that are difficult to interpret. Moreover, much of the information that is disseminated is impossible to interpret without an understanding of the budget process. For example, in Bolivia, central government spending on health and education appears very low online, mainly because transfers of funds to regional government to pay teacher and health personnel salaries are not reflected under the relevant line-agency budget. Without this kind of background information, nontechnical users would struggle to extract useful conclusions from the existing information systems. This is, to a large extent, the situation in all five countries.

Information availability on how government funds are actually spent is critical to monitoring the consistency of budgets with government strategies as well as to curbing misappropriations. The focus of the PRSP process on data production and dissemination, and on budget and outcome monitoring, has contributed to progress in these areas. For example, significant improvements have been made in generating and publicizing good budget execution data in the five countries, and pressure for further improvements is mounting. The introduction of integrated financial management systems in Bolivia and Tanzania has made real-time information on actual expenditures available; in Cambodia, execution reports are produced monthly and aggregated annually. In Vietnam, the Ministry of Finance produces provisional monthly, quarterly, and annual fiscal data on government operations shortly after the end of the reference period and posts final data for the year on its Web site. Less progress has been made in the dissemination of within-year data or year-end preliminary data. Only final budget execution data are shared with the public and only after the lengthy six-month period it takes to produce them. The 2004 PER, however, recommends that preliminary budget outturns be published, and, given the eagerness of the Vietnamese government to make progress in the area of transparency in PFM and the donor community's emphasis on this area before considering a move to budget support, progress on this front is likely. In Burkina Faso, within-year data are not shared by the Ministry of Finance with other ministries, the donor community, or the public—despite the fact that this was a condition for budget support. This is a topic of ongoing discussions between the Burkinabe government and the donor community, and it is indeed likely to result in greater publicity of budget execution figures.

Overall, despite the magnitude of obstacles still ahead, the PRSP process and its accompanying move to budget support appear to have resulted in efforts to improve the production and availability of budget data to government ministries outside finance as well as to the public.

Linking Spending with Results

Evidence from the case studies suggests that the PRSP approach has increased the focus of governments on assessing the impact of public spending on poverty reduction. For monitoring purposes, good information on inputs needs to be complemented by tracking of outputs and intermediate indicators. The PRSP process has encouraged all the countries studied to spell out more clearly the targets and indicators that could be tracked to demonstrate progress toward their poverty reduction goals.

A number of common shortcomings are also observed. First, the links between some indicators and poverty reduction outcomes should be spelled out more clearly. Second, it is not always clear which institution has responsibility for monitoring each indicator, nor how the collected information should be used to inform future policies or allocations. Third, indicators have often been selected without taking account of government capacity to collect relevant information. Moreover, there is a general overreliance on survey data while routine administrative data remain weak and underexploited.

The PRSP process has clearly fostered greater emphasis on monitoring and evaluation. However, much of this effort remains incipient, and few effective systems are operational thus far. Tanzania's is the best example in our sample of a solid monitoring and evaluation system with strong links to the PRSP and budget processes; in Bolivia, the agency tasked with tracking results has yet to become fully functional. In all five countries, results information in most ministries is still collected in an ad hoc manner. And in all, the ministries of education and health were the most advanced in establishing and monitoring targets and indicators. These ministries' good performance seems to reflect the fact that they often have sectoral programs with associated monitoring frameworks, that they are priority sectors for their countries' PRSs, and that it is easier to define and monitor meaningful targets and indicators in these sectors than others, such as the productive sectors.

Valuable information on impacts is increasingly being collected on a systematic basis, but weak coordination among collecting agencies and insufficient use by policy makers mean that its full potential is not yet utilized. Moreover, relevant information is often not available at appropriate points in the budget cycle, and line ministries receive little guidance on what information they are expected to compile as part of their budget reporting.

That said, some good practice is emerging. In Tanzania, for example, poverty data are being used for the determination of fiscal transfer formulas to local government; in Cambodia and Burkina Faso, innovative mechanisms for the joint monitoring of sectoral results frameworks have been developed, including an annual review of sector performance reports. In Cambodia, moreover, these reports—for education and health—feed into the production of revised financing frameworks for the medium-term expenditure framework (MTEF).

The results orientation of donor budget support programs seems to be increasing the attention paid by finance ministries to the links of budget inputs with outputs and intermediate indicators. For example, in 2003 in Burkina Faso, the failure of the finance ministry to provide a budget allocation for the Ministry of Basic Education to be able to produce routine data on school enrollment led the country to miss a key benchmark with the European Union. Partly as a result of this failure, the variable tranche of Burkina Faso's EU budget support program was not disbursed, causing strain in budget management. (This crisis, however, seems to have significantly increased the awareness of Ministry of Finance officials of the importance of budgeting for results and of documenting and accounting for those results in a timely manner.)

For increased data availability to result in better policy making, the data need to be used by government, parliament, and civil society. Encouragingly, the studies also show that the PRSP process has motivated new interest in how funds are spent and what results they are having. In Burkina Faso, for example, the growing participation of civil society in the PRSP process has created expectations of increased involvement in other aspects of policy making, including budgeting. Nongovernmental organizations (NGOs) are increasingly pressuring government for, at least, improved availability of budget information and, at most, increased involvement in the budgeting process. Our case studies also point to the need for capacity building to increase the budget literacy of civil society, as well as parliament and government officials. Although greater budget literacy should increase stakeholders' ability to hold governments accountable, a recent survey of monitoring and evaluation systems carried out by the German aid agency GTZ finds that the main channel for increased accountability is through greater political pressure on government by stakeholders (a channel that is not exclusively dependent on "capacity").

Over time, it is expected that the greater demand for information both from within and outside government will lead to changes in how budget data are presented and disseminated, as well as to greater consistency among goals, targets, indicators, outputs, and inputs. The PRSP process has enhanced the results orientation of budgets. In Tanzania, for example, civil society organizations are urging the government to link outputs from the PPER to the budget and the PRS cycles.

Emerging Policy Lessons

Our studies thus suggest that the PRSP process is fostering the increased production and use of strategy, poverty, and fiscal data that provide the incentives for greater results orientation and enhanced government accountability.

They also suggest that further improvements are needed for the process to realize its full potential. For example:

- The production and publication of comprehensive, sufficiently disaggregated, readable, and timely budget data need to be further improved, and effective incentives or sanctions developed, to ensure that all levels of government account fully for their spending. At the local level, this is likely to require capacity building as well as streamlining of reporting formats.
- More work is needed to develop appropriate budget classifications to allow governments to track inputs in a way that usefully informs the policy cycle. In particular, the elaboration of full functional classifications and the expansion of programmatic budgeting would allow agencies to strengthen the strategic and propoor focus of their resource allocations. Once program budgets are elaborated, they should be tracked and used by government, donors, and civil society.
- PRSP expenditures need to be properly and consistently identified in the PRSP, PRSP progress report, the MTEF, the budget, and executed budget data to allow proper monitoring of their evolution.
- Information on inputs should be complemented with more systematic efforts to develop useful indicators and collect information on results. These efforts would need to be complemented by capacity building within line agencies to interpret monitoring results and use the results to inform relevant analytical work. Moreover, line agencies could be required to report key performance data as part of their budget submissions. Similarly, capacity building for sectoral experts in ministries of finance is needed to allow them to properly interpret the performance data submitted by line ministries.
- There is a need to stimulate better understanding of the budget basics by the legislature and civil society groups. In addition, budget information could be presented to potential users in formats such as pamphlets and newsletters for readers without access to Web technology. The annual presentation and discussion of the government's budget organized by civil society groups in Tanzania is a good practice that would be very useful elsewhere.

B. Budget Formulation and the PRSP—Has the PRSP Process Increased the Openness and Transparency of the Budget Process?

The PRSP process aims to foster greater openness and transparency in policy making. This is expected to be valuable in at least two senses. First, openness, participation, and transparency are of intrinsic value, because they expand citizens' access to information on how they are governed and their ability to participate in government decision making. Second, it is assumed that openness and participation will eventually lead to more efficient, accountable, and pro-poor decision making, as the result of the involvement of the poor and other representative groups in monitoring and even in directly influencing government decisions. The ways and extent to which this potential is realized vary enormously across countries, but one would expect to see the emergence of both a more strategic approach and greater participation in budget formulation as a result of the PRSP exercise.

Below we assess the extent to which this has indeed been the case in the five countries. We look at the processes associated with preparing annual budgets and, where applicable, MTEFs, and how these have been linked to, and shaped by, PRSP processes.

Importance of Initial Conditions in PFM

The initial state of PFM differs widely among the countries in our sample. Whereas Burkina Faso and Tanzania significantly reformed their PFM systems in the 1990s, such reforms are more recent in Vietnam and only incipient in Bolivia and Cambodia (Table 9.1). The soundness of PFM systems strongly influences the ability of the budget process to determine actual resource allocation and hence to support the country's PRS. Tanzania and Burkina Faso have sound PFM systems and associated budget processes that have become more strategic with the advent of the PRSP process, but this impact has been weaker in Bolivia and Cambodia. Countries with a stronger degree of social cohesion and government control (Burkina Faso, Tanzania, and Vietnam) have also done much better at imposing fiscal discipline on the PRSP process than countries with greater social fragmentation and weaker government control (Bolivia and Cambodia).

Improvements in PFM and the PRSP Process

Dual Budgeting and Costing

An important weakness of budgetary processes in Bolivia, Cambodia, and Vietnam is that these countries have not integrated the preparation of their capital and current budgets. In Vietnam, moreover, the current and capital budgets are prepared not

TABLE 9.1 Key Characteristics of Budget Formulation

	Separate preparation of capital and current budgets	Operations and Maintenance as residual	High level of off-budget expenditures	Protected priority expenditures	History of incremental budgeting	MTEF	History of inaccurate aggregate projections	Fragmented line-ministry responsibilities	High level of fiscal decentralisation
Bolivia	■	■		■	■		■		■
Burkina Faso	■		■		■	■	■	■	
Cambodia	■	■		■	■	■		■	
Tanzania	■		■	■	■	■			■

just by different units but by different ministries. As a result, disconnects are observed, and forward projections for current expenditures are often inappropriately low. In Cambodia, necessary allocations for operations and maintenance are typically treated as a residual and hence underestimated and suffer from large cuts if revenue falls short. As a result, the sustainability of earlier investments is compromised. High off-budget capital expenditures, funded by donors, exacerbate this problem.

The PRSP process, with its focus on results, increases the pressure on governments to use an integrated planning process as the only way to assess sector program costs to achieve specific targets. Costing has received great impetus under the PRSP process. In Tanzania and Burkina Faso, for example, the costing of the PRSP continued after the initial estimates were made for the PRSP. In Vietnam, however, the PRSP seems to play a less important role in government budgeting processes. There, it is the incipient building of an MTEF that has more potential to integrate the budget process.

Strategic Planning

Tanzania, Vietnam, and, to a lesser extent, Burkina Faso seem to take a more strategic approach to planning and budgeting than the other three countries in our sample. In all three countries, this strategic approach has translated into the protection of spending priorities in times of budget crunch.

Cambodia and Bolivia, on the other hand, made mid-year expenditure increases or cuts routinely across the board without any attempt to identify priorities. Some good practice, however, was observed even in these two countries, especially in health and education, which often receive a degree of protection as a result of their use of sectorwide approaches. The greater the reliability and protection of budget allocations, the greater the incentive for line ministries and other stakeholders to invest time in good budget preparation. The reverse, of course, is also true: if line ministries know that cash flows to the sector will not reflect the budget, they are unlikely to invest time in preparing budget submissions. This was especially the case in Bolivia, where the budget is not regarded as a binding document.

To increase the strategic orientation and reliability of their budget allocations, Burkina Faso, Cambodia, Tanzania, and Vietnam have, to varying degrees, introduced MTEFs in recent years. They have made good progress on some fronts: Cambodia, for example, has developed a rolling three-year expenditure plan; Burkina Faso has introduced bottom-up planning for a sectoral MTEF in education; and Vietnam is working on introducing MTEFs in four priority sectors. However, there is still much distance to go before effective MTEFs are securely in place. In Burkina Faso, efforts are hindered by inaccurate growth estimates and large amounts of undisclosed donor finance; in Tanzania, links between the annual budget and the MTEF remain weak; in Cambodia, the MTEF excludes vital parts of the government's budget, such as the medium-term wage bill and external finance. In addition, there is no guarantee that MTEFs will reflect PRSP priorities: Burkina Faso's MTEF for 2004–06, for example, showed no discernible alignment with the PRSP.

In some cases, the PRSP process has led to an improved ability to forecast and manage public expenditure in PRS priority sectors. In Tanzania, the establishment of a system of quarterly releases to PRS priority sectors has freed priority ministries from the strictures of the cash budgeting system. Beneficiary ministries and local authorities report that the quarterly increases have greatly enhanced their ability to plan and manage their resources. In Burkina Faso, on the contrary, the special treatment of HIPC resources leads to a complex accounting system that separates regular budget resources, HIPC resources, and the consolidated budget. It also fosters a dual accounting and dual responsibility mentality according to which poverty reduction activities are funded by donors through specific funds, but the rest of the budget does not necessarily focus on these objectives.

Are Budget Processes Becoming More Open and Participatory?

Ministries of Finance

Finance ministries play a critical role in ensuring links between PRSPs and budgets. A traditional weakness of previous development strategies was that they remained strategies on paper, with extremely weak links to either sector strategies or budgets. Meanwhile, ministries of finance typically elaborated and implemented budgets with little consultation with line ministries and little regard to strategic considerations. Hence ownership of the PRSP by the ministry of finance is critical to its successful implementation. Moreover, by shaping the process of budget preparation and implementation, the ministry of finance plays the key role in determining whether the PRSP principle of "participation" in policy making—including by line ministries, parliaments, and civil society organizations—is reflected in the budget process. Conversely, we would expect the ministry of finance to be more likely to "own" the PRSP when it has been closely involved in its elaboration.

In our sample countries, the ministry of finance was generally engaged in but did not have a leadership role in elaborating the PRSP. In both Bolivia and Burkina Faso, although the unit responsible for the PRSP was initially housed in the ministry of finance, it was subsequently moved to ministries focused on planning or external finance. Likewise in Cambodia and Vietnam, the PRSP was managed by the planning ministry, and in Tanzania it was the responsibility of the Vice President's Office.

An institutional home other than the ministry of finance does not preclude strong links between the PRSP and the budget, as evidenced by Tanzania, where the budget and the PRSP processes are increasingly aligned, and Burkina Faso and Vietnam, where the PRSP and the budget processes were housed in different ministries, but budget allocations show an increasing alignment with the PRSP.[7] However, experience from our other cases suggests that there is a risk that the PRSP remains divorced from key allocation decisions if the institutional links are not strong enough. In particular, we observed that the PRSP was sometimes seen as only having traction on external finance (Bolivia) or the investment budget (Cambodia). Similarly, in Burkina Faso, the government proposed to focus donor monitoring not on the PRSP but on "the parts of the budget financed by donors."

Although some substantive congruence is observed between budgets and PRSP priorities, in practice the *processes* used are normally quite distinct. In Bolivia, Burkina Faso, and Cambodia, different timetables were followed, and as a result, useful inputs from both processes (such as costings from the budget or strategic priorities from the PRSP) were unavailable at critical points in both cycles. In Tanzania, however, the successful alignment of the preparation of the PRSP progress report with the annual budget cycle suggests that practice can be improved over time.

Line Ministries

Our case studies provide evidence that the iterative and collaborative nature of the PRSP process has strengthened the collaboration between ministries of finance and line ministries in both planning and budgeting. Along similar lines, a recent study of Bolivia concluded that "the [PRSP] preparation process opened up a certain level of inter-sectoral dialogue between ministries and government institutions that normally do not have a strong tradition of cooperation . . . and has drawn attention to need for intersectoral coordination at both a local and central level" (Entwistle 2005). Likewise, in Tanzania, the PRSP motivated the resurrection of sector working groups as part of the PPER exercise—a key forum for dialogue among the ministry of finance, line ministries, donors, and civil society.

However, a strategic approach to budgeting by line agencies continues to be undermined by some key practical issues. In Bolivia and Cambodia, for example, other ministries do not receive their budget envelopes from the ministry of finance in time to prepare realistic budget submissions. Timetables are often out of sync, and key

BOX 9.1 Fostering Intra- and Interministerial Cooperation in Burkina Faso

In Burkina Faso, the PRSP process is improving the dialogue within ministries during budget elaboration. Traditionally, budget funding requests from line ministries to the Ministry of Finance were elaborated by their financing departments without much input from the planning departments. This practice significantly impaired links between sector strategies and sector budgets. The focus of the PRSP process, related sector strategies, and donor financing on results, however, requires strong intraministerial coordination. The focus on results has led to a noticeable improvement in the coordination between planning and financing departments, in particular in priority sectors, to ensure enhanced coherence between planning and financing strategies. According to the Ministry of Finance, the better coordination has improved the financing requests prepared by line ministries and the strategic orientation of budgets.

Coordination between line ministries and central ministries is also improving. This improvement is also a consequence of the focus on results of program budgets, MTEFs, and the PRSP process. The elaboration of program budgets and MTEFs has led to the organization of interministerial workshops to discuss and, in principle, decide on proposed allocations for ministries. The interministerial workshops include a key group of ministries—Economy and Development, Finance, Basic Education, Health, and Agriculture. According to Ministry of Finance officials, the interministerial dialogue has improved since the advent of the PRSP process in 2001, and the PRSP has formed the strategic framework for the 2002–05 MTEF.

Source: Alonso and Walliser (2004).

analytical inputs from line agencies are not available at the appropriate point in the budget cycle. In Tanzania, for example, before the alignment of the PPER and budget cycles, much sector analytical work undertaken for the PRSP, MTEF, and PPER remained divorced from the annual budget process, and in Cambodia, similar disconnects continue to be observed. As a result of such gaps, much of the good analytical work now being undertaken by line ministries is not well exploited. This points to the need to rationalize roles and processes.

Local Government

Although practice varies among countries, local governments have not typically participated significantly in the PRSP elaboration process, consultations having focused on grassroots communities and NGOs. As a result, a tension is observed: the PRSP is informed by local-level inputs from civil society and is aggregated at a national level, but many of its policies (especially in the area of basic service delivery) need to be implemented by local governments, who did not play an important role in their selection and design. This disconnect reduces the chances of buy-in to the strategy from local government, and principal-agent problems arise in the implementation phase.

Similarly, local government appears to have little leverage over the preparation of the national budget, despite the fact that decisions at this level can have serious impacts for local authorities. For example, in Tanzania, a number of local taxes were abolished in the FY2004 budget with little consultation with local government. This lack of responsiveness is sometimes underpinned by practical issues: in Bolivia, for example, the format for budget preparation at the local level is not standardized, resulting in numerous incompatible submissions to national government. Moreover, few countries have a process that facilitates local government–line ministry dialogue and, as a result, sector plans and budgets are often elaborated without the input of those who are to execute much of their content. In Cambodia, for example, the ministry of finance undertakes parallel negotiations with the line ministries and local governments, resulting in divergences between sector plans and actual spending.

In Bolivia, Tanzania, and Vietnam, the case-study countries with the most extensive decentralization, the PRSP process thus far does not seem to have fostered closer collaboration between central and local governments. In Tanzania and Vietnam, for example, there seems to be a disconnect between the budgeting processes at the local and national levels. Whereas budgeting at the national level aims to link to PRS priorities and sector strategies, local government takes a bottom-up approach, starting at the village level, and there is no guarantee that both sets of priorities will match up. Moreover, local government is impaired by a limited knowledge and understanding of the strategic priorities of the PRSP. Overall, despite its importance, the interface between planning and budgeting for strategies and policies at the central and local government levels is not as tight as it should be. Moreover, local government is not much involved in the central government's budget process. This is of concern, in particular since local governments depend heavily on resource transfers from the center, and decisions on local governments' own resources are also made at the central level. Finally, none of the five countries seems to have a forum where local and central governments can discuss the role of local governments in the elaboration and implementation of sector plans.

In Bolivia, the PRSP process was the catalyst for a significant devolution of resources to the local level, invigorating the decentralization process. In particular, the National Dialogue Law (2001), a result of the PRSP process, stipulates that HIPC II resources should be transferred to the municipalities according to a pro-poor formula, and spent on health, education, and other "poverty-related" expenditures. As a result, the relative size of municipalities expanded by about 40 percent, accounting for around 13 percent of total expenditure, while prefectures have maintained their share. On the other hand, decentralization seems to have led to a reduction in the share of expenditures allocated to PRS priority sectors. Indeed, an analysis of municipal expenditures undertaken in our case study found that health, education, housing, sanitation, and rural roads all suffered drops as a share of the total municipal budget between 1998 and 2001, despite being designated as strategic priorities in the PRSP. This development appears to cast some doubt on the pro-poor impact of decentralization. This issue, as well as the potentially loose fit between national priorities and actual expenditures at the local level in decentralized countries, warrants further attention.

Civil Society Organizations (CSOs)

Many observers have acknowledged that the PRSP process has increased civil society participation in policy dialogue and that it has provided stakeholders with opportunities to influence the setting of poverty reduction priorities (see, for example, Booth [2004]). In Burkina Faso, Cambodia, and Vietnam, pressure and expectations for increased participation are building up quickly, but there has been little actual progress in increasing civil society participation in the budget process to the present. In these three countries, the scope for CSOs to engage in technical budget discussions and hence wield influence in the budget process is still very limited. In Bolivia and Tanzania, on the other hand, the process is much more advanced, reflecting these countries' more active and well-organized civil societies as well as their more receptive governments. As a result, the *Mecanismo de Control Social* in Bolivia and the NGO Policy Forum in Tanzania represent the views of their members in budget discussions with government.

In Burkina Faso, Cambodia and Vietnam, the scope for civil society to engage in technical budget discussions and hence wield influence in the budget process is still very limited. Although NGOs tend to have stronger knowledge of the sectors in which they are directly engaged, their capacity in the public finance and macroeconomic areas tends to be significantly weaker. Moreover, in countries where there is much informality throughout the budget cycle, such as Bolivia, entry points for participation are often hard to identify, and the buildup of societal demands can be hard to control. In fact, the case of Bolivia provides a stark example of the need for clear "rules of the game" to govern CSO engagement in the budget process if macroeconomic instability and social conflict are to be avoided.

BOX 9.2 Tanzania: the PPER and the PRSP Process

The PPER was introduced in Tanzania in 1997 in recognition of the fact that the traditional PER exercise conducted by the World Bank and the government allowed for scant engagement by domestic stakeholders and hence had little ownership. The PPER has three main objectives: it provides a forum for information sharing on budget issues; it identifies and undertakes joint analytical work on macroeconomic, sectoral, and structural issues of interest to its members; and it facilitates the emergence of constituencies that seek to ensure the actual budget reflects poverty reduction concerns.

Led by the Ministry of Finance, the PPER team comprises CSOs and donors as well as other members of the government from, for example, line ministries and the local level. Working groups meet biweekly, developing a work program and delivering a report intended to inform the actual budget. At this point, an "external evaluation" of the PPER outputs takes place. Chaired by the World Bank, all nongovernmental participants such as CSOs and donors review the PPER recommendations, and the process is finalized with the publication of a report, ready to feed in to the formal budget cycle.

The PRSP process has been able to build on the accomplishments of the PPER and the PRS is now the point of reference for the PPER process, which strengthens the focus of the strategy on poverty reduction and results. Moreover, in FY03, with the impulse of the PRSP process for increased dialogue in the priority sectors, PPER sectoral working groups—which had been discontinued—were reestablished. These sectoral working groups are one of the key mechanisms to strengthen the alignment of sector budgets with the PRS.

Source: Alonso and Utz (2003).

Tanzania, on the other hand, provides a welcome example of how CSOs can work with the Ministry of Finance, line ministries, and the donor community to increase the pro-poor focus and accountability of the budget process without creating social instability. In fact, CSOs in Tanzania place high value on the PPER, seeing it as their main window of opportunity for influencing the budget, sharing views, and forging and sustaining alliances with actors in government and the donor community.

Role of the Legislature

Although in principle the legislature has a mandate to approve and monitor the budget in each of the five countries, in practice its role in budget formulation is limited in all cases. We observed several practical constraints. First, the budget was often presented to parliament with very little lead time, giving insufficient opportunity for parliamentarians or any specialist committees to analyze and review the proposals. Second, parliamentarians lacked the technical capacity needed to understand the budget. Third, in countries such as Bolivia, where the budget was not perceived as binding, the incentive to engage in a serious discussion was minimal.

We also found little evidence that parliaments owned PRSP priorities, and where parliamentarians did engage with the budget and demanded amendments, the resulting allocations were less in line with the PRSP. In Burkina Faso, for example, analysis showed that over the last five years, the changes made to the budget by Parliament have consistently increased the resources allocated to nonpriority sectors while reducing priority expenditures. Interviews with high-ranking members of Parliament's Finance Committee revealed a perception that basic health and basic education are already provided for by the donor community and hence are overendowed with resources. Similar regressive amendments were also observed in Tanzania.

Despite these shortcomings, the PRSP process does seem to be generating both an increased interest in poverty issues by parliamentarians and a growing awareness of the critical role they could potentially play in budget formulation. In Cambodia, for example, the Parliamentary Commission on Banking and Finance has spent time visiting poorer areas of the country and sensitizing its members to key PRSP themes. Likewise, in Bolivia, members of the legislature made clear that they would like support to build their capacity to analyze and influence the budget. In Vietnam, the involvement of individual parliamentarians in the budgetary process and the breadth and transparency of discussion on budget allocations have both increased over the past two years. The members of Vietnam's National Assembly are increasingly questioning ministers during their appearances at the legislature and proposing amendments to proposed legislation, including budgets. For example, members of the Assembly have raised questions on the efficiency of capital expenditure as well as on governance and corruption issues. Moreover, during the last budget cycle, the National Assembly significantly increased the policy focus and allocations devoted to HIV/AIDS. This progress is seen as particularly important by those who have noted that to date the PRSP has emphasized the role of civil society with respect to the budget, and that this has sometimes led to a sidelining of elected representatives.

Emerging Lessons

Overall, the PRSP process seems to have fostered improved openness in budget formulation and to be facilitating better dialogue among all stakeholders, within and outside government. Recognition is growing that both national and local budgets need to be better connected to the government's strategic priorities and goals, and the links between the former and the latter are receiving greater scrutiny.

However, ensuring that the principles of the PRSP process—in particular, openness and transparency—further inform the budgeting process will depend on continued support of the PRSP process by governments, CSOs, and the donor community. If the PRSP process becomes institutionalized and its principles are increasingly espoused by all stakeholders, there will be significant potential for continued improvement in budgeting processes. Moreover, stronger links between budget formulation and the PRSP process depend on the clarification of both processes and improved synchronization of both cycles.

In countries with weak budget processes, the budget as an instrument needs to gain credibility so that actual spending matches planned spending, increasing the predictability of financing to spending units and enhancing the incentives of all stakeholders to engage in the budget process. This is clearly a challenging agenda that depends on governance and public expenditure management reforms. But without progress on this front, the possibilities for linking budget allocations to strategic priorities will remain limited in the countries where stronger links are most needed. Some specific suggestions include:

- Foster the joint work of planning and financing units within line ministries (or consider merging these units). Increasing the results orientation of budgets will require these units to cooperate in budget planning in order to ensure the delivery of results.
- Foster dialogue between line ministries and the ministry of finance. Again, this is fostered by increased results orientation of budgets (fostered by MTEFs and PRSPs) as well as by lending instruments, such as budget support, that focus on results.
- Enhance the capacity of the legislature to engage on budget issues and foster dialogue between governments and parliament by encouraging governments to submit readable and realistic budgets to parliament with enough time allowed for discussion.
- Consider establishing working groups along the model of Tanzania's PPER, with the assignment of channeling dialogue among stakeholders as well as examining links among PRSs, MTEFs, sectoral strategies, and budgets.
- Hold budget hearings or develop other forums for civil society and other stakeholders to express their opinions on planned budgets. Such arrangements, however, should be based on clear and agreed rules of engagement to ensure that expectations are managed and the scope for unconstructive conflict is limited. In our case studies, the best example of such hearings is the publicity and discussion forums of annual budgets in Tanzania hosted by research institutes with good ties to both government and civil society. In Bolivia, the expectations created by a preexisting national dialogue and the PRSP process proved dangerous and should carefully be avoided.
- Align PRSP and budget timelines. Both the strategic priorities of the PRSP and the results from monitoring need to be available at a time that is relevant to the annual budget process, for both inter- and intrasectoral allocations as well as for medium-term adjustments. PRSP progress reports should be timed to inform the budget process and could usefully become background papers to national budget documents.
- Streamline and integrate the multiple budget processes such as the PPER, MTEF, and annual budget in Tanzania or the Public Investment Program, MTEF, and annual budget in Cambodia and Vietnam, and work toward the integrated preparation of capital and current accounts in Cambodia, Bolivia, and Vietnam.
- Strengthen links between the PRSP process and the MTEF. Ensure that MTEFs reflect the strategic priorities of the PRSP and, conversely, that PRSPs take as their basis the overall budget envelopes determined by MTEFs. The policy orientation of forward expenditure planning requires a range of new skills, such as policy analysis, costing, and programming. Experience from Africa suggests that MTEFs may be more effective where existing departments are complemented by new units that can

fulfill these functions to provide the support necessary for implementation (Le Houerou and Taliercio 2002).

- Communicate budget ceilings and overall government priorities to all spending units within a reasonable time to allow for planning to be based on a realistic budget envelope. In addition, review the format of budget submissions and standardize the template for all spending units, and introduce incentives or sanctions for the use of this framework.
- In cases where macroeconomic stability is a particular concern, consider negotiating a fiscal pact with spending agencies that would make financing more predictable but would reduce agencies' opportunities for bargaining.

C. Accountability for Expenditures and Results

The PRSP approach places strong emphasis on monitoring and on accounting for results. The key mechanisms for fiscal accountability lie with the legislature, civil society, the donor community, and internal and external audit institutions. This section assesses whether the PRSP process has given added impetus to these institutions, and whether it has increased the accountability for government spending decisions to a broader range of stakeholders. It begins with a survey of problems encountered in the case-study countries during budget execution and then reviews the performance of various actors in enhancing accountability.

Initial Conditions in Budget Execution and Impact on Accountability

The technical ability (and political will) of governments to execute budgets as planned varies greatly among our sample countries, with an ensuing impact on accountability. In countries such as Tanzania, gaps between planned and executed budgets are relatively small, and in others, such as Vietnam, executed expenditures have consistently been above projections; in others, such as Bolivia, gaps have been large, negative, and highly variant across ministries. In Bolivia, while the government has largely maintained overall control on spending, expenditures by ministries in 2001 varied from only 20 percent to more than 300 percent of planned allocations. Deviations on this scale demonstrate the failure of the budget to perform as a planning tool, and the disconnect between planned and executed budgets seriously undermines the former as an instrument for implementing the government's strategy and policies. It also discourages any attempt at building in participation and accountability at the budget elaboration stage, as stakeholders rightly recognize the lack of binding character of the process.

The reasons for such large deviations between budgeted and executed expenditures are numerous and vary across countries. Revenue forecasts are often inaccurate, and expenditure levels typically need to be revised downward over the course of the fiscal year. Poor revenue forecasts are due to a number of reasons, ranging from high volatility of prices and quantities of crops, through weak technical capacity in macroeconomic forecasting and revenue administration agencies, to political pressures for high spending. Governments often deal with such uncertainties by establishing cash budgeting systems. Tanzania and Vietnam, which have not tended to overestimate revenue and hence have not suffered from serious cash flow problems, have a system of quarterly transfers—to PRS priority ministries in Tanzania and to all ministries in Vietnam. Bolivia, Burkina Faso, and Cambodia, on the other hand, typically overestimate their revenue and expenditure levels and need to use cash budgeting as a way to ration available funding over the course of the fiscal year. This system facilitates control, but it undermines the ability of line agencies to plan and weakens the overall credibility and accountability of the budgeting system. In some cases, these weaknesses are jeopardizing PRSP implementation. For example, in Cambodia, the education strategy contained in the PRSP has been lauded as comprehensive and coherent, outlining a range of good policies from reducing user fees to raising maintenance spending and teacher salaries. However, slow and unreliable cash flows to the Ministry of Education have undermined implementation and, as a result, many of the promises of the strategy have yet to be fulfilled. Similarly, in Burkina Faso, the spending cuts typically implemented at the mid-year budget review, combined with cumbersome budget execution procedures, lead to large gaps between budgeted and executed amounts, including in PRS priority sectors.

Another reason for gaps between budgeted and executed expenditures is limited absorptive capacity. In Burkina Faso, for example, the Ministry of Finance was reluctant to increase resources to key social sectors, because it felt that low execution rates in those ministries reflected constraints on their absorptive capacity. Staff from the line agencies, however, complained that delays in transfers and excessively tight control by the finance ministry on all transactions constrained their ability to spend effectively.

Finally, decentralization can lead to important differences between national strategies and actual implementation at the local level. As discussed in Section B, local government often has the power to spend funds in ways that are at variance with the approved budget. In Tanzania the central government maintains a degree of control over local government spending through conditional grants, but it is expected that, as decentralization proceeds, its ability to influence local spending will diminish. In Bolivia, efforts have been made to ensure that municipalities spend funds in line with overall national priorities, but this has not been without its challenges (Box 9.3).

Overall, our studies point to the contribution of the PRSP process to a strategic approach to budget execution, but they also underline the need to continue to improve macroeconomic and revenue forecasting and budget execution systems if accountability is to be strengthened and the potential of the PRSP process realized.

Legislature and Audit Bodies

The key mechanism through which the government is expected to account for expenditures is the legislature. However, in most of our case studies, parliament played only a limited oversight role, and its supervision of accounts was perfunctory. In part, this is because members of parliament have only a weak capacity for budget analysis, but

BOX 9.3 Bolivia: Incentivizing Pro-poor Spending at the Local Level

In 2001, as a result of the PRSP process, various social funds in Bolivia were reformed and merged to create two consolidated funds. It was envisaged that one of these, the Fondo de Inversión Productiva y Social (FPS), would play a critical role in ensuring the implementation of the PRSP through spending executed at the local level. The FPS was expected to set an allocation for each municipality based on a progressive formula, and municipalities could then apply for grant finance up to this ceiling so long as they could show that they had sufficient counterpart funding to implement the project. Thus the FPS was expected to provide incentives to municipalities to spend their resources in a way consistent with poverty reduction objectives that are embodied in the PRSP.

In practice, however, the FPS has been subject to many problems. Its procedures are complex and often contradictory, reflecting the requirements of the contributing donors. Many municipalities lack the capacity to navigate its systems efficiently. As a result, disbursement rates are low; in 2002, for example, only 54 percent of the agency's budget was executed. The problems encountered in accessing FPS support have an additional negative impact on municipal finance: HIPC resources remain unspent as they await counterpart finance. In addition, the grants actually made by the FPS are not well aligned with the PRSP and do not follow a clear progressive pattern.

Source: Judge and Klugman (2004).

it also suggests a lack of incentives to fulfill this valuable role. As noted above, there is some evidence that the PRSP process has stimulated the interest of parliamentarians and that they are now demanding capacity building to help them undertake more detailed budget analysis.

Effective auditing of accounts would assist legislators with such analysis, but audits by line ministries are usually weak and untimely. Even in Tanzania, which met 8 of 15 benchmarks of expenditure accountability set in the HIPC tracking system, line agencies' internal audits did not meet the benchmarks. There are also weaknesses in external audit. In Burkina Faso, an external audit office has been created but is not yet functional. In Bolivia, the independent auditor was regarded as technically competent, although its ability to scrutinize resource use across government was limited by its own lack of budget. Moreover, the reports it did produce were not passed on to Parliament, and it has few powers to enforce its own findings.

In short, both the role of parliament and other formal auditing mechanisms remain weak in our sample countries (as in most low-income countries), and the PRSP process does not seem to have made a visible impact on them.

Civil Society Oversight

Because of the implicit recognition of the weakness of formal accountability mechanisms, the PRSP process bets heavily on the accountability brought to bear by CSOs and external partners. In fact, the PRSP process has provided new opportunities for CSOs to hold governments accountable, especially through participatory monitoring and evaluation mechanisms. In Tanzania, for example, the PRSP process has added new strength to the role played by CSOs in the PPER process, which now focuses on strengthening links among the PRSP, sector strategies, MTEFs, and budgets. In addition, CSOs are seeking to strengthen their budget analysis skills and taking a leading role in public expenditure tracking surveys and in assessing service delivery.

In most of the five countries, expenditure tracking at the local level is poor, with weak sanctions for local governments who do not report in a timely and comprehensive fashion. In Bolivia, however, local groups called *Comites de Vigilancia* have been given power of oversight with respect to municipal budgets. In particular, they have the ability to request that central government freeze transfers if misappropriations are detected. But, as discussed above, the ability of civil society to engage in detailed budget analysis is still limited, both by capacity and by lack of user-friendly budget information. On the other hand, CSOs in Bolivia have been successful in finding a role in monitoring the PRSP more broadly, and in scrutinizing whether the government has delivered on its action plan. According to a recent study of monitoring and evaluation systems, it is this kind of general political monitoring that is most effective in increasing government accountability (GTZ 2004).

Finding the appropriate balance between government and civil society scrutiny, however, is difficult. For instance, some have suggested that in Bolivia the balance has tipped too far in favor of CSOs, with the result of marginalizing core government oversight functions. It is also clear that CSOs, auditors, and legislators do not collaborate effectively in any of the five countries and that there are unexploited synergies in their roles in monitoring government policies, expenditures, and impacts.

Accountability to External Partners

Because money is fungible, especially when provided as general budget support, the PRSP process has focused on general accountability in PFM and on monitoring of performance.[8] This is an enormous improvement on the previous narrow focus for accountability of moneys spent on a myriad of projects. As a result, both government and donors are focusing increasingly on *government* systems and overall results. This is a strong finding in our case studies. In Burkina Faso, for example, there is evidence that the move to budget support has promoted a more results-oriented culture in the Ministry of Finance; in Tanzania, the government is using its PRSP progress report to good effect in accounting to both internal and external stakeholders. In Vietnam, the government used the 2004 PER to show progress toward improved transparency and accountability to increase donors' willingness to provide budget support.

Progress on harmonization of PFM and monitoring requirements, however, is still limited. In most countries, donors continue to use their own targets and performance benchmarks despite the emphasis placed by the PRSP process on homegrown points of reference. In some cases, however, there is progress. In Cambodia, for example, the Consultative Group has developed benchmarks, mostly focused on policy actions and notably in areas of special concern to major partners. Some observers, however, have questioned whether it is optimal to have separate accountability mechanisms for donors in the face of limited capacity and a nationally defined set of actions set out in the PRSP. More recently, a joint donor-supported PFM strengthening program in Cambodia has been developed.

Emerging Lessons

It is clear from our studies that the PRSP process has led to increased scrutiny of budget expenditure as well as greater focus on monitoring service delivery and overall accountability. However, countries with poor budget execution need improvements in their public expenditure management systems to allow the budget to be the key instrument of strategic policy implementation it is meant to be, and to allow both internal and external actors to exercise proper accountability in budget scrutiny. Thus it is important to:

- improve budget execution at both the central and local levels through better macroeconomic and revenue forecasting and improve cash management leading to more reliable and strategic budget allocations to line agencies;
- increase the capacity of all stakeholders—internal and external audit, the legislature, and CSOs—to understand the budget process, analyze budget-related information, and scrutinize accounts. Improved capacity to track results and monitor performance is also sorely needed, including in ministries of finance; and
- explore synergies among various accountability agents/mechanisms, in particular among auditing bodies, parliament, and civil society.

D. Costing and Consistency with Overall Macroeconomic Framework

Ideally, a PRSP should provide a comprehensive cost estimate for the programs it contains, including disaggregation by sector and economic classification.[9] This estimate should be consistent with a realistic overall macroeconomic framework. In addition, the paper should indicate which programs are priorities (to receive extra funds if growth and revenues surpass expectations) and which should be cut in the case of revenue shortfalls.

Few PRSP countries provided comprehensive cost estimates of their development strategies before the PRSP process and, hence, this is not a realistic expectation for a first PRSP. Indeed, in some countries (such as Bolivia or Burkina Faso), the first PRSP took a "new project" approach that focused on costing incremental activities (linked to HIPC funding).

Therefore, the question we posed is whether, taking account of initial conditions, the PRSP has added to the impetus for better program costing and prioritization within a consistent macroeconomic framework.

In all five case study countries, the PRSP indeed came closer than previous plans or strategies to a comprehensive costing of government objectives and programs.

More importantly, as a consequence of the PRSP initiative, a process for more detailed costing of the sectoral strategies needed for PRSP implementation continued after the initial paper was elaborated. In Cambodia, for example, the PRSP developed well-costed programs in health and education, building on pre-existing strategies for these two sectors. In Bolivia, important efforts were made to link poverty reduction objectives with financing requirements, including by programming capital and some current expenditures. In Tanzania, the costing estimates in the initial PRSP were not particularly strong, but subsequent PRSP progress reports have refined and expanded them. In Burkina Faso, on the other hand, challenges to sound costing continue: the second PRSP includes a much-expanded list of priorities without a concomitant estimate of their costs.

There is less evidence of effective interaction between the PRSP's needs-based approach and macroeconomic fiscal programming. Ideally, there should be mutual feedback between PRSPs and macroeconomic projections, with the former affecting the latter in medium-term plans (for example, leading to plans to increase revenue collection to fund needed expenditure in poverty reduction programs) and the latter prevailing over the former in the short run (for example, revising the PRSP targets, programs, and expenditure levels to reflect actual resource availability). In our case studies, we found little evidence of this interaction. In particular, the domestic revenue side has been treated as a hard constraint in all the PRSPs reviewed, with the focus placed on using PRSPs as tools to increase donor funding. Similarly, although hard budget constraints as reflected in MTEFs and budgets have tended to prevail over PRSP needs in the short run, there has been no well-defined feedback loop into adjusting PRSP targets and expenditure programs. The issue of the proper fit between PRSPs and macroeconomic—in particular, revenue and expenditure—projections is one that deserves further attention if identified PRSP needs are to be taken seriously while preserving macroeconomic stability.

Pro-poor Budgeting

Has resource allocation become more aligned with PRSP priority sectors? Assessing whether any budget is progressive is inherently complex, given the methodological challenge of isolating the impact of particular programs and the significant time lags between spending and likely poverty outcomes. In several of the case study countries, this challenge was compounded by lack of information on both inputs and outcomes. Consequently, we limited our assessment to ascertaining whether spending allocations have been realigned toward PRS priority sectors, leaving aside the issue of whether expenditures have translated into more pro-poor outcomes. We also did not seek to ascertain whether PRS priority sectors are actually pro-poor in the countries studied. Although this approach has its limitations, we are comfortable with this definition of "pro-poor expenditures" since, in most PRSP countries, the sectors identified as priorities (notably primary health, primary education, rural roads) are those that benefit-incidence analysis finds to be most progressive, and that poor people perceive to be of most benefit to them, as shown by consultative processes. Ascertaining the degree of alignment of budgets with PRSP priorities is also a valuable exercise in determining whether PRSPs are strategic documents that find their reflection in actual budget allocations or whether, like many previous development strategies, they are merely vague declarations of government intent.

We begin by considering the extent to which in each country the PRSP has been used to provide direction for budget allocations. In particular, we examine whether (1) actual expenditures in priority sectors have increased—in absolute terms as well as a percentage of the overall budget; (2) there is a better balance between capital and current expenditures; and (3) priority expenditures have been protected in times of budget crunch. Subsequently, we look for evidence that allocations have shifted in favor of poorer areas of the countries concerned.

The PRSP as a Strategy for Budget Allocations

Each of the five countries' PRSPs identified priority sectors such as education and health care and, in some cases, core priority areas such as primary education and primary health care, and indicated that allocations should be redirected to these sectors and areas. Although we encountered data difficulties in all countries, we were still able to provide a good view of the evolution of resource allocations and the degree of consistency of these allocations with PRSP priorities.

Priority Sector Expenditures

Since the advent of the PRSP, absolute funding for PRSP priority sectors has significantly increased in real terms in all five countries. In Burkina Faso and Tanzania, for example, real per capita allocations to PRS priority sectors and core priority areas doubled between FY99 and FY04.

FIGURE 9.1 Tanzania: Real per Capita Expenditures in Priority Sectors, FY99–FY06

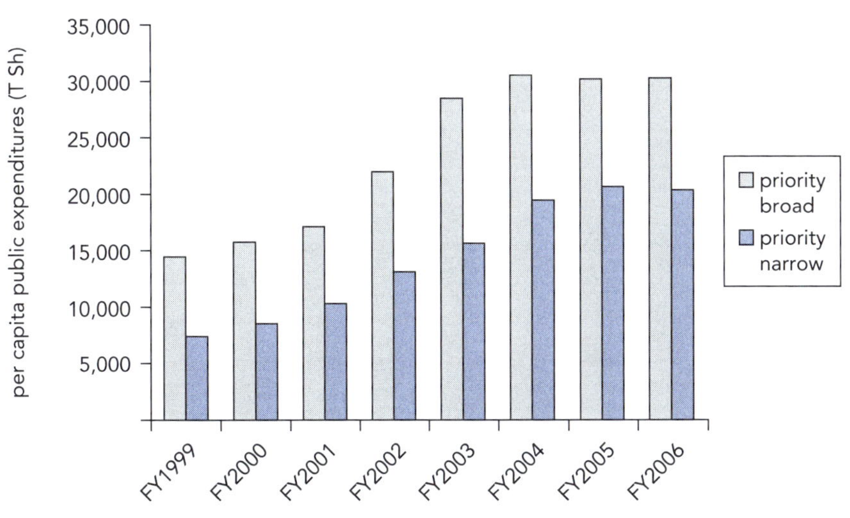

FIGURE 9.2 Burkina Faso: Real Per Capita Expenditure in Priority Sectors and Core Priority Areas, 1998–2002

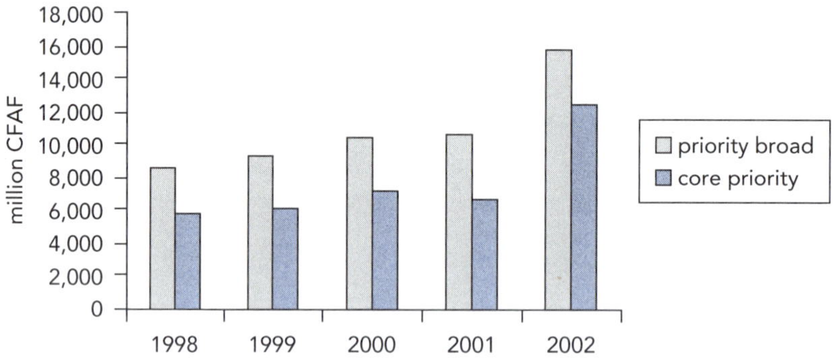

The distribution of increases across priority sectors, however, varies greatly. Education, agriculture/rural development, and transport seem to have benefited the most. Health care seems to have received much smaller increases, but this is hard to ascertain because of a move that has taken place in this sector toward vertically managed off-budget global programs.

Prioritization within sectors—to core priority areas—has also varied significantly. Primary education has tended to benefit the most from the increases in education sector spending, receiving, for example, 80 percent of the total sectoral increase in Burkina Faso. Primary health care, on the other hand, has not always received priority within the health sector and, in some cases, it has even lost relative ground. In Burkina Faso, for example, the share of the total health budget devoted to primary health

FIGURE 9.3 Tanzania: Per Capita Spending by Priority Sector, FY99 and FY03

(T Sh at constant FY03 prices)

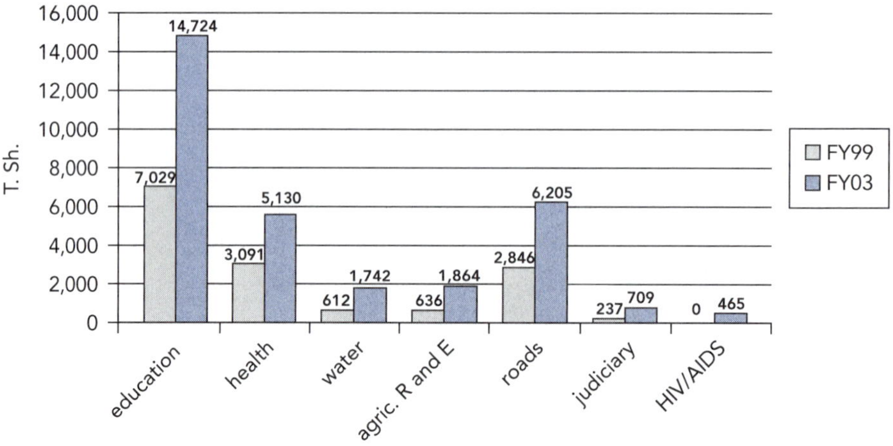

FIGURE 9.4 Burkina Faso: Real Per Capita Spending in Priority Sectors, FY1999 and FY2002

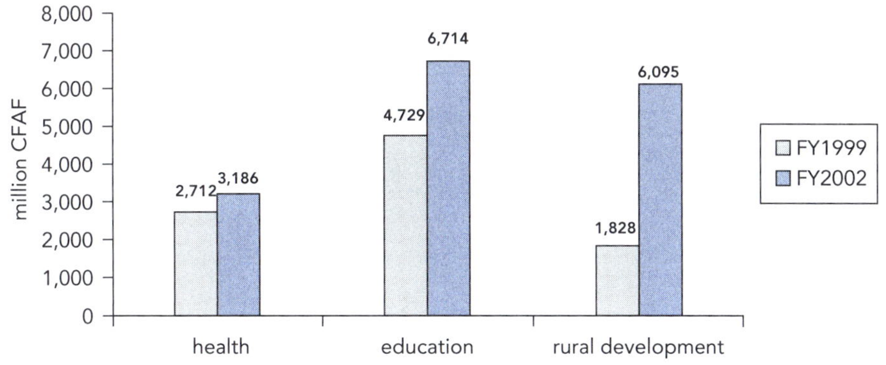

since the advent of the PRSP decreased from around 56 percent in 1999 and 2000 to 46 percent in 2001 and 2002. In all five countries, in fact, the increase in budget allocations to health care and, within health, to primary health have been quite modest, especially by comparison with the progress made in (primary) education.[10] Rural roads seem to be the most underfunded core priority area; in Tanzania and Burkina Faso, for example, they only received 4 and 3 percent of overall allocations to the transport sector, respectively.

Absolute increases in spending can be the result of a general increase in resource availability and do not necessarily represent a change in priorities. Thus we also examine the shares of the budget devoted to PRS priority sectors and compare expenditure increases in priority and nonpriority sectors. Cambodia presents the most positive picture: health, education, agriculture, and rural development all benefited from increased shares of current expenditures between 2000 and 2002, while the share designated for security and defense declined (Table 9.2).[11]

In Burkina Faso, we also find evidence of government prioritizing PRS sectors. The share of priority sector expenditure in total discretionary spending[12] seems to have increased gradually since 1998 (Figure 9.5), though with a slight setback in 2001 due to a delay in the disbursement of foreign aid and the concomitant decrease in primary education and primary health expenditure.

TABLE 9.2 Cambodia: Shares of Current Expenditure, FY2000–FY2005

(percent)

	FY2000	FY2001	FY2002	FY2003	FY2004	FY2005
Health	8.4	9.5	10.9	12.0	12.5	12.9
Education	14.0	16.2	18.2	18.5	19.5	20.0
Agriculture and rural development	2.9	4.6	3.8	3.4	3.8	6.4
Security and defence	37.1	30.1	24.7	22.0	20.8	19.4

Note: Figures for FY2003 onward are projected.

FIGURE 9.5 Burkina Faso: Shares of Priority and Nonpriority Expenditure in Total Discretionary Spending, 1998–2002

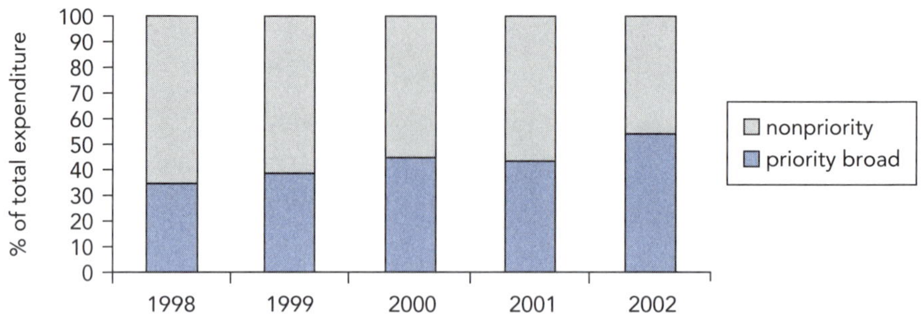

In Tanzania, on the other hand, priority sectors do not seem to have consistently received priority in budget allocations (Figure 9.6).

It is often argued that one of the main advantages of budget support is that it can produce a better balance between capital and current expenditures, by contrast with the heavy emphasis on capital expenditure typical of project-based aid. Our case studies found no consistent evidence of increased spending on operation and maintenance since the introduction of the PRSP, though an incipient trend seems to be emerging in some countries. In Burkina Faso, almost the whole increase in priority sector spending over 2000–02 is attributable to increases in development/investment spending, with only very small increases in recurrent spending. This is a

FIGURE 9.6 Tanzania: Percentage Change in Priority and Nonpriority Expenditures, FY2000–FY2006

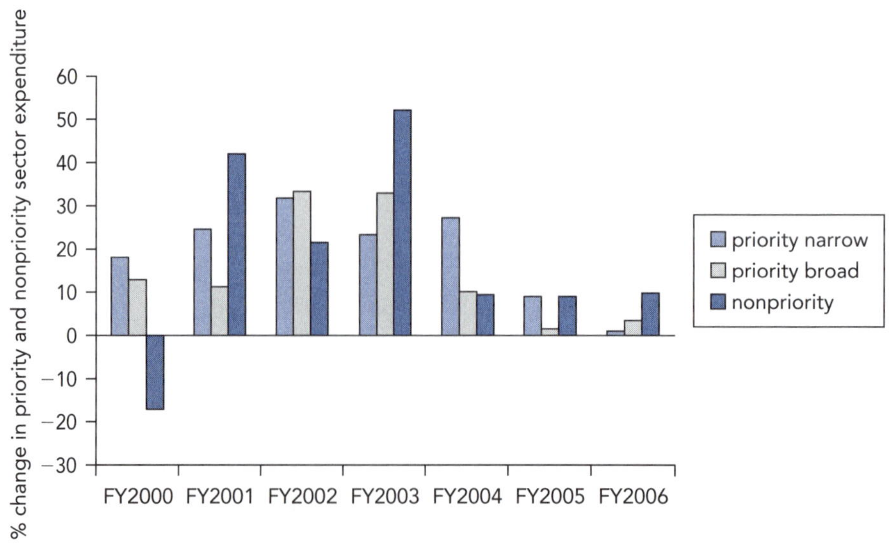

worrying trend as some of the direst needs (particularly in the social sectors) are in nonwage current expenditure (operations and maintenance and school and health center materials). Similarly, in Cambodia, the PRSP does not yet seem to have helped ministries plan their operation and maintenance requirements more strategically, although there is some evidence of good practice in education and health. In Bolivia, on the other hand, the share of the budget directed to the National Roads Authority, which is responsible for maintaining the main and trunk roads, has received increases in recent years.

Finally, the PRS process seems to be contributing to increased prioritization in the implementation of budget cuts. Four out of five case studies show strong evidence that when expenditures are cut, PRS priority expenditures are protected. In Tanzania, protection of PRSP priority sectors from budget cuts is official policy and constitutes part of the benefits entailed in the definition of being a "priority sector." In Burkina Faso, the government substituted its own funds to (partly) compensate for aid shortfalls and, to the extent possible, protect overall allocations in priority sectors. In Vietnam, revenue over the past four years has consistently overperformed, hence there have been no shortfalls. However, during the East Asian crisis, the government clearly protected allocations to what would later be PRSP priority sectors, whose share in the budget increased during the crisis (as other sectors' shares dropped). Cambodia made no budget cuts during the period reviewed. In Bolivia, on the other hand, budget cuts do not seem to reflect any strategic objectives.

Regional Targeting of Expenditures

In three of our case studies, it was possible to consider the regional distribution of spending and come to some preliminary conclusions on whether it has become more progressive since the advent of the PRSP. In Cambodia, an analysis of health and education expenditures per capita and provincial poverty data showed that, among the 14 poorest provinces, funding was above the national average in only 4. This is not surprising as, in a traditional budgeting system, increases in budget allocations are made as a continuation of historical trends. Typically, as a result, the larger increases in expenditure accrue to the regions that are endowed with larger numbers of facilities and personnel, which tend to be the wealthier areas of the country.

Bolivia shows a similar pattern. Though increases in municipal spending for housing and sanitation did go disproportionately to the poorer prefectures, no straightforward progressive relationship could be seen in the health and education sectors, despite the fact that HIPC funds devoted to these two sectors are allocated according to a pro-poor formula. In addition, a recently introduced social insurance scheme for maternal and child health was criticized for poor targeting as it provides universal coverage for a range of secondary as well as primary health care services.

However, more positive examples of successful targeting can be found. In Burkina Faso, for example, a new primary education development fund focuses on the 20 provinces with the lowest enrollment rates; in Cambodia, transfers to new local

BOX 9.4 Uganda: Poverty Criteria as a Guide to Budget Allocations

In recent years, the Government of Uganda has used seven criteria to assess the poverty focus of the budget framework papers submitted by line agencies: (1) addressing needs of the poorest 20 percent; (2) addressing gender inequalities; (3) addressing geographical inequalities; (4) HIV/AIDS; (5) environment; (6) empowerment of communities; and (7) addressing intersectoral linkages.

To increase focus and reduce workloads for sector working groups, however, these questions were narrowed down in financial year 2002–03. As a result, line agencies had to ask themselves whether they had addressed the needs of poor people in their sector, addressed geographic inequalities, and designed measures to empower poor people in their budget submissions.

A Poverty Eradication Working Group reviews and makes recommendations on the overall allocation of resources and intraresource allocations within sectors. It also considers other budget policies that have an impact on the poor and sectors that qualify as "priorities" (to be under the Poverty Action Fund), while advising the sector working groups in applying the PRSP cross-cutting principles to the budget framework papers.

Source: Klugman and Taliercio (2003).

councils are based on a formula that factors in a measure of need. In Tanzania, the government has used data from the 2002 household budget survey and census as well as analysis from its poverty monitoring system to elaborate a poverty map and a fiscal transfer system that takes account of regional diversity in poverty and social indicators. Similarly, the government of Vietnam plans to use a study of the geographical allocation of expenditure based on the 2003 poverty map to continue increasing the resources it allocates to poorer areas.

Overall, when budgets are programmed, the geographical distribution of expenditure is not systematically considered, but more consideration is being given to the geographical incidence of poverty now than before the advent of the PRSP process. International experience suggests it is valuable to explicitly include considerations of poverty impacts in budget submission guidelines, in order to ensure that line ministries consider the consequences of their spending decisions for marginalized groups and regions (Box 9.4).

Emerging Lessons

A key goal of the PRSP process was to encourage increased expenditure in pro-poor priority sectors and core priority areas. All our five case studies find strong evidence that the process has succeeded in this regard. There is also evidence (in Burkina Faso, Tanzania, and Vietnam) that these sectors receive protection in times of budget crunch, bearing testimony to real prioritization by governments. Moreover, although poverty considerations do not consistently feature in decisions on the geographical distribution of spending, there is a trend toward greater consideration of these issues in all five countries. These are very important achievements.

Some priority sectors have been more consistently well endowed (notably education, transport, agriculture) than others (health), and some priority areas have received much larger increases (primary education) than others (primary health and rural roads). These divergences seem to stem both from the behavior of the international community as well as from the true degree of ownership of priorities by governments.

There is less consistent evidence to judge whether current priorities will be sustained in the medium term. In Cambodia, medium-term projections do show a continued trend toward increasing the budget shares of PRSP priority sectors. In Burkina Faso and Tanzania, however, MTEF projections for 2004–06 reveal stagnation and even decline in the shares devoted to PRS priority sectors. This trend is worrying: in Tanzania, resources fall considerably short of the requirements in PRS priority sectors as established by careful costing work. Similarly, in Burkina Faso the new PRSP contains an expanded list of priorities which can only lead to reduced allocations to original PRS priority sectors, and indeed this is reflected in the MTEF.

While data limitations make any analysis at this stage preliminary, our findings point both to important achievements (especially for such a short period of time) and to the need for greater congruence between resource allocation and the PRSP. This could be facilitated by:

- Avoiding overexpanding the list of priority sectors and core priority areas included in PRSPs. The choice of sectors, areas, and programs to receive priority should be informed by the messages that emerge from PRSP consultations and are ratified by parliament.
- Defining which specific programs and expenditures should receive priority and consistently identifying them in PRSPs, MTEFs, and budgets. The identification process should include agreement on the criteria for assessing whether a particular program should be regarded as a priority. Ideally, the identification of specific PRSP priority programs should be led by the finance ministry but would involve the substantive engagement of line agencies as well as feedback from civil society, development partners, and possibly parliamentary review and approval.
- Developing transparent technical criteria for prioritizing major spending proposals across sectors (the criteria could be complemented by sector-specific guidelines) for use in the annual and medium-term budgeting processes, as is currently done in Uganda. Since the extent to which effective prioritization can take place depends significantly on the existence of program-based budgeting, we stress the need to expedite progress on this front.
- Re-examining existing resource allocations for their consistency with identified priorities for poverty reduction and complementing this with other kinds of analysis, such as cost-effectiveness analysis.
- Using priority criteria to guide capital spending, thereby increasing the transparency and accountability of public resource allocations.
- Using the results of the poverty-mapping work to check proposed allocations and executed expenditures against regional measures of deprivation.

E. Donor Coordination and Alignment with PRS Priorities and Predictability and Variability of External Financing

All the five countries studied except Vietnam depend heavily on aid. In Cambodia, for example, external financing exceeds domestically mobilized public resources by about 30 percent; in Bolivia and Tanzania in 2001–02, the share of the capital budget that was externally financed amounted to 49 and 90 percent, respectively. In countries with such high aid dependency ratios, the cooperation of the donor community is essential for the PRSP approach to succeed. To implement their PRSPs, these countries need aid coordination to avoid fragmented reporting of expenditures, alignment of aid instruments with PRSP priorities, and predictable and stable financing. Our case studies examine the extent to which the donor community has delivered on these fronts.

Efforts to improve partnership between government and donors often predate the PRSP. In Tanzania, for example, the Tanzania Assistance Strategy and the PPER were in place before the advent of the PRSP; in Bolivia, the New Relationship Framework launched in 1999 sought to ensure alignment with government priorities as well as manage donors' contributions in a more coordinated manner. Below we consider whether the PRSP has provided additional impetus to such initiatives, whether it has helped governments manage external finance better to deliver on their pro-poor priorities, and how this potential could be exploited further.

Donor Alignment and Aid Modalities

Most donors in the case-study countries have indicated their commitment to supporting PRSP priorities and their willingness to align their assistance accordingly. There is evidence that this is indeed occurring. In Cambodia, for example, a move away from funding core government functions and economic development to supporting the social sectors has been observed for some years, and there is evidence from the health sector that external finance is distributed progressively in regional terms.

However, PRSP priority areas in all five countries are so broadly defined as to make alignment relatively easy for donors, at least in nominal terms. In Bolivia, for example, the ministry responsible for external finance estimated that 99 percent of donor funding was aligned with the PRSP pillars in 2002. However, not all activities under each pillar could be regarded as pro-poor, and this figure also obscured the fact that aid was not ideally distributed among the various priority sectors. Further analysis of donor programming for the periods 1998–2002 and 2003–06 in Bolivia was more illuminating: it showed that donors generally tended to crowd into more popular areas, and that few were prepared to commit even new project support to PRSP priority sectors that the government regarded as underfunded.

While this lack of flexibility can be explained in part by historical commitments to specific sectors or issues, it is an obstacle to closer alignment between the PRSP and external financing. The significance of this lack of donor alignment with a country's agreed priorities becomes even more apparent when one considers the requirement of domestic counterpart funding for many donor-funded projects. Estimates from the 2003 Bolivian budget suggest that almost 20 percent of internal finance is linked to foreign financing. Thus, where donors do not program explicitly to deliver on PRSP priorities, the domestic budget is also directed away from these vital activities, making the overall alignment of the budget to PRSP priorities extremely challenging.

The PRSP approach places a premium on moving toward aid modalities that minimize transaction costs for the recipient country as well as give the government more control over how funds are spent. Thus another way to ascertain the degree of alignment of donor financing with the PRSP is to trace the evolution of budget support. A move toward budget support, however, is only feasible and desirable when a number of preconditions that give confidence in a government's ability and willingness to manage resources effectively are in place. These conditions typically include a stable macroeconomic situation; strong country ownership of the PRSP, with clearly articulated structural and sectoral policies and programs and evidence of momentum toward implementation; good progress in getting the basics right in public expenditure management; and confidence in the area of governance and PFM transparency and accountability. As much of the foregoing analysis will have shown, these conditions are not always in place in our sample countries, hindering progress toward budget support.

In addition, it has not always proven easy for donors to agree on the shared conditionalities, monitoring frameworks, and procurement plans that are needed to facilitate budget support and basket funding arrangements. In Burkina Faso, for example, tensions were observed among various donors with respect to the triggers to be used to unlock funding, while in Bolivia, the performance of the social funds testifies to a lack of progress with respect to harmonizing procedures. However, practice suggests that over time, donors can reach compromises and that streamlined aid modalities produce significant benefits for the recipient country.

In Tanzania and Burkina Faso, the PRSP approach has increased donor confidence in these governments' ability to manage resources for poverty reduction, as confirmed by large increases in the amounts of external assistance provided in the form of budget support in recent years. Between 1999 and 2002, program grants and loans as a share of GDP rose significantly in both countries, from 1.8 to 3.2 percent in Tanzania and from 2.9 to 4 percent in Burkina Faso.[13]

In Bolivia, donors have increased their commitments in the form of budget support, while suggesting that the number of projects would decline over 2003–06. In Tanzania, sectorwide approaches have been established in health, education, and agriculture, and several thematic basket funding arrangements are in place.

Predictability of External Finance

In the aid-dependent countries in our study, timely and predictable disbursements of donor commitments are critically important for effective public expenditure management and PRSP implementation. Performance in this area was mixed. In Tanzania, for example, the PRSP has given additional impetus to government efforts to collate information on donor funding, and progress has been made in capturing in-kind transfers, direct support to local governments, and funding from NGOs. Conversely, Burkina Faso appears to have made little progress in developing a comprehensive overview of donor finance, thus the understanding of the full parameters of the budget is still limited.

In general from our case studies, it seems that the PRSP process provides additional impetus and rationale for recipient country governments to request better information on aid projections and disbursements, but that only when the units responsible for external financing are strong enough to provide leadership (as in Tanzania) is this potential actually realized.

Even when an external financing unit specifies the information, frequency of provision, and format that are required, development partners have problems in supplying such information, especially for projected commitments. Few donor countries themselves undertake medium-term budgeting and hence are unable to make firm commitments beyond an annual horizon. As a result, efforts by recipient countries to develop MTEFs are undermined as resource envelopes cannot be accurately estimated without information on foreign financing commitments.

Donor flows seem to be extremely volatile. Evidence from Tanzania shows donor flows varying widely from year to year, and much more so than domestic resources. Similarly, in Burkina Faso, foreign aid has varied significantly from year to year, and has been difficult to predict, as HIPC aid was delayed for almost a full year from 2000–01. We found no clear-cut evidence as to what types of aid were more volatile.

Even within a year, aid flows are hard to predict, which significantly impairs the ability of governments to properly plan and execute budget expenditures. Analysis from Bolivia suggests that, in 1998–2002, the best-performing donors disbursed only 70 percent of their committed aid, and the poorest performers could only provide 33 percent, with the large multilaterals tending to fall into the latter category. Similarly, evidence from Burkina Faso and Tanzania shows important gaps between aid commitments and disbursements (Figure 9.7).

Evidence from Burkina Faso also points to irregular flows of external financing throughout the fiscal year, with a tendency to bunch during the last quarter (Figure 9.8).

Emerging Lessons

This section has highlighted the significance of donor financing for PRSP implementation and improved public expenditure management. It has also shown the contri-

FIGURE 9.7 Tanzania: Projected and Disbursed External Assistance

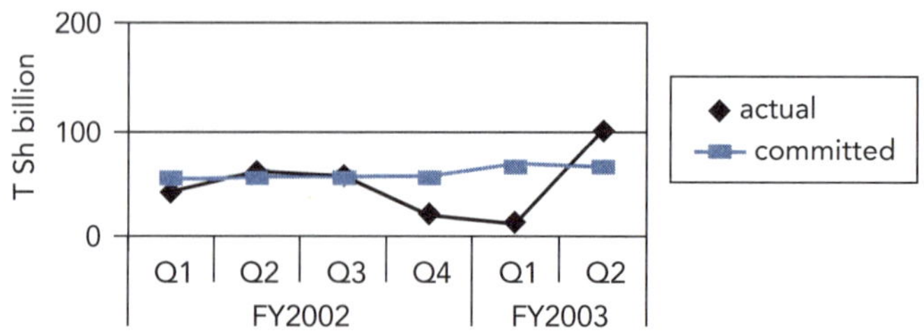

FIGURE 9.8 Burkina Faso: Budget Support—Quarterly Disbursements

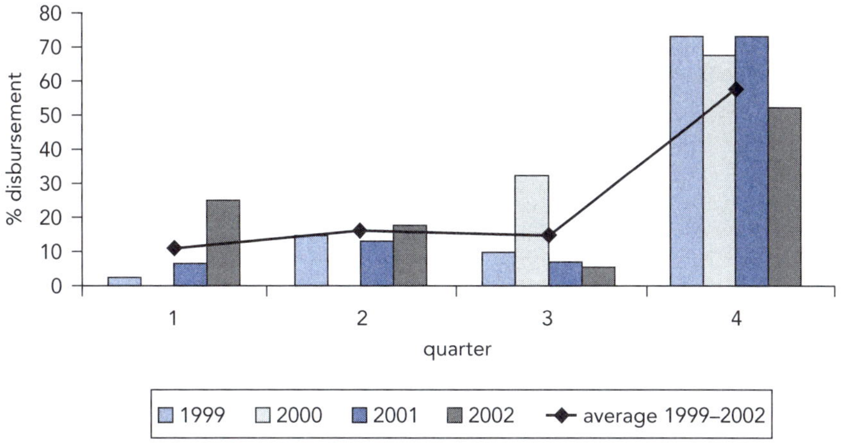

bution of the PRSP process to increased aid coordination and alignment with government priorities. Much remains to be done. In particular, the findings point to the need for:

- greater self discipline on the part of donors to ensure that all aid is on budget and is aligned first and foremost with recipient governments' rather than donors' objectives,
- aid disbursements that are synchronized with the recipient country's budget cycle to support good planning and public expenditure management,
- improved forward planning by donors, allowing them to make better estimates of their contributions over the medium term,
- improvements in channeling aid through the treasury and in reporting external finance in the budget,
- faster progress on harmonizing procedures, and
- more realistic common understanding between donors and recipient countries on conditions for aid disbursement, to help minimize gaps between committed and disbursed amounts.

F. Conclusions

Evidence from our five case studies suggests that the PRSP process is significantly affecting budget processes and budget allocations. The accomplishments are particularly impressive, given the difficult changes envisaged and the short period of implementation. Moreover, the PRSP approach attempts to affect results by influencing incentives and, in particular, by affecting the environment in which policies are made and influencing the actors who are involved in policy-making processes. This approach bodes wellfor sustainability but does not necessarily yield immediate results. In particular, our case studies show the following trends:

Accomplishments

- Greater production, use, and dissemination of strategy, poverty, and fiscal data and increased expectations that the data will inform policy-making;
- greater dialogue between planning and financing units within ministries and between line ministries and ministries of finance;
- more active involvement of civil society in budget elaboration and/or budget monitoring processes;
- significantly increased allocations to PRSP priority sectors and core priority areas in real per capita terms and, in some cases, protection at times of budget crunch; and
- a move toward general and sector budget support and greater recognition of the need for donors to align aid with recipient country priorities.

Shortcomings

- Weak evidence that data and monitoring and evaluation results systematically affect policy making;
- weak role of parliaments in the PRSP process and weak ownership of PRSP priorities by parliaments;
- uneven increases in resource allocations across priority sectors (with education, transport, and rural development faring well and health faring less well);
- uneven increases in resource allocations within priority sectors (with more consistent evidence of prioritization of primary education than primary health and very poor allocations to rural roads); and
- continued high levels of donor financing off-budget, poor forward aid commitments, poor predictability, and high variability of aid within-year.

Within a short period, the PRSP process has succeeded in difficult areas where traditional public sector reform initiatives had failed. In particular, we find evidence that it has increased the transparency, openness, and pro-poor character of budgeting processes. We also find that these reforms have a much larger impact when implemented in a context where the PFM basics are in place. Hence the types of reforms the PRSP process encourages are supplements, not substitutes, for improvements in basic public expenditure management.

The PRSP process has also helped to highlight areas where important gaps remain and has created expectations of further progress. Although some observers consider this to be a shortcoming, in our view, it is one of its strengths, as greater pressure for plans to fit budgets and for greater transparency, participation, and accountability are the engine for further progress in the future. The process has also created greater awareness of the need for capacity building in line ministries, parliaments, and civil society if these bodies are to be well-informed actors in budget processes. This is also to be celebrated. Further progress on all these fronts, however, is needed and highly dependent on the continued ownership of the PRSP process by recipient governments and the donor community alike.

Endnotes

1. On the dismal performance of public sector reform projects in Sub-Saharan Africa, see Levy and Engberg in Levy and Kpundeh (2004). Their paper finds that more technical, narrower, public expenditure management reforms had a much higher chance of success than broad public sector reforms, especially in unsupportive political environments.
2. Judge and Klugman (2004); Alonso and Walliser (2004); Klugman and Taliercio (2003); Alonso and Utz (2003); Alonso and Ngo (2004).
3. The introduction of governance finance statistics coding, still incomplete for the development budget, will further strengthen the quality of data available and allow their international comparability and consistency with the integrated financial management system.
4. Much of the information provided in the new formats is still incomplete; classification headings are often changed from year to year, thereby hindering comparisons over time; and they are rarely used to shape future policy development.
5. This problem has no easy solution. In situations where efforts are being made to extend the financial management information system to local levels, some PFM experts have questioned whether such complex and rigid systems as financial management information systems make sense in low-capacity environments. In particular, there is little encouragement for local governments to pilot systems such as SIGMA in Bolivia that are not sufficiently flexible to allow agencies to veer across budget lines. Hence improving incentives for regular reporting by local governments is probably a better alternative.
6. For instance, key documents such as the pre-PRSP National Poverty Eradication Strategy were only available in their technical version and in English. The PRSP, on the other hand, was made public in summary form and in Kiswahili.
7. In the case of Burkina Faso, the fact that donors take the PRSP as the basis for their budget support operations plays an important role in focusing the Ministry of Finance on the strategy.
8. In the context of traditional project support, external finance is treated separately from the budget and accountability for donor funds is a relatively simple accounting exercise, albeit with negative consequences for the long-term development of government systems. However, as the importance of direct budget support increases in the context of the PRSP, both accounting for and isolating the specific impacts of donor contributions become more difficult.
9. See JSA guidelines at http://poverty.worldbank.org.
10. These varying trends, which are reflected in different progress in outcomes, could be related to the different role played by the international community in both sectors—the Education for All initiative versus vertical global health programs—as well as to the recent evolution of sector policies, with an increased role of state provision in education and a

reduced state role in health. Although answering these questions falls well beyond the scope of this paper, our case studies provide some room for optimism on recent progress in the education sector and raise concerns about the lack of progress in health.

11. These findings must be seen in the light of two considerations: the broad definition of priority expenditures and the postconflict nature of Cambodia's situation. Regarding the first consideration, we need to take into account that Cambodia spends a proportion of its education budget on sports (not strictly part of the core priority area). Regarding the second, we must allow for the fact that reallocation is easier in a stabilizing postconflict situation such as Cambodia's (where the share of the budget initially allocated to security was unusually high) than in more stable situations like those of our other sample countries.
12. Discretionary spending is defined as government's own resources plus general budget support.
13. As of 2003, a decline seemed to have taken place in the share of budget support in overall grants and loans in both countries as some large projects in the infrastructure and rural development sectors got under way.

10

Reconciling Alignment and Performance in Budget Support Programs: What Next?

DAVID BOOTH, KARIN CHRISTIANSEN, AND PAOLO DE RENZIO
Overseas Development Institute

Aid alignment and development performance are friends, not enemies. Yet friends do fall out. Our starting point in this paper is that the discussion about alignment in budget support programs is moving toward a point where some serious reconciliation efforts may be required. We need to remind ourselves of the foundations of the current aid reform agenda, and offer some sympathetic warnings about some of the initiatives currently being considered.

The paper addresses the challenge of programmatic alignment between budgetary aid and country policies.[1] Our main concern is to address a specific set of problems that have arisen at the interface between the annual monitoring of poverty reduction strategy papers (PRSPs) and the joint performance assessment frameworks (PAFs) that are being used by budget support groups as the centerpiece of their conditionality. To place these problems in their proper context, we also highlight a broader set of problems in the way the alignment challenge has come to be defined in countries with PRSPs. Our examples in the paper are drawn mainly from African experience.

Section A reviews the broad problem of PRSP alignment, followed by a discussion in Section B of the monitoring of PRSs and PAFs. Sections C and D then review in turn what is wrong with PRSP annual progress reports and the current debate about PAFs (including poverty reduction support credits [PRSC] policy matrices). In Section E, we suggest an alternative way to seek a reconciliation between performance and alignment. We emphasize the need to recognize the crucial role of leadership and politics in the recipient country in determining the degree to which the Rome-Paris agenda can be implemented. Donors should stop believing that what they do is overwhelmingly important in determining what happens in countries they assist. Section F concludes.

We argue that further advances in alignment will be achieved only if more explicit attention is given to the recipient side of the relationship and to the reasons why annual

We are grateful for written comments on the conference draft by ODI colleagues Tony Killick, Laure-Hélène Piron, John Roberts, Alina Rocha, and Andrew Rogerson, and by Gilles Hervio, Riccardo Maggi, Peter Rundell, and Mailan Chiche at the European Commission. We are wholly responsible for all remaining errors.

progress reports do not have the qualities donors expect. Until this is done, there is a case for simplifying PAFs but not for making them more results-based. PAFs should build country ownership by including only the sorts of conditionalities that are likely to work, and combining these with multilevel selectivity and complementary actions to address the missing preconditions for aid effectiveness.

A. The Broad Problem: PRSPs as a Two-Sided Deal

Aid alignment is a means to an end. The final goal toward which the whole harmonization and alignment effort is oriented is better performance in meeting poverty-reduction objectives and the Millennium Development Goals. Equally, when countries perform better, aid alignment becomes easier to achieve. There is a clear mutuality behind aid alignment and performance, so long as both are correctly understood.

Background

The association of alignment with better performance has a solid empirical basis. Behind the international community's endorsement of the alignment agenda lies a substantial body of research and experience suggesting that the "ownership" of poverty reduction policies critically influences effectiveness. Neither the traditional approach to conditionality in program aid nor the typical practices associated with projects has been easy to reconcile with a high degree of country policy ownership. This has weakened development effectiveness in general and aid effectiveness in particular.

Recognizing that new approaches were needed, the PRSP initiative of 1999 took the view that PRSP processes might generate poverty reduction policies with some significant country ownership around which donors could organize their assistance, thereby reducing the need either for conditionality imposed from the outside or for donor-driven, separately managed projects. Different actors supported the PRSP initiative for a mix of reasons (Christiansen and Hovlard 2003), but most agreed that it held out good promise of solving two connected but distinct problems in the typical aid relationship, on the one hand, donors' tendency to act in ways that undermine country policy ownership, and on the other, the weak impulse on the part of many poor-country governments to assume ownership of coherent, results-oriented poverty reduction policies.

The point of insisting on an open and participatory PRSP design process was to try to obtain a significant level of country commitment to doing what is locally considered necessary to reduce poverty. With that commitment in place, it was argued, donors could reasonably be pressured to alter their behavior in ways that would further enhance both country ownership and development effectiveness.

An Emerging Imbalance

Our concern is that the two strands in the argument that made PRSPs worth trying are in danger of getting detached from each other, and that the understanding of issues and options is hindered by a lack of balance in the attention being given to the two sides of the alignment relationship.

Donors are quite rightly increasing the pressure on one another to improve aid quality. Useful efforts are in progress to monitor aid harmonization and alignment, both across the whole field of official development assistance and in respect of budget support programs in particular (OECD-DAC 2004c; Strategic Partnership with Africa [SPA] 2005). These monitoring surveys are quite rightly intended as a source of peer pressure as well as a means to track what is happening. There has also been some exploration (de Renzio and others 2004) of the factors in donor agencies that weaken organizational and personal incentives to implement harmonization and alignment principles. As reflected in the survey results, both donor and government representatives think that donors are moving too slowly to align budgetary aid with country policies and systems.

No less emphasis should be placed on improving donor practices. But this agenda will make faster progress if there is more clarity about what should count as good donor behavior, particularly in respect of policy alignment.

While donor deficiencies in respect of alignment are now well documented, nothing equivalent is publicly available about whether on the country's side the conditions for successful alignment are closer to being met. Though in many countries the PRSP initiative has improved public policy processes, PRSPs are still quite far, even in the best of cases, from delivering coherent, results-oriented policies that reflect the authorities' true preferences and genuinely govern what they do. This gap is not documented as explicitly and systematically as one might expect, partly because of the restraint than the World Bank and International Monetary Fund (IMF) have imposed on themselves in assessing PRSPs.[2]

From the wider political science literature, we know that African countries with PRSPs typically have highly Balkanized administrations, with little policy coordination at the cabinet level and downward, and almost no functioning mechanisms for rewarding or punishing ministers or officials on the basis of the performance of their departments. It is also well established that with a few marginal exceptions, voters do not assess candidates and governments in terms of general programmatic principles or performance standards. That does not mean voters are uninterested in obtaining the kinds of benefits that PRSPs promise to provide (decent schools, clean water, jobs), but only that they perceive that informal networking and patronage are more effective ways to obtain them than demanding better general standards of public service.[3]

The debate about PRSP experiences tends to ignore these essential facts about the functioning of political systems.[4] The consequences can be unfortunate. For example, without clear evidence to the contrary, donor debates at headquarters and international levels tend to assume that aligning with the country's PRSP is ipso facto aligning with a serious country commitment to achieving a set of widely shared results objectives.

Connecting with Theory

The same thing can be stated in more theoretical terms. The basic *raison d'être* of aid agencies, it has been argued, is to mediate between the disparate preferences of aid donors and recipients (Martens 2005). The underlying reason for both conditionality and ring-fenced projects is that donor and recipient interests may overlap but do not generally coincide. This is why the aid relationship is usually thought susceptible to analysis as a principal-agent problem.

Current debates on aid policy tend to sound as if the principal-agent problem were a thing of the past. Rather than seeing the PRSP initiative as a promising avenue for moderating the more seriously negative features of the principal-agent relationship, they tend to assume that the nature of the relationship has already changed.

One symptom of this tendency is the overuse of the word "partnership." In the case of budget support, there is strong reason to think that in some countries, the donor-government relationship has indeed entered a phase in which it cannot be analyzed in purely contractual terms, so that new concepts are needed to express effectively the explicit and implicit rules of the game. However, *partnership* implies a higher level of overlapping preferences and a lower level of power disparities than can safely be assumed (Oxford Policy Management–Overseas Development Institute 2003). In other words, development partnerships are a worthy aspiration, not an established fact.

Recognition is growing that to improve aid, a better understanding is required of what makes countries tick, politically and socially, and how aid features in this. Hence donor agencies are looking more rigorously not only at their own incentive structures (for example, Martens and others [2002], Ostrom and others [2002]) but also at the politics and political economy of the countries they work in. Unfortunately, most of this work is either pitched at quite a general level or is simply unavailable in the public domain.[5] Nonetheless, for thinking about the next steps toward alignment, it is no less relevant than the political economy of the donor side of the aid relationship.

B. The Particular Problem: PRSP Annual Progress Reports and PAFs for Budget Support

At the fulcrum of the current debate about programmatic alignment is the widely observed lack of correspondence between the process and content of the PRSP annual review mechanism and the process and the content of the joint review of budget support operations.

What Was Supposed To Happen But Hasn't

PRSPs were supposed to deliver a monitoring system generating annual progress reports (APRs) that budget support donors could use as the basis for regularly assessing the use of their aid. For governments, the PRSP monitoring systems were meant to provide an important new source of policy learning, and for governments, parliaments, and civil society stakeholders, a mechanism for greater policy accountability. Donors would increasingly be able to rely on these domestic learning and accountability mechanisms, so that eventually they would no longer need additional reports by government or separately negotiated conditionalities.

Even in the best of cases, PRSP monitoring arrangements have not delivered these benefits. APRs are poorly integrated into country processes and do not seem to be a strong focus for domestic stakeholders who wish to hold governments to account (Driscoll 2005; Driscoll, and others 2005). Though timing and other process issues may play a role, an important reason seems to be the content of these reports. Donors are unconvinced that the APRs constitute a robust alternative to their own reporting systems, and they are not prepared to use them as a basis for disbursement decisions (SPA 2005).[6] Instead, they have focused on working jointly and with governments on elaborating an agreed policy matrix or PAF that is broadly identified with the goals of the PRSP but quite different in character from the APR. The PAF provides the basis for quarterly or twice-yearly reviews that run parallel to the production and discussion of the APR (Chiche 2004).

Donors that are most committed to the Rome-Paris alignment agenda (OECD-DAC 2003; High-Level Forum 2005) tend to have a bad conscience about this. Although PAF matrices are usually said to be "derived from" the PRSP, in many cases they appear to be additional. PAF reviews tend to differ strikingly in both content and form from PRSP APRs. PAFs tend to be very long lists of prior actions and other policy measures,[7] along with target dates for their completion. APRs contain a good deal of descriptive reporting on activities undertaken during the past year and some indications of intentions for coming years,[8] but they are *systematic* only about a limited list of "PRSP priority indicators," most of which are measurable inputs, outputs, and outcomes rather than policies or actions.

Policy Matrices: For and Against

Donors often rationalize this situation using an argument developed by the World Bank in relation to PRSCs. This says that the PRSP provides a reasonable framework for donor monitoring and conditionality but is not sufficiently operationalized to serve this purpose on its own, and that the PRSC-PAF matrix provides some of the necessary operationalization. They emphasize that since the matrix is agreed with the government, the measures in it do not constitute old-style adjustment conditionalities. Indeed, the government's commitment to the measures listed in the matrix may be no less real than its commitment to the content of the PRSP. And the matrix is more valuable because it is more concrete and time bound.

Another donor view is that this thinking leads donors to micromanage government policies. Those in the nongovernmental organization (NGO) world who take the view that the economic policy prescriptions typically offered by the Bank and the IMF are mistaken, if not pernicious, regard it as doubly dangerous—a new way of foisting bad policies on weak countries (see, for example, Nyamugasira and Rowden [2002]).

Even those donors who broadly agree with the international financial institutions' advice on policies express several worries about how policy matrices are likely to work in practice. They argue that governments everywhere need room for policy experimentation and scope for adjusting generic ideas on reform to country circumstances, including political circumstances.[9] Governments are unlikely to get this space within the hothouse conditions of donor design and review missions. Governments that are not given a chance to work out policies for themselves may "agree" on a set of policy actions, but their real ownership of these actions may be little greater than their ownership of conditions imposed by donors.

Worse, by getting as thoroughly inside the national policy process as they now do, donors of budget support have lost the independence of judgment they had when the aid relationship was conducted at arm's length. For example, Harrison (2001) describes how the power dynamics and rules of engagement have changed in countries such as Uganda and Tanzania, where budget support groups have entered a "postconditionality" relationship with governments. In these countries, donors now have a much deeper involvement in the policy process—through budget support groups, sectoral working groups, technical assistance, and so on—that allows them to steer the process from within. Harrison argues that this situation is a potential threat to the quality of poverty reduction efforts, because donors acquire vested interests in the current policy regime and this creates perverse incentives. When things go wrong, their reluctance to blame themselves along with the government will tend to interfere with sound judgment. Thus, under a "postconditionality" regime, the donor tendency to fudge the question of what is not working and why may be even more marked than it was under arm's length conditionality.

These worries and dilemmas were very evident in the budget support group in Tanzania while the joint evaluation of the Poverty Reduction Budget Support program (Daima Associates and ODI 2005) was being conducted in 2004. Views about how the PAF should be adjusted differed among the consultants in the evaluation team as well as among the donors, suggesting that the issues are not simple.

Which Way Forward?

The principles are clear enough. We need an approach that is based on a robust understanding of the political economy of both sides of the aid relationship in PRSP countries, taking account not just of *donors'* capacity for tokenistic and self-serving adjustments, but of *country* policy processes and their shortcomings.

On the face of it, the most coherent and attractive set of proposals for more effective alignment is that from the European Commission. This favors the restriction of policy-based conditions to an essential floor of fiduciary safeguards, and a significant shift in disbursement decision making toward ex post conditionality focused on results (policy outcomes). The EC argues that an optimal combination of predictable funding flows and results orientation is pursued by providing Commission budget support in two tranches: a fixed one based on a minimal standard of macroeconomic management (the country is on track with the IMF and so forth) and a variable one whose level is decided ex post in the light of an analysis of expenditure efficiency and social service outcome indicators.

Although this approach has not yet been applied for an extended period in more than a handful of countries, it is clear in principle, strongly advocated, and beginning to be empirically documented (Adam and others 2004; EC 2003a, 2005). Budget support donors are expressing growing interest in the variable tranche approach as a means to avoid interrupting funding, with the damage that can cause. Several bilaterals, including the DFID, are also attracted by the prospect of minimizing policy conditionalities by focusing on joint assessment of results. They show increasing signs of adopting large parts of the EC thinking about the conditions for successful aid partnership[10] and are urging the World Bank to do likewise (DFID-FCO-HMT 2005).

There is some possibility, therefore, that the EC approach will prevail for lack of a coherent alternative way to salve donors' bad conscience about the alignment agenda. PAFs will become not just shorter and prioritized (as in Mozambique in 2004) but distinctly "lighter" in terms of policy specifics and much more results-oriented.

Would that be a good way to go? That is very doubtful under present conditions. The next two sections explain why.

C. Why PRSP Monitoring Is Not Working

Current debates attribute several negative features to budget support PAFs: excessive length, overelaborate content, intrusiveness, and tendency to promote micromanagement. Streamlining, results orientation, and an approach that protects "country policy space" and keeps donors out of the driver's seat are the corresponding positives that seem attractive to many. But these are loaded terms, and the degree to which they apply depends on country circumstances. In particular, it depends on the nature and role of the country's PRSP and the associated mechanisms for reporting and tracking progress.

What Is the Problem with APRs?

PAFs exist because donors do not yet feel able to base their disbursement decisions on PRSP APRs. Why is this so?[11] The reasons are diverse (Box 10.1). The survey by SPA suggests that sometimes the problem is the relatively straightforward one that donors base their financing decisions on the country's performance in meeting macroeconomic targets agreed with the IMF. These targets may appear in the APR, but the APR is not the principal vehicle for their dissemination. In other instances, the reasons have more to do with the reliability and/or timeliness of the data that are made available on the results indicators featured in the PRS monitoring matrix: APRs are often judged insufficient because the institutional arrangements for PRSP monitoring, on which they rely for data and data analysis, are perceived to be unreliable or dysfunctional. Data systems do need to be improved, but this is a long-term task that is likely to prove extremely challenging for both technical and "political economy" (vested interest) reasons.

Often, however, donors with a strong commitment to aid alignment express concern about the failure of PRSPs to specify clearly enough the policy actions that will be undertaken to meet the government's intermediate and final objectives in respect of poverty reduction.[12] PRSPs typically lack the equivalent of a well-articulated log-

BOX 10.1 Why the APR Is Not Adequate for Budget Support Financing Decisions: Examples from Africa

Burkina Faso: "The PRSP has not been operationalized in the required way, by identifying the priority policies and actions to be taken, and it lacks an analytical link between the actions and the indicators for measuring the progress made towards the objectives of the PRSP. Also, late delivery of the monitoring indicators for the sectors that have them (budget management, health, and education) made it impossible to integrate the results and their analysis into the progress report." (Switzerland)

Ghana: "Financing decisions are not based on the information from the APR. They are based on the information distributed on the progress on the benchmarks in the Multi-donor Budget Support policy matrix. Although this matrix serves as a proxy for the Ghana Poverty Reduction Strategy (GPRS), some of the benchmarks that have been defined are measured in terms of execution of a policy action that is not necessarily proposed in the GPRS." (Netherlands)

Ghana: "Annual progress report is improving but questions remain about quality of some data. Also, timelines on submitting draft and preparing final report do not leave sufficient time for development partners to fully analyze data and comment on validity. This situation is partly related to process timelines of World Bank. Annual World Bank/PRSC contributions are made on basis of performance as demonstrated in annual progress report. PRSC needs to go to board in July which means that APR process can sometimes be hurried. However, the release of the Canadian payment is based on the participating donors' consensus that a) we are satisfied with the IMF decision with respect to the Poverty Reduction and Growth Facility program which is releasing the base payment and b) we are satisfied that the Government of Ghana has met all the triggers as defined in the policy matrix for the performance payment." (Canada)

Malawi: "PRS report was only on first half of 2002/03, and was not very informative. Much improved report covering full FY 2002/03 was presented in spring 2004. However, the new report was too late to be useful, and also the information on budget implementation was still insufficient." (World Bank)

Malawi: "Malawi has only published one PRS APR (for 2002/03) to date and has yet to firmly establish the APR process. However, note that budget support financing decisions to date have NOT been linked to APRs, only to Malawi's status with the IMF PRGF." (United Kingdom)

Malawi: "Too late, too low quality. In addition, our budget support is not explicitly linked to PRS APR." (Norway)

Mali: "Few commitments to systematically improving public financial management. Insufficient information on sector policy indicators." (France)

Mali: "Report is late and not sufficiently precise for assessing real achievements." (Sweden)

Rwanda: "The APR did not contain sufficient information on the macroeconomic situation, the budget, or the education sector. We have used other government sources for all of this extra information. We do not expect it all to be adequately covered in the APR." (United Kingdom)

Rwanda: "Detailed data regarding performance under Rwanda's Poverty Reduction and Growth Facility arrangement with the Fund, not included in the PRS Annual Progress Report, are required for consideration by the IMF's Executive Board." (IMF)

Source: Strategic Partnership with Africa (2005; p. 52).

ical framework matrix. Most contain some form of monitoring matrix, sometimes referred to as a logframe. But these monitoring tools seldom have the full scope of a logframe, which would trace relationships all the way from inputs to final outcomes and impacts, and clearly articulate how the required effects will be produced in between, with an effort to record assumptions and risk factors. Usually, they are heavily skewed to the outcome end of the results chain. And though they specify indicators for the more easily measured impacts, outcomes, and outputs, they rarely do so for financial inputs (because the PRS is not costed) and almost never for specific, time-bound policy actions to be taken. In Tanzania and Uganda, for example, the reports have made real efforts to track progress on as many links as possible in the chain from PRS inputs to final impacts. However, in both these countries, the attention to the input end of the chain could only be relatively descriptive and unsystematic, because most sectors lacked a formally recognized logical framework or similar statement of the intended actions and chains of causation. Systematic treatment has been reserved for the list of PRS indicators that was agreed in the early days of the PRSP process (under the influence of the HIPC Initiative). Those indicators were rates and ratios measuring or serving as proxies for impacts, outcomes, and, in a few cases, standard sector inputs such as numbers of teachers.

There is some dispute about whether the typical "PRS indicators" are sensitive enough to capture year-on-year changes that are relevant to assessing the quality of policy. Proponents of results-based budget support insist that they are. But donors and other stakeholders want to know what a government has *done*—that is, what policy actions it has undertaken with a view to solving specific problems or removing definite obstacles that prevent the realization of PRS objectives. They will not be satisfied by an administrative description of relevant activities (workshops held and so on).

What Lies Beneath

The nature of the typical PRSP monitoring matrix reflects the fact that PRSP processes in most countries were fairly general "visioning" exercises.[13] The PRSP documents reflect a lack of clarity about the specific policy actions and intermediate results that are being pursued, and they therefore leave uncertainty about which changes would be worth monitoring regularly.[14]

In some respects the typical setup of PRS monitoring has worsened the biases created by the content of the PRSP. International influences have played a part here. At the World Bank, it is still customary to refer to the monitoring of PRSs as "poverty monitoring," as if to suggest that the impact end of the results chain is overwhelmingly important. The EC's interest in pegging some of its budget support to results has created new pressure to focus on outcome measurement. Most PRS monitoring offices originated in the poverty monitoring efforts that were launched in the early or late 1990s, and they are institutionally quite separate from any arrangements for tracking the implementation of cabinet decisions or ministerial work plans.

Given this background, it is perhaps surprising that APRs have been as good as they have been.

The Way Forward for PRS Monitoring

Until the problem of the content of PRS APRs is addressed, it is hard to see PRS monitoring serving the purpose assigned to it in PRSP theory—that of facilitating the alignment of aid with country systems and country-owned policies. A recent innovation in Uganda is relevant. The 2004 version of Uganda's PRSP, the Poverty Eradication Action Plan (PEAP), is accompanied by a policy matrix that lists actions to be taken by the government and other stakeholders, as well as a monitoring matrix of the previous type. It is not yet clear how much use will be made of the policy matrix in future annual reviews of Uganda's PEAP.[15] However, it points a way forward that other countries could usefully follow when they next revise their PRSs.

To reduce the gap between budget support PAFs and the annual monitoring of PRSPs requires action from both sides. Because budget support donors will not unilaterally give up their interest in policy, the gap will be most effectively closed if the PRSP becomes more of an action plan, preferably with a full, logical framework structure.[16] Therefore, APRs need to change, which in turn implies better PRSPs and more effectual PRSP processes or their equivalent.

Donors could certainly direct more of their influence to making those things happen. For example, those, including the UNDP, that provide technical assistance to PRSP management and monitoring offices could do more to help strengthen the action content in PRS monitoring. Aiming to develop something comparable to Uganda's PEAP3 Policy Matrix would be a sound medium-term goal in most cases.

The Politics of PRSP Strengthening

The obstacles to making PRSPs more action-oriented are primarily political, and if change comes it will be through a political process. The current state of affairs reflects deeply embedded institutional factors.

Weak engagement by parliamentarians and civil society organizations in the APR process partly reflects the general constraints that have affected participation in PRSP processes: resource and capacity shortages and—rather more importantly—weak traditions of transparency and accountability. Many PRSP countries have hardly any culture of evidence-based policy making inside government. This is related to the observation already made that the political contest in parliament and during elections is not very much based on generalized performance standards.

Where politics is mostly about personalities and patronage, not about issues, there is not a ready constituency for holding the government to account. This must be regarded as the main reason why PRS processes have not led to an upsurge of accountability to citizens. The fact that PRSPs do not lend themselves to a worthwhile tracking of performance is both a cause and a consequence of the systemic lack of demand for policy accountability.

In these circumstances, donor staffs and visiting consultants tend to underestimate, or at least not to acknowledge publicly, the true weakness of the domestic demand for good performance and the political realities that lie behind this weak demand. Their stance may have something to do with the nature of their interactions with government, which take place mainly at the senior technical levels and involve limited contact with the politicians who call the shots. Unfortunately, this blind spot tends to extend to both PRSP enthusiasts (who are taken in by their own ideology on the power of participation) and to critics from academia and NGOs, who blame PRSPs for promoting donor-led technocratic decision making at the expense of domestic politics (Craig and Porter 2003; Gould and Ojanen 2003). Both sides exaggerate the ability of external initiatives to transform the way national political systems work.

D. Reforming PAFs: Toward Results-Based Conditionality?

Most of our reasons for doubting that a more results-based approach would be appropriate for PAFs have already been stated or hinted at. In summary:

- Donor staff on the ground generally wish to know what the government has done since the last review before they report that PRS implementation is on track.
- PRS APRs do not usually provide this information because they are systematic only about "priority indicators," which tend not to include policy actions.
- Underlying this is the fact that PRSPs tend to have truncated logframe structures at best.
- PRSPs need the kind of "operationalization" that PAFs provide.
- Both the focus on policy actions that characterizes the PAFs and the donor unwillingness to rely on APRs have their origin in the characteristics of the typical PRS.
- These characteristics reflect the political conditions that shape the scope and character of policy making in the typical PRS country.

In short, there are solid grounds for PAFs to stay focused on the policy actions that need to be undertaken to meet PRS objectives.

Dissecting the Case for Results-Based Conditionality

Why then does a shift toward results monitoring seem so attractive to so many? One explanation is that many observers have fallen victim to some simple non sequiturs, which have gained credibility by sheer repetition and lack of contestation. Another is that donor staff and consultants frequently misunderstand the politics of policy in PRSP countries. The following is the typical syllogism:[17]

- Policy ownership matters for effectiveness.
- The traditional form of policy conditionality prevents ownership from developing, and anyway is often inflexible/dogmatic in content.
- Therefore we need a form of conditionality that incentivizes government to develop its own policies.
- This can be achieved by focusing conditionality on progress in meeting shared outcome objectives.

This argument is logically loose at several points. First, from the proposition that the traditional form of policy conditionality was bad for ownership, it does not follow that the focus on policies is the source of the problem, or that focusing conditionalities on something else is the solution. Second, there is no reason to restrict the alternatives to a different form of conditionality—indeed, why not consider the now-standard alternative of greater selectivity? Third, the incentive effects of focusing on results are asserted but not backed by any kind of argument from evidence.

On the first point, it is worth reminding ourselves that the research literature on adjustment lending was not comprehensively damning about policy-based conditionalities. What attracted particular criticism was the performance of complex reform measures that lacked significant domestic support. Conditionalities that are aligned with the policy preferences of significant political constituencies in the country do not necessarily do badly, especially if they involve simple, self-contained actions of the flick-of-a-switch type. Without looking more closely, then, we should not assume that actions named in PAFs are "traditional conditionalities" in the above sense.

On the second point, it may be that the EC is not attracted by the type of selectivity at the intercountry level that was mooted following the original Burnside and Dollar research on aid effectiveness (World Bank 1998) and has since been adopted in initiatives such as the U.S. Millennium Challenge Account. But the principle of selectivity can also be applied in choosing what types of assistance to use. And, most relevantly for the present argument, it can be applied to the choice of required prior actions or performance measures to be included in a budget support PAF. For example, if donors and the government fundamentally disagree on a particular proposed measure, there would be a strong case for leaving that particular measure out. Certainly no logic requires that because *some* of the policy content of a PAF is never likely to be owned by the country, *all* of the policy content should disappear.

The third point is that an extremely large body of research on political systems and policy processes in poor countries makes implausible the EC assertion about the incentives likely to arise from results monitoring. We develop this argument in what follows.

Political Naiveté of Results Conditionality

As is widely acknowledged, using results to assess performance is problematic in two respects. First, it is unreasonable to penalize a government for the effects of factors outside its control, such as a drought or a collapse in the price of a key export crop. Second, time lags in implementation imply that the most recently observed changes in outcomes may not be attributable to the most recent policy actions or resource inputs, even assuming all the data are available and reliable.

Advocates of the approach admit that these circumstances make it difficult to hold a government to account for the observed results. However, they say that what matters is the quality of the policy dialogue. The donor is expected to approach the performance data in a nonmechanical way that recognizes all the genuine difficulties of attribution, and discounts the effects of exogenous shocks, but also reinforces the general idea that the results are what matter and that it is up to the government to find the best way of achieving them. A conventional rebuttal points out that this kind of flexibility, while very necessary once one goes down the road of results-based disbursement, works against the important goal of predictability in funding flows.

So far, so good. However, the standard treatment of the attribution and accountability difficulties associated with results conditionality does not go far enough. It is shot through with unjustifiable assumptions about the aid relationship and its political basis. First, it implicitly assumes that even if the donor and recipient have different ideas about policy, they have broadly the same preferences at the level of results, so that when policy actions are to be defined, the recipient has no strong reason to subvert the donor's intentions. This notion is only superficially persuasive. Of course, politicians like everyone else favor better health and education outcomes for poor people, and may even sincerely espouse this as an objective. But the test is whether in practice they choose actions that would promote that objective over actions that correspond to any of the other objectives they have as participants in a particular political and social system.

Second, the argument implies a picture of the recipient government as a well-coordinated, rational actor, such that policy dialogue with the government has real incentive effects where it matters. As we have already said, however, political science research does not support that picture. Under the conditions reported in a large literature, it seems quite unlikely that a focus on results would ever give a government a strong incentive to improve its policies. Even less persuasive is the suggestion that the use of outcome indicators serves to hold the government accountable before its electorate (Zongo and others 2000, p. 5).

Under the actual conditions of African politics and public administration, the only accountabilities with a chance of being effective are those where attribution is utterly straightforward and the time lags nonexistent. When well-specified, policy actions and other inputs meet these criteria; some outputs may meet them, but outcomes will almost never meet them. The situation might differ if the government were working with policies that had all the features of a well-worked logframe and were the subject of general agreement. Then some tracking back of poor results to the actions and persons specifically responsible might be possible. But that is to assume that a host of well-known problems have already been solved.

Under present conditions, therefore, it would be irresponsible to abandon the current approach to PAFs in favor of results monitoring. If giving governments more room for policy innovation were really likely to lead to the flowering of national development initiative that the EC argument implies, there would hardly be any principal-agent problem and barely a need for conditionality of any sort. But the world is not yet like that.

E. The Alternative

Instead of pretending that donor and recipient interests closely coincide, so that "micromanagement" can be safely abandoned, budget support donors should seek to learn what parts of policy action monitoring are producing useful results and what parts are not, and why. Our general position is that a way forward should be sought in three areas:

- identifying policy and process conditionalities that are more likely to work because they are built on and serve to buttress policy options adopted by (sections of) government, with support from outside government;
- greater selectivity, both in the choice of budget support partners and in the selection of policies that are to be advanced by means of budget support; and
- more deliberate and coordinated use of complementary measures to help create the conditions for wider application of the budget support modality.

Conditionalities that Are More Likely to Work

Views about the effectiveness of conditionalities of different sorts are still mostly based on an era of arm's length adjustment lending that is now past in many countries, and there has been very little systematic study of these issues during the relevant time period.[18] As Killick has argued (2004), this part of the aid policy agenda gravely needs a stronger empirical basis provided by systematic research.[19]

What hypotheses might such a research program test? Nothing we have said implies any reason to doubt the finding (from the research on adjustment lending) that externally imposed policies tend to fail, especially where complex institutional reforms are concerned. One implication is that conditionalities should not be multiplied without good reason. This creates a prima facie case, which could be tested, for thinking that PAFs containing 100-plus items cannot be good and for strongly advocating both streamlining and consolidation of conditionalities.

A second hypothesis is the suggestion, from research on adjustment lending, that emphasis should be placed on desirable policy measures that are easy to implement and benefit from real commitment on the government side, whether this is because they are in the PRSP (when it is thought that this benefits from some political backing), because they have the active support of the president or a significant section of the political leadership, or because they have been the subject of a genuine internal policy debate, creating a real potential for policy change. These seem to be the conditions under which PAFs and PAF reviews have served to stimulate policy actions in Mozambique, Tanzania, and Uganda, for example.[20]

A third element whose importance might be explored is the willingness of donors—particularly the World Bank's country director—to employ a *style* that is sensitive to the political acceptability or otherwise of particular policy actions. The relevance of operational style seems well-supported by the experience in Tanzania (International Monitoring Group 2002) and Uganda in recent years. An effective style may well include a willingness to lend support to policy proposals that are not first-best solutions in terms of current international thinking but are feasible and command a growing local consensus. All this may have some of the dangers that Harrison (2001) associates with a "postconditionality" approach (compromised judgment), but if it works to get good, or good enough, measures implemented, that trade-off might be acceptable.

Research is needed to confirm these hypotheses, but the challenge of alignment cannot be put on hold until the research is done. This said, it would be a serious mistake to rush headlong in the direction of a "light" PAF and results conditionality before trying to assemble some conclusions on what has worked and what has not in the recent past. Without delay, a serious collective reflection should be undertaken on the experience of each country with a budget support program. Several countries have quite a rich body of experience to draw on; the main concern is that experience has not been recorded, so that given typical rates of staff turnover, institutional memory will be quickly lost.

Selectivity and Complementary Actions

A serious enquiry into the above topics would probably vindicate, at least partially, some forms of policy conditionality under some sets of circumstances. If it did not, the only other option would be some form of selectivity.

Selectivity in the management of general budget support could consist of a decision to focus on policy actions that have enough domestic support for conditionality to work in the way described above. Other policy actions would be excluded from the scope of the budget support operation, but that would not necessarily mean ignoring them altogether, especially if they are thought to be among the critical preconditions for better developmental performance. It might mean—for those donors that are allowed to do so—engaging actively in the public intellectual life of the country with a view to shifting public opinion in a new direction. This is one of several ways in which greater selectivity should imply complementary action to work on the conditions that make selectivity necessary.[21]

For example, it seems unlikely that a sensible approach to institutions for agricultural growth in Tanzania will be achieved by technocratic policy dialogue on the margins of the budget support review. The whole climate of opinion in Tanzania on issues such as this, where not only ideology but also important vested interests are involved, is far from what modern research-based knowledge would suggest is a sound basis for policy. New sources of intellectual conviction as well as political arguments of an unfamiliar sort would be needed to create the essential ingredient of country policy ownership. Budget support donors should use other means to pursue the crucial topic of institutions for agriculture.

In some countries, such selectivity in the policy conditions linked to budget support would rapidly reduce the PAF to an extremely slim affair. That too should probably be countenanced. The option of not providing budget support at all, even if there is a PRSP, should also be on the agenda wherever there is no real coincidence of objectives or potential for domestic accountability. And, of course, where policy debate of any kind is impossible because basic freedoms are not respected in the country, the donor agenda has to concern itself with helping to alter some of the political fundamentals.

Getting to Grips with Politics and the State

Finally, it is time to see whether the debate about aid selectivity among countries can be given a new twist. Country selectivity has acquired a bad name for two reasons. First, it seems morally distasteful to deny aid to countries with abysmal policy regimes and very poor populations, given the evidence that aid yields benefits of some kinds to some degree whatever the policy regime. Second, the criteria currently in use for distinguishing between "good" regimes and "bad" are the subject of considerable debate. Even supporters of the various measures for assessing governance standards concede that they are only weakly grounded in the lessons of international development experience.

Both objections have recently begun to be addressed. For example, Lockwood (2005) makes a compelling case for focusing aid policy more deliberately on what he considers the key missing ingredient of poverty reduction in Africa: the developmental state. He argues that the first objection could be handled by separating country assistance into the provision of a floor component based on need alone and a variable component allocated selectively (but in a coordinated way, not by one donor acting alone). After noting the shortage of robust selectivity criteria, Lockwood is led down a path back to outcome-based measures. For the reasons given above, we think this choice is a mistake. However, Lockwood's plea for a radical reconsideration of these issues remains compelling, and is supported by other recent work (for example, van de Walle 2005).

The elements of an alternative approach are still being formed. Along with the coordinated and well-publicized selectivity advocated by Lockwood and van de Walle, recent suggestions include the construction of a new type of "compact" between the international community and forces within countries that are committed to the long-term goal of constructing a developmental state. Where such forces can be identified, the contents of the compact would be negotiated in a strategic process, "backward mapping" from the agreed final objective, rather than based on current conventional wisdom about good governance (Ghani and Lockhart 2005). For such an approach to succeed, the requirements are quite stringent. Many of the details are still being worked out. However, this is the kind of radical proposal that merits discussion alongside the more immediate tasks in trying to reconcile alignment and performance in budget support programs.

F. Conclusion

PRSPs are a two-sided deal: if countries come up with viable, locally owned policies to deal with poverty, they will be entitled to receive a less intrusive form of international support, delivered in a more helpful form. It is correct for the donor community to keep up the pressure on itself to improve aid quality, including alignment with country systems and policies. But there is a danger of slipping into a simplistic understanding of the policy alignment challenge that ignores the substantial deficiencies of real-world PRSPs and their monitoring systems. Symptoms of this danger, we have suggested, include the use of words like "partnership" in ways that imply that power differences have disappeared and that the preferences of donors and recipients coincide perfectly.

An important manifestation of this problem is the current discussion about the relationship between budget support PAFs and PRS annual reviews and progress reports. We have observed that PAFs and APRs tend to differ in both content and form. This is rightly seen as a difficulty in the context of the Rome-Paris commitments on alignment. But although there are some real worries about the practices of budget support groups around PAFs, it would be a serious mistake to seek the solutions only on the PAF side of the relationship. A key obstacle is that APRs have not delivered the robust tracking of performance against a plan that would be required to make PAFs and their review unnecessary. The APR problem, moreover, is not so much a lack of technical monitoring capacity; in the typical PRSP country, it is much more a matter of the lack of bureaucratic and political commitment to a rigorous, goal-oriented policy-making process. There are only a few things that budget support donors can do about this, but they should at least recognize it as a major dimension of the alignment problem.

These being the circumstances, we have argued that reforming PAFs to make them more results-oriented is the wrong thing to do. At best, it would be an act of faith, based on no clear evidence that results monitoring encourages better policy thinking. At worst, it flies in the face of abundant political science research into the causes of inferior policy making and weak accountability in poor countries. Our argument implies that a focus on policy measures that are agreed to be conditions for achieving better results is one of the things that are *good* about current PAFs, and one of the things that are unfortunately missing from most PRS monitoring matrices.

This does not mean that we favor heaping large volumes of policy content into PAFs. Conditionalities do need to be streamlined and consolidated. They also need to be used much more carefully than in the adjustment era, taking into account the goal of encouraging country policy ownership and the available evidence on the types of conditionality that have some chance of working. These strictures imply using a limited form of conditionality in conjunction with greater selectivity—about what to include in the PAF, when to provide budget support, and which countries to assist at levels above the minimum demanded by humanitarian considerations. It is important that budget support donors should also be taking measures to complement this multilevel selectivity. They should be prepared to participate actively in a country's intellectual life, to help create the conditions in which essential but complex policy measures have some chance of being implemented consistently and with conviction.

For budget support groups, the most important practical implication of this argument is the urgency of investigating systematically what seems to have worked well and badly during the several years in which PAFs and/or PRSC matrices have been in operation. Ideally, this should take the form of a new generation of research studies, as proposed by Killick (2004). But failing that, donor groups should agree to undertake their own exercise, and do it while the leading actors are still in their posts and institutional memories are still fresh. The object would be to provide an evidence base for applying selectivity to conditions, and to suggest ways of strengthening local policy processes or engaging with opinion formers.

Another and more difficult challenge is to make a real difference to the quality of the development policy making that is reflected in countries' PRSPs. The World Bank and IMF are not mistaken in showing restraint in dealing with the content of PRSPs; this restraint has increased somewhat the chances that heterodox and locally adapted policy proposals will get some airing. But being restrained about content should not imply making excuses for flabby, inconsequential thinking about how to address the problems that lie behind an abysmal poverty reduction performance.

Efforts to raise the level of policy debate need to be guided by an excellent understanding of the local political context. They also call for willingness to be more open in discussing the political and social factors underlying weaknesses in policy processes. A minor international industry is now producing country-level political analysis and political economies of reform for different donors, including the World Bank. Most of its products are not in the public domain. That is wrong. It is time to go public, globally and locally, about the obstacles to the emergence of effective developmental states in poor countries. Discussion of this challenge should become an explicit component of the framework in which budget support and other aid agreements are negotiated and published. Anything less is an affront to the poor people that are supposed to benefit from these agreements.

Endnotes

1. It is not centrally concerned with systems alignment, although the argument has some implications for that debate. Nor is it much concerned with harmonization (among aid donors) as a distinct issue.
2. The vast PRSP literature focuses almost exclusively on assessing processes or analyzing the content of the documents.
3. Good overviews are provided by Chabal and Daloz (1999) and van de Walle (2001, 2005).
4. Some useful efforts to inject more political realism into the assessment of PRSP experience are synthesized in Piron (2004) and Dijkstra (2005).
5. The second category includes the country studies undertaken in the last few years for the DFID's Drivers of Change program, Sida's "power analyses," and the range of exercises on the political economy of reform and macrosocial analysis undertaken at the World Bank.
6. According to the 2004 SPA survey, an overwhelming majority of budget support donors now regard annual PRSP reviews and progress reports as insufficient for their information needs. The proportion considering PRS reporting inadequate rose from 57 percent in the 2003 survey to 71 percent in 2004 (SPA 2005, p. 50).
7. The number of indicators (including conditionalities, benchmarks, prior actions, and monitoring indicators) contained in the matrices ranges from 19 (Malawi) to 100+ (Tanzania and Uganda), according to Chiche (2004).
8. This is how we would characterize the "review of key policy measures undertaken last year" and "to be undertaken next year", which the 2004 SPA survey (SPA 2005, p. 10) found to be included in most of the surveyed APRs. This sort of reporting is notoriously easy to manipulate and very hard to use to hold anyone responsible for actions not taken, or not taken on time. This is what we mean by contrasting it with a systematic approach.
9. The new recognition now being given to the institutional diversity of successful economic growth models (for example, Rodrik [2003]) reinforces this concern.

10. Although with an additional concern to set a floor in terms of human rights conditions.
11. The following paragraphs draw freely on Driscoll and others (2005, p. 17–21) and indirectly on Booth (2005) and Booth and Nsabagasani (2005).
12. Once again, the issue is not whether APRs contain reporting on policy actions taken, with some reference forward to plans for the next year, but whether actions are clearly specified in advance, with a definite rationale in terms of objectives, so that the monitoring can be rigorous and reasonably foolproof.
13. PRSPs have been improving, particularly where well-run joint working groups have been operating at the sector level. It could be argued that an innovative sector policy, capable of being expressed in a well-worked logframe, is a precondition for a sound PRSP. This means that in some cases "second-generation" and "third-generation" (Uganda) PRSPs are more sophisticated in the respects that concern us here. But strengthening PRSP content takes time, and many weaknesses endure.
14. In most cases, these weaknesses in the PRSP stem from the long-term processes that have undermined whatever capacity once existed for effective policy making. Without getting into details, the erosion of the capabilities of the senior civil service by the poisonous combination of economic decline and political corruption is an obvious factor. So is the way aid, during the structural adjustment period and since, has eroded the policy and planning functions in recipient countries by delivering predetermined policy packages.
15. The institutional arrangements for annual monitoring are in a state of flux following the launching of a new National Integrated Monitoring and Evaluation Strategy and other initiatives (Booth and Nsabagasani 2005). However, an annualized version of the three-year PEAP policy matrix has now been prepared, suggesting that serious use may be made of it (Sudharshan Canagarajah, personal communication).
16. Some readers see our advocacy of logframes as conflicting with our insistence that policy processes in PRSP countries are embedded in political systems. However, what we are advocating is not the particular technical instrument, but the principles it embodies (relating means to ends, anticipating risks, and so on), which do not seem inherently alien to the political level of policy debate. Others think that knowledge about "what causes what" in development is so limited as to make the whole idea of a PRSP logframe absurd. We disagree.
17. This is based on the argument of the report on the Burkina Faso conditionality reform pilot exercise for the SPA (Zongo and others 2000), which has been reiterated in most subsequent EC statements.
18. However, Koeberle and others (2005) provide an excellent overview of the issues and the state of debate.
19. The current round of evaluations of general budget support includes some thematic work on PAFs that will be relevant, but was not set up to fill this gap in our understanding.
20. Note that the actions do not need to be the subject of a *consensus* within government. This is also suggested by the findings of the last generation of research on adjustment conditionality as represented by Killick (1998). Killick saw a residual role for just two types of conditionality: a "pro forma" conditionality, which simply smoothes the path of agreed policy reforms, making them more orderly and assured, and a limited application of "hard core" conditionality, where it serves to "tip the balance" between reformers and opponents of reform within the government. Killick (1998, p. 188–89).
21. Killick's (1998) plea for an intelligent *combination* of encouragement of country ownership selectivity, technical assistance, and efforts to change the country-level intellectual climate, remains as relevant as his defense of a residual use of conditionality. It has to be recognized that this approach risks promoting incoherent policy packages and creating sequencing disorders. Such possibilities would need to be taken into account in selecting the mix of conditionalities and topics to be addressed by other means.

PART IV
Predictability of Budget Support

11

Predictability of Budget Aid: Recent Experiences

OYA CELASUN
International Monetary Fund
and
JAN WALLISER
World Bank

Aid predictability has become a central issue in the quest to make aid more effective. This paper reviews aspects of aid predictability using a newly constructed dataset for eight African countries with longstanding IMF engagement during 1994–2004.

Predictability of resource flows has taken a particularly important place in the discussion on how untied budget aid can be delivered most effectively. For countries whose budgetary spending depends heavily on disbursements of untied aid, volatile and unpredictable aid disbursements can undermine the credibility and reliability of short- and medium-term budget planning processes by rendering original allocations obsolete and forcing expenditure adjustments during budget execution. These adjustments, in turn, can hamper the attainment of government objectives, most importantly by disrupting the implementation of poverty reduction strategies. Moreover, to the extent that budgets cannot be significantly adjusted during the budget year, lack of predictability can result in deviations from macroeconomic targets, with potentially important consequences for macroeconomic stability.

Definitions of aid predictability vary, and misinterpretations can arise as a result. The Development Assistance Committee (DAC) of the Organisation for Economic Co-operation and Development (OECD) in its guidelines for harmonizing donor practices for effective aid delivery defines aid as predictable if "partner countries can be confident about the amount and timing of aid disbursements" (OECD 2005a). DAC's broad definition encompasses short-, medium-, and long-term disbursements, as well as intra-annual disbursements.

For the purposes of this paper, we primarily define predictability as the government's ability to limit the forecasting error of budget aid disbursements based on the information it has available at the time of budget preparation. Statistically speaking, our concept of predictability focuses on the difference between expected values and outcomes, with expected values being conditioned on the set of information that is available before budget implementation begins. This definition is narrower than that of OECD (2005a), since it focuses only on disbursement during the following budget

The authors thank Naomi Griffin and Russell Lundberg for research assistance.

year. Nonetheless it follows the notion of "confidence in disbursements" by implicitly allowing for a discounting of commitments that are not credible for recipient or borrowing governments. We also focus on budget aid, or "general budget support," rather than overall aid, since it is budget aid whose lack of predictability tends to have the most immediate impact on budget implementation and macroeconomic stability. (By contrast, project aid generally is committed for several years in advance and is lumpier, given the varying implementation speed of investment projects.)

The most elaborate recent study of aid volatility and predictability is that of Bulíř and Hamann (2003), who find that aid flows are volatile and largely unpredictable. Drawing on aggregate commitment data and long-term disbursement data, originating from OECD-DAC statistics, that cover both budgetary support and project aid as reported by donors, they conclude that (1) aid is more volatile than fiscal revenue and volatility increases with aid dependency; (2) commitments consistently exceed disbursements; and (3) disbursements cannot be reliably predicted on the basis of commitments alone.[1] In a recent update (2005), the same authors not only confirm this finding but conclude that volatility and lack of predictability have worsened in recent years despite efforts to harmonize aid.

As regards the predictability of aid in the context of IMF projections, which reflect judgments about the credibility of disbursements, Bulíř and Hamann (2003) provide some evidence from a survey of IMF desk economists for 37 countries. These data permit a distinction between project aid and budget aid and show that IMF program projections for 1998 overestimated disbursements of untied budget aid by about 25 percent on average, with the one-year-ahead IMF projections overestimating disbursements by more than 30 percent. Within-year disbursement predictions also performed poorly. Surprisingly, the study also finds that IMF staff consistently predicted disbursements of project aid more accurately than disbursements of budget aid.

A survey of donors and governments conducted in 15 African countries in 2003 and 2004 by the Budget Support Working Group (BSWG) of the Strategic Partnership with Africa (SPA 2005) broadly confirms the magnitude of the shortfalls found by Bulíř and Hamann (2003).[2] This survey found that on average 81 percent of 2003 commitments were disbursed during 2003, with an additional 10 percent being disbursed in 2004. Nine percent of commitments were lost. Large differences across countries were observed, with less than 25 percent of resources disbursed on time in Senegal and 100 percent disbursed on time in Ethiopia and Niger.

The same SPA survey also offers some explanations for the delay in disbursements. Donors responded that unmet policy conditions accounted for 40 percent of delays or lost disbursements, followed by administrative problems on the donor side (29 percent), government delays in meeting processing conditions (25 percent), and political problems on the donor side (4 percent). Again, the reasons varied widely by country and donor group. International financial institutions, for their part, cited unmet policy conditions as the reason for disbursement difficulties in more than 60 percent of the cases, followed by delays in governments meeting processing conditions (about 25 percent).[3] For the European Commission (EC) and bilateral donors, administrative and political problems on the donor side ranked first with about 40 percent of the cases, followed by unmet conditionality with about 35 percent.

Below we cast new light on the predictability of budget aid in eight African countries—Benin, Burkina Faso, Ghana, Mali, Mozambique, Senegal, Tanzania, and Uganda—using information on IMF projections and actual outturns.[4] Our focus on countries with long-standing IMF engagement minimizes the importance of unmet policy conditionality for disbursement shortfalls, allowing us to focus on donor behavior. The data are measured consistently in a unified setting of macroeconomic and fiscal accounts, thus avoiding potential inconsistencies between donor-reported data on aid flows and the national and fiscal accounts of recipient countries. On this basis, we are able to test whether other types of information that are available to country authorities and IMF staff would allow better prediction of outturns than information on donor commitments alone.

Section A describes the dataset and its main characteristics. Section B explores different aspects of budget aid predictability by country and region and over time. We find that for any given year, errors in projecting budget aid arising from both disbursement shortfalls and excesses remain large, at close to 1 percent of GDP on average. Adjustment needs in the case of aid shortfalls are exacerbated by the fact that they are accompanied by tax revenue shortfalls and current expenditure overruns. Section B also discusses potential costs from low predictability as displayed by the data. Section C concludes and proposes areas for future research.

A. Data on Budget Aid

To gauge some characteristics of the predictability of budget aid, we explore projections and outturns reported in IMF staff reports from 1992 to 2004 for a sample of eight African countries. The eight countries each have (1) long-term program relations with the IMF, albeit not always without minor program interruptions or delays; (2) relatively large external aid flows; and (3) at least one poverty reduction support credit from the World Bank—except for Mali, which instead received large World Bank adjustment aid flows in 2001–03. The eight countries thereby provide consistent data for disbursement projections. They are receiving budget aid from a variety of donors in a medium-term programmatic framework defined by their poverty reduction strategy papers (PRSPs), as also evidenced by their inclusion in the recent SPA survey. It is therefore reasonable to expect that the most important progress with predictability of budget aid could be observed in these countries.

In constructing the dataset, we identified, to the extent possible, IMF projections that governments are likely to have used to underpin their budget allocation decisions for the following year. In line with our definition of predictability, our aim was to simulate as well as possible the information set available to policy makers and IMF staff at the time of budget preparation. Untied general budget aid, which helps to close the fiscal gap and thereby is central for financing IMF programs, receives considerable attention in projections of external aid for the next budget year, presumably resulting in maximum use of information by government and IMF counterparts on the volume and likelihood of disbursements. We usually chose projections made between zero and six months before the start of the budget year. In a few cases, however, we used staff reports finalized as much as three months after the beginning of the government's fiscal year to avoid using projections that were established more than 12 months before the beginning of the budget year.[5]

It should be noted that IMF projections may differ from countries' actual budgetary frameworks. In recent years, much care has been taken to more fully align IMF programs with countries' budgets, but for political reasons projections of budgetary spending and revenue have often exceeded those agreed under IMF programs. Nonetheless, in most cases ministers of finance have used their powers to restrict spending items to stay within IMF program targets. Thus programs agreed with the IMF usually provided the guideposts for budget implementation.

In our dataset, we contrast projections for a range of variables with outturn data for the same variables. We draw most of the outturn data from the latest available staff reports reporting on that year to ensure that original preliminary data have been firmed up. The data include a consistent set of information on fiscal revenue, current and capital spending, and financing items. By drawing on these items from internally consistent fiscal accounts, we ensure that we can identify how governments adapted to changes between projection and outturns. (For a few years, we could not find sufficiently detailed fiscal data to derive projection and outturn data. Notably, for 1993–97 in Ghana and 1994–97 in Mozambique, the breakdown between budget aid and project aid was not reported.) Overall, we obtain 84 observations for the dataset.

In compiling the dataset, we corrected and adapted the raw data from the staff reports as follows:

- A few of the projections identified a financing gap without indicating how it would be filled. In these cases, we first narrowed the gap with the debt relief that could be expected based on other external financing tables or the text of the report and then distributed the remainder of the gap among budgetary grants and loans in accordance with historical patterns.

- In some cases, project grant information had to be derived from other variables, such as foreign-financed investment spending and project lending contained in fiscal and balance of payments data.

- We reclassified certain expenditure and financing categories to derive a fairly small set of consistent fiscal accounts across countries and over time. For example, privatization was consistently classified as nonbank financing, arrears fluctuations were treated separately from domestic or external financing, and debt relief, including all relief under the HIPC Initiative, was treated as external financing.

- Large spending on commercial bank restructuring, which entered fiscal accounts simultaneously as an expenditure and a financing item, was omitted.

- Obvious arithmetical errors in fiscal accounts were corrected, if necessary by including discrepancies in the nonbank financing item.

- Where fiscal accounts showed a discrepancy between items above and below the line, we included this discrepancy in nonbank financing.

To ensure the comparability of data across countries and over time, we normalized all data originally collected in nominal values and local currency by actual GDP as reported in the IMF staff reports. The effect of this procedure is to give a greater weight to shortfalls of aid where the shortfall is important relative to a country's GDP.[6] It also avoids other potential problems related to exchange rate conversions that would be necessary for other presentations of the data.

The data are fairly straightforward to interpret, given that they relate directly to differences within the same consistent fiscal framework. Differences between actual budget aid disbursements and original targets, both expressed in terms of actual GDP, can be attributed to aid disbursement shortfalls or excesses as well as to possible variations in exchange rates for which donors do not compensate.

The projections lay out expected values for aid, revenue, spending, and domestic financing in local currency that were established before the beginning of the budget year by country authorities and IMF staff. They reflect commitments made by donors as well as judgments by the authorities about the likelihood of disbursements. In agreeing with the IMF, governments may anticipate delays in meeting certain conditions or processing requirements, but this information may not be available to donors. Similarly, a country may include less than the full potentially available disbursement of a variable performance tranche if it considers full attainment of agreed targets to be unlikely. Given that IMF reviews normally take place every six months, IMF programs can revisit these targets during implementation, and as a result the final IMF program targets for the whole year may not coincide with the original projections. However, the original projections used herein would usually drive original fiscal and budgetary planning.

As shown in Figure 11.1, in most countries selected for this study, total aid flows as a share of GDP have not increased since the adoption of PRSPs, and project aid remains the predominant form of aid. Aid inflows have varied from 4 percent of GDP in recent years in Benin to almost 20 percent of GDP in Mozambique. Only Uganda and Tanzania show fairly significant increases in overall aid volumes since 1999–2000, and this picture does not change if we include debt relief under the HIPC Initiative in the aid figures. Moreover, except in Uganda and Tanzania, project aid remains the predominant aid delivery mechanism, particularly in member countries of the West African Monetary and Economic Union (WAEMU).

The eight countries show remarkably different patterns of budget aid delivery over time. Notable characteristics are the large budget aid inflows in the WAEMU member countries after the 50 percent devaluation of the CFA franc in 1994, the increase and stabilization of budget aid in Burkina Faso (at about 3.5 percent of GDP) and Uganda (at about 5 percent of GDP) since 2000, the large scaling up of budget aid in Tanzania from about 2 percent to 5.5 percent of GDP since 1999, and the recent decline in the importance of budget aid in Benin and Senegal.

FIGURE 11.1 Program versus Project Aid

(percent of GDP)

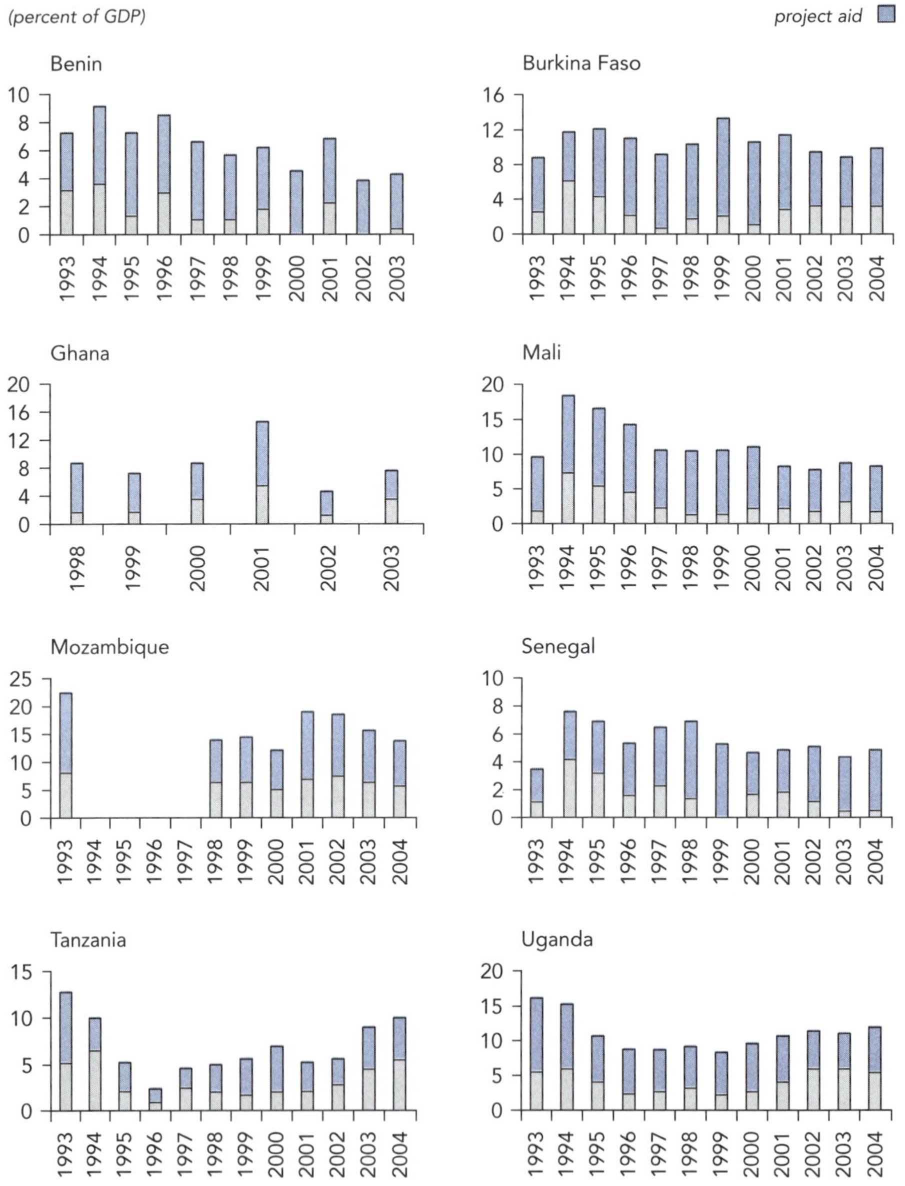

B. Budget Aid Flows: How Unpredictable Are They?

Both negative and positive errors in projecting budget aid disbursements are large and thus impose burdens on budget management. On average, the mean absolute error in projecting budget aid has been about 1 percent of GDP during 1993–2004, indicating that on average disbursed aid differed by 1 percent of GDP from projections (Table 1.1). Mean absolute errors in projecting budget aid correspond to about 40

TABLE 11.1 Budget Aid and Tax Revenue Deviations from Projections,
(Percent of GDP)

	Budget aid projections				Tax revenue projections			Correlations
	Average budget aid	Average deviations	Mean absolute projection error	Standard deviation	Average deviations	Mean absolute projection error	Standard deviation	Budget aid and tax revenue rrojection errors
Benin								
1993–2003	1.74	−0.38	0.90	1.12	0.61	0.66	0.74	−0.16
1993–1999	2.27	−0.70	1.18	1.23	0.88	0.88	0.78	0.11
2000–2003	0.80	0.17	0.41	0.69	0.13	0.27	0.39	−0.42
Burkina Faso								
1993–2004	2.93	−0.63	1.01	1.18	−0.34	0.88	1.13	0.49
1993–1999	2.96	−1.07	1.40	1.32	0.00	0.93	1.36	0.89
2000–2004	2.87	−0.01	0.46	0.61	−0.82	0.82	0.51	0.05
Ghana								
1993–2004	3.02	0.28	0.87	1.10	0.60	1.24	1.61	0.88
1993–1999	1.85	–	–	–	–	–	–	–
2000–2004	3.61	0.56	1.17	1.30	1.26	1.51	1.60	0.88
Mali								
1993–2004	3.05	0.48	1.05	1.20	−0.29	0.88	1.10	0.32
1993–1999	3.52	0.12	1.06	1.29	−0.01	0.97	1.17	0.76
2000–2004	2.41	0.99	1.03	0.96	−0.69	0.75	0.95	−0.13
Mozambique								
1993–2004	6.67	0.81	1.71	1.99	0.39	0.76	1.33	−0.85
1993–1999	6.93	0.54	2.93	3.60	1.14	1.27	2.00	−1.00
2000–2004	6.52	0.98	0.98	0.58	−0.06	0.46	0.63	−0.17
Senegal								
1993–2004	1.67	−0.16	0.89	1.06	−0.21	0.64	0.94	0.47
1993–1999	2.04	0.05	0.87	1.13	−0.33	0.68	1.06	0.48
2000–2004	1.14	−0.42	0.92	1.04	−0.05	0.59	0.86	0.68
Tanzania								
1993–2004	3.25	−0.37	0.57	0.55	−0.51	0.99	1.81	−0.07
1993–1999	3.08	−0.51	0.58	0.48	−1.06	1.38	2.24	−0.42
2000–2004	3.49	−0.17	0.57	0.63	0.26	0.44	0.44	0.49
Uganda								
1993–2004	4.28	−0.67	1.32	1.64	−0.20	0.41	0.53	0.51
1993–1999	3.85	−0.27	0.84	1.08	−0.09	0.40	0.48	−0.01
2000–2004	4.89	−1.23	2.00	2.22	−0.36	0.44	0.61	0.76
Whole Sample								
1993–2004	3.21	−0.14	1.03	1.31	−0.06	0.78	1.20	0.17
1993–1999	3.16	−0.34	1.13	1.33	−0.04	0.90	1.39	0.17
2000–2004	3.27	0.10	0.95	1.25	−0.08	0.65	0.94	0.30
WAEMU								
1993–2004	2.36	−0.17	0.97	1.18	−0.07	0.77	1.04	0.27
Non-WAEMU								
1993–2004	4.26	−0.11	1.10	1.46	−0.05	0.80	1.39	0.05

Note: Projections are usually established in the three- to six-month period before the start of the budget year.
– not available.
Source: Authors' calculations based on IMF Staff Reports, various issues.

percent of actual aid in the WAEMU countries, and 25 percent in the non-WAEMU countries in our sample. Errors have declined very little over time, from 1.13 percent of GDP during 1993–99 to 0.95 percent of GDP during 2000–04. Similar information is conveyed by the standard deviation of the differences between aid projections and disbursements reported in the fourth column of Table 1.1.

Budget aid disbursements remain difficult to predict on a year-by-year basis, and they carry large prediction errors. But, unlike other authors, we find no evidence that in the aggregate and over time, aid disbursements have systematically fallen short of aid projections by large amounts. In other words, it does not appear to be the case for our sample that aid is systematically over- or underpredicted by a large margin. During 1993–2004, on average, actual disbursements were smaller by 0.14 percent of GDP than predicted (Table 11.1). Splitting the sample into pre-PRSP (1993–99) and post-PRSP periods (2000–04) shows that on average, budget aid disbursements fell short of budget aid projections by 0.34 percent of GDP in the earlier years, but since 2000, budget aid disbursements on average have exceeded projections by 0.1 percent of GDP.

Our findings from comparing IMF projections and disbursements overall are broadly consistent with the SPA survey results. The SPA survey (2005) showed that 80 percent of commitments are disbursed and another 10 percent of disbursements are postponed rather than lost. If projections for the following year are established by the third quarter of the previous year, a postponed disbursement could lead to an overstatement of aid in the current year and an understatement in the following year. This finding follows from the fact that at the time the projection for the following year is made, decision makers still assume that the disbursement will arrive in the current rather than the following year. On average, given the trend rise in GDP over time with which aid flows are normalized, one could expect that postponed disbursements would result in a slightly negative average deviation of actual disbursements from originally projected figures. However, the average positive deviation in recent years points to some additional discounting of aid flows by governments in recent projections.

Aggregate figures mask considerable variation between countries, as also illustrated in Figure 11.2. For some countries, both average deviations and absolute errors have declined, indicating that projections have better captured overall aid volumes and reduced the error in predicting the timing of disbursement. Benin and Burkina Faso fall into this category. In Tanzania, average deviations have declined but prediction errors have remained large, indicating that difficulties remain in pinning down the timing of disbursements. In Senegal and Mali, average deviations have increased while prediction errors have remained largely unchanged. In Mali, this can be attributed to the large unanticipated additional transfers that followed the cotton crisis (2001) and Ivorian crisis (2003), whereas in Senegal, the shortfalls were related to delayed reforms in 2001–02. In Uganda, surprisingly, average deviations as well as errors have increased in recent years. In Mozambique, projections have consistently understated disbursement volumes, pointing to deficiencies in communicating aid volumes. Looking at the experience of country groups, WAEMU member countries tend to have somewhat smaller projection errors. This fact may reflect the better local currency aid projections as a result of the peg of the CFA franc to the euro, which is the currency for aid disbursements by the EC and most bilateral donors.

FIGURE 11.2 Deviations between Actual and Projected Budget Aid

(percent of GDP)

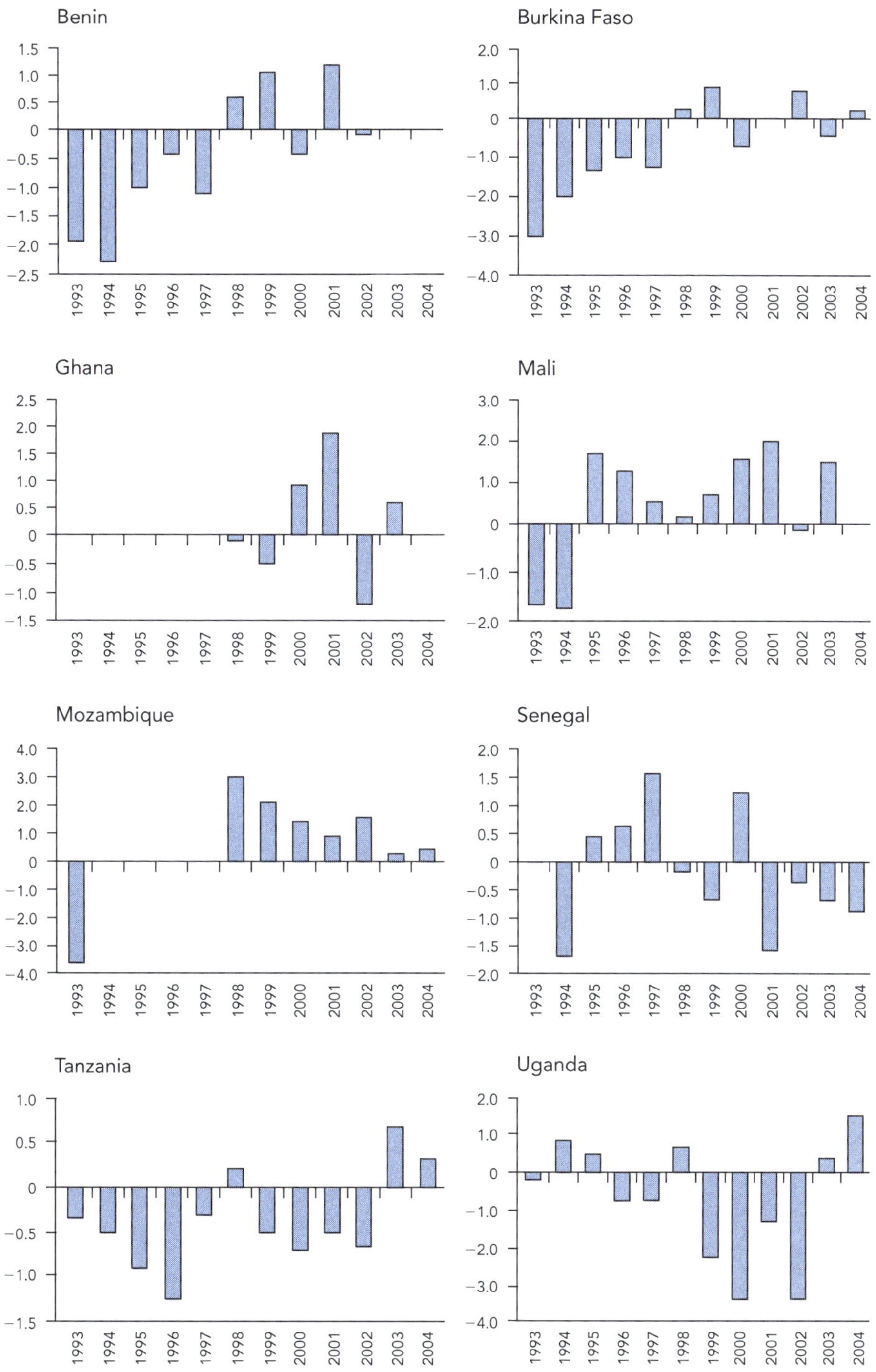

Regressing aid disbursement outturns on projections underscores a strong relationship between the two. Table 11.2 reports the results of a simple regression of disbursed aid on projections. In line with the averages discussed above, for the whole sample we find that, as a share of GDP, disbursements have been 11–12 percent smaller than projections, with a 95 percent confidence interval ranging from 0.80 to 0.97. These findings correspond fairly well to the magnitude of "lost disbursements" in the SPA survey. Projections explain 87 percent of the variation in disbursements, which overall is not a bad record.

Another issue we can tackle with the dataset is that of whether aid or tax revenue is more stable in African countries. Collier (1999) provided some evidence that U.S. dollar–denominated tax revenue flows were just as unstable as aid. We take a related approach below in comparing deviations between projections and outturns for both aid and tax revenue that were reported in Table 11.1.

Tax projection errors on average have been important at 0.8 percent of GDP, but smaller than aid prediction errors. In fact, errors in projecting tax revenue as a share of GDP have been consistently smaller by about 20 percent than errors made in projecting budget aid disbursements. This finding indicates a higher overall predictability of tax revenue compared with budget aid—in contrast to the argument put forward by Collier (1999). Average projection errors have declined substantially, to 0.65 percent of GDP during 2000–04 from 0.9 percent of GDP during 1993–99.

Overall, the statistical evidence emphasizes that budget aid flows as a share of GDP remain difficult to predict and certainly more difficult to predict than tax revenue. There are also some signs of improvement both in declining average deviations and in average prediction errors. Nonetheless, experiences have varied across countries, with some countries facing increasing difficulties in predicting budget aid and thus executing their budgets.

The contrasting experiences of the Sahelian neighbors Burkina Faso and Mali vividly convey the potential benefits of harmonized budget aid. In Burkina Faso in 2001, based on an early adoption of the poverty reduction strategy paper (PRSP) in 2000, several bilateral donors, the EC, and the World Bank moved to provide regular annual budget support and jointly preannounced their forthcoming disburse-

TABLE 11.2 Regressions of Actual Budget Aid on Projected Budget Aid

	Coefficient	Robust standard error	95% confidence interval	R squared	Number of observations
Whole sample	0.884	0.042	[0.801, 0.968]	0.87	84
Benin	0.695	0.052	[0.581, 0.810]	0.88	11
Burkina Faso	0.770	0.061	[0.635, 0.905]	0.93	12
Ghana	1.140	0.165	[0.724, 1.574]	0.92	6
Mali	0.972	0.123	[0.700, 1.244]	0.87	12
Mozambique	1.01	0.173	[0.601, 1.420]	0.81	8
Senegal	0.778	0.081	[0.597, 0.959]	0.82	11
Tanzania	0.924	0.038	[0.839, 1.009]	0.98	12
Uganda	0.819	0.089	[0.623, 1.014]	0.90	12

ments in the context of the annual PRSP review. Budget aid to Burkina Faso improved; the remaining volatility of budget aid in 2001–04 can be largely ascribed to the uncertain timing of disbursements by the African Development Bank and, to a fairly minor extent, to the size of the EC's variable performance tranche.[7] Mali, by contrast, suffered from recurrent financial pressures related to the cotton sector and the Ivorian crisis, leading many potential budget support donors to "wait and see." Although Mali eventually mobilized more budget aid than originally projected, this aid has not been predictable or stable and it has been used largely to cover additional recurrent spending, such as transfers to the cotton company. Macroeconomic and budget management in Mali therefore remain subject to much larger uncertainties than in Burkina Faso.

Aid shortfalls are made more difficult to manage by being associated with shortfalls in tax revenue. Our data show that aid shortfalls (or excesses) are on average associated with tax revenue shortfalls (or excesses), as reflected in the positive correlation coefficient of 0.17 of projection errors for aid and tax revenue for the sample as a whole. However, as Table 11.1 also shows, the correlation has varied considerably over time and across countries. For example, Tanzania moved from a negative correlation of 0.42 during 1993–99—indicating that aid shortfalls were on average offset by overperformance of tax revenue—to a positive correlation of 0.49 during 2000–04. Overall, the positive correlation of aid and tax revenue projection errors, which has become even stronger in recent years, implies that governments that suffer a shortfall in aid must find ways to adjust not only to less aid but also to tax revenue shortfalls at the same time.

The main objective of enhanced predictability of budget aid is to allow smooth budget implementation, avoiding the costs associated with abrupt adjustment of spending or increased domestic borrowing. In most cases, we find that governments cope with shortfalls in budget aid by accessing additional domestic bank financing and cutting domestically financed investment spending. Excess budget aid leads to a reduction in domestic debt, but we do not find any evidence that governments increase domestically financed investment spending, suggesting an asymmetric response. These preliminary findings warrant further studies of aid dynamics to better gauge the potential gains to be made from improved predictability.

C. Intrayear Predictability of Budget Aid

In addition to their overall financial needs, governments also need to manage their cash flows within a given budget year. Domestic financing constraints may make it difficult to smooth fluctuations in disbursements during the year, especially if budget aid is large relative to tax revenue. Unfortunately, IMF staff reports offer only an incomplete look at this issue as they do not systematically report quarterly projections and outturns. However, in the case of Burkina Faso and Mali, performance criteria tables allowed us to reconstruct not only the series of actual disbursements but also quarterly projections.

In Burkina Faso and Mali, budget aid disbursements were often heavily back-loaded, and these patterns changed over time (Figure 11.3). Up until 2001, Burkina Faso received 80–90 percent of its annual budget aid during the last quarter of the year. Since then, as budget aid has become more predictable, donors have made an effort to more evenly spread their disbursements over the budget year. Still, only in 2004 did the bulk of disbursements to Burkina Faso move from the fourth to the third quarter. For Mali, by contrast, a rather smooth disbursement pattern of budget aid in the mid-1990s has been replaced since 2000 by a pattern under which at least 80 percent of disbursements are made in the last quarter. These developments can be largely attributed to the diverging paradigm of budget aid in these two countries, with Mali's donors showing reluctance to move to regular and predictable budget support. The potential gains to be reaped from moving from a "structural adjustment" to a "budget support" paradigm of budget aid thus go beyond the size of resource flows.

To the extent that disbursement of budget aid within the budget year remains uncertain, governments who draw on bank financing or accumulate payment backlogs while awaiting aid incur large risks of undermining macroeconomic stability and thereby deviating from program targets. Our comparison of projections of quarterly budget aid disbursements and actual outturns reveals that in both Burkina Faso and Mali—even when for the year as a whole outturns exceeded projections—disbursements during the first three quarters generally fell significantly short of projections (often by between 30 and 100 percent) and thus made it very difficult to execute the budget smoothly without accessing other financing sources. Fiscal accounts reveal that shortfalls in budget aid often slowed down budget execution, notably for domestically financed investment spending.

We conclude that additional gains for managing the budget could therefore be achieved by further limiting the intrayear variability of budget aid disbursements. The latter appears to be easier within coordinated budget aid settings.

D. Conclusions

During 1993–2004 within the countries studied, projection errors (positive and negative) were about 1 percent of these countries' GDP, corresponding to about one-third of actual budget aid. Over the same time period, budget aid projections deviated by about 0.1–0.2 percent from outturns when averaged over time. The costs of aid shortfalls are exacerbated by their tendency to be accompanied by tax revenue shortfalls, creating a double adjustment burden for governments. Preliminary indications are that most adjustments to aid shortfalls take place through higher domestic financing and lower investment spending.

Intrayear predictability remains an important issue for countries facing external financing constraints. Coordinated budget support frameworks seem likely to also improve the intra-annual disbursement patterns and help avoid the typical "year-end rush" of aid disbursements. Reaping these gains, however, depends on creating the environment for a reliable medium-term engagement by budget support donors.

FIGURE 11.3 Burkina Faso and Mali: Pattern of Budget Aid Disbursements over the Year

(percent of annual disbursements)

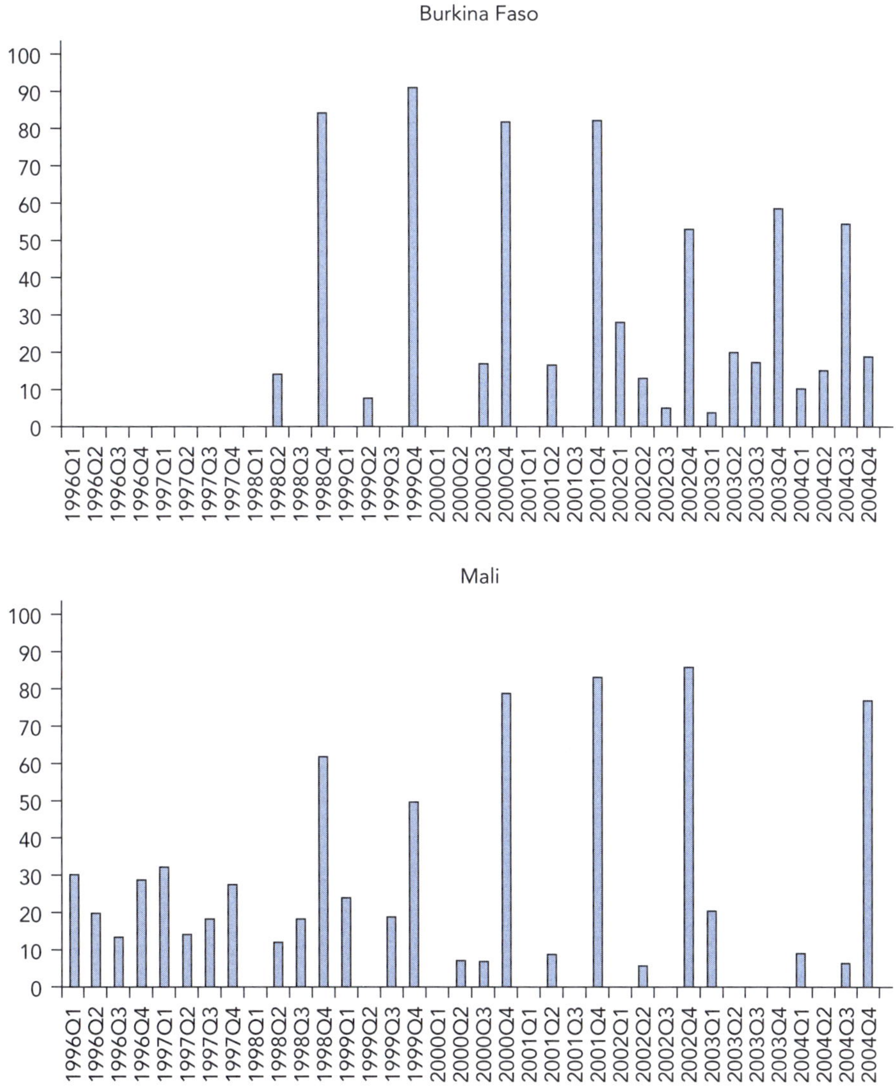

Endnotes

1. Bulíř and Hamann contrast total aid commitments with disbursement of long-term aid.
2. The countries covered in the survey are Benin, Burkina Faso, Ethiopia, Ghana, Kenya, Madagascar, Malawi, Mali, Mozambique, Niger, Rwanda, Senegal, Sierra Leone, Tanzania, and Uganda.

3. The SPA survey notes that all poverty reduction support credits from the World Bank were disbursed on time. Experience with poverty reduction support credits is also reviewed in a stocktaking paper (World Bank 2005e and Chapter 3 in this volume).
4. The macroeconomic framework under programs supported by the Poverty Reduction and Growth Facility is a crucial determinant for overall spending levels, tax targets, and financing needs.
5. The number of the originating staff report has been recorded in the database to be able to trace the origin of each projection.
6. By contrast, Bulíř and Hamann (2003) report on shortfalls from the survey of IMF desk economists as a percentage of IMF program projections, thereby giving equal weight to each percentage point of nominal U.S. dollar aid shortfall.
7. Although the exact size of the performance tranche was usually unknown at the beginning of the budget year, historical data allowed us to fairly accurately project a disbursement rate of 66–70 percent. See also EC (2005).

12

Improving the Dynamics of Aid: Toward More Predictable Budget Support

BENN EIFERT AND ALAN GELB
World Bank

Unpredictability and pro-cyclicality of aid can impose high costs for vulnerable, aid-dependent economies. Like changes in private capital flows, changes in aid can occur exogenously or in response to perceived changes in a country's governance and economic management. Aid cannot be completely stable if it is to respond to performance and also provide disaster relief, but studies suggest that predictability is surprisingly low, even for nonemergency flows. They also suggest that aid has tended to be mildly pro-cyclical, moving in the same direction as GDP and domestic revenue.

This paper considers ways to improve the predictability of aid, in particular program aid delivered in the form of budget support. The predictability of aid in general is becoming a more urgent issue as the donor community moves to increase aid flows, strengthen donor coordination, and tighten selectivity—all of which are likely to make aid flows more volatile. The predictability of program aid is particularly important, as donors have been shifting toward budget or sector support. The shift toward budget support promises to reduce the transaction costs of aid and offers an incentive to strengthen country systems. But program aid also has disadvantages: it tends to be more vulnerable to fluctuations than project support, which is usually committed upfront and disbursed on a multiyear basis. The problem of predictability will become more serious as aid is sought to underpin longer-term recurrent spending commitments such as recruiting teachers and raising the pay of medical personnel.

If aid does not become more predictable, countries moving from uncoordinated project support to coordinated program support may see any resulting decline in transaction costs offset by an increase in the costs of volatility. This shift away from projects then increases the risk of countries slipping into a low-level equilibrium: to budget prudently within a sound medium-term fiscal framework, countries will discount pledges of assistance; in turn, donors will see few funding gaps, and this in turn will cause pledges and commitments to fall. Among the many countries that reportedly discount aid commitments heavily in formulating their budgets, some already see signs of this happening.

To make aid more predictable, several problems must be solved. First, progress is, of course, needed to extend the funding horizon on the donor side. This entails finding ways to make multiyear commitments, possibly underpinned by mechanisms like the proposed International Financing Facility, or moving to the three-year framework of IDA or the Millennium Challenge Account, and extending these facilities for longer periods. More streamlined processes could help disbursements to better reflect pledges and commitments. Strengthening the annual review and aid programming cycle at the country level can also improve predictability.[1]

However, even if progress is made on these fronts, three major issues will remain:

- First, how can countries deal with residual "exogenous" short-run volatility of disbursements relative to commitments?
- Second, can donors lengthen commitment horizons from one year to several, without excessive risk of misallocating aid between countries?
- Third, within the overall aid envelope, how should donors respond to levels of performance versus changes in performance when setting the shares of project aid and program or budget support?

This paper addresses these topics, with emphasis on the dynamics of aid flows. Section A summarizes the basic stylized facts emerging from the literatures on volatility and aid instability, focusing on the magnitude and the determinants of past aid volatility, the degree of pro-cyclicality in disbursements, and the likely economic costs of volatility and uncertainty. Sections B–D address these three questions in a forward-looking framework.

Section B addresses the exogenous component of aid volatility. We consider how to integrate aid volatility into fiscal programming and reserve management to buffer development spending against exogenous aid shocks and allow time for donors to compensate for under-or overdisbursement relative to commitments. This requires appropriate rules for spending and reserve management. Simulations of a simple system suggest that for most countries a buffer on the order of three months of import coverage can enable a smoothly functioning corrective feedback loop. Naturally this is not the end of the story: domestic revenue shocks might need to be buffered also, and pooling buffer reserves across countries could reduce the overall stock of reserves needed. But estimates of need and rules for access would still need to be considered at the country level.[2]

Section C considers the trade-off between predictability and performance-driven aid. Can donors' commitment horizons be lengthened to several years, or is this too risky, given that the quality of policies and governance can drift over time? Taking IDA as an example, and using only very general assumptions, we estimate the deadweight losses that would have resulted over 1999–2003 from precommitting allocations to countries for periods of five years rather than annually. Losses are modest in most cases, and they become very small with a "flexible commitment" rule where changes kick in only when governments' performance ratings rise or fall substantially. Indeed, the losses are smaller than those due to the likely error in measuring performance. This suggests that aid can safely be committed with a multiyear horizon, subject to provisions related to catastrophic performance failure or quantum improvements.

Section D turns to the place of budget support within the overall aid envelope and the role of conditionality in setting the breakdown of total assistance into budget support and project support. Taking IDA as an example again, why should prior actions and triggers be used to determine this breakdown? Are they just a hangover from the previous conditionality of structural adjustment programs? Why not just set budget support as some proportion of the overall allocation, perhaps determined by a performance benchmark such as the country policy and institutional assessment (CPIA) used by the World Bank? We suggest an explanation for the continued use of triggers: that budget support is also an investment in improving country systems. Triggers and prior actions signal the return to this investment by showing countries' commitment to improve their performance in return for donors agreeing to channel funds through their still fragile country systems.

The question then is how sharply budget support should respond to changes in performance versus levels of performance. We argue for establishing a code of good practice where core budget support is stable for several years, complemented by graduated performance-levels-based changes in the share of aid that is provided as budget support, together with deep, periodic assessments of changes in budget management and the efficiency of service delivery. In interim years, prior actions or other indicators of performance change could trigger modest incentive payments, along the lines of frontloading or backloading in a country assistance strategy (CAS). "Catastrophic" breakdowns in financial management, budget discipline, or macromanagement that compromise the effectiveness of budget support would warrant sharp responses, both for budget support and for overall assistance. Of course, the graduated response raises the need for donors to be able to decide where macroeconomic slippage is "catastrophic" rather than relying only on an on-off judgment from the IMF.

In Section E, the paper considers the other main approach to budget support, the outcomes-driven approach of the European Union (EU). We do not debate whether budget support is better determined by assessments of policies and institutions (as in the current World Bank approach) or service delivery or other outcome targets. Indeed, these approaches should be complementary; tracking outcomes is essential for assessing policies, and understanding the causes of the outcomes, including the underlying policies, is essential for using targets intelligently to guide resource use. What is relevant to this paper is that the EU framework provides a useful approach to the trade-off between predictability and performance. However, while the final relationship between outputs and disbursements in EU programs is clear, the determination of the size of the fixed tranche and the crucial question of how to set the targets for the indicators remains less well-determined. Countries setting "stretch goals" will be more likely to be penalized than countries with more modest objectives, so that setting targets requires some comparative reference.[3] We consider how service delivery and progress norms could be derived from the historical experience of developing countries to help interpret a country's goals and improve the foundation for outcome-based assistance. This is illustrated using the examples of gross primary enrollment and infant mortality. The results suggest that goal setting in EU programs is indeed ambitious.

One important issue is the implications of performance measurement errors for fine-tuning support. CPIA ratings and outcome data are subject to error, and even if not very large, such errors can obscure the true size of changes over the short run. Optimal control theory suggests that responses should be dampened when noise/signal ratios are high; this provides an additional argument for not leveraging modest changes in performance into major swings in assistance.

Section F concludes with a summary of implications.

A. Aid Instability: Some Stylized Facts

The issue of aid instability has a number of dimensions. Volatility and unpredictability often go together, but volatility is sometimes predictable (as with the reliable provision of emergency food aid). Volatility can be endogenous (performance-related) or exogenous. Unpredictability can be very short-term (intrayear), short- to medium-term (one to three years), or long-term in nature. Aid instability can have microeconomic and macroeconomic implications and can also influence institutions by changing the rules and incentives affecting behavior. Not all studies of aid instability cover all dimensions, but together they offer a reasonably clear picture of experience.

How Volatile Is Aid?

In the aggregate, aid looks quite stable; looking at the period 1970–97, Osei, Morrissey, and Lensink (2002) suggest that the sum of official development assistance to low-income countries was less variable than the sum of either foreign direct investment or other private capital flows. The volatility of aid flows to individual countries is much greater, and it also varies significantly among countries, with aid to better-managed countries often less volatile. Standard deviations around time trends and autoregressive forecasts are generally smaller than the coefficients of variation. In Indonesia, for instance, the coefficient of variation is 78 percent of the mean aid flow, but the standard deviation around an autoregressive forecast is only 19 percent.

Though predictability based on past trends is therefore not quite as poor as measurements of overall volatility suggest, volatility is substantial according to both measures: the median standard deviation of disbursements is 37 percent of the mean, and it is 34 percent relative to an autoregressive predictor of the expected level. Bulíř and Hamann (2003, 2005) find that the volatility of aid is very large—with coefficients of variation usually in the range of 40–60 percent of the mean aid flow—and that it exceeds the volatility of fiscal revenues. They find that volatility rises with the level of aid dependence: among the 33 countries with aid to revenue ratios of 50 percent or more, the median volatility of aid is almost five times as high as that in their entire sample of 72 countries. They also find that aid volatility tends to be higher in those countries that also have higher revenue volatility, and that program aid tends to be more volatile than project aid.

Underlining the seriousness of the volatility problem is another finding: in most aid-dependent countries, commitments convey no more information on future disbursements than do past disbursements. This is disturbing, given the importance placed on commitments as an input into medium-term fiscal frameworks.[4]

Is Aid Volatility Declining?

Recent reassessments suggest that, despite efforts to harmonize aid around the poverty reduction strategy paper (PRSP) process and to improve predictability, progress has not been made on the latter front. Gabriele, Baratav, and Parikh (2000); Osei, Morrissey, and Lensink (2002); and Bulíř and Hamann (2005) all find evidence that all types of flows to both low- and middle- income countries became more volatile in the 1990s. As commitments have risen, disbursements have fallen behind, to about 60 percent of commitments. Though aid patterns in the post–Cold War era should in principle have become more development-friendly, the title of the Bulíř-Hamann (2005) paper is suggestive: "Volatility of Development Aid: From the Frying Pan into the Fire?"

How Much of Aid Volatility Is "Exogenous" and How Much Is Directly Performance-Related?

It is difficult to disentangle these factors because donors are not always clear why they change their levels of support. Performance-related factors influence project disbursements, but their impact on overall volatility is unclear. Bulíř and Hamann (2003) show that, as might be expected, IMF program status does not affect project aid. However, it does influence program aid: off-track countries receive 33 percent of commitments, and on-track countries receive 75 percent. This result crudely suggests that about 70 percent of the volatility of program aid might be due to performance-related issues, and 30 percent to other factors. A 2005 assessment of donors' views (SPA 2005) indicates that 40 percent of nondisbursements were considered to be due to failure to meet policy conditionality, 25 percent to recipient governments' delays in meeting administrative conditions, 29 percent to administrative problems on the donor side, 4 percent to political problems on the donor side, and 2 percent to other factors.

A rough rule of thumb might therefore be that around half of the volatility in program assistance might be performance related, and half reflects administrative delays and other exogenous factors.

Is Aid Pro-cyclical or Countercyclical?

Several studies, including Bulíř and Hamann (2003), Gemmell and McGillivray (1998), and Pallage and Robe (2001), find that aid is mildly pro-cyclical, tending to move in the same direction as GDP and domestic revenue.

Various factors have been put forward to account for this. Some observers have hypothesized that pro-cyclicality arises from correlated business cycles in the North and the South which cause aid budgets to tighten during downturns, but this proposition finds no empirical support (Pallage and Robe 2001). A more interesting argument revolves around the complementary role of counterpart funds. Pallage and Robe (2003a and b) develop a model in which the pro-cyclicality of aid results from the divergence of preferences between donors and recipients. If recipient governments value both the social returns of projects and some other output (for instance, disproportionate benefits to favored constituencies), it is rational for donors to require counterpart funds to reduce the fungibility of resources to "low-return" projects that would otherwise accompany increased aid. Shocks or economic downturns that cut counterpart funds then cause aid flows to projects to fall—an especially likely outcome in the poorest and most vulnerable countries. Another donor-discretion-based hypothesis that has not yet been explored concerns the imperfect observability of policies followed or "effort" made by recipient governments.

If economic performance is a function both of governments' overall development efforts and other factors, and if "effort" is difficult to observe, donors will associate an observed improvement (deterioration) in economic performance with an improvement (deterioration) in effort, and pro-cyclical aid flows will result. Countries doing well "must be doing something right" and therefore get more aid. While facilities including the Compensatory Financing Facility and Stabex have been developed to provide countercyclical finance, studies suggest that their effectiveness has been undermined by decision delays, slow procedures, and lags in information (particularly about the coming impact of newly identified terms-of-trade shocks).[5]

Do Political Explanations of Aid Allocations Account for Aid Volatility?

Cross-country evidence suggests weak performance-based patterns in aid allocation. Neumayer (2003a) investigates a broad set of governance variables, finding that none shows a consistent pattern of significance across the group of donors, though for some donors, democracy, human rights, corruption, military expenditure, the rule of law, and regulatory burden are all significant. Alesina and Dollar (2000) note that, for major bilateral donors, political-interest variables like colonial history and voting similarity in the UN General Assembly are more important determinants of aid allocation than are governance and policy. Andersen, Hansen, and Markussen (2004) find that voting similarity to the United States in the UN was a significant determinant of World Bank *commitments* (not disbursements) during 1991–2000, while Andersen, Harr, and Tarp (2004) also find that "political concessions"[6] in UN votes that are identified as important by the U.S. State Department are significant determinants of IMF loans. Interestingly, Neumayer (2003b) finds that several UN agencies, as well as the African and Inter-American Development Banks, tend to counteract certain biases of bilateral donors, giving less to former colonies of large donor countries. Dollar and Levin (2004) find that, for many donors, aid has become increasingly selective on the basis of policies, governance, and poverty over the 1990s: their top performers (as defined by the selectivity of their aid programs) are IDA, the IMF, the United Kingdom, and the Scandinavian countries; the exceptions unfortunately include some of the largest donors, such as the United States and France. There is somewhat less work on changes in aid over time, but Alesina and Dollar (2000) find that, while donors respond to democratization with large surges in aid, the same pattern does not hold for economic reform.[7]

None of these studies focuses on the predictability of aid, and the mechanisms that they document are unlikely to cause short-run unpredictability. Most political-interest variables change slowly, and aid fluctuations based on votes in the UN General Assembly are a predictable element of international relations. Similarly, since movements into and out of democracy are uncommon, it is unlikely that they constitute a major cause of aid instability in most countries. Nevertheless, the studies point to the continued medium-run vulnerability of aid flows to political factors and the significance of explicit or implicit political conditionality. This becomes more important in the context of efforts to provide larger, and more stable, aid flows in support of efforts to meet the Millennium Development Goals, since the share of aid in such high-case scenarios rises to more than half (and sometimes up to two-thirds) of overall budgets.

Is Volatility Really Costly?

Most studies on the impact of volatility have been carried out at the macroeconomic level, looking at changes in growth or indicators of consumption and risk aversion to estimate the impact. Whereas the costs of volatility seem to be modest for diversified, high-income countries, those for poor, undiversified economies with greater rigidities and tight liquidity constraints appear to be considerable: the welfare costs of output instability in Sub-Saharan Africa might be 15–20 times those in the United States (Pallage and Robe 2003a). The same study suggests that moderately risk-averse consumers in Africa might be willing to trade off an extra 1 percent annual improvement in living standards to eliminate volatility. Collier and Dehn (2001) show that a 40 percent negative price shock to exports reduces growth by 1.5 percent per year, for a 5.5 percent loss over a four-year period.

These results echo those of simulations undertaken for resource-rich economies seeking to manage volatile natural resource rents: Gelb and associates (1990) show that the costs of volatility induced by errors in projecting oil prices can easily overwhelm the benefits of export-driven spending booms, even assuming optimal savings and spending profiles along the projected oil price trajectory. Loss functions are not symmetrical: the losses from big adverse shocks exceed the gains from big positive shocks.

For lack of consistent data, there are no comparable estimates of the efficiency cost of unstable budgetary revenues. But anecdotal evidence suggests that this cost is very large. On the upside, rapid spending increases are often wasteful; on the downside, governments lack the recurrent resources needed to complement capital investments and to complete unfinished projects. Spending rigidities, especially for salaries, crowd out other essential inputs; cash-strapped governments turn to thin domestic financial markets, crowding out the private sector and sparking high-interest domestic debt spirals that threaten macroeconomic stability. In addition, high volatility in fiscal resources undermines results agreements and accountability mechanisms between donors and governments and among ministries within governments. Kostopoulos (1999) found that budget instability in Africa was very high: only 45 percent of countries experienced less than 10 percent deviation of aggregate spending from projections; 33 percent experienced deviations of 10–30 percent, and 22 percent experienced deviations from projections of more than 30 percent. Because certain expenditures are less compressible than others, deviations are magnified at the sector and program levels: about half of all spending programs at the sector level deviated from projections by

30 percent or more. Unstable aid was of course not the only—or perhaps even the main—cause of deviations. But the results suggest how far the combination of improved budget management and more predictable resource flows needs to improve if it is to provide a stable base for development spending.

B. Cushioning Expenditures through Reserve Management and Fiscal Rules

Reserves represent countries' first line of defense against shocks. The extensive literature on central bank reserve management focuses mainly on middle-income countries and their responses to commodity price shocks and private capital flows. Some studies provide strong arguments for ample reserves. They include Aizenman, Lee, and Rhee (2004), who study a model of exposure to sovereign risk. In their model, downside output risk associated with a costly debt crisis implies a relatively high optimal level of reserves.[8] General reserve management principles can be adapted to particular contexts of instability using specific institutional mechanisms. The most commonly cited in the developing world is Chile's copper revenue stabilization fund.[9]

We use a simulation model to study the potential of a parallel mechanism for managing the *exogenous* volatility of aid inflows. We highlight three main points. First, a relatively simple scheme based on a reserve tranche of 50–100 percent of annual aid-financed spending (two to four months of import cover in a typical aid-dependent low-income country) can be effective in smoothing expenditure in most periods under a range of levels of aid instability. Second, while our simulated stabilization fund does in some cases go "bankrupt," this usually requires three to five years of large negative shocks to aid flows. During this lead time, countries and donors should have enough time to organize an emergency response. Third, for instability in the high end of the range that we consider, the reserve levels required are significantly higher. With moderate reductions in instability, the necessary reserve cover could be cut substantially.

Our simulated stabilization fund is a simple one. Unplanned deviations from aid-financed spending targets should be kept within a small percentage of target levels. When the reserve buffer exceeds its long-run target, the fund operates in "high mode," protecting against downside shocks more vigorously. When the fund's reserve stock is below its long-run target, the fund operates in "low mode"—a more cautious framework that attempts to maintain spending levels while replenishing its reserve stock. One could imagine much more sophisticated mechanisms for managing aid volatility, but this simple instrument suits our illustrative purposes here.

Suppose that donors agree to finance a recipient government's medium- to long-term development plan, but their commitments are subject to a stochastic shock. That is, $a_t = \tilde{a}_t + \theta_t$, where θ_t is potentially serially correlated, for example, $\theta_t = \lambda\theta_{t-1} + \varepsilon_t$, where $\varepsilon_t \sim N(0, \sigma^2)$.

We define a target path for aid-financed spending, G_t^*, which donors commit to finance with aid a_t, such that $G_t^* = \tilde{a}_t$. We denote actual program spending as G_t. The buffer stock S_t is designed to smooth G_t in the face of fluctuations in a_t.

A simple rule for a buffer mechanism is as follows:

- Target an equilibrium buffer stock level S^* equal to a share s of targeted aid-financed spending G_t^*, such that $S^* = sG_t^*$.
- Designate a program spending floor $\underline{G}_t$, and spending ceiling $\overline{G}_t$.
- In year t,
    - if last period's year-end buffer stock level $S_{t-1} < S^*$, then:
        - If $a_t < \underline{G}_t$, then $G_t = \underline{G}_t$, with the deficit financed by the buffer stock.
        - If $\underline{G}_t < a_t < G_t$, then $G_t = a_t$, so no change in the buffer stock.
        - If $a_t \geq G_t^*$, then $G_t = G_t^*$, and the surplus replenishes the buffer stock.
    - If $S_{t-1} > S^*$, then:
        - If $a_t > \overline{G}_t$, then $G_t = \overline{G}_t$, and the surplus augments the buffer stock.
        - If $G_t > a_t > G_t^*$, then $G_t = a_t$, so no change in the buffer stock.
        - If $a_t \leq G_t^*$, then $G_t = G_t^*$, with the deficit financed by the buffer stock.
    - If $S_{t-1} = S^*$, then:
        - $a_t <$, $\underline{G}_t$, then $G_t = \underline{G}_t$, with the deficit financed by the buffer stock.
        - $\underline{G}_t < a_t < \overline{G}_t$, then $G_t = a_t$, so no change in the buffer stock.
        - $a_t > \overline{G}_t$, then $G_t = \overline{G}_t$, and the surplus augments the buffer stock.

Simulating the Performance of the Buffer Stock

We randomly generate 1,000 successive observations of θ, based on parameter choices discussed below, and then impose the spending rule under its own range of parameters to see what the performance of the buffer fund is. A key metric of performance is the percentage of years in which the buffer fund's balance runs negative. We also produce graphs of the buffer fund's balances over time and investigate the characteristics of negative shocks: what does it take to drive the fund into the red, and how predictable would the bankruptcy of the fund be?

The standard deviation of program aid flows from their targets (σ) is of crucial importance to the viability of buffer mechanisms. Following Bulíř and Hamann (2003), we take the endogenous-exogenous breakdown as 70:30, which suggests that an appropriate range of σ to consider for historical exogenous aid shocks is 0.12 – 0.18 of mean aid flows. To this range we add a lower bound (0.10) and an upper bound (0.20) for sensitivity analysis.[10]

For the size of the equilibrium buffer stock, we consider the range from 50–100 percent of the annual aid flow. For an aid-dependent low-income country receiving 10 percent of GDP annually in budget support aid and with annual imports of close to 40 percent of GDP (the average for poverty reduction support credit [PRSC] countries), this corresponds to two to three months of import cover—less than their current average cover of almost five months' imports. The spending floor and spending ceiling determine both the usefulness of the model in smoothing expenditure and the vulnerability of the buffer stock to persistent shocks. The closer the floor and ceiling are to the target expenditure level, the greater the expenditure-smoothing effect, but also the more easily the fund can be depleted by persistent negative shocks to aid flows. For illustrative purposes, we use plus and minus 5 percent of the spending target to designate the floor and ceiling.[11]

Finally, perhaps most important is the nature of the variability in aid flows. If aid evolves according to a stationary process, such that $\lambda = 0$ (that is, aid shocks are not auto-correlated) and θ_t is purely stochastic, simple buffer stock mechanisms may be quite effective. In the best of all scenarios, if donors offset unreasonably weak aid flows in time *t* by increasing aid in *t+1* (for example, $\lambda < 0$), a simple buffer mechanism would be highly effective in smoothing spending, but the more persistent are aid shocks, the more vulnerable the buffer mechanisms will be. We consider four values of λ: −0.25, 0, 0.25, and 0.5.[12]

The benefits of the buffer fund are clear from the simulation. While the fund retains positive balances, its operation reduces the standard deviation of actual spending to 2.8–3.3 percent of mean spending under all parameter configurations. By definition, spending never falls below its target level by more than 5 percent.

The problem that must be contained is the vulnerability of the buffer stock to persistent negative shocks. Table 12.1 shows the percentage of years in which the buffer stock has a negative balance, under a range of parameter values for σ (overall aid volatility levels), λ (autocorrelation in aid shocks), and *S* (target stock as share of aid-financed spending). Taking a negative balance rate of 10 percent of years or below as an adequacy benchmark, if aid shocks are negatively autocorrelated ($\lambda = -0.25$), our smallest fund ($S = 0.5$) can easily dampen anything less than the highest volatility we consider ($\sigma = 0.20$). Serial independence of shocks implies very low vulnerability as well, particularly for the larger funds. The more positively autocorrelated are aid shocks, the more vulnerable is the buffer fund, because bad shocks tend to be persistent. With $\lambda = 0.5$, even the largest buffer fund we consider ($S = 1$) can only keep the years of negative balance less than 10 percent of all years in the mildest volatility environment we consider ($\sigma = 0.10$). For a milder level of autocorrelation ($\lambda = 0.25$), however, the larger buffer stocks can successfully dampen moderate levels of volatility ($\sigma = 0.12$ for $S = 0.75$, $\sigma = 0.15$ for $S = 1$).

TABLE 12.1 Percentage of Years with Negative Buffer Stock Balance

S	0.5				0.75				1.0			
σ	λ = −0.25	0	0.25	0.5	λ = −0.25	0	0.25	0.5	λ = −0.25	0	0.25	0.5
0.10	1	3	6	24	0	1	3	11	0	0	2	6
0.12	3	6	14	34	0	3	5	24	0	2	3	16
0.15	7	14	26	41	3	5	15	35	2	3	8	28
0.18	9	21	31	42	5	10	25	38	3	5	17	33
0.20	16	30	38	47	7	18	31	43	4	10	24	39

To illustrate the functioning of the buffer stocks, Figures 12.1–12.4 trace the 1,000-year simulations for the smaller fund ($S = 0.5$) in a country receiving 10 percent of GDP in aid. The illustration shows the middle ranges of volatility ($\sigma = 0.12, 0.15$), across the range of possibilities for autocorrelation. Zero or negative autocorrelation ensures that the fund's balance fluctuates fairly closely in the range of 0–10 percent of GDP, turning negative only in the case of persistent large negative shocks (for example, around year 100), but in the higher autocorrelation cases, the small fund is more vulnerable.

FIGURE 12.1 Buffer Stock Trajectory, $\lambda = -0.25$, $S = 0.5$

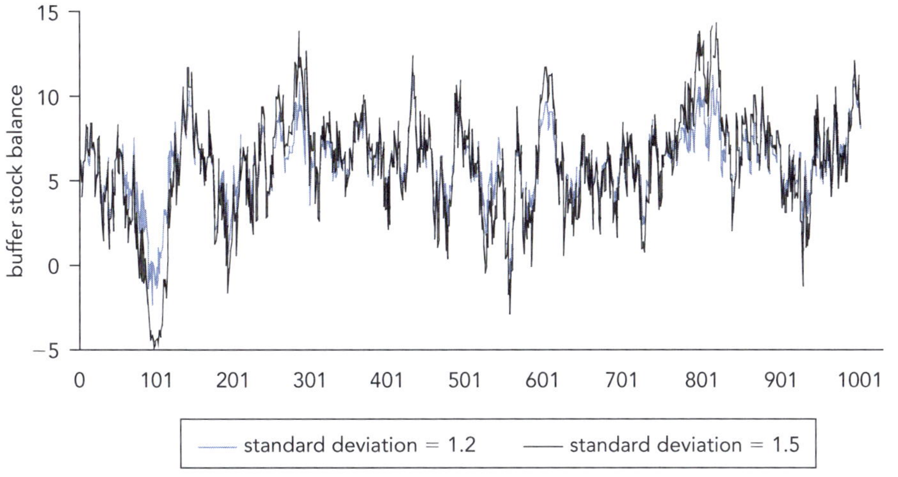

FIGURE 12.2 Buffer Stock Trajectory, $\lambda = 0$, $S = 0.5$

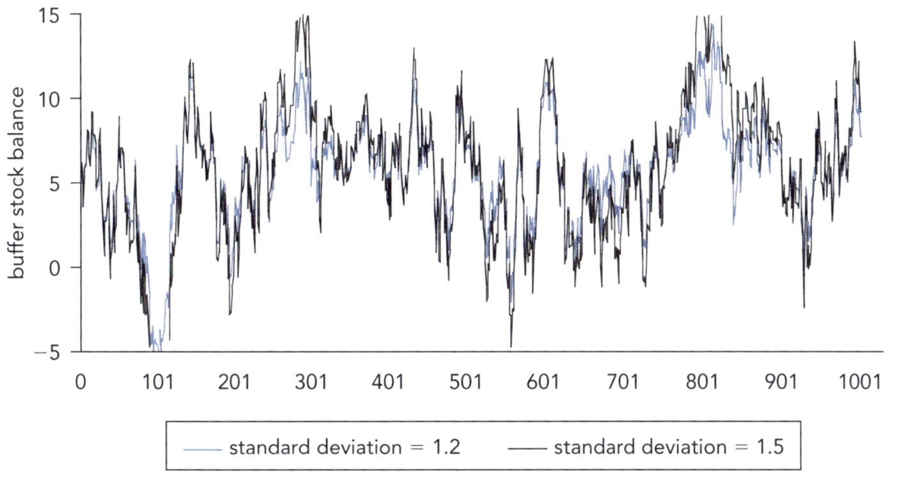

FIGURE 12.3 Buffer Stock Trajectory, λ = 0.25, *S* = 0.5

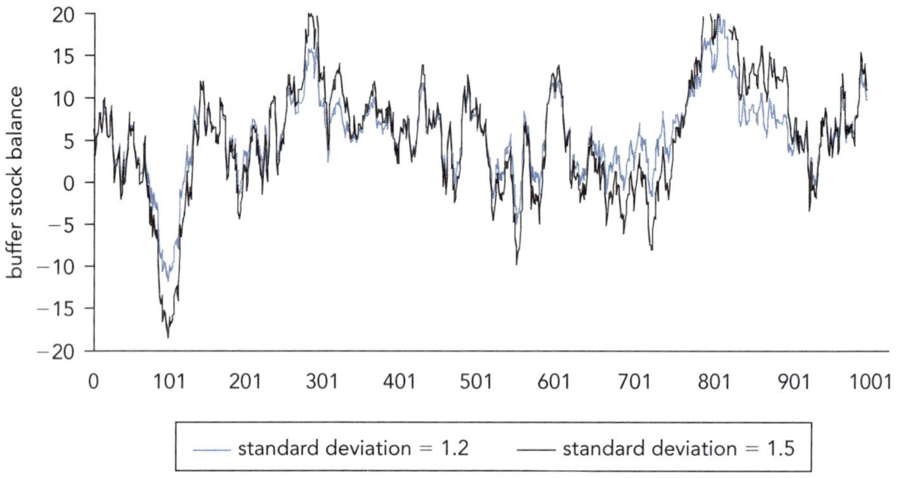

FIGURE 12.4 Buffer Stock Trajectory, λ = 0.5, *S* = 0.5

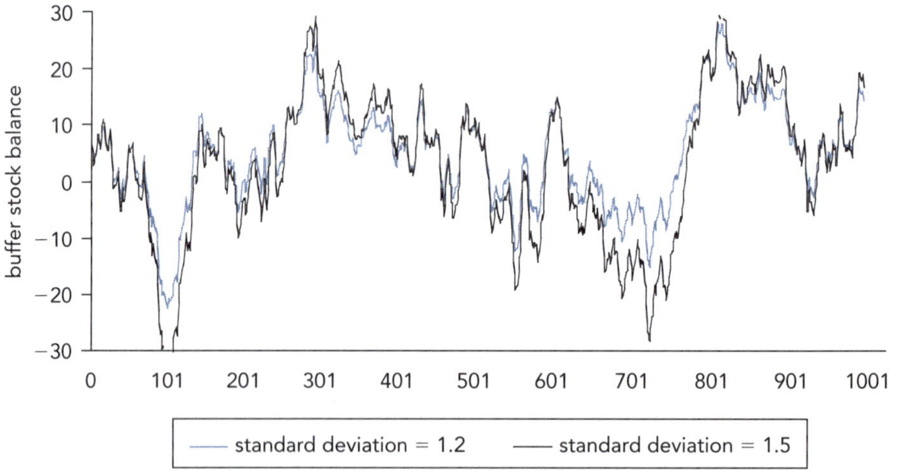

Figure 12.5 zooms in on the episode of shocks concentrated in the simulation years 21–59 to investigate the anatomy of the worst series of shocks generated by the simulation under the strongest autocorrelation ($\lambda = 0.5$). In the worst episodes, 25–30 and 54–59, the buffer fund has a reasonably positive balance to begin with, and even the $\sigma = 0.20$ cases require three to four years of sustained large negative shocks before the buffer fund is depleted.

This is comforting. It implies that countries and donors will have plenty of lead time before a full rundown of reserves occurs. If consultative group arrangements can

FIGURE 12.5 Anatomy of Major Shocks

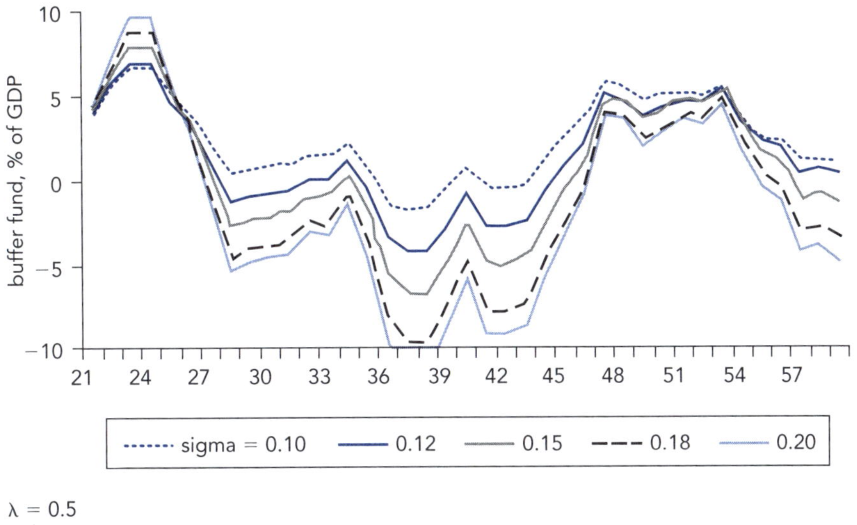

work reasonably well, and if there is a clear performance framework to help define when aid shocks are exogenous, countries should be able to avoid severe crises. The better such processes work, the smaller the reserve fund can be.

Aid-dependent low-income countries, together with donors and the international financial institutions, may therefore wish to consider more active fiscal programming and reserve management arrangements to reduce the negative effect of exogenous volatility in aid flows. Such instruments can work well as long as volatility does not become too extreme and negative shocks are not too persistent, and they can also underwrite an effective consultative process to correct disbursement levels to better reflect trends in commitments. Our simulation suggests that the upper range of current levels of purely exogenous volatility (equivalent to 18–20 percent of mean aid flows) would be difficult to buffer effectively. Yet even here it still takes several years of large negative shocks to exhaust a buffer fund, which in principle allows for a compensatory feedback process to work well. Relatively modest decreases in exogenous volatility (to 10–15 percent of mean aid flows) have high returns in lowering the vulnerability of the buffer fund.

C. How Risky Are Multiyear Aid Commitments?

The issue of multiyear aid commitments is controversial. On one hand, they can introduce a greater degree of stability into fiscal programming. On the other, long-horizon commitments run the risk of over- or underproviding aid in the event of significant changes in country performance. This section lays out an approach to thinking about the efficiency losses associated with suboptimal aid allocations. It then simulates this model to ask the following questions: given countries' actual scores on the CPIA (our proxy for performance) over 1999–2003, how large would the efficiency losses from aid misallocation have been if five-year donor programs had been implemented in 1999 under different precommitment rules? And how large a reduction in aid volatility results from these rules?

A Simple Model of Aid Effectiveness

We start from two main propositions. First, there is some optimal allocation of a given total of aid across countries that depends on poverty levels, population, and a measure of "absorptive capacity" or "performance." Second, the optimal allocations to individual countries are independent of total aid.

Though not too restrictive, these assumptions do have some implications. One is that aid does not have increasing marginal returns over any range; another is that all countries, even if poorly governed, will still have some aid opportunities with high social returns. The problem in poorly governed countries is that these opportunities run out quickly, and the possibilities for more complex interventions, which depend on domestic management and complementary public sector actions for their effectiveness, are scarce. Such countries therefore receive less, though not zero, aid.

It follows from the first and second assumptions that the marginal value of aid decreases linearly with the level of aid, whether expressed as aid per capita or aid as a share of GDP. A number of studies have estimated the returns to aid using functions that are compatible with the above propositions, including Burnside and Dollar (2000), Collier and Dollar (2002), Denkabe (2003), and Clemens, Radelet, and Bhavani (2004).

At the point where aid tends to zero, the marginal product of aid will then be equal for all countries (k), but its slope β_i will vary according to the measure of performance or capacity of country I, C_i.[13] If O is a measure of social outcomes and a is aid,

$$\frac{\partial O_i}{\partial a_i} = k - \beta_i a_i \tag{1}$$

$$\beta_i = \alpha(C_i)^{-\gamma} \tag{2}$$

Where $\alpha > 0$ and $\gamma > 1$ are scalars.

To take a specific example, we depart from the IDA allocation formula. At the margin, the cost of raising one dollar of IDA is one dollar; it is therefore reasonable to assume that at the optimal level and allocation of IDA, its marginal product will be one in all countries.[14] The optimal level of aid a_i* is then given by equation (3), where C_i is country i's CPIA score. Given a fixed stock of available aid,[15] the optimal aid allocation is fixed in proportion across countries according to the quality of policies and institutions, as in equation (4).

$$a_i* = (k - 1)\alpha^{-1}(C_i)^{\gamma} \tag{3}$$

$$\frac{aid_1^*}{aid_2^*} = \left(\frac{C_1}{C_2}\right)^{\gamma} \tag{4}$$

The marginal product of aid falls to zero at some multiple $m = k/(k - 1)$ of the optimal aid level.

This parameter, m, is central to the global debate over scaling up aid: how much can aid flows expand in the short term while maintaining positive returns, given the current quality of policies and institutions? The estimates of Clemens, Radelet, and Bhavani (2004) suggest that the marginal product of aid falls to zero when aid is doubled from present levels: we term this the "optimistic" scenario. Skeptics who emphasize absorptive capacity constraints may believe that little productive increase in aid is immediately possible: for them, m is much closer to one. World Bank studies of absorptive capacity suggest that many countries are now able to productively absorb substantially more aid, say 50 percent above present levels. Without intending to imply a judgment, we term these the "realist" estimates.[16]

Figure 12.6 shows the marginal productivity of aid as k at $a = 0$ and falling at the rate $\beta_i(C_i)$. Optimal aid allocations a_1*, a_2* and a_3* correspond to C_1, C_2, and C_3. In high-performing countries ($C_i = C_3$), the slope β is relatively flat, so that a large quantity of aid can be absorbed productively. In poorly governed countries ($C_i = C_1$), the marginal product of aid drops rapidly. If actual aid allocations a_1, a_2, and a_3 differ from optimal allocations, this causes efficiency losses of two types: countries may get too much aid, such that the marginal product is less than one (type 1 error), or too little, such that the marginal product is greater than one (type 2 error). These triangular losses are easily quantifiable:

$$L_i(a_i, a_i*, m) = 0.5\ |1 - MPa_i|\,|a_i - a_i*| \qquad (5)$$

This model provides a framework for thinking about the trade-offs between "optimality" and the stability of aid flows (Figure 12.6). Precommitment that guarantees

FIGURE 12.6 Aid Allocation and Efficiency

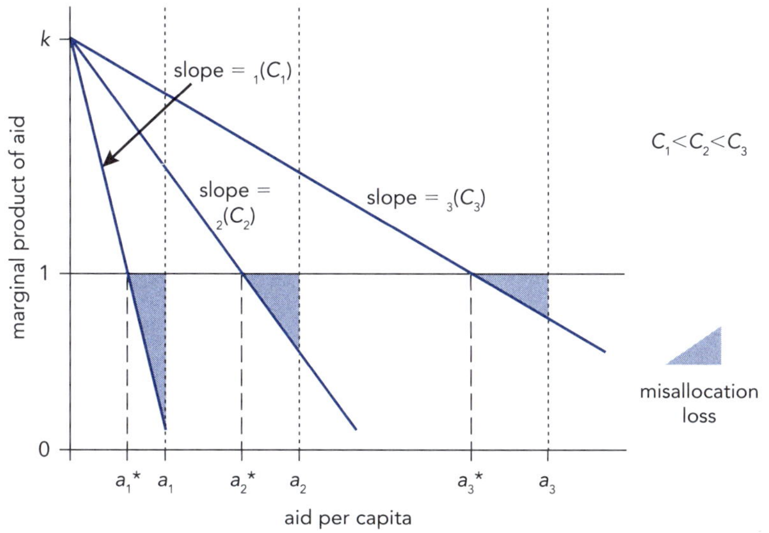

a certain level of aid over several years is desirable in terms of stability and predictability, but it can generate efficiency losses if policies deteriorate during the life of the aid program. Even if country performance deteriorates sharply, aid will flow despite its falling social impact. Similarly, if precommitments are upwardly rigid, countries that rapidly improve their performance may be denied funds that they otherwise might use well. Because rising aid levels confront absorptive capacity constraints more slowly in better-governed countries, both types of losses are smaller in such countries for misallocations of similar magnitudes.

Simulating Trade-Offs in Aid Predictability

We use five years of CPIA country performance ratings, for 1999–2003. Given this record, how much more stable would aid flows have been under a purely performance-oriented regime based on the model above, or under a modified regime with a flexible precommitment rule to improve predictability? How large would efficiency losses have been if five-year forward-looking aid programs had been enacted in 1999 according to various precommitment rules?

Table 12.2 and Table 12.3 list the countries considered in the exercise, arranged by CPIA quintiles for 1999 and for 2003 over the five-year period. Roughly half of the countries remain in the same quintile, one quarter move up, and one quarter move down. Most movements are across a single quintile, but some countries slip more (for example, Côte d'Ivoire, Eritrea, Zimbabwe).

Patterns of year-on-year changes in performance are important for the design of mechanisms to improve aid predictability. If one-year drops in CPIA scores tend to signal subsequent declines, the type-I losses from not responding to initial signs of deterioration of performance could be substantial. Similarly, large type-II errors may

TABLE 12.2 Countries by CPIA Quintiles, 1999

1	2	3	4	5
Armenia	Benin	Burkina Faso	Azerbaijan	Angola
Bangladesh	Eritrea	Cameroon	Cambodia	Burundi
Bhutan	Ethiopia	Gambia, The	Chad	Central African Republic
Bolivia	India	Georgia	Djibouti	Comoros
Côte D'Ivoire	Kyrgyzstan	Kenya	Guinea	Congo, Dem. Rep. of
Estonia	Lesotho	Madagascar	Indonesia	Congo, Rep. of
Ghana	Malawi	Mali	Kiribati	Equatorial Guinea
Guyana	Mozambique	Moldova	Lao PDR	Guinea-Bissau
Honduras	Nicaragua	Mongolia	Nepal	Haiti
Mauritania	Tanzania	Pakistan	Niger	Papua New Guinea
Senegal	Yemen	Rwanda	Nigeria	São Tomé & Príncipe
Sri Lanka	Zambia	Solomon Islands	Togo	Sierra Leone
Uganda		Vietnam	Zimbabwe	Sudan
				Tajikistan
				Ukraine
				Uzbekistan

TABLE 12.3 Countries by CPIA Quintiles, 2003

1	2	3	4	5
Armenia	**Azerbaijan**	Cameroon	Cambodia	Angola
Bhutan	*Bangladesh*	*Ethiopia*	Chad	Burundi
Estonia	Benin	Georgia	**Congo, Dem, Rep. of**	Central African Republic
Honduras	*Bolivia*	*Guyana*	**Congo, Rep. of**	Comoros
India	**Burkina Faso**	Kenya	*Côte D'Ivoire*	Equatorial Guinea
Mauritania	*Ghana*	*Kyrgyzstan*	Djibouti	Guinea-Bissau
Nicaragua	Indonesia	*Lesotho*	*Eritrea*	Haiti
Senegal	Madagascar	*Malawi*	*Gambia, The*	*Lao PDR*
Sri Lanka	Mali	Moldova	Guinea	*Nigeria*
Tanzania	Nepal	Mongolia	Kiribati	Papua New Guinea
Uganda	Pakistan	**Mozambique**	Niger	São Tomé and Príncipe
Ukraine	Yemen	Rwanda	**Sierra Leone**	*Solomon Islands*
Vietnam		*Zambia*	**Tajikistan**	Sudan
				Togo
				Uzbekistan
				Zimbabwe

Notes: Quintile unchanged; **quintile improved**; *quintile worsened.*

occur if one-year improvements tend to foreshadow sustained improvements. On the other hand, if movements in the CPIA tend not to be autocorrelated (so that last year's change is not a good predictor of this year's change), then the case for not placing great stress on small year-on-year falls in CPIA scores may be strong. Indeed, this is more typically the case: initial changes in ratings are often reversed and are not a good guide to future movements.

One reason for the random nature of short-term changes in performance rating can be measurement error. Using the natural experiment of two similar and independent performance assessments, one by the African Development Bank and the other by the World Bank, Gelb, Ngo, and Ye (2004) estimate the standard error of a CPIA estimate as about 2.4 points. While not large in relation to the overall rating scale, this exceeds the typical annual change of plus or minus 0.1 point seen in the country sample. Most countries' annual changes are therefore within the range of measurement error, with a typical country requiring two, three or four years of sustained change to pull its rating outside this range. This has implications, discussed below, for the design of budget support.

Another reason for small movements can be changes in the survey instrument. Donors will want to take advantage of the best knowledge to allocate their assistance, and any assessment mechanism can be expected to evolve over time as knowledge accumulates. Even if the changes are gradual (as in the case of the CPIA), they can shift the relative position of countries slightly. This is an inevitable feature of a living assessment system.

We consider three values of m: the skeptic (1.25), the optimist (2), and the realist (1.5) values. Each doubling of the distance between m and 1 (that is, from 1.25 to 1.5, from 1.5 to 2) is associated with a halving of type-I and type-II losses. The "skeptic" will thus see efficiency losses twice as large as does the "realist," and the "optimist" will see them half as large as does the "realist."

The other parameter of interest is λ, the relationship between country performance (as proxied by the CPIA) and the slope of the marginal product function with respect to aid, β. The IDA allocation formula has a CPIA-aid elasticity of roughly 3; therefore we use $\gamma = 3$ throughout. We could also consider the case of direct budget support. There is no formula here, but because the better-performing countries tend to receive budget support, its allocation is more sensitive to performance than overall aid. We could take an approximate performance elasticity for budget support to be four.

We can now fit the approximate IDA allocations in per capita terms. Figure 12.7 shows the relationship among the CPIA, the slope of the marginal product of aid (β), and the optimal level of aid in per capita terms (aid^*).[17] The graph on the left is parameterized and scaled for overall IDA flows, and the graph on the right is closer to budget support. The midpoint of the CPIA scale, 3.5, is associated with overall aid flows of roughly US$10 per capita and budget support of US$4 per capita; both overall IDA and the share provided as budget support rise with the CPIA.

Simulating Losses from Precommitment

The CPIA has been broadly consistent over periods of time, but has changed slightly from year to year. There is some slight upward drift in the 1999–2003 ratings, and we normalize the scores for each year so that the means are consistent across years.[18] We assume that aid in 1999 reflects the optimal allocation from equation (3) and consider three types of programs for 2000–03. The first, the annual performance-based system, sets $aid_{it} = aid_{it}*$ for each country and year. The second, the pure precommitment system, holds each country's aid level in 2000–03 at its (optimal) 1999 level. The third, the flexible precommitment rule, adjusts aid levels if and only if a country's CPIA score drifts to a point that is well above or below its 1999 level. Here, this

FIGURE 12.7 Optimal Aid Allocations and the Quality of Policies and Institutions

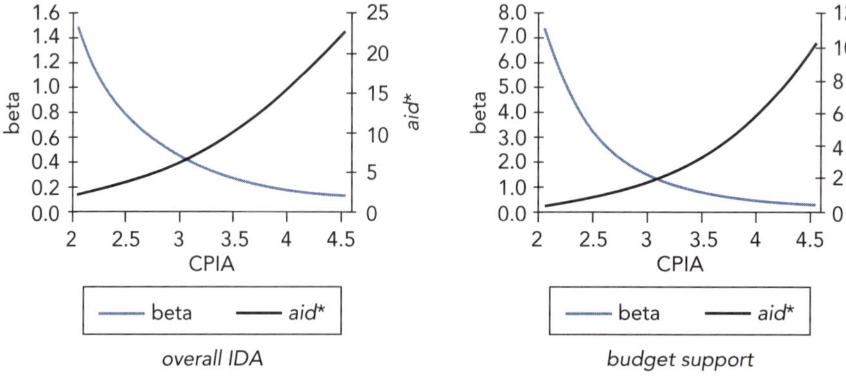

critical point corresponds to +/− 0.33, around a 92 percent confidence interval associated with the estimated standard error of the CPIA.[19] This rule will not adjust aid flows unless a country has had a rather clearly observable performance improvement or a major performance deterioration.

For each of these three programs, we perform two sets of analyses. First, we compute the degree of volatility inherent in the "optimal" performance-based aid flow. If we had a purely performance-based system without additional safeguards for predictability, how stable would aid flows be? How does this level of stability compare to the stability of aid in recent years? How much is stability further improved by the flexible precommitment rule? Second, we compute the implied efficiency losses from aid misallocations over 2000–03 arising from the pure and flexible precommitment rules given countries' actual CPIA trajectories.

Stability of Aid Flows

Performance-based aid should be volatile if country performance is volatile. Using the model laid out above, we simulate the volatility of an optimal performance-based system with no stability safeguards and compare it to that of the system with the flexible precommitment rule. (Of course, this question is irrelevant for the full precommitment rule, which eliminates all variability.)

Under the optimal allocation system with no precommitments, aid allocations have an average standard deviation of 17 percent of 1999 levels. Much of this volatility comes from the lowest-performing countries; for those in the first four 1999 CPIA quintiles, the standard deviation is between 0.12 and 0.14, compared to 0.31 for the poorest-performing quintile (Figure 12.8). Being in the highest CPIA quintile does not make much of a difference for a country's simulated volatility; over the last five years, a number of countries in the top two quintiles have slipped badly (Table 12.2 and Table 12.3). Countries that perform consistently—whether first quintile or third—ben-

FIGURE 12.8 Stability of Aid Flows, Standard Deviation 1999–2003, Share of 1999 Aid Flow

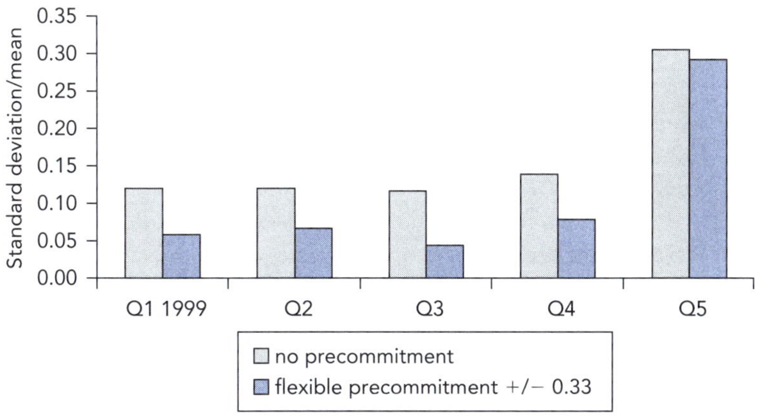

efit from low volatility. In countries with initially worse performance, subsequent improvements result in rapid increases in aid flows and hence greater volatility.

In comparison, the estimates of historical volatility for most low-income countries from Bulíř and Hamann (2003) are in the range of 0.40 – 0.60, or 0.30 – 0.40 around an autoregressive forecast, and they suggest that these trends extend through recent years as well. This implies that a purely performance-based system, even without precommitments, would be much more predictable than the current aid regime: reductions in volatility for most countries would be on the order of two-thirds of their past levels.

As Figure 12.8 also shows, the flexible precommitment rule is quite successful in reducing volatility where performance deviations are modest. Our simulations suggest that it is capable of delivering another 50 percent reduction in average variability for countries in the top four quintiles. For those countries which stay on track throughout the program, it reduces variability all the way to zero. Of course, where programs go rapidly off track (as in several of the quintile-five countries), the flexible rule has little effect. One reason for not providing budget support, or much budget support, to low-performing countries is that it is harder to reconcile stable financing with performance-based allocation.

In summary, the use of a performance-based allocation mechanism based on the model developed above would have substantially improved the predictability of aid allocation, reducing the variability of flows to a third of their historical level. The addition of a flexible precommitment rule, in which five-year forward-looking aid programs are guaranteed on the basis of current performance as long as performance does not vary outside the 92 percent confidence interval, would have further reduced the variability of aid flows by half.

The Efficiency Trade-Off

We now impose pure and flexible precommitment rules on the 2000–03 programs, and compute the efficiency losses from aid misallocations over 2000–03 arising from the rules' responses to divergence between original and subsequent performance.[20] Table 12.4 and Table 12.5 present the results for the pure precommitment rule, where $a_t = a^*_{1999}(C_{1999})$ for all t. For simplicity, the discussion will use the "realist' assumption that $m = 1.5$; "skeptics" can double the estimated losses and "optimists" can halve them.

More than half of type-I losses are moderate, equivalent to less than 5 percent of the total aid flows to the recipient country. Better-performing countries in 1999 are not necessarily less likely to incur moderate losses than their worse-performing counterparts, in part because their potential mobility is mostly downward. In fact, substantial type-I errors can occur where strong performers suddenly deteriorate. For example, Côte d'Ivoire's slip into conflict pushed it from the first quintile to the fourth, and Guyana slid from the first quintile to the third. Precommitments in these countries would have engendered large efficiency losses. However, large type-I efficiency losses are rare and occur only in countries that were initially not highly rated but slipped further (Solomon Islands, Zimbabwe). The sum of type-I losses generated by

TABLE 12.4 Type-I Losses under Pure Precommitment

Loss, percent of aid	Q1 1999	Q2 1999	Q3 1999	Q4 1999	Q5 1999
0–2		India	Gambia, The		
2–5	Bolivia	Lesotho, Malawi, Mozambique, Nicaragua, Zambia		Togo	
5–10	Bangladesh, Ghana		Cameroon	Lao PDR, Nigeria	
10–25	Cote d'Ivoire, Guyana	Eritrea, Ethiopia, Kyrgyzstan			
25–100					
>100			Solomon Islands	Zimbabwe	

TABLE 12.5 Type-II Losses under Pure Precommitment

Loss, percent of aid	Q1 1999	Q2 1999	Q3 1999	Q4 1999	Q5 1999
0–2		Tanzania	Burkina Faso, Madagascar, Pakistan		
2–5			Vietnam	Indonesia	
5–10					Tajikistan
10–25				Nepal	Sierra Leone
25–100					
>100					Congo Dem. Rep. of; Congo, Rep. of; Ukraine

TABLE 12.6 Simulated Efficiency Losses, Percent of Aid Flows for 2000–03, Pure Precommitment

Quintile	Type-I			Type-II		
	m = 1.25	1.5	2	m = 1.25	1.5	2
1	9.2	4.6	2.3	0.3	0.1	0.1
2	7.4	3.7	1.8	0.1	0.1	0.0
3	3.5	1.8	0.9	2.4	1.2	0.6
4	12.9	6.5	3.2	7.0	3.5	1.7
5	10.1	5.0	2.5	107.7	53.8	26.9
All	8.3	4.2	2.1	13.0	6.5	3.8

the pure precommitment program, weighted by the amount of aid received in 1999, is about 4.2 percent of total aid flows, with no strong pattern by initial CPIA score (Table 12.6).

Type-II errors are less common than type-I errors, but often larger. This is because on average the improvements were larger than the slippage. Large type-II errors never occur in well-managed countries, first because of the flatness of their marginal productivity curves (β_i), and second because these countries have little upward mobility on the CPIA. In contrast, type-II errors can be very large in initially poor performing countries that make progress over the horizon of the five-year program. Almost half of type-II errors occur in countries which started in the fifth CPIA quintile in 1999, and several are equivalent to more than 25 percent of aid flows, including those in the Democratic Republic of Congo, the Republic of Congo, and Ukraine. The sum of type-II losses generated by the pure precommitment program, weighted by the amount of aid received in 1999, is about 6.5 percent of total aid flows and incurred almost entirely in countries with low initial CPIA scores (Table 12.6).

The sum of type-I and type-II errors under full commitment is therefore 10.7 percent of aid flows, a not insignificant number.

Table 12.7 and Table 12.8 present the results for the flexible precommitment rule. This rule cuts efficiency losses dramatically. No country generates losses equivalent to more than 10 percent of its aid flow, and most of the losses lie between 0 and 5 percent. Countries that experienced rapid deterioration in governance, and thus generated large losses under the pure precommitment rule, now go off track for most or all of the program. The flexible aid system also scales up assistance to countries which see major improvements in performance from a very low level.

The sum of type-I losses falls to 1.3 percent of total aid flows, or less than a third of its level under pure precommitment (Table 12.9). Type-II losses are very small (0–2 percent of aid flows) and are concentrated in the bottom three quintiles. Total losses using the flexible precommitment rule are only 2.3 percent of aid flows.

Measurement Error in the CPIA Process: Implications for Efficiency

As noted above, even if the CPIA is the "right" measure of country performance and is estimated through a rigorous process of judgment, like any other performance estimate (whether policy-based or output/outcome-based), it will be subject to measure-

TABLE 12.7 Type-I Losses under Flexible Precommitment

Loss, percent of aid	Q1 1999	Q2 1999	Q3 1999	Q4 1999	Q5 1999
0–2		India, Kyrgyzstan	Gambia		Sierra Leone
2–5		Eritrea, Lesotho, Malawi, Mozambique, Nicaragua, Zambia	Vietnam	Togo	Tajikistan
5–10	Bangladesh, Ghana			Lao PDR, Nigeria	

TABLE 12.8 Type-II Losses under Flexible Precommitment

Loss, percent of aid	Q1 1999	Q2 1999	Q3 1999	Q4 1999	Q5 1999
0–2		Tanzania	Burkina Faso, Madagascar, Mali, Pakistan	Nepal	Congo, Dem. Rep. of
2–5	Bolivia			Azerbaijan, Indonesia	

TABLE 12.9 Simulated Efficiency Losses, Percent of Aid Flows for 2000–03, Flexible Precommitment

Quintile	Type-I			Type-II		
	m = 1.25	1.5	2	1.25	1.5	2
1	5.4	2.7	1.3	0.2	0.1	0.05
2	3.8	1.9	0.9	0.2	0.1	0.05
3	0.6	0.3	0.2	2.5	1.2	0.6
4	1.6	0.8	0.4	4.4	2.2	1.1
5	1.0	0.5	0.2	2.8	1.4	0.7
All	2.7	1.3	0.7	2.0	1.0	0.5

ment error. This fact nuances the task of aid delivery significantly. It creates the potential for misallocation even without precommitment rules, because ratings may be too high or too low. It also obscures the judgment of whether country performance has improved or worsened.

How large are the potential efficiency losses from misallocations of aid which arise from errors in the measurement of the CPIA? To estimate them is simple: for each level of the "true" or underlying CPIA, we consider the efficiency costs of providing aid at the inaccurate levels around the "true" CPIA (within the 92 percent confidence interval). Figure 12.9 shows the results, with $\gamma = 3$ and $m = 1.5$. The inverse relationship between performance levels and losses from misallocation is evident: even at the maximum misjudgment (+/− 0.33), losses are only 5–6 percent of aid flows for countries in the high CPIA range (4–4.5), compared to 10–20 percent in the low range (2–3) and even higher on the type-II side for very weak performers.

FIGURE 12.9 Potential Efficiency Losses in Optimal Allocation System from Errors in the CPIA

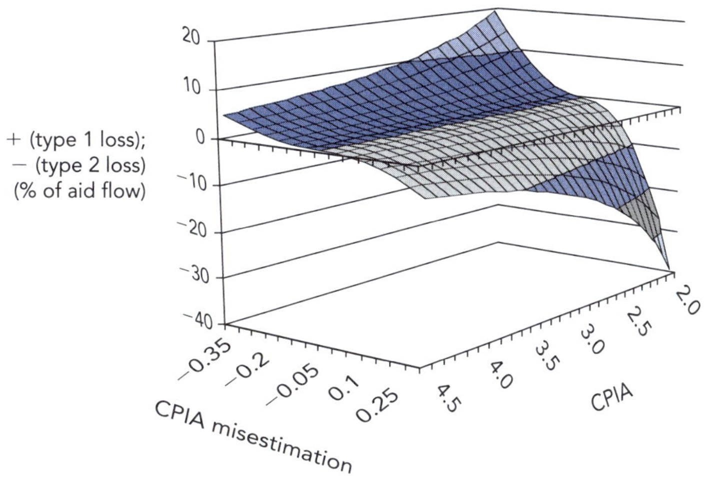

Note: $\gamma = 3$; $m = 1.5$.

Figure 12.10 shows the expected value of type-I and type-II efficiency losses stemming from misestimating the CPIA, assuming that errors follow a normal distribution. For the poorest-performing countries the efficiency losses add up to more than 10 percent of the value of the total aid flow. For most of the countries, clustered in the range of 3.25–3.75, expected efficiency losses are roughly 3–4 percent of the aid flow.

The likely efficiency losses from mismeasurement are therefore larger than the previous estimates of efficiency losses from misallocation under the flexible precommitment rule. This result suggests that, since performance is difficult to measure precisely, there is little to gain from continually fine-tuning aid levels in response to minor year-on-year performance changes. On the other hand, such a graduated response needs to include a mechanism to reassess the level of support when performance clearly improves or worsens by a large margin.

D. Calibrating Budget Support: Performance Levels versus Changes?

Given a system for allocating overall aid, how should the fraction going through budget support, rather than project support, be determined? Country circumstances will partly shape the answer, but some common principles may apply. Most donors, including the World Bank, tend to channel more aid to better-performing countries through budget support. A recent review of PRSCs shows quite a high degree of selectivity, with most recipients of budget support being in the top three quintiles of the CPIA ratings and only one (Guyana) in the third quintile.[21] Budget support may amount to up to half of total aid for high-performing countries and to little or nothing in the low performers.

FIGURE 12.10 Expected Value of Efficiency Losses from Misestimation, by CPIA Level

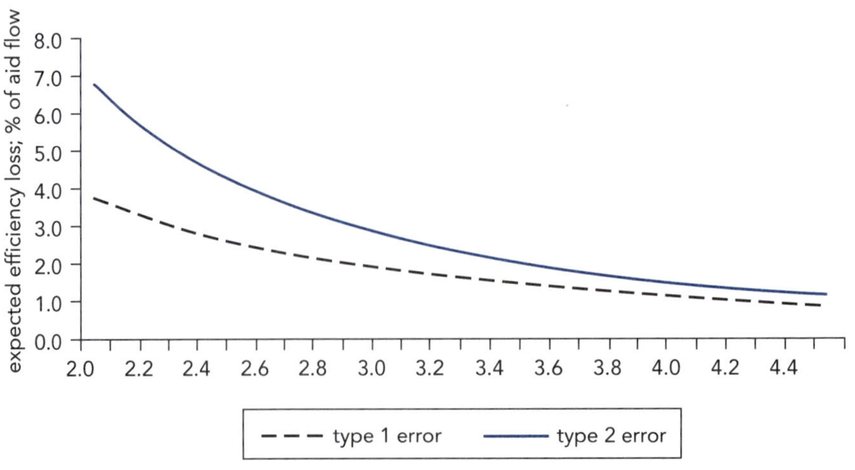

Such selectivity in the allocation of budget support can be implemented in several ways. One approach would be formula based, where countries become eligible above a certain performance cut-off, and where the maximum share increases with a country's level of performance. With overall IDA allocations proportional to the third power of the CPIA (CPIA cubed, as in the previous section), setting budget support proportional to the fourth power of the CPIA would approximate IDA's current practice. Assuming budget support is valued highly by recipients relative to project support, this would also provide an additional incentive for countries to move up the performance rankings. The costs of precommitment using a fourth-power allocation system can also be considered using the model of the previous section; they too are modest, especially for the higher-rated countries, and using the flexible precommitment rule that responds to only major performance changes. Budget support, too, could be committed based on performance levels, with a provision that enables a reassessment in response to major changes.

However, such an approach may not fully capture the important role of budget support as an investment in country systems. In some cases, donors agree to channel funds through still-fragile country systems with the expectation that countries will use this opportunity to strengthen their own systems of budget and financial management and service delivery. At very low levels of country capacity, the expected cost in terms of ineffective or corrupt use of funds exceeds the likely benefits (and it will be more difficult to reconcile performance-based assistance with stable financing). But as country capacity increases, donors will find it appropriate to encourage capacity improvements through budget support in countries on a promising trajectory, even if they are not comfortable with the existing levels of budget and financial management and service delivery. The more rapid the capacity gains, the greater is the return on donors' willingness to take risks. Without demonstrated improvements in capacity that are large enough to yield an acceptable return on their financial and reputational investment, donors can credibly withdraw from budget support back toward projects, but only if the level of capacity is still below their comfort threshold. For very high-capacity clients, donors can provide assistance through budget support simply by "certifying" country systems.[22] Unless they observe a large deterioration in country performance, it is not credible for them to threaten to return to projects in such countries.

This notion of budget support as an investment in country systems suggests that criteria for budget support should reflect both levels and trends in performance. This stands generally in contrast to the CPIA and similar systems, including the indicator-based Millennium Challenge Account criteria, which focus exclusively on levels. There are two exceptions, however. First, levels of performance tend to be interpreted in a comparative context, so a country that lags behind all others in improving performance will see its allocation fall even if there is no absolute change in its performance. Second, depending on progress against CAS triggers, countries can move between low, base, and high cases in the IDA system, with variations of up to about 30 percent of the base case over a three- to four-year CAS period; countries can also see commitments frontloaded or backloaded in response to anticipated changes in their performance and allocations. Such changes can be interpreted as compensating, to a degree, for the backward-looking nature of the CPIA process. This approach can be consistent with seeing budget support as an investment in country systems in response to positive trends.

This story is illustrated in Figure 12.11. With assistance delivered through traditional project mechanisms, capacity improves slowly along the line ABC. Only at time T2 does it reach the level C* at which donors feel fully comfortable in channeling assistance through the budget. At some earlier time, T1, however, the country's track record is strong enough for donors to begin to shift to budget support, hopefully creating a "virtuous circle" that will further strengthen country capacity, as along ABDC. The risks to the donors of providing support during the time when capacity lies below their level of comfort are offset by the potential gains from the more rapid increase in capacity levels to above their comfort threshold. The slope of BD determines the return to the donors' investment, so that the speed of improvements in country systems (not just the level) is an important indicator of effectiveness for budget support. Of course, the slope of BD is unknown a priori; donors' decision to take the risk of providing budget support will depend on the country's previous track record and evidence of government commitment.

The question then arises of the relative weighting of performance levels and trends. Too small a response to positive trends might not reinforce the need to improve systems and coordinate ministries to implement agreed programs: such reinforcement is welcomed by some clients.[23] But too strong a response reduces predictability, thus undermining the value of the budget support instrument and eliminating its potential incentive effects. There is no simple answer, especially given that it is not always easy to distinguish trends in performance from temporary changes or measurement errors. But the analysis above of the likely size of error in measuring performance and the benefits and costs of flexible precommitment suggest ways to approach the problem.

FIGURE 12.11 Balancing Risks and Gains from Budget Support

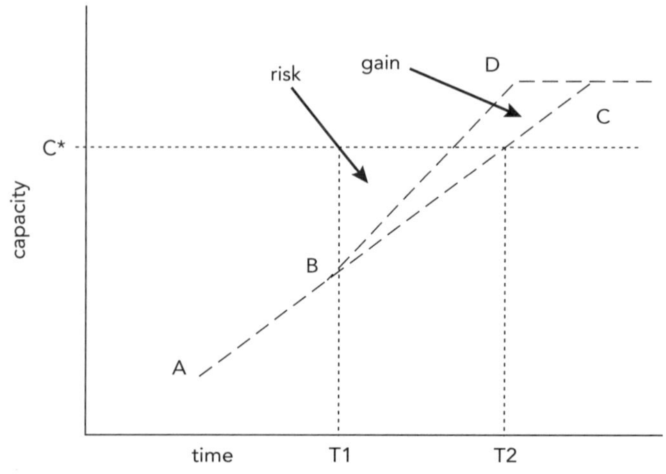

One approach would be for donors to establish a code of good practice. This would set a base level of budget support for several years at a time and supplement it by incentive payments based on agreed actions or other interim assessments of performance. These payments would be modest, perhaps up to 10 percent of base support, corresponding to the modest changes in overall assistance that would follow "normal" (if uncertain) annual changes in a CPIA. They would thus anticipate future changes in the aid envelope and be applied to the next year's support rather than to the current level to further improve the predictability of assistance.

Every three years or so, there would be a deep, systematic review of progress in strengthening country systems of budget and financial management and service delivery, support by independent assessment, and comprehensive output measurement. This would feed back into the CPIA and help shape the decision on how much to channel through budget support in future. As in the case of overall aid, major performance changes, whether positive or negative, should trigger a comprehensive review, informed by neutral external assessment. The results reported above suggest that flexibly committing support forward in this way will involve little efficiency loss while greatly increasing predictability. [24]

E. Developing Performance-Based Norms to Guide Aid Allocations

A further issue concerns the distinction between policy-based and results-based aid allocations. In recent years, the development community has shifted away from emphasizing only policy actions and toward including a focus on results. The European Commission's budget support programs represent the most ambitious move in this direction: they combine a fixed tranche, which is delivered as long as a set of basic conditions are met, with a variable tranche which disburses at a level determined by the recipient country's success in meeting a set of mutually agreed targets for service delivery and public financial management. As shown in the recent assessment of experience (EC 2005), the approach has been quite successful in combining a reasonable degree of predictability with performance-based incentives.

At the core of outcome-based approaches is the set of targets that determine the disbursement of performance-related assistance. As emphasized by the European Community's evaluation of its programs, there is as yet no analytical framework to guide the setting of targets. For example, what is an appropriate three-year target for improvements in the primary enrollment rate, given the current enrollment rate and possibly other variables like income? How rapidly can schooling quality improve or child mortality decline? Little research has been done on the pace of change in outcome, output, and service delivery indicators. The EC evaluation identifies the issue of target setting as one of the most important remaining issues for its new framework.

This section considers how targets might be set with reference to historical evidence. EC programs use indicators for direct government outputs (school enrollment rates, number of children immunized) rather than for broader impacts such as infant mortality, but we take the examples of primary enrollment and under-five and infant mortality because data are available on these indicators.[25]

Primary Enrollment

Clemens (2004) assembles evidence on the speed with which countries have moved from low to high levels of primary enrollment, fitting rates of improvement to a logistic function. He finds a strong pattern of regularity in their transitions, with a typical country taking 115 years to move from enrollment rates of around 10 percent to 90 percent. Without considering the influence of income-related and other factors, the normal speed of increase in enrollment is:

$$N = a\,(s)(1 - s)$$

where s is the current enrollment share. The parameter a is estimated at 3.8, with standard deviation 0.33.

This means that, for a country starting off with 50 percent enrollment, "normal" progression is at 0.95 percentage points annually, with a 95 percent confidence interval of 1.12 percent, 0.78 percent. This can be further refined by allowing a to vary among countries according to exogenous characteristics and policy-related factors. Clemens finds some sensitivity to income levels but little response to indicators of education policy. He further suggests that observed episodes of extremely fast enrollment expansion relative to the norm are likely to reflect wrong or misleading data (for instance, in one example, enrollment rates rose rapidly because large numbers of children were not allowed to exit from the system) or to be associated with a sharp deterioration in indicators of educational quality.

Clemens's norms do not show that rapid progress is impossible, but they can provide a useful reality check on the goals embedded in country programs. The targets embedded in the EU's budget support programs for Burkina Faso and Ethiopia, for example, are set at about 350 percent of the Clemens norms for these countries. Recent trends suggest that, while Burkina Faso's "slow" performance has been quite close to the norm, Ethiopia has expanded enrollment far more rapidly than the Clemens norm. The past might not be a good guide to the future, but experience suggests that sustaining progress at the rates targeted will be very challenging, especially if countries are to maintain educational quality.

Infant and Under-5 Mortality

In this exercise, we compare mortality rates (for infants and children under age 5, respectively) with subsequent (annualized) changes in mortality rates. Observations for mortality rates are for all countries for the years 1960, 1970, 1980, 1990, 1995, and 2000; the subsequent changes are measured as the average annual rate of change between those one-year observations. Clearly, where mortality rates are already low, subsequent changes tend to be small, but at higher mortality rates, we see the subsequent rates of change diverging among countries. In poorer countries with high mortality rates, improved living standards or strong efforts to improve health outcomes can cause declines in mortality rates in the range of 3–5 per 1,000 per year. In other countries, rates stagnate or even rise further, generally because high mortality rates are a symptom of persistent problems (conflict, poor governance) and/or because new challenges are emerging (HIV/AIDS).

Quantile regressions examining the relationship between current mortality levels and subsequent changes in mortality rates were executed at the 10th, 25th, 50th, 75th, and 90th percentiles.[26] Table 12.10 and Table 12.11 report the results. The coefficients α are high at the 90th percentile (−1.1 and −1.7) and fall with lower percentiles until the 10th percentile, where there is no relationship. Coefficients are all statistically significant at the 99.9 percent level, except of course the 10th.

Table 12.12 illustrates the implications for improvements in mortality rates. It suggests that countries with relatively high mortality rates, if performing well, can rapidly reduce both infant and under-5 mortality. These estimates can be used to suggest appropriate target rates of improvement for forward-looking programs. Countries with infant mortality rates above 100 (as per most African countries) can reduce mortality at a rate of 2.5–3.5 per 1,000 per year with strong efforts (75th percentile) and even faster (3.5–4.5 per 1,000 per year) at the 90th percentile. These might be suit-

TABLE 12.10 Quantile Regressions on Annual Rate of Change in Infant Mortality

Percentile %	90		75		50		25		10
		T		T		T		T	
log infant mortality	−1.07	18	−0.8	22	−0.58	24	−0.29	11.6	0
constant	1.5	6.6	1.33	8.9	0.99	10.4	0.50	5.1	0
R^2	0.28		0.28		0.26		0.06		0

TABLE 12.11 Quantile Regressions on Annual Rate of Change in Under-5 Mortality

Percentile %	90		75		50		25		10
		T		T		T		T	
log infant mortality	−1.7	24	−1.27	23	−0.88	30	−0.36	18	0
constant	2.84	10	2.3	10	1.77	15	0.65	8	0
R^2	0.34		0.31		0.22		0.06		0

TABLE 12.12 Annual Rates of Improvement in Infant Mortality (per 1,000)

Initial mortality rate (per 1,000)	Subsequent annualized change in infant mortality, at percentile...					Subsequent annualized change in under-five mortality, at percentile...				
	90th	75th	50th	25th	10th	90th	75th	50th	25th	10th
300	4.6	3.4	2.3	1.2	0	6.9	4.9	3.2	1.4	0
200	4.2	3.1	2.1	1.0	0	6.2	4.4	2.9	1.3	0
150	3.9	2.8	1.9	1.0	0	5.7	4.1	2.6	1.2	0
100	3.4	2.5	1.7	0.8	0	5.0	3.5	2.3	1.0	0
80	3.2	2.3	1.6	0.8	0	4.6	3.3	2.1	0.9	0
70	3.0	2.2	1.5	0.7	0	4.4	3.1	2.0	0.9	0
60	2.9	2.1	1.4	0.7	0	4.1	2.9	1.8	0.8	0
50	2.7	1.9	1.3	0.6	0	3.8	2.7	1.7	0.8	0
40	2.4	1.7	1.1	0.6	0	3.4	2.4	1.5	0.7	0
30	2.1	1.5	1.0	0.5	0	2.9	2.0	1.2	0.6	0
20	1.7	1.2	0.7	0.4	0	2.3	1.5	0.9	0.4	0

able goals for countries with sufficient capacity to receive budget support. For countries with particularly weak systems and difficult circumstances, the median may be more appropriate, where infant mortality rates improve by 1.7–2.3 per 1,000 per year.

Patterns in the estimates for improvement on under-five mortality are similar. The 90th percentile of countries in the 100+ range historically have seen improvements of 5–7 per 1,000 per year in under-five mortality, 3.5–5 at the 75th percentile, and 2.3–3.2 at the median.

Firgure 12.12 and Figure 12.13 illustrate the estimated paths from high to low mortality rates for countries at different performance percentiles. The 90th percentile paths, for instance, suggest that a very strong performer starting with an infant mortality rate of 150 and an under-5 mortality rate of 250 could reduce those mortality rates to 80 and 135, respectively, in 20 years. Over the same period, the 75th percentile paths would bring a country to 100 and 165, respectively.

F. Conclusion

This paper has considered three problems that will remain even if donors are able to lengthen their funding horizons to create multiyear aid budgets:

- First, how to deal better with exogenous factors that cause disbursements to diverge from commitments in the short to medium term?
- Second, how to commit aid forward in a multiyear framework that balances the need for predictable funding against the risk of misallocating aid as countries' performance changes?
- Third, within the overall aid envelope, how to shape the breakdown of assistance into project support and budget support in a way that responds to performance yet provides the degree of funding predictability needed for budget support to be effective?

FIGURE 12.12 Infant Mortality Rates, Estimated Paths for Different Performance Quantiles

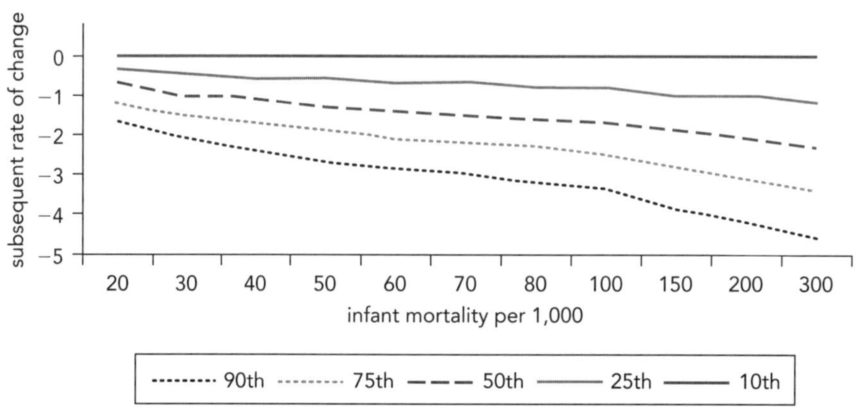

FIGURE 12.13 Under-5 Mortality Rates, Estimated Paths for Different Performance Quantiles

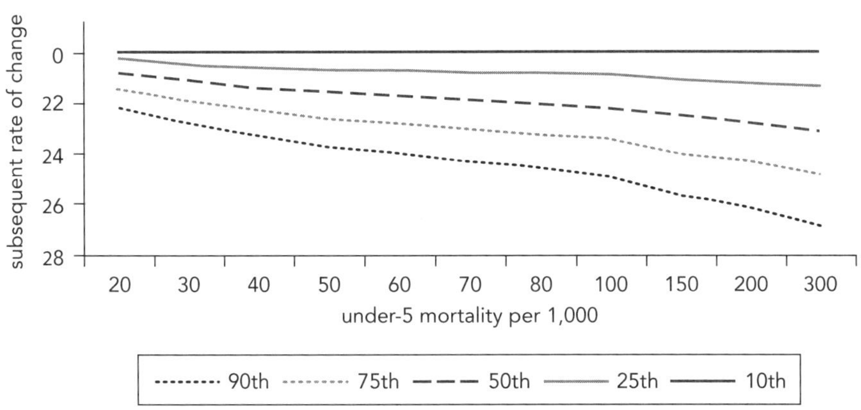

On the first topic, we show that much could be done using active reserve management and fiscal rules to cushion spending against fluctuations in disbursements that are not directly attributable to performance-related factors. Moderate reserve levels, on the order of two to three months' imports for most countries, can help to buffer a good deal of exogenous volatility in aid. Since, on average, PRSC countries now hold close reserves close to five months' import cover, some are already in a position to begin to use such an approach. Assuming that donors do indeed have longer aid horizons and that they are committed to following through, the success of this approach depends on two interrelated factors.

First, the reserve cushion works best when fluctuations in disbursements are serially independent or tend to offset each other in subsequent years. Such a pattern would be expected to result from administrative factors that cause uncertain delays. The cushion is most vulnerable when disbursement shocks are autocorrelated, since countries will tend to experience a series of negative shocks over several years. Even in the worst cases, however, the size of the reserve provides a clear signal to donors over several years that disbursements are falling below anticipated levels. This provides ample time for consultative groups to address the funding issue. The better the groups work, the lower the reserve target can be set.

Second, a clear performance framework will be needed to enable such a process to work smoothly. Donors are being asked, in effect, to fund a country's holding of reserves as insurance against shortcomings in disbursements that are not performance driven. Lack of agreement on the performance framework will undermine such a system, as donors will see the fund as an escape valve for performance-related shortcomings. Inadequate budget discipline in the country will also undermine the system. Mutually agreed independent performance review, as pioneered in Tanzania and more recently extended to other countries such as Mozambique, can strengthen consensus around the performance assessment.

In short, if donors are able to extend their horizon for aid funding and are really committed to following through their commitments with disbursements, and if a clear performance framework can be agreed, nothing stands in the way of solving the problem of short-term exogenous volatility in development assistance.

The second problem, of whether it is possible to precommit aid for several years at a time without incurring high risks of misallocation, is more complex. It can only be addressed quantitatively within a specific framework for aid effectiveness and allocation, and most of the basic assumptions underlying the IDA-based model used here are common to many other approaches. Fully applying a performance-based allocation rule such as used for IDA can cut aid volatility considerably relative to historical levels, and precommitting aid for several years ahead can further increase predictability. However, the losses from precommitting aid to all countries for several years can be substantial. Depending on assumptions about absorptive capacity, the losses could be more than 10 percent of total aid over a five-year period, with a plausible loss range between 5 percent and 21 percent.

These losses can be cut dramatically using a flexible precommitment rule, where levels of assistance are revised sharply only in response to major changes in performance. Such a rule can increase predictability, especially for the more stable countries, while avoiding serious prolonged misallocations to countries experiencing "catastrophic" change or rapid improvements. Indeed, a flexible commitment rule results in smaller losses, over time, than those that result from the likely measurement error in the performance ratings themselves. This makes it a very attractive option. Observed small performance changes frequently reverse themselves, possibly because they partly reflect measurement error. Another advantage of the flexible precommitment rule is that, by focusing on large and clearly observable changes, it reinforces the credibility of performance-based allocation. Looking at the countries concerned, major performance changes within a short period very often seem linked to factors concerning political governance. Other studies show, and we assume, that aid in itself does not drive performance.

The third problem, of how to determine the share of budget support within an overall aid envelope, introduces a further degree of complexity. Budget support represents an "investment" of funds and reputation by donors to give client countries the opportunity to develop stronger systems of budget and financial management and service delivery. More so than for project aid, indicators of changes in country performance, rather than just levels of performance, are then important indicators for justifying budget support. Changes can partly be taken into account by increasing the share of assistance provided through budget support as the country's performance improves. This approach would make budget support almost as predictable as the overall aid envelope. But if indicators are also considered necessary to signal the speed of change, the question is what the indicators should be and how changes and levels should be weighted in determining disbursements.

Donors use different approaches to these questions. The World Bank, for example, has a tight, formula-driven method to determine the overall envelope but no formulaic approach to set either the desired level of budget support within the country program or the way in which levels of budget support will change in response to the fulfillment of prior actions. As a result, although in practice disbursements of PRSCs have been close to anticipated levels because the countries chosen for such operations have managed to sustain good track records, budget support from IDA is not explicitly predictable, except to the extent that countries higher in the ratings scale are more likely to receive it than those low down. The EU, on the other hand, uses a tight formula linking variable tranche levels of budget support to indicators of effectiveness, including service delivery targets. Because the fixed tranche is usually large, the variability of EU budget support has been modest, at about 8 percent of the mean level.

This paper does not take a position on whether prior actions or specific service indicators are better ways of conditioning changes in budget support levels on country "effort." Indeed, it is interesting that the weights placed by the EU on public and financial management indicators (45 percent) and health and education indicators (25 percent and 22 percent) differ little from the corresponding sectoral weights in PRSCs. We see the two approaches as complementary but imperfect ways to form a view on changes in the effectiveness of budget and financial management, service delivery systems, and in some cases, wider-ranging policies that affect private sector development and growth. Unless these changes are "quantum" or "catastrophic," the analysis of the CPIA shows that they cannot easily be observed from year to year.

This then argues for an approach closer to that of the EU, delineating a base level of support over a multiyear programmatic framework and using variable disbursement levels as incentive payments to encourage performance improvements. For overall allocations, IDA already uses such mechanisms including frontloading, backloading, and in more extreme cases, the high-low CAS scenarios. Similar approaches for PRSCs, holding incentive payments to around 10 percent of the base value, would enable disbursements to reflect trends in budget support that would be expected from positive or negative changes in CPIA scores over time.

This graduated approach would need to be complemented with two more processes. First, as for overall aid, budget support needs a reassessment trigger in response to major performance changes, equivalent to those that would result in a 0.3–0.4 point change in the CPIA, or an equivalent change in its governance and service delivery–related components, which are more critical for budget support.

Second, every three years or so, progress should be assessed in the key areas, buttressed by output, financial management, and service delivery indicators. This would both feed into the assessment that determines overall aid and shape the decision on how much to provide in the form of budget support in the following multiyear period.

As for overall aid, these approaches can help to make budget support more predictable and more credible, while containing the losses from large changes in performance.

A final issue is whether budget support can be used to strengthen the countercyclical potential of aid flows. The regular annual cycle of disbursements makes budget support potentially useful, since funding can be increased or reduced in response to exogenous fiscal shocks. Natural disasters are often easy to identify at the country level, but this is less true for terms-of-trade and other worldwide changes, which may not be reflected at the country level for several months after they become apparent at the global level. To increase the feasibility of providing countercyclical support, we suggest adding a global monitoring variable to IDA's CPIA ratings for poor countries.[27] This variable would be the joint responsibility of the World Bank and the IMF, be updated quarterly, and would indicate to donors whether global developments promised to deliver a negative, neutral, or positive shock to the country. This would cut down the information lag and help mobilize support more quickly than in the past, with the goal of adjusting support levels to partially offset the impact of shocks on the budget. With such a system in place, the concessionality of compensatory financing would also be less of an issue, since donor grants could be used to pay off higher-cost finance more quickly.

Endnotes

1. For recent approaches to improving the quality of aid, see OECD-DAC (2004a, 2005a).
2. Another issue, touched on in Section E, is how aid could be made more countercyclical by shortening information lags on the country-level impacts of global trends.
3. One of the strengths of the CPIA system is its explicit attempt to be comparative.
4. In a simple autoregressive model of disbursements, the coefficient on commitments is significant at the 5 percent level in only one-third of all countries. In these cases, the coefficient is around 0.4 on average and 0.3 at the median, suggesting that even here commitments contain only partial information. The only countries for which the coefficient is larger than 0.7 are Argentina, Mexico, Panama, Turkey, and República Bolivariana de Venezuela, which are all low-aid-dependency countries. Among the high-aid-dependency countries, the coefficients on commitments are significant in only one-fifth of cases.
5. Rapid countercyclical disbursement mechanisms are difficult to implement, both because of performance criteria and because shocks are not always easy to recognize as such when they occur. The EU Stabex and Sysmin programs operated between 1975 and 2000 and disbursed €6.1 billion in total. Stabex increased conditionality and payment justification schemes in the wake of the collapse of most domestic microstabilization schemes in an attempt to ensure that benefits reached farmers, but this slowed disbursements badly, such that assistance actually became pro-cyclical, amplifying the effects of commodity cycles (Hermann, Burger, and Smit 1990). The EU Flex scheme began in 2000, aiming at fast-disbursing aid in response to two conditions: losses of overall export earnings from goods by more than 10 percent and 10 percent worsening in the programmed public deficit. So far, six countries have been declared eligible for support and €36 million has been disbursed. The IMF used the compensatory financing facility (CFF) 344 times in the 1970s and early 1980s, mostly for export revenue shortfalls; it has not used the CFF since its 2000 review. Because the CFF was not concessional, it was not particularly attractive for LICs, the IMF has recently proposed changes to create more consistent responses to shocks in LICs, including augmenting existing on-track poverty reduction grant facilities and subsidizing some General Resources Account facilities in countries that do not have PRGFs or are off track. The IMF is recommending that for the weakest countries, its role should be to draw attention to needs, cooperating with donors capable of providing grants. The World Bank has occasionally provided supplemental financing to countries that are already on a multiyear adjustment program and experiencing adverse trade shocks.
6. These are measured as movement from a country's "bliss point" toward the U.S. position.

7. Consistent with literature that finds that aid has not "bought" reform, the authors also find no tendency for policy reform to follow surges in finance.
8. One important caveat is noted by Aizenman and Marion (2004). A greater chance of corruption and opportunistic behavior by future policy makers reduces the demand for international reserves and increases external borrowing, such that a high debt-to-reserves ratio is a symptom of poor governance. They suggest that, in such cases, the traditional policy recommendation to increase international reserve holdings may be welfare reducing.
9. Together with Chile's Structural Balance Rule, the stabilization fund has enabled the conduct of credible countercyclical fiscal policy. See Perry (2003).
10. Note that this may be interpreted as an upper-bound estimate for the share of exogenous causes in the variation of aid, because performance can still vary over a significant range without causing an IMF program to go off track.
11. The 5 percent limit is arbitrary, but would represent a large improvement over current conditions.
12. To our knowledge, no work has estimated the degree of autocorrelation of aid disbursements relative to commitments. Future research could help to underpin forward-looking plans for volatility management.
13. This implies that returns to aid can be negative where the quality of policies is low and aid is high. One mechanism could be through Dutch disease, if large aid inflows cause significant real exchange rate appreciation, which has high costs in terms of competitiveness if aid is not used effectively. Another mechanism can be the effects of high aid flows on governance in weak institutional environments in propping up poor policy regimes and unaccountable governments.
14. This assumption could be relaxed to set the marginal product of aid equal to the donors' shadow cost of aid, which may be higher or lower than one, depending on the political pressures their governments face.
15. Alternatively, this could be the globally optimal level of aid if the marginal product indeed equals one.
16. The parameter m should be distinguished from scaling-up proposals that allow some time for absorptive capacity and performance ratings to increase, thus opening the way for further productive increases in aid.
17. These "normal" allocations abstract from special allocations to postconflict countries. The approximation to the IDA rating system used also abstracts from the super-weighting of the governance-related component and the weighting on portfolio performance.
18. Normalization is needed to eliminate biases from changes in overall performance trends over time. To some degree, these changes are real, but they can also result from slow evolution in the rating instrument. Some degree of evolution is inevitable in any rating scale and is considered part of a normal process of reassessment.
19. The one-tail significance level is appropriate here.
20. A further concern may be the influence of aid on the quality of policies and institutions. On one hand, aid in the form of budget support and public sector management projects might plausibly be used to support programs to improve government capacity. On the other hand, aid that does not respond adequately to government performance might plausibly have a negative influence on the quality of policies by softening the government budget constraint. We return in part to this relationship in Section E.
21. World Bank (2005e). See also the progression of support instruments set out in World Bank (2003b).
22. This approach has been suggested for IBRD support to some middle-income countries with high-quality policies and institutions.

23. Surveys conducted by the SPA Working Group on Budget Support (SPA 2005) suggest that recipients are not necessarily opposed to conditionality. For instance, conditions can bolster the positions of ministers to pursue needed reforms, and create incentives to work across ministerial lines. On a 1–5 scale, the usefulness of conditionality was rated as 3.1 in 2002–03 and as 3.6 in 2003–04. The intrusiveness and specificity of some conditions may cause concern, as can an excessive number and the instability of financing that can result from high leverage on conditionality. The last is an issue of instrument design, however, rather than one of conditionality per se.
24. This approach could be implemented in a number of possible ways. One would be to separate budget support into a set of well-defined segments, each responding to performance assessments for a given sector (World Bank 2003b). The difficulty of leveraging this strongly on an annual basis is that one year provides a only a short interval for definitively assessing efficiency changes.
25. Infant mortality is not strictly speaking a service delivery indicator and is therefore not used in the budget support operations of the EU. However, data on this variable are easily and consistently available across countries and over time, and it is therefore used as an additional illustration. With more data effort, norms could be derived for a number of service delivery indicators, such as immunizations or performance on standardized educational tests. For an assessment of the linkages between governance, spending, growth, and some of the variables related to the Millennium Development Goals, see Baldacci and others (2004).
26. See Koenker and Basset (1978).
27. These will become public in spring 2006.

PART V
Budget Support Coordination and Conditionality

13

World Bank Conditionality: Trends, Lessons, and Good Practice Principles

STEFAN KOEBERLE AND JAN WALLISER
World Bank

Conditionality is a key implementation challenge for budget support and has been a subject of debate ever since policy-based lending became an important instrument of World Bank financial support in the early 1980s. Many donors and lending institutions use conditions, often with different objectives. The World Bank does so for two reasons: to ensure that the assistance it provides contributes to the country's development objectives (development effectiveness rationale) and to ensure that the resources are used for the purposes intended (fiduciary rationale). The challenge is to find a set of conditions that meets these objectives and can be monitored with little ambiguity.

The conditions in the structural adjustment programs of the 1980s and 1990s generally addressed short-term macroeconomic imbalances and economic distortions by focusing on policies to resolve some of the imbalances and create potential for higher growth. In many cases, conditionality was critical for the advancement of first-generation reforms. However, at times, the reforms were insufficiently owned by the country, subject to policy reversals, and perceived as excessive or intrusive.

Reviews of the effectiveness of development assistance have shown that reforms are more likely to be sustained when they emerge from a country's own domestic political process and are suited to its own specific circumstances (World Bank 2005a). As a result, the past few years have seen the emergence of new approaches to policy-based lending, and the practice of conditionality itself has evolved with increased efforts by the International Monetary Fund (IMF), the World Bank, and other development partners to analyze and improve the effectiveness of their support.

These efforts have been reflected in improvements in the compliance, outcome, and sustainability ratings of policy-based lending during the past decade, as measured by the World Bank's independent Operations Evaluation Department (OED) (World Bank 2005b). However, the development community continues to face practical questions about what conditions to attach to support for development programs.

In this context, in October 2004 the Development Committee of the World Bank and IMF requested a review of the Bank's "policy and practice on conditionality" and a "report on the continued efforts by the Bank and the Fund to streamline their aggregate conditionality" (Development Committee 2004, para. 7). Undertaken over an eight-month period during 2004–05, this review involved workshops, a survey of country authorities, and discussions with executive directors, governments, donors, development practitioners, civil society organizations, and other parties interested in contributing to the debate.[1]

This paper summarizes the findings of the review that relate to the World Bank's policy-based lending.[2] Section A discusses definitions, modalities, and approaches to conditionality; Section B presents recent trends in the World Bank's conditionality; and Section C frames the key implementation challenges that arise in the practice of conditionality. Section D presents key messages of the review, and Section E proposes good practice principles to guide the future use of conditionality.

A. Conditionality: Definitions, Modalities, and Approaches

Definitions

After a quarter century of policy-based lending by the World Bank and of structural adjustment programs supported by the IMF, the term "conditionality" has been interpreted in different ways by country authorities, staff, academics, and outside observers (World Bank 2005a). Some have associated it with all types of activities a country may need to undertake to gain access to or influence the level of financing—including, for example, actions that borrowers need to take to meet the World Bank's operational policies or the selectivity embedded in performance-based aid allocations. Others consider the country policy and institutional assessment (CPIA)—a summary rating of a country's policy environment that affects IDA aid volumes—as additional conditionality. In the extreme case, any interaction of the Bank with country authorities on economic policies and outcomes has been seen as conditionality, in the sense that the outcome of these interactions affects ultimate financing decisions and borrower behavior. For the purpose of this paper, it is therefore necessary to define the use of the term "conditionality" and distinguish it from other considerations.

Definition of World Bank Conditionality

Conditionality in the World Bank context and for the purposes of this paper is defined as the set of conditions that must be satisfied for the Bank to make disbursements in a development policy operation (World Bank 2005d, para. 9). These conditions are maintenance of an adequate macroeconomic policy framework, implementation of the overall program in a manner satisfactory to the Bank, and implementation of the policy and institutional actions that are deemed critical for the implementation and expected results of the supported program. Only conditions meeting these criteria are included in the Bank's loan agreements.

Selectivity Criteria

Conditionality applied at the level of the specific lending operation is distinct from other, broader considerations in Bank lending (World Bank 2005c). These considerations are generally associated with selectivity criteria for making resources available to borrowing countries. Such criteria are based on broad assessments of a country's policy environment rather than the implementation of any specific policy or institutional action, and often change only slowly. In particular, accessing Bank lending requires that:

- the country has its own development program (reflected in government strategy documents, especially—in low-income countries—a poverty reduction strategy paper [PRSP]) that sets out the country's development priorities and strategy;
- the Bank's country assistance strategy (CAS) defines a results framework for CAS outcomes to which the Bank's interventions contribute and indicates a notional lending envelope and instrument mix, including development policy operations where appropriate (World Bank 2005e); and
- the country is considered sufficiently creditworthy for additional lending if it is an IBRD borrower or—for low-income countries—additional resources are available from IDA on the basis of a formula that takes into account population, per capita income, CPIA ratings, a governance factor, and the country's implementation of its existing Bank portfolio.

Considerations specifically concerning development policy lending also include the assessment of ownership of the program of policy or institutional actions, the country's track record, analytical underpinnings, poverty and social impact analysis, environmental considerations, adequacy of fiduciary arrangements, and participatory processes (World Bank Operational Policy (OP) 8.60, *Development Policy Lending,* para. 3).

Modalities

The Bank applies conditionality in a variety of settings.

Prior Actions and Tranche Release Conditions

Policy-based loans can be structured as either single-tranche or multitranche operations. In either case, the funding is available only when the borrower accomplishes critical policy and institutional actions, or loan conditions.

- In a *single-tranche operation*, a program's critical conditions are usually met before the operation is presented to the Bank's Board of Executive Directors for approval. These conditions are referred to as "prior actions" and are listed in a schedule accompanying the legal agreement.
- In a *multitranche operation*, the borrower complies with certain conditions after Board approval and effectiveness. These conditions are in addition to any conditions the borrower must meet for the operation to be presented to the Board. They are termed "tranche release" conditions because they must be satisfied before a tranche may be released, and they are listed in a schedule accompanying the legal agreement. If they are not satisfied, the tranche may be released only if the Board approves a waiver of the conditions.

Triggers and Benchmarks

Aside from the critical policy and institutional actions that constitute loan conditions, a policy-based operation usually includes other substantive elements that embed the operation in a medium-term framework of government policies:[3]

- *Triggers.* Triggers are an important design element of programmatic policy-based lending, which usually consists of a series of single-tranche operations in support of a government's medium-term program (World Bank 2004a). Triggers represent a notional set of expected prior actions for future operations that are critical for achieving and sustaining the results of the medium-term program. Compliance with triggers indicates that sufficient progress has been made to move from one operation to the next (as long as the satisfactory macroeconomic policy framework and program implementation requirements are met). Using triggers as indicative measures of progress provides greater operational flexibility than using tranche release conditions, because triggers can be adapted more easily to a changing program environment. Bank operational documents are expected to explain how triggers were adapted and modified to support program objectives before being converted into the prior actions of a follow-on operation.
- *Benchmarks.* Benchmarks in program matrices describe the contents and results of the government's program in areas monitored by the Bank. They are often used to describe small steps in a reform process (such as the preparation of studies and action plans) that represent significant though not necessarily critical progress markers for the implementation of the program. Although they help define an area of the Bank's policy involvement, they do not determine disbursements of Bank loans or grants and are not intended to become prior actions for future support.

Triggers and benchmarks are not reflected in a lending operation's legal agreements as "conditions." They represent an indicative understanding of measures under the overall policy program that a country intends to implement and are used as a reference framework and management tool.

Conditionality in Investment Lending

The Bank generally discourages the use of conditionality in investment lending. Nonetheless, investment projects may sometimes include agreements on particular policy undertakings that are important for achieving the project's objectives. In particular, sectorwide approaches and adaptable program loans may involve an understanding between the Bank and the recipient government on a sectoral development program. Such cases are outside the purview of this review, but some of its conclusions and principles may be broadly applicable to them.

Changing Approaches

The Bank's understanding of conditionality has changed significantly over time—from the early emphasis on actions for macroeconomic adjustment and growth to more recent attention to the different design aspects of conditionality, including those associated with initiatives to enhance country ownership of programs and streamline conditionality and with Bank-Fund collaboration (Stiglitz 1998; Wolfensohn 1999).

Today the Bank takes a flexible approach to conditionality as evidence of a borrower's commitment to its program suitably combined with capacity building. This approach has been embedded in programmatic lending and the new operational policy for policy-based lending (World Bank 2004e).

Emergence of Programmatic Lending

The Bank increasingly uses a programmatic approach for its policy-based lending (World Bank 2004a). This approach involves a series of single-tranche operations that are presented sequentially to the Bank's Board of Executive Directors, with a medium-term framework specified at the outset that includes completed prior actions, monitorable progress indicators, and expected prior actions (triggers) for subsequent operations.

This approach combines the discipline of a medium-term framework with triggers for subsequent operations that offer the flexibility to accommodate the unpredictability and uncertainty of complex policy reforms. Unlike traditional multitranche operations, which relied on promises of future actions to justify disbursements, each single-tranche loan under a programmatic approach is approved following actual performance—that is, on the basis of already completed actions—and it thus contributes to systematic policy implementation.[4] Typically, programmatic lending is used to support complex medium-term institutional reforms. To the extent possible, programmatic approaches align disbursements with the borrowing country's financing needs during the annual budget cycle. In low-income countries, the poverty reduction support credit (PRSC) is a programmatic development policy loan designed to assist countries that are performing well to implement their poverty reduction strategies (PRSs) (World Bank 2005e).

From Adjustment Lending to Development Policy Lending

In September 2004, the Bank issued a new operational policy statement for use by Bank staff (OP 8.60, *Development Policy Lending*). In replacing the previous guidelines, the Bank retired prescriptive passages on specific policy areas, such as privatization, financial sector reform, and public sector reform, because it had recognized that generalized prescriptions often fail and policies need to be country and time specific.

The new development policy lending explicitly aims at supporting a country's program of policy and institutional actions to promote growth and achieve sustainable reductions in poverty. These lending programs are expected to be based on country and sectorwide analytical work; in addition, operations need to assess the country's fiduciary arrangements; the policy effects on its environment, including forests and other natural resources; and the likely poverty and social impacts of key policies supported by the operation. As regards conditionality, the new operational policy mandates that conditions should be confined to those actions that are critical for implementing the country's program to achieve the expected results. Programs under the new operational policy are expected to reflect programs that have been developed in consultation with stakeholders in the country, and to include a results framework that allows adequate monitoring and evaluation.

B. Trends in World Bank Conditionality

Discussions of conditionality frequently focus on the average number of conditions per loan or tranche. The number of conditions and benchmarks has raised concerns of "overloading" the policy agenda and "intrusiveness," notably in low-income countries. But although the number of conditions may suggest the breadth of engagement and program monitoring, it says little about the actual use of conditions, their content, or their potential impact. For example, neither the number of conditions nor the size of the policy matrix would necessarily represent an additional burden for governments if the conditions were fully aligned with the government's own intentions and timing. The relevance and impact of conditions also can differ greatly depending on the modality (for example, tranche release conditions or future prior actions), the thematic areas of engagement, and the specific formulation of conditions. This section therefore not only reviews trends in the numbers of conditions in Bank loans but also reviews conditionality content and quality.

Number of Conditions

World Bank conditionality as measured by the number of conditions has been sharply reduced. The average number of conditions per World Bank policy-based operation has declined from more than 35 in the late 1980s and early 1990s to about 12 in FY05 (Figure 13.1).[5] This trend can be found in all regions and in all types of borrowing countries, whether IBRD or IDA borrowers (World Bank 2005b).

Number of Benchmarks

By contrast, the number of indicative benchmarks in Bank-supported policy-based operations has increased from an average of about 15 in the early 1990s to around 23 in FY05. The increased use of benchmarks is highly concentrated in programmatic operations in IDA countries, in particular in PRSCs; in core IDA countries, the use of benchmarks per lending operation has risen from 5–10 in the mid-1990s to more than 35 in recent years.

Aggregate Bank-Fund Conditionality

The combined conditionality in programs supported by the IMF and the World Bank has declined, and there is no discernible evidence of a systematic gap in covering key areas of the country policy dialogue (World Bank 2005b). The framework for Bank-

FIGURE 13.1 Average Number of Conditions and Benchmarks per Lending Operation, FY1980–2005

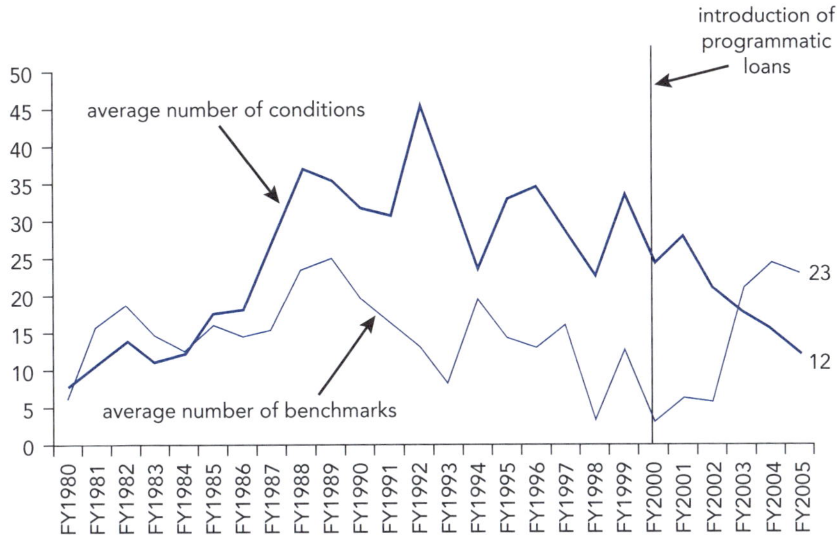

Source: World Bank Conditionality Database.

Fund collaboration introduced in 2001 (World Bank and IMF 2001) encourages the staffs of the two institutions to provide more coherent support to countries through early and systematic coordination on programs and conditionality, with each institution focusing its conditionality on those areas that are deemed critical for the success of its own program (IMF 2001, 2005b).

Looking at the periods before and after 2000 among 30 countries with parallel Bank- and Fund-supported programs, aggregate conditionality (measured per program year for comparability reasons) declined by 25 percent for middle-income countries and by 14 percent for low-income countries.[6] In middle-income countries, the decline in aggregate conditionality mainly reflected a halving of the number of conditions in World Bank programs. In low-income countries, by contrast, it was due more to a fall in the number of conditions in IMF operations.

The decline in conditionality in both Bank and IMF programs can be attributed to both institutions' concentration on their core areas of expertise. When accounting for the Bank's extensive policy dialogue, there seems to be no evidence of systematic gaps in coverage across both institutions. This issue will be kept under review through regular reviews of Bank-Fund collaboration.

Content of Conditions

The lessons of the 1990s show that generalized policy prescriptions often fail, and that no single model of development is appropriate (World Bank 2005f). Difficult institutional reforms such as privatization and trade reform are unlikely to succeed unless strong political commitment is combined with wider public understanding of and support for the process (Nellis and Kikeri 2002; Winters, McCulloch, and McKay 2004). However, development research recognizes that sustainable growth and development are usually based on indispensable foundations: namely, institutions that provide dependable property rights, manage conflict, ensure the rule of law, and align economic incentives with social benefits and costs. To build up these institutions often requires experimentation, willingness to depart from orthodoxy, and attention to local conditions (Rodrik 2003). These lessons are being reflected in the evolving content of conditionality.

Trends

Over the past two decades, the content of the Bank's conditionality in policy-based lending has broadly moved away from its traditional focus—on short-term macroeconomic adjustment and removing major economic distortions—toward support for medium-term institutional changes that are complex and often inherently unpredictable (Figure 13.2).

To some extent, these shifts reflect the changing focus of many countries' policy agendas. Trade policy issues, for example, have become less important, following the significant reduction of trade barriers across the world. In recent years, the content of conditionality has strongly emphasized improvements in public sector governance: support for government efforts to strengthen public financial management, fiduciary arrangements, public expenditures, and public sector reforms now account for the largest share of conditionality. The use of conditionality has increased in the social sectors and declined in the areas of environment, rural development, and urban development, as well as in trade and economic management. Reforms in the financial sector and private sector development continue to be important areas of Bank engagement, but with a focus on improving business environments rather than on privatizing state enterprises.

Sensitive Structural Policy Areas

In particularly sensitive policy areas, the use of conditionality has declined and now focuses more on long-term institutional issues (World Bank 2005g).

- *The emphasis on privatization has strongly declined since the 1990s.* The shift away from privatization is related to the increased attention to the quality of the investment climate as a whole. In noncompetitive sectors, independent of the ownership structure, the institutional framework has become central to the design of reforms.
- *Conditionality on user fees is extremely limited.* Conditions on user fees figure more prominently in the electric power sector (Eastern Europe and Latin America). There are virtually no such conditions in basic health, education, and water; when such conditions are used, they may actually call for the removal of user fees or the design of targeted schemes to improve access for the poor.
- *Conditionality on trade has declined significantly since the mid-1980s* with the increasing importance of international bodies, notably the World Trade Organi-

FIGURE 13.2 Trends in the Share of Conditions by Thematic Area, FY1980–2005

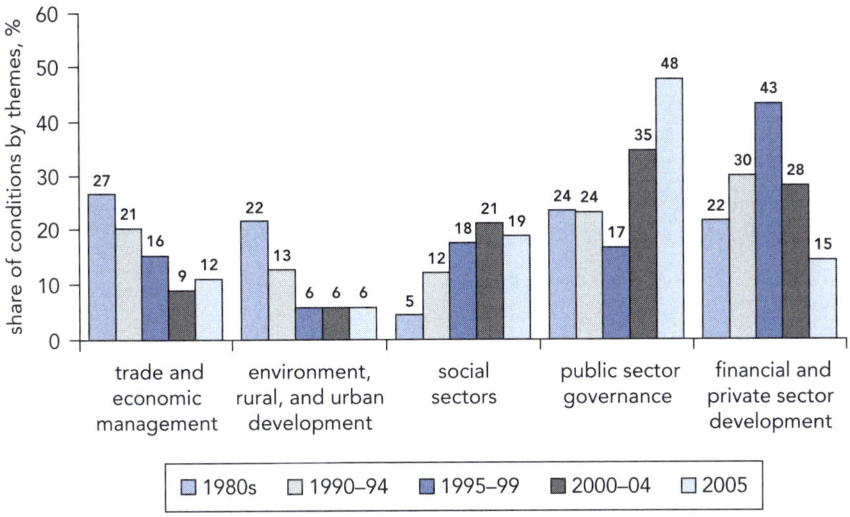

Source: ALCID, World Bank.

zation, in the trade area. The focus of remaining conditions is on institutional issues, such as the performance of customs agencies, product quality, and certification, rather than on tariff rates or trade liberalization.

Compliance and Quality

Development Impact of Conditionality

Several indicators point to improvements in the development impact of Bank support through policy-based operations (World Bank 2005b).

In a survey of country authorities conducted for the conditionality review (World Bank 2005h), 88 percent of the respondents agreed that Bank-supported programs have a positive overall development impact; large proportions of respondents also felt that Bank-supported programs improve growth prospects (82 percent) and contribute to poverty reduction (66 percent), and that the Bank is helpful in setting up systems to monitor and evaluate program outcomes.

Similarly, evaluations by the World Bank's OED indicate that policy-based operations increasingly meet their development objectives: the OED's satisfactory outcome scores for policy-based lending increased from 60 percent in the 1980s to 68 percent in FY90–94 and then rose to 82 percent in FY00–04.[7]

Finally, a recent review of PRSCs (World Bank 2005e; see also Chapter 3 of this volume) finds that only 5 percent of triggers were not met at the time of Board approval of the subsequent operation.

Sustainability and Institutional Development Impact

Most of the governments surveyed for the conditionality review responded that the implementation of policy reforms continues after Bank operations close (77 percent) and that Bank work on institutions has a positive impact (83 percent). According to OED ratings, the likely sustainability and the institutional development impact of policy-based operations have increased considerably. The share of policy-based operations rated sustainable rose from 31 percent of those implemented in FY85–89 to 83 percent of those implemented during FY00–04. Meanwhile, the share of policy-based operations with an institutional development impact rose from 26 percent to 50 percent.

C. Applying Conditionality

The conditionality review examined a number of tensions or implementation challenges in the application of conditionality. These relate to the objectives of country ownership, which may not always align with the Bank's responsibility to ensure that scarce financial resources are used effectively; the notion of performance orientation of financial support, which could test the predictability of resource flows; and the importance of flexibility to respond to unforeseen circumstances in the context of difficult policy changes, which may lead to divergences from a consistent and specific plan. The review also examined the issues of reducing the transaction costs of conditionality through improved coordination with financial partners, designing the scope and specificity of the policy matrix, aligning conditionality with countries' accountability frameworks, and customizing programs to country circumstances.

Implementation Challenges

Country Ownership and Fiduciary Accountability

A critical lesson of the research on aid effectiveness is the importance of country ownership: financial partners can advise on and support, but cannot buy, economic reforms (see, for example, World Bank [1998]; Dollar and Svensson [1998]; Devarajan, Dollar, and Holmgren [2001]). Development financing with strong conditionality but without strong domestic leadership and political support has generally failed to produce lasting change (World Bank 1998, p. 4). Where there is ownership, conditionality allows the borrowing country and the Bank to develop and nurture mutual trust and commitment. The Bank's operational policy recognizes the importance of country ownership, requiring that the Bank's decision to extend development policy lending to a country take into account the country's commitment to and ownership of the program and its track record of reform.

In practice, the level of ownership is not easy to assess. A careful review of the country's political economy and of stakeholders' concerns is required to identify the scope for a sustainable reform program. Given the complexity of country situations, such an assessment goes beyond a simplistic notion of ownership that presupposes a uniform government position or a full consensus. It would not be sensible to suppose that all recipient countries are functioning democracies, respond to the interests of the majority of the population, avoid elite or foreign-interest capture, and maintain a stable course on reforms. A realistic assessment of ownership relies on the government's track record of reform and acknowledges that reforms may be owned by some constituencies and opposed by others who stand to lose from them.[8]

During consultations for the conditionality review, a strong degree of country ownership was widely seen as key to successful policy implementation, with some criticism that conditionality tends to undermine rather than strengthen ownership when it is perceived as imposed (World Bank 2005j). Countries perceive conditionality as less of a burden if the Bank program has been embedded in their own economic policies and programs. Most developing countries see themselves as taking charge of their development strategies and in general welcome access to the global development knowledge of the Bank and other development partners through a process of dialogue. However, some people—particularly representatives of civil society—are concerned that, given the power imbalance, this dialogue itself can become controlling and intrusive, undermining ownership.

Sixty-nine percent of survey participants reported that their country has a development strategy that is widely owned, and 85 percent agreed that the Bank-supported program was well aligned with their country's own medium- and long-term development strategy (World Bank 2005h). A large majority (82 percent) also felt that Bank-supported programs help their government focus on policy actions that support the country's medium- and long-term development strategy. Moreover, 77 percent noted that the implementation of policy programs continues even after the completion of Bank operations. However, there is still room for progress: 50 percent felt that the Bank introduced elements that were not part of the country's program, and 40 percent thought the Bank was not sensitive to political constraints. Thirty-seven percent of respondents to the survey said that negotiations with the World Bank significantly modified their original policy program.[9]

Predictability of Resource Flows and Performance Orientation

In aid-dependent countries, unpredictable fiscal cash flows can lead to macroeconomic instability or inefficient expenditure allocation and execution (Bulíř and Hamann 2003). Recent evidence suggests that unforeseen variations in budget aid disbursements in aid-dependent countries remain large, at about 1 percent of GDP, undermining budget planning (see Chapter 11 of this volume).

Ensuring the predictability of budget support for low-income countries has gained particular relevance in the context of potentially larger aid inflows for achieving the Millennium Development Goals (see Chapter 1 of this volume). Participants in consultations for the conditionality review expressed concerns about the predictability of flows in low-income countries. In the context of developing new approaches to conditionality, one suggestion is to enhance the medium-term predictability of aid by conditioning levels of policy-based aid on a country's overall performance (including fiduciary management) in implementing its program, without tying conditions to specific policy actions (DFID/FCO/HMT 2005).[10]

In middle-income countries, external support typically accounts for a much smaller proportion of budget spending. During the consultations for the conditionality review, middle-income countries expressed less concern about the exact timing of resource flows but wanted clarity on the conditions to be met in multitranche operations and expected prior actions (or triggers) in programmatic operations (World Bank 2005j).

The Bank's programmatic approach to policy-based lending—based on a limited set of completed (as opposed to promised) critical actions that reflect country priorities—has contributed to establishing a regular review cycle that is aligned with the country's processes and provides a more predictable medium-term flow of resources. In low-income countries, the PRSC has helped improve resource predictability and, where early disbursement is critical, the Bank attempts to accelerate the PRSC preparation and negotiation process to improve alignment with the government's domestic timetables (World Bank 2005e). Deeper policy changes to address aspects of medium-term predictability, such as moving from policy actions in individual operations to country-level conditionality through the country assistance strategy (CAS) and the CPIA, would involve complex legal, institutional, and operational changes to the Bank's existing framework for appraising and approving policy-based lending.[11]

Flexibility and Consistency

The Bank applies conditionality flexibly: for example, Bank teams can modulate or postpone disbursements of subsequent programmatic operations as a response to a country's underperformance or to an assessment of the adequacy of the macroeconomic policy framework or the overall progress of the program. Similarly, some programmatic loans contain an element of discretion when their triggers are not precisely defined.

While there may be an advantage to Bank teams in having flexibility to address concerns about underperformance, undue discretion also carries the risk of uncertainty. The challenge for the Bank is to exercise this discretion consistently and transparently.

The Bank and other financial partners have developed a variety of ways to address the issue of excessive flexibility (World Bank 2005e); among them, transparent decision rules and clearly specified triggers can help set out clear expectations of financial partners and recipients and clarify their mutual accountability.

During the consultations for the conditionality review, participants expressed broad support for using a series of programmatic operations, with judgments made on overall progress toward medium-term program results rather than, as traditionally, on compliance with ex ante conditions (World Bank 2005j). However, middle-income participants, in particular, suggested that the Bank consider the issue of consistency in making judgments, requesting that an objective way be defined to measure results and compliance with lenders' expectations for future support.

In programmatic operations, triggers (or expected prior actions) help reconcile the tension between flexibility and discipline in multiyear programs. Triggers allow the Bank to make an overall assessment of whether enough progress has been made to move to the subsequent operation. Good practice suggests that triggers should be formulated in a clear and precise manner to be useful as a performance measure, unless they explicitly refer to the outcome of transparently conducted sector reviews.

In principle, failure to meet triggers could result in a reduction of the commitment amount or a delay in the next operation. In most PRSCs, triggers were converted into prior actions and met before approval of the next operation, indicating that the programs were progressing as intended. Nonetheless, in some cases, implementation deviated significantly from expectations (5 percent of triggers were not met at the time of Board approval), and the Bank responded in a graduated manner. In most of these instances, the Bank determined that enough progress had been made in other areas to justify moving to the next operation. But in some cases, lending volumes were reduced or the operation was delayed until corrective measures had been implemented. Finally, a few PRSC-supported programs went entirely off track, and the programmatic series was interrupted (World Bank 2005e).

The Bank has an exceptional record of transparency. For all development policy operations, it discloses program documents (which set out the country context, the entire program supported by the operation, the specific conditionality, and the indicative benchmarks and triggers), tranche release documents, and legal documents.[12] Decisions on the loan amount and timing of programmatic operations are transparently reported on the basis of an assessment of progress against specific triggers.

Outcome-Based Conditions

The *Annual Review of Development Effectiveness 2003* called on the Bank to "experiment with approaches that would complement intermediate indicators and conditions with indicators of direct poverty reduction results or other outcome-related indicators" (Operations Evaluation Department 2004b). During the consultations underlying the World Bank's conditionality review, there was a rich debate about the potential role of outcome-based conditions, with a universal recognition of their importance for monitoring and evaluation to ensure that programs reach their intended results over the medium term (World Bank 2005j). Of particular interest is the emerging experience with an approach of the European Commission to condition variable tranches on service delivery indicators (EC 2005).

Linking annual disbursement volumes directly to outcome indicators faces a number of practical challenges, such as unavailability of suitable short-term outcome indicators (for example, for public finance management and private sector development), substantial time lags in data availability, unreliability of data, and the risk of penalizing governments for outcomes that are outside their control (World Bank 2005e). A formulaic application of outcome-based conditionality could also reduce the flexibility and adaptability of the programmatic approach.

Country experience therefore suggests that outcome-based indicators are an essential tool for measuring results but that their use as conditions for disbursement should be approached with caution (World Bank 2005c, 2005e).

Improving Coordination with Financial Partners

Harmonization of financial support holds the promise of reduced transaction costs and a reduced burden of conditionality for the recipient country, particularly in aid-dependent low-income countries. However, policy matrices may expand as a variety of financial partners ask a government to reflect their focal areas in a harmonized framework. Hence, as more financial partners participate in the design of a unified program, the number of conditions could increase, and the quality and relevance of the substance could suffer. Moreover, bilateral partners' use of political conditionality in unified policy matrices will require careful allocation of oversight responsibility among partners for different areas of the policy matrix, particularly for those, such as the Bank, whose Articles of Agreement prohibit political involvement.[13]

Consultation Feedback on Harmonization and Alignment

All parties agree on the need to encourage development partners, including the Bank, to make further progress in aligning aid with country priorities, harmonizing practices, and reducing transaction costs. Most believe that to make progress in this respect will require strong leadership by recipient governments. To a large extent, therefore, the question of alignment is associated with strong country ownership and with financial partners' respect for that ownership.

Improving Harmonization and Support for Country-Owned Strategies

It is important to minimize the risk that the conditions used by development partners and the Bank will contradict or impair each other. If there is a clear division of labor among the partners, each partner's approach to conditionality can be effective and can reduce transaction costs. Assigning specific areas to lead partners that have a comparative advantage can help. In low-income countries, the common framework provided by countries' PRSs and annual progress reports has become a useful platform on which to facilitate donor coordination and harmonization. The aim is for governments to negotiate a single, comprehensive reform program, with lower costs in time and effort, preparation, reporting, and monitoring. The content of all donor programs should be consistent with the priorities of the country's PRS and with each other, and should be streamlined.[14] The challenge for the Bank is to conduct its due diligence and coordinate its conditionality with that of other development partners while aligning operation-specific conditionality with the results framework set out in the CAS and retaining its own distinct accountability.

Scope and Specificity of the Policy Matrix

The presentation of a country's policy program that is supported by a development policy operation can draw on existing policy matrices if a government's development strategy is well articulated and prioritized. Where this is not the case, policy matrices tend to go well beyond simply listing conditions for disbursement, to serve as a reference framework for a subset of government policies supported by the Bank. They also help to spell out implementation steps for achieving program objectives. Governments have often found it useful to have Bank assistance in operationalizing a more detailed framework for implementation and results—particularly when this serves as a vehicle for conducting substantive sector dialogue and addressing cross-sectoral issues.

Length of the Policy Matrix

The average policy matrix—which includes prior actions, triggers, and indicative benchmarks—has expanded over time, even though the number of prior actions has decreased (World Bank 2005b). The main reason seems to be that the sectoral coverage of PRSCs, and therefore the scope of the policy program, typically broadens as the program matures, and thus the number of indicative benchmarks increases. Country authorities themselves may at times prefer to rely on a detailed matrix that helps them implement the sectoral agenda of the PRSP. In countries where several donors are providing budget support, the proliferation of benchmarks has also been driven in part by efforts to include specific donor preferences in a harmonized framework.

Consultation Feedback on Scope of Conditionality

During the consultations for the conditionality review, some stakeholders pointed to the length of the policy matrices in Bank-supported operations, criticizing them as intrusive micromanagement that is inconsistent with national PRSs (World Bank 2005j). Others, however, stressed that World Bank conditions, triggers, and benchmarks need to be seen in the wider context of the country's own development program and the conditionality set by other development partners. They recognized that countries need to focus attention on a few actions that are critical to success, particularly where capacity is weak—and that development partners, including the Bank, should do likewise.

Survey Results on Conditions and Benchmarks

Authorities responding to the survey did not seem to recognize the strong distinction the Bank makes among conditions, triggers, and benchmarks (World Bank 2005h). Seventy-five percent of survey respondents believed that their countries must comply with *all* the policy actions listed in the policy matrix. At the same time, 74 percent believed that the government only needs to meet those of the actions in the matrix that it has agreed with the Bank to be critical. These seemingly inconsistent responses may be partly explained by the fact that the number of benchmarks varies widely across the countries covered by the survey, with fewer in IBRD countries than in IDA countries.[15]

Many respondents felt that the size of the policy matrices was determined more by the inclusion of multiple sectors (79 percent) than by collaboration and harmonization among external development partners (38 percent). Borrowers generally agreed (72 percent) that policy matrices include measures that complement those necessary to achieve the program's outcome, and that in multisectoral operations the number of actions a government needs to take to obtain financial support increases significantly (77 percent).

In addition, 21 percent of respondents thought that some critical actions were not included in matrices. Finally, respondents saw little difference in the flexibility to obtain formal waivers (in multitranche operations) or adapt triggers (in programmatic operations).

Avoiding Matrix Overload

The clear challenge for the Bank is to avoid overloading the policy matrix. While advice to Bank teams has emphasized the need to focus on a few critical conditions and triggers that are truly essential for the achievement of the program results, teams have had considerably more latitude regarding benchmarks and outcome indicators. In addition to further clarifying its approach, the Bank can do better at choosing actions that are critical for achieving the outcomes and thus limiting the proliferation of measures in multisectoral settings.

Aligning with Countries' Accountability Frameworks

For greatest aid effectiveness, the monitoring of policy-based support should be aligned with a country's own processes. Experience has shown that when conditionality and results monitoring are based on a country's own accountability arrangements, they can make a substantial contribution toward greater alignment across different dimensions, particularly in countries where budget support supplies a significant share of total budgetary resources. In better-performing low-income countries, PRSCs help align the Bank's policy-based financing with other donor budget support programs, and budget support with the government's annual PRS, budget, and planning cycles (World Bank 2005e).

Consultation Feedback on Accountability and Monitoring

During the consultations, participants stressed the need for stronger domestic arrangements for financial management and accountability, transparency, and monitoring of progress and results (World Bank 2005j). Donors providing direct budget support in low-income countries see such improvements as important for reducing their own fiduciary risk—and they, and recipient countries, also see a major payoff in increasing the coherence of countries' budget processes and strengthening budget execution.

Survey Results on Designing and Implementing Programs

Country authorities suggest that the Bank can simplify the preparation, negotiation, and implementation of programs it supports (World Bank 2005h). The greatest preparation challenges are poverty and social impact analysis (58 percent), prior analytical work (57 percent), and consultations with stakeholders (51 percent), which respondents viewed as more burdensome than fiduciary aspects (30 percent).

Budget and Planning Cycles

Programmatic support is expected to be closely aligned with the government's budget and planning systems and timetables. The aim of facilitating the government's ability to plan and execute the budget could be met by confirming commitment amounts at a time when the government is finalizing the budget and then disbursing when the resources are needed for program implementation. Governments are particularly interested in having the implementation reviews with the Bank (and other financial partners) take place in line with established internal accountability cycles—such as the annual performance review for the PRS or the government's internal reporting cycle during the budget process.

Customizing to Country Circumstances

Many development issues and questions have no single answer, and to a large extent the relevance of any issue and the response to it seem to depend on country-specific circumstances (World Bank 2005f). The *Annual Review of Development Effectiveness 2003* (OED 2004b) identified strong analytical underpinnings as a major factor contributing to the success of policy programs, but noted that the Bank had not always paid enough attention to alternative perspectives or to individual country circumstances. The review said that generic "best practices" should give way to intensified efforts to customize and adapt knowledge to specific localized problems, taking country experience into account.

Variety of Experiences

Much of the debate on conditionality over the past few years—and much of the consultation for the conditionality review—revolved around the notion of regular budget support for well-performing low-income countries (see Chapter 1 of this volume). Middle-income countries, despite their obvious differences from low-income countries, also endorsed many of the concepts and possible best practices that emerged from these debates (World Bank 2005j). However, the approach to conditionality clearly must vary with the circumstances of recipient countries, including their implementation capacity and aid dependency, degree of commitment and reform readiness, effectiveness of resource use, fiduciary framework, macroeconomic stability, and financial vulnerability to crises. In particular, the conditionality review singled out the case of development policy lending to fragile states and subnational entities in middle-income countries.

Conditionality in Fragile States

While participants in the consultations agreed that the role for policy-based support in fragile states (also termed low-income countries under stress) is limited, but they also recognized that in some cases it can play a critical role. The World Bank and other donors have been providing budget support for poverty reduction and reconstruction in such fragile states as Afghanistan and Timor-Leste, and in the West Bank and Gaza. In post-conflict transition situations, there are some good examples of the use of policy-based financing to structure donor dialogue on priorities and leverage complementary capacity building (World Bank 2005l).

Lessons of good practice in conditionality are emerging from this experience: particularly, the need for the design of conditionality to take into account a broad assessment of progress and the country's limited institutional and implementation capacity. Conditionality can be helpful if it bolsters the government's case for implementing policy measures to which it is already committed, and it helps operationalize its strategy. But the imperfect policy analysis of underlying transition programs, the fluctuating policy environment, implementation constraints, and high cost of disbursement delays all call for building flexibility into program design.

Conditionality for Subnational Lending

Some World Bank borrowers, including most of its large borrowers, have a federal or quasi-federal structure of government, in which states or provinces have legislative and administrative autonomy in various areas and independent budgetary authority, including the right to raise revenues and issue debt. The performance of such state or provincial governments can matter greatly for the country's macroeconomic stability, growth, and poverty reduction.[16] The Bank can provide development policy operations to subnational units in support of state-level programs of fiscal and sectoral policy and institutional actions if these units have satisfactory fiscal relations with the central government and a sovereign guarantee. General design considerations for conditionality also apply to operations in support of state-level reforms (World Bank 2005m).

A specific issue for subnational development policy lending concerns the actions the central government should take to allow the state's program to succeed (for example, actions to tighten budget constraints for states). Such actions are neither under the control of the state government nor limited to the state that receives the loan proceeds. Hence they should typically be part of the prior actions to be taken before the loan is presented to the Bank's Board for approval.

D. Key Messages of the Conditionality Review

Operational Policy Framework

The findings of the literature and feedback received during consultations confirm that the Bank has the capacity to apply best practice under the umbrella of its existing operational policy. OP 8.60 is consistent with a view that conditionality is not a coercion to undertake reform and does not prescribe policy content. The policy includes the principles of country ownership, selectivity in Bank support, strong analytical underpinnings for policy choices, alignment of Bank operations with a country's own development strategy, customization of support to country circumstances in the context of the CAS, criticality of conditions for program results, harmonization of support and conditions, alignment of support cycles with a country's monitoring and evaluation cycles, and transparency of Bank documentation. The operational policy also allows a variety of lending approaches, in line with borrower preferences and needs.

Ownership

In its operational work, the Bank has fully recognized the importance of ownership for development effectiveness—but, like other development partners, it is grappling with the practical challenges of assessing ownership and responding to changing policy environments. To ensure country ownership of Bank-supported programs, the Bank is systematically aligning its CASs with countries' development strategies.[17]

Rather than imposing a burden, conditionality in development policy lending should help measure progress. In addition, the Bank provides analytical work and advice on policy options and recognizes that borrowers require policy space to make their choices and seek the support of stakeholders. Difficulties can arise where ownership issues are blurred, since different groups in government and in the country may support the program to different extents. Generally, the operational policy therefore advises staff to make judgments on the basis of the country's track record. However, further study of political economy considerations and indicators of ownership for Bank operational purposes is typically needed. When the Bank does not see enough evidence of ownership, it normally chooses not to engage in development policy lending, rather than attempting to substitute conditionality for ownership. Applying selectivity may not always be easy, especially in genuine turnaround cases and fragile states, where the Bank often needs to weigh the risks of engagement carefully against the potential for large impact.

Matrices in Multisectoral Programmatic Operations

The Bank has made important strides in adapting its lending practices to complex reform programs and focusing conditions on critical actions—but as policy matrices in multisectoral programmatic operations expand, they are perceived as unduly complex and intrusive. Although the Bank has reduced the number of conditions and moved to programmatic lending operations in which conditionality is based on completed actions, the programmatic support of broad multisectoral government programs—particularly in low-income countries—has given rise to increasing numbers of benchmarks in the policy matrices that describe and operationalize the program supported by the Bank. Although these benchmarks are considered indicative milestones to gauge progress and help manage program implementation, and are not critical actions that could hold up disbursements, there is a perception of Bank intrusiveness and the risk that capacity in low-income countries may be strained as matrices become more complex.

Balancing Predictability and Performance

The Bank has applied conditionality in a clear and transparent fashion, but it needs to exercise the flexibility of programmatic approaches cautiously to balance predictability with performance. Bank conditionality is generally set out clearly in advance through conditions or anticipated prior actions (triggers) for future support, which are transparently disclosed to a wider public through the documentation available on the Bank's external Web site. However, particularly in programmatic operations, the Bank's approach allows discretion in the design of prior actions and a gradual adjustment of support volumes in response to performance. This flexibility must be applied in a disciplined setting of progress evaluation, or the Bank may be seen as "raising the bar" or announcing support volumes late and forcing borrowers to find alternative financing arrangements. Borrowers need clarity about conditions and level of support at a sufficiently early stage to adjust their budgetary planning. Although the Bank has delivered predictable budget support for well-performing low-income countries through PRSCs, its practice of adjusting development policy lending volumes annually on the basis of performance evaluations has also raised questions by some governments and other financial partners about medium-term predictability.

Balancing Harmonization and Accountability

The Bank's approach fully supports international efforts to harmonize financial support while retaining its own distinct accountability. In the context of harmonization, borrowers are concerned about the expanded or inconsistent conditionality that may be involved in dealing with a large number of development partners, and the consequent transaction costs. While the Bank's governance structure and review processes require separate accountability for making independent assessments, its approach to conditionality encourages harmonization around a unique and coherent set of performance measures, in line with the Paris Declaration on Aid Effectiveness and good practice developed by the Development Assistance Committee of the Organisation for Economic Co-operation and Development (OECD-DAC 2005). At the same time, to avoid the perception of collusion and to reduce the risk of greater aid volatility, some borrowers may prefer "diversifying" the risk of disbursement shortfalls by allowing development partners to disburse against different indicators in the single framework.

E. Good Practice Principles

The messages emerging from the conditionality review are an important input for disseminating and reinforcing good practice in the Bank's development policy operations. Building on these messages, the review yielded a set of good practice principles as guidance for Bank staff in the preparation of development policy lending operations and application of conditionality (Table 13.1).

These principles build on the foundation laid by the new operational policy for development policy lending, which will continue to guide the Bank's policy-based sup-

TABLE 13.1 Good Practice Principles

Ownership	Reinforce country ownership
Harmonization	Agree upfront with the government and other financial partners on a coordinated accountability framework
Customization	Customize the accountability framework and modalities of Bank support to country circumstances
Criticality	Choose only actions critical for achieving results as conditions for disbursement
Transparency and predictability	Conduct transparent progress reviews conducive to predictable and performance-based financial support

port (World Bank 2004e), and on the findings of the 2005 review of the poverty reduction strategy approach (World Bank and IMF 2005). The latter identifies and discusses in detail how the PRS approach can reinforce domestic accountability mechanisms in low-income countries and help balance them with external accountability. In particular, it notes the importance of functioning domestic mechanisms to ensure that external accountability frameworks do not overwhelm domestic settings. It also emphasizes the importance for functioning domestic accountability mechanisms of sufficient support for country analytics, monitoring and evaluation, participation, and space for policy dialogue. The good practice principles outlined below build on these findings and emphasize how conditionality and approaches of the Bank's policy-based lending can be mindful of striking a balance between internal and external accountability needs.

Although they are generally applicable across the Bank, the principles may translate into different forms of engagement depending on country circumstances. (Box 13.1, for example, describes the Bank's experience in two different countries.)

Ownership: Reinforce Country Ownership

Bank operations and conditionality should actively contribute to broad ownership of the programs, policies, and institutional actions undertaken by the government. To this end, the Bank's development policy lending should support only policies and programs for which there is clear evidence of ownership. In low-income countries, the policies that are described in a PRS adopted by the government after broad-based consultations typically meet that expectation. In other countries, the Bank may ascertain, for example, that the government's proposed policies and programs gained strong support through an election or parliamentary process. In all cases, evidence of a track record of sound policy implementation strengthens the articulation of government programs.

Assessing Country Ownership

Political economy analysis may give additional insights into the program's likelihood of success and could be employed both at the CAS level and the level of the individual operation.[18] It may also be necessary for the Bank to allow sufficient time for coun-

BOX 13.1 Good Practice in Different Country Circumstances

Low-income country—Mozambique: In Mozambique, the Bank is engaged in a series of programmatic development policy credits and grants, including a PRSC. Mozambique adopted a PRSP in 2001 and has prepared annual updates of the government's implementation plan for the PRSP, a retrospective on PRSP implementation, and a budget implementation report. The preparation of these reports is closely aligned with the government's own budget cycle and internal accountability process. Drawing on these documents, in 2004, the government began to agree annually with a group of donors (numbering 17 in 2005) on a maximum of 50 actions and results indicators in a performance assessment framework (PAF). Progress made under the PAF is reviewed twice a year, in April-May and September-October, with the first review focusing on achievements in the previous year and the second on mid-year implementation and the draft budget for the following year. Donors use the April-May review to announce financial support for the following fiscal year (starting in January), and each donor can modulate or withhold support based on this evaluation of performance. Proposed donor financing is firmed up in September-October, once the final budget for the following year has been presented, and, in the Bank's case, the Board has approved the loan. The Bank has aligned its disbursement conditions and triggers for future PRSC support with the PAF, drawing a set of six to eight measures from this internally coherent framework, and has aligned its disbursement cycle with the PAF review cycle.

Middle-income country—El Salvador: The Salvadoran government, elected on the basis of a strong electoral platform, requested Bank support for its agenda in the form of a series of programmatic development policy loans under the 2005–08 CAS. A first development policy loan was approved in early 2005 on the basis of the strong policy actions the government had already taken toward trade integration and competitiveness, fiscal reform, and better governance. Discussions with the government identified an additional set of 10 follow-on actions in these areas as key progress indicators for future support. In addition, the government identified its targets for results indicators in these policy areas for the CAS, which were also reflected as expected results of the development policy loan. The Bank has aligned its review of progress under the series with the parliamentary budget approval cycle to permit ratification of future loans in conjunction with future budgets. The close link of the intended reforms with the country's growth potential and fiscal performance also implies that the Bank's assessment of creditworthiness and thus the overall volume of future fast-disbursing lending during the CAS period are tied to progress made under the program.

try processes, such as parliamentary debate, to be completed before establishing the details of its support. If the government's own policy agenda is insufficiently owned or weak, the Bank would now choose not to provide development policy loans rather than substitute conditionality for ownership.

Supporting Analytics and Capacity Building

Efforts to reinforce ownership need to rely strongly on country-tailored policy and institutional analysis and, as appropriate, enhancement of country leadership capacity. Through the CAS and in consultation with country authorities and other financing partners, the Bank should identify any relevant analytical gaps, which can be filled by the Bank itself (through analytical and advisory activities and economic and sector work), the country, or third parties. This work should then feed into the country's policy-setting mechanism, such as a PRSP process. Further, if gaps exist, the Bank should seek to support the country in building its institutional capacity for leadership in policy formulation, implementation, monitoring, and evaluation through joint analytical work or targeted technical assistance and capacity-building operations.

Harmonization: Agree Upfront with the Government and Other Financial Partners on a Coordinated Accountability Framework

Under the leadership of country authorities, Bank staff should reach understandings with the government and other partners on a single, internally coherent framework for measuring progress under the government's program. Typically, such an accountability framework should comprise actions, outputs, and outcome indicators drawn directly from the government's own program over a medium-term period. As appropriate, depending on the type of Bank intervention, the accountability framework could apply to the overall program or to a sector program. In countries with support from a multitude of partners, the accountability framework should be used to foster coherent interventions: all financial partners would support a set of policies that aim at achieving a single set of results agreed under the accountability framework. Typically, harmonized and coordinated support for government policies would include an upfront division of labor, under which the Bank could follow the lead of others in specific areas, as appropriate, but without jeopardizing quality standards.

Customization: Customize the Accountability Framework and Modalities of Bank Support to Country Circumstances

Accountability frameworks should never be used to add policy actions to the government's agenda, or to leverage outside preferences. Any agreed accountability framework should be fully consistent with the government's expressed policy intentions and internal accountability mechanisms.[19] Moreover, the detail, size, and frequency of review of progress under government programs should fully reflect country circumstances, such as country capacity and reform readiness. For example, in countries that have already undertaken a substantial reform process, reviews would typically focus on sustained policy implementation rather than on new reform actions, and an accountability framework would contain only a few critical steps or indicators to track broadly whether sustained policy implementation is having the intended results. By contrast, if substantial reform efforts are still under way, the accountability framework could reflect a closer tracking of policy actions and results over time and contain a limited set of additional benchmarks relevant to the program.

The modalities and timing of support should respond to country- and program-specific needs. The choice of lending design—whether the Bank engages through single or multiple tranches, in a programmatic or short-term fashion, in a broad or focused manner, or on a national or subnational level—should reflect country preferences and needs. Policy-based support in fragile states requires particular attention to country circumstances and institutional capacity. The Bank's support for sensitive policy reforms (such as privatization, trade liberalization, and user fees) should be based on an understanding of the country-specific political economy of reform and may be warranted when such reforms are part of a well-designed and broadly owned government strategy. Similarly, the timing of Bank operations should be aligned with the country's financing requirements and its internal approval processes, such as the budget session of parliament.

Criticality: Choose Only Actions Critical for Achieving Results as Conditions for Disbursement

In establishing the conditions for lending, Bank and country staff should choose, from within the agreed accountability framework, those policy and institutional actions that are critical for achieving the results of the program and are aligned with the CAS results framework. These actions could serve as prior actions for single-tranche operations, conditions for tranche releases under multitranche operations, or indicative future prior actions (or "triggers") for follow-on operations in a programmatic support framework.

Triggers in programmatic operations should be clearly marked and identified to country authorities and in Board documents. The flexibility gained by specifying only triggers should not be used to introduce unexpected new disbursement conditions, nor to lower performance standards.

If the government agrees, triggers can, if necessary, be modified or replaced with alternative prior actions to achieve the intended results. However, this change should not be used to "leverage" other reform areas by adding new conditions from within or outside the accountability framework. For example, the benchmarks contained in many policy matrices to describe the broader policy program should generally not be used as additional prior actions for disbursements of subsequent loans. At the same time, once an area has been identified as critical through the choice of a trigger, the Bank should clearly indicate in follow-on operations how the intended results are being achieved, even if sometimes the original actions have been modified to reflect changes on the ground.

Presentation of Program

Bank operational documents should rely to the extent possible on the government's existing presentation of programs and policies. If the agreed accountability framework coherently sets out actions, outputs, and outcomes for the government program, there is no need to include more than a few conditions and triggers, as well as a set of related results indicators, in the Bank's Board documentation. These conditions or triggers and results indicators would identify how the Bank follows progress under the program and clearly set out expectations of the Bank for making resources available. Results indicators would also serve as tools to evaluate to what extent Bank operations achieve their intended development outcomes, and they should be equivalent to those reflected in results-based CASs. The accountability framework—that is, a set of actions, outputs, and outcomes—could be used as an attachment to the letter of development policy (LDP) to define government intentions under the program, and the text of the LDP could become a short and focused summary statement of policy intentions that cross-references the accountability framework. In this case, there would be no need to include a separate Bank policy matrix in program documents.

Outcome Indicators

Outcome indicators are important for measuring results. For Bank operations, output and outcome indicators with clear baselines and targets should be included in performance frameworks as key instruments to measure results under the government's program, and they should be monitored closely. Selected indicators from the performance framework could also serve to measure results in the Bank's CAS and lending operations. However, they should be used only cautiously as disbursement conditions or triggers. To serve as conditions or triggers for Bank disbursements, indicators would need to be reasonably responsive to government actions within a short timeframe and able to be measured with satisfactory timeliness and accuracy. A few service delivery indicators in the social sectors (such as the vaccination rate or the completion rate for primary education) may meet these criteria, but generally institutional reforms, notably in public financial management, are less amenable to such an approach.

Transparency and Predictability: Conduct Transparent Progress Reviews Conducive to Predictable and Performance-Based Financial Support

In the context of medium-term Bank support, progress should be reviewed regularly and in line with a country's monitoring and evaluation cycle. In many countries, such reviews take place in the context of the budget preparation or the preparation of annual PRS progress reports, and the review may build on several staggered sectoral review processes. To the extent possible, the government's own internal accountability processes (such as required reporting to parliament) and reporting systems and monitoring frameworks should be used to meet the Bank's and others' information needs.

In addition, the Bank should actively encourage governments to strengthen their own internal accountability mechanisms and monitoring systems. Transaction costs of reviews should be minimized by harmonizing with the reviews of other interested partners, reducing the number of individual requests for information.

On the basis of the review of progress, which should draw on implementation of triggers and conditions, and an evaluation of the overall advancement toward anticipated results, the Bank should adjust financing levels to performance. In this regard, recent experience with graduated responses under PRSCs offers useful lessons on the modulation of financial support. Any financial support decisions should be announced early enough to be taken into account in the country's own decision-making and budget allocation processes.

Results Management and Measurement

Performance reviews should actively promote a culture of results management and measurement. Using the policy actions and indicators in the accountability framework as the basis, the performance reviews should not only report on policy implementation and progress made, but also foster analysis and feedback on improving the impact of government policies.

Endnotes

1. The background papers of the review have been published as *Review of World Bank Conditionality*, Operations Policy and Country Services, Washington, DC: World Bank, September 2005, and are also available at http://www.worldbank.org/conditionality.
2. The term "policy-based lending" is used here to denote financial support through loans or grants given by the World Bank in the form of the now-retired adjustment lending (under OD 8.60) and development policy lending (since the introduction of OP 8.60, *Development Policy Lending* in September 2004).
3. The Bank's OP 8.60 (para. 14) requires that stand-alone single-tranche operations be embedded in a medium-term framework.
4. Experience with the programmatic approach to date suggests that it has been robust and effective in a wide range of country circumstances, largely because of the design features that provided sufficient flexibility to facilitate a stronger focus on results, participation, and harmonization (World Bank 2004a).
5. Conditions here include prior actions (preceding Board presentation), effectiveness conditions, and conditions for tranche release, which are set out in the Bank's legal agreements.
6. In view of the methodological difficulties in comparing conditionality of the two institutions and the small sample, these results should be interpreted with some caution. For the Bank, the numbers differ little from previously reported figures of conditions per operation.
7. Survey results suggest that, although borrowers' overall evaluations of development outcomes are in line with the OED's findings, improvements could be made in linking Bank activities directly to poverty reduction.
8. For a discussion of conceptual frameworks for assessing ownership, see World Bank (2001a, p. 73), Johnson and Wasty (1986), and World Bank (2005i).
9. A recent survey of 15 African countries (SPA 2005) finds that depending on the policy area, 20–30 percent of conditions were not literally drawn from the PRS but consisted of measures that were either drawn from other government documents or were considered broadly consistent with the PRS.
10. Eifert and Gelb (Chapter 12 this volume) examine the costs of potential aid misallocations arising for IDA from a move to CPIA-based development policy lending volumes.
11. Such a change could imply, for example, that (1) the CAS becomes a Board-approved document allocating resources over a three- to four-year period based on CPIA scores or creditworthiness criteria, (2) a larger part of financing is delivered through fast-disbursing operations, (3) the Board drops its prerogative to review individual lending operations during the CAS period, and (4) annual disbursements are automatic, absent major changes in policy implementation.

12. The Bank's OP for disclosing program documents and tranche release documents of development policy loans is specified in OP 8.60, paras. 29 and 31, respectively. Disclosure of legal documentation after loan effectiveness is described in the World Bank's Disclosure Policy, para. 72.
13. IBRD Articles of Agreement, Article 4, Section 10; and IDA Articles of Agreement, Article 5, Section 6.
14. In a number of countries, budget support donors have signed formal memoranda of understanding with the government and donor partners to clarify the rules of the game, including mechanisms for the resolution of differences (World Bank 2005k).
15. Of the survey respondents, 33 percent were from core IDA countries and 14 percent were from Africa, where most PRSCs are being implemented.
16. In India, for example, state-level deficits account for almost half of the consolidated fiscal deficit, and achieving country-wide objectives relies on significant policy and institutional reforms at the state level.
17. In IDA countries, all CASs are now based on the PRSP (World Bank 2005n).
18. For a set of indicators to gauge the ownership of PRSs, see World Bank (2005i).
19. As noted under OP 8.60, development policy lending is only extended to countries with sufficiently strong programs. For example, a country would be expected to address identified fiduciary weaknesses under its own program.

14

Budget Support, Conditionality, and Impact Evaluation

JAN WILLEM GUNNING
Free University, Amsterdam, and Tinbergen Institute

The perceived failure of aid conditionality has led to proposals to tie aid to results achieved rather than to policy changes. Results-based aid has now started to be implemented, and this paper reviews some of the implications for the relationship between aid donors and recipients.

The structure of the paper is as follows: Section A sketches the background for results-based aid. In an extreme form of selectivity, aid allocation is based on measured performance. This is not expected to change the incentives of recipient governments, yet most donors do expect their allocation decisions to have incentive effects. Section B therefore considers aid as a contract, examining how performance targets should be set and whether governments should be compensated for adverse events beyond their control. Section C discusses the experience of the European Union (EU) with results-based aid. Section D considers the effects of shocks and the possibility of introducing an insurance element in aid contracts, and also addresses the question of whether making aid results-based introduces undesirable volatility in aid flows. Section E, on aid evaluation, discusses the implications of the switch to budget support and the growing reliance on performance indicators. Section F concludes.

A. The Case for Results-Based Aid

The idea for results-based aid grew out of the critique of conditionality. Donors have always attached conditions to aid, often at the level of individual projects. Sometimes the objective was to promote donor interests (for example, by requiring that bidding for procurement for a project would be restricted to firms in the donor's country). More commonly, the donor was convinced that imposing conditions will raise the project's returns and therefore be in the interest of the recipient government. Such paternalism might be a source of friction, since obviously the two parties could disagree on what best serves the government's interests (Collier and others 1997).

Ex ante conditionality at the project level has been criticized on many different grounds. The fungibility critique is the most important one. It argues that if aid is fungible, the donor deludes himself: what his aid makes possible is the government's marginal project, which may be very different from the project the donor thinks he is financing. In this situation, "what you see is *not* what you get" and conditionality makes little sense (World Bank 1998).

The importance of aid as project finance receded in the 1980s, when donors tried to use structural adjustment lending to change the policy environment in developing countries. Conditionality was increasingly applied at the national level—for example, to trade policy, fiscal reform, or privatization—rather than at the level of individual projects. A substantial empirical literature, using case studies or growth regressions, has shown that the type of conditionality used under structural adjustment lending did not work.[1]

In some cases, as in Zambia under Kaunda, the reforms required by donors simply were not implemented, in spite of conditionality. More commonly, as in Vietnam and Uganda, the reforms were implemented, but as the result of a domestic policy debate rather than donor pressure. Finally, there are many instances, such as the famous case of food marketing liberalization in Kenya, where conditionality did succeed in bringing about reforms but these were not maintained.[2]

The experience with aid for structural adjustment revealed the ineffectiveness of ex ante conditionality where aid was contingent on *promises* of reform. In the 1990s, ex post conditionality was proposed as an alternative. Under ex post conditionality, sometimes called results-based or performance-based aid, the amount of aid depends in a previously agreed way on progress realized over a given period and measured by an agreed set of indicators (see, for example, Collier and others [1997]).

Performance-based aid could easily have remained a pipe dream of academics. That it was implemented owes much to the conjunction of two developments. First, the *Assessing Aid* report (World Bank 1998) became extraordinarily influential, spreading the message of the failure of conditionality very widely. Second, rational choice models of government behavior in response to aid contributed to a growing awareness that the effectiveness of aid depended crucially on the incentives for governments to use aid in desirable ways.

A well known example is the political economy model of Adam and O'Connell (1999). Here private agents choose a level of savings and allocate their savings between an informal sector, where they escape taxation, and a formal sector, where they are taxed. By its choice of a rate of taxation, the government determines the growth of the economy through the incentives thereby provided to private agents for investing in the formal sector. The government serves the interests of a subset of the population: it uses the aid it receives and its tax revenue to finance an amount of government spending (which is fixed in this model) and transfers all remaining resources to the favored subset of the population.[3]

The size of the subset whose interest the government serves determines the nature of the state. If the subset is very small, the government has strong incentives to tax. At the margin, all additional tax revenue accrues to the favored group while the cost of taxation—lower growth—is borne by the entire economy. The cost-benefit ratio becomes less favorable for taxation if the subset expands, because there is then less scope for letting the excluded group bear the costs. At some critical level, the state will be "sufficiently representative": it will still serve the interests of a subset but will find it optimal to reduce taxes and thereby promote growth.

It is easily seen that these two regimes have radically different implications for the effects of aid. If the regime is narrowly based (that is, if the favored subset is very small), then aid will be used entirely to increase transfers to the favored group. Aid is then ineffective in raising growth. If the state is sufficiently representative, however, it will act as a "developmental state": at the margin aid is then used to reduce the tax rate. This gives private agents an incentive to invest in the formal sector. As a result of this incentive effect, aid increases growth. Such models help to explain the increasing support for selectivity in the allocation of aid. Apparently there are countries in which aid cannot be effective, simply because the government has no incentive to use it in a way that would make it so. According to this argument, since the evidence from the conditionality literature suggests that donors cannot "buy" reform, donors should simply accept that they have no role in such countries. Selectivity then implies that aid is allocated only to those countries where it can be effective.

The selectivity approach does not rely on incentive effects. However, selectivity will of course be reinforced if recipient governments strive to satisfy the criteria that would qualify them for aid. In addition, if the amount of aid is a function of performance and the government knows this, then the government may have an incentive to improve its performance, as perceived by the donor. Such incentive effects are central in the discussion on the design of the "aid contract."

B. Aid as a Contract

While the language of "cooperation" and "partnership" suggests that donors and recipient governments pursue common goals, the reality of aid relationships is, of course, often very different. Once it is recognized that the two parties—donors and recipient governments—may have very different aims, it makes sense to see their relationship in contractual terms.

The challenge is to design what economists call an incentive-compatible contract. This is an arrangement in which one party (the principal) has imperfect control over the other party (the agent), but the terms of the contract give the agent an incentive to behave in a way that promotes the interests of the principal.[4] Contract theory focuses on situations in which the interests of the two parties diverge and where the principal can only imperfectly observe the actions of the agent. In the political economy literature on aid, this principal-agent framework is applied with the donor as the principal and the government as the agent.

As the Adam-O'Connell (1999) model clearly illustrates, aid will be wasted (from the donor's point of view) when it is unconditional and the government has no incentive to promote growth and reduce poverty or to pursue other objectives that donors cherish.

Selectivity in aid allocation can be seen as a radical response to this situation: if aid is likely to be wasted in such environments, then it should be allocated exclusively to countries where governments have an incentive to use aid in a poverty-reducing way.[5] Since donors have been singularly unsuccessful in "buying policy reform," the argument runs, there is no point in trying to use aid to promote policy change. In this view, aid is therefore tied to success, not as an incentive for governments to choose policies that might generate success, but simply to ensure that aid is not wasted but allocated to countries where it can be productive.

A less extreme view would leave some room for an incentive effect of aid. Donors may succeed in influencing government behavior if they tie aid to results *and if that link is perceived as credible*. The emphasis on incentives implies that the relationship between donor and recipient government is indeed seen as a contract.

Performance-based aid ("ex post conditionality" in the jargon) can be seen as a practical way of implementing this moderate version of selectivity. The donor provides aid in the form of budget support and the amount of aid increases with performance as measured by a set of agreed indicators. Clearly, the framework of contract theory is very relevant for the analysis of such budget support. Here, we briefly consider four issues of contract design for budget support: completeness of the contract, the choice of target levels for the various indicators, procedures for audit and evaluation, and risk sharing between the contract partners.

Completeness of Contracts

Donors and governments typically set multiple targets. This raises the question of to what extent aid will be reduced if one or more of the targets are not met. In ex ante conditionality, a similar situation arose: in principle, all conditions had to be met, so that failure to meet any one of them would result in *all* aid being withheld. In practice, such a drastic response seemed so inappropriate that this all-or-nothing aspect of ex ante conditionality came to be seen as lacking credibility.

A similar issue arises for ex post (performance-based) conditionality: if all targets are to be met, then a single failure would jeopardize the entire aid budget. As before, this uncompromising approach would make the aid contract less than credible. Alternatively, then, the contract would have to specify a formula, indicating how much aid is to be "earned" with progress on each of the indicators. Such a formula would indicate trade-offs: superior progress in one dimension would offset disappointing outcomes in another dimension.

So far, many donors (with the notable exception of the European Union, discussed in Section C) have been rather reluctant to specify such trade-offs and commit themselves to a "mechanistic" formula. As a result, the early use of performance-based lending was remarkably vague: targets were specified, but it was unclear how much money was riding on them. Obviously, such an incomplete contract cannot provide effective incentives (Collier and others 1997; Adam and Gunning 2002).

Choice of Target Levels

Consider how the targets set in the contract can be made realistic. Where there is uncertainty over what is feasible, there may well be a danger that the recipient government will try to set unambitious targets. As the EU recognizes, if a country sets modest targets it may get more aid than a country that is making more progress but had set more ambitious targets (European Commission [EC] 2005, p. 40). The incentive to play safe is not just a theoretical possibility. In Uganda in 2001, when targets in the education sector were missed, the government reacted by lowering the targets (Adam and Gunning 2002).[6]

Making targets realistic would require some international comparability. Collier and others (1997) proposed a regression-based approach to set growth targets. A growth regression with various controls for initial conditions and geographic growth determinants such as landlockedness could be used to derive an estimate of a "normal" growth rate, in the sense of the expected value for a country with a particular set of characteristics. Targets could then be set in such a way that the "normal" amount of aid would be disbursed if this average performance were realized, with revisions upward or downward for better or worse performance.

Clearly, this approach can be extended to other performance indicators (see, for example, Chapter 12 of this volume). Targets derived in this way would be seen as fair since they would incorporate all available information on the difficulty of progress in a particular set of circumstances. It would be difficult to argue that an international average, corrected for observable intercountry differences, sets too high a standard. Such an approach would remove the incentives for donors and governments to set low targets so as to avoid acrimonious debate when targets are not met. It might also introduce an element of international competition. This could well provide a powerful incentive, as did the comparisons of India with China in the debate on economic policy in India prior to the liberalization.

Procedures for Audit and Evaluation

If aid is tied to measured performance, then a key question is who collects the performance data. Obviously, measured outcomes may be inconvenient both to the government and to donors. Leaving the responsibility for verification to the contract partners therefore raises a moral hazard issue. As yet, there are few indications that data have been withheld or altered, but incentives to do so clearly exist. There seems to be a strong case for independent data collection: once indicators are agreed, the audit function could be assigned to independent consultants or researchers. Just as donors have come to recognize the need for independence in evaluation, they should now recognize the case for independence in data collection.

Risk Sharing between Contracting Parties

Should results-based aid allocations be corrected for circumstances over which the government has little or no control? This is a perennial question (Collier and others 1997; EC 2005, p. 49).

For example, suppose the donor has tied its aid disbursements to reductions in infant mortality, and infant mortality rises as a result of a drought. Should aid be cut because the infant mortality target has not been reached and, if so, by how much? Or should the donor in fact offer insurance, compensating for the drought by raising aid above the level the government would otherwise be entitled to?[7] The answer depends on whether the government can mitigate the impact of the drought on infant mortality and, in addition, whether its efforts to do so can be reliably monitored by the donor. Very likely, there is considerable scope for government action (for example, through targeted drought relief, food storage programs, and development of credit and insurance markets). But it is also likely that such government actions can at best be only imperfectly monitored by the donor.

In the debate on aid effectiveness, one can distinguish two radically different solutions to problems of this kind. One school argues that the extent to which the government has affected the outcome is a matter for ex post negotiation between the two parties. In effect, this amounts to abandoning results-based aid, because under such an arrangement there is no contract ex ante specifying state-contingent aid disbursements. Since the terms of the contract are left unspecified, they can have no incentive effects. In effect, this school argues for a return to ex ante conditionality. Since there now is overwhelming evidence that such conditionality is not effective, this solution is simply not credible. However, it enjoys considerable popularity.

What is the alternative? Analyzing the problem in terms of contract theory, it is readily seen that the situation is analytically equivalent to the case for partial insurance. The argument is straightforward.[8] Taking the case of infant mortality, suppose the outcome depends both on exogenous shocks and on efforts of the government. In particular, the government is able to reduce, though not to zero, the probability of a bad outcome. However, the donor is unable to monitor the government's efforts. Hence the donor observes outcomes but is unable to determine to what extent these are due to exogenous events beyond the government's control or to the government's actions (or lack thereof) in response to the *possibility* of events such as a drought.

Since the donor cannot observe the government's efforts, the contract can only be written in terms of outcomes. Though both parties recognize that a bad outcome may not be the government's fault, they understand the contract must be written in terms of outcomes. How much aid will be disbursed is therefore mechanistically determined by the observed outcome. The contract would provide full insurance if aid were independent of the outcome; the donor would then in effect fully compensate the government for a poor outcome. Clearly, this would remove any incentive for the government to exert itself so as to reduce the probability of a bad outcome.

Under an efficient contract, however, the government will make that effort even though its efforts cannot be observed. Partial insurance achieves this by imposing risk sharing on the two parties. Technically, the contract must satisfy the *incentive constraint*. This means that when the government chooses to allocate resources to, say, programs affecting child health, it thereby reduces the probability of high infant mortality sufficiently to make this worth its while, through the increase in *expected* aid. Under such a contract, the government will receive *less* aid (compared to a simple results-based aid program) when the measured results are good and *more* aid when they are poor. In this sense, the aid involves an element of insurance.

The first point to note is that this insurance is partial. Complete insurance is not incentive compatible under asymmetric information: the government would become passive. This point is relevant for the case of budget support. It is often suggested that results-based budget support should be amended in such a way that governments are *fully* compensated for events beyond their control. But, as the example of drought illustrates, the issue is not whether an event is beyond the government's control, but rather to what extent a performance indicator such as infant mortality is affected by such an event. Clearly, this is a very difficult question, and in this area, the perfect may well be the enemy of the good.

Even so, there is some scope here for advancing beyond pure guesswork. For example, cross-country regressions can be used to estimate the effect of various easily observable variables (such as the occurrence of a drought) on infant mortality.[9] This goes some way toward estimating the impact of government actions. Alternatively, and more convincingly in my view, one can use microstudies (impact evaluations) to estimate this effect more directly. This information can then be used as input into the design of the aid contract.

Implications for Performance-Based Aid

As the discussion above shows, the design of aid contracts involves two information problems. One can be called model uncertainty: we do not know the effect of the government's actions on the chosen performance indicators. The other information problem is that the government's actions themselves are not known, at least to the donor: this is the standard case of informational asymmetry in contract theory.

A second point to note is that some of the risk is borne by the donor. That this is efficient seems to be insufficiently appreciated by the donor community. Donors understandably want to keep aid contracts as simple as possible, and they are therefore reluctant to make contracts state-contingent. In practice, their choice leaves all risk with the government, giving the government the maximum incentive to take measures that increase the probability of good outcomes. However, such an arrangement may hold little attraction for a risk-averse government.

Where recipient governments typically have very limited scope to deal effectively with risk, refusing to extend insurance is unlikely to be an effective aid policy. To take an example, the empirical literature on the effect of trade shocks shows that positive shocks contribute very little to growth in developing countries, and negative shocks substantially reduce growth.

This suggests that there is a case for aid as insurance.[10] The donor could use the regression evidence to derive an estimate of the effect of a particular event (a drought) on an indicator (an increase in infant mortality by x). It would like to give the government an incentive to take measures that reduce the impact. Probably it lacks the information (for example, on how much compensation is needed to induce the government to take additional measures) that is needed to design an efficient partial insurance contract. What it can do offer partial compensation (a fraction of x) in the aid contract contingent on the occurrence of a drought.

The question of whether performance-based aid should be designed so as to offer an element of insurance is one to which we return in Section D.

C. Implementing Results-Based Aid: Design and Experience

The implementation of results-based aid owes much to the EC.[11] The key characteristic of European budget support to African, Caribbean, and Pacific countries is that part of it is a fixed tranche and part a variable tranche. Payment of the fixed tranche is tied to satisfactory macroeconomic performance and retains the all-or-nothing character that belied the credibility of traditional ex ante aid conditionality: that is, in principle, a failure on any aspect of macroeconomic performance would justify withholding the entire tranche. The obvious comparison is with a nuclear threat: if the only options are doing nothing or imposing enormous damage, the threat to "go nuclear" for any, possibly minor, infringement is not credible. At present, the variable tranche is still fairly modest, accounting for about 35 percent of the total amount.

In its review of 34 programs, the EC (2005) found that the percentage of the variable tranche disbursed ranged from 65 to 85 percent.

The EC distinguishes four types of performance indicators: those measuring input, output, outcome, and impact. Input measures the resources provided, such as the budget allocation for primary schooling. Output measures the direct results of the activities financed. For example, output in the education sector can be measured by the number of schools built, schoolbooks delivered, or teachers trained. Outcome is vaguely defined as "results at the level of beneficiaries"; examples include school enrollment. Impact measures ultimate objectives—for example, poverty, literacy, or morbidity rates.

The EU approach is gradually gaining wider support. For example, both the Swedes and the Swiss are experimenting with variable tranches tied to performance in Mozambique. It may be that as more donors shift to budget support and, through better coordination, increasingly agree on the indicators to be used to measure success, they will find the all-or-nothing alternative to a graduated system increasingly untenable. At the limit, when donors fully agree on the indicators, either all donors will cut off aid or none will. Coordination therefore very much worsens the "nuclear threat" aspect of all-or-nothing systems. Hence such aid systems become less credible as donor coordination improves. As donors become aware of this growing credibility problem they are more likely to adopt graduated response systems (EC 2005, p. 47).

In practice, this means that performance is measured on the basis of a small number of indicators, that these are scored (0, 0.5, or 1), and that a weighted average of the scores is calculated. This then determines what fraction of the variable tranche is disbursed.

A number of aspects of the European system are worth noting. First, the system is entirely transparent: the government knows how much it will receive, depending on the performance indicators. The link between results and disbursements is, in the phrase of the EU's critics, mechanistic. During an unfortunate episode, "grossing up" was applied (scores were multiplied by 1.25 after the fact to be able to disburse higher amounts), but this practice was quickly abandoned (EC 2005, p. 39).

Second, the indicators used are measures of output or outcome, not of impact. Indeed, the EC insists that the indicators used for the variable tranche need to be measured annually (EC 2005, p. 7).

Third, about two-thirds of the aid provided belongs to the fixed tranche and is tied to satisfactory macroeconomic performance. My interpretation is that the EC is gradually moving from one system to another and that eventually the entire aid program will be of the variable tranche type. However, the present hybrid is difficult to understand. Since the fixed tranche has the old all-or-nothing character, an entire aid program (rather than just the fixed tranche part of it) should cease if the macroeconomic conditions are not satisfied. More important, as in our earlier examples for Uganda and Zimbabwe, the "show-stopping" conditions that donors have in mind are typically outside the macroeconomic domain.

This suggests that recipient governments face a complicated and potentially confusing set of signals: (1) there are circumstances, apparently not clearly spelled out, that will stop the entire program; (2) there are macroeconomic events that might stop the disbursement of the fixed tranche, but it is difficult to believe that the donor would choose such a drastic approach if all the conditions associated with the fixed tranche were not violated; and (3) there is a category of events that affect the performance indicators with precisely known consequences for the disbursement of the variable tranche.

An additional concern is that the macroeconomic conditions are often rather vaguely specified, leaving much room for interpretation, disagreement, or negotiation (EC 2005, Table 3a.). For Malawi in 1999, for example, what was required was "adherence to the structural adjustment program's macroeconomic framework and ESAF benchmarks." For Uganda in 2000, the EC required a "satisfactory macroeconomic background;" for Benin in 2003, "*conclusions positives à l'issue des revues de la FRPC,*" and for Rwanda in the same year, "*le gouvernement doit poursuivre avec le FMI son programme de réformes macro-économiques.*" Adam and Gunning (2002), in their preliminary assessment of the experience with the EU's system in Uganda, concluded that the aid contract had as yet changed little.

D. Shocks, Results, and Predictability

A key concern in the debate on aid effectiveness is the predictability of resource flows. Particularly in African countries—where aid often finances a very large part of public spending—there is a concern that effective management of public spending requires long-run commitments. It is sometimes suggested that this need may be difficult to reconcile with results-based lending where, at least in principle, aid flows can suddenly diminish if targets are not met.

This concern confuses *volatility* with *predictability*. Certainly aid flows can be volatile under results-based lending. This would happen if the achievement of targets varied substantially from year to year. However, to the extent the government can influence the outcomes, aid flows are predictable. (This is, of course, the very idea of results-based lending: the contract has an incentive effect only if the government knows exactly how much aid it will receive as a result of the outcomes as measured by an agreed set of performance indicators.) In these circumstances, aid flows can diminish but this would not come as a surprise. Obviously, this is only part of the story: outcomes are also affected by events that are beyond the control of the government, and this does introduce an element of unpredictability.

However, it is a mistake to view this unpredictability as a disadvantage of results-based aid. Presumably the counterfactual would be a situation in which aid was stable (not being tied to possibly volatile outcomes) whereas outcomes were not. Given a choice, the government would *prefer* the unstable aid flows under the results-based aid contract if the latter were designed as a partial insurance contract, as discussed in the previous section. Indeed, if the aid-cum-insurance contract is well designed, the government has no incentive to reject it in favor of an arrangement with stable aid but no insurance.

Hence it is misleading to emphasize that resource flows may be *less stable* under results-based aid. The point is rather that under this system, the government will face *less risk* than under stable aid flows. A risk-averse government will therefore prefer the unstable aid flows implied by the partial insurance contract. Once it is recognized that the aid contract involves insurance, the apparent contradiction is easily resolved: the contract enables the government to share some of the risk it faces with the donor.

The EU takes quite a different position on this issue. In response to the question "Should the government be penalized for something for which it is not solely responsible?" the EC (2005, p. 49) makes two points. The first is that although the chosen performance indicators "are not directly within government's control, they are measures over which the government has very large leverage, for good or ill: if primary enrolment is low, for example, while it is true that government cannot (and probably should not) force children into schools, enrolment is probably low because schooling is unaffordable, inaccessible, or of such low quality that parents see no point in sending their children to schools. All of these are factors within government's control. Hence in general the kinds of indicators used are readily susceptible to government action."

This is obviously true for outcome indicators such as school enrollment, but it is not true for impact indicators. These measure progress toward higher-level targets such as the Millennium Development Goals for reducing poverty or under-five child mortality. Government control over the achievement of such targets is only partial. This poses a dilemma. Either results-based lending should be gradually shifted toward reliance on impact indicators—in which case the claim that the measures are within the government's control is no longer valid. Or the aid contract should continue to be defined in terms of measures that are under government control—in which case the contract gives the government no incentive to strive for higher-level development goals. Before long this dilemma will have to be faced.

The EC (2005, p. 50) summarizes its position on general (as opposed to sector-specific) budget support as follows:

> . . .we judge it appropriate to use a small number of results indicators, at outcome level, recognizing that this strikes the best balance between what is swift-changing enough to be meaningful annually, close enough to Government control to be relevant to public decision-making, but sufficiently synthetic to capture a wide range of actions sufficiently closely linked to actual outcomes (indeed, often being desired outcomes themselves) to be strong measures of poverty reduction itself.

Note that here it is taken as self-evident that indicators should be "swift-changing enough to be meaningful annually." At the same time, these will be "strong measures of poverty reduction itself."

This combination is neither feasible nor desirable. It is not feasible, because poverty reduction is typically a slow process that proceeds in fits and starts; annual observations vary too much to give a meaningful indication of long-run trends. Nor is it desirable. In a hypothetical world without uncertainty, the results of aid would be produced fully predictably from inputs via outputs and outcomes to impact. Given such a mechanistic "production process" one could measure results just as well at the beginning as at the end of this process (Adam and Gunning 2002, p. 2053). Clearly, as soon as uncertainty is introduced, early indicators become imperfect predictors of final results. It is then sensible to monitor intermediate results. However, such monitoring is intended to establish whether the country is still on track. It cannot be a substitute for measuring final results—that is, impact. Indeed, ownership is considered important precisely because there is no unique way to reach particular targets. Basing aid allocation on inputs, outputs, or outcomes is therefore fundamentally inconsistent with ownership.

Here donors are caught in a dilemma. They have tried to resolve the dilemma by denying it, as in the EC's statement, which in fact asserts that the two functions *are* compatible. Adam and Gunning (2002) proposed a distinction between, on the one hand, those indicators designed to form the basis for the donor's aid allocation decisions, and, on the other, those designed to monitor interim progress. That proposal is still relevant.

Trying to combine the two functions, as in the EU practice, is undesirable for two reasons. First, as noted, it undermines ownership. If an intermediate indicator shows a deterioration, that calls for an audit to establish the reason. If instead the deterioration triggers a reduction in aid, the incentive effect may be perverse, with the government being punished even though it was on track toward the ultimate objectives.

These questions have a bearing on the emerging practice of selectivity. Under selectivity, donors active in a particular country are, by definition, in broad agreement over the government's policies as these affect poverty: without such agreement, there would be no justification for aid. In addition, they need assurance that the government's general policy stance will not change fundamentally in the short run. In these circumstances, donors must make two very different decisions: whether the country still qualifies for aid and how much aid it should get.

The first decision requires a judgment as to whether an event has occurred indicating that the government's general policy stance is no longer the one the donors agreed with. Adam and Gunning (2002) described this as a "show-stopping" condition. The important point to note is that performance indicators are *not* designed for that purpose. Measuring achievements in terms of school enrollment, vaccinations, or the number of teachers trained makes sense only if the government's policy stance is one that ensures the good policy environment in which donors are willing to support the country. For example, school enrollment in Zimbabwe might be quite satisfactory, but donors have decided that the country does not qualify for aid.

As Adam and Gunning stressed in the case of Uganda, one needs to distinguish clearly between indicators that inform the decision whether or not to support the country and indicators that inform the decision about the scale of that support. Ironically, Uganda's donors were quite clear on the former, but extremely vague on the latter. It was clear in 2001 that continued donor support depended on the extent of corruption in Uganda and the country's involvement in the war in Zaire. By contrast, no "transparent mechanism exists to allow donors to sign clearly the conditions under which the country may expect increased or decreased support even though such a mechanism may be implicit in the thinking of many donors" (Adam and Gunning 2002, p. 2052). The government may find the resulting vagueness annoying.

The donor position is consistent if one adopts the extreme form of selectivity, whereby the donor does not believe that he can influence the government by building incentives into the aid contract. However, donors do seem to believe in incentive effects. This makes their position incoherent: the vaguer the link between aid and performance, the weaker the incentive offered to the government.

The EC's second reaction to the objection that its system may penalize a government for an outcome beyond its control is to recognize that "an exogenous shock" may disrupt a government's plans. In this case the indicator concerned is "excluded from the calculation" (EC 2005, p. 49). As a practical solution, this is impeccable. However, it implies that the insurance function of aid is abandoned.

The EU uses no impact measures. To some extent, this is understandable. As has long been recognized, long lags may occur between government actions and, say, poverty reduction. Tying aid to its impact on poverty would then reward (or punish) a government for the actions of its predecessors, while giving it little incentive to reduce poverty if it does not expect to be still in power when the results of its actions show up as a reduction in poverty. But using no impact indicators distorts incentives. For example, in education a typical indicator is enrollment, but there is no attempt to assess what children learn at school. Where, as in many countries, enrollment has expanded very rapidly, educational quality may have deteriorated.[12] A well-known example is that when the number of boreholes drilled in rural areas was selected as a performance criterion, more effort was expended on drilling boreholes and less on maintenance, so that water quality suffered.

These observations have implications for auditing and evaluation. First, the two functions must be independent to reduce manipulation of the performance indicators as much as possible. Second, they should move beyond the agreed performance indicators to investigate the relationship between these indicators and final objectives.

E. Impact Evaluation

Aid-supported development activities are evaluated to an unusual extent; indeed, it is difficult to think of public sector activities on which more information is collected for taxpayers. In most donor agencies, however, evaluations have focused on process. Evaluation reports indicate whether planned activities were undertaken as envisaged, whether objectives (often formulated in vague terms) were reached, whether problems were encountered, and, if so, what action was taken. There is much to be learned from such reports, but most are silent on what taxpayers really want to know: did the aid work?

Increasingly, formal econometric techniques are used to address just that question. Such impact evaluation tries to establish a convincing counterfactual so that measured results can be compared with what would have happened without the aid-supported activity. Where randomization is involved (as when a schooling program was implemented gradually and participating schools were chosen randomly), impact evaluation is very similar to the experimental designs used in the sciences. In the absence of randomization, statistical techniques need to be used to construct the counterfactual. Impact evaluation was first developed in labor economics. Recently, it has become very popular in development research,[13] and in the last few years, donors have started experimenting with impact evaluations. In part this reflects their growing awareness that traditional evaluation methods, while certainly useful, do not address the issue of aid effectiveness.

The recent emphasis on budget support, ownership, and results-based lending affects the development of aid evaluation in several ways. First, as donors switch from financing projects to budget support, they may come to feel that the effectiveness of aid should no longer be assessed at the micro level but at the macro level instead, as in the growth regressions that are used to derive efficient aid allocations. Second, donors might come to feel that if the aid is tied to outcomes, there is no need for impact evaluation.

Both of these reactions would be mistaken. To start with the latter point: if performance indicators record progress—for example, a fall in poverty—aid may still be ineffective, for two reasons. First, the fall in poverty may have nothing to do with the aid; without impact evaluation, it would be impossible to avoid falsely attributing the success to aid. Second, when the success is in fact correctly attributed to aid, it is possible that the fall in poverty was achieved at very high cost. This points to the need for cost-benefit analysis. This is rare in modern impact evaluations, which usually are content to establish whether or not aid has a statistically significant effect. By contrast, cost-benefit calculations are becoming more common in the macro literature on aid effectiveness. For example, Collier and Dollar (2002) calculated that on average US$1 million of aid had the effect of reducing poverty (as measured by the headcount) by 300 people. Such an average then can be used as a benchmark by which the poverty impact of aid in particular countries can be judged.

How is aid to be evaluated if it is given in the form of budget support rather than project finance? This is a fundamental problem. The methodology of impact evaluation is suitable only for activities with homogeneous output, such as an increase in the school enrollment of poor children. It is not designed to evaluate the aggregate of government activities in, say, the health sector. But if donors contribute to a common pool in that sector, aid effectiveness obviously requires an assessment of the effectiveness of all activities in the sector. Given the heterogeneity of such activities, the sector cannot be treated as a single project for the purpose of evaluation.

What is the alternative? In principle, given a reliable description of the activities within a sector, it should be possible to draw a representative sample and apply impact evaluation to each of the activities in the sample. Aggregating the results of the evaluations, one would arrive at an estimate of the average effectiveness of aid to this sector. (Note that this approach will not establish the marginal effect, which may well differ substantially from the average effect.) Organizing such a sectorwide evaluation is complicated, costly, and unattractive for a single donor to undertake. The logic of the common pool approach suggests that such activity should be undertaken jointly by the government and all donors involved in the sector. After all, the average effect of a sector activity is the same, irrespective of the source of financing. These issues are beginning to be discussed, though as far as I know, no such sector evaluation has yet been undertaken.

F. Conclusion

The proposal for results-based aid was a response to the failure of conditionality. While selectivity in aid allocation does not rely on any incentive effects, the question of how aid affects the incentives facing the recipient government has recently become prominent, partly as a result of the work of political scientists in the rational choice tradition. In addition, as results-based aid is beginning to be implemented, questions about the appropriate design of the aid contract are becoming urgent.

We have noted that in practice the aid contract is incomplete. Many donors have agreed on the performance indicators to be used, but they have been reluctant to spell out how much aid would fall or rise with performance. If the contract is to affect incentives, then such vagueness must be avoided.[14]

A key issue in the design of results-based aid contracts is, of course, the setting of targets. To affect incentives, targets must be set at realistic and sufficiently ambitious levels. Thus far, this task has been left to consultations between donors and the individual recipient governments. We have suggested that the target-setting process could be improved by using cross-country regressions to introduce international comparability. The regressions would show the level of progress that could reasonably be expected on a particular performance indicator in a country with a particular set of characteristics. The aid contract could then specify how much more the country would receive if this expected level were exceeded or, conversely, how much aid would be cut if performance fell short of this average.

We have suggested that there is a need for independent measurement of performance. This need has not yet come to prominence, precisely because the aid contract has usually been left vague. However, as the relation between performance and aid begins to be specified more precisely, there are strong incentives to manipulate the data. Independent verification of the performance indicators is therefore becoming increasingly important.

There is a case for including partial insurance in the aid contract. The key issue here is that the impact of a negative shock on performance indicators is rarely known and that it depends in part on actions undertaken by the government, both before and in response to the event. International evidence can be used to reduce uncertainty about the impact of the shock. Incentives for the government to mitigate that impact can be built into the aid contract by offering partial insurance rather than full compensation.

The aid contract could therefore be improved in four ways: by (1) indicating precisely how much aid a country will get, depending on performance; (2) basing target levels on international average performance, controlling for relevant country characteristics; (3) ensuring independent data collection and auditing of a country's performance; and (4) including partial insurance for particular shocks such as droughts.

A corollary is that aid may well be volatile. This would be the case if it included an insurance element. If the aid contract were well designed (in the sense that the government has no incentive to reject it), the government would see the volatility of aid as beneficial rather than detrimental.

Donors have attempted to use performance indicators for two very different purposes: to indicate whether the country still maintains a policy environment in which aid can be used productively, and to measure progress toward ultimate objectives such as poverty reduction. We have argued that these two functions cannot be combined: donors will need to distinguish the monitoring variables from the performance indicators to which they tie their aid.

Though it is tempting to view results-based lending as a guarantee for aid effectiveness, this would be mistaken. There remains a need for impact evaluation (in the econometric sense of the word) to assess whether aid actually makes a difference in the chosen impact indicators. Much of the impact evaluation literature stops at that point. There is a need to move beyond establishing impact toward cost-benefit analysis. And a further and much more difficult challenge is to use impact evaluation to evaluate budget support at the sector or national level.

Endnotes

1. See, for example, Gunning (2001) for a review of this literature.
2. In Kenya, the reform of maize marketing was a condition of World Bank assistance. The Kenyan government agreed, implemented the reform, and subsequently reversed the liberalization. Eventually the reform was implemented and reversed seven times. The episode has been cruelly but accurately summarized by the saying that the Kenyan government sold the same reform to the World Bank (indeed to the same Bank vice president) seven times in a row.
3. One could interpret the fixed amount of government expenditure (other than transfers) as a reflection of the participation constraint of the excluded part of the population. They will consent to the regime's policies provided they receive a particular amount of public goods.
4. Contract theory has become very influential in development economics. For a textbook example, see Ray (1998). Azam and Laffont (2003) is an example of the use of contract theory to analyze conditionality.
5. The most influential statement of the case for selectivity is probably the *Assessing Aid* report (World Bank 1998).
6. The EC somewhat downplays the issue, stating that "Revisions of target levels made so far do not seem unduly lacking in ambition" (2005, p. 43).
7. There is an old literature on the use of aid to compensate developing countries for trade shocks through mechanisms such as the European Stabex program. See, for example, Collier and others (1999). Guillaumont and Chauvet (2001) revived the case for aid as insurance, in the context of the debate on criteria for the allocation of aid across countries. Cf. Gunning (2001, 2004).
8. See, for example, Ray (1998, p. 602–605), for a formal treatment.
9. This is the approach advocated by Collier and others (1997) to correct for, say, the impact of trade shocks.

10. See Collier and Gunning (1999) on the trade shocks evidence and Collier and Dehn (2001) on the impact of aid and shocks on growth.
11. See Adam and Gunning (2002) and Adam and others (2004) for early assessments of the EU's performance-based lending in four African countries. For a more recent and much more comprehensive assessment, see EC (2005).
12. There is shocking evidence on this for Uganda. See Adam and Gunning (2002, p. 2050).
13. For an entertaining and fairly nontechnical introduction, see Ravallion (2001). One of the most famous applications is Miguel and Kremer (2004). See Duflo (2004) for an overview of recent developments.
14. This is an instance of the irony of aid: donors often shy away from the very measures that would make aid effective. Gunning (2004).

15

Trust, Conditionality, and Aid Effectiveness

PAUL MOSLEY AND SULEIMAN ABRAR
University of Sheffield

Recent literature on aid effectiveness has been very skeptical about the power of conditionality to increase aid effectiveness. Verdicts such as "the failure of [conditional] program aid" (Collier 1997; Collier and Dollar 2001, 2002; Svensson 2000, 2003) have become common. In a context where the main goal of aid is poverty reduction, such a negative judgment of a key element of aid is more than unfortunate.

The paradox is that conditional program aid, or budget support, in fact has numerous successes to report. A number of poor developing countries—including Ethiopia, Mozambique, Tanzania, Uganda, and with certain reservations, Ghana, Nicaragua, and Rwanda—have restored reasonably sustained pro-poor growth, and the role of budget support aid in this process has clearly been substantial. The jury is still out on what differentiates these cases from the still distressingly common cases of failure, but an increasingly distinctive characteristic of the success cases is the transformation of the old conditionality game into looser *trust-relationships* between the providers and the users of budget support aid, which are often linked to an emerging agreement on poverty strategy. Within this "new conditionality" (Mosley, Hudson, and Verschoor 2004), slippages on some performance criteria are condoned so long as trust remains about fundamentals. What is at issue, and has not properly been examined by the large literature on conditionality and budget support, is how such trust, or social capital between donor and recipient representatives, is formed and sustained. More technically, this requires an explanation of how the modeling of relationships in which trust is a key variable needs to diverge from standard models of the "game" between aid donor and recipient.

This paper seeks to answer this question and to trace its implications for policy makers. In Section A, we argue that a major determinant of aid effectiveness is the element of trust—or social capital—that builds up between representatives of the donor and recipient. In Section B, we model the conditionality processes attending budget support aid, not purely in the conventional way as a noncooperative two-person game, but rather as a noncooperative game which may mutate into a collaborative equilibrium if sufficient trust builds up between the negotiating parties. Whether or not this happens is, we argue, fundamental to the effectiveness of conditionality and of budget support aid. This idea then requires us to examine the determinants of donor-recipient trust and possible mechanisms for cultivating it, which we do within a social capital framework. We find that trust derives from the experience of the negotiating parties with one another, from the incentives they are able to provide to trust one another, and from the processes within which their negotiations are conducted. The model is tested in Sections C and D against two country samples: extensively, in Section C, against a broad sample of all African countries undergoing budget support operations and intensively, in Section D, against a narrow sample of Ethiopia, Uganda, Malawi, and Zambia. Section E concludes, drawing implications for policy.

A. Intuitive Foundations

We start from one of the key dilemmas of budget support aid—which is that this form of aid is often unsuccessful in achieving a sustained improvement in economic performance, because the performance criteria attached to it are breached, even though both donor and recipient agree that observing the criteria will be in the recipient country's interest. The reasons why this breach occurs are various, but a common one is the threat of disruptive and possibly violent political opposition from interests that oppose the reforms on which budget support aid is conditioned. Thus, even though the receiving government believes that the country will benefit economically, in the long run, from implementing a particular reform condition attached to a budget support loan[1]—say an increase in income tax—it fails to implement it, because it fears the political consequences of doing so; as a consequence, the reform is not implemented, and budget support aid looks as if it is unsuccessful. (This sequence of events took place in Bolivia. In February 2003, despite the withdrawal of the politically sensitive income tax increases, further riots followed, and neither political nor economic stability has yet been restored.)

Analytically, the problem has analogies with the basic prisoner's dilemma (Figure 15.1(a)) in the sense that there are elements of both common interest and conflict between donor and recipient, and one element of conflict is that each party benefits from exploiting the other and breaking an agreement that the other player has honored, as is the case when a donor continues to lend but a recipient fails to comply with conditions because he fears the political consequences.

But, as is well known, with the structure of payoffs depicted in figure 15.1(a), the equilibrium is in the bottom right-hand corner: in practical terms, untrusting behavior on both sides dominates trusting behavior, and the loan process collapses, because the donor implements his threat to not disburse the loan. Hence the illustration only describes a rather atypical case of budget support lending, in which relations between donor and recipient quickly break down and the flow of funds dries up.

Such a case differs from the one we wish to examine, in which lending continues but at low efficiency because the reforms in policy instruments that are essential to make the loan effective have not been implemented. For these, another approach is needed.

A possible approach, which we have previously taken in Mosley, Harrigan, and Toye (1995), is to model conditional program lending as a one-sided prisoner's dilemma

FIGURE 15.1 Two Illustrations of "Failed" Program Operations

(a) The conventional, symmetric prisoner's dilemma: equilibrium at bottom right

		Player 1 ("donor") behaviors	
Player 2 ("recipient") responses		Trusting (e.g., "disburse next installment of loan")	Untrusting (e.g. "not disburse next installment of loan")
	Trustworthy (e.g., " comply with conditions")	1,1	2,−2
	Untrustworthy (e.g., "not comply with conditions")	−2,2	0,0

(b) The one-sided prisoner's dilemma: equilibrium at bottom left

		Player 1 ("donor") behaviors	
Player 2 ("recipient") responses		Trusting (e.g., disburse)	Not disburse
	Trustworthy (e.g., " comply with conditions")	2,2	0, −1
	Untrustworthy (e.g., "not comply with conditions")	1,3	0,0

Note: Payoffs are given in order (player 1, player 2). They are defined in terms of additional years of detention in relation to the "norm" in the bottom right-hand corner.

(Figure 15.1b). Here it is acknowledged that (1) the donor derives utility from a continued lending relationship—hence the payoff to continuing to lend rather than breaking off lending in the bottom left-hand cell is one rather than minus two; (2) the dilemma is asymmetric, because although the recipient gains from being able to exploit the donor (in the sense of achieving both finance and noncompliance with conditions), it is not clear what a donor would gain from refusing to lend to a recipient who complies with conditions. Accordingly, the top right-hand cell in Figure 15.1(b) has been amended so that the donor derives no utility from exploitative behavior of this sort.

With these altered parameters, the dominant strategy equilibrium of the game moves to the bottom left-hand corner, in which lending continues even though conditions are not complied with. Empirically, this is a commonly observed outcome with both the World Bank and the IMF; however, it is also an inefficient outcome, because the recipient is not managing policy instruments in a way that at least the donor considers to be vital for the success of the loan operation, and because failure is being openly indulged, with a consequent loss of donor credibility. The calls cited earlier for abandoning conditionality, possibly in favor of "selectivity"—the giving of aid to recipients whose policy and institutions are already acceptable—derive from a logic of this type.

However, there are reasons to doubt that selectivity will resolve the problems represented by Figure 15.1(b). One of them is moral hazard: once selected to receive long-term budget support, any recipient is contractually insured against punishment for poor performance, and hence discouraged from performing well. Worse, probably too few aid recipients, certainly in Africa, are performing well enough to spend even the existing aid budget, let alone the expanded aid budgets for the next few years that are being urged through programs such as the International Financing Facility (HM Treasury 2004), the Strategic Partnership with Africa (SPA), and other aid flows earmarked for the continent on the basis of unchanged policies. Thus donors, if they wish to maintain disbursements even at existing levels, need to work out some incentive for improving policy frameworks that is not supplied by the selectivity approach. Moreover, conditionality, as previously discussed, has produced some notable successes. The question is how these successes have materialized, and what differentiates them from cases where conditionality has achieved no improvement.

Our provisional answer is that the successes derive from the collapse of noncooperative games such as those represented in Figure 15.1 into *trust games* or *quasi-trust games,* as represented by the parameters of Figure 15.2.

In these ways, we are modeling the formation of a type of *social capital*—the formation of linkages within a specific network, consequent on the reduction of perceived risks within that network. Social capital in general has been found capable of explaining intercountry variations in growth, even when conventional causal influences such as policy physical and human capital are held constant (Knack and Keefer 1997; Whiteley 2000). What we are suggesting here is simply that the social capital that exists between just two entities—negotiators for the donor and recipient authorities—is a factor of production that is particularly important for explaining the productivity of resources invested in aid negotiations.

However, as a factor of production, trust has a number of peculiarities. In particular, unlike physical and human capital, it cannot be bought and sold in a market. How then can it be accumulated?

We argue that the dynamics by which social capital is created in this context—by which the type of game in Figure 15.1 metamorphoses into that in Figure 15.2—typically

FIGURE 15.2 The All-in Matrix: Trust Made Rational

		Player 1 ("donor") behaviors	
Player 2 ("recipient") responses		Trusting (e.g., disburse)	Not disburse
	Trustworthy (e.g., " comply with conditions")	3,3	2,−2
	Untrustworthy (e.g., "not comply with conditions")	−2,2	0,0

contain some or all of the following four features, any or all of which can cause the game represented in Figure 15.1 to collapse. In each of these cases, we shall give an example from the recent history of conditionality negotiations and show how the application of the example brings about a parameter change that causes the equilibrium of the model to shift from conflict to trust.

- *Increasingly "trusting" behavior by the truster, or donor, in which some slippage is not punished.* That is, the link between trustworthiness and trust becomes more flexible, because the donor sees a long-term payoff from condoning minor forms of untrustworthiness. Examples include Uganda between 1987 and 1995, where donors tolerated fixed exchange rates and the reimposition of export taxes on coffee, and Ethiopia, throughout the period since 1991, where donors tolerated the maintenance of state ownership of land and even a return to war with Eritrea in 2000, in each case because there was a fundamental meeting of minds between donor and recipient over poverty strategy.
- *Behavior by the trustee, or recipient, that is seen as increasingly trustworthy by the truster.* This can take several forms. An important form is when the recipient undertakes positive initiatives, such as providing evidence-based signals about future behavior, possibly with a view to influencing the donor's perception of his long-term payoff, and often deflecting attention from cases of slippage on nonfundamentals. We call these *bona fides*: a form of forward-looking moral collateral. One prominent illustration is Tanzania between 2000 and 2005, where various surrogate signals of recipient commitment to pro-poor reform, including the setting up of rigorous poverty monitoring procedures, were offered in place of evidence of actual poverty reduction (interviews with DFID staff, Cape Town, May 2005). Another example is Ethiopia in 1997–98, where the World Bank was willing to continue to lend even though fiscal conditions had been breached, because the president on his own initiative had set out a recovery plan that the Bank saw as coherent (see Section D).
- *Measures to improve the channels of communication between donor and recipient.* Examples include increased frequency of meetings or the setting up of a donor office in the recipient country, rather than relying on visiting missions.
- *"Insurances" to protect the donor in the event that his trust is misplaced*—for example, the use of nongovernmental organizations rather than governments as alternative channels for aid flows. This kind of switch has occurred in Bangladesh, Kenya, and Zambia, where donors have felt able to take greater risks in indulging government slippage on performance criteria (notably in health and agriculture) because those countries have vibrant NGO sectors that are able to incentivize, or deliver in place of, the government sector. Because a substitute for pure trust in the recipient existed and was increasingly implemented, the vulnerability associated with trusting was reduced. Measures of this kind, of course, represent the building of substitutes for trust rather than the growth of trust, and so we call relationships that contain this feature *quasi-trust games*.

Our thesis is that each or any of these processes may cause a distrust equilibrium to mutate into a trust equilibrium, just as the reversal of any of them may cause a shift back from trust to distrust. An important feature of an increase or decrease in trust is the interaction between its backward-looking ("affective") and forward-looking ("predictive") components. An initiative in any of the four areas mentioned above may potentially act as a forward-looking incentive for trusting behavior, compensating for a negative "social history" and vice versa. The task of our empirical section will be to assess which, if any, such initiatives work well in which contexts.

Once trust is built up, it has consequences that go beyond the restoration of aid flows. It alters behavior: if donors are more trusting, aid flows are more stable, and they thus come to be treated as permanent rather than transitory income. This expectation influences investment rates, with consequent benefits for the recipient economy. And if donors become less trusting, then instability in aid flows prejudices the stability and also the *level* of domestic development spending, which then has an important bearing on poverty levels (Mosley and Suleiman 2004; Bulíř and Hamann 2003, 2005).

In Section B, we seek to convert these considerations—both the determinants of trust and its consequences—into a testable model.

B. The Model

In Figure 15.3, we sketch the structure of a simple model that reflects these considerations. Although the centerpiece of the structure is a conventional noncooperative game between a "donor" and a "recipient" of conditional program aid, what drives aid effectiveness in this context is the breakdown of the game and its replacement by a trust relationship between those parties, as in the main metaphor of Section A: the transition from Figure 15.1(a) to Figure 15.1(b).

The Standard Conditionality Game, without Trust

We may begin by considering the objectives of lender and recipient. The recipient government has a financial motive to maximize the inflow of finance and a political motive (as illustrated by Figure 15.1) to resist at least some elements of conditionality. The recipient's utility function is therefore:

$$U_j = f(t,p,X);\ f_t < 0,\ f_p < 0,\ f_x > 0 \tag{1}$$

Without loss of generality, we can write this as a linear function:

$$U_j = X - \beta t \tag{1a}$$

where the notation is as set out in Table 15.1. The utility function is negative in the number of conditions *(t)* and the proportion of them that is implemented *(p)* because if any policy conditions are necessary, it can be assumed that a recipient facing no pressure has no wish to implement any of them.[2] The utility function is presumed positive in x (the value of finance provided) because of an expectation that such finance will reduce the cost to the recipient of achieving its developmental and other objectives; in the limit, if such finance cannot be secured from any other source, the country simply runs out of reserves.

The utility of the lender is expected to vary positively with volume of lending: in particular because the donor perceives economic performance in the recipient country as varying positively with the amount of lending achieved, and because the reputations and control over resources of donor staff working in operational departments increase as their department's volume of business grows (Mosley, Harrigan, and Toye 1995, Chapter 3). But sustained growth of lending, of course, requires that clients remain able to repay loans, and this requirement limits the implementation of conditionality, since the interruption of a loan may prejudice the borrower's ability to repay loans to the lender and all other creditors.

In consequence of this conflict between lending and leverage—which we refer to as the *creditor's dilemma*—the lender's utility function will be influenced not only by the amount of lending and the conditions implemented, but also by the recipient's ability to repay debt (q):

$$U_i = g(tp, q, X); g_t > 0, g_x > 0, g_p > 0, g_g > 0 \quad (2)$$

FIGURE 15.3 Model Structure

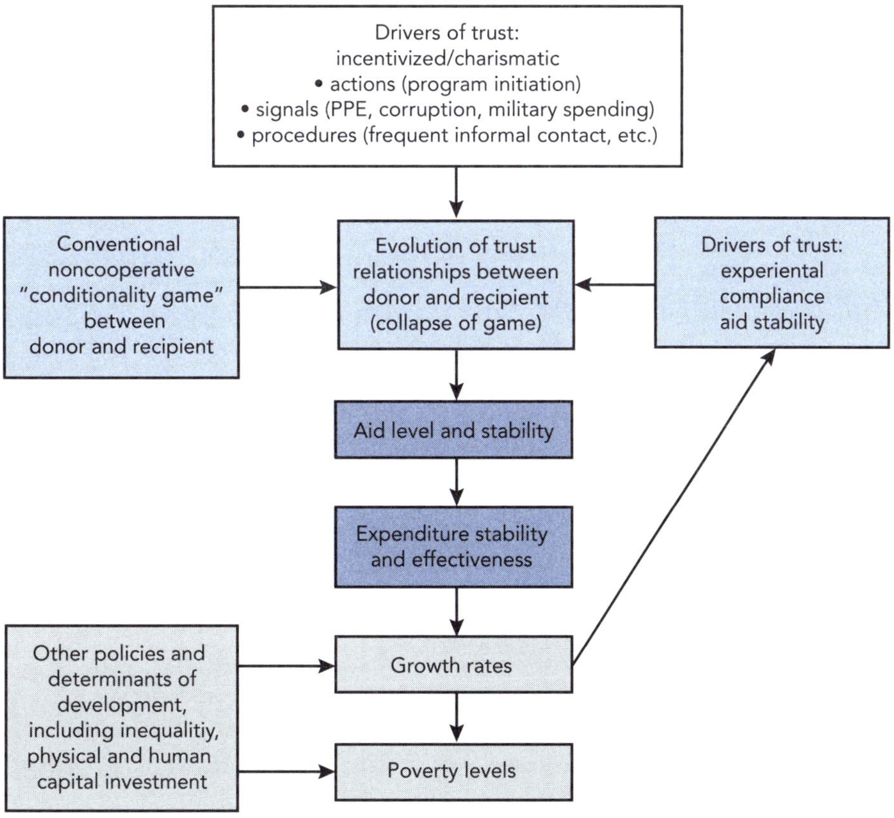

TABLE 15.1 Notation

Symbol	Meaning	Empirical specification
U	Utility	
X	Volume of lending (aid)	
OFF	Volume of other (nonaid) financial flows	
t	Number of conditions attached to a budget support loan	
p Hence 1 −*p*	Proportion of conditions implemented Proportion of conditions not implemented (slippage)	Implementation rate on World Bank adjustment loans and IMF ESAFs
q	Recipient's ability to repay debt (debt-service ratio)	
S	Trust (social capital) between donor and recipient	Frequency of interrution of lending, controlling for slippage (1 − *p*)
A	Vector of factors that determine affective (incentivized) trust	Bona fides: •PPE • military expenditure • corruption Initiator dummy Procedural variables (frequency of contact, etc.)
P	Vector of factors that determine predictive (experiential) trust	Compliance with conditions Aid instability
Pov	Poverty indicator	Headcount Under-five mortality
T	Inequality indicator	Gini coefficient

which by analogy with equation (1) can be linearized as:

$$U_i = X + \alpha tp \tag{2a}$$

Using these utility functions, the "tree" of the game between donor and recipient can be drawn as a three-act game, as in Figure 15.4. The matrix of payoffs in Act 3 corresponds exactly to the one-sided prisoner's dilemma in Figure 15.1(b),[3] and it can be readily shown that in the equilibrium solution of this game, the volume of lending depends on tightness *t*, implementation *p* (the negative of slippage), and the parameter of the recipient's utility function *β*. In a linearized version, the reduced form of the game's solution may be written as:

$$X = constant + a_1 t + a_2 p + a_3 \tag{3}$$

The Determinants of Trust

The conditionality game described above is played as a noncooperative game, unclouded by any concerns of reciprocity, friendship, or trust. However, as discussed, trust may indeed be present between the participants in conditionality negotiations, and in the transition from Figure 15.1 to Figure 15.2, trust was fundamental

FIGURE 15.4 The "Game" between Donors and Recipients of Conditional Aid

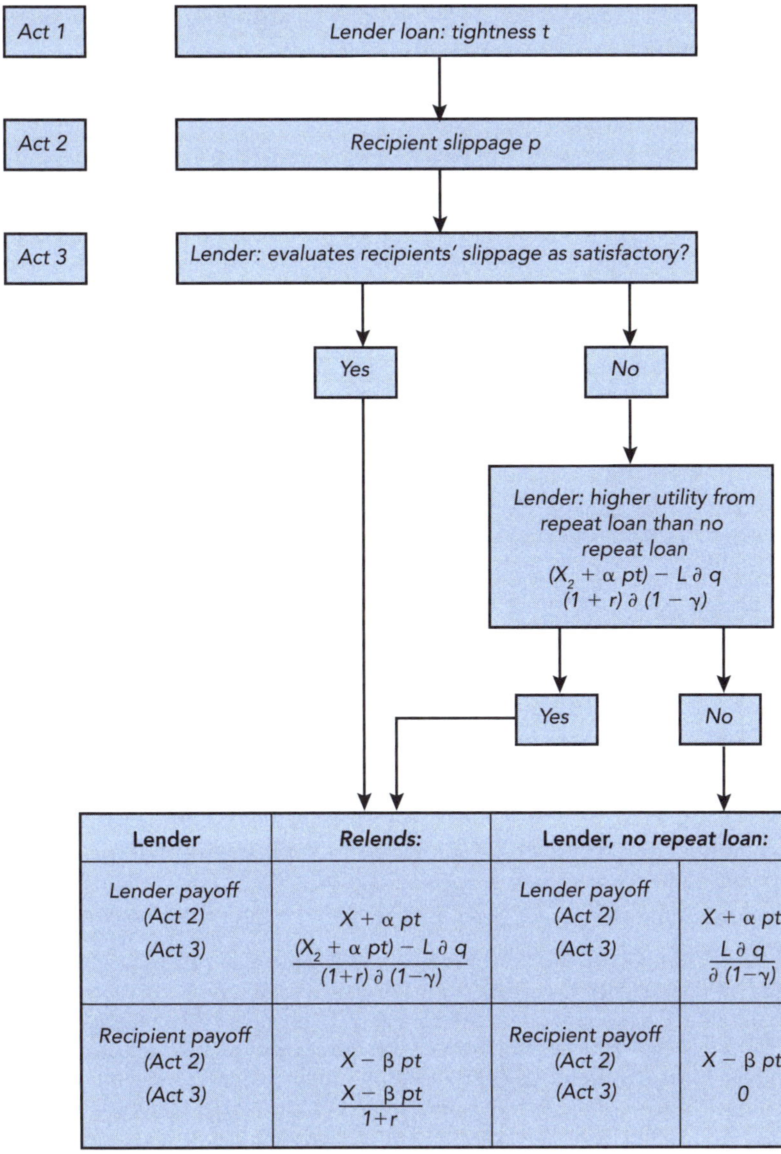

Lender	Relends:	Lender, no repeat loan:	
Lender payoff *(Act 2)* *(Act 3)*	$X + \alpha pt$ $\frac{(X_2 + \alpha pt) - L \partial q}{(1+r) \partial (1-\gamma)}$	*Lender payoff* *(Act 2)* *(Act 3)*	$X + \alpha pt$ $\frac{L \partial q}{\partial (1-\gamma)}$
Recipient payoff *(Act 2)* *(Act 3)*	$X - \beta pt$ $\frac{X - \beta pt}{1+r}$	*Recipient payoff* *(Act 2)* *(Act 3)*	$X - \beta pt$ *0*

to causing the game to break down, and thence to the volume, stability, and thus the effectiveness of the concessional resources transferred. Analytically, what we visualize is that the parameters α and β (donor and recipient utility) will in practice vary not only with the factors described above, but also with the trust that each party has in the other.

This immediately raises the questions of how trust is measured, determined, and created, all of which have proved contentious within the social capital literature.[4]

At the level of measurement, our response is to represent the level of trust between donor and recipient in terms of the stability or frequency of interruption of the relationship. At the level of prediction, as discussed, we partition trust into predictive and affective elements:

$$\beta = a_5 + a_6P + a_7A \tag{4}$$

where P and A are vectors of "experience" variables that respectively explain experiential trust (explicable in terms of past experience of the other party) and predictive incentivized trust (explicable by other factors, including interpersonal affect, and opportunities for insurance and verification).

Once we investigate by case-study methods the processes by which trust appears to be effectively built up in international negotiations (Section D), we encounter some surprises. For example, a good track record in complying with conditions—low slippage $(1 - p)$, in the notation of equations (1) and (2)—does not necessarily build up trust, nor does a poor record of compliance with conditions destroy trust. As noted above, Uganda in the late 1980s and early 1990s persisted with fixed exchange rates and with export taxes on coffee, both of which were anathema to the World Bank, and Ethiopia, in addition to fixed exchange rates, kept land and agricultural credit within the public sector against the Bank's advice.

What mattered was that the governments of those countries, at a time when the donor community was moving to adopt the poverty targets of the Millennium Development Goals as primary beacons for development policy, not only adopted but initiated poverty reduction strategies of their own. This generated predictive trust: in additional cases, other factors were also crucial, including personal warmth between the negotiators for the donor and the recipient.

The blending of the two types of trust—in the case of the World Bank and Ethiopia—is nicely illustrated by Joseph Stiglitz's account of his meetings with President Meles Zenawi in the mid-1990s, which helped to achieve one of the transformations of a confrontational game into a trust equilibrium that we have been discussing:

> A doctor by training, Meles had formally studied economics because he knew that to bring his country out of centuries of poverty would require nothing less than economic transformation, and he demonstrated a knowledge of economics—and indeed a creativity—that would have put him at the head of any of my university classes. He showed a deeper understanding of economic principles—and certainly a greater knowledge of the circumstances in his country—than many of the international economic bureaucrats that I had to deal with in the succeeding three years. Meles combined these attributes with personal integrity: no-one doubted his honesty and there were few accusations of corruption within his government. . . . His political opponents raised questions about his commitment to democratic principles, but he was not an old-fashioned autocrat. Both he and the government were generally committed to a process of decentralization, bringing government closer to the people. . . [and] the World Bank had direct evidence of the competence of the government and its commitment to the poor. Ethiopia had formulated a rural development strategy, focusing its attention on the poor, and especially the 85 percent of the population living in the rural sector. It had dramatically cut back on military expenditure. . . because it knew that funds spent on weapons were funds that could not be spent on fighting poverty. Surely, this was precisely the

> kind of government to which the international community should have been giving assistance.[5] (Stiglitz 2003, p. 26–28)

In the empirical work reported in Sections C and D, we discover that procedural factors (such as the frequency of meetings between donor and recipient, and whether the donor had an office in the recipient country), as well as policy and experiential factors, help to determine the buildup or otherwise of affective trust between donors and recipients of conditional program assistance.

Conditionality and Aid Flows

We expect that where trust is low and program aid flows are often interrupted, those aid flows will have less impact on growth:

$$G = a_8 + a_9 X + a_{10}\sigma_x (P, A) + a_{11}OFF \tag{5}$$

Note the role of aid instability σ_x, driven by predictive and affective trust between the aid donor and recipient P and A.

Determinants of Poverty

Finally, poverty (equation (6)) is driven by growth and other factors that influence the growth elasticity of poverty reduction in particular countries. Some of the factors that influence this elasticity will be policy variables, including those such as pro-poor expenditure that influence affective and predictive trust. Other proven "confounders" of the growth-poverty relationship include inequality (Hanmer and Naschold 2000) and corruption (Mosley, Hudson, and Verschoor 2004). We have included these confounders in the specification of equation (6).

$$Pov = a_{12} + a_{13}G + a_{14}I \tag{6}$$

These six relationships (the last specified with two different definitions of poverty, the headcount and infant mortality), plus an equation to endogenize the Gini coefficient of inequality in (6), make up the model that is estimated in the next section.

C. Econometric Tests

As there are simultaneities in the system, we estimate the model consisting of equations (3), (4), (5), and (6) by three-stage least squares regression, with allowance made for country and time fixed effects. The estimation is made for the period 1985–2004 in relation to a group of 14 countries in Africa that received budget support aid under the guidance of both the Bank and the IMF: the ESAF (Enhanced Structural Adjustment Facility) countries, now known as PRGF (Poverty Reduction and Growth Facility) countries.[6] The results are shown in Table 15.2.

Two points should be noted before the results are discussed. First, budget support aid, as portrayed here, is simply concessional support provided by the IMF (through SAF, ESAF, PRGF, HIPC) and the World Bank (through structural adjustment

TABLE 15.2 Results of SE Regression Analysis: Poverty, Growth, and Aid Characteristics

Independent variables	Dependent variable (1) Trust variables		(2) Compliance	(3) Budget support aid
	Frequency of breakdown of negotiations (expected sign − ve)	Forgiveness of slippage (expected sign + ve)		
Constant	8.09 (0.95)	−764.3** (2.56)	−20.9 (6.26)	85.5** (4.65)
Trust variables Distrust parameter (program interruptions)				-0.97** (9.93)
'Bona fides': Compliance with conditionality	−0.19** (2.52)	27.08* (2.34)		1.71** (6.64)
Ln (PPE)	−0.52** (12.22)	14.90** (3.65)	0.118** (5.82)	−0.30** (4.99)
Ln (military expenditure)		−4.73* (2.08)	−0.073* (2.33)	0.58** (6.94)
Compliance*PPE		14.24** (4.09)		
Corruption	−0.24 (2.23)	−1.11 (0.15)	0.65** (14.06)	−1.21** (9.77)
Corruption *PPE		4.44* (2.30)		
Financial flows				
Aid			0.015 (1.72)	
Aid instability		−0.015 (0.51)	−0.062** (3.45)	
GDP per capita				
Process variables:				
Recipient-initiator dummy	−1.89** (14.08)	9.88* (2.33)	0.48** (7.26)	
Residence dummy	0.13 (1.74)	8.56** (4.52)	0.20** (6.54)	
Need indicators				
Ln (infant mortality)				
Debt service				
Total population				
GDP/capita		0.25** (7.37)		
Other indicators:				
Openness dummy		5.77** (6.38)	0.093** (4.75)	0.42 (4.14)
Log (Gini coefficient of inequality)				
Time fixed effects	−0.0051 (1.20)	0.45** (2.97)	0.011** (6.90)	−0.045 (4.99)
Country fixed effects	0.058** (6.88)	1.22** (6.85)	0.004 (1.40)	0.043* (2.03)
No. observations	215	350	215	215
(Pseudo)R^2	0.7888	0.3508	0.6038	0.4923
P	0.0000	0.0000	0.0000	0.0000

Notes: Estimation method. 3SLS. Data set consists of panel data running from 1986 to 2004. T-statistics in brackets below coefficients.
Variable definitions (source is World Bank World Development Indicators CD-ROM unless stated):
Budget support aid: gross annual disbursements, from World Bank and IMF *Annual Reports* and project performance audit reports.
Aid instability: coefficient of variation of disbursements, from World Bank and IMF Annual Reports and project performance audit reports.
Compliance with conditionality: percentage of conditions implemented. From miscellaneous sources.

TABLE 15.2 *(continued)*

Dependent variable

(4) Aid instability	(5) Log GDP/capita	6 Gini coefficient of inequality	(7) Poverty headcount	(8) Infant mortality
13.19 (1.23)	−34.5** (6.57)	-43.5** (3.56)	-18.20** (3.40)	6.97** (2.61)
0.098** (2.85)	−0.22** (7.78)		0.011 (0.39)	-0.039** (2.62)
	0.42** (5.81)	−1.60** (9.69)	−0.41** (5.49)	−0.19** (5.10)
−0.30** (4.99)	0.24** (8.00)	−0.20** (2.65)	−0.10** (3.04)	−0.008 (0.49)
0.58** (6.94)	−0.38** (8.80)	1.41** (13.49)	0.20** (3.78)	0.077** (2.83)
−1.21** (9.77)	0.59** (7.56)	-1.19** (6.55)	0.15* (1.89)	0.10 (1.52)
	0.038** (2.81)	−0.27** (8.58)	−0.13** (9.40)	−0.01 (1.50)
	−0.17** (6.89)	−0.49** (8.47)	0.24** (8.71)	−0.005 (0.39)
		−0.13 (1.19)	−0.53** (10.78)	−0.275** (11.04)
				−0.275** (11.04)
−0.44** (8.18) 0 .	21** (7.75)	−0.16 (2.55)	0.19 (6.62)	−0.035* (2.44)
0.23**			0.17** (8.10)	0.058** (5.32)
−0.004 (0.87)	0.02** (7.90)	0.021** (3.47)	0.012** (4.70)	−0.0003 (0.27)
0.054** (4.80)	−0.007 (1.43)	0.026* (2.11)	0.071** (13.26)	0.002 (0.002)
215	215	215	215	215
0.6084	0.3576	0.7967	0.6989	0.7272
0.0000	0.0000	0.0000		0.0000

Residence dummy: 1 if IMF maintains a resident mission in country stated, 0 otherwise. From Mecagni (1999), table 9.
Recipient-initiator dummy: 1 if the recipient government initiates significant components of the government's poverty reduction strategy paper, 0 otherwise.
Openness index: the Sachs-Warner indicator.
PPE: "pro-poor expenditure", consisting of the share of primary health and education, rural water and sanitation, agricultural research and extension, and social protection, less military expenditure, in total government spending. For full details of the construction of the index see Mosley, Hudson, and Verschoor (2004), Appendix 1.

operations, sectoral adjustment operations, and other policy-based operations such as reconstruction loans). No program assistance from regional development banks or bilateral donors is included, although this assistance is generally provided in support of operations by the Washington institutions and so can be expected to correlate strongly with their disbursements.

Second, compliance with conditionality, measured here as the proportion of conditions that is implemented, needs to be understood as an attempt to hit a moving target. Whereas the performance criteria (policy conditions) imposed by the IMF have gently evolved over the 20 years of our survey in the more micro direction of greater use of tax increases and public enterprise reform, those imposed by the Bank have evolved very radically from market liberalization into the much broader territory of, in particular, governance and poverty reduction. In the process, the Bank's yardstick for the assessment of policy has evolved into the multifaceted country performance and institutional assessment (CPIA) index, which has been used for compliance assessments since 2001.

The main inferences from Table 15.2 are the following.

First, trust, whether measured by the frequency of program interruptions or by the sense of forgiveness of slippage, is heavily influenced by recipient charisma and initiative (the initiator dummy); by various process variables, including frequency of contact; and by several signals of good intent, including pro-poor expenditure and low levels of corruption.[7] Both measures of trust are more robustly associated with these bona fides than they are with compliance with conditionality, which is barely a significant influence (at the 5 percent level).

Second, the results from equations (3) and (4) strongly support our hypothesis that trust and not just compliance matter for the level and stability of aid disbursements. In the aid flow equation (3), the (dis)trust variable impacts with greater significance than the compliance variable.

Third, not only the level but the stability of aid flows strongly influence welfare outcomes, and in particular growth and poverty. In these regressions, aid is a strongly negative influence on both inequality and headcount poverty (controlling for the level of bona fides, openness, and country and time fixed effects).

Putting these findings together, it can be said with some confidence that the achievement of higher levels of mutual trust between aid donors and recipients would be good for aid effectiveness and poverty reduction: but this begs the question of how this can be achieved, and how, in what are still scarce cases, it has achieved in practical terms. The next section considers these issues in relation to a small subset of our main sample.

D. Evidence from Case Studies

In this section, we elaborate on our econometric work by presenting evidence of a more qualitative and anecdotal kind. In Table 15.3, we present evidence of this type for 6 of the 39 countries in Section C: three (Ethiopia, Ghana, Uganda) whose relationships with donors became trusting and stable and three (Malawi, Kenya, Zambia) for whom they were less so. The discriminators presented as explanations of performance in the left-hand column are the same as those used in Table 15.2.

At first sight it might seem from Table 15.3 as though the principal difference between the three cases of pro-poor growth on the left-hand side of the table and the three cases of lower growth, and increasing poverty, on the right-hand side of the table consisted of worse policies, reflected in lower compliance with conditionality, which then led to lower and more unstable aid flows. And indeed, there is quite a significant

TABLE 15.3 Case-study Countries: Experience of Budget Support Operations, Determinants of Trust and Aid Effectiveness

(data period: 1980-2003)

	High trust, low volatility			Low trust, high volatility		
	Uganda	Ghana	Ethiopia	Malawi	Zambia	Kenya
Aid indicators:						
Aid/GDP%	9.2	5.6	12.1	16.6	11.6	6.5
Aid volatility parameter (sd) (c of v)	6.49 69.5	4.1 73.2	5.44 44.6	8.90 53.6	12.90 111.2	3.55 53.8
Indicators of relationship with aid donors and of performance:						
CPIA(2002)	Very good	Good	Good	Moderate	Moderate	Poor
Conditionality on adjustment lending:						
Agricultural policy						
Privatization	**		***	**	**	**
Governance	**		*	*	**	*
Public expenditure prioritization	**		***	**	*	*
PRSP	***					
Overall score for slippage on conditionality (1-p)	yes	yes	yes	yes	yes	yes
Trust score% (number of program interruptions; high level denotes low trust)						
Expenditure stability (pro-poor sectors)%	26.7		26.9		(44.3)	
Outcome indicators:						
Poverty reduction 1990-2000 (or nearest available period)	Decline from 56%(1992) to 35%(2000), possible increase thereafter	Minor decline	Decline from 51% (1992) to 44% (2000)	Increase from 54% (1990) to 65% (1998)	Increase 68% (1991) to 72% (1996)	Increase 46% (1992) to 50% (1998)
Annual average GDP growth 1990-2000 (or nearest available period)	7.2	4.3	4.8	4.0	1.0	2.2

Sources: Aid data from OECD Development Assistance Committee database. Trust score is a measure of interruptions on IMF and World Bank budget support lending, see notes to Table 15.2 above. CPIA (Country Policy and Institutional Assessment) score from Collier (2001), table 3, p. 1796. All other data from World Bank, *World Development Indicators* 2003 CD-ROM.

correlation, between low implementation of conditionality and high volatility of program aid (Figure 15.5). This appears, on the surface, to support the recommendation of IMF staff members Bulíř and Hamann (2003, 2005), that "a higher degree of compliance with conditions attached to aid is likely to lead to a smoother path of [aid] disbursements" (2003, p. 82) and thence, by implication, to a more effective and pro-poor pattern of growth.

This recommendation is superficial, however, because it conceals the dynamics by which rapid and stable growth of aid flows has been achieved in some countries and not in others with very similar initial conditions. In Figure 15.6 and Figure 15.7, we contrast four of these countries, whose compliance with loan conditionality in the mid-1990s was very similar, at about 50–60 percent, but whose economic performance, and relationships with aid donors, evolved in highly contrasting fashion. The first two appear in the "poverty reduction" group in Table 15.3: Uganda, where compliance increased over time but aid volatility was always moderate, and Ethiopia, where compliance increased over time but aid volatility diminished dramatically. The next two appear in the "increasing poverty" group: Zambia, where compliance was moderate and aid volatility high throughout, and Malawi, where compliance improved and yet volatility worsened after a bad start. Why these differences?

We hypothesize that the key variable in determining the trajectory and effectiveness of aid flows, and specifically budget support aid, was the emergence or not of trust relationships between representatives of the aid donor and recipient. We have further argued in the econometric analysis of Section B (see also Mosley and

FIGURE 15.5 Aid Volatility in Relation to Compliance with Conditionality

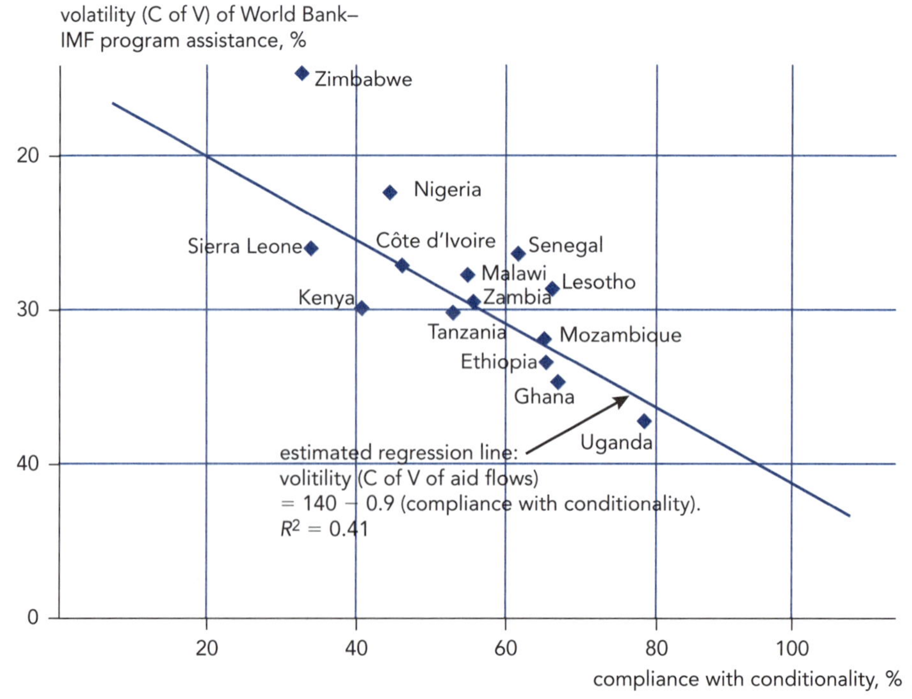

FIGURE 15.6 Ethiopia and Uganda: Volatility of World Bank–IMF Program Assistance in Relation to Compliance with Conditionality

aid (left scale, %)
compliance (right scale, %)

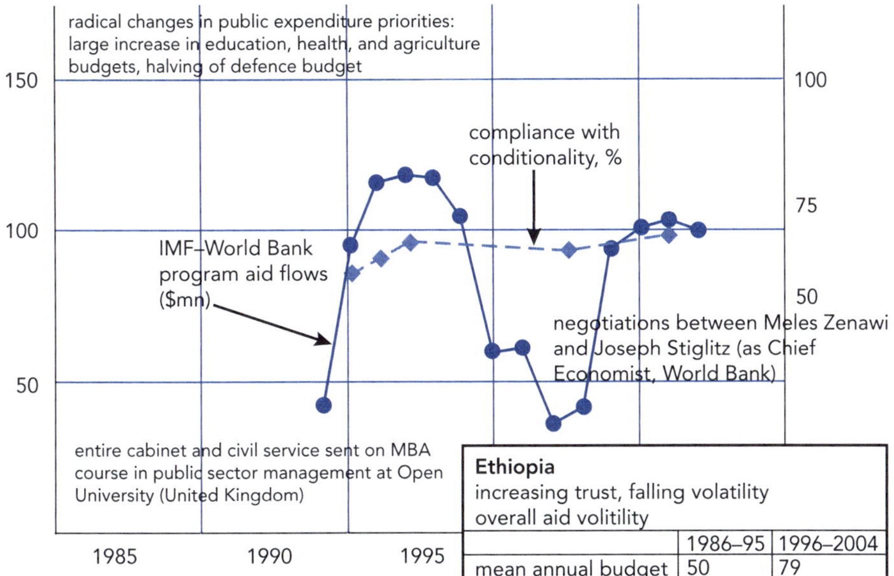

Ethiopia
increasing trust, falling volatility
overall aid volitility

	1986–95	1996–2004
mean annual budget support aid (Smn)	50	79
C of V of aid flows	112.6	34.7
conditionality compliance index (whole period)	67%	

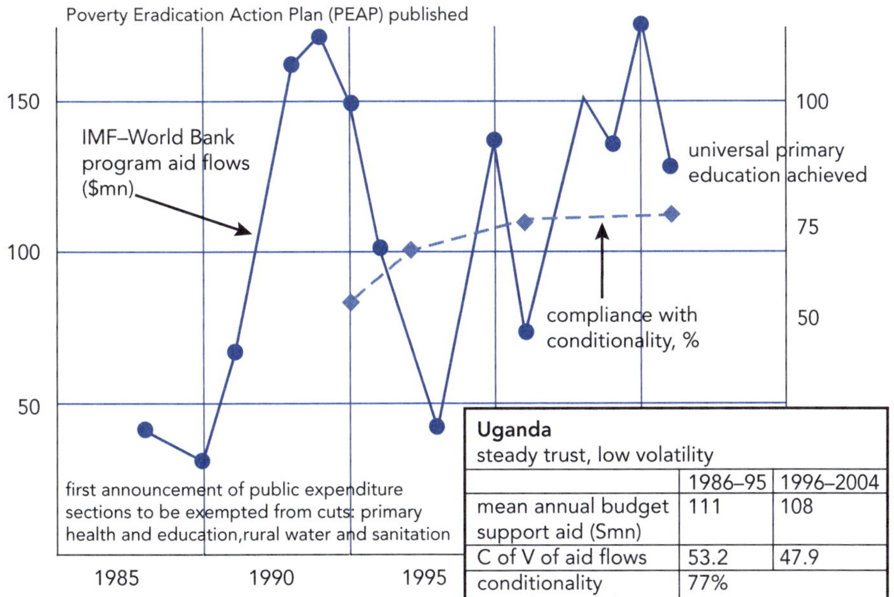

Uganda
steady trust, low volatility

	1986–95	1996–2004
mean annual budget support aid (Smn)	111	108
C of V of aid flows	53.2	47.9
conditionality compliance index (whole period)	77%	

FIGURE 15.7 Malawi and Zambia: Volatility of World Bank–IMF Program Assistance in Relation to Compliance with Conditionality

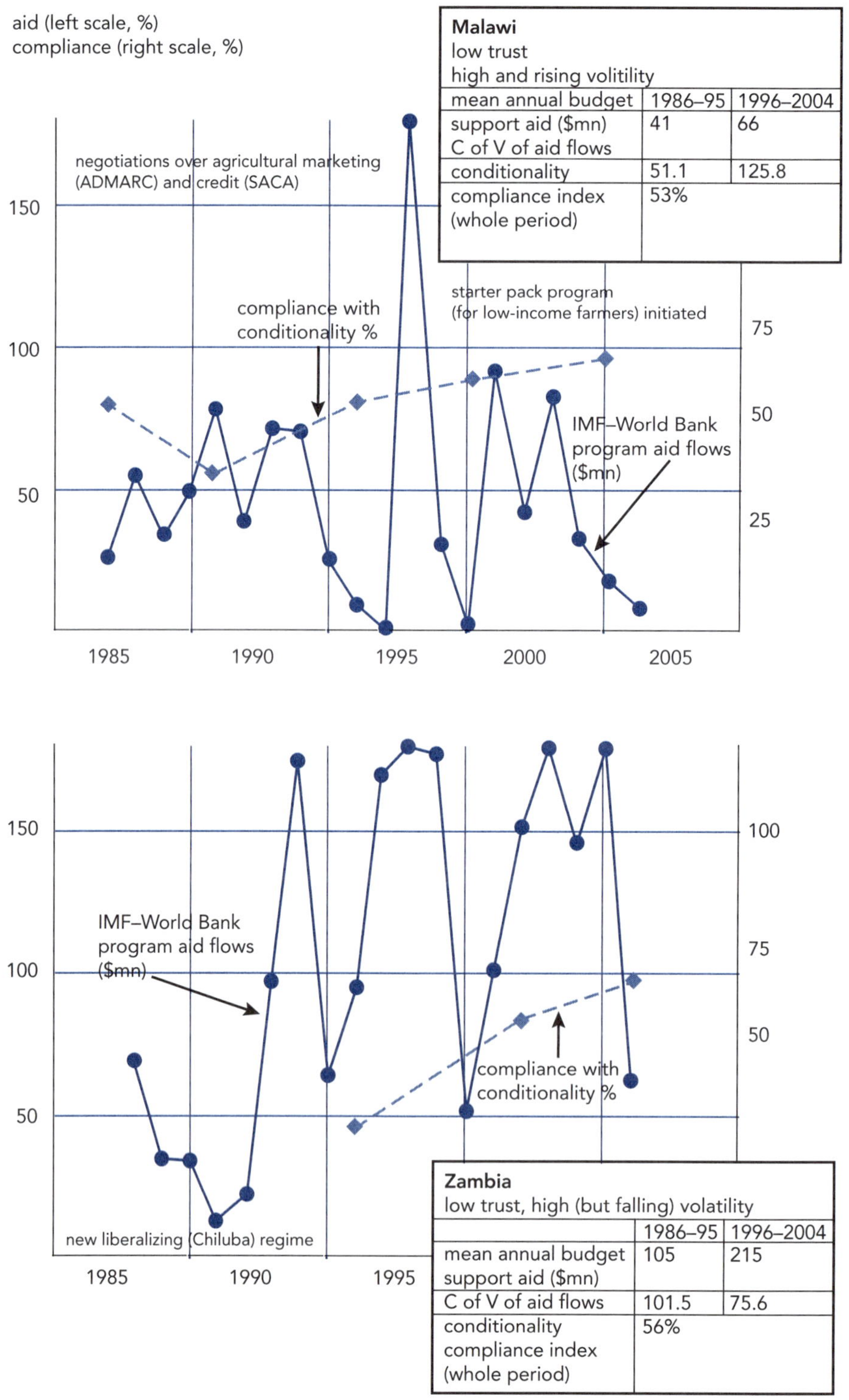

Suleiman [2005]) that certain key factors caused these trust relationships to develop or disintegrate:

- willingness(or lack of it) to target public expenditure in a pro-poor direction;
- levels of corruption in the public service;
- willingness (or lack of it) on the part of the recipient to take initiatives in policy formulation, rather than strike a passive attitude in relation to the donor;
- the personal charisma of, and chemistry between, negotiators on behalf of the donor and recipient.

These four causal factors can be seen at work in the case-study countries depicted in Figure 15.6 and Figure 15.7. In the early 1990s, as mentioned, all these countries were complying with about 50–60 percent of their loan conditions.

Uganda was still adhering (in defiance of the advice of the Bank and IMF) to export taxation on coffee and elements of a fixed exchange rate, while Ethiopia (equally defiantly) retained state control over land and rural microfinance. In the pivotal year of 1994, however, both countries took key initiatives, not paralleled by other recipients, in the field of public expenditure programming. Uganda articulated public spending priorities that favored sectors designated as pro-poor (primary education and health, agricultural research and extension, rural water and infrastructure), and Ethiopia began a more radical reform of public spending,[8] more than halving the military budget in favor of education, agriculture (with an emphasis on vulnerable environments and drought mitigation) and infrastructure. These signals of good intent, portrayed in Figure 15.6, won the trust of donors, despite the low rates of formal compliance on the budget support programs at the time. This trust sustained itself in spite of (prima facie) grave breaches of performance criteria, such as the Ethiopian government's return to war with Eritrea, and consequent military overspend, in 2000.

Trust in Ethiopia and Uganda was won and sustained through two channels, first by identifying a coherent strategy toward pro-poor growth (with, in both cases, a strong pro-agriculture bias, somewhat against the prevailing current of poverty advice within international financial institutions) and second by doing so proactively—the factor that we have attempted to reflect in the initiator dummy in Table 15.2. Trust has been reinforced by results, notably the evidence of a long-term decline in poverty in each of these countries over the 1990s. Certainly in Uganda, a level of trust has been reached where, in the case of the World Bank, performance criteria are jointly determined by recipient and donor rather than being imposed by the donor (Adam and Gunning 2002); this arrangement of course gives a recipient still more room to maneuver.[9]

By contrast, in both Malawi and Zambia, the obligatory poverty reduction strategy was prepared as a response to a donor demand, so that the recipients lost the initiative and encouraged the donors to focus on skeletons in the cupboard, such as corruption and other problems of governance. In the process, aid flows lost momentum and became volatile, with stoppages in the overall flow to Malawi in 1995 and Zambia in 1998. The erosion of mutual trust meant that even genuine pro-poor initiatives by government, such as the Malawi government's Starter Pack program for small farmers in 1999,[10] did not increase either the size or the stability of aid flows;

donors were divided about the proper manner in which to respond (Harrigan 2003). The discord between the donors then compounded the existing distrust between donor and recipient.

Various lessons emerge from these case studies. The first is that the social capital between donor and recipient is influenced not only by the behaviors of individual donors and recipients but also by the coherence or otherwise among the behaviors of the donors. In all of the countries examined, but especially in Malawi, the discord among the donors left the recipient unable to satisfy all of them by any set of policy actions. Malawi, classically—and to a lesser extent, Zambia and Kenya also—was a country where the donors could not agree, and because they did not agree, the relationship between donor and recipient, and the stability and effectiveness of the aid flow to the recipient country, suffered badly.

A second lesson is that there is no direct mapping from any of the bona fides that we have identified to mutual trust: perceptual factors matter, and, as happened in Malawi, even genuine pro-poor initiatives may fail to break the cycle of low trust, aid instability, and low support expenditure if they are not given the right packaging.

A third lesson is that where aid was severely unstable—as in Malawi and Zambia—the impact fell directly on the effectiveness of public spending and the level of net inward investment. The latter is fragile everywhere in Africa, but particularly in those countries marked by instability in the large component of public spending that is financed by aid.

E. Policy Conclusions and Recommendations

In the wake of the shift from generalized "adjustment lending" to a framework of program aid centered on long-term poverty reduction operations, critiques of conditionality have gathered strength. Proposals for reform range from abandonment of conditionality in favor of outright selectivity (Collier and others 1997; Collier and Dollar 2002) to reduction of the number of conditions within a long-term framework and their unbundling into "policy clusters" such as macro, budget, and equity (Leandro, Schafer, and Froutini 1999) to joint determination of performance criteria on the Ugandan model (Adam and Gunning 2002).

Our approach in this paper rejects the first of these proposals, and we argue that the second and third are already on the way to being realized through the new conditionalities that the World Bank and the bilaterals are currently practicing.

What is important for the effectiveness of budget support aid is not only aid volume and targeting, but also stability; and for all of these objectives and especially the last, trust is the crucial variable—indeed, more crucial, on the evidence we present, than compliance with publicly stated conditions. Where trust is effectively built up, much of the conflictual basis of conventional conditionality disappears, and with it many of its efficiency costs.

We argue that trust has in practice been achieved not only through a positive "social history" but by the transmission of forward-looking signals or bona fides concerning fundamentals, which we infer, on the strength of our statistical analysis, to be high pro-poor expenditure, low military expenditure, and low corruption. If these are present, trust builds and budget support aid is stable, and slippage on overt conditionality is generally forgiven. But there are outliers to this trend, as our case-study analysis shows: some countries have sent pro-poor signals but been rebuffed by donors, resulting in stop-go. More positively, initiative taking and charisma in defense of pro-poor options have often been effective in keeping aid stable despite massive noncompliance; so too have procedural reforms such as the spread of IMF resident missions.[11] High trust makes for stability of aid, and stability of aid, in conjunction with its level and its targeting, significantly influences growth and poverty outcomes.

The implication is that well-designed shifts in public expenditure are capable of reducing poverty, and that contrary to Collier's proposals (1999, 2002), conditionality has been instrumental in bringing these shifts about. The conditionality in question, however, has not been orthodox conditionality but a kind of shadow conditionality, focused on targets other than those formally announced as performance criteria, and requiring recipients to be able to read between the lines (Mosley, Hudson, and Verschoor 2004). Those recipients that have been able to master this art have earned impressive rewards. A further dividend for growth and poverty could be achieved by better aligning the formal criteria with the true performance criteria that effectively earn trust.

Endnotes

1. Throughout the paper, we use the word "loan" to describe budget support operations, which in practice may be loans, low-interest credits (as in the case of the IMF's Poverty Reduction and Growth Facility, for example), or outright grants (as in the case of most bilateral donors).
2. This does not imply that there are no gainers from conditionality. Rather, such gainers (for example, people working in exporting industries) are typically scattered, unorganized, and receive their gains in the long rather than the short term, so that the government has little political interest in trying to satisfy them.
3. With $\alpha = \beta = p = (0.5)$, $X = t = (2)$, the game payoffs are as specified in Figure 15.1(b).
4. Glaeser (2002, p.p. 437), for example, reports that "there does not yet exist a commonly accepted theoretical framework... for thinking about the determinants of investment in social capital."
5. That this subsequently happened was partly due to Stiglitz's advocacy. The phrase "should have been" relates to the IMF's initial reluctance to come on board because fiscal conditions had not been met.
6. The data collated for this paper are available from the authors.
7. Corruption, in the sense of frequency of program interruptions, is significant only at the 5 percent and not at the 1 percent level. The impact of corruption on this form of aid does, however, have the "right" sign, somewhat at variance with the findings of Brautigam and Knack (2004), who find a positive association between corruption and the level of aid.
8. This was accompanied by a training program in the form of a master's degree (MBA) in public sector management, commissioned by the Ethiopian government from the Open University for 1995–99 and compulsorily taken by all senior managers in the government from the President downward.
9. The IMF, however, does not yet take the approach that conditions are negotiable.

10. In many ways the Malawi government was the victim of poor representation rather than poor policy. Despite World Bank opposition, it had fought through the 1980s to retain a fertilizer subsidy and a smallholder rural credit administration that were both intended to overcome capital market constraints in favor of low-income farmers. But it had no spokesperson—let alone a high-level one such as Tumusime-Mutabile in Uganda or Meles in Ethiopia—to show how these initiatives could be viewed as part of a poverty strategy. Rather, the battle was fought purely on grounds of fiscal feasibility. Thus, when the even more pro-poor Starter Pack initiative was mooted in 1998, the Malawian government had no basis of pro-poor credibility with which to build in relation to most donors.

    The Starter Pack provided "enough free seed and fertilizer along with extension advice for all smallholders to cultivate 0.1ha of staple grains... and legumes" (Harrigan 2003, p. 856). But the World Bank did not support the program, neither did any other donor subscribe to it except, briefly, the DFID, and the program had to be drastically scaled down from the year 2000 onward. This was the year when a high-water mark of nearly two tons per hectare maize yields was reached, and hybrid seed planting was abandoned. Smallholder yields then fell progressively and had halved by 2003. Much of the recent increase in poverty in Malawi (Table 15.3) can be explained in these terms. Malawian smallholders, after 1994, had no structure of state support with which they could form a trusting partnership, and being unable to exercise voice or loyalty, they responded largely by means of exit: migration to modern sector employment, where possible, or, more commonly, retreat into the subsistence economy.

    What also failed in Malawi was the lack of a long-term preventive vision. Smallholders in many parts of Malawi, notably the south, are extremely vulnerable to drought. This had been repeatedly exposed every few years, with particular force in the famine year of 1949 (Vaughan 1987) and again in 1992. Yet investments were never made to reduce the vulnerability of the south to drought, so that when the drought of 2002 hit, the fall in output was the same as 10 years previously. The contrast with Ethiopia, which had also experienced famine and learned from it, was eloquent.

11. This suggestion has been made by the IMF internal evaluation of the ESAF. See IMF (1998, p. 22).

16

Fungibility, Prior Actions, and Eligibility for Budget Support

OLIVER MORRISSEY
Center for Research on Economic Development and International Trade, and School of Economics, University of Nottingham

The basic principle of general budget support, as an alternative to aid financing of projects or sector programs, is that if donors approve of a recipient's spending allocation plans, it is appropriate to provide aid as budget support. This begs the question of how donors determine which recipients should be eligible for budget support. Typically, recipients are required to demonstrate for a period that they can and do allocate spending in the way agreed with donors, and they then become eligible. This practice can be termed "selectivity," where the recipient's prior actions are used as conditions to determine eligibility for budget support.

This paper addresses two issues related to providing aid in the form of general budget support. First, is conditionality (requiring prior actions by the recipient) an effective mechanism for selecting which recipients should be eligible for this support? Second, are concerns about fungibility solid reasons for not providing general budget support? Aid makes up a large share of the budget in poor countries, and clearly the impact of aid on fiscal behavior is an important determinant of the development effectiveness of aid (McGillivray and Morrissey 2004). Section B of the paper addresses the question of how donors decide which recipients should receive general budget support. Donors often resolve this problem by using a form of conditionality, selecting those recipients that implement required prior actions. A simple model shows that this practice imposes excess costs on deserving recipients and may not generate the efficiency gains in aid allocation that are posited by proponents of targeting. These features weaken the argument for selectivity in this form. Section C assesses whether concern with fungibility is a valid argument against general budget support. Section D concludes that budget support can safely be granted if recipients allocate spending in a manner broadly agreed with donors. Donors should focus on the effectiveness of spending, not on conditionality or fungibility.

A. Approaches to Improving Aid Effectiveness

Most aid is given to the governments of recipient countries and is used to finance public expenditure. In the poorest countries, aid accounts for a large share of government spending. For example, in low-income countries in 1997, aid accounted for almost a third of general government consumption on average—and was more than 100 percent in African countries such as Ghana, Senegal, Tanzania, and Uganda—whereas in lower-middle-income countries, the share was about 6 percent (McGillivray and Morrissey 2004, p. 74).[1]

Clearly, the impact of aid in developing countries depends on how it affects government spending and fiscal behavior more generally. Two issues are especially important: the effect of aid on the allocation of spending, and the effectiveness of that spending in delivering public goods and services—for example, whether health sector spending delivers improvements in health. For example, aid has a greater impact on growth if it increases spending on public investment, even though the productivity (effectiveness) of public investment in Sub-Saharan Africa is low (Gomanee and others 2006). Recent research shows that aid raises spending on social sectors (health, education, and sanitation), and that this contributes to poverty reduction (Mosley and others 2004) and helps to improve aggregate welfare, although again in the poorest aid-recipient countries the effectiveness of social spending in delivering welfare improvements is low (Gomanee and others 2005).

To enhance the effectiveness of aid, it is important to allocate aid to the most appropriate areas of spending and increase the effectiveness of such spending. Donors have tended to be most concerned about allocation (although recent work has addressed the effectiveness of spending—see Devarajan and Reinikka [2004] and Reinikka and Svensson [2004]). They have adopted a number of approaches to restrict or influence the areas of spending financed by aid. At one extreme is the creation of a special ring-fenced fund that can only be used for designated expenditures. For example, under the Heavily Indebted Poor Countries (HIPC) Facility II, the aid and savings from debt relief may be placed in a Poverty Action Fund to be spent on budget headings identified in the country's poverty reduction strategy paper (Morrissey 2004b). At the other extreme, donors may give aid in kind (such as medicines) or stipulate that recipients must match aid-financed spending in specified areas, through matching grants or counterpart funds (McGillivray and Morrissey 2000, 2001). Underlying all of these measures to influence the allocation of aid to expenditures is donors' concern with fungibility: is aid allocated to the areas of spending that donors want to support?

Three elements of fungibility can be distinguished (McGillivray and Morrissey [2004] provide a review). General fungibility arises where aid intended for a general purpose, investment spending, is actually used for a different purpose, consumption spending. If donors believe that aid must finance investment if it is to have an impact on growth, they will believe that redirecting aid to recurrent spending undermines the (growth) effectiveness of aid. A second element is categorical fungibility, where aid intended for a particular use, such as health, is used for another, in particular one that the donor does not intend to support, such as security or wages. Again, donors will believe that this undermines the development effectiveness of their aid. The third issue is additionality: even if the recipient government allocates all the aid to the donor's intended expenditure, the government's own (tax) resources previously allocated to that expenditure may be reallocated elsewhere so that spending on the donor's intended purpose does not increase by the full amount of the aid (McGillivray and Morrissey 2000). It is important to note that fungibility per se is not concerned with the misuse of aid (such as corruption), but simply with misallocation, or specifically nonadditionality. The misuse of aid is a concern, but it is relevant to the effectiveness of aid and spending rather than to fungibility.

Concern about fungibility is one reason why many donors are reluctant to provide aid in the form of general budget support. Cordella and Dell'Ariccia (2003) use a "fungibility model" to compare general budget support, where donors influence the overall allocation of resources (through conditionality) but fungibility may arise, to project aid, where donors can target an area of spending but do not influence overall allocation. In an environment where only some expenditures are subject to conditionality, these authors argue that budget support is preferred if (1) aid levels are low relative to the budget and (2) donor and recipient preferences are aligned. In practice, these conditions may not often hold simultaneously in the poorest countries for which aid is most important. For example, aid is significant in Uganda, so the first condition is not met even if the second is. Furthermore, as White and Morrissey (1997) show, the latter condition is only one of at least four possible cases (if preferences are defined over both aid levels and conditions).

A core argument of this paper is that this fungibility critique of general budget support is misplaced. If donor and recipient preferences on allocation are aligned, then fungibility is not an issue. Irrespective of the importance of aid in spending, recipients will allocate aid broadly in the way that donors desire, and general budget support is appropriate. Further, as White and Morrissey (1997) show, conditionality serves no useful purpose in this case and may be counterproductive (because unintentional noncompliance with conditions may appear intentional). On the other hand, if donor and recipient preferences are not aligned, conditionality is ineffectual (White and Morrissey 1997), and fungibility is less likely to undermine general budget support if aid is a *large* share of the budget. The intuition here has two elements: (1) it is easier to monitor the allocation of spending over broad budget headings than to monitor actual spending on many particular projects, and (2) if aid is a large share of the budget, recipients have fewer of their own resources to reallocate. Thus fungibility arguments do not undermine the case for general budget support to poor countries; fungibility is a "red herring," in the words of McGillivray and Morrissey (2000).

B. A Model of Selectivity through Prior Actions

Assume that donors only want to give general budget support to those countries that will allocate aid and government spending in a manner that donors approve of and in which government spending is effective. Assume further that some recipients are less able than others to monitor and guarantee the allocation and effectiveness of spending because of factors they cannot alter (at least in the medium term), such as administrative inefficiency or low-level corruption, and that donors cannot identify those factors with certainty. Thus donors believe that among the potential recipients of general budget support, at least some may not use this support appropriately and effectively. Our interest is in how donors can use information on countries' prior actions to acquire information on the distribution of types of recipients so as to allocate support to the most deserving. We are not concerned here with how prior actions are decided; we assume countries will comply if they perceive a benefit, and not otherwise. Thus "undeserving recipients" will not commit to prior actions and will not receive general budget support, and in this way, general budget support is targeted to the most deserving recipients.

Assume that the benefit of general budget support is maximized only if spending is effective and allocation is as agreed with donors (one could think of this as maximizing joint utility from spending). Taking an interpretation of the model proposed in Bougheas, Dasgupta, and Morrissey (2005), consider three types of developing country recipient (D) about which donors are uncertain (that is, donors do not know if the recipients would allocate expenditure properly or use it effectively):[2]

- Countries of the first type (s) have strong capacity, so that expenditure is allocated as planned and is effective, implying the ability to use general budget support effectively.
- Countries of the second type (w) are willing to allocate general budget support as planned but have only weak capacity to ensure allocation and effectiveness.
- Countries of the third type (u) are unwilling to allocate spending as donors wish, and their expenditure tends to be ineffective; they can be treated as undeserving of general budget support.

Conceptually, at the beginning of the period, recipients face an *expenditure allocation* (e) financed by aid. If s countries implement e, they receive a return of X at the end of the period, whereas if w countries invest e their return is X-α (where α is a measure of their expenditure inefficiency, in allocation and effectiveness, relative to s types). However, if w countries undertake adjustment by implementing a set of *prior actions*, which cost c, then they can increase the return from their expenditure. The parameter c measures both the extent and the cost of these actions, such as costs of improving expenditure monitoring and management systems. Specifically, if w countries spend e, having implemented the prior actions, they receive

$$(X - \alpha + g(c)),\ g(0) = 0_1\ g' > 0_1,\ g'' < 0,\ g'(\bar{c}) = 1,\ g(\bar{c}) = \alpha$$

Evidently the efficient level of adjustment is at cost $\bar{c}$; at this level, spending by w countries yields the same return as spending by s countries. Adjustment activities must be performed at the beginning of the period, *prior* to spending (hence, in this model, prior to receiving aid). Type u economies receive zero benefit if they spend, regardless of whether or not they undertake prior actions (zero benefit is the extreme; it is only necessary that the benefit of general budget support is very low).

Donors do not know which type a given developing country recipient falls into. For any $k \in \{s, w, u\}$, the proportion of k countries in the pool of D countries, assumed to be constant over time, is π_k. N, X, and e are common knowledge, as is the function $g(\bullet)$, but individual outputs are unobservable (for example, even if expenditure allocation can be monitored, effectiveness is not observed). Adjustment cost, c, is only observable over intervals, either because government actions exhibit indivisibilities or because a donor's ability to measure a country's adjustment activities is imperfect. As ($\alpha > \bar{c}$), adjustment is worthwhile for *w* countries, but for *s* countries, prior actions impose a net cost because they are unnecessary.

The donor knows some upper bound for $\pi_u > 0$, that is, it knows some value $\lambda \in (0,1)$ such that $\pi_u \leq \lambda$. This also implies knowledge of some lower bounds for the deserving types, that is, that $\pi_s, + \pi_u) \in [1-\lambda, 1)$. The donor does not know the actual proportions but has prior beliefs about these proportions, given by a subjective distribution function $H(\pi_s, \pi_u)$, which need not correspond to the objective distribution.

Let $\theta = \frac{\pi_s}{\pi_u}$, and let $F(\theta, \pi_u)$ be the donor's subjective distribution function for θ, generated from H, and assume that F is independent of π_u. In simple terms, donors can have separate views about the proportion of *u* types and about the distribution of types. This implies that the support of F must be some subset of $\left[0, \frac{1-\lambda}{\lambda}\right]$.

$$E(\theta, \pi_u) = \theta_E \in \left[0, \frac{1-\lambda}{\lambda}\right] \tag{1}$$

The donor has a total budget of:

$$B = \kappa Ne, \text{ where } 0 < \kappa = \delta(1-\pi_u) < 1-\lambda \tag{2}$$

Since the donor knows $\pi_u \leq \lambda$, it knows $\delta \in (0,1)$, though it does not know its exact value. Thus the donor knows its budget is not large enough to award general budget support to all effective economies.[3] Note that the donor would not know this unless she knew some upper bound for π_u. The donor's objective is to distribute the budget among *D* countries so as to maximize their expected total (or average) benefit.

Suppose the donor offers general budget support of *e* provided that the recipient carries out prior actions costing $\bar{c}$. All *u* countries will reject this, but all *s* and *w* countries would be willing to implement the adjustment, accept the aid, and use it for spending with a return $[X - \bar{c}]$. As $\delta < 1$, not all potential recipients can be funded. Assuming funds are allocated randomly, the average conditional benefit (G_C) therefore is:

$$G_C = \delta[(1 - \pi_u)(X - \bar{c})] \tag{3}$$

Thus prior actions succeed in screening undeserving applicants out of the application process and thereby eliminate "leakage." This efficiency in targeting general budget support (implementing selectivity, albeit of a self-selection form) comes at the cost of unnecessary adjustment by *s* types, which leads to a total wastage of $\delta\pi_s\bar{c}N$.

If *e* is distributed nonselectively, all *D* economies will then wish to receive general budget support, and the equilibrium involves pooling. Given the donor's budget constraint in equation (2), only $\delta(1 - \pi_u)$ proportion of each type will receive the aid. The average realized benefit (G_R) is:

$$G_r = \delta(1 - \pi_u)[(X - \bar{c}) + \bar{c}\pi_s + e\pi_u] \tag{4}$$

Thus nonselective general budget support diverts resources away from some *s* or *w* types, but eliminates waste from unnecessary adjustment. Note that equation (3)−(4) yields:

$$G_R - G_C = \delta\pi_u(1 - \pi_u)[,\backslash\theta c - (X - e - \bar{c}), \text{ where } \theta = \frac{\pi_s}{\pi_u}] \tag{5}$$

If the term in square brackets is zero, $G_R = G_C$; if positive, $G_R > G_C$; and if negative, $G_R < G_C$. We can define the value of θ for which the term in brackets is zero using equation (5) to get:

Proposition 1. Let $\hat{\theta} = \dfrac{X - e - \bar{c}}{\bar{c}}$. Given the assumptions:

(a) There exist distribution functions for θ that would make a risk-neutral donor prefer prior action selectivity.

(b) If λ is believed to be high, then θ_E is expected to be low (π_u high relative to π_s), therefore $\theta_E < \hat{\theta}$ (implying $G_R < G_C$), and the distribution function for θ would make a risk-neutral donor prefer prior action selectivity.

(c) If λ is believed to be low, then θ_E is expected to be high (π_u low relative to π_s), therefore $\theta_E > \hat{\theta}$ (implying $G_R > G_C$), and there exist distribution functions for θ that would make a risk-neutral donor prefer nonselective allocation.

By Proposition 1(a), regardless of the values of the known parameters X, e, $\bar{c}$, and λ, there will always exist prior beliefs that would justify selectivity. Intuitively, the donor need only expect the proportion of s countries to be sufficiently small. If the upper bound for the proportion of u countries is sufficiently high, then it is not possible to hold beliefs involving very high proportions of s countries. Consequently, all possible prior beliefs regarding the distribution of θ, which are independent of the proportion of u countries, must justify selectivity (Proposition 1[b]). If it is believed that the proportion of u countries is relatively low—that is, λ is low—then one may expect the proportion of s countries to be high. Such beliefs would justify nonselectivity (Proposition 1[c]). Proposition 1(a) implies that other beliefs exist in this situation that would justify selectivity.

Under plausible restrictions on the prior distribution of beliefs, when individual outputs are unobservable and recipient costs are sufficiently indivisible, donors favoring prior action selectivity would not receive any additional information from the equilibrium. They may learn which recipients are of the u type, but they would not get information on the distribution of the other two types. Consequently, they would have no reasonable grounds for revising their beliefs, and requiring prior actions becomes self-perpetuating. The implication is that allocation according to prior actions reveals no objective information on country characteristics that would facilitate more efficient selection of eligibility for general budget support.

In this context, a donor's decision on whether to advocate prior actions will depend on its beliefs about the proportion of recipients for which these actions imply significant net (excess) costs and about the proportion of recipients that would not use this support effectively. If a donor believes that the first proportion is small (that is, prior actions impose few excess costs on the countries whose spending is productive), and/or that the second is large (that is, the potential gains from targeting are large), it would advocate prior actions. It is donors' beliefs regarding the distribution of types of recipient that lead donors to prefer prior action selectivity for the allocation of general budget support (that is, certain beliefs imply they will require prior actions, but different beliefs may imply that that eligibility is not based on required prior actions). Evidently, the first-best allocation involves ensuring that as many of the *s* countries are covered as possible, without any adjustment. All the remaining aid available for general budget support should be used to cover as many *w* countries as possible, with adjustment being required only of these *w* countries. However, as donors do not know what type each potential recipient is, the first-best allocation cannot be attained. The simple point is that requiring prior actions may deliver the targeting benefit of excluding *u* countries, but does so by imposing an excess cost on *s* countries.

A solution is possible if donors could identify some observable recipient characteristic that is common and specific to each type.[4] What information on performance and characteristics of recipients would allow donors to identify those that can make the greatest use of such support? This is the issue we now address by considering fungibility. Note that if one has such information, this determines eligibility, and prior actions (conditionality) are not required.

C. Government Spending: Fungibility, Allocation, and Effectiveness

In the context of broad conditionality and policy reform, it may be reasonable to assume that donors are relatively uncertain about the type of (most) recipients. But in the case of budget support, donors may have enough information at least to classify potential recipients under one of the three types considered above.[5] Of course, if they can do so, prior action conditionality is not required. In principle, donors are reasonably well informed about how well recipients monitor and allocate expenditure, and are party to the monitoring process; they know where aid goes, even if they do not know how effective spending is. In practice, however, it may only be the World Bank and IMF, and those large bilateral donors that engage with ministries of finance (such as the British and Dutch), that feel well-informed about expenditure allocation and monitoring.

Even if donors collectively are fairly well informed about expenditure management, many have reservations about budget support. Typically, as argued above, these reservations relate to concerns about fungibility. This section argues that such concerns are misplaced and may even be misleading. There are two elements to the argument. First, fungibility is a very static concern; it ignores the dynamics of the evolution of spending and the broader context of the effects of aid on fiscal behavior (spending, taxation, and borrowing). This literature is reviewed in McGillivray and Morrissey (2004), and we consider only the core issues below. Second, fungibility is assumed to be an *action* taken by recipients: they decide to use aid to allocate spending in a way that differs from what donors intended. McGillivray and Morrissey (2001) show that what appears to be fungibility can arise for a variety of reasons and may not be due to deliberate actions by recipients. We sketch their model as they specifically consider ways of delivering aid, such as in kind or matching grants, that are intended to minimize fungibility.

Studies of fungibility have many problems (McGillivray and Morrissey 2000, 2004). Typically, analysts focus on the sector allocation of aid in a particular year, ignoring dynamic (or lagged) effects. Given the problems of measuring sector aid (good data are rarely available on how donors intended the aid to be allocated), slow disbursement, and the many implementation problems that occur in spending ministries, it is not surprising that studies find a weak correlation, if any, between sector aid and sector spending in any given year. The studies do not explicitly allow for the effects of aid on tax effort or borrowing (the fiscal effects) or on the evolution of total or sector spending. "It may well be the case that in any given year expenditure outcomes by sector do not correspond closely to aid allocations. If, over time, spending on the headings favored by donors does increase, then how much of a concern is fungibility?" (McGillivray and Morrissey 2004, p. 80). If one takes a longer-term view, it is the evolution of expenditure that is important, and whether this is in the direction (and at a speed) acceptable to donors. Donors only need to monitor expenditure, rather than exercise concerns over fungibility.

Building on the public choice literature on fiscal illusion, McGillivray and Morrissey (2001) propose the concept of "aid illusion," whereby failures in the transmission of information from donors through government policy officials to spending officials (often at the local government level) weaken the links between aid and spending. They propose two levels: negotiating the "parameters" of aid (for example, block grants versus matching grants) between donors and recipient policy makers and implementing associated spending (a relationship between recipient policy and spending officials). Aid illusion can be shown to generate, among other things, apparent ex post fungibility even where preferences are aligned (that is, policy officials did not intend fungibility) or overspending (that is, total spending increases by more than the amount of aid).

Conventional treatments of fungibility consider interaction between donors and recipients, where the latter include officials who make spending plans, and in doing so may treat aid as fully fungible, as well as officials who implement the plans. A richer analysis is provided by distinguishing these two levels of decision making: McGillivray and Morrissey (2001) focus on the actions of the implementing officials with ultimate responsibility for expenditure on specific headings. These officials are responsible for allocating a given amount of aid within a spending category, but they need not know the share of aid in the total revenue pool at their disposal and may not be fully informed of the budget terms on which aid was granted. The finance ministry, or policy officials, draw up the budget and set expenditure plans; they may or may not wish to treat aid as fully fungible. That paper allows for possibilities that have been observed in empirical research on the impact of aid on public sector fiscal behavior. Aid can lead to greater than proportional increases in total expenditure, while tax and other recurrent revenue can rise or fall simultaneously, and the conditions for full fungibility can be present. The authors consider aid in kind and two scenarios for matching grants:

- Donors give aid in kind (such as medicines) to ensure it is allocated in the intended area. Policy officials intend fungibility by planned reallocation of their own resources. However, spending officials perceive aid in kind as reducing the price of a good they require or distribute, so they increase their demand, and overall spending on the sector increases by at least the amount of the aid. Ex post there is no fungibility, although it was intended.

- Donors offer a matching grant, and policy officials agree with the donors' spending allocation. However, spending officials misperceive the matching grant as a block grant and therefore spend less than intended. Ex post there is apparent fungibility, although it was not intended; apparent fungibility can arise from implementation rather than intentions.
- Donors offer a matching grant, but policy officials intend fungibility. However, spending officials perceive the matching grant correctly, and spending increases by more than the value of the aid. Again, ex post there is no fungibility, although it was intended. This highlights that it is the action of the spending officials that really matters.

The aim of this analysis is to show that unintended outcomes can result from misperceptions or illusions regarding either the real or nominal value of the aid inflow or the way in which the aid is delivered. The analysis is not intended to describe what happens but rather to highlight the complexity that arises when many levels of officials are involved.[6] Specifically, it emphasizes that observed fungibility may not be due to deliberate actions.

The above arguments thus imply that a focus on conditionality may lead donors to (a) incorrectly infer that aid is misallocated, because it discourages them from considering the evolution of expenditure allocation over time, and (b) attribute misallocation to the intentions of officials, when it is actually due to the complexity of expenditure management and implementation. The analysis does not suggest that intentional fungibility never occurs (there will be cases where recipients use aid in a fungible manner), but it does imply that donors should focus their monitoring on the evolution of expenditure plans and outcomes rather than on static (annual) allocations.

D. Conclusions and Policy Implications

Section B demonstrated that, when donors are uncertain about recipient types, the requirement for prior actions (conditionality) is an imperfect selection mechanism. It may exclude the least deserving recipients but does so by imposing an excess cost on the most deserving, and does not help in identifying the latter. Section C showed that undue focus on the fungibility of aid resources can detract a donor's attention from what is really happening. It is useful to draw a distinction between fungibility, where donor and recipient spending preferences differ (by definition), and aid illusion, where both donors and recipients have imperfect processes for allocating and monitoring aid expenditures. The analysis highlighted that what really matters is to ensure that the officials responsible for spending have full and correct information.

Taken together, these conclusions imply that donors need only be concerned that recipients share their spending allocation preferences. They can determine whether this is the case by observing expenditure allocation plans and outcomes in a monitoring process that has become almost a routine feature of donor-recipient relations. If donors and recipients do have the same preferences, general budget support can be granted: conditionality is not required (and is not even helpful), and fungibility concerns are not relevant. If preferences are not aligned, then general budget support is not appropriate, and again conditionality is unlikely to serve a useful purpose (because it will not align preferences). If donors want to deliver aid through the budget, they can use mechanisms such as aid in kind or matching grants to minimize fungibility (though it is important to ensure that spending officials are fully aware of the aid modalities). Alternatively, donors could choose to fund projects directly.

The argument made in Section C is an example of a more general critique of conditionality for selection. Morrissey (2005b) uses the model to discuss conditionality and selectivity more generally, and builds on Morrissey (2005a) to argue that a partnership built on dialogue and monitoring the use of aid is preferable to selectivity based on conditionality. The World Bank is adopting more flexible, simple, and transparent approaches to conditionality, advocating ownership and partnership and "an approach based on reputation and results" (Koeberle 2005, p. 66). However, a recipient's prior actions are still viewed as an important element of conditionality, if only to signal commitment to a particular direction of policy. Emphasizing ownership does not necessarily resolve the inefficiency of prior actions as a basis of conditionality outlined in Section B. For example, a recipient may commit to a particular policy action not because it believes it is the best option but because it knows the donor favors that action. Further, although monitoring is seen as important, it is not usually interpreted simply as monitoring the way in which aid is used. Rather, "monitoring has typically focused more on compliance with ex ante conditionality than on progress, outcomes, and poverty impacts" (Koeberle 2005, p. 74). Conditionality may have a role to play, but it should not have a role in determining eligibility for general budget support.

Even if donor and recipient preferences are aligned, general budget support is not necessarily better than project aid. In poor countries, donor projects may be more effective than government spending. For example, Gomanee and others (2005) show that although aid raises government spending on social sectors in low-income countries, government social spending is not effective in delivering welfare improvements, whereas aid is effective (perhaps through projects). In middle-income countries, on the other hand, government social spending is effective, but aid has no discernible effect on the level of social spending (perhaps because aid is a small share of spending). The relative effectiveness of government versus direct donor social spending is an empirical question, and we are not aware of much evidence comparing the effectiveness of donor project spending with that of government spending. The practical implication is that donors could continue with project aid (where they can demonstrate that it is effective) even where much aid, or some donors' aid, is channeled through general budget support. Relying on project aid may appeal to some small donors that are reluctant to commit to budget support. Belgium, for example, prefers project aid because that is where its aid agencies' experience lies, and because they feel unable to influence recipient countries' general budget allocation (Holvoet and Renard 2005, p. 143).

In conclusion, it is appropriate to give aid as general budget support in those countries where expenditure allocation is monitored and seen to be broadly aligned with donor preferences. Donors should have enough experience and information to be able to identify such countries. Prior actions or conditionality for receiving general budget support are unnecessary, and there is no need to be concerned with fungibility. However, it is important that donors focus on improving the effectiveness of government spending to ensure that general budget support is used effectively. Donor project aid will continue to have a role in countries where government spending has low effectiveness, although donors should be able to show that their project spending is effective. In countries where donor and recipient expenditure preferences are not aligned, there is little justification for general budget support; in these countries, more effort and dialogue are needed to align spending and, most likely, to improve expenditure planning and monitoring. Conditionality will not necessarily improve this process. There are still ways that donors can influence where aid is spent, such as by providing aid in kind and matching grants, but the success of this will depend on getting correct information to officials responsible for spending. Budget support is not appropriate always and everywhere, but increasing the effectiveness of spending is a priority in all recipients.

Endnotes

1. Aid may be equivalent to more than 100 percent of government spending if the measure includes aid that is not delivered through the budget, such as technical assistance or donor-financed projects.
2. We assume only three types for convenience; adding more types increases complexity without providing new insights. Note also that the discussion here is a specific interpretation of a quite general model in Bougheas, Dasgupta, and Morrissey (2005).
3. This simplifies exposition, but we only need the budget to be insufficient to cover all D recipients, that is, $\kappa < 1$.
4. Of course, if unique indicators could be identified for each type, donors would face no uncertainty regarding recipient type and this model would not apply. Bougheas, Dasgupta, and Morrissey (2005) argue that it is not generally possible to identify such indicators for aid or charity in general, but perhaps it is easier in the case of general budget support.
5. Although aid modalities and the nature of donor-recipient relations have changed over the past two decades, donors have well-established working relationships with most recipients. And while governments may change, the same senior officials usually remain in place, at least in ministries of finance. Policy reform is a slow and difficult process influenced by many economic and political factors, but budget and expenditure processes are more clearly defined, both in terms of what is done and who is responsible. Such processes have also been improved over the past 10 years or so—for example, with the widespread adoption of medium-term expenditure frameworks.
6. Note that complexity is increased when there are many donors with different preferences and requirements for aid delivery and monitoring, and also when spending is more decentralized.

Good Practice Note on Harmonization

*Lessons from OECD Development Assistance Committee on Harmonizing Donor Practices for Effective Aid Delivery**

How can donors best deliver budget support in ways that maximize its developmental benefits while reinforcing partners' capacity to achieve aggregate fiscal discipline, strategic allocation of funds, value for money, and probity in the use of public monies—key objectives of public financial management (PFM) systems? Experience suggests the following are good practices.

Supporting Ownership

- *Refrain from targeting support.* As a norm, there should be no restrictions on the use of funds once these are transferred to a partner country's treasury account following the fulfillment of agreed conditionality.
- *Reflect partner country priorities.* Conditionality should draw as much as possible on the partner country's policy agenda and objectives, as reflected, for example, in the programs and targets set out in national development strategy documents (particularly the poverty reduction strategy paper and its annual review).
- *Focus on results.* Budget support should focus on results, that is to say, the outputs and outcomes that are linked to the policies pursued by the partner government.

Enhancing Performance and Accountability in PFM

- *Follow good practices in PFM diagnostic and assessment work.* Donors should avoid burdensome and costly duplication of work by sharing the results of their own diagnostic and assessment work and basing their decisions on the results of work conducted by others.
- *Directly support the capacity development of partners' PFM systems.* Budget support should directly encourage improvements in partners' PFM systems, including transparency and accountability to the legislature and civil society at large.
- *Avoid undermining country systems.* Given the varying standards of expenditure management among partner countries and the accountability requirements of donors, budget support providers cannot always fully rely on partner countries' systems for expenditure and control. Ex ante and ex post assessments, safeguards, and additional reporting requirements can therefore be justified. They should, however, be carried out in a way that strengthens partner country systems rather than replacing them with temporary and/or donor-specific parallel arrangements.

* This note summarizes key principles and good practices identified in OECD-DAC (2005a).

Reducing Transaction Costs

- *Streamline conditionality.* Partners should have a single, comprehensive national budget and a single national strategy, and budget support providers should link funding to a single framework of conditions and/or a reduced set of indicators. This does not mean that all donors should have identical conditions, but rather that each donor's conditions should be derived from a common framework. Donors should seek, whenever possible, to draw conditions from a partner's poverty reduction strategy (PRS), its annual PRS review, or an equivalent national framework.
- *Rationalize fiduciary assessments.* When providing budget support, donors have different accountability requirements and fiduciary concerns. In doing so, they should reduce the burden on partner countries through fewer, better-coordinated, and, to the extent possible, common diagnostic reviews.
- *Align processes.* Donors should individually and collectively align their dialogue and monitoring processes with the partner countries' national budgetary cycles of policy formulation and implementation, and rely as much as possible on the partners' reporting and monitoring systems for their own reporting purposes.
- *Tap the potential of joint donor frameworks.* The drive toward increased harmonization has led to the creation of donor groups on a country-by-country basis. These are often formalized through the drafting of "joint partnership frameworks" that outline the basic principles of donor collaboration and often contain a "common assessment framework" as the basis for reviews and disbursements. Frameworks should be streamlined and made as simple as possible. Particular attention should be paid to the risk of creating additional layers of institutional processes, and of reaching agreement on common assessment frameworks simply by creating a single list of all partnership members' individual concerns.
- *Time disbursements to facilitate the smooth execution of budgetary payments.* Donors should agree with a partner country's budgetary authorities on the most appropriate timing for the planned release of budget support resources, particularly if there are significant fluctuations in the country's budgetary cash flows during the year.

Enhancing Predictability and Reducing Volatility

- *Program budget support over several years.* Donors should increase their efforts to program and commit budget support (subject to performance) over a rolling multiyear framework to match the timeframe for partner countries' medium-term budgetary planning. Indications of the overall envelope of this medium-term support should be provided as early as possible.
- *Align support with partner country budget cycles.* Donors should align budget support commitments as closely as possible with partner countries' budget cycles. They should provide early indicative commitments to facilitate budget planning and

strive to complete negotiation in time to permit final commitment before the start of the new budget year.

- *Design conditionality to enhance the predictability of disbursements.* To effectively design conditionality to enhance the predictability of disbursements, one should consider:

    - *The timing of the review of performance.* The sooner the fulfillment of conditions can be verified, the sooner a partner country's budgetary authorities can be sure of the amount of budget support that will be disbursed. When possible, zero in-year variability should be sought—for example, by specifying in year n disbursements for year $n + 1$.

    - *The clarity of conditionality and its evaluation process.* The conditions attached to disbursements, and the process through which their fulfillment is assessed, should be clearly specified and leave little margin for interpretation.

    - *Political conditionality.* This should not be specifically linked to budget support or any individual aid instrument, but rather should be handled in the context of the overarching political dialogue between a partner country and its donors.

- *Time disbursements in a predictable manner.* Following the positive review of conditionality, disbursements should occur promptly or at least within a well-defined timeframe.

- *Avoid stop-go cycles and allow for graduated responses.* Depending on the share of a country's public expenditures financed through budget support, the suspension of aid by donors can be particularly disruptive, leading to an unintended excessive response to the underlying policy slippage and introducing significant additional macroeconomic volatility. To help mitigate these risks:

    - Avoid bunching conditionality around a limited number of common criteria.

    - Avoid institutionalizing the principle of unanimous donors' agreement.

    - Identify potential underperformance early on.

    - Allow for partial disbursements in cases of partial fulfillment.

- *Build public support.* Donors should communicate actively with their political constituencies and civil society to enhance the understanding of budget support, its opportunities, and the related risks. A better understanding of budget support and of the related importance of partner countries' own systems and priorities will provide an incentive for donors to move the policy dialogue away from narrowly defined individual agendas.

Good Practice Note on Memorandum of Understanding

*Use of the Memorandum of Understanding**

The memorandum of understanding (MOU) is an informal tool used to document government and donor partner commitments on harmonization and alignment of budget support programs. One of its main purposes is to help strengthen donor coordination and harmonization, with a view to enhancing the effectiveness and efficiency of budget support programs to achieve governments' poverty reduction goals.

Donor Harmonization and Budget Support Groups

At the 2005 Paris High-Level Forum, donors reinforced their commitment to working toward common arrangements for financing, disbursements, monitoring and evaluation, and the reduction of duplicative missions and diagnostic reviews by introducing a series of indicators to track progress on these and other areas.[1] MOUs and budget support groups, particularly in IDA-eligible borrowers, are expected to play a key role in furthering progress on the donor harmonization agenda.

Characteristics of Donor Harmonization

Harmonizing budget support entails a concerted effort between budget support donors and the government to reduce transaction costs in terms of time, effort, reporting, and monitoring. Key characteristics include:

- assessing country performance and making subsequent disbursements against a common evaluation framework (often called a performance assessment framework[PAF]) that draws the performance benchmarks and targets from the PRS,
- participating in joint donor missions,
- harmonizing donor reviews and simplifying procedures, and
- aligning disbursements to correspond with recipient countries' budget cycles.

In this respect, MOUs outline mutual obligations of countries and their partners in the PRS process.[2] MOUs aim to facilitate early commitments of aid, integration of these commitments into the budget formulation process, and predictability of aid disbursements within the fiscal year.

Budget Support Groups

Where multiple donors provide budget support in selected countries, budget support groups may provide a degree of harmonization of donor efforts around country-led programs. Emerging good practice principles for the operation of budget support groups include:[3]

* This note summarizes key principles and good practices identified in World Bank (2005k).

- *MOU.* An MOU or similar document may be a useful approach to formalizing the objectives and procedures of the budget support group, particularly if there are many donors. However, it is not a necessary document if a country already has a robust division of labor among donors or there is a clear but informal understanding among donors.
- *Donor alignment.* Donors in budget support groups should, as far as possible, harmonize with each other, align their budget support processes with the national PRS and budget calendar, and draw monitoring indicators and prior actions and triggers (conditions) for disbursement from the PRS or annual PRS progress report.
- *Alternative programs.* Where PRSs and their annual progress reports are not sufficiently operational and prioritized, or where the government seeks a more specific implementation framework, more specific programs need to be agreed as the result of a transparent and coordinated process.
- *Actions/triggers.* Disbursement actions/triggers and monitoring indicators may be policy actions, inputs, outputs, or outcomes. They should be incorporated in a single matrix—often referred to as a PAF—ideally drawn from the government's PRS. Actions/triggers and monitoring indicators in the PAF should be limited in number, including only those crucial to the government's implementation of its program. They should be as specific, credible, and easily monitorable as possible.
- *Program assessment.* Donors should be clear about how they will assess progress against disbursement actions/triggers and how they will respond to performance and underperformance. Allowing flexibility for different donors to respond differently to performance mitigates the risk of all aid flows to the recipient government being simultaneously delayed or suspended.
- *Rotating chairmanships.* Rotating chairmanship arrangements, an annual report to government on donor compliance with MOU principles, and establishment of a (donor-funded) group joint secretariat may improve efficiency and reduce transaction costs.
- *Membership rules.* Establishing rules for membership of the budget support groups is useful. Typically, it makes sense to focus on donors that are actually providing budget support.

Remaining Challenges

Budget support groups face many challenges, including limiting the size of the PAF, handling governance and PFM concerns and designing measurable indicators or benchmarks in this area, providing transparent and predictable mechanisms for reaction to underperformance, and managing tensions between "big" and "small" donors within the group.

Operating Principles for MOUs and Budget Support Groups

MOUs have been agreed in a variety of countries, and each takes a slightly different approach based on country circumstances. However, some emerging good practice principles are outlined below.

Objectives and Participants

Overall, the MOU should focus on the procedural and economic development aspects of the provision of budget support. Teams should consider the following areas when developing an MOU:

- *Objectives.* Include a clear statement of objectives. The MOU should aim to enhance the harmonization of budget support programs to help the government achieve its poverty reduction goals.
- *PRS as basis for support.* In line with the objectives, indicate that the country's PRS or equivalent national development strategy serves as the foundation upon which donors agree to base their provision of budget support.
- *Participants.* Spell out the criteria for participation in the MOU. Consideration should be given to defining carefully the roles and responsibilities of "full members" of the budget support program versus those of observers, which may include nonbudget and nonfinancial contributors and/or the IMF.

Operating Principles

In developing an MOU, budget support groups should incorporate the following operating principles:

- *Precedence of bilateral and multilateral agreements.* Respect institutional governance structures and binding institutional constraints. Indicate that bilateral or multilateral agreements take legal precedence over the MOU and that agreements reached within the MOU framework are subject to review and revision until approved by relevant authorities.
- *Government responsibilities.* Spell out clearly and succinctly the responsibilities of the government. This includes, among other things, reporting requirements, such as annual progress reports under the framework of the poverty reduction strategy paper.
- *Donor responsibilities.* Spell out clearly and succinctly the distinct accountabilities of donor partners in relation to the government and each other. Sharing information on relevant operations with other donors and clear agreement on roles should be an integral part of donor responsibilities
- *Timing of disbursements, commitment levels.* Donor partners should seek to indicate as clearly as possible the timing/cycle of budget support to improve the in-year, short-term, and medium-term predictability of funding.

- *PAF.* The MOU should include a process to develop a PAF, setting out an internally consistent, concise, and monitorable set of key policy actions and output and outcome indicators with which to gauge successful implementation of the government's program.
- *Adjusting disbursements to country performance.* Improving predictability requires donors to be transparent about the circumstances/criteria under which aid flows may be withheld or reduced.
- *Reviews.* Donor reviews should ideally be carried out jointly and be rationalized in the context of the PRS annual preformance reviews and preparation, as well as sectoral and other relevant reviews.
- *Reporting.* The MOU should spell out clearly the reports to be used as a basis for reviews and performance assessment. Reporting requirements should be kept to a minimum, harmonized among donors, and, to the extent possible, linked with the annual performance and budget reviews.
- *Provision of capacity building/technical assistance.* To address the challenge of weak institutional and human capacity, MOUs can indicate donors' intentions to provide specific assistance for capacity building and technical assistance in line with the government's program.
- *Calendar.* MOUs commonly include a generic calendar showing the timing of reporting, reviews, assessments, disbursements, commitments, and so on.
- *Audits.* MOUs often specify whether the regular audits of the budget are to be furnished by the country, and include the possibility for signatory donors to request external audits.
- *Evaluation.* MOUs could indicate how progress in implementing the MOU will be evaluated, by whom, and at what frequency, including whether the MOU will be regularly reviewed and updated (for example, annually, every three years, and so on).
- *Entry into operation and amendments.* MOUs should indicate the date the MOU becomes effective and how the MOU may be amended.
- *Termination.* MOUs need to spell out procedures for termination of membership/participation in the MOU.

Endnotes

1. See High-Level Forum (2005); for more information on the donor harmonization agenda, see www.aidharmonization.org
2. For a more extensive discussion, see World Bank (2005e).
3. Drawn from Strategic Partnership with Africa, "Budget Support Working Group, Report on Kigali Workshop, June 16–18, 2004."

PART VI
Country Experiences

17

Budget Support, Aid Dependency, and Dutch Disease: The Case of Uganda

MICHAEL ATINGI-EGO
Bank of Uganda

Uganda's commitment to economic reforms and macroeconomic stability has given confidence to major donors, which have provided project aid, budget support, food aid, and emergency relief. Uganda now depends on budget support to finance nearly half its total government expenditures, most of which are used for nontraded goods and services. Budget support provides substantial injections of Ugandan shilling liquidity into the economy, and to prevent inflationary pressures arising, the monetary authorities have sought to reduce the shilling injections to levels that are consistent with demand conditions in the economy. But because Uganda's financial markets are thin and the country has only a limited range of monetary policy instruments, the sterilization efforts put upward pressure on the interest and exchange rates. However, large-scale sterilization in thin financial markets could become detrimental for the competitiveness of an economy, raising fears of Dutch disease.[1]

Some recent studies on Uganda have suggested these fears might be unfounded. Some have argued that Uganda has idle capacity that could be drawn into production to satisfy the demand for nontradable goods and services that is induced by increased aid inflows. Simulation results suggest that the supply of nontradables would increase strongly enough to almost entirely satisfy the additional demand arising from increased aid flows and, consequently, that the pressures for exchange rate appreciation would be reduced or even reversed—thus enhancing the performance of Uganda's exports.

Other observers, however, emphasize that there is a limit to the amount of aid that can be sterilized by the monetary authorities, and that aid above this limit can render macroeconomic management difficult or even undermine a country's growth prospects.

This paper analyzes the growth of budget support to Uganda and its implications for the economy. Section A discusses the patterns and composition of budget support to Uganda. Section B analyzes the implications of increased budget support inflows to the economy and for macroeconomic policy. Section C discusses the evolution of prices for tradables and nontradables in Uganda and what this could mean for export sector competitiveness. Section D presents summary findings of the recent Uganda shilling appreciation and its impact on exports. Section E provides conclusions and policy recommendations.

A. Patterns and Composition of Budget Support to Uganda, 1993–2003

In 1991 and 1992, the Ugandan government implemented wide-ranging policies intended to eliminate structural bottlenecks (Holmgren and others 1999). Partly on account of these reforms, inflation was contained at low levels, and with the coffee boom of the mid-1990s, economic growth averaged 10 percent in 1994–95. The restoration of macroeconomic stability ushered in increased flows of aid, notable among which were a three-year Enhanced Structural Adjustment Facility (ESAF) program with the International Monetary Fund (IMF) and the second Structural Adjustment Credit from the World Bank (both in 1994); these were followed in 1997 by a new ESAF and the approval of a third Structural Adjustment Credit by the World Bank.

The overall trend in budget support to Uganda reflects donor support for the country's economic reform effort. Until 1999, budget support flows to Uganda were relatively small, averaging less than US$200 million a year (Figure 17.1), or about 3 percent of Uganda's GDP. After 1999, this started to change, with total budget support almost doubling to 6 percent of GDP in 2000 and peaking in 2001 at about 8 percent. The increase was a result of the development of the first Poverty Eradication Action Plan (PEAP) (1997–98), which led to the introduction of the Poverty Action Fund in 1998–99 in support of the PEAP, and Uganda's resulting qualification for debt relief under the Heavily Indebted Poor Countries Initiative (HIPC) in 1998–99.

Budget support has supplied a growing share of Uganda's total aid receipts, rising from an average of about 28 percent during the 1990s to a current level of about 42 percent after peaking at 52 percent in 2001–02. This trend has been largely due to the government's continued efforts to achieve the Millennium Development Goals (MDGs)[2] as embodied in the PEAP.

The ratio of grants to total budget support has risen from an average of 44 percent in the 1990s to 73 percent today, partly to address the increasingly worrisome growth of Uganda's stock of external debt and partly to address the problem of debt sustainability. Government has set a ceiling on how much aid (both budget support

FIGURE 17.1 Budget Support Disbursements to Uganda, 1993–2003

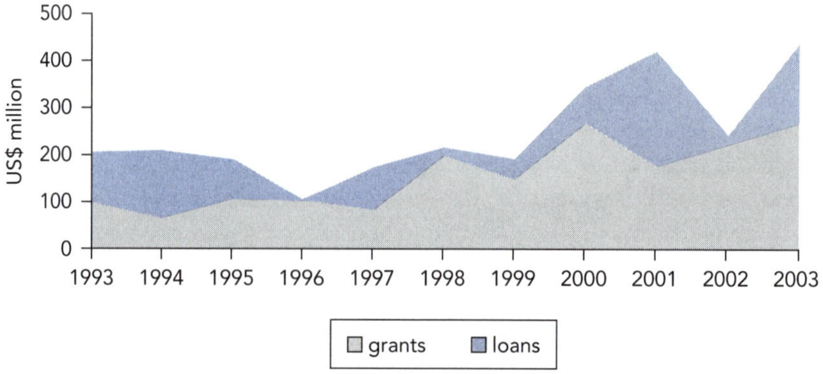

and project aid) it can source in the form of loans; only after assessing that both domestic revenues and grants are insufficient to finance the national budget has government contracted loans, but only on highly concessional terms.

Bilateral budget support as a share of total budget support rose from about 20 percent in 1993 to 60 percent in 2003 (Figure 17.2). The major bilateral donors include the United Kingdom, Ireland, Denmark, Japan, Netherlands, Germany, Sweden, Norway, Austria, and the United States. The United Kingdom has consistently been the largest donor, accounting for more than 40 percent of total budget support from bilateral creditors.

Among the multilateral donors of budget support, the World Bank has consistently been the largest; its support peaked in 2001 at US$225 million (current prices), or more than half of the total budget support disbursements that year. IMF credits, which were also quite high in the early 1990s, have dropped from an average of US$53 million in the 1990s to an average of US$7 million in the early part of this decade. This is partly explained by the conclusion of the structural adjustment credits.

In Uganda as in most HIPC countries, budget support commitments have historically been higher than disbursements. In 1999–2000, only 27.4 percent of the loans committed were disbursed—a disparity that was largely caused by delays due to different donor disbursement procedures and conditionalities. Nonetheless, there has since been a marked improvement and in 2002–03, disbursements exceeded commitments for the first time, by about 6 percent (Table 17.1). The improvement reflects the streamlining of donor disbursement procedures as well as the depreciation of the U.S. dollar (the reporting currency) against other currencies in 2002–03 and 2003–04. Loans have generally had lower disbursement ratios than grants, except in fiscal year 2002–03.

A large portion of budget support for poverty-reducing expenditures has been channeled through the Poverty Action Fund, which has directly benefited poverty-reducing sectors such as health, education, agriculture, water and sanitation, roads, and works. The increase in budget support resources has therefore resulted in an increase in the share of Poverty Action Fund in total spending from 17 percent in 1997–98 to 23.5 percent in 2002–03.

FIGURE 17.2 Share of Multilateral and Bilateral Disbursements to Total Budget Support, 1993–2003

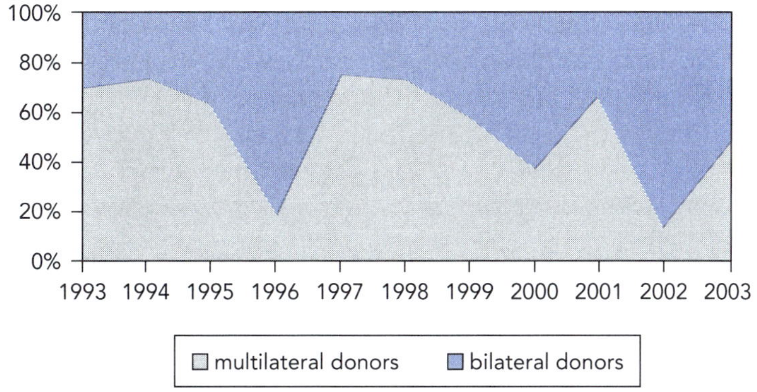

TABLE 17.1 Budget Support Commitments/Disbursements in US$ Millions, 1999–2000 to 2003–04

	1999–2000		2000–01		2001–02		2002–03		2003–04	
	Projection	Outturn	Projection	Outturn	Projection	Outturn	Projection	Outturn	Projection	Outturn
Loans	140.60	38.50	180.40	83.40	373.80	198.90	179.44	191.20	187.76	30.67
Grants (excl HIPC)	181.50	109.09	156.10	153.00	193.30	154.60	177.39	173.90	245.76	358.97
Total	322.10	148.40	336.50	236.40	567.10	353.50	356.83	365.10	433.52	389.64
Ratios of loans outturns to commitments (%)		27.38		46.23		53.21		106.55		16.34
Ratios of grants outturns to commitments (%)		60.55		98.01		79.98		98.03		146.00
Ratios of total outturns to commitments (%)		46.07		70.25		62.33		102.32		89.88

B. Implications of the Increase in Budget Support

The issue of whether increased budget support to finance Uganda's poverty reduction has resulted in Dutch disease has been much discussed.

Adam and Bevan (2003) developed a simple model of aid and public expenditure in which over time, investment in public infrastructure improves productivity in both the tradable and nontradable sectors. Contemporary conditions in Uganda were calibrated in this model to simulate the effect of increased aid. The results show that those public expenditures whose productivity effects are skewed toward the nontradable sector deliver the highest growth in exports and total output, besides sustaining high aggregate real income. The effect of public expenditure on productivity raises the supply of nontradable goods by almost enough to match the additions to demand that are caused by increased aid flows. Further, the authors also show that exchange rate appreciation is reduced or even reversed, enhancing the performance of the export sector. However, their results show that income gains largely accrue to urban skilled and unskilled households, leaving the rural poor relatively worse off.

Given that aid in the form of grants used to finance government expenditure results in a rise in the recipient country's disposable income, the effects on the real exchange rate (RER), and subsequently on the trade balance largely depend on the country's supply and demand elasticities with respect to income (Adam and Bevan 2003; Nkuzu 2004). If the income elasticity of demand for nontradables is high, a large appreciation of the RER could result, while a high price elasticity of supply and demand for nontradables would result in a smaller RER appreciation.

Both these studies suggest that the fears that aid will induce Dutch disease in Uganda may be unfounded. Nkuzu (2004) advances three reasons for this.

First, Uganda's economic structure differs from the key features assumed in the Dutch disease model. Unused or inefficiently used factors of production could be combined with the increased financial flows and brought into better use, preventing the economy from degenerating into Dutch disease. The probability of Uganda producing within the production possibility frontier is high. The large scale of unutilized land resources supports this,[3] while imperfections in the labor market and its segmentation weaken the likelihood of meaningful upward flexibility in real wages.

Second, Uganda has undertaken economic liberalization, and its terms of trade have deteriorated in the recent past. The combination of a relatively stable political environment and economic liberalization has encouraged crop production and investment in various sectors of the economy. Uganda's trade deficit has widened since the aid flows increased, partly reflecting increased absorption of government spending.[4] The increased aid flows to a large extent offset a shortfall in export proceeds that followed the deterioration in Uganda's terms of trade; it could, however, be argued that the aid inflows slowed down the rate of depreciation that resulted from the terms-of-trade deterioration.

Third, Uganda's monetary and exchange rate management have been prudent, resulting in low and stable inflation, in turn exerting depreciation pressures on the real effective exchange rate (REER).

Nkuzu (2004) argues that Uganda's experience confirms that developing countries with relatively large aid inflows can escape Dutch disease if they can (1) draw upon their idle productive capacity to satisfy the demand for nontradables that is induced by the aid inflows, (2) undertake reforms that support structural transformation so that resources move into areas where they can earn a higher rate of return, and (3) pursue prudent macroeconomic policies that deliver low and stable inflation in order to support the depreciation of the REER. However, Nkuzu emphasizes that there is a limit to the level of aid that the monetary authorities can sterilize, and that aid above this limit could render macroeconomic management difficult or even undermine growth prospects. She also raises the question whether the successful experience with large ODA flows masks weaknesses that could be storing up trouble for years to come.

To examine issues raised by the above authors, the next section takes stock of the buildup of upward pressures on Uganda's exchange and interest rates that began in 1998–99, and of the developments in export sector performance in 2003–04.

Upward Pressures on Exchange and Interest Rates

The increase in budgetary allocations toward the poverty-reducing sectors led to a reduction in the share of population living below the poverty line: from 56 percent in 1992 to 44 percent in 1997 and to 35 percent in 2000, before the proportion rose again to 38 percent in 2002. The reduction was welcome, but there are concerns that the resultant complications in macroeconomic management could easily negate the benefits. The increasing disbursements of budget support geared to reducing poverty levels have widened Uganda's budget deficit, and since the poverty reduction expenditures have been directed toward nontradable goods, they have created a need to sterilize the resultant shilling liquidity to ward off inflationary pressures caused by the increase in money supply.

Fiscal Deficit

The increase in government expenditure and the associated fiscal deficit have become contentious issues in Uganda. By six different measures,[5] fiscal deficits have risen. The increase is largely attributed to the increased availability of donor aid—mainly in the form of budget support, including debt relief—which has been used to expand the government budget (Brownbridge 2000). Large aid-funded increases in expenditure, equivalent to some 8 percent of GDP, occurred from 1999–2000 while domestic revenues rose by barely 2 percent of GDP. As a result, the fiscal deficit excluding grants doubled from 6.3 percent in 1997–98 to 12.8 percent of GDP in 2001–02 before slightly improving to a deficit of about 10.5 percent of GDP in the years thereafter (Figure 17.3).

As noted, donor support of one form or another now accounts for nearly half of Uganda's government expenditure. Uganda's budget is vulnerable because the government has no direct control over its financing, and any interruption to this flow can be very disruptive to the budget and the broader economy. Realizing the implications of such donor dependence, Uganda's long-term expenditure framework envisages a gradual fiscal consolidation, which should ease the upward pressure on the exchange and interest rates and thereby "crowd in" the private sector in the medium term.

Shilling Liquidity Injections

With the rise in the fiscal deficit, the net liquidity injections created by fiscal operations—government domestic expenditure less domestic revenues—rose massively, from a mere U Sh 63 billion in 1997–98 to U Sh 640 billion in 2001–02, and have averaged U Sh 400 billion in the last two financial years. This has resulted in a big burden on the Bank of Uganda (BOU) to ensure that all this liquidity is sterilized to ensure price stability.

Monetary and Exchange Rate Policies

Monetary Aggregates

Uganda's large fiscal deficits have been funded through budget support in the form of external loans and grants. This has resulted not only in upward pressures but also

FIGURE 17.3 Liquidity Created by Fiscal Operations and the Fiscal Deficit, 1997–98 to 2003–04

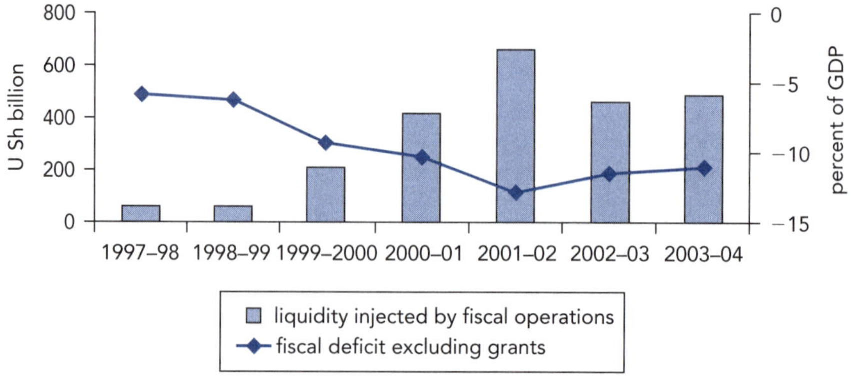

Note: The figure shows the impact of growing donor resources (a large portion of which is budget support) on the fiscal deficit excluding grants and the shilling liquidity injections on account of fiscal operations.

TABLE 17.2 Outstanding Stock of Treasury Bills and Bonds and Foreign Exchange Sales to the Interbank Foreign Exchange Market, 1993–94 to 2003–04

	93–94	94–85	95–96	96–97	97–98	98–99	99–00	2000–01	01–02	02–03	03–04
Total stock of treasury bills (U Sh billions)	45.80	62.80	93.83	95.01	143.24	214.48	361.77	589.44	928.50	1202.60	1247.96
of which holdings by commercial banks	32.71	42.94	70.36	73.25	109.14	144.68	273.77	466.12	721.18	880.80	819.04
Total stock of treasury bonds (U Sh billions)											105.00
Forex Sales (US$ millions)[a]	25.79	6.91	44.47	41.53	5.44	−24.84	−117.25	−174.28	−198.99	−246.59	−140.80

a. A plus is a purchase and a minus is a sale.

Source: Bank of Uganda.

in the volatility of the exchange and interest rates, presenting significant challenges to monetary and exchange rate management. To the extent that the monetary authorities use a monetary targeting framework, sterilizing shilling liquidity of anything up to 6 percent of GDP is a tall order.

The BOU has engaged in a combination of open-market-type operations and foreign exchange sales to manage liquidity in order to contain underlying inflation to 4–5 percent. Sterilizing this much liquidity in thin financial markets is difficult. Because money demand has not risen as fast as money supply, interest rates have been higher and more volatile than they might otherwise have been. Commercial banks have to be enticed into taking growing quantities of treasury bills (TBs), while increased sales of foreign currency to the domestic market have caused the exchange rate to appreciate.

On account of the increasing injections by government, the stock of TBs grew rapidly from U Sh 45.8 billion in 1993–94 to U Sh 1,247.96 in 2003–04, while the stock of treasury bonds, which were introduced in January 2004, had already hit U Sh 105.00 billion by June 2004 (Table 17.2).

As the stock of treasury bonds and TBs continues to grow, so does the worry about the impact of domestic interest costs on the fiscal deficit, apart from other macroeconomic effects. The commercial banks hold a large share of the stock of TBs, because nonbank demand for TBs is very limited; their holding of TBs have risen in tandem with net TB issues. Consequently, commercial banks' holdings of TBs increased from 23 percent of their assets to 32 percent between June 2000 and June 2002. This period was marked by slow growth in private sector credit. The fiscal deficit is directly crowding out private sector borrowing; the huge increase in TB sales has squeezed the funds available in the banking system for lending to the private sector.

Reasons independent of the widening fiscal deficit, such as weak demand for credit from creditworthy borrowers, might explain the stagnation of private sector credit in the recent past (except for last two years). But it is reasonable to conclude that even if demand for private sector credit had been strong enough to support the anticipated growth in private sector credit, banks would not have had enough resources to supply this credit because of their increased holding of TBs, and therefore growth in PSC would have still been choked off.

As part of the liberalization process, the restrictions on the capital account were removed in 1997. The reform meant that Ugandans could now hold foreign-denominated financial assets both domestically and abroad, while nonresidents could also hold shilling-denominated assets in Uganda. In 2003, following the worldwide decline of interest rates, the interest rate differential widened in favor of financial assets denominated in Uganda shillings, because of the high government expenditures that had to be sterilized by the BOU. As a result, in that year, Uganda received portfolio investment flows into the domestic money markets to acquire government securities (Figure 17.4). The portfolio inflows lasted from August 2003 until February 2004, after which there were outflows. This raised policy makers' concern about the potential disruption to the foreign exchange market.

Both the upward pressure on the exchange rate and the high interest rates are inconsistent with the government's development objectives of increasing exports and increasing the role of the private sector in economic growth. The long-term solution to this policy conflict lies in gradual fiscal consolidation, while in the near term, the best the BOU can do is try to pursue a balanced approach to TB and foreign exchange sales.

Getting this balance right can be very challenging. Improvements in liquidity management, together with the introduction of longer-maturity government paper, have succeeded in lowering and reducing volatility in the money market interest rates in the period beginning March 2004 to date. However, the nominal exchange rate appreciation of more than 11 percent year-on-year in 2004—not all of which could be blamed on a weaker U.S. dollar—is a source of concern.

Exchange Rate Effects

Since 1999–2000, the BOU has increasingly mopped up shilling liquidity by selling foreign exchange to the interbank foreign exchange market (IFEM). Previously, from 1993–94 to 1997–98, the Bank's participation in the IFEM was on the buy side. It reversed its position partly because of the unwinding of the coffee boom but largely because of the need to sterilize the shilling liquidity that was injected by budget support for government expenditure (as seen in Table 17.2). In 1998–99, the BOU sterilized the equivalent of US$24.84 million, which has since risen to about US$140.85 million in 2003–04 having peaked at US$246.59 million in 2002–03. The decline in the use of foreign exchange for sterilization in 2003–04 was due to the growing appreciation pressures on the Uganda shilling, thus limiting its usefulness as an instrument for mopping up shillings.

To fully appreciate the impact of the recent increase in shilling liquidity sterilization using foreign exchange sales, a discussion is necessary of the evolution of the exchange rate in relation to Uganda's terms of trade and the performance of its exports.

Terms of Trade[6]

The continued decline in the coffee price since the boom of 1994–95 has caused a general decline in Uganda's terms of trade (Figure 17.5). The decline in terms of trade highlighted the risks of Uganda's overdependence on a single export commodity and exposed the country's vulnerability to external shocks. The government has since

FIGURE 17.4 Net Government Portfolio Liabilities to Nonresidents, February 2003–June 2004

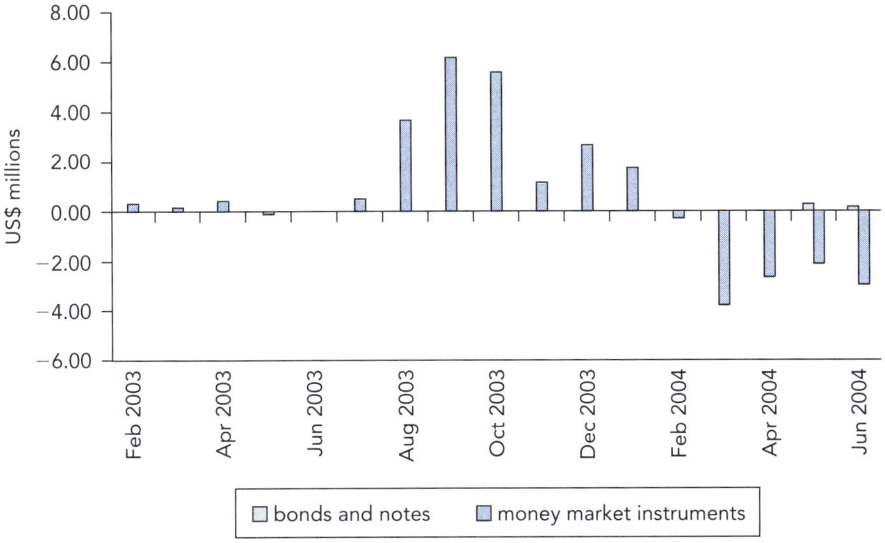

FIGURE 17.5 Terms of Trade and Coffee, US$ Export Price, 1992–93 to 2003–04

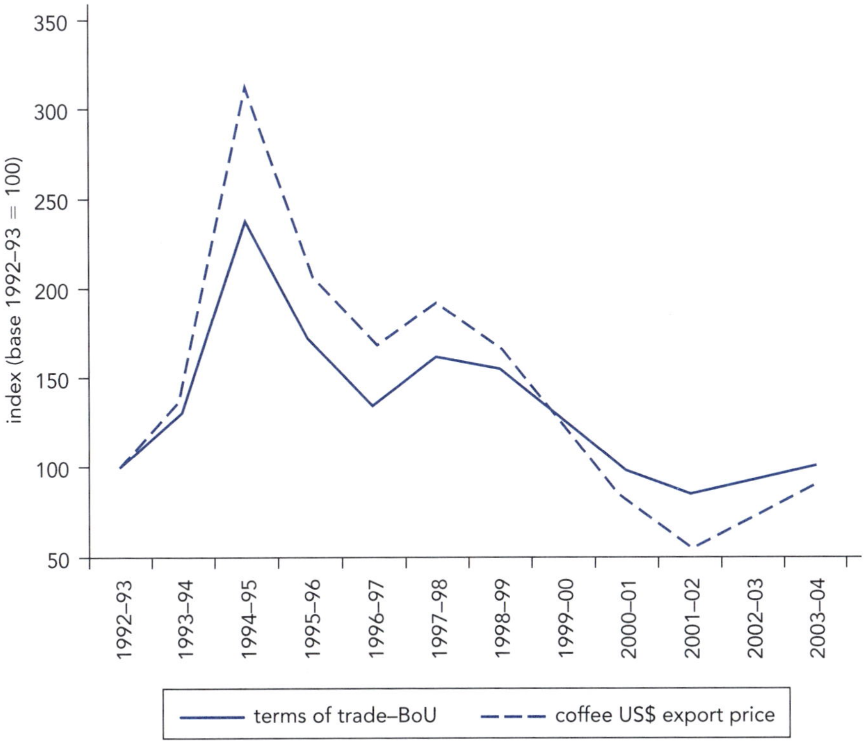

Source: BOU.

taken strong policy measures to diversify exports by reviving other traditional exports such as cotton, tea, and tobacco and promoting nontraditional exports such as fish, flowers, vanilla, and tourism services.

These efforts paid off: total exports of goods and services increased from US$665 million in 1994–95 to almost US$1 billion in 2003–04 (Figure 17.6). The contribution of coffee to total exports has fallen from more than half in the mid-1990s to just 12 percent today.

The export developments in 2003–04 could to a large extent support the findings of Adam and Bevan (2003) and Nkuzu (2004) that increased spending on nontradables in the presence of idle productive capacity need not result in Dutch disease. However, the continued sterilization using foreign exchange sales in 2003–04, and its impact on export sector performance, are revisited in Section D.

The policy measures credited with diversifying Uganda's exports include the pursuance of prudent macroeconomic policies and reforms in the marketing, payments, and exchange systems. Increased competition in marketing significantly reduced the distortions in resource allocation and raised the incentives to produce. A rise in farmgate prices helped make production profitable. In addition, the restoration of peace in

FIGURE 17.6 Export Diversification, 1992–93 to 2003–04

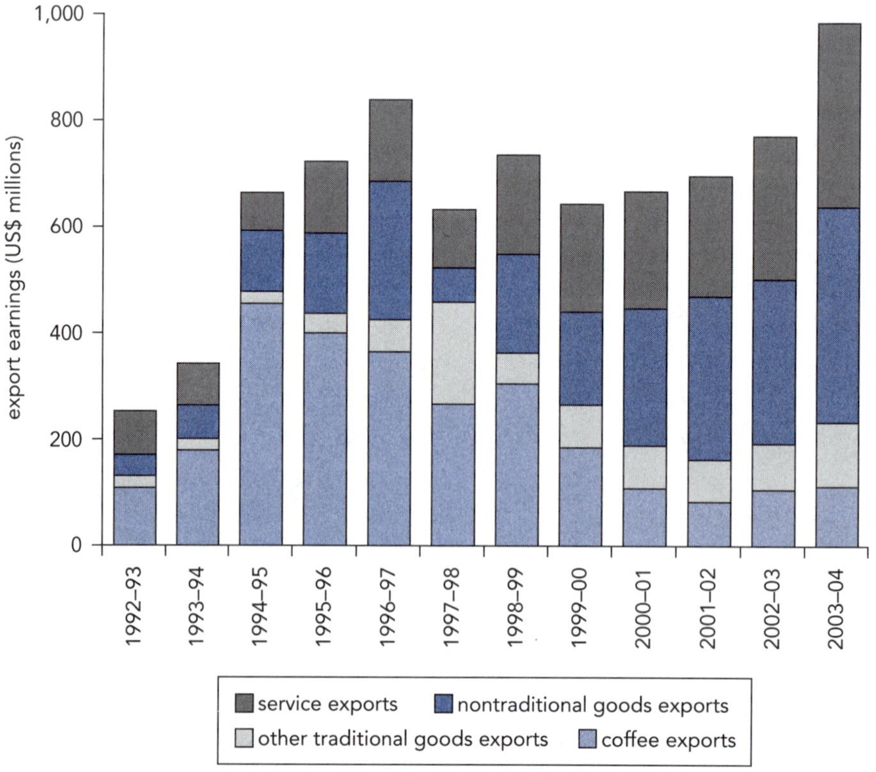

Source: BOU.

the greater part of the country resulted in more production. Productivity-enhancing measures such as increased availability of seeds and fertilizers, progress in planting practices, and the replacement of old coffee trees with new, clonal ones with higher yields have reduced coffee production costs.

As Uganda's terms of trade deteriorated, the market-determined exchange rate depreciated, and given the low inflation rates, so did the REER, thus making Ugandan noncoffee exports more competitive. Consequently, maintaining low and stable inflation has been crucial to keeping the cost of inputs low, thereby increasing profit margins as the exchange rate depreciates. This is in line with the observation by Nkuzu (2004), which urges aid-recipient countries to pursue prudent macroeconomic policies that deliver low and stable inflation in order to support the depreciation of the REER.

Historical Exchange Rate Movements

The competitiveness of the shilling, as measured by the REER, has improved since 1995–96, depreciating by about 50 percent up to 2002–03 largely on account of deteriorating terms of trade and low and stable inflation. Over this period the nominal effective exchange rate (NEER) and shilling–U.S. dollar nominal exchange rate (NER) depreciated by 68 percent and 86 percent respectively (Figure 17.7)

FIGURE 17.7 NEER, REER, and Shilling/US Dollar Exchange Rates, 1992–93 to 2002–03

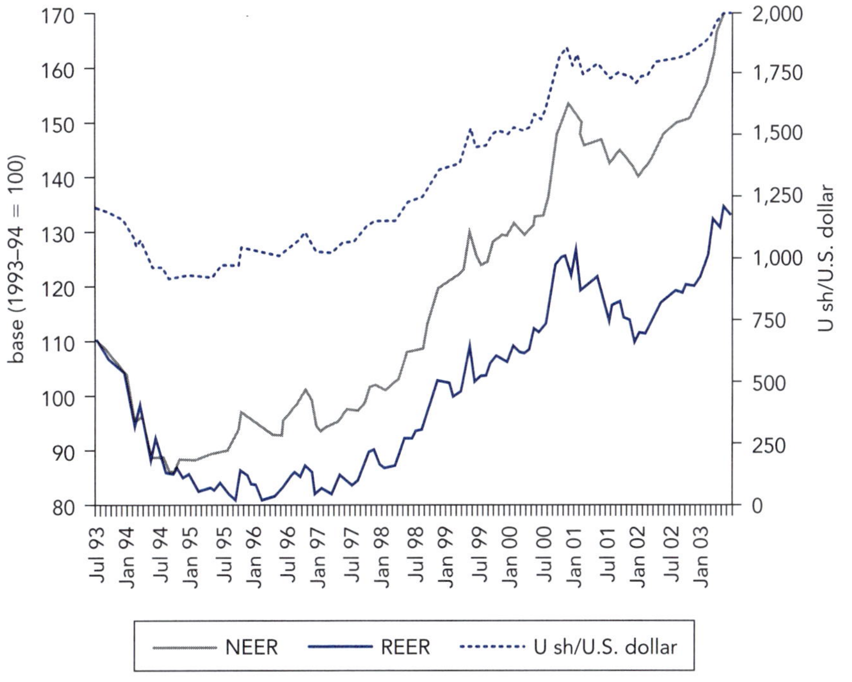

Source: BOU.

In 2003–04, however, the depreciating trend in the NER and the REER reversed. Between August 2003 and September 2004, the shilling appreciated against the U.S. dollar, from U Sh 1,998–US$1 to U Sh 1,721–US$1, marking an overall appreciation of 13.9 percent. From July 2003 to June 2004, the REER appreciated by 4 percent to its least competitive level since February 2003 (Figure 17.8).

The recent appreciation pressures must be attributed at least partly to the strong efforts to sterilize the shilling injections associated with the donor-supported fiscal deficit.[7] As noted above, an upsurge in offshore investor inflows to purchase TBs, attracted by high returns and widening interest rate differentials against global government securities, took place in the first half of 2003–04. These inflows placed additional appreciation pressures on the exchange rate, causing the Bank of Uganda to increase its sales of securities and reduce its sales of foreign exchange. This, however, created a vicious circle as interest rates rose, in turn attracting more inflows from offshore investors and exerting more pressure on the exchange rate.

To halt these portfolio inflows required a reconstitution of the monetary policy instrument mix for liquidity management. The Bank of Uganda increased its sales of foreign exchange and scaled back its sales of government securities, but with more emphasis on longer-term bonds in the second half of the year. The BOU sold more than US$120 million in the second half of 2003–04, which is three times the amount

FIGURE 17.8 NEER, REER, and Shilling/US Dollar Exchange Rates, January 2002 to September 2004

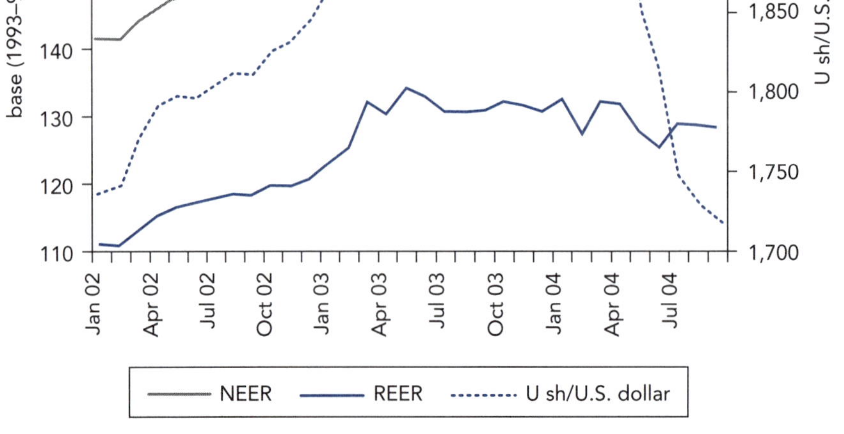

Source: BOU.

sold in the first half of 2003–04. Coupled with strong private transfer inflows in the first half of 2003–04 and 28 percent growth in export earnings in 2003–04, appreciation pressures became inevitable.

C. Prices of Tradables versus Nontradables

Prices for nontraded goods and services in Uganda have grown much faster than prices for tradables (Figure 17.9). This implies that the price incentives within the domestic economy have shifted away from traded goods production toward nontraded goods production in the last few years, on account of the increased demand for nontradables that arises from increased government spending. Given the fixed supply of nontradables in the short run, price increases have been inevitable.

Uganda's trade deficit rose from 7.2 percent of GDP in 1997–98 to 10.1 percent of GDP in 2003–04, possibly pushed up by the aid-funded expansion in government spending. It would be difficult to ignore the fact that a shift in relative prices from tradables to nontradables will undermine the government's objective of creating a dynamic export-led economy. Private sector–led export promotion is central to Uganda's Medium-Term Competitiveness Strategy, and this objective should not be compromised by an excessive fiscal deficit.

FIGURE 17.9 Prices of Tradables versus Nontradables, 1997–98-2002–03

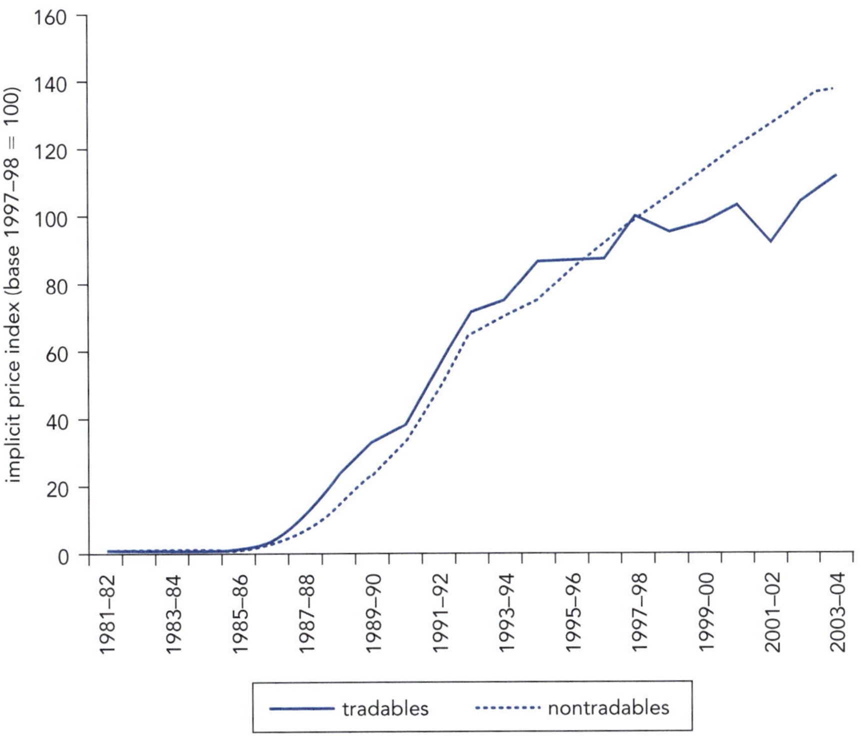

The developments in prices of tradables and nontradables (Figure 17.9) seem to run counter to the findings of Adam and Bevan (2003). (As noted above, these authors argue that public expenditures skewed toward the nontradable sector can deliver productivity effects that increase the supply of nontradable goods by an amount sufficient to reduce or even reverse pressures for exchange rate appreciation and hence enhance export performance.)

The relative increase that has taken place in the prices of nontraded goods might be because donor-funded increases in government spending have generated a high income elasticity of demand for nontradables, resulting in the appreciation pressures in the REER that were seen in 2003–04. Alternatively, the price increase might be because both supply and demand for nontradables are price inelastic, with the result that the REER appreciated on account of increased government spending.

To the extent that the price elasticity of supply of nontraded goods appears to be low in Uganda, the observations made by Nkuzu (2004) need to be revisited. The appreciation pressures arising from the relative increases in prices of nontradables raise the question of why idle capacity was not drawn into use to satisfy the demand for nontradables that is induced by aid inflows.

D. Exchange Rate and Export Sector Competitiveness

On account of the sharp appreciation pressures in 2003–04 and subsequent concerns about competitiveness that were raised by exporters, a joint study was undertaken by the Macroeconomics Department of the Ministry of Finance, Planning, and Economic Development and the Research Department of the Bank of Uganda to investigate the impact of the appreciation on a number of key export sectors (Uganda Ministry of Finance and Bank of Uganda 2005). A break-even exchange rate[8] for each of the major export items was calculated, and the study showed that at an exchange rate of U Sh 1,700 per U.S. dollar, a number of export items were not breaking even. These included fish, tea, tobacco, and maize. The study found the general negative consequences of the recent appreciation to be:

- reduction in export profitability (and even large losses in some sectors) and/or reduction in farm-gate prices, with reduced incentives having major implications for future production and value addition;
- reduced export competitiveness and loss of major contracts to foreign competitors; and
- reduced investment in the export sector.

These short-term consequences also have significant longer-term implications for the wider economy, in that a permanently appreciated REER will discourage export diversification and export-led growth in general, in addition to shifting incentives toward the nontradable sector and encouraging imports. Lower farm-gate prices also reduce rural incomes and thus reduce demand for locally manufactured goods and services. The increase in poverty between 2000 and 2003 is partly attributed to the fall in farm-gate prices of several export crops, and it coincided with a slowdown in the growth of formal manufacturing. It should be borne in mind that the resources of the rural poor in Uganda engaged in the production of export crops are limited and cannot easily substitute to other profitable crops. If left on their own, poverty levels are likely to increase further.

These findings partly contributed to Uganda's scaling back of attempts to sterilize liquidity through foreign exchange sales in 2003–04. This action was in line with the caution by Nkuzu (2004) that over a certain limit, aid can exceed a government's sterilization capacity and render macroeconomic management difficult or even undermine growth prospects.

E. Policy Recommendations and Conclusions

Uganda depends heavily on budget support to finance nearly half its government expenditure, which is largely used for non-traded goods and services. To reduce inflationary pressures, the authorities attempt to reduce the local currency injections arising from aid-supported spending to levels that match demand conditions in the economy. But on account of thin financial markets and the limited range of monetary policy instruments, this has exerted upward pressure on the interest and exchange rates. The lesson clearly emerging is that large-scale sterilization in thin financial markets is detrimental for the competitiveness of the economy.

Uganda's experience also highlights the fact that unless domestic resource costs are coming down, appreciation pressures on the exchange rate will erode profitability and reduce investment, and may also lower the incomes of the rural poor engaged in the export sector—thus working against the reason why government spending has been increased in the first place.

The above suggests the following recommendations for aid-recipient countries:

- For the short run, consider taking aid only in amounts that will not overwhelm the sterilization capacity of the monetary authorities, because of the risk of compromising export and private sector growth.
- Undertake productivity-enhancing public expenditures that are designed to raise output by providing public goods and raise the productivity of the rural poor by measures such as increasing the availability of higher yielding seeds and encouraging progress in planting practices and the use of fertilizers. These policies have a cost-reducing impact on production and thus raise the competitiveness of producers.
- Reduce domestic resource costs through investing in public goods with a high import content—such as power generation, water harvesting, and transport and communications. Automatic sterilization through imports here would not exert pressures on monetary policy instruments but would go a long way to reduce the cost of doing business. Simply put, absorb what government spends on productive infrastructure.

- Deepen the financial sector. Though a long-term goal, this will increase the demand for money and thus sterilize some of the increased money supply. This goal calls for continued financial sector reforms.
- Strengthen institutions to increase absorptive capacities, as these institutions would increase the value obtained for government expenditure. Increased absorption and value for money will also lower the cost of doing business and ultimately help to raise factor productivity. These gains will raise the profitability of producers without requiring a depreciation in the nominal exchange rate.

Endnotes

1. Dutch disease was named after the effects of natural gas discoveries in the Netherlands. It refers to the adverse effect on a country's other industries that occurs when one industry substantially expands its exports. The expansion causes a real appreciation of the country's currency and hence a decline in the worldwide competitiveness of the country's other industries. Dutch disease is defined here as the appreciation of the RER arising from a particular inflow of a resource (export or service) that causes a decline in the performance of the rest of the other exports.
2. With effect from 1999–2000, the government of Uganda achieved the 20/20 initiative under the MDGs, which stipulates that an average of 20 percent of budgetary expenditure and 20 percent of aid flows should be allocated to basic social services that include education, health, and water infrastructure.
3. The 1997 version of Uganda's PEAP estimated that only one-third of available land was currently under utilization.
4. See IMF (2005a) definition of absorption.
5. These measures are overall deficit (including grants), primary deficit (including grants but excluding domestic and external interest payments), overall deficit (excluding grants), current deficit (current revenue minus current expenditure), government of Uganda budget deficit (excludes the externally financed development expenditures and defined as domestic revenue minus the government budget), and domestic deficit (defined as the government deficit excluding the interest payments on external debt and government imports financed directly through the BOU but including arrears and promissory notes payments).
6. Terms of trade are defined as the ratio of export prices to import prices and measure the volume of imports that can be bought with one unit of exports. The unfavorable movement in Uganda's terms of trade indicates that fewer imports can be bought for a given level of exports, in other words, the purchasing power of Uganda's exports (in terms of imports) has fallen. The progressive decline in prices paid for agricultural commodities such as coffee is one of the major reasons why Uganda is focusing on value addition. Exports of simple commodity products such as Robusta coffee, which are undifferentiated and indistinguishable to customers, are normally sold to markets with sole purchase criteria of minimum acceptable quality and low cost. Such commodity products are also vulnerable to a long-term decline in prices when new entrants start producing, as has happened with the start-up of large scale Robusta coffee production in Vietnam. In value addition markets, determining purchase factors go far beyond simply providing commodities at the lowest cost. An industry that provides a high-value differentiated product can generally obtain higher or at least more stable prices and profit margins, and finds it easier to defend its competitive position.

7. Exporters note that the current strength of the shilling does not reflect the export performance of the economy but the high level of aid dependency.
8. The calculation of break-even exchange rates was extremely difficult, partly because the quality of data provided by each export sector varied significantly. As such, the figures presented should be treated with caution, but they still serve as a useful guide on how vulnerable sectors are to adverse exchange rate movements. See Section IV of Uganda Ministry of Finance and Bank of Uganda (2005) for the assumptions made for individual sectors in arriving at the break-even exchange rates.

18

Budget Support in Mozambique

GREGOR BINKERT
World Bank
and
JOSE SULEMANE
Ministry of Planning and Development, Mozambique

For Mozambique, budget support represents about 19 percent of budget expenditures and about 35 percent of the total external resources—grants and loans—that flow into the budget. Donors' disbursements to Mozambique for general budget support were US$240 million in 2004, and their pledges for 2005 were US$270 million. This is one of the largest joint programs in Africa, both in volume and in the number of donor agencies involved.

Budget support has brought many advantages for Mozambique, but institutional weaknesses need to be addressed to increase its effectiveness. Particularly, improvements are needed in the quality of planning and budgeting, definition of clear priorities, and costing. This brief note outlines aspects of Mozambique's experience that may have relevance for other countries.

A. MOU, Dialogue, Trust Building, and Harmonization

Mozambique's dialogue with donors is reflected in the memorandum of understanding (MOU) signed in 2004 (Box 18.1). The MOU specifies the modalities and conditions under which each of the partners will disburse funds, and any future partner that may want to provide direct budget support will be expected to respect the MOU.

The monitoring and dialogue processes are now aligned with the government's planning, budgeting, and monitoring cycle. A joint review takes place each year in April to assess the performance of the government and the donors in the previous year and provide the basis for commitments in the following year. A mid-year review takes place in September, focusing on forward planning and agreeing on the performance assessment framework (PAF) matrix. Formal performance assessments are undertaken jointly by the government and donors.

In this context, the most important initial step in a budget support program is to accept the principle that all conditions for disbursing funds should derive from documents approved by a country's parliament. Members of parliament, for their part,

BOX 18.1 Budget Support and the Aid Relationship in Mozambique

Coordinated general budget support to Mozambique started in 2000 with six donors disbursing US$98 million. In 2004, a new MOU was signed between the government and 15 donor agencies, and 2 more joined in 2005.

The MOU defines commitments to improve aid effectiveness and provide general budget support. It clarifies the performance, reporting, and auditing commitments of the government as well as the program aid partners (PAPs) in the spirit of mutual accountability.

The signing of the MOU has had a far-reaching impact on the way budget support is provided and on the relationship between the government and its partners. Four dimensions stand out:

1. The timing of the dialogue follows closely the national cycle of budget preparation, approval, and execution. This alignment is not perfect yet, but it is a big step forward. It also enhances the predictability of the resource flow to the budget.
2. Only documents are used that are also submitted to parliament. This enhances government ownership and accountability to domestic institutions.
3. There is no separate policy dialogue between an individual agency and the government. The dialogue is carried out jointly, and all PAPs are requested to draw their conditionality from the PAF, which in turn is a subset of the government economic and social program (PES) that is approved by parliament.
4. The dialogue on sector issues has become much more structured as a result of the work of sector working groups, which discuss all issues related to projects, sectorwide approaches, and common funds; these groups also provide the technical input to the joint and mid-year reviews that are part of the general budget support process.

Formalizing the new relationship and methodology of donor harmonization in the MOU was a significant step forward. But equally important for the effectiveness of budget support has been the growing trust between donors and the government. The government's far-reaching public financial management reforms had an important impact on donors' trust. These included a complete overhaul of the legislation and regulations for public financial management and profound changes in the approaches to planning, budget execution, accounting, reporting, and auditing, including doing performance audits. Their most visible aspects were the introduction of an electronic integrated financial management system and a single treasury account. From the donors' side, these reforms required a commitment to accept, strengthen, and reform national systems, rather than circumventing them and/or creating parallel structures.

should understand that donors' release of the funds needed to support the budget depends on the country's performance on a number of indicators.

B. Planning and Budgeting

In Mozambique, the two key policy documents submitted to parliament are used in the dialogue between the government and its international partners. One is the economic and social program (PES by its Portuguese acronym), which lists activities and targets; the other is the annual budget, which parliament approves as a law.

Because of the weaknesses in Mozambique's capacity for planning and budgeting, the economic program and the budget are still not fully linked, but the government recognizes this as a priority for the near future.

For a country to accomplish such a link, it will be helpful to agree on the overall framework and basic principles through a consultative process. For example, if a country has a credible poverty reduction strategy that sets the overall framework, donors and the government should base their work on the key elements of the strategy, regardless of whether their cooperation is related to budget support or project support.

One of the related objectives is to include the PAF as a subset of indicators within the government's PES and in the budget and other documents that are approved by parliament. In other words, there is no need for a country to have a PAF as a separate document—everything covered by the PAF should be part of the normal activities of government institutions. The basic indicators and conditions included in the PAF should be limited to those that are important for the development process, and they should be linked with disbursements. In Mozambique, the PAF matrix is annexed to the PES as submitted to parliament, in order to keep parliament informed on which subset of indicators will receive more attention from budget support donors. Mozambique's PAF contains 50 major indicators of the more than 200 targeted by the government's PES.

A serious challenge is the perception that the PAF and the conditions in it are set by donors. In Mozambique, this perception is present even in the dialogue within government. It is important for all development partners—government and donors—to understand that the indicators that appear in the PAF must be derived from the country's regular planning and budgeting process.

C. Monitoring and Evaluation of Budget Support

Presents other potential problems. Monitoring and evaluation are inherently associated with the planning and budgeting process, but in some cases there are differences between what annual reports provide and what donors want. The solution is to use a single document to evaluate performance. Again, this should be something that a country's parliament should be aware of.

D. Accountability

Government's main accountability is to parliament. In Mozambique, as mentioned above, a major breakthrough was achieved when the budget support donors agreed to use only documents submitted to parliament for their assessment of the performance of the executive. In addition, government must be accountable to the civil society. During joint review exercises, government and donors decide among policies that will ultimately affect the civil society, private sector, and all other constituencies, including public servants. These constituencies should take part in the discussion of the policies. This is not the case yet in Mozambique. Within the joint review process in 2005, the government tried to incorporate civil society representatives in discussions of different policies with technical teams. This was the first such exercise; all the stakeholders probably need more experience, but this is a process that should be further developed, taking into account the experiences of other countries, such as Uganda and Tanzania.

Mozambique faces a challenge in the political economy of public finance and policy design. The challenge encompasses the relationship among executive government, parliament, civil society, and donors. High interdependency and the complexity of interactions sometimes leads to a situation where the executive branch is more accountable to donors than to parliament. Sometimes this reflects the weak capacity of parliament, but the approach is wrong and should be changed. Currently, Mozambique has 17 donors that have signed the memorandum of understanding and are working with the government on the joint annual review. This exercise should be performed in a way that provides for more accountability of the executive branch to parliament, even though parliament's capacity is still relatively weak.

While the MOU has formalized a very positive change in Mozambique's traditional relationship with donors, the process of building mutual trust continues, and there are, of course, things that can be improved on the side of both the government and the donors. Donors and international financial institutions are now asking governments of developing countries to proceed with a second generation of reforms. These reforms may require changes in behavior and performance also from the donors' side, including a reduced number of missions and harmonized analytical work, reforms at headquarters and in the field, transfer of more staff to the field, and more coherent efforts for capacity building. Sometimes there is a lack of coordination among donors, or between the International Monetary Fund and bilateral donors. Development partners still need to find better ways of dealing with such issues.

In Mozambique, donors have agreed on a set of indicators for improving their behavior, which imply:

- the need to align with government's instruments, processes, and systems of financial management, shifting accountability from donors to the Mozambican citizens through the National Assembly;
- more strategic, ongoing dialogue with government on those instruments and systems;
- all assessments of performance, including sector and cross-cutting issues and strategic policy dialogue with the government, must be done jointly;
- the signatories of the memorandum of understanding committed themselves not to use any kind of conditionality outside the PAF framework;
- commitment to greater transparency, predictability, and harmonization; and
- commitment to reduce administrative burden.

These do not constitute a really binding commitment for donors, but are more of a moral nature. Still, they are a move in the right direction.

E. Institutional and Human Capacity Building

Mozambique's planning and budget institutions are severely short of experts in fields relevant for budget support. The challenge is what process to use to upgrade their institutional and human capacity in order to move toward more budget support. In this context, technical assistance and aid in general should be treated as part of a growth and development strategy, rather than as an exercise of funding financial gaps. This requires continuing changes in the current aid paradigm.

19

Afghanistan: Budget Support in a Postconflict Environment

WAHIDULLAH SHAHRANI
Deputy Minister of Finance
Afghanistan

Afghanistan is totally dependent on foreign aid. About 93 percent of its total budget, and half of the ordinary budget and total development budget, have been financed by aid. In fiscal year 2005, the ordinary budget is $680 million, and the size of the development budget is $4.3 billion.

In this context, Afghanistan faces four particular challenges:

1. *Control over the use of finance.* The government has made good progress in the past three and a half years. It has demonstrated strong fiscal discipline and sound budgetary management, and has promoted the national budget as the anchor of all international assistance. However, despite enormous international goodwill and generous financing, the government is still being bypassed in the development process. There is also a need for better aid coordination among donors in order to avoid duplication. For that purpose, Afghanistan has established a donor database in the budget department, and a number of consultative groups for each sector, in order to avoid duplication and achieve greater efficiency.

2. *Achievement of a balanced program of investment.* Over the past few years, Afghanistan has had an obvious urgent need for the international community to focus resources on the humanitarian and security sectors. The country now needs donors to shift their emphasis and finance a number of core infrastructure projects. The country is currently considering an infrastructure investment plan that will create more favorable conditions for the private sector and foreign direct investment. The national development strategy should embody a balanced approach to growth. Ensuring that all participants in the economy benefit from the growth is particularly important for Afghanistan, which has 1 million disabled people, 500,000 internally displaced people, 3 million refugees living in neighboring countries, and, overall, a very high vulnerability to natural disasters. In this regard, the country's national solidarity program has achieved international recognition for its ability to reach marginalized rural communities. However, much more needs to be done to strengthen the coordination and use of resources, at both the local and national levels, to ensure that projects are well planned and targeted toward local needs and that the benefits are distributed evenly.

3. *National capacity building.* Many of the difficulties Afghanistan faces in its fourth year of reconstruction and development stem from a lack of attention to national capacity development. Capacity is especially limited in the public sector, where it is badly needed, and can only be increased if donors direct their assistance toward government organizations rather than to third-party organizations. Otherwise, a culture of substitution will prevent needed institutional development in the public sector and lead to a loss of its professional-grade workers. International assistance needs to be refocused to assist long-term capacity building in the public sector and help national and provincial institutions to work more effectively.

4. *Stimulation of foreign direct investment and private sector investment.* The private sector should and will be the real engine for economic growth in Afghanistan. This requires acceleration of reforms for strengthening a legal and institutional framework that promotes enterprise development. Trade relations with neighbors in the region are increasing steadily, but Afghanistan faces considerable obstacles in tapping private sector investment. While the internal security risks in Afghanistan have significantly decreased, the country must also win the war of perception that it is a safe and stable place in which to do business.

Finally, some donors' commitments have fallen well short of disbursements. The disbursement rate needs to be accelerated.

20

Budget Support and Poverty Reduction in South Asia

SHANTAYANAN DEVARAJAN AND SHEKHAR SHAH
World Bank

South Asia's rapid growth over the past decades has highlighted both the opportunity and the challenges of reducing poverty in our lifetime. There is no question that economic reforms, often supported by external assistance, have contributed to the region's 3 percent average per capita GDP growth (Figure 20.1). Sri Lanka began liberalizing trade and deregulating industry in the 1980s, India and Bangladesh in the 1990s, and Pakistan in the late 1990s and early 2000s. All four countries have seen an acceleration in their growth rates.

If present trends continue, South Asia will achieve the Millennium Development Goal of halving income poverty by 2015 (Figure 20.2).

But to significantly alleviate poverty—say, to reduce the number of people living on one dollar a day by 200 million—South Asia would need to raise its growth rate to more than 8 percent a year. Further, despite the recent growth, many forms of human deprivation in the subcontinent remain deep. India's child mortality rate is stagnating. Malnutrition is pervasive throughout the region. Some of Pakistan's social indicators are lagging, starting from a low base. Illiteracy in this nation of 152 million people is among the highest in the world: half the adult population is illiterate, and more than two-thirds of Pakistani women cannot read or write. The net primary school enrollment ratio for girls is barely 50 percent. Even Sri Lanka and Bangladesh, which have made significant progress in human development, are facing serious problems with the quality and equity of education and health care.

In addition, the governance problems that have plagued many parts of South Asia are not abating. Bangladesh continues to top the charts on worldwide ratings of perceived corruption. Afghanistan, Sri Lanka, and Nepal face simmering conflicts that flare up from time to time. And governance problems lie at the heart of the diverging fortunes of regions within South Asia's larger countries. Bihar, mired in corruption and weak governance, has stagnated while most of the states of South India have grown at 7 percent a year; in Pakistan, Punjab province is growing and improving human development while Sindh is not.

We are grateful to Ahmad Ahsan, Rocio Castro, Amit Dar, Manuela Ferro, Stephen Howes, Tahseen Sayed, Vinaya Swaroop, and Hassan Zaman for helpful comments on an earlier draft.

FIGURE 20.1 Growth in South Asian Countries, 1981–2000

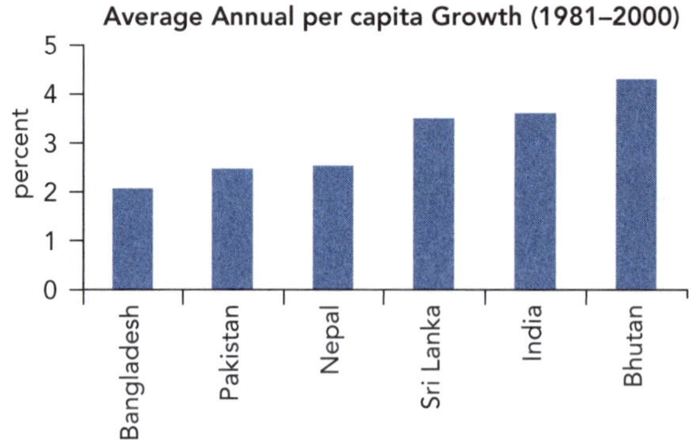

To achieve higher growth rates, accelerate human development, and contain governance problems, the region is attempting "second-generation" reforms. These are proving to be politically much more difficult than the reforms of the first round. Several Indian states are divesting loss-making public enterprises and reducing untargeted subsidies, such as those on power and water for farmers, only to see incumbent governments lose elections. Pakistan and Bangladesh are privatizing banks, but with mixed results in Bangladesh. To improve service delivery by strengthening accountability to local citizens, India and Pakistan are devolving responsibility for health, education, and other public services to local governments. The transition is turning out to be tricky, with weaker local administrative capacity (and political interests) sometimes overcoming the benefits of greater accountability. In countries from Afghanistan to Sri Lanka, the capacity of the public sector remains a major binding constraint on implementing these second-generation reforms.

FIGURE 20.2 Poverty Trend in South Asia, 1990–2015

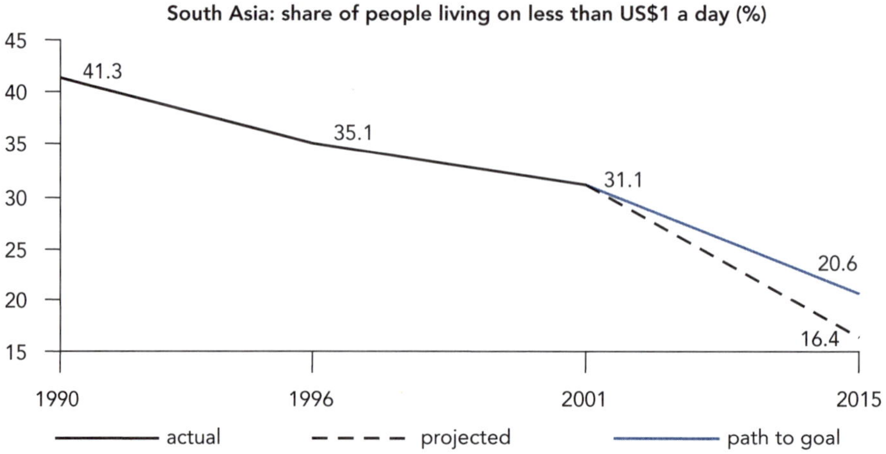

Along with other development partners, the World Bank has supported South Asian countries' poverty reduction strategies through a mix of knowledge and finance. The financial assistance, especially to support first-generation policy reforms, has taken the form of old-style, conditionality-based adjustment lending. But as the countries move beyond first-generation reforms, this phase of adjustment lending is coming to an end. More recently, the Bank has increased the use of programmatic instruments, including development policy credits, to accelerate growth and human development in the subcontinent. It has provided budget support to states in India and provinces in Pakistan, as well as for reform programs in a particular sector, education. Weak governance in some countries and regions in South Asia, as well as difficulties in implementing second-generation reforms, have led to a discussion of the pros and cons of budget support.

This paper reviews the recent experience with budget support in South Asia. It argues that the challenges facing South Asia today strengthen, rather than weaken, the case for budget support, in high-capacity and low-capacity reform settings alike. At the same time, the use of budget support raises certain new issues that need to be addressed if the international community is to help South Asians realize their dream of eliminating poverty. One of these issues is to understand why budget support makes sense in both high-capacity and low-capacity settings.

A. Addressing South Asia's Development Challenges with Budget Support

How does budget support foster policy and institutional change in South Asia? The answers to this question depend partly on two fundamental characteristics of the region. First, many parts of the region—such as Punjab province in Pakistan and several states in South India—have substantial administrative capacity relative to other countries at similar levels of income. But, in the large-country setting of South Asia, these better-endowed regions coexist alongside lagging regions, such as Balochistan and Bihar, as well as countries such as Bangladesh and Nepal, with their huge concentrations of poverty and more limited capacity for reform. In short, South Asia represents both extremely strong and weak reform settings.

Second, the presence of some form of democracy and the resulting political contestability make policy reforms and institutional change in the region intensely political. Since party politics tends to be more clientelist than programmatic in South Asia, even reformers may, and indeed do, lose elections.

In both types of reform settings, client ownership, deep local knowledge, and the ability to make careful political choices with regard to the sequencing and pace of public sector reforms are critical to successful development outcomes. Client ownership is important in more mature reform settings because reformers are typically dealing with long-haul, second-generation reforms—such as the delivery of quality education services—that require ideas, resources, and well-functioning public sector management practices to sustain them. In more fragile, low-capacity settings, there is first the need to assess whether *any* financial support (as opposed to knowledge assistance) is warranted. If the answer is yes, then client commitment and ownership need to be strengthened, together with a focus on measurable outcomes. As we show below, budget support provides superior approaches for revealing and then strengthening these attributes of client ownership, local knowledge, politically sensitive reform design and implementation, and the focus on measurable outcomes.

Supporting Second-Generation Public Sector Reforms

By supporting the whole budget and the internal workings of the government's policy-making and implementation apparatus, budget support first and foremost allows reformers to make choices for which voters and legislatures can hold them accountable. This is in contrast to investment projects, which are typically added on to the domestic budget process and, once approved, typically cease to attract attention at high political and administrative levels.

Budget support also contrasts with stand-alone technical assistance projects that focus on inputs—a focus that makes it difficult for them to measure or sustain their impact. Bangladesh, for example, has a long tradition of technical assistance projects designed to build capacity. These have yielded mixed results because they have often been overdesigned and inflexible, and ad hoc and fragmented in their coverage, or implemented in the absence of institutional changes that might have produced better incentives for sustainable government performance (World Bank 2002b). More recently, budget support in the form of two multisector Development Support Credits (DSC) (and a third one in preparation), aligned with the Bangladesh government's interim poverty reduction strategy paper (PRSP), has improved the prospects for better performance in a number of areas, including the financial sector, state-owned enterprises, energy, public administration, and governance. Indeed, these credits are providing the justification for an Economic Management Technical Assistance Program that will build capacity in Bangladesh's core institutions for economic and public management and contribute to better functioning of public administration across a range of sectors. Linking the policy reform agenda supported by the credits with the technical assistance is expected to help address some of the policy and structural impediments necessary to realize the benefits of such technical assistance.

Budgets that Matter

If countries are to reach the Millennium Development Goals, they need policies and institutions that contribute to, among other things, better health and education. In large, federal countries, the responsibility for health and education is often devolved to subnational governments. Programmatic support to states and provinces provides incentives for reformers to focus on budgets that matter directly for growth and poverty alleviation. A series of policy-based loans to Andhra Pradesh and Karnataka states in India and the Punjab and North West Frontier provinces in Pakistan have supported each subnational entity's medium-term reform framework, particularly as it relates to the acceleration of human development and the provision of basic services such as health, education, and infrastructure.

Budget support to subnational entities in India has made it possible to focus on the poor fiscal situation of several Indian states. A slow secular deterioration in state fiscal performance over the 1980s and 1990s was transformed into a crisis by the pay awards of the Fifth Central Pay Commission. A sharp increase in spending alongside declining revenues led to much higher deficits and debt accumulation. Off-budget liabilities increased sharply. Real growth in priority spending areas such as education and health slowed or halted. The quality of spending worsened as expenditures became more salary-intensive, especially in the poorer states. In response, a series of six structural adjustment loans to four Indian states by the end of 2004 have sought to help these states reform their public finances. There are strong signs of improved fiscal performance in recent years (Figure 20.3). The intensified revenue effort appears to be paying off, and the wage bill is being restrained. Interest costs are falling, in part through a debt swap scheme, and liquidity has improved. Karnataka's fiscal performance in 2003–04 was particularly good: the state lowered its deficit considerably ahead of the target originally set in 2001. Had the World Bank provided investment operations only during this period, the fiscal adjustment would probably not have been achieved. And achievements including deregulation, poverty monitoring, and governance reform across multiple sectors would have been hard to come by.

Flexibility

Quick-disbursing budget support based on prior actions has provided a number of advantages in supporting complex, second-generation, public sector reforms in areas that are dominated by political concerns. The assistance has provided flexibility in terms of timing; it has typically supported the governments' own reform programs; and it has provided a learning process to understand better the political constraints on reform. In those instances where politics discouraged early adoption of reforms, analytical work done as part of a knowledge partnership underlying potential budget support has facilitated domestic debate and the creation of a climate for reform.

FIGURE 20.3 Fiscal Deficits of Indian States, 1985–86 to 2003–04

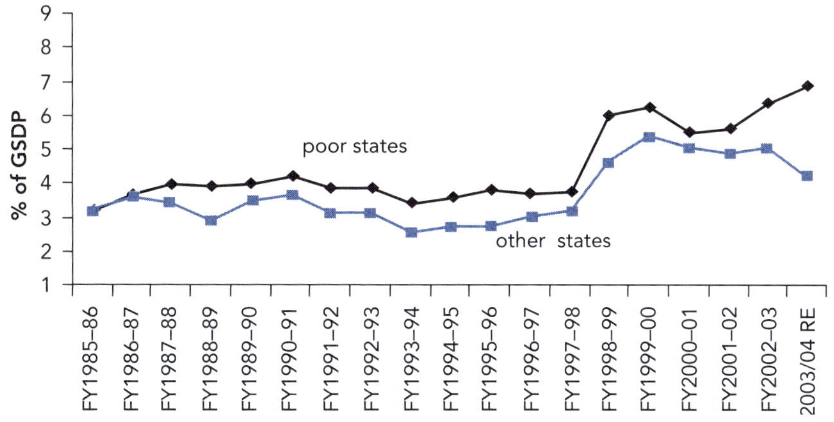

In India, Pakistan, and Bangladesh, a series of budget support operations—including the Karnataka Economic Reform Loans, the Andhra Pradesh Economic Reform Loans (APERLs), the poverty reduction support credit (PRSC) in Pakistan, and the Bangladesh DSCs—have been calibrated to match the direction and pace of ongoing reforms. The Pakistan PRSC and the APERL amounts have been adjusted to reflect reform progress. Bank privatization has been politically charged in both Pakistan and Bangladesh; in Pakistan, the banking sector loan was made only after successful privatization, and the preparation of the third Bangladesh DSC has been slowed down because of slow progress on bank privatization.

More important, the flexible "new-style" budget support operations have incorporated an important lesson from the new growth economics. The binding constraint on growth in a particular country can be very different from that in other countries, or even in the same country at a different point in time (Haussmann, Rodrik, and Velasco 2004). Often, external actors do not know precisely what the binding constraint is. By designing the budget support operation around a flexible set of reforms, rather than using the "hard conditionality" of the past, donors are allowing for learning and adapting to circumstances. For instance, many observers had believed that governance was the binding constraint on growth in Bangladesh. Yet that country's GDP grew at nearly 6 percent a year, and human development indicators improved at even faster rates. A strict conditionality approach that insisted on improvements in governance before supplying any further budget support would have missed the opportunity to reinforce and strengthen some of the ongoing reforms in Bangladesh. To be sure, governance may *become* the binding constraint in Bangladesh, especially as it attempts to reach its poverty reduction strategy target of 8 percent growth.

Ownership

Budget support operations in South Asia have provided a platform to map closely into governments' own poverty reduction strategies. In Andhra Pradesh, the APERLs have been based on the government's Andhra Pradesh Vision 2020, a 20-year strategic vision for that state. In Bangladesh, Pakistan, and Sri Lanka, the World Bank's PRSCs are similarly mapped into the country's equivalent of the PRSP. In Sri Lanka, the second poverty reduction support credit (PRSC2) has been delayed because the new government initially rejected the existing PRSP, "Regaining Sri Lanka." The Punjab Education Sector Adjustment Credit and the Punjab Education Development Policy Credit fully support the three pillars of the multiyear Punjab Education Sector Reform Program: public finance reforms to increase public spending for education and other pro-poor services and ensure their fiscal sustainability, reforms to strengthen devolution and improve the fiduciary environment and governance, and education sector reforms to improve quality, access, sector governance, and public-private partnerships.

Even where budget support operations have faltered, not been fully successful, or been delayed, they have provided valuable opportunities for understanding the politics of difficult second-generation reforms, as in the case of power sector reforms in

India or merit-based teacher recruitment in Sindh province of Pakistan. In the Indian state of Tamil Nadu, the intense knowledge partnership and analytical work underlying the preparation of budget support operations have helped public debate on policy issues even as political constraints have stalled key reforms such as those in agricultural power subsidies. The contribution of this jointly conceived analytical work to public debate and its impact on the climate for reform hold the promise of faster convergence on difficult political issues and a shared understanding of the way forward that would be supported by future budget support operations. In fact, the government of Tamil Nadu has so valued this work that it is formalizing the knowledge partnership with the Bank independently of whether a loan is made.

Strengthening Public Sector Management Practices

In several countries and states of South Asia, especially those with weak governance or low administrative capacity, core public sector management practices such as budget formulation, financial management, and procurement remain fragile. In these settings, once the decision to provide financial support has been made, budget support more readily reveals gaps in capacity and provides an entry point for creating ownership and incentives to initiate reforms. It focuses attention on outcomes that are often lost sight of in fragile settings. Equally important, it promotes the sustainability of public sector management reforms by helping coordinate them with sector reforms designed to implement poverty reduction strategies.

In Bangladesh, for example, budget formulation remains problematic. An annual routine with little policy orientation, the budget process lacks a coherent, strategic medium-term framework in which to link sector policies to resource allocation. A key constraint is that the budget for investments (the so-called development budget) is prepared separately from the budget for recurrent expenditures (the revenue budget). The overall budget classification structure does not apply identically to investment spending, undermining the effectiveness of such expenditures and making it difficult to improve budget and service delivery outcomes. Through development support credits, the World Bank is working with the government on its public expenditure program to achieve priority improvements in health, education, infrastructure, and public administration. Similarly, in the North-West Frontier province of Pakistan, two of a series of three planned structural adjustment credits have supported upfront actions on public financial management and accountability.

An important aspect of budget support operations in relatively difficult settings has been the willingness of all parties to remain engaged in policy dialogue, and to search for solutions as problems emerge in implementation. In Bangladesh through the 1980s and 1990s, before the Bank started its DSCs, there was a strong tendency toward an "on-again, off-again" relationship on core public sector practices. Intense dialogue around the preparation and approval of old-style, multiyear adjustment credits gave way to a distinct absence of such dialogue once the credit was approved. Not surprisingly, many of the adjustment credits failed to achieve their sector objectives and did not strengthen core public sector management. In Indian states receiving budget support, work has continued on poverty monitoring to increase the focus on measurable outcomes, even in those states where for other reasons the processing of a loan has been delayed or halted.

Similarly, once a reform process has begun, budget support can strengthen its momentum. Despite three changes in the top civil servant in charge, Bangladesh's secondary education program has continued reforming, thanks to broad buyin by the government, strong analytical work, and a successful program of communicating the reforms to the public.

Scaling Up Human Development

Budget and programmatic support have provided incentives to governments to adopt holistic approaches to social sector reforms. Besides providing vital links to the allocation of resources for human development in the budget—and in part because of these links and the need to make public expenditures more effective—this approach has brought welcome attention to both supply- and demand-side considerations in service delivery.

In Pakistan, under the Punjab Education Sector Reform Program supported by a series of three budget support operations, the government is reallocating public spending toward education and other pro-poor programs.[1]

Punjab is also implementing national initiatives on decentralization and the accompanying public management reforms, using education as a leading sector. An indirect but important benefit is the strengthening of decentralization by increasing the role of district authorities and promoting accountability between service users (parents and students) and service providers (schools and teachers). To improve teacher accountability and performance, there has been a major policy shift toward hiring new, better-qualified teachers with school-based term contracts. More than 30,000 qualified contract teachers have been hired so far. Before the reform program, 1,300 of the schools were empty school buildings without any students. Surveys show that after the recruitment and posting of contract teachers to these schools, half of the former non-functional schools have now become functional. And interim analysis based on the latest school census survey data from October 2004 shows an increase in enrollments of 13 percent in government primary schools in Punjab, as compared to the annual 1.5 percent increase documented during the past decade (Figure 20.4). These findings have been validated through independent third-party surveys.

Most schools in Punjab have school councils, but these have been largely ineffective. The government of Punjab is now revitalizing these councils. A watershed in this effort has been the direct provision to school councils of funds for development. In pilot districts, nongovernmental organizations have been hired to revitalize local school councils by increasing their level of involvement in a range of activities, such as helping to identify new infrastructure needs and monitoring teacher absenteeism. Besides providing free schooling to all children until matriculation (grade 10) and providing free textbooks up till grade 5 (which has now been extended to cover middle school in the second year of the program), the government of Punjab is implementing a female middle-school stipend program in 15 low-literacy districts to enhance access to education for girls. Under the program, all girls in grades 6–8 in government schools in the 15 target districts receive a monthly payment as long as they main-

FIGURE 20.4 Primary Enrollment in Punjab, Pakistan, 1996–2004

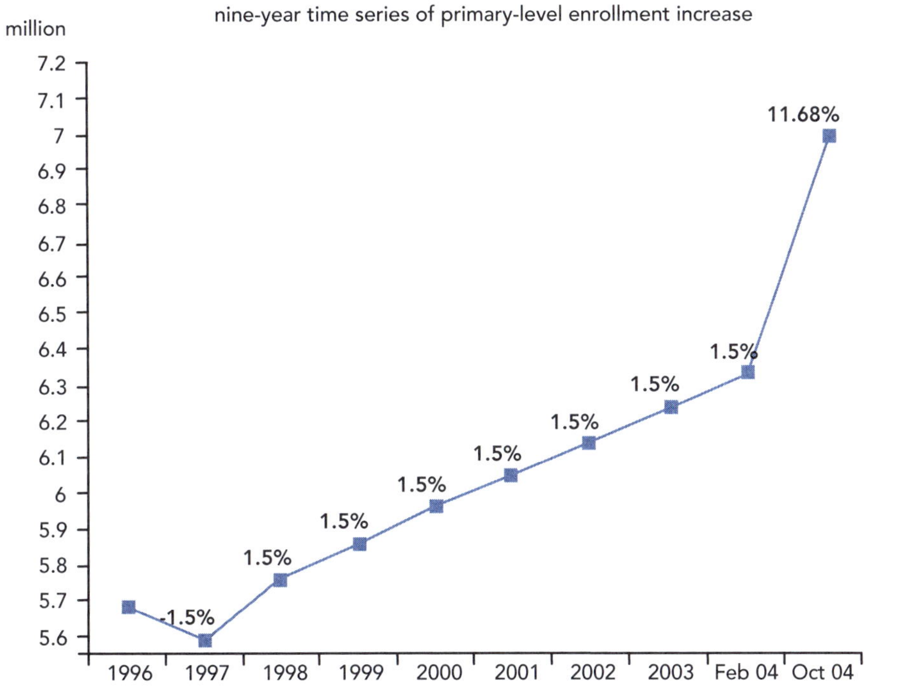

tain an 80 percent attendance record. Initial results are impressive, with increases of about 20 percent in girls' middle-school enrollment in the target schools.

Other countries in South Asia have also focused their education reform programs on demand-side issues with considerable success. Bangladesh has been a pioneer in increasing girls' secondary-school enrollment. The Bank has been its main partner through projects that have provided cash stipends to girls, based on their continuous enrollment, and associated capitation grants to secondary schools. Under the first project, enrollment in project areas more than doubled from 462,000 in 1994 to slightly above 1 million in 2001. The second project, approved in 2002, is expected to reach an additional 1.5 million girls by 2007. The third "project" was a budget support operation that, among other things, provided support for privatizing the procurement of textbooks—which was previously a major source of corruption in the country. The program also set up a Teacher Registration and Certification Authority to reduce the rent-seeking, nepotistic capture by the elite and political interference that had been associated with the hiring of teachers. Learning from these initiatives that strengthen the accountability between service providers and clients, the government of Andhra Pradesh has introduced a reduction in teacher absenteeism as a monitorable indicator of its reform program, which will be part of the next budget support operation.

Budget support operations are helping ameliorate thorny political constraints on strengthening human development and service delivery. These constraints are often not specific to the education or health sector but nonetheless pose important barriers to reform. In several instances, budget support operations are generating relevant information that can shape the domestic debate on reforms and transfer knowledge to other sectors of the economy. Nepal, despite the administrative limitations imposed by its Maoist insurgency, is moving forward with returning primary schools to local community control. The results-focused Nepal PRSC is helping make the case for this by systematically evaluating the impact of community management of schools and potentially demonstrating its value in conflict situations.

Budget support operations in Pakistan to support the Punjab Education Sector Reform Program are showing the political potential and pitfalls of decentralization—the role of the full fungibility of funds in financial devolution, the importance of strengthening the monitoring and evaluation capacity of the government, and the use of performance indicators at local levels to allocate resources. The lessons from the education program on performance-based resource allocation have been adopted by the Punjab Provincial Finance Commission, which has introduced a performance-based window for its awards to the districts.

Finally, key elements of programmatic approaches derived from budget support operations are cross-fertilizing traditional investment projects. The US$500 million IDA credit for the Sarva Shiksha Abhiyan, the Indian National Program for Universal Elementary Education, has for the first time in India adopted a sectorwide approach. The program's goal is to ensure that all children between the ages of 6 and 14 will eventually receive eight years of education in India. External partners pool funds with the government, rely on the government's own rules and procedures in procurement and financial management, and work jointly in improving institutional capacity during implementation of the project. This is likely to enhance the development effectiveness of the Bank's support for this compact among the central government, Indian states, districts, and civil society.

Also in India, the World Bank's second HIV/AIDS Control Project finances institutional strengthening by enhancing planning, management, implementation, and monitoring capacity at the national, state, and local levels; supports operational R&D; and encourages broad social mobilization through locally appropriate information, communication, and awareness campaigns. The Bank has also supported analytical work on modeling the cost and consequences of HIV/AIDS treatment and prevention in India. This work has informed the Indian government's recently adopted AIDS financing policy and its plans to scale up the existing treatment program, adopt a more cost-effective mix of components, and design monitoring and evaluation measures that provide feedback on program performance.

In a similar use of programmatic elements, the US$50 million Bank project assistance to Nepal's health sector program seeks to increase the use of essential health care services, especially by underserved populations. It is doing so by helping to develop and disseminate services standards, employ behavior change communication to affect care seeking and the attitudes of providers, decentralize responsibilities and authority to districts and communities, contract the private sector to complement public sector services, improve Nepal's planning, budgeting and fiduciary management, and closely monitor and evaluate the impact of these initiatives on access, utilization, and coverage.

B. Challenges Facing Budget Support in South Asia

Despite the encouraging early results, the increased use of budget support operations in South Asia faces some important challenges. These fall under two categories: decentralization and weak governance.

Decentralization

As we said above, budget support operations enable a focus on budgets that matter, such as those of subnational governments that are responsible for human development. But problems arise when the budget support is directed to second-tier, subnational entities in countries where responsibility is being devolved to the third tier. In Pakistan, education services are the responsibility of the districts, which receive transfers according to a formula determined by the Provincial Finance Commission (PFC). The Bank's second credit stipulated that the additional financing be allocated by the province to the districts, according to a formula that put a 30 percent weight on performance and a 70 percent weight on need. This led to the concern that the Bank's credit was circumventing, and possibly undermining, devolution in Pakistan. In fact, the additional conditional grant formula seemed to be working so well that the PFC adopted the performance-based formula for its conditional grant awards. The experience of the education sector is now prompting the Punjab political and administrative leadership to develop a similar program for the health sector.

The traditional trade-off between long-term, capacity-strengthening budget support and quick and tangible results from investment operations is being played out at the subnational level in a set of operations in Karnataka, India. Karnataka is one of the states that are furthest along in implementing the 73rd Amendment to the Indian Constitution, an amendment that devolves responsibility to *panchayati raj* institutions (third, fourth, and fifth tiers of government). Yet the devolution is proving difficult because capacity is weak at these lower tiers of government, which previously had no say in the allocation of public resources. To strengthen these institutions, the Bank is preparing a loan that will provide budget support and capacity-strengthening to *panchayats*. Alongside this operation, however, the Bank is preparing a health sector loan to Karnataka that will pass funds through the budgets of the *panchayats*, but give them no discretion over their use. Thus while one loan is aiming to strengthen the lower-tier institutions by giving them incentives to allocate resources according to local preferences, another operation is earmarking the funds that the *panchayats* spend on a particular sector—and running the risk of weakening the incentives that the first operation is trying to strengthen.

Budget support operations to states must also deal with the issue of symmetry in treatment across states. These operations were initiated in India under the explicit policy that they go to "reforming states." The idea was to create competition among states for these scarce loans, and thereby accelerate reforms in the states. One particular target of reform was subsidies for electric power, and especially the policy of free power to farmers that many states had introduced, which was seen as a litmus test for reforms. But all subsidies are deeply political, particularly those provided to farmers in India. As political fortunes change, specific policy reversals can happen even in states that are performing well above the average on other reforms, and decisions on who is to receive budget support can then pose issues of symmetry. For example, Andhra Pradesh eliminated free power to farmers and received two World Bank budget support operations. The chief minister lost the next election. His opponent ran on a platform of reintroducing free power and, when he was elected, did just that. The World Bank suspended discussions on the next operation. While the suspension was consistent with the policy of lending to "reforming states" as indicated by the litmus test of no power subsidies, the fiscal impact of the new free-power policy was likely to be minimal, and, most important, Andhra Pradesh was embarking at that very time on a large number of other second-generation reforms.[2]

There is a related issue in Pakistan where, in contrast with a successful (thus far, at least) budget support operation for education in Punjab, the Bank is designing an investment operation in education in Balochistan. Many of the conditions for making budget support operations feasible in Punjab (strong government commitment to reform, relatively good financial management practices, monitoring and evaluation capacity) do not exist in Balochistan.

Governance

The second area of difficulty has to do with weak governance. Though, as argued above, weak governance does not diminish the case for budget support in principle, in practice certain problems arise. One is the ability to respond to crises or unanticipated events. In Nepal, for example, the February 1, 2005, coup caused many donors to rethink their strategy of assistance to the country, including (where applicable) the strategy of budget support. On the one hand, most of the reforms underpinning the budget support operation could be described as "governance-independent"—reforms, such as those in customs, labor laws, and telecommunications, that would have a high payoff regardless of the governance situation. If these reforms were on track, a case could be made to proceed with the budget support operation. On the other hand, in light of the royal takeover of the government, there is the question of whether reforms are still "owned" by the larger government. If parliament passes a bill that was part of the reform program, is it doing so under pressure, or as a result of genuine debate among the various stakeholders?

A similar issue arose with a World Bank loan to Sri Lanka in the wake of the tsunami relief operation. Typically, emergency loans of this type are budget support operations—the whole point is to get the money disbursed as quickly as possible. However, in light of Sri Lanka's history of ethnic conflict, and the fact that both Tamil and Sinhalese communities were affected, it was decided that this would be an investment operation—to ensure that the credit was allocated according to the needs of the two communities. Weaknesses in the government's allocation mechanisms meant that emergency relief had to satisfy the various safeguard and fiduciary regulations of investment operations—even though Sri Lanka had a long history of budget support operations.

Politics in Donor Countries

Perhaps the biggest difficulty for budget support operations comes from the effect of weak governance on politics in donor countries. In addition to the widespread view that, in recipient countries with high levels of corruption, budget support is "pouring money down a rat hole," there are some donor countries where special-interest groups hold the country's entire aid program hostage to the budget support that goes to certain weak-governance countries. For example, in some OECD countries, human-rights activists are lobbying for the whole aid budget to be cut unless the countries stop giving aid to Bangladesh. Yet, to the extent that health and education are human rights, Bangladesh's track record is much better than that of all other South Asian countries (except Sri Lanka). Recent events in Nepal are eliciting a similar reaction from donors—again while Nepal has been making significant progress in health and education.

The general problem here is one of perceptions. Of course, providing budget support to a country that Transparency International has labeled the most corrupt in the world "looks bad." But if the decision has already been made to transfer *some* money to Bangladesh, then the question is, what type of instrument will produce the best results?

As we have argued above, by focusing on the whole of the public sector and providing incentives for economy-wide reform, budget support operations have a better chance of addressing the very governance problems that plague a country. And considering the evidence on the fungibility of project funding, there is no difference in the actual use of external funds between the two types of instruments—only a difference in perceptions. Moving the debate from these perceptions to the reality of results on the ground is the biggest remaining challenge for budget support operations in South Asia.

Endnotes

1. Interestingly, the Punjab government informed the Bank that it would raise its spending on primary education whether or not it obtained the World Bank credit. This led to some concern that the Bank's finance would not be additional. Eventually, the benefits of prospective results on the ground outweighed the concern about fungibility, and the Bank went ahead with the operation. Promising results after the first year led to a second budget support operation.
2. An underlying issue may be that, since the same World Bank country director deals with all the states in a federal country, there is a high premium on uniformity of policies and consistency of dialogue. If Andhra Pradesh and Maharashtra were different countries, with different country directors, it might be easier for each country director to have his or her own view of the overall policy framework in the country, taking into account the underlying politics of the situation.

PART VII
Donor Perspectives on Budget Support

21

International Monetary Fund Perspective on Conditionality

ATISH GHOSH
International Monetary Fund

Although the IMF is not a donor and does not, per se, provide budget support,[1] it has long confronted many of the issues discussed in this volume, including the purpose of conditionality and whether disbursements should be conditioned on actions or on outcomes (so-called "results-based" conditionality). As a result of its continual thinking about these issues, and as part of an effort to streamline conditionality in IMF-supported programs, the IMF undertook a major review of its conditionality starting in 2000, culminating in a new set of Conditionality Guidelines in 2002.

Before examining what lessons can be drawn for donors providing budget support, it is useful to step back and recall what are the main purposes of IMF conditionality and the principles that are stressed by the new guidelines.

A. Purposes of IMF Conditionality

IMF conditionality is intended to:

- provide assurances to the Fund that the member (borrowing) country is addressing its balance of payments problems in an appropriate way and that it will be in a position to repay the Fund upon maturity of the loan; and
- provide assurances to the country that, as long as the agreed policies are implemented, the Fund will provide financing. Conditionality thus reduces uncertainty for the borrower about the availability of financing.

The purpose of conditionality is therefore *not* to get the country to implement policies that it would not otherwise want to adopt. This also means that the IMF should seek to *finance* rather than *buy* reforms. When a country is not committed to adopting policies that are likely to achieve the program's goals, the guidelines require that the IMF exercise *selectivity*—that is, decline to provide financial support for the program.

These remarks draw on van der Willigen and others (2005), and in particular, conversations with Tessa van der Willigen as well as Elliott Harris.

In fact, these principles may represent some evolution in the thinking about the underlying "model" of what conditionality is supposed to achieve (or at least, in how it was applied). At the risk of some oversimplification, two alternative views might be considered here:

- Conditionality is intended to induce the government to adopt measures beneficial to the economy (or to the poor or other vulnerable groups).
- Conditionality is intended to interrupt IMF financial support when the program is unlikely to achieve its goals and until corrective measures have been taken.

The second view represents the traditional thinking about the purpose of conditionality, as it was constructed in the 1950s. But starting in the late 1980s, as IMF-supported programs (charged with being excessively oriented toward expenditure reduction and expenditure switching) started tackling structural bottlenecks to growth and to balance of payments viability, the objectives of programs became blurred, and conditionality was expanded to include measures that were deemed beneficial to economic performance even if not crucially related to the program's goals. In practice, the first view started gaining greater currency.

This tendency was reinforced with the IMF's involvement in Eastern Europe and the former Soviet Union, where programs were intended to help the transformation from centrally planned to market economies. Providing further impetus for the expansion of structural conditionality were the Fund-supported programs in the Asian crisis countries, where the crises were driven less by traditional sources of macroeconomic problems (such as unsustainable fiscal deficits) than by a lack of market confidence reflecting deep-rooted structural problems in the financial and corporate sectors. The key to resolving these crises was to restore market confidence, but it was less clear which structural reforms were required to turn the markets around—in turn, arguing for a very broad structural reform agenda.

By the late 1990s, as observers took stock of the evolution of structural conditionality over the previous decade, recognition was growing within the IMF that conditionality might have become too much of an intrusion into national policy making and too burdensome for the implementation capacity of national authorities. There followed a period of "streamlining" conditionality as the IMF, in broad consultation with national authorities, other multilateral organizations, bilateral donors, and elements of civil society, thought through how best to return toward the second of the views above—that is, that conditionality should act as a "tripwire" to signal when a program is unlikely to meet its well-defined objectives and interrupt IMF support until corrective measures have been taken. This perspective led naturally to the "criticality" test for conditionality—that conditions should be applied only to those measures that are critical to the achievement of the program goals (but should be applied to all such measures)—codified in the 2002 Conditionality Guidelines.

B. 2002 Conditionality Guidelines

The IMF's 2002 Conditionality Guidelines emphasize five principles: national ownership of policy programs, parsimony in the use of conditions, coordination with other multilateral organizations, tailoring policies to circumstances, and clarity in specification of conditions.

Without *national ownership*, a program is unlikely to be implemented, or may be implemented purely nominally. The flip side of ownership is selectivity—the IMF can only provide financial support if it is satisfied that the member is sufficiently committed to implement the agreed policies. How to test for ownership, however, and whose ownership—the authorities, parliament, or civil society more generally—is required for implementation to be assured and is a difficult judgment. Moreover, although conditionality should not substitute for ownership, it need not be entirely independent of it: indeed, conditionality can help strengthen ownership by demonstrating the authorities' commitment to a course of action.

The guidelines implement the principle of *parsimony* by applying a "criticality" test—conditions should be applied only to measures that are critical to the program that the IMF is supporting, but they should be applied to all such measures—where "critical" means that if the measure is not implemented, it is expected that the program objectives will not be attained.

A key question, of course, is how to make the concept of criticality operational—is it an entire reform that is critical (perhaps with several measures that are not in themselves, but only in aggregate, critical), a specific measure that is critical, or a specific measure to be undertaken on a specific timetable that is critical? The guidelines adopt the first of these interpretations, but by allowing individual measures that are not critical to be part of conditionality, they do make the concept of criticality a little fuzzier.

One possible implication of applying conditionality only to critical measures is declining waiver rates: if conditions are applied only to measures that are truly critical, the Fund should only grant a waiver of a condition if the country adopts the measure or an equivalent measure.

The criticality principle also has implications for *coordination* with other institutions because the criticality test applies to all measures—whether in the IMF's core areas of expertise or not, and regardless of whether other institutions (such as the World Bank) apply conditionality on the same measures. Of course, the IMF may, and should, draw on the expertise of other institutions in helping to design the conditionality on measures outside its areas of expertise.

Tailoring of conditionality means, among other things, setting conditions that are appropriate to the specific circumstances of the member requesting IMF support and the economic program for which it is seeking support.

Clarity of conditionality is required, so that there is no confusion between the measures that the member must adopt in order to maintain its access to IMF resources and additional measures that the authorities might want to adopt as part of their broader agenda.

C. Lessons for Donors Providing Budget Support

For donors providing—or contemplating moving to—budget support, three lessons come to mind:

First, an important purpose of conditionality is to provide assurances to the borrower that, as long as the agreed policies are implemented, the funds will be available. Unlike bilateral donors and creditors, multilateral organizations such as the IMF cannot withhold disbursement for political reasons unconnected to the program conditionality. Nevertheless, to the extent possible, in order to make flows predictable—or "provide assurances to the recipient" in the IMF's parlance—bilateral agencies should make such "political" conditionality clear upfront and distinguish it as much as possible from "program" conditions.

Second, again since part of the purpose of conditionality is to provide assurances to the borrower (or recipient) that the funds will indeed be available, there is an inherent tension between using more "outcomes-based" conditionality (in order to leave the national authorities greater "policy space" and enhance their ownership) and providing financing assurances, since the more conditionality is based on outcomes, the greater the risk of that financing will be interrupted due to reasons outside the borrower/recipient's direct control. One way to help resolve this tension is to examine, ex post, whether less than satisfactory outcomes were the result of poor policy implementation or unforeseen events (either a different link between policies and outcomes than expected or exogenous shocks), and in the latter case, to disburse at least part of the funds.

Third, donor support should not be subject to so much conditionality that taking the necessary measures overwhelms the implementation capacity of the country—here the IMF's "criticality" concept can be a useful guide—and where there are multiple donors, there may usefully be complementarities in the coverage of the reform agenda by the various donors. This brings two advantages: first, it allows donors to focus their efforts on areas where they may have particular expertise; second, it means that if there are slippages or disappointing outcomes in one reform area, this need not spill over into a complete cutoff of support from all donors simultaneously, which may severely undermine the ability of the government to maintain macroeconomic stability.

Perhaps the most important lesson is that all these choices involve important tradeoffs. There is probably no "right" answer—certainly not one that is universally applicable—and what has to be done is to find what works best for donor and each recipient.

Endnotes

1. The IMF provides balance of payments support to both the private and the public sectors. The part of the support that goes to the public sector has some similarities to "budget support" in that it is not earmarked for specific expenditures but rather helps to finance the government budget in general.

22

Ending Policy Conditionality: The Recent Shift in the United Kingdom's Aid Policy

NICK AMIN
UK Department for International Development

Evidence shows that coercive conditionality does not achieve sustainable change (Koeberle 2003; Koeberle and others 2005; Killick 1998; Kanbur, Sandler, and Morrison 1999; Morrissey 2004a; White and Morrissey 1997). Lines of accountability that are established mainly to emphasize relations between donors and partner governments distort the accountability of partner governments to their domestic constituencies.

In a major change in policy, the UK government has formally acknowledged the limits of conventional approaches to conditionality. Its recent policy paper (DFID-FCO-HMT 2005) recognizes both country ownership of the policy process and partnership as critical for improving aid effectiveness. The new policy requires conditionality solely to ensure accountability for UK resources to the UK Parliament, and not to leverage policy change in partner countries.

The principal reason for this changed approach to conditionality is to increase partner countries' ownership of the policy process. The UK will contribute to this by sharing evidence and lessons learned from experience. It will respect a partner government's prerogatives to set priorities, formulate policies, and respond to the views and demands of its constituents. At the same time, the UK will make clear to its partners the basis on which it will provide aid and the framework by which it expects itself to be held accountable to the UK Parliament. By increasing mutual accountability for aid, the hope is that partner governments will be more accountable to their citizens and the UK government will be more answerable to its public. Strengthened accountability is crucial for ensuring that aid is directed toward poverty reduction.

The main features of the UK's new aid policy are summarized in Box 22.1. The intent of the policy is to make aid more effective by supporting policy leadership and to help governments build stronger institutions of public accountability. It recognizes that the basis for demonstrating the accountability of aid to citizens should be the progress made in reducing poverty, gauged against benchmarks agreed with partner governments. The DFID's conditionality policy applies to all aid; it is applied to influence the whole aid relationship with a country, and will not necessarily attach to specific instruments, such as budget support and/or project investments.

This paper outlines emerging thinking and UK practice, rather than articulating definitive guidance, which is being prepared by the UK (DFID) and is likely to evolve

BOX 22.1 Essential Elements of the UK Policy

Good policy matters for development. Macroeconomic stability, growth, good governance, and social inclusion are all important for long-term poverty reduction. We believe that developing countries must be able to determine their own policies for meeting the MDGs. We are committed to supporting greater country ownership, especially of the policy process, and better mutual accountability.

The UK government believes that an effective aid partnership should be based on a shared commitment to three objectives:

- reducing poverty and achieving the MDGs;
- respecting human rights and other international obligations;
- strengthening financial management and accountability, and reducing the risk of funds being misused through weak administration or corruption.

So as to ensure that a partnership is achieving these shared objectives, agreement will be reached for assessing progress in these three areas. The poverty reduction strategies of developing countries should specify progress benchmarks and clarify to all stakeholders the intended results of the program.

In its aid relationships, the UK will be guided by five principles:

Developing country ownership. DFID will support nationally owned poverty reduction plans that take account of the views and concerns of poor people. We will not make our aid conditional on specific policy decisions by partner governments, or attempt to impose policy choices on them (including on sensitive economic areas such as privatization and trade liberalization). Instead, we will agree with partners on the purpose for which aid is being given, and will agree benchmarks to assess progress. We will draw these from countries' own plans, where available, and these benchmarks will relate to the impact and outcome of countries' overall programs in reducing poverty, rather than to specific policies.

Participatory and evidence-based policy making. Both donor and developing countries should be accountable, to their citizens and to the wider global community, for showing how aid is improving the quality of life for poor people. The UK supports participation and the use of evidence in policy making and will press for the use of poverty and social impact analysis (PSIA). We will also encourage national debate—including in parliaments—on the relative impact of different policy choices.

Predictability. Developing countries can use aid most effectively if they can rely on it as part of their long-term budget plans. The UK will seek to make aid more predictable by being clear in advance about how much aid will be given and the basis on which funds will be reduced or stopped. We will talk to partner countries before any interruption of aid and assess the impact that reducing or interrupting aid would have on the poor.

Harmonization. The UK will work with other donors to improve aid harmonization and limit the overall burden of conditionality. In particular, we will encourage the World Bank and the IMF to use conditionality in accordance with the principles in this paper and continue to press them to monitor and streamline their combined terms and conditions. DFID will use analysis from the IMF and World Bank in making its assessment of progress toward poverty reduction. However, an IMF or World Bank program going off track will not automatically lead the DFID to suspend its assistance.

Transparency and accountability. Both partners—donors and developing country governments—should be committed to transparency and should make public their decisions and the evidence on which they are based. The UK aims to increase transparency around the process of decision making on conditions, the conditions themselves, and the process

BOX 22.1 *(continued)*

for deciding to reduce or interrupt aid. The UK will use conditionality to ensure that aid is not used corruptly or for purposes other than those intended. In giving aid, we will also take account of countries' commitment to universal human rights standards and other international obligations.

The circumstances in which the UK will consider reducing or interrupting aid are if:

- countries move significantly away from agreed poverty reduction objectives or outcomes or the agreed objectives of a particular aid commitment (for example, through an unjustifiable rise in military spending or a substantial deviation from the agreed poverty reduction program);
- countries are in significant violation of human rights or other international obligations; or
- there is a significant breakdown in partner government financial management and accountability, leading to the risk of funds being misused through weak administration or corruption.

Source: DFID-FCO-HMT (2005).

as experience accumulates in different countries. Section A lays out the rationale for the change in policy emphasis. Section B presents emerging thoughts on implementation and how donor coordination might work in practice. This includes a discussion of the circumstances when aid might be interrupted, cut back, or withdrawn. Section C traces the implications of such actions, especially for aid modalities and donor cooperation mechanisms. Section D concludes, suggesting that the change in approach to conditionality should encourage the donor community to provide more long-term, predictable aid flows. This should help to build better partnerships and enhance accountability.

A. Rationale for a New Conditionality Framework

In its aid relationships, regardless of the specific form in which funds are made available, the UK will emphasize discussion and dialogue with partners rather than imposing change coercively. The emphasis of the aid relationship, and of conditionality in particular, will not be to press recipient governments into behaving differently. Rather, it will focus on agreeing with partner governments, and where possible with other donors, on a mutual set of commitments for (1) reducing poverty and meeting the Millenium Development Goals (MDGs), (2) respecting human rights and other international obligations, and (3) reducing the risk of funds being misappropriated and/or misused.

If a partner government shows little or no commitment to the above three objectives, the UK will not provide it with aid directly. Instead, different kinds of engagement will be sought for promoting peace and development: for example, working more effectively with nongovernmental or other organizations delivering services and advocating change, promoting better analysis of the circumstances that might lead to development and change, discussing the range of possible improvements with various key stakeholders, and supporting the private sector. In situations where support might lead to a significant turnaround of circumstances for poor people, early engagement with authorities will be sought, recognizing that this will involve making difficult judgments about the trajectory of change and the potential for reform.

As far as possible, the basis for the aid engagement with partners will be formalized in an agreed document designed to make clear the mutual commitment and partnership for reducing poverty. Given the varied circumstances in which the UK provides support, the form of agreement will vary but without diluting adherence to the abovementioned objectives and principles.

The desire is to support countries' endeavors to reduce poverty over the longer term. Decisions on whether, how, and when to provide assistance will be based on information that partners make available on the progress made toward reducing poverty and building stronger institutions of accountability. As much as possible, this evidence will be gathered from regular monitoring and assessment exercises that rely on national systems and procedures. Benchmarks for tracking progress will be agreed in advance with partners. Where information systems allow, these benchmarks will be drawn from a set of national indicators used by partners to assess and report progress in reducing poverty. Additional monitoring mechanisms will be applied only where local information systems generate inadequate information for progress monitoring.

B. How Will the New Policy Be Implemented?

The UK is already implementing significant elements of the new policy in several countries. In some, this is being done by way of a memorandum of understanding that sets out the overarching principles of the aid relationship. In countries to which it provides budget support, performance assessment frameworks (PAFs) are used (closely synchronized with those of other providers of assistance) for monitoring progress against commitments to reduce poverty. These performance frameworks draw on indicators defined by partner countries.

New practices are throwing up significant implementation challenges, not least regarding the transparent links between benchmarks used for monitoring progress and factors that lead to decisions to suspend aid. The current approach to conditionality centers on monitoring and measuring the progress of reform *processes* (that is, *inputs*), whereas the new policy encourages a focus on *outcomes*.

In countries to which the UK is not providing budget support, monitoring is more often concerned with the implementation of fairly specific elements of the reform program and with tracking sector results. In such situations, the intent of the new policy is not to raise the burden of conditionality but to require only a small number of benchmarks to monitor overall progress toward poverty reduction objectives.

The new policy will not require complex benchmarking exercises to enable assessments in respect of commitment to human rights and other international obligations and/or for strengthening financial management and accountability. The following discussion therefore relates primarily to assessing partner governments' commitment to poverty reduction.

A range of indicators will be used to assess the overall impact of a government's poverty reduction program. The emphasis will be on measuring outputs and outcomes transparently, not just tracking the actions of government. This approach should allow a fuller picture to be formed of progress being made, and thereby provide a sound basis for engaging in policy dialogue with partner governments. Progress indicators will be drawn from national poverty reduction programs, and they will have been agreed and selected through a domestic policy process.

Where donors establish a parallel or supplementary set of indicators, a time-bound transition process should be agreed with government to encourage progression to stronger national determination. Such processes are already current practice in some countries where budget support arrangements are operating and where governments and development partners use a common PAF. PAFs normally comprise a range of indicators. They have the virtue of encouraging donors to subscribe to a common set of objectives in supporting a partner's development efforts, while allowing various donors to track different performance criteria and meet their own unique requirements for accountability.

As is emerging practice, procedures for assessments should be agreed with partner governments in advance. As much as possible, reviews should be done jointly, and with other partners, so as to avoid adding to governments' transaction costs. If credible domestic review processes are in place, these should be relied upon and strengthened where need be. Use of donor-generated supplementary review processes should be kept to a minimum and should work toward establishing solid national systems. In such situations, the DFID will consider support for building capacity and hasten the transition to government-led processes.

The purpose of monitoring through benchmarks will be to assess progress against the core commitment to reduce poverty. The disbursement of UK funds will not be mechanically linked to progress against poverty reduction benchmarks; a failure to meet specific indicators will not automatically trigger interruptions to, and/or reductions in, aid disbursements in the period that the UK will have agreed to commit its aid (commonly three years).

Perceptions of insufficient progress will lead to dialogue with partner governments. This will involve a consideration of constraints stalling progress and a discussion of how difficulties might be resolved. Conditions will not be used to lever policy change. If there are concerns with the policy formulation process, these will be discussed with the country authorities in ways that do not crowd out the articulation and discussion of policy options among key domestic stakeholders. A government's commitment to poverty reduction will be reviewed where there is continued failure to achieve results and where extensive dialogue with government signals a high risk of deviation from agreed objectives.

As indicated above, the UK will consider reducing or interrupting committed aid when:

- partner countries are perceived to have moved significantly away from the agreed poverty reduction objectives;
- partner countries are considered to be violating human rights or other international obligations; or
- partner governments' financial management and accountability systems deteriorate to an extent that funds risk being misused and/or misappropriated through corruption.

By a process of regular monitoring and dialogue, and by acquiring a thorough understanding of the political, economic, and social context, suspensions and reductions in aid disbursements will hopefully be avoided. But the possibility of a breakdown in relations will always remain. Unanticipated political events and a progressive deterioration in political governance could lead to a breakdown in relations if dialogue does not achieve progress or does not help to address a critical concern. For example, there might be a violation of civil and political rights through election rigging, the violent suppression of political protests, and/or the placing of reporting restrictions on the media. Alternatively, financial management and accountability might break down, whether because of political patronage or because of a capture of state institutions by nonrepresentative ethnic/social groups. Or, as mentioned above, a departure from poverty reduction objectives may arise from a large increase in military spending and/or aggression toward neighboring countries.

If the UK has to decide on a sudden suspension or reduction in aid, the process for doing so will be agreed in advance with all partners. The process will include agreeing a substantial period for making an assessment and discussing how to resolve matters. During that period, planned disbursements will continue, although decisions will inevitably be shaped by the context and gravity of the circumstance leading to a breakdown in relations. A structured approach to addressing problems should significantly enhance the predictability of aid.

A decision to reduce or terminate financial support will not be taken without considering the longer-term effects on poor people of a sudden and substantial withdrawal of funds. Where possible, the UK will seek to resolve difficulties multilaterally with partners. It will do this by drawing on existing procedures such as the provisions outlined in the EU's Cotonou Agreement, which proposes a series of actions that partners might wish to implement when things go wrong.[1]

In the event of the UK taking an unavoidable decision to stop or reduce aid, its response will be proportionate. The response will reflect the extent of breakdown in relations and be considered within the context of the overall partnership established with the country. It would be impractical to outline in advance the precise ways in which a partnership might be in breach. But in instances threatening a collapse in relations, judgment will be needed to gauge the seriousness of specific events and the circumstances surrounding them. Decisions to cut back aid will not be based on a predetermined formula but on a careful review of case-by-case evidence.

Any decision to restrict disbursement will be based on evidence that shows that continuing to provide aid will violate the three fundamental objectives agreed with the country regarding the aid partnership. It will not be assumed that a substantial reining-in of UK funds will produce a turnaround in a partner country's policy.

The objective of a suspension and/or reduction in finance will not be to punish partner governments, but to respond to a strong perception that a policy to continue providing aid will not produce worthwhile results. The response to a deteriorating situation will be commensurate with, and reflective of, the deterioration in the aid relationship, and graduated so as not to damage unnecessarily partners' public expenditure plans. Consequently, the UK will aim not to cut back funds within a country's financial year, and will give advance notice of planned reductions in the outer years of an aid agreement. Alternatively, the form of aid might be adjusted—say, by commuting flexible general budget support into sector-specific investments or redirecting support from governments to nonstate organizations.

Greater transparency regarding aid disbursement decisions will affect how conditionality succeeds in improving aid accountability. To enable better dialogue with government, and to encourage wider debate on key development issues, the UK will ensure that all critical decisions and background information regarding aid commitments and disbursements are publicized. More transparency, discussion, and debate will not only increase societal scrutiny over key aid and public finance decisions, but also help to gauge the level of public opposition (or support) there might be to specific aid-related actions.

C. Implications for Budget Support and Cooperation with Development Partners

Recent discussions in the OECD-DAC regarding aid effectiveness have influenced the UK's policy on conditionality. As Box 22.1 made clear, harmonization and predictability are key principles of the new policy. Although aid donors have made some advances in harmonizing aid practices and in aligning procedures with national systems, considerably more progress is needed to make aid more effective and to reduce the burden of transaction costs on partners (High-Level Forum 2005).

Donors' basis for moving in the same direction is now much stronger with the wider acceptance of country-led approaches involving alignment with partner governments' own policies, processes, indicators, and targets. Donors should be considering partners' preferences when deciding how to design interventions and how to harmonize their activities with others'.

It is not clear how the UK's new conditionality policy will affect donors' disbursement policies—how they link together within a common frame, and how flows will be delivered predictably to partners. Donors should be moving toward making more predictable disbursements within a framework of medium-term commitments, while avoiding within-year financial cutbacks. Not all donors will be able to progress at the same rate, and the same set of conditions will not meet all donors' accountability requirements. (Recipients may also not want all donors to apply the same conditions, as this might make aid flows highly volatile.) It seems likely that budget support partners will continue applying different conditions but do so within a common framework.

To move forward with the alignment and harmonization agenda at the country level calls for a pragmatic approach. Alignment will be achieved by making more use of governments' own indicators and targets when setting disbursement conditions and assessing progress. Similarly, alignment will entail making more use of national policy, planning, financial management, accountability, and assessment processes. Reduced use of disbursement triggers should also help to achieve closer alignment by providing governments more space for implementing national policy priorities.

Harmonization represents a greater challenge. Given differences in their accountability frameworks (either to shareholders or to parliaments), donors may not be able to harmonize their conditionality requirements in all contexts. Judgment will be required in assessing how to apply the new UK conditionality policy to strengthen harmonization objectives within different aid modalities. Where harmonized conditionality cannot be achieved, donors should carefully manage their use of conditionality to minimize transaction costs for partner governments.

In the context of working within common budget support frameworks, the UK will harmonize with other donors in the way most appropriate to the specific country's budgeting arrangements. There may be transitional issues to address in coordinating with other donors, such as the adjustment of PAFs so as to ensure compatibility between the aid policies of the UK and other partners. The solutions sought should not undermine the government's ownership of the framework. Over time, outcome indicators should come to dominate the mix of indicators that make up PAFs.

The biggest differences in approaches among budget support donors are likely to arise in the use of indicators in PAFs. While some donors will use these indicators to monitor progress, others will use them to make decisions regarding the disbursement of funds. Two of the UK's key multilateral partners, the World Bank and the EC, share the UK's preference for alignment, but both use indicators and targets in the PAF as triggers for signaling disbursement (the World Bank focuses attention on policy actions, and the EC tends to emphasize results). Such differences need not prevent donors from agreeing with government a harmonized framework of indicators that each donor can then use to meet its own requirements. With the World Bank now acknowledging that, barring exceptional circumstances, forcing policy choices on countries through conditionality is likely to be suboptimal, the basis for a shared approach with the World Bank and the EC is even stronger (World Bank 2005p).

In future, it should be possible for all partners to (1) agree on a common set of progress benchmarks and how these will be measured, (2) be clear about how the benchmarks will be used as disbursement triggers or how the information they generate will influence aid allocation decisions in the longer term, and (3) establish the time horizon for when, and how, each contributing donor will make disbursements into the common budget support pool. Mechanisms arranged between budget support donors and country authorities in response to the new conditionality environment should reflect specific circumstances. These will include how donors historically have cooperated and have established partnership agreements with recipients, including at the sector level.

The UK intends to make clear to partners how its budget support commitments will be made. It will notify partner countries about the expected flow of funds and the circumstances when this might be interrupted. As noted above, it will aim to provide firm commitments for three years and only interrupt aid within the partner government's financial year in exceptional circumstances.

Establishing closer links and coordination with the World Bank in budget support settings has been made much easier by the use of ex post conditionality in poverty reduction support credits (PRSCs). The recent removal of prescriptive approaches to policy choice from the World Bank's Operational Policy with regard to development policy loans (DPLs) is welcome, but implementing this more flexible, hands-off approach remains a challenge. World Bank conditionality in PRSCs and DPLs is still perceived by borrowing countries, and some sections of the international development community, as too onerous, intrusive, and complex. It will be important to ensure that World Bank conditionality is not invasive and is not used to leverage reforms from reluctant governments. PRSC frameworks should be congruent with poverty reduction strategies and domestic policy processes. In countries with an established track record of programmatic lending, a shift to three-year PRSCs would do much to increase predictability.

The operational relationship between progress benchmarks and disbursement criteria (prior actions and triggers) in World Bank PRSC matrices also requires clarification. Within the World Bank's conditionality framework, the precise role to be played by progress benchmarks, and whether and how they influence disbursements (and future aid allocations), must be made clear to borrowing country authorities. The simplification of World Bank conditionality should help signal to other development agencies the need for them to do the same.

Simplification should be sought not just at the instrument level (in PRSCs, DPLs, and investment loans), but between these instruments and the World Bank's country assistance strategies (CASs). It is the latter that should be the fundamental means to secure congruence and consistency between the results sought by Bank programs and those that are specified in borrowing countries' poverty reduction strategies. With the rising use of outcome indicators in World Bank CASs, it should become easier for the Bank to monitor progress toward overall poverty reduction.

D. Conclusion

The fundamental change in the UK's conditionality policy has been motivated by the desire to make aid more effective and accountable. The latter is critical if sustained progress is to be made in reaching the MDGs. Stronger partnerships are required between donors and aid-recipient countries to ensure that the vision and responsibility for achieving results is shared. Mutual accountability should make it possible for donors to support national development efforts and build institutions in contexts where good policies are strongly owned, and it encourages growth and development.

The shift in focus in conditionality, from coercion to partnership, should make donor assistance less volatile and more effective in supporting national poverty reduction efforts. More predictable aid should be delivered to partner countries for flexible use. But to ensure lasting impact, harmonization of policies and actions among donors will be needed. Unless all donors reform their conditionality, it will be difficult to align the bulk of external assistance behind developing countries' national poverty reduction efforts, and for it to work in ways that strengthen accountability systems in both donor and partner countries.

Endnotes

1. For African, Caribbean, and Pacific (ACP) countries, the Cotonou Agreement provides an overall framework for assessing political, aid, and trade relationships. For non-ACP countries, separate regulations are agreed. Article 8 of the Cotonou Agreement defines how political dialogue might be conducted between the EC and ACP member states. Article 9 focuses on "essential" (human rights, democracy, and rule of law) and "fundamental" (corruption) elements of a partnership with the EC. Articles 96 and 97 outline the process which should be followed in the event of one of the above elements being breached. The agreement indicates that if consultations do not lead to a mutually acceptable solution, appropriate measures may be taken, including suspending aid if necessary.

23

Germany's Perspective on Budget Support

INGRID-GABRIELA HOVEN
Ministry for Economic Cooperation and Development, Germany

Germany, among other countries, was perceived until quite recently as reluctant to place full attention and high priority on budget support. Though Germany started using policy-based approaches to its aid in 2001, the volume of aid affected was originally quite small. This was because in the German aid cooperation system, there was a feeling that budget support was highly risky, given that many partner countries still lacked the institutional basis for effective use of this form of aid.

This approach has changed in the past two years. Germany fully supports the vision developed since Rome in 2003 and documented in the Paris agenda on aid effectiveness with respect to the opportunities that budget support provides for development cooperation. Today, Germany provides budget support to 18 countries and contributes €300 million through budget support operations. The benchmarks agreed by Germany and its partners for the coming years mean that starting in 2006, Germany will channel about one-fourth of its financial cooperation through contributions to budget support programs and other forms of program-oriented joint financing. For Sub-Saharan Africa, Germany aims to provide up to half of its bilateral financial assistance as program-oriented joint financing (including budget support) by 2007, provided that conditions are favorable in the recipient countries.

Experience with budget support operations is still new. Germany is participating in evaluations of this experience, and probably will refine its position on the basis of evaluation results. An issue that Germany considers to be of high priority is the expectation that with program-oriented joint financing, an incentive system will be created that initiates and encourages reform. In that way, the financing will contribute to creating government structures and institutions. The main objective is good governance: with governments that are able to operate on a sustainable basis and to plan, implement, and account for policies that are relevant for the Millennium Development Goals. Strengthening cooperation countries' sense of responsibility and ownership is a very important goal for Germany.

Looking to the future, Germany's Ministry for International Cooperation and Development sees six important challenges:

- *Poverty reduction strategy papers (PRSPs) as the orientation for donor operations.* Recent evaluations have shown that in many countries, PRSPs have not yet provided a specific planning framework or a sufficient basis for the design of budget support or donor policy alignment. As a result, it is quite difficult to establish the needed direct link between the PRSP, budget operations, and development cooperation. This reflects the fact that partner countries' main objective in drafting PRSPs is to qualify for debt relief or poverty reduction support credits, or the Poverty Reduction and Growth Facility of the International Monetary Fund, and not to provide a basis for medium-term, results-oriented development cooperation. Therefore, in many countries, there is a gap between the PRSP orientation and the concrete measures that are to be supported by budget support programs. The donor community runs the risk of pushing certain goals that are not directly linked to the longer-term policy framework of the respective partner countries. The only way to avoid this risk is to strengthen the recipient country's capacity to design policies and create a medium-term framework that provides guidance for providing donor support and development cooperation.
- *Public financial management.* From the point of view of German development cooperation, a major goal of budget support programs is to help enhance public financial management—an area where progress has been relatively limited. Efforts to improve public financial management and develop relevant capacity should receive more support in budget support programs and more attention in the policy dialogue. In the past, donor support has not been sufficiently coordinated or based on government programs. One reason for the slow progress may be donors' past tendency to stick to project aid, deflecting partner countries' attention from public financial management issues. If a signal could be sent that the donor community, in accordance with the Paris agenda on aid effectiveness, is moving ahead with the budget support agenda, it could create a new impetus for moving forward. Quicker progress on public financial management is necessary for expanding budget support more swiftly and for including even donors that are still hesitant to fully implement the Paris agenda for aid effectiveness.
- *Capacity development.* Budget support makes the need for capacity development or institutional reforms even more evident, not only for public financial management, but also for sectoral ministries and decentralized government structures and at the local level. In addition, donors are tempted to focus exclusively on the executive branch of government. But the benefits of budget support can only fully unfold when a capable parliament and a well-informed public can take part in setting priorities and monitoring their execution. Strong domestic ownership is a key for effective implementation of policy reforms and a precondition for efficient budgetary aid. Donors should selectively focus their aid in countries that have committed to agreed reforms.

- *The need to disburse funds against results achieved rather than against agreed inputs.* A consensus is emerging that donors and partner countries need to move away from input conditionality to much more results-oriented accountability frameworks. They must find ways to reconcile predictability with the accountability framework, and here some proposals have already been advanced for consideration. The reduction and harmonization of different sets of conditionalities are also of particular importance if we want to reduce transaction costs for our partner countries in line with the spirit of the Paris agenda.
- *A need for stronger mutual accountability.* Collective action is needed by donors and recipient countries. Mutual accountability also implies the need for a much more rigorous review of donors' performance in implementing the commitments made under the Paris agenda. If donors compete as much as they did with respect to project aid, the hopes that budget support will improve the efficiency and effectiveness of aid will not be fulfilled.
- *Donor coordination.* Even under donor budget support programs, a greater division of labor is still needed. Budget support programs must not be conceived as add-ons to a typical project-related lending portfolio, or transaction costs will not be lowered in the medium term. Donors must use such instruments as delegated cooperation and silent partnership. This requires, in many cases, that they reflect on their comparative advantages in respect of providing certain assistance to specific countries and refrain from getting involved in an additional sector if it is already sufficiently covered by other donors.

24

Direct Budget Support, Disbursement Mechanisms, and Predictability

Norwegian Agency for Development Cooperation (NORAD)

For this paper, the Norwegian Ministry of Foreign Affairs has requested NORAD to discuss different aspects of direct budget support, including a discussion of graduated response as a possible measure for increasing predictability while maintaining reform incentives and recipient ownership.

This concern falls in line with the ongoing international discussion on conditionality and graduated response. Many donors are searching for new approaches to conditionality, recognizing that reforms cannot be "bought" or imposed by donors, but rather have to be "owned" by the recipient country to be successful and sustainable. The discussion on graduated response is largely dominated by the European Commission (EC) model, which has been in use for five years and is the most formal graduated response mechanism. Both the World Bank and the UK Department for International Development (DFID) have stated that they will explore the potential to link aid to performance results or outcomes rather than to partner governments' policies, referring to the EC model (DFID 2004a; World Bank 2005o), among others. Other donors too are increasingly turning to graduated response mechanisms. Norway, for its part, is discussing a possible graduated response together with other donors in Uganda, Zambia, Malawi, and Tanzania.

The general principles governing Norwegian budget support are ownership, a close link to the poverty reduction strategy paper (PRSP) process, harmonization with other donors, and alignment with the recipient's budget cycle.

These principles also guide the design of a graduated response and form a starting point for the discussion in this paper. Section A gives an overview of the use of direct budget support by Norway and some other donors. Section B discusses some of the underlying incentive problems connected to aid in general and budget support in particular and to the causes and consequences of lack of predictability. Section C discusses different graduated response mechanisms. With the EC model as a point of reference, we, also raise some questions and concerns as to the design of a graduated response. In section D, we make some recommendations and discuss the way forward.

This paper is also available at http://www.norad.no.

A. The Use of Direct Budget Support

Norway may give budget support to main partner countries or to countries in post-conflict and peace-building processes. In Report No. 35 to the Storting (2003–04), *Fighting Poverty Together* (p. 97), the Norwegian government expresses a clear ambition to increase the share of direct budget support and general sector support in Norway's bilateral aid—an ambition that has broad political support.

The budget support to several of Norway's partner countries has developed from earlier types of general support, such as balance of payments support and import support.[1] Figure 24.1 shows Norway's use of different types of budget support and debt relief in 1990–2003. The change in the use of aid modalities during this period reflects the change in aid policy and dialogue: whereas the focus in the early 1990s was on structural adjustment programs aimed at macroeconomic stability, liberalization, and privatization, today's discussions on budget support focus mainly on poverty reduction and the recipient countries' "ownership" of reforms.

Debt relief has features in common with budget support, because it releases funds that the recipient country otherwise would have to spend on interest payments and amortization.[2] Norway gives debt relief both bilaterally and multilaterally. A part of our bilateral debt relief is given within the Paris Club debt relief forums.[3] Between 1998 and 2003, Norway relieved some of the world's poorest countries of 1.6 billion Norwegian Kroner (NKr) in debt to Norway in connection with the debt plan, but this was not posted as aid and is therefore not included in Figure 24.1.

Norway's general aid in terms of debt relief, import support, and balance of payments and budget support was only slightly higher in 2003 than in 1990. The total declined during the first half of the 1990s, mainly because of the reduction in import support. Between 1995 and 2003, the total increased, reflecting the stepped up use of multilateral debt relief and balance of payments and budget support. The increase in balance of payments and budget support is partly explained by the introduction of budget support programs in Norway's main partner countries (Mozambique in 1996, Tanzania in 1998, Uganda in 2002, and Malawi in 2002, with the first disbursement in 2003), but also by the increase in budget support to countries in postconflict and peace-building processes. An example is the budget support to Afghanistan, which accounted for more than a quarter of the total balance of payments and budget support in 2003.

The share of direct budget support in Norway's total bilateral support has grown steadily during the last few years. In 1999, Norway gave NKr 180 million in direct budget support, representing 2.5 percent of total bilateral support. This share increased to almost 5 percent in 2003, when Norway gave NKr 480 million in direct budget support. Although the total share of budget support still is relatively low, the share at the individual country level can be quite high. For Tanzania, Mozambique, Uganda, and Malawi, the share of direct budget support in total bilateral support was 20–23 percent in 2003.

Table 24.1 shows the share of direct budget support for Norway and some other donors during the last few years. Norway's increasing share of direct budget support follows a trend among donors. In the United Kingdom, the share of direct budget

FIGURE 24.1 Norwegian Debt Relief, Import Support, Balance of Payments, and Budget Support, 1990–2003

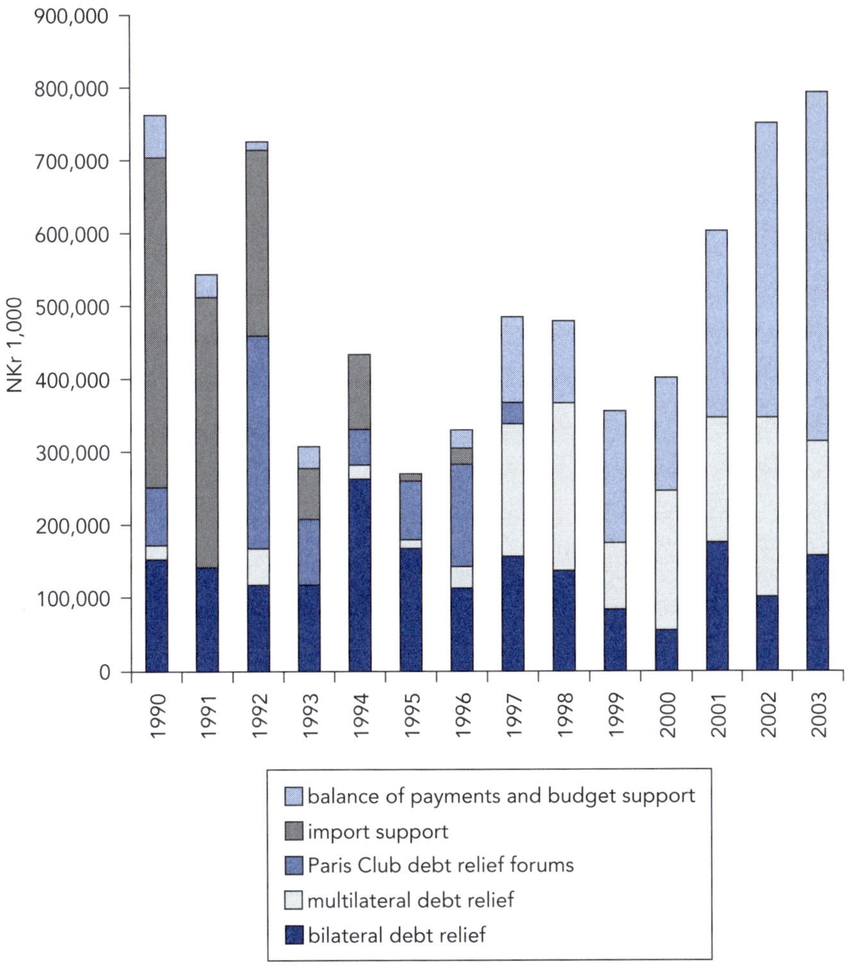

TABLE 24.1 Direct Budget Support in Percent of Total Bilateral Support from Norway and Some Other Donors, 2000–03

	2000	2001	2002	2003
Norway	2.0	3.2	4.7	4.9
Sweden	5.8	4.4	4.6	5.2
Netherlands	-	8.5	11.3	20.4
United Kingdom[a]	24.0	24.0	18.0	22.0

a.Includes general and sector budget support.
Note: The table is based on information from the respective development agencies, whose definitions of budget support may vary.

support in total aid has fluctuated around 20 percent, whereas in the Netherlands it has risen significantly, from 8.5 percent in 2002 to 20.4 percent in 2003. Sweden has signaled an intention to increase budget support to countries that have the capacity to manage this type of assistance. According to Sida, partner countries' efforts to formulate and implement poverty reduction strategies (PRSs), together with the ongoing work on harmonization and coordination of budget support, increase the opportunities for providing a larger share of development assistance in the form of budget support.[4]

B. Causes and Consequences of Lack of Predictability

Generally, aid is less predictable than other types of government revenue, for instance tax revenues, and direct budget support is less predictable than other types of aid. In a recent study, Bulíř and Hamann (2003) found that aid is substantially more volatile than domestic revenues, and that the relative volatility of aid grows with aid dependency.[5] For the most aid-dependent countries, these authors found that aid is more than seven times as volatile as domestic revenues. They also showed that aid cannot be predicted reliably on the basis of donor commitments, which have a systematic tendency to exceed disbursements. Further, the predictive power of donors' commitments tends to be lower in poorer and more aid-dependent countries.

Unpredictable aid inflows make it very difficult for the recipient government to plan the next year's budget and the allocation of resources. As an example, Uganda's Ministry of Finance "discounts" donor aid projections when preparing its budget. The current discount factor is set at 35 percent, corresponding to the average level by which disbursements have fallen short of donor commitments over the last five years.[6] The difficulty in forecasting aid inflows weakens the national budget as a tool of government policy and a basis for a meaningful parliamentary discussion on the allocation of resources.

The typical aid-dependent country has few options available to offset an unexpected nondisbursement of aid. Unpredictable aid inflows therefore can lead to budgetary and overall economic instability, especially when budget support is a significant share of government inflows. Expenditure cuts necessitated by nondisbursement of aid can affect the poorest in particular. If the disbursements, on the other hand, should exceed the planned amount, there is a risk of inefficient spending.

The causes of lack of predictability in budget support can be divided into two main categories:

- *Technical and administrative matters.* This includes poor alignment with the recipient's national processes and budget cycle and disbursement delays due to administrative problems, bureaucratic procedures, or time-consuming coordination between donors.
- *Conditions set up by the donor.* Lack of fulfillment of economic or political governance conditions may lead the donor to hold back planned disbursements. Unclear conditions or unclear consequences when conditions are not met aggravate the predictability problem caused by conditionality.

It is useful to distinguish between these two categories. Disbursement delays caused by technical and administrative matters are largely unintended and should, according to best practices, be avoided whenever possible. A recent survey by the Strategic Partnership with Africa Budget Support Working Group (SPA 2005) indicates substantial scope for improvement in this area. The recipient governments that were interviewed in the survey felt that the most important way to improve predictability was to make multiyear commitments and provide information about future disbursements in time for inclusion in budget preparation.

By contrast, the lack of predictability caused by conditionality is partly deliberate. In the eyes of the donor, conditionality is needed to underpin reforms and ensure that the budget support is used as intended. Donors must be able to react if the recipient country is not making enough progress in critical areas like macroeconomic management, governance, public finance management, and PRS implementation. Further, the taxpayers of the donor country require some reassurance that their financial contributions to another country are achieving their intended purpose.

The incentive problem is connected to the latter category. It arises from the conflict between securing reform incentives through conditionality and the recipient countries' need for predictable funding.[7] If reform incentives were our only concern, the disbursement of budget support could in principle be made completely dependent on the recipient country achieving agreed targets, and the choice of policy action to achieve this goal could be left entirely up to the recipient country. This would maximize reform incentives and recipient responsibility. However, there may be a large degree of uncertainty as to what is the right policy action, and how well the selected policy action will achieve the agreed goal. With completely results-based conditionality, aid inflows would be reduced or even eliminated completely if agreed conditions were not met. Thus, with this model, the recipient country would bear all the risk connected with selecting the right policy action. At the other extreme, if predictability were our only concern, budget support could be a fixed amount with no conditions.

Both effort (incentives) and risk (predictability) must be considered when choosing a disbursement mechanism for budget support. The preferred mechanism should reflect the relative weight attached to predictability and reform incentives. A graduated response with a combination of fixed and variable components is only an instrument for balancing conflicting concerns; it does not remove the basic dilemma.

A graduated response can be a means to avoid an "all-or-nothing" or a "stop-go" approach to budget support, which may undermine the intended incentive effects of conditionality. Well aware of the political pressure in the donor country to "spend the money," the recipient government may not take seriously the donor threat of holding back disbursements. Further, the economic and social consequences of holding back disbursements (which may constitute a substantial part of the national budget) may be so harmful that, at the end of the day, the donor does not want to go through with it. This is sometimes referred to as the "nuclear deterrent effect," describing a situation where the sanctions would be so disproportionate to the alleged failure of the government that they are impossible for the donor to carry through. This can especially be the case if there is "herd behavior" or peer pressure on the donor side—that is, if several donors (more or less uncritically) follow one donor's disbursement decision. The more flexible approach of graduated response mechanisms can thus make threats of sanctions more credible.

C. Graduated Response Mechanisms

Current Donor Approaches

The use of graduated responses is not new. Donors have different methods for graduating their reactions if the recipient country fails to fulfill conditions: they can reduce the future level of budget support, delay or suspend payments, or terminate the agreement altogether.

Norway

All these reactions are permitted by Norway's present guidelines for budget support, and in recent years, several such measures have been used or considered by Norway and other donors of budget support to Norway's partner countries (see the annex to this paper for a more detailed description of the country cases):

- In *Malawi*, when the IMF's Poverty Reduction Growth Facility (PRGF) program was off track in 2001–03, budget support disbursements from the IMF, the World Bank, and the Common Approach to Budget Support (CABS) partnership (consisting of the EU, the UK, Sweden, and later Norway) were stopped. Norway's disbursements were not contingent on the IMF program being on track, but in response to the government's lack of fiscal control, Norway decided to follow the other members and withhold disbursements (under the budget support agreement signed in February 2002 with planned disbursements for 2002 and 2003). In October 2003, when the IMF resumed its loan disbursements under the PRGF, the CABS partners resumed their budgetary support. In 2004, the IMF program again went off track, but a nevertheless positive development led most donors, including Norway, to continue disbursements.
- In *Mozambique*, the donor community delayed disbursements for some months in 2001 as a reaction to a corruption scandal and crisis in the banking sector. After discussions with the donors, the Mozambican government committed itself to four follow-up actions related to the banking crisis. The donor community regarded this as a satisfactory response and thus donor funds were released as planned toward the end of the year.
- In *Uganda*, Norway has chosen to earmark budget support to the Poverty Action Fund instead of providing general budget support, partly as a reaction to the government's increased military spending in 2002–03. The Poverty Action Fund budget support has, however, been disbursed as planned. The three bilateral donors of general budget support (Ireland, the Netherlands, and the UK) cut their budget support for fiscal year 2002–03 because of the disagreement with the government on the level of military spending. Ireland decided to reassign the rest of its general

budget support funds to the Poverty Action Fund. The World Bank delayed disbursements for some months in 2003 and 2004, due to administrative problems, the need to verify budget execution, and questions regarding the implementation of the Leadership Code (an anticorruption measure requiring high-level government officials to declare their assets). The UK also withheld budget support for some months in 2004 because of discontent with the dialogue with the government on the defense review.

- In *Tanzania*, several donors, including Norway and DFID, questioned the government's decision in 2002 to purchase a US$40 million radar system for air traffic control, and decided to postpone budget support disbursements until the terms and conditions of the purchase had been clarified and a solution acceptable to the donors had been found. During the mid-year review in April 2004, donors expressed concern about Tanzania's slow progress in establishing the Public Financial Management Reform Program (PFMRP). Norway concluded that the release of the tranche for fiscal year 2004–05 would depend on the progress in the PFMRP and that the Ministry of Foreign Affairs should be consulted before disbursement.

The problem with these approaches is that the consequences of nonfulfillment of conditions may be unclear in advance, resulting in inconsistent donor reactions and lack of predictability for the recipient country. This problem has drawn the attention of many donors and has led them to review their methods for implementing conditionality.

EC

Many donors are showing interest in the EC's graduated response model, which combines fixed and variable components. The fixed components are basic resources for macroeconomic support, disbursed in an "all or nothing" form depending on broad macroeconomic conditions (for example a satisfactory implementation of an IMF program) or specific conditions connected to, for example, fiduciary risk. The variable components are additional resources that are released in a graduated form, depending upon performance on selected sectors, usually health, education, and public financial management. The model allows for partial disbursements in case of partial fulfillment of conditions: 50 percent fulfillment of the agreed indicator goal leads to a 50 percent disbursement. Table 24.2 illustrates how the disbursement of a variable tranche is calculated in the EC model.[8] Characteristic of the EC model is the focus on impacts and outcomes instead of policy actions. The EC applies this model to most of its budget support programs.

World Bank

The World Bank's poverty reduction support credits (PRSCs) involve a series of single-tranche operations with a medium-term framework specified at the outset. A number of policy actions are selected as "prior actions" and triggers for disbursement. The World Bank's approach has broadly moved away from traditional conditionality, which focused on short-term macroeconomic adjustment and removing major eco-

TABLE 24.2 Example of a Variable Tranche Calculation in the EC Model

Indicator[a]	Weight	Score	Weighted score
Education			
Primary enrollment	0.1666	1	0.1666
Gender balance in primary enrollment	0.1666	0.5	0.08333
Primary completion rate	0.1666	0	0
Total education	0.5		
Health			
Vaccination coverage	0.125	1	0.125
Births attended by trained staff	0.125	0.5	0.0625
Attendance at operating department practice(ODP)	0.125	0	0
Gender balance of ODP attendance	0.125	0.5	0.0625
Total health	0.5		
Total	**1**		**0.5**

a. Only for illustration.
Note: Since the total weighted score is 0.5, in this example, the actual disbursement would be 0.5 times the tranche total. The example does not include public financial management indicators, but the process of calculation would be analogous.
Source: EC (2003a, Annex, 3).

nomic distortions. The current focus is on the implementation of the recipient countries' own national strategies for poverty reduction.

The World Bank has prepared a review of its conditionality (see Chapter 13 of this volume), including a discussion of the role and scope of outcome-based conditionality as well as a discussion of variable budget support components as a way to make resource flows more predictable.

For PRSC5 in Uganda, the World Bank is discussing a graduated approach with a core component subject only to basic requirements for the provision of budget support, to be confirmed annually through a joint government–development partners' review of the PRS, and a variable component that would be performance related, as defined by the prior actions and other performance triggers.

The World Bank has also used so-called floating tranches to increase country ownership. A floating tranche is disbursed when a specific condition is fulfilled—that is, the timing of the disbursement is flexible. The principle of floating tranches was used for HIPC (highly indebted poor countries) completion point disbursements.

Bilateral Donors

Several bilateral donors have introduced graduated responses in some countries, and intend to or consider extending the practice to other countries.

The United Kingdom (DFID) is revising its approach to conditionality, and is actively considering graduated response mechanisms as well as the scope for incorporating outcome benchmarks as part of an approach harmonized with other donors.

Sweden (Sida) is elaborating new guidelines for budget support. These are expected to be "cautiously positive" toward a graduated response, but are not expected to include a firm position on this issue, since Sida believes that more methodological work is needed in this area.[9]

At the country level, Sweden has introduced performance-based tranches in its budget support to Mozambique and Bolivia. In Mozambique, part of the budget support has been linked to the preparation of the forensic audit of Banco Austral. In Bolivia, one tranche has been linked to progress in public financial management, fiscal policy, and progress under the national poverty reduction policy. Sweden is currently considering variable tranches linked to performance in public financial management and social sectors in some countries, including Tanzania. In Zambia, Sweden has taken part in designing a graduated response model (together with Norway, for example), but this model has not yet been implemented.

In Uganda, bilateral donors (the Netherlands, DFID, Ireland, Sweden, and Norway) are discussing a graduation of disbursements both as a possible response to non-performance within public reform programs linked to budget support and as a more general response to deterioration in governance. The bilateral donors intend to link variable tranches to political governance indicators beyond the scope of the PRSC.

The Netherlands has some experience with graduated response mechanisms in relation to multiannual budget support (Burkina Faso and Mozambique), in the sense that disbursement in a given year depends on the progress made in the previous year on previously agreed upon indicators and measures as well as on a sufficient track record. The Netherlands seeks to avoid a "stop-go" policy. When progress looks bleak or performance is deteriorating, this is primarily addressed through dialogue—in which governance issues are very important. In Uganda, for example, rising doubts about the quality of reforms and political commitment has led the Dutch embassy to intensify the dialogue with the government. Dutch budget support in 2005 has been made conditional upon visible improvements, notably in the area of governance.

Switzerland is currently adopting a "multiple flows" arrangement. In the case of Mozambique,[10] for instance, half of the funds provided through budget support are disbursed as a fixed tranche, based on an assessment of macroeconomic developments and, more generally, performance against commitments in the performance assessment framework. The remaining funds are disbursed through thematic subtranches linked to performance in public financial management (20 percent), revenue mobilization objectives (15 percent), and performance in private sector development (15 percent).

Issues in the Design of a Graduated Response

Graduated response mechanisms have several merits:

- They provide a way to balance the conflicting concerns of predictability and reform incentives.
- By avoiding "all or nothing" decisions, they make threats of sanctions more credible.
- They provide a framework for clarifying conditions for disbursement and consequences when conditions are not fulfilled.

However, a number of complicated choices must be made when designing a graduated response mechanism. Some of these are discussed below, in the case of a graduated response with a combination of fixed and variable components. The EC model is used as a point of reference.

Triggers for Disbursements of the Fixed Component

Important issues in the design of a graduated response are what should be the triggers for disbursement of the fixed component and whether the disbursements of the variable components should be made conditional on the disbursement of the fixed component.

The fixed component is supposedly linked to some basic conditions that are likely to be met. The EC refers to the fixed-tranche components as "basic resources in terms of macroeconomic support...disbursed in 'all or nothing' form depending on the fulfillment of the general conditions (typically, satisfactory implementation of the program for the IMF) and specific (typically fiduciary) conditions," whereas the variable-tranche components "account for additional resources that are released in a graduated form depending upon the achievements of targets and indicators agreed with the government" (EC 2005).

One of the principles governing Norwegian budget support is the close link to the PRSP process. As implementation of the PRS is the objective of budget support, disbursement of the fixed component should somehow be linked to performance in overall PRS implementation. The question is how explicit this link should be. Best practices according to OECD-DAC (2005b) say that "specific conditions should be chosen over those that are vaguely defined, e.g. 'the successful conclusion of a joint-donors' review of PRSP implementation.'" There could, however a trade-off between simplicity and predictability, on one side, and a focus on overall PRS implementation, on the other.

Two alternatives stand out:

- *The fixed component is linked to a successful conclusion of the PRS review.* To increase predictability, donors should select areas for specific attention that are known to the recipient government.
- *Successful implementation of PRS is stated as an underlying principle* (in the bilateral agreement or joint MOU) in the implementation of a budget support program and is an important concern of an appraisal for renewal of the agreement. In this case, the fixed component could have simpler conditions with a low risk of nondisbursement. Norway should still take an active part in PRS reviews, and concerns about the PRS implementation should be addressed in the donor-government dialogue.

There is also a question of how explicit political conditions should be linked to disbursements of budget support. Severe breaches of political conditions could lead to the interruption of budget support—in principle, both its fixed and variable components—as well as influence the total aid volume and the selection of aid modalities.

All conditions should be clearly defined and leave little margin for interpretation, and factors influencing fulfillment should be under government control. Political conditions—for instance, related to the human rights situation and democratization—are very difficult to formulate according to these principles. Therefore, such conditions should preferably be handled in the context of the political dialogue between a partner country and its donors instead of being a trigger for budget support.

If the recipient country fails to meet the conditions connected to the fixed component, an option should probably be retained to delay conclusion (disbursement) in order to allow more time to fully implement the agreed actions or to await the development of the issues in question.

There are arguments for separating the disbursement of the fixed and variable components, and allowing for the disbursement of the variable components although the disbursement of the fixed component is delayed or stopped. If all the support is withheld simultaneously, then some of the advantages of a graduated response might be lost. The consequences of, for instance, an IMF program going off track might be as in Malawi, where budget support disbursements from the IMF, the World Bank, and the CABS partnership stopped altogether for a period of three years (2001–03).[11]

OECD-DAC (2005b) addresses this when discussing the possibility of a graduated response:

> While some funds could then, for example, be withheld in the case of a delay in an IMF program review, the remaining funds could still be disbursed if sectoral conditionality was being met, thus allowing the continued financing of a sector despite the existence of some problems at the macroeconomic level.

Combination of Fixed and Variable Components

The relative share of fixed versus variable components decides the relative weight of predictability and reform incentives. Greater variable components increase the incentive effects at the expense of predictability of resources for the budget.

The fixed component is set to two-thirds in most of the EC programs. In Uganda, the two-thirds share is being discussed by the World Bank (and the donor group), and in Zambia, donors are discussing a 50–50 combination. The preferred combination of fixed and variable components may vary from one recipient country to another. Factors that should be taken into account are:

- the scale of the budget support program (in relation to the national budget);
- the degree of aid dependency (how dependent is the recipient country of budget support for financing basic public services?);
- the scale of earmarked support;
- macroeconomic and public financial management (does the recipient country have a positive track record on its IMF program?); and
- the importance of providing incentives for specific reforms if fiduciary or other risks are considered high.

The appropriate share of the fixed component is partly a question of how much confidence the donor has in the recipient government. A weak track record or high fiduciary (or other) risks would generally reduce the size of the fixed component. On the other hand, if the recipient country is highly aid dependent and the budget support constitutes a significant part of the budget, this could in itself be an argument for putting extra weight on predictability and enlarging the share of the fixed component. The existence of earmarked programs on a large scale could reduce the need for a large fixed component.

Selection and Weighting of Sectors/Areas for the Variable Components

A graduated response gives the opportunity to provide strong reform incentives in selected sectors. It is therefore a mechanism for maintaining a focus on particular sectors and maintaining a sector dialogue within a general budget support framework. Donors are currently discussing the transfer of earmarked sector support to non-earmarked budget support (NORAD 2004). The discussion is motivated by the need to strengthen the recipient country's budget process and the fact that funds are fungible. Graduated response can potentially ease the transition from sector support to general budget support.

The variable components in a graduated response can in principle be connected to any sector (such as health, education, water and sanitation) or to cross-cutting initiatives—for example, in public financial management or gender. The variable component in the EC's programs is mostly connected to performance in public financial management, health, and education. Sectors or areas can be selected according to the need for reform in each individual country.

The priority of the selected sectors/areas will be reflected in the relative weight attached to each. In most of its programs, the EC has weighted the different sectors equally, except in Burkina Faso, where public financial management receives more weight than others.

Selection of Indicators

Critical to the success of performance-based budget support is the selection of indicators for assessing performance. An important question is at what level of the results chain the indicators should be, ranging from input and output indicators reflecting policy choices and concrete measures to outcome and impact indicators seeking to estimate the effects on intermediate or ultimate policy goals.

In the view of the EC, impact and outcome indicators would be the ideal for results-based conditionality. The EC does, however, recognize the practical difficulties that can make indicators of impact, especially, less useful as indicators of the results of government efforts:

- Impact indicators are extremely difficult to measure without knowledge of the counterfactuals (what is a meaningful benchmark?), and often the relevant data are poor.

- The influence of factors beyond the government's control (exogenous factors) gets stronger the further the indicator is from the concrete policy measure.
- Impact indicators normally evolve slowly; several years may elapse from the time the policy action is taken to the time the effects appear on ultimate or even intermediate goals.

The EC concludes that it is best to use outcome-level indicators, which should be measured annually and sensitive to policy action as well as plausibly linked to the long-term goal. An example would be to apply the use of health services as an outcome indicator, rather than to apply the ideal impact indicator, life expectancy. In practice, however, the EC applies indicators at all levels, including process indicators.

According to the EC, performance-based conditionality with indicators of outcome and (if possible) impact is most coherent with the objective of ownership. The idea is that the recipient government can choose whichever policy measure it prefers in order to achieve the agreed goals. Also, OECD-DAC (2005b) emphasizes ownership in its recommendation to increase the focus on results:

> Budget support should increasingly focus on results, that is to say policy outputs and outcomes, rather than policy measures and inputs. This creates decision-making space for partner governments, enhances accountability, and gives partners an incentive to monitor and reflect on the progress achieved towards stated goals. It also shifts the focus from inputs and policy design to outcomes. Increasing focus on results complements, rather than substitutes for, the dialogue between donors and partners on the underlying policies and the related provision of technical assistance. Increased focus on results can be achieved in several ways, including, but not exclusively, through the use of service-delivery indicators and/or conditionality. However, the move towards greater focus on results is a difficult issue in practice, not least because of the need to identify clearly monitorable indicators.

The increased flexibility that comes with results-based conditionality does, however, involve increased risk for the recipient country, and risk-sharing considerations should also be taken into account when discussing the optimal indicator level. If the disbursement of a variable component is conditioned on the success of a policy measure, then the recipient country bears all the risk connected to selecting the right policy measure. If the disbursement depends on the recipient country carrying through some agreed policy action, but not on the actual results of the policy, the risk is partly shifted over to the donor.

While the problems with impact (and outcome) indicators discussed above are essentially practical, the increased risk for the recipient country is a more fundamental argument against outcome- and impact-based conditionality. An important question is whether risk sharing is an objective in itself also for the variable component of the budget support. If the answer to that is yes, then process- or action-based indicators may still have a role to play. It will be important to hear the recipient countries' view on this. Do they want the increased risk that comes with the increased flexibility?

According to best practices as defined by the OECD-DAC, conditions and indicators (at whatever level) should be drawn from the PRSs or related documents, so as to help advance the objectives of ownership and harmonization. This is not possible in all cases, however. Political governance conditions are the most evident examples.

Another important question is to what extent donors should coordinate their use of indicators, and whether it is detrimental if some donors use input and process indicators while others use results indicators. One view is that the use of different indicators spreads the risk for the recipient country. However, the desired flexibility for the recipient country of linking disbursements to results indicators can be undermined if other donors establish input conditionalities in the same area. The EC also points to results-based approaches as a means to "... reduce tension among donors over controversial actions featuring in policy-based conditionality (e.g. privatization of public utilities), thus easing some aspects of joint donor processes" (EC 2005). The potential conflict between different donors' use of input and result indicators should in principle be reduced if donors adhere to the principle of drawing indicators and conditions from the recipient's PRS.

D. The Way Forward

The increasing use of direct budget support by Norway and other donors stresses the need for disbursement instruments that are flexible, recognizing the inherent uncertainties about the future, yet transparent and predictable. A graduated response mechanism is a possible way to balance these concerns. Many donors are developing new guidelines for budget support and/or reconsidering the content of conditionality and giving the EC model serious consideration in the process.

A graduated response is not synonymous with the EC model. Section C gave a picture of the different choices in designing a graduated response model. Both at the country level and at the policy level, it is important to consider the strengths and weaknesses of outcome- and impact-based indicators as triggers for disbursement. A cautious use of outcome-based conditionality does not preclude an increased focus on results in the donor-government dialogue and in monitoring and evaluating the effects of budget support on poverty reduction.

The discussion on graduated response has a close link to the ongoing discussion on integrating sector programs into general budget support, thereby delinking sector dialogue and funding modalities. A combination of fixed and variable components is an instrument for doing this, without making the sector support much more volatile (risky). This presupposes that the disbursement of components linked to sector performance is made independent of the disbursement of the fixed component.

In summary, the following factors should be emphasized when considering and designing a graduated response with fixed and variable components:

- Disbursement delays caused by technical/administrative matters should be solved.
- Performance indicators should preferably be derived from the PRSP, should not be too numerous, and should be relatively easy to monitor and evaluate.

- The conditions must be reasonably under the control of the authorities, so that governments are not unduly punished for exogenous shocks. Outcome-based conditionality should be used with caution.
- At the local level, it is important to consult with the recipient countries on the choice of indicators and the use of performance-based conditionality as well as on the division between fixed and variable components.
- The very nature of political conditionality, which for instance covers issues related to the human rights situation and democratization, makes it difficult to formulate clear conditions that leave little margin for interpretation. Human rights and democratization issues should therefore preferably be handled in the context of the political dialogue between a partner country and its donors.[12]
- Disbursements of the fixed component should be linked to performance in overall PRS implementation—either explicitly, by linking the disbursement of the fixed component to a successful conclusion of the PRS review, or implicitly, by stating successful PRS implementation as an underlying principle for the budget support agreement. In the latter case, the fixed component could have simpler conditions with a low risk of nondisbursement. Norway should still take active part in PRS reviews, and concerns about the PRS implementation should be addressed in the donor-government dialogue.
- Greater variable components increase the incentive effects at the expense of predictability. Sectors or areas where the need for reform—and thus strong incentives—is the largest could be selected for the variable components.
- The disbursement of the variable components should not be automatically linked to the disbursement of the fixed component.

Annex to Chapter 24

Country Cases

Malawi

Malawi embarked on the PRSP process in 2000 and presented its PRSP in April 2002. In December 2000, Malawi agreed with the IMF on a PRGF program. However, the PRGF went off track in 2001, mainly because of overspending by the administration of ex-President Muluzi.

In November–December 2001, the members of the CABS, then consisting of the UK and Sweden, decided to suspend budgetary support to Malawi "in view of the Government's consistent failure to implement agreed economic reforms and follow a sound macroeconomic policy, therefore hampering economic growth necessary for sustainable poverty reduction."

Norway signed a budget support agreement with the Malawian government in February 2002 with planned disbursements of NKr 40 million in 2002 and NKr 20 million in 2003. But Norway withheld its disbursements of budget support until October 2003, when the IMF resumed its loan disbursements under the PRGF. Norway's decision to withhold funds was made in close consultation with the other CABS members (the EC joined CABS in February 2002), which did not disburse as their budgetary support was conditioned upon the existence of an IMF program.

After the 2003 disbursements, the IMF again considered Malawi to be off track, on the grounds of fiscal slippages during March–May 2004. The two most recent IMF assessments of Malawi have, however, been positive, and the IMF has stated that continued positive performance under the Staff Monitored Program (SMP) would provide a basis for a new financial arrangement under the PRGF in the course of 2005. Norway released the second tranche of NKr 20 million in October 2004, in support of the SMP and following strengthened fiscal control. Norway signed an addendum to the agreement in December 2004 and disbursed NKr 17.33 million. In October 2004, the UK disbursed a £5 million tranche withheld from their 2000–03 agreement. The EU is in the process of agreeing on a new budget support agreement, and Sweden is considering whether to release its SKr 40 million tranche withheld from 2001.

The World Bank released US$25 million to Malawi in September 2004 "on the basis of an encouraging three-month track record, and the recently presented budget for the current fiscal year—which is in line with the macroeconomic program that was agreed with international finance institutions." The disbursement was the first tranche of the Fiscal Management and Accelerating Growth Program in support of Malawi's PRSP.

Critics (for example, Krakowski [2004]) have argued that the Malawi example illustrates that "automatic" donor coordination implies a risk of "overshooting" if disbursements from a significant number of donors are directly or indirectly linked to the performance of the program with the IMF. In the course of 2001–03, budget support disbursements from the IMF, the World Bank, and the CABS partnership were stopped in Malawi. This made it impossible to fully implement the PRSP. On the other hand, the firm and coordinated response from donors may also have put pressure on the government to change its "policy" of weak fiscal control.

Mozambique

Mozambique's rapid economic growth and increased exports made it an example of successful reform in Africa in the 1990s. The other side of the picture was an increasing level of corruption, from relatively low in the 1970s to widespread in the 1990s. The Mozambican financial system faced a crisis in 2000, when it became clear that two of the country's largest banks were undercapitalized, mainly due to large non-performing loan portfolios. In 2000 and 2001, a newspaper editor and the government's head of banking supervision were assassinated because they knew too much about the fraud and corruption in the Mozambican banking system.

In the international debate, donors were criticized by some (including Hanlon 2004) for not adequately addressing the issue of corruption, allegedly because they wanted to maintain the donor "success story" of Mozambique. Under the previous agreement with the Mozambican government (2001–03), Norway, like other donors, decided to disburse its programmed budget support, despite the banking crisis. The possibility of putting pressure on the Mozambican government by holding back budget support was, however, discussed in the donor group, with Norway and Sweden as the main advocates for this view.

In April 2001, when the Banco Austral crashed, the budget support providers collectively decided to keep back disbursements for a period. In the Consultative Group meeting of October 2001, the Mozambican government committed itself to four follow-up actions related to the banking crisis: (1) prosecute wrongdoing in the financial sector to the full extent of the law, (2) make purposive and equitable efforts to recover outstanding debts, (3) divest the government's interests in banks, and (4) strengthen banking supervision. The donor community regarded these commitments as a satisfactory response to the banking crisis, and donor funds were released as planned.

Norwegian budget support under the present agreement (2004–06) started with the disbursement of the first tranche of NKr 60 million in November 2004. The second disbursement of NKr 65 million was requested by the Ministry of Finance and Planning (MFP) in early January 2005, but its release is still pending. The reason is that the MFP, since the first deadline of April 2004, has failed to submit an agreed report documenting that the budget support in the period November 2000 to August 2002 entered into the main treasury account and was formally registered in the state accounts (Conta Geral do Estado).

Before Norway entered into the joint donor program for budget support (consisting of the World Bank, the EC, and 13 bilateral donors) in November 2000, there were instances of delayed Norwegian disbursement of budget support. In 1999, Norway held back budget support because the audit report of the budget support was considered inadequate. The audit reports were improved the following years.

Uganda

The level of development assistance to Uganda is relatively high, amounting to approximately half the country's budget. Uganda was one of the first countries to have a workable PRS—the Poverty Eradication Action Plan—and the country's economic performance has been outstanding during the past decade, with a growth rate above the African average and relatively good progress toward the Millennium Development Goals. Recent household surveys seem, however, to indicate a decline in certain poverty indicators, which is of concern to the donor community. Another issue of concern is the government's military approach to the war in northern Uganda, where the Lord's Resistance Army rebels have waged an 18-year war with brutal methods and gross human rights violations, including the targeting of children for forced recruitment.

Donors are inclined to accept that the military is inevitably part of the solution to the conflict in northern Uganda, but do not agree with the government's balance between a military and nonmilitary solution. The three bilateral donors of general budget support, Ireland, Netherlands, and the UK, withdrew a total of US$25 million in general budget support for the Ugandan fiscal year 2002–03 as a reaction to the government's substantial increase in defense spending after the budget had already been appropriated. The UK and the Netherlands cut their disbursements (the UK paid only 50 percent of the programmed disbursement), and Ireland reassigned the rest of its general budget support funds to the Poverty Action Fund. In February 2003, after an extensive dialogue with the Ugandan government, the donors agreed to accept an increase in defense spending of US$17.5 million, and this was entered into the PRSC as Prior Action 1 (budget execution).

The World Bank delayed its Executive Board discussions and disbursements for some months both in 2003 and 2004, due to administrative problems, the need to verify budget execution (Prior Action 1), and questions regarding the implementation of the Leadership Code. US$50 million of the second PRSC was in fact a floating tranche, as it was made contingent on the Parliament passing the Leadership Code. In April 2002, when the code was passed by Parliament, the US$50 million tranche was disbursed together with the PRSC's remaining US$100 million.

At the beginning of 2004, the UK withheld a disbursement of £10 million because of discontent with the dialogue with the Ugandan government about the defense review, which was supported by the UK. The review aimed at defining Uganda's defense priorities and the optimum size and capability required for Uganda's armed forces. The disbursement was made later that year.

Norway's reaction to the increased military spending has been to earmark budget support to the Poverty Action Fund, and await the intentions of giving general budget support to Uganda. The Poverty Action Fund budget support has been disbursed as planned under Norway's first agreement with the government in Uganda (2002–04), with disbursements of NKr 50 million in each of the Ugandan fiscal years 2002–03 and 2003–04.

Tanzania

In November 2000, NORAD entered into a three-year poverty reduction budget support (PRBS) agreement of a maximum of NKr 150 million. The agreement did not specify the annual disbursement amount, only a total amount for the period 2000–02. This allowed for a flexible disbursement schedule that took into account both over- and underperformance and lower disbursement than anticipated in other Norwegian-funded programs.

Based on overall satisfactory progress in implementing the PRBS policy matrix, the first tranche of NKr 50 million was disbursed in December 2000. The second disbursement was also based on overall positive progress. Due to lower than anticipated disbursement in other programs, the disbursement in December 2001 was NKr 80 million.

As the Norwegian embassy wanted a higher annual disbursement in 2002 than the remaining NKr 20 million that was unallocated under the agreement then in force, a one-year addendum of maximum NKr 100 million was signed and fully disbursed in December 2003.

Disbursement of the first tranche in 2002 of NKr 20 million was planned for March 2002. However, as several donors questioned the government's decision to purchase a US$40 million radar system for air traffic control, Norway decided to postpone the disbursement until the terms and conditions of the purchase had been clarified and a solution acceptable to the donors had been found. Norway had close contact with the other donors, and the decision to postpone planned disbursements was made by several donors, among which DFID took the lead in the dialogue with the government on the issue.

A new three-year contract of NKr 300 million was signed in 2003. The agreement did not specify the annual total disbursement, but only the total amount for 2003–05.

The disbursement for 2003 was NKr 96 million. The progress of PRBS implementation was considered satisfactory. The disbursement of slightly less than one-third of the total amount reflects the slight overspending in some of the other programs supported by the embassy. The disbursement for 2004 was NKr 104 million (one-third of the total amount plus the reduced amount in 2003).

During the mid-year review in April 2004, donor partners expressed concern about Tanzania's slow progress in establishing the PFMRP. This program is a central part of the Tanzanian performance assessment framework, and its establishment has been long delayed. Norway concluded that the release of the tranche for fiscal year 2004–05 would depend on the progress in the PFMRP and that the Ministry of Foreign Affairs should be consulted before making disbursements. In June 2004, the government of Tanzania launched the PFMRP, and Norway decided to disburse, as scheduled, NKr 100 million for 2004.

The World Bank delayed its PRSC of US$150 million to give the government more time to implement the needed reforms set as conditions for disbursement. The same situation occurred in 2004. The EU reduced the variable tranche of its budget support to Tanzania due to the underperformance in the PFMRP. Denmark, which was in the process of signing a new bilateral agreement on budget support, deferred the final signing until the PFMRP was established. Denmark then disbursed as planned.

Endnotes

1. Import support was introduced in the 1970s in order to improve the balance of payments in the recipient countries. Import support takes the form either of in-kind support, where the donor country offers the recipient country raw materials or other commodities, or of financial support earmarked to the import of specific goods. At the end of the 1990s, import support lost its desired effect as many recipient countries switched to floating exchange rates.
2. This presupposes that the country actually pays interest and amortization without the debt relief, which is not always the case.
3. The Paris Club is an informal group of 19 creditor countries "whose role is to find coordinated and sustainable solutions to the payment difficulties experienced by debtor nations."
4. As expressed by Sida in a memo to NORAD dated January 21 2005, contributing to the preparation of this paper.
5. The database for their study covered 72 countries from 1975 to 1997.
6. The example is taken from OECD-DAC (2005b).
7. This dilemma is known from economic theory as the "principal-agent problem." Agency theory is about structuring monitoring and compensation systems to induce effort- and risk-averse agents (in this case, the recipient country government) to act on the principal's (in this case, the donor's) behalf without shifting too much risk onto them.
8. Many donors, including the EC, use the term "tranche." In this paper, "tranche" and "component" are used interchangeably.
9. As expressed by Sida in a memo to NORAD dated January 21, 2005, contributing to the preparation of this paper.
10. The example is taken from OECD-DAC (2005b).
11. See the annex to this paper for details.
12. This is similar to the recommendation in OECD-DAC (2005b).

25

Budget Support and Aid Effectiveness: Experience in East Asia

HIROTO ARAKAWA
Japan Bank for International Cooperation

Budget support has attracted great attention as a new aid modality for achieving the Millennium Development Goals and for increasing the effectiveness of aid.[1] In Africa in particular, aid efforts have been highly fragmented, with donor-driven approaches imposing a considerable burden on the administrative resources of partner countries (Johnston and Manning 2005).

Today there are more than 60,000 aid projects under way in the developing world, often with different administrative procedures set up by the donors. Eighty-five percent of these projects cost less than US$1 million. This places a heavy burden on poor countries that lack the administrative capacity to handle these demands, and does not help them build their own systems. So when the project ends, the results are often not sustained.

A conservative estimate for a typical African country is that this way of delivering aid translates into thousands of new reports and more than 1,000 new annual missions to appraise, monitor, and evaluate. Each mission asks to meet with key officials, and each will ask the government to comment on its reports. Strong evidence supports that these donor-driven approaches are one of the reasons development assistance has been underperforming.

Such fragmentation may not apply to aid to East Asia, where attempts are being made to enhance aid effectiveness by linking assistance for individual projects, fostering ownership by partner countries, and not merely offering aid but collaborating in foreign direct investments and private funds.

This paper reviews efforts by the Japanese government and the Japan Bank for International Cooperation (JBIC) in East Asia, especially in Vietnam, as examples of such attempts and draws out their practical and policy implications. East Asia provides an aid model that is characterized by harmonization processes within the donor community and respect for ownership by the governments of partner countries. The goal is both to enhance and extend the partner country's capacity for system operation through official development assistance for projects and apply policy leverage through program assistance in the form of budget support and poverty reduction support credits. Section A of the paper defines the terms used, Section B looks at the role played by budget support in Africa and East Asia, and Section C describes efforts being made to coordinate and harmonize aid in Vietnam and the Philippines. Section D concludes, drawing general lessons and some implications for aid to African countries.

A. Definitions

At the outset, some terms must be clearly defined. First, the characteristics of bilateral aid are defined by the Development Assistance Committee (DAC) as follows (OECD-DAC 2004b, p. 40):

- *Project support* tends to identify a manageable set of problems and prescribe the inputs needed to foster local development. To contribute more significantly to poverty reduction, projects should be situated within the broader development framework, address the multiple concerns of the poor, and strengthen the capacities of the poor to achieve sustainable livelihoods.
- *Sector support* or sectorwide approaches (SWAps) contribute, under partner government leadership, toward a single sector policy and expenditure program and should, where possible, use common management and reporting procedures to disburse and account for all funds. Sector programs imply a different approach to aid management, calling for greater modesty, an acceptance of a slow process of change, and partnership building.
- *Program aid* consists of financial contributions, not linked to specific project activities, that are extended to a partner country for general development purposes, such as balance of payments support or general budget support. Program aid is often associated with the promotion of policy reforms at the macroeconomic level and/or in specific sectors.

The official development assistance (ODA) modalities specified by DAC are described in Table 25.1.

The JBIC makes several types of ODA loans, both project-type loans and sector-targeted or program-based loans.[2] To maximize the effectiveness of its assistance the

TABLE 25.1 Modalities for ODA

Project assistance	
Program assistance	
General program assistance	Program assistance made available to a developing country, without specific sector allocation, for development purposes, i.e., balance of payments financing, general budget support, and commodity assistance, (cf. structural adjustment loans with World Bank-IMF).
Sector program assistance	Program assistance directed to a specific economic or social sector, such as agriculture, education, community development, and transport.
Program food aid	
Debt relief	

Source: OECD (1992).

TABLE 25.2 Types of ODA Loans from the JBIC

OECD-DAC categorization	JBIC loan types
Project assistance	Project loans Engineering service loans Financial intermediary loans (two-step loans)
Program assistance	Structural adjustment loans Commodity loans Sector program loans
Debt relief	

Source: http://www.jbic.go.jp/english/oec/yenloan/kind/index.php.

JBIC also has a technical assistance (TA) facility to complement project management efforts.

Highly concessional ODA loans have four advantages for enhancing aid effectiveness (Ojima 2004):

- *Sustainability*. They can create incentives for appropriate aid management as they foster cost recovery mechanisms within the partner country government.
- *Continuity*. They support the seamless transformation of an economy from dependence on aid (100 percent grants) to dependence on the financial market (100 percent private funding).
- *Stability*. Those that are based on large multiyear commitments can mitigate the volatility and unpredictability of aid funds, helping to stabilize the partner government's budget process.
- *Ownership*. They can foster the ownership of the partner government, because each project is officially screened for its consistency with the government's policy.

With these advantages, even project assistance can exert effective policy leverage at the project implementation level.

B. Roles of Budget Support

We can identify differences between the roles and significance of budget support in Africa and those in East Asia.

The *Joint Evaluation of General Budget Support* (DFID 2005), in which the Japanese government and JBIC participate, defines budget support as follows:

- *Budget support* is channeled directly to partner governments using their own allocation, procurement, and accounting systems and is not linked to specific project activities. All types of budget support include a lump-sum transfer of foreign exchange; differences then arise on the extent of earmarking and on the levels and focus of the policy dialogue and conditionality.

- *Sector budget support* is distinguished from *general budget support* by being earmarked for a discrete sector or sectors, with any conditionality relating to these sectors. Additional sector reporting may augment normal government accounting, although the means of disbursement is also based upon government procedures.

The roles and practices expected of budget support are specified by the DAC as follows (OECD-DAC 2005a):

- *Budget support should reinforce partner countries' ownership.* When providing fungible resources in the form of budget support, donors should support a partner country's overall development policies and priorities. While this requirement raises a justifiable need to discuss budgetary goals (and related funds allocation decisions) with the partner government, sustained policy implementation ultimately depends upon strong political commitment. Budget support should therefore not attempt to leverage policy actions where such commitment does not exist.
- *Budget support should help to enhance the performance and accountability of partner countries' public financial management (PFM) systems.* Budget support provides donors with a legitimate interest in strengthening the PFM systems through which their funds are spent. For both developmental and fiduciary reasons, donors should use the provision of budget support to foster the improvement of partners' PFM systems, including transparency and accountability to their legislatures and civil society at large.
- *Transaction costs incurred by budget support should be minimized.* Channeling budget support through national procedures is a way to reduce transaction costs. Additional transaction costs associated with budget support, such as those incurred through multiple and large-scale PFM assessments, should be kept to a minimum.
- *Budget support should be delivered in a way that enhances the predictability of resources and reduces their volatility.* When planning their budgets, partner countries' authorities should be able to count on reliable estimates of the amount of budget support, the timing of its disbursement, and clear conditions for its release. Predictability is an important requirement for partner countries' budgetary authorities, particularly with respect to the short-term disbursements of committed aid and the early commitment of future aid flows in the medium term. Higher predictability and lower volatility facilitate the implementation of policies geared toward macroeconomic stabilization, the design (and implementation) of medium-term expenditure frameworks (MTEFs), the strategic allocations of funds across policy priorities, and the rational choice of the most cost-effective financing strategies. However, experience shows that the actual timing and size of budget support commitments and disbursements are variable. While this may be partly due to partner countries' behavior, donors should seek to eliminate the sources of volatility that are under their control.

The question arises whether budget support is a panacea to any country or not. We look at the experience of two countries, Tanzania and Vietnam, to compare the different roles that budget support assistance has played.

In Tanzania in 2003, aid accounted for 75 percent of government spending, about 14 percent of GDP, and more than 80 percent of investment (Ohno and Niiya 2005). Tanzania has received debt relief under the Heavily Indebted Poor Countries (HIPC) Initiative, and thus efficient aid management is a critical component of its fiscal management. Private sector finance is still only a small share of Tanzania's economy. Though historically stand-alone/off-budget/in-kind assistance prevailed, Tanzania's approach since the introduction of the national poverty reduction strategy has been to (1) channel aid in accordance with the priorities outlined in the poverty reduction strategy paper (PRSP), (2) harmonize donor procedures with its own government systems, and (3) channel aid increasingly through program aid, particularly general budget support (Ohno and Niiya 2005). Now Tanzania is often cited as a model of donor-government partnership. The important characteristic of general budget support in Tanzania is that it supports the government's budget implementation process directly, along with SWAps in important social sector programs.

In Vietnam, we see a different picture. Aid in 2003 accounted for about 18 percent of government spending, about 5 percent of GDP, and about 15 percent of investment. Vietnam has not applied for HIPC debt relief. Private sector finance plays an important role in the country's economy, and private sector development is the priority agenda for the transition to a market economy. A specific line ministry coordinates the overall development budget, and thus development planning, promotion of foreign direct investment, and aid coordination are led by strong government ownership. Three-fourths of the total aid to Vietnam comes from the World Bank, Asian Development Bank, and Japanese government–JBIC, and since large-scale project assistance constitutes a major share of aid, procedural harmonization among donors has advanced and transaction costs are relatively low. Project assistance dominates Vietnam's development effort, and budget support functions as a complementary tool to disseminate and replicate concrete outcomes from individual project assistance toward the achievement of growth-oriented structural reform processes (Ohno and Niiya 2005).

The above comparison shows that the role and significance of budget support differs between Tanzania and Vietnam because of the differences between the two countries' development agendas, including foreign aid management reflecting their aid dependency. It is also important to note that in Vietnam, the Comprehensive Poverty Reduction and Growth Strategy (CPRGS) is growth oriented (Ohno 2002), and thus the country's development agenda and programs have been supplemented with budget support.[3]

How can a country efficiently and effectively use the various aid modalities, including budget support, to address its development agenda? Ohno and Niiya (2005) developed a development policy matrix as a tool for specifying the relationships between aid modalities and development agendas (Figure 25.1). The matrix can indicate the position of certain project or a program on the Y axis, representing policy and institutional level versus project implementation level, as well as on the X axis, representing macroeconomic policy versus sector and local administration.

C. Aid Coordination and Harmonization in Vietnam and the Philippines

This section describes the latest results of aid coordination and harmonization in Vietnam and the Philippines mainly from the viewpoint of the Japanese government–JBIC, before offering an analysis of JBIC assistance to Vietnam using the matrix in Figure 25.1.

Vietnam

Box 25.1 outlines the chronological efforts to harmonize aid and enhance its effectiveness in Vietnam, in association with the commitment of the Japanese government–JBIC to the CPRGS development process.

FIGURE 25.1 Development Policy Matrix

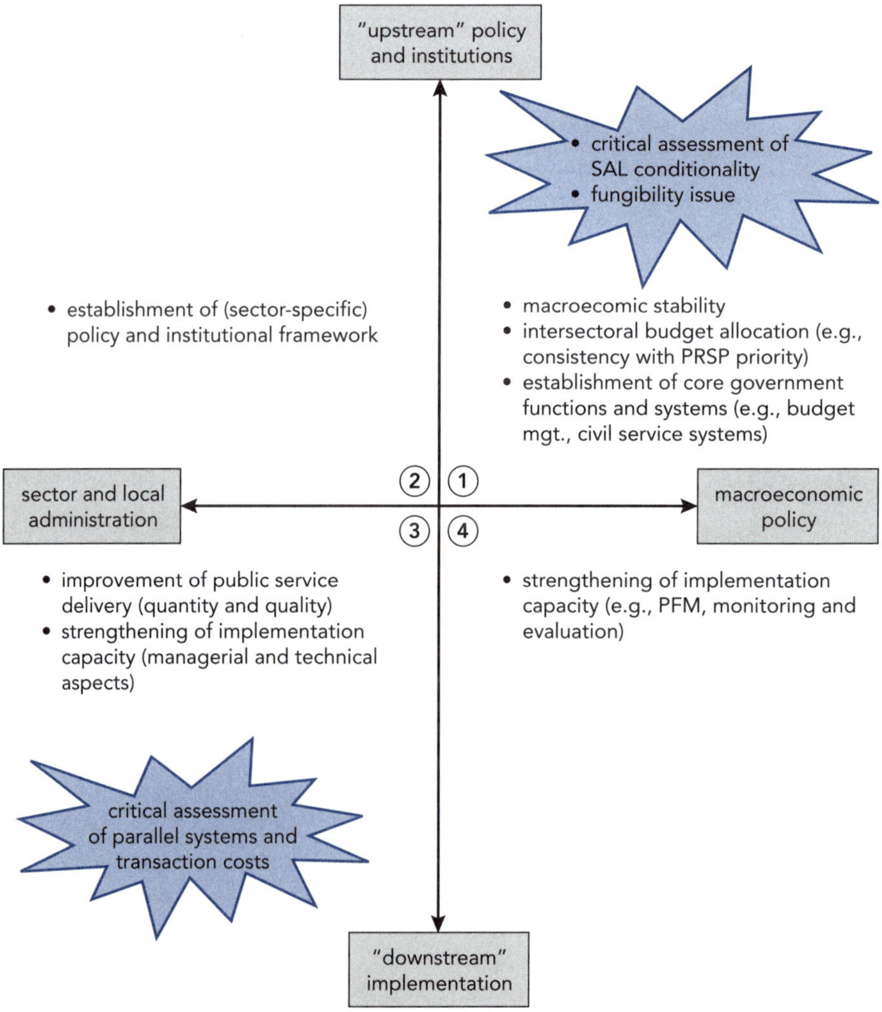

Source: Ohno and Niiya (2005).

BOX 25.1 Aid Enhancement Efforts in Vietnam

Before May 2002
Vietnam requested harmonization through Joint Portfolio Performance Review (JPPR), separately from international discussions.

May 2002 (Interim Consultative Group) to February 2003 (Rome Declaration)
In the wake of an approach by the World Bank, three banks (the World Bank, Asian Development Bank, and JBIC) agreed on the three areas of procurement, financial management, and environment in the harmonization action plan.

February 2003 (Rome Declaration) to December 2003 (Harmonization Action Plan)
Two more banks, Agence Française de Développement (AFD) and Kreditanstalt für Wiederaufbau (KfW), joined the project in May 2003. The JPPR was implemented. During this period, an initiative for harmonization was developed throughout Vietnam. Vietnam proposed the issues of harmonizing harmonization and aid modalities (including financial aid and migration) to sectorwide approaches.

December 2003–February 2005
Group on Aid Effectiveness (GAE) was established.

Based on the experience of the five banks, in procurement, for instance, the JBIC presented the view that harmonization only among donor countries or harmonization of ODA-related projects would not lead to solutions, but that it is much more essential to improve public investment systems developed by the governments of partner countries. (If they were improved, donor countries would be able to fully utilize the systems of the partner country.) The issue of country systems presented by the World Bank and the importance of building capacity were integrated.

A mutual understanding between Vietnam and donors was promoted from the view that improvement in overall management of development funds would be necessary and that utilization of country systems would not be viable without capacity building.

The Vietnamese government identified two main headings and contents of activities of local projects in Vietnam:

- reinforcement of procurement systems → capacity building
- Intensification of PFM → development of MTEF, PFM Intensification Project, integration of reporting systems for ODA projects.

Japanese government–JBIC efforts to PRSC3 assistance can be summarized as follows:

- *Focus on public expenditure management and improvement of business and investment environments*: The proposals by Japan were reflected in the policy matrix. The Japan-Vietnam Joint Initiative Action Plan was reflected in the matrix for improvement of business and investment environments in April 2003.
- *Improvement of business and investment environments*: This was based on the awareness of the problem that foreign capital investments were not advanced due to regulations regarding foreign capital, flaws in fundamental rules and administration, lack of support industries, and other underdevelopment factors in the investment environment.
- *Public spending management:* For implementation of individual infrastructure development and enhancement of public spending efficiency, pursuit of consistency between investment budget and ordinary budget, appropriate examination of public investment programs, and establishment of evaluation frameworks were included as future tasks. The chapter for the roles of large-scale infrastructure in poverty reduction was added to the CPRGS as proposed by Japanese government–JBIC.

The five banks' initiative described in Box 25.1 was primarily launched on the assumption that harmonization (integration of the five banks' systems with the country systems of Vietnam) for financial management and safeguard policies could be realized first at the project level.

The prime example of accelerating policy reform through individual projects under the five banks' initiative was the improvement of public procurement systems. Vietnam's donor countries accepted, with certain conditions, the draft standard documents for local competitive bidding (LCB) that had been prepared under the current framework (Procurement Ordinance #88/66) for the procurement reforms initiated by the Vietnamese government. At the same time, as discussions were in progress on redrafting the LCB standard documents for use in the country's overall procurement system, the five banks also continuously sought improvement (from a medium-term perspective) in the course of developing the government's new procurement ordinance. The Japan International Cooperation Agency (JICA) also contributed significant TA for capacity building in public expenditure management. This was a notable collaborative contribution by the Japanese government as a whole, in addition to the harmonization process among the donor community.

The Philippines

Box 25.2 outlines the efforts for harmonization and enhancement of aid effectiveness in the Philippines.

Findings and Lessons

The above comparison yields two major findings:

- The experiences at the project level have led to capacity building and the establishment of comprehensive country systems at the national level.

BOX 25.2 Aid Enhancement Efforts in the Philippines

Aid coordination and harmonization efforts have strengthened since 2002 and are ongoing.

Reinforcement of public procurement systems through individual projects:

- More than two years of intensive policy dialogue to start up the Procurement Harmonization Program.
- Harmonized standard bidding documents for national competitive bidding for works, goods, and consulting services are now being used.

Intensifying financial management through individual projects.

The three banks' (World Bank, Asian Development Bank, and JBIC) initiative has led to harmonized drafts of (1) private auditor's terms of reference, (2) auditor's qualification questionnaire, (3) executing agency's qualification questionnaire, and (4) financial management reports by executing agencies.

Support to Commission on Audit for implementation of new government accounting system.

- Standardizing the use of country systems in the implementation of ODA projects has created incentives to implement necessary policy reforms under the budget support framework.

These findings suggest four lessons with regard to enhancing aid effectiveness through harmonization:

Importance of Short-Term Outcomes

- Prompt production of tangible outcomes in the short term is important because it will encourage both partner countries and donors to make progress toward harmonization.
- To this end, donors should harmonize those of their methods and processes that differ unnecessarily. Also, harmonization and simplification should be implemented at an early stage in the areas where both donors and partner countries can implement harmonization and simplification easily and effectively reduce administrative costs.

Cost of Harmonization

- Because harmonization requires coordination among different organizations within both the donor and partner countries, it tends to raise administrative costs. Therefore the efficient and cost-effective processing of harmonization is critical.

Areas of Harmonization

- While procedures must be simplified to reduce partner countries' administrative costs and harmonize aid, safeguard policies and transparency must meet international standards. The task is to provide a method to fulfill these two requirements simultaneously. But the areas where both are easily fulfilled are limited.

Consistency with Partner Country Systems

- Adoption of higher standards for ODA-funded activities than those for domestic operations is not always sustainable.
- Harmonization in ODA may enhance operational efficiency and reduce processing costs, but entrenched differences in rules and methods between domestic operations and ODA operations may push up the administrative costs of the partner countries.

As regards the selection of aid modalities and the need to control administrative costs, Japanese government–JBIC's harmonization experience suggests the importance of the following (Ohno and Niiya 2005):

- country-specific approaches that respect the ownership and leadership of the partner country;
- respect for the diversity of aid modalities;
- respect for capacity building and participation of civil societies; and
- no a priori preference for specific modalities.

In Vietnam, budget support (in the form of PRSCs) significantly affects policies and systems, and individual infrastructure projects also affect policies and systems through project implementation (Figure 25.2). In addition, the conditions attached to budget support affect the mobilization of private resources for each sector and the structural reforms of the financial sector.

Vietnam's experience also shows that project assistance and budget support (PRSCs) can complement each other. While PRSCs support the improvement of institutional frameworks, project loans provide replicability at the micro level to individual projects.

In this context, one could argue that the JBIC's ODA loans incur extensive transaction costs, considering that the average project is quite large in both physical and money terms. The costs of learning by doing should be regarded as constructive investment in human resources, but needless to say, minimizing the administrative costs of the JBIC's projects is important in general.

In Tanzania, priority is placed on general budget support and pooled finance. In this case, project assistance (small-scale) has comparative advantage, as long as such assistance is on budget and therefore aligned to Tanzania's development strategies (Figure 25.3).

D. Conclusion and Implications for Future Assistance to Africa

From Projects to the National Level

The experience in East Asia emphasizes the need for:

- a balanced response to conflicting demands, such as simplification of ODA project procedures and introduction of international standards for improvement of transparency, and
- strong respect for ownership by the governments of partner countries.

FIGURE 25.2 Vietnam: Effects of Different Aid Modalities on Policies and Systems

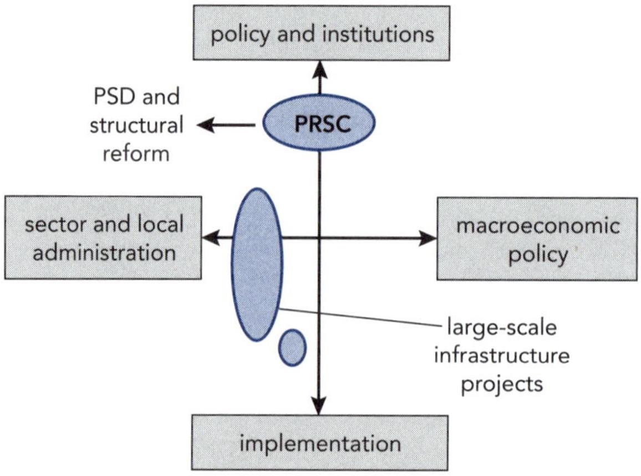

Vietnam: general budget support (PRSC) and infrastructure projects

- General budget support is designed to (a) promote policy and structural reforms for private sector development and (b) complement the investments in infrastructure projects.
- Low aid dependence.
- Weak linkage among PRSP, budget allocation, and performance monitoring (absence of MTEF).
- Broad but restrained partnership. Limited introduction of new aid

Source: Ohno and Niiya (2005).

FIGURE 25.3 Tanzania: Effects of Different Aid Modalities on Policies and Systems

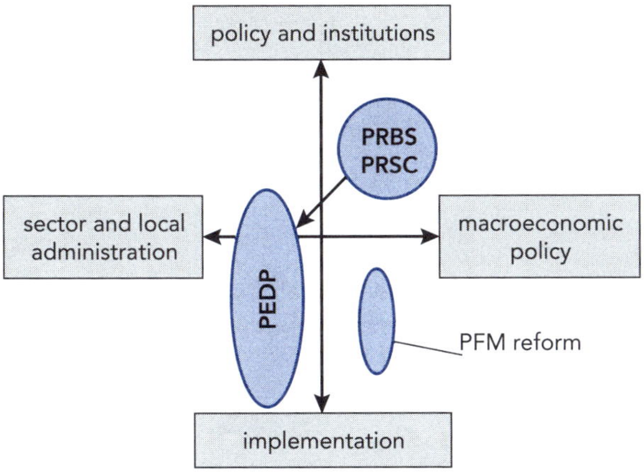

Tanzania: general budget support (PRSC/PRBS) and primary education SWAp (PEDP)

- General budget support and SWAp intend to address (a) macroeconomic policy and institutional framework and (b) the implementation of priority sector reform (e.g., budget allocation, quantitative expansion of social service delivery).
- High aid dependence.
- Shared understanding between recipient and donors of the problems of transaction costs and aid fragmentation.
- PRSP-MTEF-PAF linkage established.
- Open and extensive partnership, active introduction of new aid modalities.

Source: Ohno and Niiya (2005).

Both of the above lessons have been applied in the JBIC's ODA lending at the project level. The experience suggests that ODA loans will lead to capacity building at the national level as well as to the establishment of comprehensive country systems. Standardizing the use of the country system through the implementation of projects will automatically provide an incentive to partner country governments to accelerate the reforms that they encourage through budget support.

The harmonization process in East Asia does not merely seek efficiency in ODA projects and speed in ODA disbursements. It has also been implemented to assist the capacity development of partner countries, for example, improving the overall public expenditure system and replicating the best practices learned under ODA projects.

As seen from the examples above, "good projects" are premised on respect for ownership by the governments of the partner countries, consistency with the development plans of the countries and their domestic projects, investment/maintenance costs that are within budget, and effective replication of institution building. The effects expected from these "good projects " may be similar to the four effects expected from budget support that were outlined above (OECD-DAC 2005a). The JBIC considers that budget support can be an effective tool for supporting such good projects.

Therefore a comparison between preferable characteristics of budget support and the JBIC's modality of assistance through project-type loans and program-based loans can be summarized as in Table 25.3.

Swift transfer of aid resources from donors to partner countries is not a sufficient condition for enhancing aid effectiveness. As long as the ODA funds transferred are

TABLE 25.3 Achieving the Goals of Budget Support through Project and Program Lending

Preferable characteristics of budget support	JBIC's assistance in east asia (The project loans and program loans)
• On budget; partner country's ownership	• Yes (single line ministry, relatively small number of major donors)
• Alignment to partner country's policy and practice	• Yes (PRSP, programmatic approach, use of improved country systems)
• Enhance the performance and accountability of partner country's PFM systems	• Yes (harmonization among donors, use of improved country systems)
• Reduced transaction cost	• Yes (harmonization among donors, use of improved country systems)
• Predictability of aid	• Yes (multiyear commitment and disbursement)

converted into services and delivered to the beneficiaries through the public expenditure system of the partner countries, the efficiency of the entire public disbursement system of the partner countries may be more important than the facilitation of fund transfers to the partner countries.

From a mid- and long-term perspective, donors should support the development of human resources and institutional capacity in the partner countries and encourage the greater use of countries' own systems in channeling ODA. These processes should be implemented at a pace appropriate to the administrative or social capacity of the partner countries, according to their degree of ownership.

Need for Customization of Project and Program Assistance

No single model exists for enhancing aid effectiveness. A major premise is that aid should respond to local characteristics, historical politics/economics/social structure, donor structure, and the historical reality of aid acceptance. Based on these features, it is important to improve the budget expenditure system, which enables efficient distribution of aid funds, so as to engender synergy through the effective use of aid modalities.

Implications for Future Assistance to Africa: The Way Forward

What does East Asia's experience imply for future assistance to Africa?

The choice and sequencing of aid modalities should cater to the country's priority development agenda. The significance and appropriateness of budget support to Africa should be assessed based on political/economical/social conditions and the environment that is fostered by the use of country-by-country approaches. Development will be a mid- and long-term continuous process involving economic and social changes in the partner countries. Thus it will be essential to respond from a mid- and long-term perspective, based on changes in development needs of the partner countries.

Facilitation of fund transfer mechanisms is necessary but not sufficient for aid effectiveness. Ways should be explored to improve the overall public expenditure system (planning system, procurement system, integration of capital expenditure and current expenditure, project evaluation and selection, budget management, individual project management). Experience with the use of various frameworks such as PRSCs, portfolio performance review, and harmonization of procurement procedure can be applied.

Development is not a linear process from aid dependence to dependence on the market. The viewpoint that the ultimate goal is to free the partner country of dependence on aid is an important one, and very relevant in the ongoing debate on budget support and aid modalities. And the extent to which the priority problems of partner country governments can successfully be addressed by public expenditures and policies (such as primary education and health issues), rather than by private sector activities, is a critical point to begin with. Pro-poor growth requires growth promotion and development of private agriculture, industry, and business, for which both public actions and the behavior of private agents such as firms and farmers matter. The importance of economic growth through private sector development cannot be overemphasized. Moreover, to foster productivity and thereby accomplish the Millennium Development Goals and alleviate poverty in Africa, the creation of network infrastructure, agricultural development, private sector development, and improvement in the investment environment are critical.

In this connection, the Strategic Framework for Assistance to Africa of the World Bank–IDA (Figure 25.4) is promising for identifying good projects in future assistance to Africa. It is based on the premise of various aid modalities dependent on the partner country policy/system and reflects lessons from past assistance for structural adjustment.

An efficient aid environment needs to be built to promote good projects, recognizing that private sector development and investment need to play a key role. The weight of each aid modality will also naturally change depending on country circumstances.

For Tanzania, as seen above, the Japanese government and JICA have been providing assistance to the first-generation poverty reduction budget support (PRBS) process with a combination of approaches according to the progress of its funding, that is, participation in forming a poverty reduction strategy system to execute the PRBS and a sectorwide approach to aid in the agricultural sector. Now the Tanzanian government and donors (including Japan) are establishing a second-generation PRBS framework, which puts more emphasis on growth aspects. The first-generation (social sector–oriented) PRBS is being transformed into the second-generation (growth–oriented) PRBS in accordance with Tanzania's current developmental needs.

Within the framework of Figure 25.4, then, Tanzania's position will shift further to the right. The key element is whether the shift reflects a growth-oriented process or not. The shift seems to be similar to the above-mentioned process in East Asia. Also, a critical view of the World Bank–IDA framework indicates that the issue of repositioning budget support will acquire major significance as the development process becomes growth–oriented.

FIGURE 25.4 World Bank–IDA Strategic Framework for Assistance to Africa

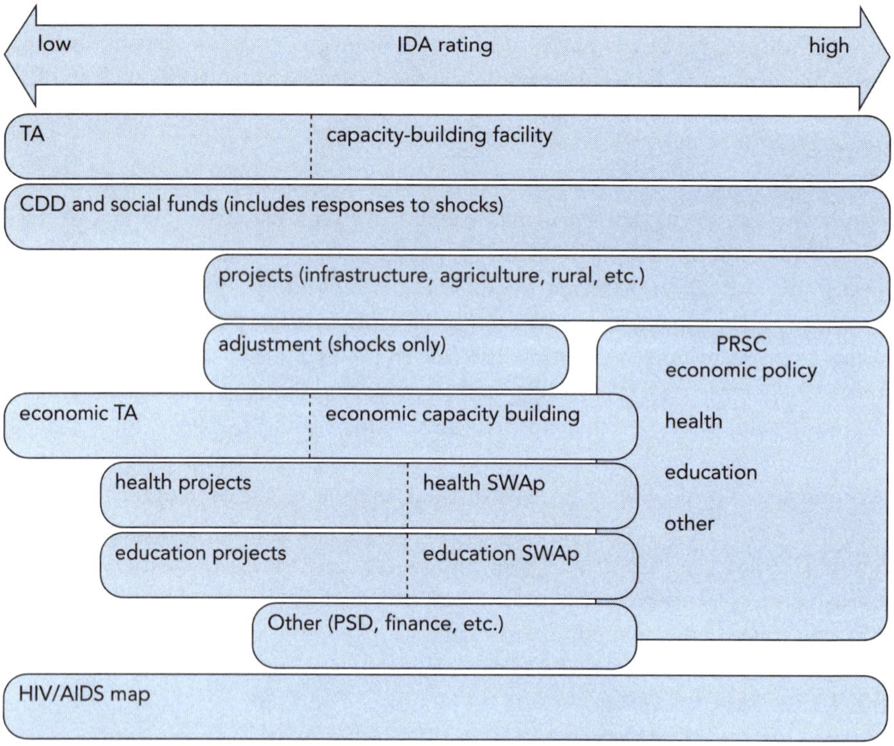

Source: World Bank (2003b).

Last, *sufficient time and patience are required to achieve concrete development results*. The following remark from a partner country seems to sums up the essence of the overall endeavor of achieving aid effectiveness (Duong 2005):

> Since the reforms of the country system would have significant effect not only on ODA-related stakeholders but on a full range of others as well, the recipient government's strong ownership and leadership is essential. Reforms may take a long time, but their impact would be much greater than any impact gained from establishing a dual system. Respecting the government's ownership and self-determination, a patient approach is necessary in implementing or supporting these capacity developments.

Endnotes

1. This interest arose out of the discussions of the late 1990s on aid effectiveness, which in turn arose from several different perspectives, including (1) the argument that aid works in a good policy environment; (2) greater focus and linkage between debt relief (HIPC Initiative) and poverty reduction (PRSPs), such as allocation of HIPC relief funds to pro-poor expenditures; (3) greater focus on aid that supports effective processes based on the recip-

ient country environment; (4) greater focus on aid effectiveness (ownership, alignment, harmonization, and so on and the trend toward SWAps, program-based approaches; and (5) volume of aid to meet the Millennium Development Goals.

2. http://www.jbic.go.jp/english/oec/yenloan/kind/index.php.
3. A comparative study between Ghana and Vietnam (Ozeki 2004) suggests similar observations.

26
The Netherlands: Country Selectivity and Aid Modality Choices

MAARTEN BROUWER
Ministry of Foreign Affairs, the Netherlands

Donors have three key decisions to make in designing their assistance programs: (1) which countries to assist (the selectivity issue), (2) how much aid to provide (the allocation decision), and (3) what aid modalities to use. It is important that both donors and partner countries make decisions using this holistic perspective, rather than focusing on one or two of these decisions alone.

Each of the decisions in turn involves three basic principles, derived from a needs-based, an incentive-based, or a performance-based perspective. As a donor country, the Netherlands has been struggling to decide on the relative weights to give these principles. The terminology of conditions, which is often used to refer to each of the criteria for decision making as mentioned above, has been confusing.

Criteria used for selecting countries for assistance seem to pose the hardest conditions. They involve such considerations as good macroeconomic policy, human rights conditions, or other aspects of good governance. Such considerations are in practice a combination of political choices by the donor country with its assessment of the opportunities for effective cooperation, and as such they continue to be relevant after the selection has taken place. They can be considered as underlying principles for good cooperation. What "good" cooperation entails is primarily defined by the individual donor, with discussions in the Development Assistance Committee on good donor practices providing some standards of reference. From the Netherlands' selection of countries for assistance, the relative weight given to perspectives based on needs, performance, or incentives is not at all clear. Political considerations seem to imply that incentives, especially with regard to the scope for fruitful cooperation, have in fact weighed strongly.

The allocation of aid is currently decided by individual donors, and a framework for joint decision making has been lacking. Recent undertakings to look at the aggregate outcome of individual donor decisions on the access to assistance by so-called fragile states are in their infancy. In the Netherlands, allocation decisions have been made largely on the basis of performance and need. The latter is assessed through a general model in which poverty data, size of population, and scores on the country policy and institutional assessment index provide a point of reference. The trigger for decision making is actual performance, measured through internal assessments. A more transparent assessment process may be needed. The IDA practice of using high and low case scenarios, based on the assessments we already undertake, could be helpful in bringing individual donors' decisions into the dialogue with the partner country, bilaterally as well as multilaterally.

The choice of aid modalities is generally perceived as a highly technical issue. Performance measurement has been at the center of the debate. However, harmonization and alignment processes have made clear that performance measurement in itself is not the decisive factor. More and more, we have come to understand that shared goals, flexible cooperation, and informed decision making are the key elements that determine what modalities are most suitable in specific circumstances. Not best practices, but best fits need be sought.

To decide on what aid modalities to apply, the Netherlands uses the type of trust relationship model described by Paul Mosley and Suleiman Abrar (Chapter 15 of this volume). According to Mosley and Abrar, the trust relationship has four triggers, or building blocks: willingness to undertake pro-poor expenditures, level of control of corruption (in terms of public financial management, but also in terms of broader governance issues), willingness to take initiative, and personal rapport between negotiators. In our assessment tool, the Netherlands similarly looks carefully at whether the quality of poverty reduction policies, the practice of pro-poor choices, and the macroeconomic framework include policies addressing the economic structure and the degree of government control over the economy. We look at public finance issues and broader issues of governance in terms of legitimacy and efficiency. Finally, we assess the relationships with recipient government and other donors, in terms of the quality of dialogue and harmonization. As such, Mosley and Abrar's four building blocks have operational significance. However, it is crucially important that our assessments, preferably undertaken with other partners, are seen as inputs for the dialogue with our partners.

It is during dialogue that partners assess the trust they have in the forward-looking elements in the debate, and the outcome of this dialogue is the basis for the decision whether or not to finance and a trigger for disbursement. Three categories could be used to structure the dialogue much better: process conditions, action-oriented conditions, and results. If partner countries and donors were to organize the dialogue around those three elements, the issue of trust would then come out strongly.

In summary, decisions on allocation and modalities involve much less hard conditions in terms of cutoff points than those on country selection. The latter decisions do not leave much space for influence by other partners. To form an overall picture of aid flows and identified needs, donors' individual decisions need to be aggregated. In the former two sets of decision making, more decisions are left to be made as the aid relationship unfolds. Conditions are in fact indicators for measurement. The need for more equal partnership, transparency, and trust requires us to be consistent in each of the three sets of decisions identified.

As an aid modality, budget support gives a recipient country a good deal of freedom and is a modality preferred by the Netherlands and by recipient countries, as evidenced by the discussion at the Strategic Partnership with Africa conference. However, countries must be very transparent in their choices in order to become reliable partners, and thus the choice of aid modalities and the level of discretion to be accorded to a recipient country need to be debated with our partners. As the internal debate within the Netherlands about preferred modalities and the underlying assessment of trust in our partners continues, we need to work harder with our partners to open up dialogue and deepen it in terms of the underlying principles of the aid relationship, in order to be able to show that trust is justified and performance is improving.

PART VIII
Practitioners' Forum on Budget Support: Discussion and Concluding Remarks

PRACTITIONERS' FORUM
on
BUDGET SUPPORT

May 5-6, 2005
Cape Town, South Africa

27
Summary of Discussion

To exchange and disseminate emerging lessons on budget support, the World Bank sponsored a practitioners' forum on budget support in Cape Town, South Africa, on May 5–6, 2005. The forum brought together 140 participants representing 20 IDA countries, 15 bilateral donors, the African Development Bank, the European Commission, the International Monetary Fund (IMF), the New Partnership for Africa's Development (NEPAD), and the World Bank. The discussions in Cape Town built on evidence presented in different chapters of this volume, and also drew on a preceding technical workshop conducted by the Budget Support Working Group of the Strategic Partnership with Africa (SPA). The discussions covered the following themes: conceptual issues and the choice of aid instruments, fiduciary issues, alignment with government programs, macroeconomic issues, aid predictability, conditionality, and donor coordination.

A. Budget Support: Concept, Instrument Choice, and Fiduciary Aspects

On the concept of budget support and conditions for its effectiveness, the discussion drew particularly on chapters 1 (Koeberle and Stavreski), 2 (Shand), 5 (Hammond), and 23 (Hoven). Participants noted that the increased use of budget support was a response to some disillusion with the sustainability of developmental outcomes of traditional project aid. Budget support was generally seen as an effective aid instrument for countries with a good track record: in such an environment, budget support could provide flexible medium-term support for complex institutional and policy reforms, improve the predictability of aid flows, and increase the results focus of government activities. The use of a country's own planning and budget systems was also welcomed as a means to foster ownership of government policies and replace traditional conditionality concepts with a mutual accountability framework for partner governments and donors. Many of these themes were echoed repeatedly during the two days of the forum.

Louis Kasekende (Deputy Governor, Bank of Uganda) raised a number of issues that further shaped the debate. First, he noted that an appropriate mix of budget and project aid was needed since line ministers did not wish to surrender authority in all cases to the finance minister. In this respect, line ministers were often tempted to accept offers of additional project aid even for projects that did not represent strong priorities for the government. Second, Kasekende noted the importance of the limits to aid absorption that are imposed by macroeconomic conditions and debt sustainability considerations. He argued that budget support would therefore need to be provided in an appropriate mix between grants and loans, and with sufficient fiscal space to attain the Millennium Development Goals. Third, he raised the question of to what extent postconflict countries and weaker performers should be eligible for budget support and could effectively use this instrument. Finally, he noted the challenges that arise for macroeconomic management if budget support is delayed or reduced within a fiscal year. In this regard, he argued for a move away from traditional conditionality (including signaling by the IMF) to a setting based on mutual accountability, noting the failure of past attempts to "buy" reforms. He also called for replication of good examples in donor harmonization, realignment of donor procedures, and the design of comprehensive strategies for joint donor support.

On the choice of aid instruments, Stefan Koeberle (Adviser, World Bank) voiced the broadly held view that budget support is appropriate if the government has articulated and owns an adequate policy program. He suggested that if a government has not articulated a clear strategy or is not in a position to implement its program on a sustained basis, more traditional instruments might be more appropriate. Other participants noted the need to establish upfront criteria for the performance of a country, and to link the level of aid and the choice of aid instruments to these criteria. Some participants argued that the "mix of instruments" debate was somewhat misplaced and that a broad move to budget support, at least in well-performing countries, was hampered more by donor reluctance to give up sectoral project funding than by aid efficiency concerns.

Several participants raised questions about selection criteria for engagement in budget support, particularly in countries without a track record of reforms; they noted that budget support in weaker environments, such as postconflict countries, remained controversial. Alan Gelb (Director, World Bank) suggested that even if different criteria were applied for postconflict countries, without a strong indication that there were forces for improvement in such countries, it would be difficult to achieve stable budget financing, and thus it might be difficult for them to meet agreed performance targets. Wahidullah Shahrani (Deputy Minister of Finance, Afghanistan) stressed the importance of having performance benchmarks and fiduciary criteria set by donors in a postconflict setting. In his view, meeting performance benchmarks allowed Afghanistan to establish trust for flexible budget financing, while external audits supported a rapid improvement in expenditure transparency and efficiency.

In discussing selectivity criteria for budget support, forum participants also examined the issue of public financial management (PFM). They noted that knowledge about country PFM systems has improved, but that different donors have different risk thresholds for engaging in budget support. Most agreed that, as long as there is a firm commitment to strengthen a PFM system, the existing weakness of PFM should not preclude budget support. Ingrid-Gabriela Hoven (Deputy Director General, German Ministry for Economic Cooperation and Development) emphasized the important role of capacity building to improve PFM systems and planning in sectoral ministries. She noted the importance of coordinated and well-prioritized technical cooperation, which should give the recipient country the right incentives to strengthen its own capacity. Another participant argued that the "technocratic" PFM reforms that are often included in budget support programs—such as introduction of a medium-term expenditure framework or results-based management—often fail to deliver on their promises. He noted that the inefficiencies and shortcomings of existing budget systems and processes may well reflect existing institutional frameworks and lack of capacity, but may also reflect internal political incentives to perpetuate weak systems; the latter would need to be analyzed more deeply to identify the best way to support change.

B. Programmatic Alignment, Ownership, and Accountability

Drawing on the presentation of Chapters 9 (Alonso and others) and 10 (Booth and others), and some country examples (Chapter 20 by Devarajan and Shah, and Chapter 25 by Arakawa), the forum debated the issues of ownership, accountability, and programmatic alignment of budget support.

There was general agreement that the ownership and leadership exercised by the recipient government play a critical role in achieving programmatic alignment. Strong ownership is of key importance for ensuring quality dialogue between partners about policies and priorities, and for successful implementation of the reform program.

One of the strong messages from the debate was the importance of solid accountability systems within countries, rather than just accountability to donors. Budget support is expected both to rely on and reinforce a country's own accountability systems. This includes the accountability of the government to its own citizens, but also the accountability within government—most notably between the line ministries and the ministry of finance. Participants from recipient countries noted that donors should give governments enough room to work within the local accountability mechanisms that enable them to build consensus with parliament and population.

In this regard, Akoto Osei (Deputy Minister of Finance and Economic Planning, Ghana) stressed the role of parliaments in the process of holding governments accountable for results, as well as the role of the head of state in holding members of government accountable. He emphasized the strong commitment of his own government to poverty reduction and the central role played by the annual progress report (APR) on the poverty reduction strategy (PRS). But he also noted the need for donors to help strengthen technical capacity at the lower levels of the civil service, to reduce the burden placed on high-level government officials in managing donor relations and the design of reform programs.

Discussions of donor alignment with national processes stressed the key role of the PRS APR. This report would ideally contain a review of policy implementation and results as well as an analysis of successes and failures, a description of planned policy actions to advance the policy agenda, and some discussion of cross-cutting issues—for example, PFM reforms. However, there was also agreement that the format and timing of the report should represent country circumstances and priorities. The risk was that the APR process might have too many stakeholders and audiences, internal and external, who would overburden it with their differing expectations. In this regard, participants agreed that APRs should in the first instance be directed to domestic audiences for domestic accountability purposes, although the reports could be used by donors. It was problematic that many APRs were still seen as donor-imposed and remained heavily focused on donor processes and external accountability needs to justify aid disbursements. Thus, although the presented case studies (see Chapter 9 by Alonso and others) confirmed that the PRSP process had helped to improve budgetary programming and the alignment of the APR with donor processes—Uganda, Mozambique, and Burkina Faso were cited—the tension between domestic and external accountability often remained unresolved, with external accountability still frequently gaining the upper hand. APRs were therefore still treated separately from national budget planning and execution processes.

Gilles Hervio (Unit Head, Directorate General for Development, European Commission) challenged some of the contents of Chapter 10 (Booth and others). In his view, that chapter was based on a vision of weak recipient governments—lacking capacity and commitment to poverty reduction—faced by donors able to correctly identify policy actions leading to poverty reduction. He disagreed with this vision, and with the paper's notion that the annual progress reports on PRSs tended to be too heavily skewed to the outcome end of the results chain and needed more details on priority policy actions to be truly operational. He pointed to recent PRS annual reports—of Rwanda, Madagascar, Mozambique, Uganda, Burkina Faso—that included a systematic analysis of key policy actions taken over the past year and contained details of actions planned for the future. Hervio also disagreed with the notion that donor performance assessment frameworks (PAFs) and APRs on PRSs showed striking differences. He noted that a comparison between donor policy matrixes and existing PRS-APR policy matrixes showed an impressive similarity of issues addressed, even if the detail of policy actions differed. He did not believe that donor-driven PAFs were the only solution to the lack of operationalization of APRs of PRSs, and in his view, such a conclusion did not match the evidence. PRS processes in many cases provided a clear, time-bound update on key policy actions taken and envisaged by governments, even if donors did not use them. Furthermore, if a government was able to produce or negotiate a PAF with donors, it was also able to do so in the context of its own national process and the APR of its PRS. Instead, he was more concerned that separated donor PAFs have in many cases slowed or hampered countries' process for developing their own time-bound operational plans for implementing the PRS.

The discussion on alignment was complemented by summary conclusions from the preceding workshop held by SPA. That workshop had concluded that budget support donors need to align behind nationally owned processes, give space for the role of parliament, and ensure that mechanisms for accountability to donors do not bypass or undermine the role of democratic institutions. Where the APR is not well linked to the PAF or policy matrix associated with budget support, and where governments view the APR as a key instrument to mobilize and align budget support, they should ensure that the report also meets donor needs (for example, for information and reporting on key policy actions, key indicators). Governments should generally define their own timing alignment agenda, based on their budget cycle/planning processes, and should encourage donors to adapt their program cycles (for example, for reviews, commitments, disbursements, or timing of board approval) accordingly. Appropriate timing of IMF missions and of IMF provision of macroeconomic assessments to donors was also crucial to facilitate timing alignment.

C. Predictability and Macroeconomic Impact of Aid

The discussion of predictability of aid flows and their macroeconomic impact drew on presentations of Chapters 11 (Celasun and Walliser), 12 (Eifert and Gelb), and 17 (Atingi-Ego). Participants stressed that budget support must be predictable to be truly effective, and that despite some small improvements in recent years, the predictability of disbursements remains a problem, even in stable environments. In fact, as a number of participants noted, volatility can actually increase in some cases, when aid is disrupted suddenly as a result of uneven performance.

Participants emphasized the importance of both short-term and long-term aid predictability for budget planning processes to work and deliver results. A medium-term perspective was necessary for a country to prepare realistic medium-term expenditure frameworks. Short-term and within-year predictability mattered to ensure delivery of funds at a time when the government can still spend them effectively—especially on investment projects that have a longer gestation period.

Many participants from recipient countries stressed that donors should make greater efforts to firmly commit resources for the following budget year before the budget is finalized and adopted. Equally important, donors should live up to these commitments and agree on a regular disbursement schedule within the budget year that is conducive to sound treasury and economic management. Donors were seen to have increased the predictability of their support to Tanzania and to some extent Burkina Faso. The case of Mali was highlighted as a counterexample, where more than 90 percent of the budget support resources were routinely made available only in the last quarter of the budget year. A participant from Madagascar explained that a delay in the disbursements of budget support had undermined the confidence the government had established through timely payment of its obligations to suppliers, and that this experience reinforced the importance of aligning disbursements to the planned budget cycle. Agreeing with some of these observations, donor representatives noted that predictability depended on both donor and recipient behavior and implied timely program implementation and exchange of information.

Some participants noted a need to make resource flows predictable over longer periods, including more than five years. However, the practical difficulties in doing so were also recognized. These included how to react to policy failures and how to deal with fragile states. Participants welcomed the proposal for a buffer fund to manage aid volatility (Chapter 12 by Eifert and Gelb), but also saw their individual constraints—

such as the need to get more frequent approval from parliaments or boards—as obstacles to moving to such a rules-based system of longer-term commitment.

Participants recognized that ensuring the predictability of aid in fragile states poses additional challenges. Since these countries could easily be thrown off the planned development path, the difficulty was how to find an appropriate response when performance criteria were not fully met and the country's track record was not good. There was a tension in these cases between the need to provide a stable and predictable flow of resources and the need for consistency with performance agreements.

Anupam Basu (Deputy Director, African Department, IMF), also welcomed the Eifert-Gelb proposal for a buffer fund to manage aid volatility, but wondered about the governance structures and institutions that would be needed to manage such a fund effectively. He also questioned whether such a buffer fund should respond symmetrically and within a narrow band to aid shortfalls and excess aid, and noted the need for further adjustment measures if aid volatility and revenue volatility were not independent. Basu asked whether a fund that only responded to exogenous aid fluctuations, and with a heavy weight of administrative delays, would truly be helpful in practice, and whether donors should not make stronger efforts to tackle the root cause of such volatility instead of financing a buffer fund. He also expressed concern about a buffer fund's viability should assumptions about the correlations of aid deviations over time turn out to be wrong. He noted the fairly large required size of the buffer fund, equivalent to 9–12 months of aid inflows, and raised issues regarding the fund's impact on domestic banking sector operations. On the links between predictability and budget execution discussed in Chapter 11 (Celasun and Walliser), Basu noted that the expenditure program could suffer if it needed to deviate from the PRS as a result of aid shortfalls. Drawing on this chapter's finding that government investment spending responds asymmetrically to aid shortfalls and excess aid, he suggested that it was important to recognize the complementarity of investment and recurrent spending both in reducing and increasing spending in response to aid volatility. The scope for protecting investment spending could also be increased by phasing the reduction of debt and domestic arrears accumulated in periods of aid shortfalls.

Richard Manning (Chairman, Development Assistance Committee, Organisation for Economic Co-operation and Development) observed that donors have few excuses for poor performance regarding in-year predictability and that OECD-DAC had developed good practice guidance to improve behavior. Aid recipient countries should continue to press for improved practice and for disbursements earlier in the budget year. Manning noted that managing medium-term predictability was a more difficult issue. In his view, a feasible model, across a reasonable slice of the donor community, was needed to make progress in medium-term predictability.

Conclusions from the SPA Budget Support Workshop also stressed that unpredictability of budget support could cause serious difficulties for recipient governments. To improve short-term predictability, donors should make firm commitments at the start of the budget preparation cycle. To facilitate medium-term planning, donors should give at least indicative medium-term allocations or commitments. Progress had been made in some countries in relation to the within-year and short-to medium-term dimensions of budget support predictability. However, little progress had been made in providing predictability over the long term (more than five years). Currently, no instrument apart from debt relief delivered long-term predictable financing. Participants at the SPA Workshop also noted that graduated responses could avoid all-or-nothing effects on disbursements when problems arose or performance was weaker than expected, and that political conditionality was a major source of unpredictability and needed further attention.

Based on the findings of Chapter 17 (Atingi-Ego) that Uganda faced increasing pressures in keeping its export sector competitive, the importance of aid-induced Dutch disease was widely debated, with a variety of opinions expressed on how real the risk was in the context of budget support. Jan Willem Gunning (Free University of Amsterdam) felt that applying Dutch disease arguments to aid inflows was not helpful, since aid inflows were not a temporary effect. Any real exchange rate appreciation as a result of aid inflows had to be compared with the counterfactual of not getting aid and evaluated against a very small risk of a sudden stop in aid inflows. Most of the participants noted that there was little evidence for the risk of Dutch disease, given current levels of budget support, but some pointed out that the risk might rise if aid increased in line with donors' commitments made at Monterrey. The complex interaction between aid sustainability, aid dependency, volatility, and scaling up of aid was debated alongside the important challenges for the concomitant management of aid inflows.

D. Donor Coordination and Conditionality

Coordination and conditionality were debated, drawing on Chapters 14 (Gunning), 15 (Mosley and Abrar), and 22 (Amin). Participants noted that borrowing countries still faced duplicity in conditionality across donors, along with high transaction costs, and that they needed to hold donors to account for their commitments to harmonization and alignment. Governments should take the lead in addressing the need for coordination with donors as well as coordination between ministries of finance and sector ministries. Experience showed that donors are more likely to coordinate their activities in the framework of robust, credible, coherent, and synchronized government-led processes and systems. Evidence from Mozambique was cited as a positive example in this context.

Referring to transaction costs, participants from recipient countries suggested that donors should review issues of common interest through joint missions. In addition, they should make more use of silent partnerships and be willing to delegate responsibility to lead donors for particular tasks, issues, or sectors. A donor representative from Tanzania noted that silent partnerships seemed like a good suggestion, but in practice tended to be hard to operate.

Many participants noted the importance of effective coordination within the host country. Tertius Zongo (Ambassador to the United States, Burkina Faso) stressed that it was a matter of political will to coordinate the activities of different domestic and external stakeholders who were often focused on their own specific areas of expertise or interest. To coordinate development initiatives, action at the government-wide level was needed, since line ministries sometimes did not fully grasp the full set of activities that are part of a broader program. Government leadership needed to impose a modicum of discipline. A participant from Mozambique emphasized that the need for coordination did not only concern the government, but extended to the legislature, civil society, and the private sector. The challenge in this regard was how to associate these constituencies with the government program and establish sustained dialogue, which would in turn ensure broader support for reforms.

Participants stressed that better donor coordination was also needed on capacity building. Donors should provide coordinated support for capacity development, preferably aligned around a clear framework owned by the government. In particular, donor support for improving statistical and monitoring and evaluation systems was considered to be of high priority by many participants.

Chapter 15 (Mosley and Abrar) generated a lively exchange on the role of the trust developed between recipients and donors through policy signals and conditionality, local presence, and effective communication. Trust was seen to be particularly important in the budget support context because of its significant potential impact on the regularity and predictability of flows. Manning added to the discussion the dimension of trust among donors, noting that more trust among donors would allow for more progress on coordination and harmonization. He also stressed the need to move away from dependence on a few personal relationships and instead build systems that are robust and country owned, and into which donors can fit. Maarten Brouwer (Ministry of Foreign Affairs, the Netherlands) suggested another side to the issue of trust: namely, the attitude within the donor community toward risks. In many cases, direct budget support started after a breach of trust—and the move to budget support signaled that a number of donors were now willing to take greater risks in their choice of instruments for aid delivery.

Moving from traditional conditionality to a concept of mutual accountability was also stressed as important for making budget support more effective. Many participants noted the progress achieved in this area but emphasized that the remaining challenges required further efforts from donors and governments. Some participants also suggested that conditionality should identify key actions, be kept to a minimum, and evaluated in the medium term, rather than on an annual basis.

There was broad agreement that the indicators monitored by budget support donors and used as disbursement conditions should be drawn from a single PAF. The indicators in the framework should preferably be based on the PRS or the PRS APR. However, since donors' full harmonization of disbursement triggers could make budget support flows more volatile, many—though not all—participants thought that donors could reduce these risks by each choosing different areas of the PAF as disbursement conditions.

There was an extensive debate on which indicators were appropriate to use as disbursement triggers: policy actions, outputs, or outcomes. A wide range of views was expressed on this issue. Some participants from recipient countries stressed that impact indicators were not fully within government control, and could only be measured on a long-term basis, and therefore posed great operational challenges as disbursement triggers. The vulnerability of outcomes to exogenous shocks was also noted. In general, participants felt that monitorable outcome indicators suitable for PAF use were easier to define in the health and education sectors than in some other areas, such as PFM or private sector development.

Regarding the danger that PAFs may be too light on concrete policy actions and too heavy on outcome indicators, noted in Chapter 10 (Booth and others), Gilles Hervio emphasized that information is lacking on the exact actions and actors needed for policies to be effective. In this context, the only feasible solution was to create incentives for processes that analyze the most relevant information available and provide due feedback into policy making. Hervio also stressed that the European Commission accepts that PAFs will contain a small number of key policy measures, but seeks to ensure that these measures are as concrete and as transparently measurable as possible and are discussed in the light of the analysis of the results obtained.

Speaking about progress with the World Bank's review of conditionality, Stefan Koeberle addressed the question of graduated responses. Poverty reduction support credits had allowed the Bank a certain discretion in responding in a graduated way to uneven performance. The Bank could wait with an operation, reduce the amount of financing, or proceed if it thought that performance had been adequate. However, one of the key challenges for the Bank was to learn from the experience of the European Union and consider whether a more formal graduated approach might be more appropriate in some cases.

Regarding macroeconomic conditionality, donors explained that their actions are now less rigidly tied to the status of IMF programs. Still, they considered signals from the IMF as very important. The IMF representative noted that the Fund is considering how it might give donors timely, clear, and more nuanced signals, including through a new nondisbursing policy support instrument.

28

Forum Participants' Concluding Remarks

LOUIS KASEKENDE
Bank of Uganda

Budget Support Is Appropriate for Some Countries

The debate on budget support has made clear the expectations and challenges associated with this aid modality. The overall conclusion is that budget support has many advantages and is an appropriate resource for some countries, but not for all.

Donors take a risk by moving to budget support as they lose certain controls over the use of resources. Recipient governments too take some risk, because they accommodate some additional expenditures, notably recurrent expenditures, and there is a risk that donors might withdraw or delay disbursements. Therefore both donors and recipient governments need to consider risk-mitigating factors.

Capacity Needs to Be Improved

Overall, the issue of capacity presents a serious challenge. Statistical capacity in recipient countries is often weak. Providing more aid in the form of budget support requires additional data to be generated, to be able to gauge whether the country's program is moving in the right direction. Improving recipients' statistical capacity is important for donors, because it allows accounting for the resources they have provided; it is also good for recipient countries because it permits them to monitor progress. This said, monitoring and evaluation should not impose too high a burden on recipient countries; it should be tailored to the capacity that is available. Given the weak statistical capacity in recipient countries, annual reviews may not be possible in some cases.

Budget support also requires strengthening countries' capacity for public financial management. The relevant issue here is the transparency of budgets and their implementation, which is often the subject of discussion by stakeholders.

Development partners need to look at capacity building in a wider perspective, taking a more holistic approach than at present. Capacity building is important for designing and negotiating programs and for implementation, and developing countries need to improve their capacity not only in ministries of finance but across the board. Institutions in recipient countries need more training and exposure and a better ability to retain their staff. Our experience at the Bank of Uganda shows that it is extremely difficult to retain highly capable people without a reform. The salaries in the Central Bank are much higher than in the public service, but it is still extremely difficult to hold on to accountants and IT staff because of the competition for staff from the private sector and from donors.

Conditionality and Political Economy Factors

Countries certainly need conditionality and have to provide assurances on the macroeconomic environment. There is an ongoing debate on the extent of conditionality, and it is important to consider the conditionality that is derived from the PRSPs. However, not all countries are the same in this context. Though there are situations where conditionality could be reduced, overall it is necessary for promoting effectiveness. And there are situations when conditionality may be particularly necessary and useful, as when the position of reformers needs to be strengthened against some interest groups.

Political conditionality presents a serious challenge for both recipients and donors. Technocrats have very little to contribute to discussions on political conditionality, and in most cases, donors need to go to the president or other politicians for such discussions. This is certainly an area that partners need to look at in more detail, to ensure that political considerations do not become a source of additional conditionality. The experiences of South Asia presented at this conference remind us again how important political economy factors and political conditionality can be.

The Lead Donor Concept Is Useful

There are times and situations, especially at the beginning of the budget support process, where it is appropriate to have a lead donor. The UNDP has played this role in some countries, and other donors have played this role across Africa. For example, the United Kingdom played a very big role in Sierra Leone and is currently playing a very big role in Nigeria. In some countries, the lack of a lead donor to guide the process has had negative implications for budget management and the dialogue between donors and governments.

Intrayear Predictability Is of Utmost Importance

Donors reserve the right to withdraw assistance in case of nonperformance, as is recognized by recipient countries. However, donors must do more to protect intrayear disbursements, because countries have very limited flexibility once they have made allocations and committed on their expenditures. We have discussed a proposal by Alan Gelb for establishing a buffer stock—which is actually a similar idea to what the International Monetary Fund proposed a few years ago—in order to prevent delays in disbursements from affecting government programs and macroeconomic management. Still, development partners need to find ways of ring-fencing disbursements, or at least some of their disbursements, to ensure that these cannot be withheld during an ongoing budget year. Trust is very important in this context: sometimes donors need to trust that a government will eventually get back on track with its program, and therefore continue providing resources.

Tertius Zongo

Ambassador of Burkina Faso to the United States

Agreement on a Mix of Instruments; Importance of Predictability and Ownership

Our debates have resulted in agreement on several elements:

- Countries need a mixture of instruments: budget support is important, but attention should also be paid to project aid.
- Predictability of resources is essential, both for the success of reforms and to support and consolidate results. Partners should find a mechanism to ensure that the resources they provide on an annual basis as budget support are predictable. With regard to medium-term commitments, a flexible approach is needed, based on best practices, that communicates clearly to partner countries the medium-term commitments of donors and attached conditions. Partner countries, in turn, should also know which procedures and mechanisms they need to use if the disbursement of resources is blocked. Lack of predictability tends to be the major element hindering the alignment of aid with national processes, and it undermines the credibility of public expenditure management.
- Successful reform requires national political authorities to have the necessary ownership. Nonetheless, ownership on its own is not sufficient. On the technical side, partner countries should be able to translate development goals into policies and programs with clearly defined objectives. Subsequently, capacity should be improved in order to enable countries to design and implement their budgets, and to improve monitoring and evaluation of activities that will lead to achievement of stated objectives and results.

Open Dialogue, Confidence, and Stakeholder Participation Matter

There is much debate on aid modalities and models of cooperation. Though no modality or model of cooperation is perfect, what matters is to have continuing cooperation resulting in a sustained dialogue. It is also important to recognize that development partners are learning throughout this process.

Another important component of the dialogue is confidence between the parties. This kind of trust can come through joint activities such as these exchanges. All partners need to stay the course: recipients of aid would like donors to consolidate the dialogue and adhere to a regular and coordinated performance assessment process. This process should shape the dialogue, which in turn will help consolidate mutual trust and confidence. In this context, partners need to find a way to ensure that performance indicators are derived from the same documents that governments submit to parliament. The dialogue and agreement on the indicators are no longer a matter between the government and partners, but a national issue, and there is therefore a need to provide a link that enables parliament and other stakeholders to be informed and participate in selecting these indicators.

Budgetary Frameworks as Well as Regional and National Institutions Need to Be Strengthened

Strengthening a country's budgetary framework is very important. Actions that will be undertaken by development partners should help to strengthen the budgetary framework and lead to an increase in national revenues. This process, in turn, will increase the responsibility and accountability of the government to citizens. It is also very important to reinforce the legal framework related to the implementation of the budget; this framework should be explicitly approved and actively implemented by the government. Such an approach would create credibility and sustainable dialogue that will enable countries to make sustained progress and maintain donors' trust.

The regional framework was rightly highlighted in our discussions as important for many countries in Africa for creating sustainable development. Unfortunately, regional approaches have been notably absent in previous discussions among development partners, so this is a welcome addition to our exchanges on how to make aid, and budget support in particular, more effective.

Finally, it is necessary to support sustainable changes in countries' institutional structures in order to promote economic growth and democracy. An economic environment based on free competition, competitiveness, and functioning markets will enable countries to attract more private investors, reduce government involvement in economic choices, and accelerate growth. These objectives could be supported through direct budget support instruments.

Nick Amin

UK Department for International Development (DFID)

Budget Support Contributes to Increased Aid Effectiveness

Budget support and aid effectiveness are strongly linked. In recent years, donors have expressed a preference for providing more support directly to national budgets, recognizing that assistance in this form may be a more effective way of helping countries to implement their poverty reduction strategies (PRSs). The motive underlying the switch to budget support is the expectation that aid is likely to be more effective when it is provided to countries programmatically, is harmonized with that of other donors, and is aligned with national processes. Evidence to show the beneficial links between PRSs and budget support is starting to emerge from academic studies and evaluation reports.

At least two presentations at this conference have already alluded to the presence of positive links between budget support, PRSs, and better budget management practices. These links have been shown in the South Asian context, and the cross-country information gathered by Rosa Alonso provides reinforcing evidence. The benefits of assisting PRSs via the budget include increased public expenditure benefiting poor people, better practices in public financial management, greater flexibility to governments in managing budgets, more focus on priority expenditures, better dialogue between partner governments and donors, strengthened country ownership of policy processes, and an increased focus on achieving results. While much progress is evident at the country level, considerably more remains to be done.

Attention to Results Is Crucial for Increasing Accountability

An emphasis on results is required for improving accountability and is critical for continuing to show that budget support and programmatic approaches help countries to enhance economic growth and reduce poverty. The OECD-DAC's evaluation of general budget support should help to strengthen the evidence base in this regard. A more determined change in the incentive framework is needed, however, to bring about a bigger shift in focus toward results. This might be done by allocating more aid to countries that are making faster progress in reducing poverty. Concentrating donor conditionality more on the achievement of results would also be helpful.

It is necessary to avoid a clash of paradigms between aid efforts focused on capacity building and efforts focused on achieving results. A complementary approach among budget support donors would allow the two types of efforts to work alongside each other. The DFID's new policy paper on conditionality puts greater emphasis on assessing the impact of various interventions. But, apart from the European Commission, donor agencies still seem reluctant to stress a strong link between aid allocation and countries' performance in achieving results. Given the poor measurement systems in most low-income countries, an overly mechanistic link between results and disbursements would be inappropriate. But without a stress on results, it is difficult to imagine how a focus on better performance might be brought about.

Sector Emphasis in the Budget Support Context

Donors are providing budget support simultaneously with other forms of assistance, including targeted assistance to sectors. The DFID's experience in some countries suggests that when general budget support becomes the main mechanism for channeling concessionary finance to partner governments, continuing project-based support to sectors could risk undermining the opportunities that budget support seeks to create with regard to institutional development (for example, improving public financial management and increasing accountability within government). The risk arises because line ministries may come to depend on donor funds for financing priority activities.

If some donors prefer to finance sector-based activities, they should channel their sector support in ways that complement budget support and strengthen national institutional development. This would mean ensuring that lines of accountability between line ministries and finance ministries do not get blurred by sector support (say, with respect to budget planning and expenditure control, performance accounting, reporting, and auditing). In such instances, targeted (that is, sector budget) support is probably the form of sector aid that is least likely to cause damage, but even in this case, explicit awareness of the advantages and disadvantages that this brings is required in justifying the continued use of targeted interventions alongside budget support.

Division of Labor in Aid Architecture

Recent years have seen much discussion about streamlining the international aid architecture. Globally, attention has focused on clarifying the respective roles of key players within the multilateral and bilateral aid system. But while progress is evident in illuminating some of the key issues at the international level, the application of good-practice lessons at the country level still has a long way to go. A clearer division of labor among development partners is required at the country level. This should seek to rationalize and streamline donors' engagement in supporting national development efforts (for example, at the sector level, budget support, or with respect to cross-cutting capacity-building work). Attention should also be given to tackling difficult issues regarding particular kinds of donor support of country-led processes. In some areas, such as budget support, it may be appropriate to have a critical mass of donors (rather than including all donors) assisting governments to implement their PRS. By narrowing and limiting the engagement of donors to a smaller, and possibly more specialized, set of activities, it may be more possible to realize greater gains in efficiency and achieve more effective results. One option for streamlining donor activities might be to separate out donors according to their main areas of focus and principal support modalities, and to set clearer rules of engagement.

Mutual Accountability

Although the reality of harmonization and alignment at the country level still lags far behind some of the rhetoric, acceptance is emerging within the donor community of the basic principles and virtues of common approaches. Recent OECD-DAC work shows that progress is being made, but that much more remains to be done. It may be possible to accelerate progress if partner countries hold donors more accountable for their behavior. Under current arrangements, it should be possible for donors to be assessed on their progress in harmonizing and aligning more effectively with PRS processes. Yet, it seems, this form of mutual accountability is being practiced in only a few countries, such as Tanzania and Mozambique. Governments do need to hold donors to account for the commitments they have signed up to internationally. Stronger mechanisms of mutual accountability would allow partners the opportunity to look periodically at the progress being made in achieving results by both donors and government. In turn, these mechanisms would enable stronger incentives to be put in place for strengthening implementation.

More Technical Assistance Is Needed for Strengthening Public Financial Management Systems in Low-Income Countries

Compared to five years ago, there is now much more recognition of the need to improve national financial management systems. Given the role these systems play in ensuring that budget resources are channeled effectively to key expenditure needs, the current level of attention and resources directed to upgrading them seems woefully inadequate. To speed progress, it may be useful for donors to consider providing more dedicated support (in the form of pooled technical assistance) for upgrading financial management and accountability systems. This would bring the added benefit of encouraging more partners to channel funds through the budget.

Alan Gelb
World Bank

Trust Is Important in Budget Support

The move from project support to budget support is fundamentally an issue of trust: trust needs to be placed in country systems and country processes and in the internal accountability of countries, and the level of trust has implications for conditionality and the structure of operations and measurement issues.

One way of thinking about trust is to see it as an extension of selectivity in making lending decisions, albeit an intangible element. There are certain tangible criteria for selectivity in lending, such as the World Bank's country policy and institutional assessment (CPIA), and there is in addition an intangible element of whether, to what degree, and in what way partners trust each other.

Conditionality, Trust, and Performance

The existence of conditionality does not necessarily imply there is no trust between donor and recipient country. If the conditions are truly expressions of what the country says it wants to do, there is no adverse reflection on trust. It is also unrealistic to expect any form of support to be completely without conditions. There will always be some conditions, and it is better if those are drawn from activities that countries are willing to implement.

One of the areas where progress could be made is to reframe the issue of conditionality toward the concept of performance incentives for countries implementing their development programs. These performance incentives can be set either as outcomes or actions and should be seen as signals that countries are able to send to donors as to which direction they are moving in.

The real conditionality lies not in these performance incentives but in the basic factors that make the partners willing to engage in budget support in the first place. Only major deviations in these basic factors, such as deviations from macroeconomic stability, will result in the European Union withholding its fixed tranche, or cause the World Bank and other donors to decide to radically scale back their budget support.

The conditionality issue could therefore be diffused by considering so called "petty" conditions as performance incentives, and focusing on the positive achievements, which would be linked with increased financial support, rather than always focusing on the negatives—the failure to achieve progress. Especially when targets are ambitious, this has advantages. The factors that cause a reappraisal of the program would then be "big" factors, clearly observable whether couched in terms of changes in the CPIA or other major developments that affect performance.

How to Measure Progress

Donors and recipient countries should put more effort into finding ways to measure the progress achieved. This applies not only to the progress toward the Millennium Development Goals or outcomes, but also to the effectiveness of public resource management systems, basic systems of service delivery, and so forth. After three or four years of budget support, a country ought to be able to say whether and how its systems are improving, whether funds are flowing better through the education system, whether teachers are attending their schools, or whether rural areas are being served well or not. This is an area where better donor coordination can help, including to strengthen statistical capacity and help institute regular rounds of surveys. If donors can work together with countries on those assessments, they can cut down on unnecessary, short-term, intrusive engagement, while relying on a few signals that in turn are treated as performance incentives for their financial support.

Mark Plant
International Monetary Fund (IMF)

The IMF Has a Role in the Budget Support Debate

In many ways, the Fund stands with one institutional foot in the debate on budget support and the other one outside it. The IMF is clearly not a bilateral donor, and it does not provide budget support. Neither is it a developmental institution; its expertise lies in macroeconomics and financial matters. Nonetheless, it is engaged in the Monterrey Consensus and the international effort to help low-income countries grow more rapidly and reduce poverty. The IMF is therefore very much involved and plays an important role in the budget support process.

There are three areas in which budget support is linked to IMF engagement. First is a set of macroeconomic and financial management issues. Second is in the area of shocks. The third is what kind of signals the Fund sends to the donor community and to low-income countries

Macroeconomic Stability Sets the Stage for Budget Support

On macroeconomics, there is broad agreement that to a large extent, the 1980s and 1990s were about macroeconomic stabilization in low-income countries. One of the major lessons learned, which has now largely been implemented, was that macroeconomic stability is a necessary precursor to growth and poverty reduction. That understanding set the stage for the possibility of budget support. Without a modicum of macroeconomic stability and predictability, it would be impossible for donors to proceed to support a national budget financially as a whole and have confidence that the funds will be used in a reasonable way. Only with inflation largely stabilized, balance of payments gaps under control, and exchange rates stabilized is the scene set for the widespread use of budget support.

Budget Support Creates Some Macroeconomic Risks

When budget support makes up a significant share of the total budget, it poses a different set of macroeconomic challenges. On a very basic level, the Fund welcomes the efforts of the donor community to help low-income countries achieve sustainable growth and poverty reduction. However, as more aid flows in, countries may see balance of payments gaps rising instead of falling. Dealing with this requires a very different approach from the type of "stabilization" we have seen in the past, which focused on lowering current account balances. Thus aid will force us to think about the macroeconomics in these countries differently.

First of all, there is a risk of so-called Dutch disease. As with any disease, prevention is better than the cure. While there may not be much evidence of Dutch disease due to aid, the potential for this problem will increase as the amount of aid increases, especially if aid becomes as large as called for in the Monterrey Consensus. Low-income countries and their partners need to understand what that potential risk is and how they can act to prevent it. This is a new challenge that is not fully understood.

Volatility is another problem. One of the risks of budget support is that it could increase rather than decrease the volatility of aid flows, because budget support can be cut off more quickly and in larger amounts when things go wrong. That behavior could pose a very serious macroeconomic management challenge for some governments. At the same time, donors need to think together how to modulate budget support up and down and under what conditions.

Budgetary and Financial Management Issues

Budget support also poses a new set of budgetary and financial management problems for a government in its dealings with the central bank and the financial markets. There is a general sense that budget support should arrive at the beginning of a fiscal year, so that funds will be available and the country can spend them over the course of the year. However, this arrangement could put a strain on the banking system and the central bank in managing the inflow of foreign exchange if the new inflows arrive at a time when they are not matched by imports and payment outflows. (In some sense, this is a "desirable" set of problems to have because it is a step beyond the basic stabilization problem that we were addressing in the past.)

Debt Sustainability and Fiscal Sustainability

Another set of long-term challenges is associated with increased aid in the form of budget support. A first challenge is debt sustainability. To the extent that the inflows take the form of loans, there is a need for consistent monitoring of aid's impact on debt sustainability. This need will feature more and more in the IMF's advice to low-income countries. There is a constant need to look at debt sustainability and make projections, which however uncertain will still give donors and the government an idea of where the country is heading.

Closely related to the problem of debt sustainability is the question of fiscal sustainability. There has been much debate about the increased financing of recurrent costs as partners move forward with budget support. The question is what fiscal precedents and future fiscal obligations the donor community is setting up through its support at this time.

Low-Income Countries Are Particularly Vulnerable to Shocks

The other issue that has to be noted on the macroeconomic front is the lack of economic diversification in low-income countries. These countries have limited financial reserves. More importantly, they have limited and "shallow" markets. They also have limited capabilities for insurance and regulatory frameworks to prevent the types of flows that could be destabilizing. They have limited accounting capacity and limited capacity to track the various financial and macroeconomic indicators that warn that trouble is ahead. As a result, a quick change of circumstances—such as a commodity price shock or a change in a particular donor's attitude toward a country—can drastically alter the macroeconomic framework.

What Role for the IMF?

There is an ongoing debate within and outside the IMF about what role the Fund should play in low-income countries. While there is agreement that the Fund should help countries maintain macroeconomic stability and solid financial management, there is a question as to what extent these responsibilities and duties are linked to the microeconomics of development. There is also a dilemma about the extent to which the IMF can set the macroeconomic environment and let other agencies do their work on the various pieces of growth and development.

Given the vulnerability of the economies of low-income countries, a closer relationship is needed between macroeconomic and microeconomic analysis. Donors need to understand what the macroeconomic impact of their aid flows will be. The flows that donor groups are managing are large, and there has to be an understanding of the impact of the changes in those flows beyond their impact on the projects and budget expenditures they are supporting. At the same time, the IMF needs to understand what donors' efforts to support growth will mean for the economy. If budgets and projects are tightened, what will happen to the long-term growth prospects that donors are supporting? What is the potential growth impact of certain microeconomic changes supported by donor interventions?

It is important for donors and the Fund to better understand each other's signals and to deepen the IMF-bilateral dialogue. One area the IMF has been reflecting on in the last few years is how it interacts with the donor community—both in the field and at headquarters level, but particularly in the field. The increased interaction by donors in the budget support mode—that is, through local donor groups—requires better understanding by the IMF of its role in that effort.

Signaling Instead of Show-Stopper Role for the IMF

There will be less and less of a role for the IMF as the so-called "show stopper" for aid. Most of the countries have achieved a certain level of macroeconomic stability and the basic tenets of how to manage an economy financially are well understood. In this context, it will be relatively rare for the IMF to say it will withdraw support or stop a country's program with the Fund. Donors and countries will see more and more forward-looking signals from the IMF, such as warning signals related to sustainability. However, these subtle signals are very difficult for IMF to send and for donors to receive. For instance, if the IMF suggests that to ensure sustainability, donors should start reducing loans and increasing grants in a particular economy, donors may be hard pressed to react and adjust their pipelines quickly.

We are currently working within the IMF on signaling and interaction with donors. We have done a survey about the signals that our programs send, and the feedback is that poverty reduction and growth facility–supported programs or other arrangements that countries have with the Fund are very blunt on-off signals. The survey shows that donors, while appreciating an on-off signal, also need more nuances—they need to understand why it is on and why it is off. Some also complain that the IMF never really sends an off signal clearly; it is pretty clear to outsiders when it is on, but it is less clear when the signal is off. The IMF is working on reshaping some of its instruments in order to send better signals in a world that increasingly relies on budget support to deliver aid and where the Fund is much more involved with donors than donors with the Fund.

Shocks, Surprise, or Scarce Resources

Many donors also plead for the IMF to return to its more traditional role of helping countries ensure against shocks. The Fund is considering ways to do that, particularly in low-income countries that cannot afford high interest loans. However, there are difficult problems to confront. The frequency, duration, and permanence of the shocks are very varied in low-income countries, so it is hard to design one instrument that works for all countries in the group. And while it is useful to have financing available, there are moral hazard problems that come along with the financing. In conclusion, more thought has to be given to shocks, particularly because budget support could make the countries more vulnerable to the external environment and to our own behavior as donors.

Jerome Morris Wolgin
World Bank, Secretariat of the Strategic Partnership with Africa

Areas of Agreement

The whole debate on results versus policy actions has become sterile. It is now time to get beyond that. We should no longer be discussing whether or not to move toward results-based disbursements: clearly both results and policy actions have a place in performance assessment frameworks, and both may actually add value.

There is also agreement that in-year predictability is a particularly important issue, and that in principle, there should be no problems in dealing with it. Donors should disburse according to a predictable schedule. They should front-load, which means they will need to make disbursement decisions for year *n* in year *n* minus one. Some donors may have an institutional problem in achieving this, but the principle is not in dispute.

A remaining issue that creates difficulty is political conditionality.

Areas that Need Further Work

Four areas require hard implementation work. The first is operationalization of the poverty reduction strategy papers (PRSPs)—the need to create within the PRSP a framework that lays out the policy actions the country is going to take, so that the performance assessment framework can be drawn directly from a government document. We learned, for example, that in Ethiopia there is a very clear log-frame in the annual progress review documents, which is helpful. However, there is a need for operationalization of the PRSP that will continue to add ownership to this process. This seems to be happening in a number of countries now.

Second, a very difficult implementation problem is to synchronize calendars and budget cycles, so that reviews take place at a time when information is available, sector reviews take place before national reviews (but are linked to national poverty reduction strategy reviews), and reviews take place in a timeframe in which they can affect donor decisions and the national budgeting process.

The third problem area is medium-term predictability. It is recognized that for long-term programs of poverty reduction, countries that are aid dependent need a commitment of long-term dependable resource flows from their partners. At the Strategic Partnership with Africa, an attempt was made to get from donors some notion of what their commitments would be over a three-year period. This turned out to be extremely difficult to do. This is an area in which donors need to make a concerted effort over the next years, in order to be able to increase medium-term predictability. The schema suggested by Alan Gelb is helpful, but it is a second-best solution. The first-best solution is providing medium-term dependable financing so that governments will have some predictability in their resource estimates and thus make rational spending decisions.

Fourth, on the coordination issue, very little has been done so far to reduce transaction costs. There is some isolated progress, which is not sufficient. This is an area where a lot of hard implementation work needs to be done, together with some changes in policies, programs, and procedures. It will have a big impact.

Areas of Evolving Agreement

The area of evolving agreement is a movement toward ex post conditionality. Poverty reduction support credits are ex post. The European Community fixed tranche is largely ex post. The ideas emerging from Mozambique, as well as the agreement to make disbursements in year *n* dependent on performance in year *n* minus one, are ex post. As the "trust" issue becomes clearer, we might begin to see more disbursements based on a review of what has already happened rather than on what is going to happen.

Further Issues

There are two further issues. One is how to deal with poorly performing countries, and whether to bring them into the ranks of budget support recipients. Where does it make sense, and where doesn't it make sense to engage? A smaller, but still important, issue is how to transit from sector programs to more general budget support.

James Adams
World Bank

Conditionality Works in Support of Reformers

Conditionality is about triggering and supporting dynamic processes of reform. The focus on reform takes place in the context of ensuring development impact, which has a direct link to poverty reduction. This is not to say that donor support does not fill financing gaps or compensate for the costs of change. However, the time of thinking that donors could "buy reform" is over. The message on conditionality should be about reform and leadership at the country level.

Opinions differ on the effectiveness of conditionality—including the view that it is ineffective overall. However, it is important to take a step back and recognize some of the critical results produced by policy change related to conditionality. For example, in my personal experience, conditionality was very effectively used in Uganda to support reformers. In Tanzania, the government would have found it very difficult to privatize the National Bank of Commerce without World Bank—IMF conditionality. More broadly, the reform of exchange rate regimes in Africa is a case where conditionality was effective. Fifteen years ago, there was a widespread practice of manipulating and overvaluing exchange rates. The transformation that has happened in this area is a result of the determination of governments and a strong push by bilateral and multilateral donors (with the IMF playing the leading role). This reform has probably been the most important step in fighting corruption as well. Improvements in fiscal discipline and governance are other examples of the successful application of conditionality.

However, traditional concerns about paying for reforms that were not implemented should also be acknowledged. This issue has certainly affected conditionality and needs to be recognized. In addition, we now recognize that the tendency to impose more conditionality when working with poorly performing countries was a mistake. There is no need to be defensive about conditionality as it was implemented in the past, or to say that changes are not necessary.

Recent practical experience has shown some new problems emerging with the increased delivery of aid through budget support, such as the expansion of donor-coordinated performance assessment frameworks and long matrices. The donor community needs to assess how effective budget support is as an instrument, taking into consideration all these aspects. A case in point is a recent situation in Mozambique, where the government limited the number of indicators to 50. In addition to the number of indicators, there are serious challenges related to capacity for implementation and monitoring, quality of selected indicators, and so on.

Donors need to constantly reevaluate the effectiveness of their conditionality and make sure it does not create new types of problems for recipient countries. The World Bank's review of its experience with conditionality refers to how the Bank approaches conditionality, identifying what is needed to increase its effectiveness. We have also been summarizing some of the emerging advice on good practices in the use of memoranda of understanding (MOUs) among budget support groups.

Selectivity, Trust, and Contractual Approach to Conditionality

Providing governments with a set of policy options, putting these options in a political context, and coordinating support among the donors are complex issues that are typically discussed among budget support practitioners. The debate has also identified a powerful message about the need for selectivity and for a focus on policies where the impact is largely predictable, while policy decisions are informed by sound analytical work.

Trust is a subject rarely discussed among development partners. It deserves more attention not only at the theoretical level but even more at the country level, so that development partners come to understand better how to build trust and reinforce it. Clearly, when a government does a good job, it increases the confidence of the development community that the country does meet the test and that donors should provide needed support for the budget.

Delegation of authority to the field is a related issue. There has been an enormous improvement in this area and more initiative and decision-making power have been delegated to the field level. This reinforces the notion about the importance of trust.

The concept of a contractual relationship, too, has implications for conditionality and for how the dialogue between partners is managed. For example, reaching an agreement between the partners when there is a track record of solid implementation, and then releasing the tranches as agreed, reflects the contractual sense of the relationship between donors and recipient countries.

Country Performance

Based on country performance, three groups of countries can be distinguished in the African context. The first group includes postconditionality performers: Mozambique, Tanzania, Uganda, and perhaps Ghana and Ethiopia, where there is very strong evidence of leadership and progress. Some of the countries in this group have made more progress than others. It is very important to understand *how* these countries made progress and how their experiences could be transferred to other countries.

The intermediate group of countries—mid-performers—includes Zambia and Malawi. The issue of trust is particularly relevant to these two countries, related to the risk of donors becoming part of the problem rather than part of the solution. These are countries where there is a possibility of expanding support, provided this is done correctly and within a more robust framework.

The third group of countries includes weaker performers and fragile states, which are often not thoroughly discussed. There are credible arguments that economic policies are key constraints on development and poverty reduction in these countries. Emerging experience suggests that these are countries where project-level work is not going to solve the underlying problems. However, due to the complexity of the work with these countries and frustrations with their lack of progress, they have rarely received the attention they deserve.

Consistent Approach to Strengthening Financial Management Is Needed

Financial management is very important in the context of budget support. Donors as a group should make additional efforts to support more consistent performance at the country level. The resources devoted to this purpose seem adequate, but donors have too often approached the reform of public financial management in a piecemeal way, from the perspective of their individual institutional requirements, rather than taking a more coherent and demand-driven approach that would support governments' efforts to put in place stronger public financial management systems.

Good Financial Management Reinforces Credibility

The need for credibility and control of fiduciary risks requires some basic conditions to be put in place in order for donors to proceed with budget support. Sound financial management plays a key role in the credibility of programs. The issue of a minimum standard has often featured in the debate on this topic. The World Bank's approach in countries with deficient fiduciary systems has been to support government measures to address those weaknesses, including through budget support where appropriate. Other institutions have other processes, but we all have to recognize that sound financial management is an important factor in the credibility of an overall program.

Donors need to consider constantly how they can work with these countries and limit the risks to acceptable levels. In certain circumstances, the donor community has been prepared to take such risks. Timor-Leste has been one example, and Afghanistan is a case where a much larger risk was taken by the World Bank. These cases are now seen as success stories. Their experience could be used for exploring the possibility of piloting the approach with some African countries, even in those with some major fiduciary challenges, always provided that governments have a credible program to address them.

Progress in Donor Harmonization Is Evident

Views differ on what donor harmonization has achieved thus far. In my view, the evidence shows that while many challenges remain, significant progress has been made in this area in a number of countries. The opinions of many practitioners from recipient countries have confirmed that progress on harmonization and budget support has been much faster than in some other areas of work.

Good Coordination and Planning Can Contribute to Better Predictability

Governments themselves can do a lot to improve the predictability of resources received as budget support. Coherent and clear signals from government about when it needs to receive the resources, and for what exact purposes, would provide clear incentives for donors to reorganize themselves and deliver financial support as planned. This does not remove the pressure on donors to make their assistance more predictable. To achieve this goal requires a more systematic and robust longer-term framework for aid delivery.

Results-Based Approach Reinforces the Need for Better Coordination

Both recipient countries and donors are engaged in ensuring that an agreed program produces results. Though the two groups have approached this goal in different ways, both face substantial pressure to deliver results. This is a key challenge for the World Bank, related to its development policy lending as well as its sector and project lending. There is strong determination within the institution to make the links with results. Achievement of results has an important broader context. Ultimately the question of attribution to an individual organization does not make much sense, because in many of the areas where the Bank is involved, the overall success is a result of joint efforts by donors, and the government is the most important actor.

References

Adam, C. S., and S. O'Connell. 1999. "Aid, Taxation, and Development in Sub-Saharan Africa", *Economics and Politics* 11: 225-254.

Adam, C. S., and Jan Willem Gunning. 2002. "Redesigning the Aid Contract: Donors' Use of Performance Indicators in Uganda", *World Development* 30: 2045-2056.

Adam, C. S., and David Bevan. 2003. *Aid, Public Expenditure, and Dutch Disease.* United Kingdom Department for International Development-Uganda.

Adam, C. S., G. Chambas, P. Guillaumont, S. Guillaumont Jeanneney, and J. W. Gunning. 2004. "Performance-based Conditionality: a European Perspective", *World Development* 32 (6): 1059-1070.

Aizenman, Joshua, Yeonho Lee, and Yeongseop Rhee. 2004. "International Reserves Management and Capital Mobility in a Volatile World: Policy Considerations and a Case Study of Korea." UCSC Center for International Economics Working Paper 04-10.

Aizenman, Joshua, and Nancy Marion. 2004. "International Reserve Holdings with Sovereign Risk and Costly Tax Collection", *The Economic Journal* 114 (497): 569-91.

Alesina, Alberto, and Dollar, David. 2000. "Who Gives Foreign Aid to Whom and Why?" *Journal of Economic Growth* 5: 33-64.

Allen, Richard, Salvatore Schiavo-Campo, and Thomas Columkill Garrity. 2004. "Assessing and Reforming Public Financial Management: A New Approach." Washington, DC: World Bank.

Alonso, Rosa, and Hoa Ngo. 2004. *Vietnam's Comprehensive Growth and Poverty-Reduction Strategy and the Budget.* Washington, DC: World Bank.

Alonso, Rosa, and Jan Walliser. 2004. *Fiscal Aspects of PRSP Implementation in Burkina Faso.* Washington, DC: World Bank.

Alonso, Rosa, and Robert Utz. 2003. *Fiscal Aspects of PRSP Implementation in Tanzania.* Washington, DC: World Bank.

Andersen, Thomas, Henrik Hansen, and Thomas Markussen. 2004. "US Politics and World Bank Lending." http://www.econ.ku.dk/okotand/images/IDA050804.pdf.

Andersen, Thomas, Thomas Harr, and FinnTarp. 2004. "US Politics and IMF Lending." Discussion paper 04-11, Institute of Economics, University of Copenhagen.

Arrow, Kenneth. 1972. "Gifts and Exchanges", *Philosophy and Public Affairs* 1 (4): 343-362.

Asian Development Bank/Japan Bank for International Cooperation/World Bank. 2005. "Aid Effectiveness in East Asia – Joint Efforts of Partner Countries, Asian Development Bank, Japan Bank for International Cooperation and the World Bank." Distributed at the Second High-level Forum on Aid Effectiveness, February 28-March 2, 2005, Paris, France.

Azam, J.-P., and J.-J. Laffont. 2003. "Contracting for Aid", *Journal of Development Economics* 70: 25-58.

Baldacci, Emanuele, Benedict Clements, Sanjeev Gupta, and Qiang Cui. 2004. "Social Spending, Human Capital, and Growth in Developing Countries: Implications for Achieving the MDGs" IMF Working Paper 217. November. Washington, DC: International Monetary Fund.

Barr, Abigail. 2003. "Trust and Expected Trustworthiness: Experimental Evidence from Zimbabwean Villages", *Economic Journal* 113: 614-631.

Besley, T., and N. Roberto Zagha (eds.). 2005. *Development Challenges in the 1990s: Leading Policymakers Speak from Experience.* Washington, DC: World Bank.

Booth, David. 2004. ODI. *Fighting Poverty in Africa: Are PRSPs Making a Difference?*

Booth, David. 2005. *Poverty Monitoring Systems: An Analysis of Institutional Arrangements in Tanzania.* ODI Working Paper 247. London: Overseas Development Institute.

Booth, David, and Xavier Nsabagasani. 2005. *Poverty Monitoring Systems: An Analysis of Institutional Arrangements in Uganda.* ODI Working Paper 246. London: Overseas Development Institute.

Bougheas, S., I. Dasgupta, and O. Morrissey. 2005. "Tough Love or Unconditional Charity?" CREDIT Research Paper 05/08. University of Nottingham, School of Economics.

Brautigam, Deborah. 2000. *Aid Dependence and Governance.* Stockholm: Almqvist and Wiksell International.

Brautigam, Deborah, and Stephen Knack. 2004. "Foreign Aid, Institutions, and Governance in Sub-Saharan Africa", *Economic Development and Cultural Change* 52 (2): 255-286.

Broback, Ulrika, and Stefan Sjolander. 2002. "Program Support and Public Finance Management: A New Role for Bilateral Donors in Poverty Strategy Work." Sida Studies No. 6. Stockholm: Swedish International Development Agency.

Brooks, Peter. 2003. "Study of Measures Used to Address Weaknesses in Public Financial Management Systems in the Context of Policy-based Support." April. Bannock Consulting for the Public Expenditure and Financial Accountability (PEFA) Program. www.pefa.org.

Brown, A., F. Naschold, T. Conway, and A. Fozzard. 2000. "Aid Transaction Costs in Vietnam." Report for DFID. London: Overseas Development Institute.

Brownbridge, Martin. 2000. "Is Budget Deficit Reduction Necessary?" Uganda Ministry of Finance, Planning, and Economic Development. Mimeo.

Bulíř, A., and A. J. Hamann. 2003. "Aid Volatility: An Empirical Assessment." *IMF Staff Papers* 50 (1): 64-89.

Bulíř, A., and A. J. Hamann. 2005. "Volatility of Development Aid: From the Frying Pan into the Fire?" Paper presented at the Conference on Foreign Aid and Macroeconomic Management, Maputo, March 14-15.

Burke, Robert V., David Colin, Aldén J. Jirón Z., and Lissette González. 2005. "General budget support: An alternative assistance approach. Nicaragua country case study." Final draft report. Washington, DC: USAID.

Burnside, Craig, and David Dollar. 2000. "Aid, Policies and Growth," *The American Economic Review* 90 (4): 847-868.

Canadian International Development Agency (CIDA). 2004. "CIDA's Action Plan to Promote Harmonization, 2004-2005." September 2004. Ottawa: CIDA.

Cashin, Liang, and C. J. McDermott. 2000. "How Persistent are Shocks to World Commodity Prices?" *IMF Staff Papers* 47 (2): 177-217.

Chabal, Patrick, and Jean-Pascal Daloz. 1999. *Africa Works: Disorder as a Political Instrument.* London: James Currey.

Chiche, Mailan, with Gilles Hervio. 2004. "Budget Support Donor Groups: Summary Analysis". Report by the EC Co-chair of the Budget Support Working Group of the SPA, Brussels.

Christiansen, Karin, with Ingie Hovland. 2003. *The PRSP Initiative: Multilateral Policy Change and the Role of Research.* ODI Working Paper 216. London: Overseas Development Institute.

Clemens, Michael A. 2004. "The Long Walk to School: International Education Goals in Historical Perspective." CGD Working Paper No. 37. Washington, DC: Center for Global Development.

Clemens, Michael A., Charles A. Kenny, and Todd J. Moss. 2004. "The Trouble with the MDGs: Confronting Expectations of Aid and Development Success." CGD Working Paper No. 40. Washington, DC: Center for Global Development.

Clemens, Michael A., Steven Radelet, and Rikhil Bhavani. 2004. "Counting Chickens When They Hatch: the Short-term Effect of Aid on Growth". CGD Working Paper No. 44. Washington, DC: Center for Global Development.

Collier, P. 1997. "The Failure of Conditionality." In C. Gwin and J. Nelson (eds.), *Perspectives on Aid and Development.* Washington DC: Overseas Development Council.

Collier, P. 1999. "Aid Dependency: A Critique," *Journal of African Economies* 8 (4): 528-45.

Collier, P., P. Guillaumont, S. Guillaumont Jeanneney, and J. W. Gunning. 1997. "Redesigning Conditionality", *World Development* 25: 1399-1407.

Collier, P., and J. W. Gunning and associates. 1999. *Trade Shocks in Developing Countries.* Oxford: Oxford University Press.

Collier, P., P. Guillaumont, S. Guillaumont Jeanneney, and J. W. Gunning. 1999. "Reforming Stabex", *The World Economy* 22: 669–82.

Collier, P., and J. Dehn. 2001. "Aid, Shocks, and Growth". Policy Research Working Paper No. 2688. Washington, DC: World Bank.

Collier, P., and D. Dollar. 2001. "Can the World Cut Poverty in Half? How Policy Reform and Effective Aid Can Meet International Development Goals", *World Development* 29: 1787-1802.

Collier, P., and D. Dollar. 2002. "Aid Allocation and Poverty Reduction", *European Economic Review* 46: 1475-1500.

Commission for Africa. 2005. *Our Common Interest.* www.commissionforafrica.org.

Cordella, T., and G. Dell'Ariccia. 2003. "Budget Support vs. Project Aid", IMF Working Paper WP/03/88. Washington, DC: International Monetary Fund.

Corre, G. 2004. "Parliaments and Development: The Icing on the Cake?" *InBrief*, No. 9, October. Maastricht: European Centre for Development Policy Management (ECDPM).

Craig, D., and D. Porter. 2003. "Poverty Reduction Strategy Papers: A New Convergence", *World Development* 31 (1).

Crown Agents Institutional Development Group. 2001. "Donor Accountability Study." http://www.crownagents.com/psr/default.asp?step=4&pid=876.

Daima Associates and Overseas Development Institute (ODI). 2005. "Joint Evaluation of General Budget Support: Tanzania 1995-2004." Report to the Government of Tanzania and PRBS Development Partners. Dar es Salaam: Daima Associates Ltd., and London: Overseas Development Institute.

Danish International Development Cooperation Agency (DANIDA). 2003. "Methodological Guidelines for Budget Support: Guidance Note on the Provision of Budget Support." October. Copenhagen: DANIDA.

de Renzio, Paolo, David Booth, Andrew Rogerson, and Zaza Curran. 2004. "Incentives for Harmonization and Alignment in Aid Agencies", Report to the DAC Working Party on Aid Effectiveness. November. London: Overseas Development Institute.

Denkabe, Philip. 2003. "Policy, Aid, and Growth: A Threshold Hypothesis." Center for Global Development seminar paper, http://www.cgdev.org/Events/Index.cfm?EventID=66.

Department for International Development, UK (DFID) 2002. *Mozambique country assistance plan 2002–2007. (Interim.)* www.fco.gov.uk/Files/kfile/MZ%20Country%20Assistance%20Plan.pdf.

Department for International Development, UK (DFID). 2004a. "Partnerships for Poverty Reduction: Changing Aid 'Conditionality'". Draft (October).

Department for International Development, UK (DFID). 2004b. "Managing Fiduciary Risk When Providing Direct Budget Support." How-to Note, 22 September. www.dfid.gov.uk/pubs/files/pfma-fiduciaryrisk.pdf.

Department for International Development, UK (DFID). 2004c. "Terms of Reference for the Joint Evaluation of General Budget Support." Final version, 5 May.

Department for International Development, UK (DFID). 2004d. "Poverty Reduction Budget Support". Policy Paper. London: DFID.

Department for International Development, UK (DFID). 2005. *Joint Evaluation of General Budget Support 1994-2004 – Inception Report.* London: DFID.

Department for International Development (DFID), and HM Treasury, UK. 2003. "International Finance Facility". January. London: HM Treasury and DFID. http://www.hm-treasury.gov.uk/media/790/14/ACF6FB.pdf.

Department for International Development (UK), Foreign and Commonwealth Office, and HM Treasury (DFID/FCO/HMT). 2005. *Partnerships for Poverty Reduction: Rethinking Conditionality.* DFID/FCO/HMT: London.

Deutsche Gesellschaft für Technische Zusammenarbeit (GTZ). 2004. "National Monitoring of Poverty Reduction Strategies/PRSPs." Governance and Democracy Division, GTZ.

Devarajan, S., D. Dollar, and T. Holmgren. 2001. *Aid and Reform in Africa.* Washington, DC: World Bank.

Devarajan, S., and R. Reinikka. 2004. "Making Services Work for the Poor", *Journal of African Economies 13 (supplement 1)*: 142-166.

Development Committee. 2004. Development Committee Communiqué, Joint Ministerial Committee of the Boards of Governors of the World Bank and International Monetary Fund on the Transfer of Real Resources to Developing Countries. October 2. Washington, DC: World Bank.

Dijkstra, Geske. 1999. *Program Aid, Policies and Politics. Program Aid and Conditionality.* Sida Evaluation 99/17:10. Stockholm: Sida (Swedish International Development Cooperation Agency).

Dijkstra, Geske. 2005. "The PRSP Approach and the Illusion of Improved Aid Effectiveness: Lessons from Bolivia, Honduras, and Nicaragua", *Development Policy Review* 23 (4).

Doan Hung Minh and de Lestrange, Alexandre. 1998. "Politique économique et emergence de groupes industriels au Viêtnam," *Revue économique* 49 (1) : 291-302.

Dollar, D., and L Pritchett. 1998. *Assessing Aid: What Works, What Doesn't, and Why. A World Bank policy research report.* New York: Oxford University Press.

Dollar, D., and J. Svensson. 1998. *What Explains the Success or Failure of Structural Adjustment Programs?* World Bank Development Research Group. Washington, DC: World Bank.

Dollar, David, and Victoria Levin. 2004. "The Increasing Selectivity of Foreign Aid, 1984-2002." Policy Research Working Paper No. 3299. Washington, DC: World Bank.

Driscoll, Ruth, Karin Christiansen, and David Booth, with Paolo de Renzio, Samantha Smith, and Katarina Herneryd. 2005. *Progress Reviews and Performance Assessment in Poverty*

Reduction Strategies and Budget Support: A Survey of Current Thinking and Practice. London and Tokyo: Overseas Development Institute/Japan International Cooperation Agency.

Driscoll, Ruth, with Alison Evans. 2005. "Second-generation Poverty Reduction Strategies: New Opportunities and Emerging Issues", *Development Policy Review* 23 (1).

Duflo, E. 2004. "Evaluating the Impact of Development Aid Programs: the Role of Randomized Evaluations". Paper presented at the Second Annual AFD-EUDN Conference: Development Aid: Why and How? November 25, Paris.

Duong Duc Ung. 2005. "Vietnam's Experience in Strengthening Procurement and Public Financial Management Systems in Harmonization, Alignment, and Capacity Development." Presented at the Second High-level Forum on Aid Effectiveness, February 28 – March 2, 2005, Paris, France.

Edwards, Sebastian, and Sweder van Wijnbergen. 1989. "Disequilibrium and Structural Adjustment." In Hollis Chenery and T. N. Srinivasan, eds., *Handbook of Development Economics, Vol. II.* Amsterdam: North-Holland.

Entwistle, Janet. 2005, forthcoming. *Country Ownership of Poverty Reduction Strategies: The Experience of Five Countries.* Washington, DC: World Bank.

European Commission (EC). 2000. *Cotonou Partnership Agreement.* Art. 60: Scope of financing; Art. 61: Nature of financing; Art. 66: Support for debt relief; Art. 67: Structural adjustment.

European Commission (EC). 2001. "Special Report on the Use of Counterpart Funds from Structural Adjustment Support Earmarked for Budget Aid," *Official Journal of the European Commission* September 14.

European Commission (EC). 2003a. "Variable Tranches in General Budget Support: Implementation Guidelines and Evaluation". Brussels: EC, Directorate General for Development.

European Commission. 2003b. "Guide to Programming and Implementation of Budget Support for Third Countries." Internal document prepared by EC-AIDCO, DEV, and RELEX. March. Brussels: EC., Directorate General for Development.

European Commission. 2005. *Budget Support: An Innovative Approach to Conditionality.* http://www.spa-psa.org/resources/2005/EC_GBS_VT_Review.pdf.

Evans, A., and E. Coyle. 2002. *Donor Alignment with the PRSP: Progress with Programmatic Support.* DAC Task Force on Donor Practices, 5th Plenary Meeting, October 8-9.

Faulkner, Paul. 2004. "A Problem of Trust." Unpublished paper. Department of Philosophy, University of Sheffield.

Foster, Mick. 2005. *Improving the Medium to Long-term Predictability of Aid.* London. Overseas Development Institute

Fozzard, Adrian. 2002. "How, When and Why Does Poverty Get Budget Priority? Poverty Reduction Strategy and Public Expenditure in Mozambique." *ODI Working Paper* 167. London: Overseas Development Institute.

Frantz, Brian. 2004. *General Budget Support in Tanzania: A Snapshot of its Effectiveness.* Washington, DC: USAID. http://pdf.dec.org/pdf_docs/PNADA029.pdf.

Gabriele, A. K. Baratav, and A. Parikh. 2000. "Instability and Volatility of Flows to Developing Countries," *The World Economy* 23 (8): 1030-56.

Gambetta, Diego. 1988. *Trust: Making and Breaking Co-operative Relations.* London: Basil Blackwell.

Gelb, Alan, and associates. 1990. *Oil Windfalls, Blessing or Curse?* Oxford University Press.

Gelb, Alan, Brian Ngo, and Xiao Ye. 2004. "Implementing Performance-based Aid in Africa." Africa Region Working Paper No. 77. Washington, DC: World Bank.

Gemmell, N., and M. McGillivray. 1998. "Aid and Tax Instability and the Government Budget Constraint in Developing Countries" CREDIT Research Paper 98/1, University of Nottingham.

Ghani, Ashraf, and Clare Lockhart. 2005. "Closing the Sovereignty Gap." Presentation to Senior-level Forum on Development Effectiveness in Fragile States (Organization for Economic Cooperation and Development, European Commission, United Nations Development Program, World Bank, UK Department for International Development), London, 13/14 January.

Gill, I. S., and T. Pugatch (eds.). 2005. *At the Frontlines of Development: Reflections from the World Bank*. Washington, DC: World Bank.

Glaeser, Edward, David Laibson, Jose Scheinkman, and Christine Soutter. 2000. "Measuring Trust", *Quarterly Journal of Economics* 115: 811-845.

Glaeser, Edward, David Laibson, and Bruce Sacerdote. 2002. "An Economic Approach to Social Capital", *Economic Journal* 112: 437-458.

Gomanee, K., O. Morrissey, P. Mosley, and A. Verschoor. 2005. "Aid, Government Expenditure, and Aggregate Welfare" *World Development* 33 (3): 355-370.

Gomanee, K., S. Girma, and O. Morrissey. 2006 (forthcoming). "Aid and Growth in Sub-Saharan Africa: Accounting for Transmission Mechanisms", *Journal of International Development.*

Gould, Jeremy, and Julia Ojanen. 2003. *'Merging in the Circle': The Politics of Tanzania's Poverty Reduction Strategy*. Policy Paper 2/2003. University of Helsinki, Institute of Development Studies.

Guillaumont, P., and L. Chauvet. 2001. "Aid and Performance: a Reassessment", *Journal of Development Studies* 37: 66-92.

Gunning, J. W. 2001. "Rethinking Aid." In Boris Pleskovic and Nicholas Stern, eds., *Annual World Bank Conference on Development Economics 2000*. Washington, DC: World Bank.

Gunning, J. W. 2004. "Why Give Aid?" Paper presented at the Second Annual AFD-EUDN Conference: Development Aid: Why and How? November 25, Paris.

Hanlon, Joseph. 2002. "Are Donors to Mozambique Promoting Corruption?" Paper submitted to the conference, Towards a New Political Economy of Development, 3–4 July 2002, Sheffield, UK. www.ipocafrica.org/cases/cardoso/mozcorr/hanlon.pdf.

Hanlon, Joseph. 2004. "How Northern Donors Promote Corruption – Tales From the New Mozambique" October. Corner House Briefing Paper 33, UK.

Hanmer, L., and F. Naschold. 2000. "Attaining the International Development Targets: Will Growth Be Enough?" *Development Policy Review* 18 (December): 11-36.

Hansen, Henrik, and Finn Tarp. 2000. "Aid Effectiveness Disputed," *Journal of International Development* 12 (April): 375-388.

Hansen, Henrik, and Finn Tarp. 2001. "Aid and Growth Regressions," *Journal of Development Economics* 64 (April): 547-70.

Harrigan, Jane. 1995. "Malawi." In P. Mosley, J. Harrigan, and J. Toye, *Aid and Power*. 2 vols. London: Routledge.

Harrigan, Jane. 2003. "U-turns and Full Circles; Two Decades of Agricultural Reform in Malawi, 1981-2000", *World Development* 31: 847-863.

Harrison, Graham. 2001. "Post-conditionality Politics and Administrative Reform: Reflections on the Cases of Uganda and Tanzania", *Development and Change* 32 (4).

Harvey, Charles. 2002. "Review of Swiss Budget Support to Mozambique." Institute of Development Studies, University of Sussex.

Hauck, V. O. Hasse, and M. Koppensteiner. 2005. *EC Budget Support: Thumbs Up or Down?* ECDPM Discussion Paper 63. Maastricht: European Centre for Development Policy Management.

Haussmann, R., D. Rodrik, and A. Velasco. 2004. "Growth Diagnostics." John F. Kennedy School of Government, Harvard University.

Hermann, R., K. Burger, and H. P. Smit. 1990. "Commodity Policy: Price Stabilization versus Financing." In Sapsford, David, and L. Alan Winters, eds., *Primary Commodity Prices: Economic Models and Policy.* Cambridge: Cambridge University Press.

Hicks, Norman. 2004. "Monitoring Performance in Poverty Reduction Support Credits: A Note on Best Practice." Poverty Reduction and Economic Management Network. Washington, DC: World Bank.

Hicks, Norman, and Klia Bassing. 2004. "Monitoring Performance in Poverty Reduction Support Credits: A Note on Best Practice." Washington, DC: World Bank.

High-level Forum (2005), "Paris Declaration on Aid Effectiveness: Ownership, Harmonization, Alignment, Results, and Mutual Accountability". DCD/DAC/EFF. Paris: Organization for Economic Cooperation and Development. http://insightstage01/policydivision/teams/prs/harmonization/FINALPARISDECLARATION2005.pdf.

HM Treasury. 2004. 'The International Finance Facility', *Journal of International Development* 16 (August): 865-879.

Holmgren, Torgny, Louis Kasekende, Michael Atingi-Ego, and Daniel Ddamulira. 1999. "Aid and Reform in Uganda." Country Case Study. Washington, DC: World Bank. http://www.worldbank.org/research/aid/africa/uganda.pdf.

Holvoet, N., and R. Renard. 2005. "Belgian Aid Policies in the 1990s". In Hoebink, P., and O. Stokke (eds.), *Perspectives on European Development Co-operation.* Research EADI Studies in Development. London: Routledge.

International Monetary Fund (IMF) and World Bank. 2003. *A Concept Note on Aligning Donor Budget Support with the PRSP Process.* (February.) Washington, DC: IMF and World Bank.

International Monetary Fund (IMF). 1998. "External Evaluation of the Enhanced Structural Adjustment Facility: Report by a Group of Independent Experts (K. Botchwey, P. Collier, J. Gunning, and K. Hamada)." Washington DC: IMF.

International Monetary Fund (IMF). 2001. *Streamlining Structural Conditionality: Review of Initial Experience.* Washington, DC: IMF.

International Monetary Fund (IMF). 2004. *Increasing the Predictability of Flows of Donor Budget Support.* Washington, DC: IMF.

International Monetary Fund. 2005a. "The Macroeconomics of Managing Increased Aid Flows: Experiences of Low-income Countries and Policy Implications." SM/05/306. Washington, DC: International Monetary Fund.

International Monetary Fund (IMF). 2005b. *Review of the 2002 Conditionality Guidelines.* Washington, DC: IMF.

International Monetary Fund (IMF) and World Bank. 2004. *The Republic of Tanzania: Tracking Poverty-reducing Spending: Second Assessment and Action Plan.* Washington, DC: IMF and World Bank.

International Monetary Fund and World Bank. 2005. "Update on the Assessments and Implementation of Action Plans to Strengthen Capacity of Heavily Indebted Poor Countries to Track Poverty-reducing Spending." April.

International Monitoring Group. 2002. "Enhancing Aid Relationships in Tanzania: Report of the Independent Monitoring Group". Dar es Salaam: Economic and Social Research Foundation.

Ivanova, A. 2005. *Outcome-based Conditionality: the Role and Optimal Design.* International Monetary Fund, Sixth Jacques Polak Annual Research Conference, November 3. www.imf.org.

Japan Bank for International Cooperation (JBIC). 2005. *Medium-term Strategy for Overseas Economic Cooperation Operations by the Japan Bank for International Cooperation.* April. http://www.jbic.go.jp/english/oec/policy/index.php.

Johnson, J., and S. Wasty. 1986. "Country Commitment to Development Projects." World Bank Discussion Paper No. 4. Washington DC: World Bank.

Johnson, J., and S. Wasty 1993. "Borrower Ownership of Adjustment Programs and the Political Economy of Reform." *World Bank Discussion Paper* No. 199. Washington, DC: World Bank.

Johnston, Donald J., and Richard Manning. 2005. *Doing Aid Better – A Comment Piece.* Paris: Organization for Economic Cooperation and Development.

Judge, Lindsay, and Jeni Klugman, 2004. *The PRSP and Budget Linkages: The Case of Bolivia.* Washington, DC: World Bank.

Kahneman, Daniel. 2003. "Maps of Bounded Rationality: Psychology for Behavioral Economics", *American Economic Review* 93 (December), 1449-1475.

Kanbur, R., and T. Sandler, with K. Morrison. 1999. *The Future of Development Assistance: Common Pools and International Public Goods.* Policy Essay No. 25. Washington, DC: Overseas Development Council.

Kanbur, R., and M. Tuomala. 2003. "Incentives, Inequality, and the Allocation of Aid when Conditionality Doesn't Work: an Optimal Nonlinear Taxation Approach". Mimeo (June). Cornell University.

Kaufmann, Daniel. 2003. "Rethinking Governance: Empirical Lessons Challenge Orthodoxy." Discussion draft. Washington, DC: World Bank www.worldbank.org/wbi/governance/pubs/rethink_gov.html.

Killick, T. 1998. *Aid and the Political Economy of Change.* London: Routledge.

Killick, Tony, with Ramani Gunatilaka, and Ana Marr. 1998. *Aid and the Political Economy of Policy Change.* London: Routledge/Overseas Development Institute.

Killick, Tony. 2004. "Politics, Evidence, and the New Aid Agenda." *Development Policy Review* 22 (1): 5–29.

Klugman, Jeni, and Robert Taliercio. 2003. *The PRSP and Budget Linkages: The Case of Cambodia.* Washington, DC: World Bank.

Knack, Stephen, and Philip Keefer. 1997. "Does Social Capital Have An Economic Payoff?" "A Cross-country Investigation" *Quarterly Journal of Economics* 112: 1251-1288.

Koeberle, Stefan. 2003. "Should Policy-based Lending Still Involve Conditionality?" *World Bank Research Observer* 18 (2): 249-273.

Koeberle, Stefan. 2005. "Conditionality under What Conditions?" Chapter 5 in Koeberle, S., and others (eds.), *Conditionality Revisited: Concepts, Experiences, and Lessons.* Washington, DC: World Bank.

Koeberle, Stefan, Harold Bedoya, Peter Silarszky, and Gero Verheyen (eds.) 2005. *Conditionality Revisited: Concepts, Experiences, and Lessons.* Washington, DC: World Bank.

Koenker, Roger, and Gilbert Basset. 1978. "Regression Quantiles," *Econometrica* 46 (1): 33-50.

Kostopoulos, Christos. 1999. "Progress in Public Expenditure Management in Africa: Evidence from World Bank Surveys," Africa Region Working Paper Series No. 1. Washington, DC: World Bank.

Krakowski, M. 2004. *Pitfalls of "Automatic" Donor Coordination – The Malawi Experience 2000-2004.* Hamburgisches Welt-Wirtschafts-Archiv (Hamburg Institute of International Economics), Report No. 242.

Kreps, David, Paul Milgrom, John Roberts, and Robert Wilson. 1982. "Rational Cooperation in the Finitely Repeated Prisoner's Dilemma", *Journal of Economic Theory*. 27: 245-252.

Lanser, P. 2004. "Inventory of Program Aid 1992-2001; Preparatory Study for the Planned Joint Evaluation of General Budget Support." Rotterdam: ECORYS-NEI Research and Consulting.

Lavergne, Réal. 2003. "Program-based Approaches: A New Way of Doing Business." *Development Express 3*, Canadian International Development Agency Policy Branch.www.acdicida.ru/publications/EExpress_Dec03.pdf.

Lawson, A., D. Booth, M. Msuya, S. Wangwe, and T. Williamson. 2005. *Does General Budget Support Work? Evidence from Tanzania*. London: Overseas Development Institute.

Lawson, Andrew, and David Booth. 2004. *Evaluation Framework for General Budget Support. Report to Management Group for the Joint Evaluation of General Budget Support.* London: Overseas Development Institute. www.odi.org.uk/pppg/activities/aid/budget/Evaluation_of_General_Budget_Support-Evaluation_Framework.pdf.

Le Houerou, Philippe, and Robert Taliercio. 2002. "Medium-term Expenditure Frameworks: From Concept to Practice: Preliminary Lessons from Africa". Africa Region Working Paper Series No. 28. Washington, DC: World Bank.

Leandro, J., H. Schafer, and G. Frontini. 1999. "Towards a More Effective Conditionality: An Operational Framework", *World Development* 27: 285-300.

Lensink, Robert, and Oliver Morrissey. 2000. "Aid Instability as a Measure of Uncertainty and the Positive Impact of Aid on Growth," *Journal of Development Studies* 36 (3).

Levy, Brian, and Sahr Kpundeh (eds.). 2004. *Building State Capacity in Africa: New Approaches, Emerging Lessons*. Washington, DC: World Bank.

Lieberson, Joseph. 2004. *What Conditions Favor the Success of General Budget Support? Mozambique Country Case Study.* Evaluation Brief No. 11. Washington, DC: USAID. http://pdf.dec.org/pdf_docs/PNACU999.pdf.

Lieberson, Joseph, Diane Ray, and Brian Frantz. 2004. *What Conditions Favor the Success of General Budget Support and Sector Program Assistance? Malawi Country Case Study.* PPC Evaluation Working Paper No. 12. Washington, DC: USAID. http://pdf.dec.org/pdf_docs/PNADA356.pdf.

Lieberson, Joseph, Diane Ray, and Brian Frantz. 2004. *General Budget Support and Sector Program Assistance: Malawi Country Case Study.* PPC Evaluation Working Paper No. 12. Washington, DC: USAID. http://pdf.dec.org/pdf_docs/PNADA356.pdf.

Lieberson, Joseph, Diane Ray, and Maxine Lunn. 2004. *General Budget Support: An Alternative Assistance Approach. Mozambique Country Case Study.* PPC Evaluation Working Paper No. 18. Washington, DC: USAID. http://pdf.dec.org/pdf_docs/PNACW878.pdf.

Lister, S., T. Williamson, J. Steffensen, and W. Baryabanoha. 2005, forthcoming. *Joint Evaluation of General Budget Support, 1994–2004: Uganda Country Report.*

Lockwood, Matthew. 2005. *The State They're In: An Agenda for International Action on Poverty*, London: ITDG Publishing.

Luthra, M. 2004. *Alternative Perspectives on the Role of Trade, Investment, and Business Solutions in Poverty Reduction in Africa.* London: Department of Trade and Industry, UK Trade and Investment. <www.uktradeinvest.gov.uk>

Malick, Jeff, Anne Beasley, and Andrew Melnyk. 2005. "Program Assistance: The Democratic Republic of Timor-Leste Country Case Study." USAID, Washington, DC.

Martens, Bertin. 2005. "Why Do Aid Agencies Exist?" *Development Policy Review* 23 (6).

Martens, Bertin, Uwe Mummert, Peter Murrell, and Paul Seabright. 2002. *The Institutional Economics of Foreign Aid.* Cambridge: Cambridge University Press.

McGillivray, M., and O. Morrissey. 2000. "Aid Fungibility in *Assessing Aid*: Red Herring or True Concern?" *Journal of International Development* 12 (3): 413-428.

McGillivray, M., and O. Morrissey. 2001. "Aid Illusion and Public Sector Fiscal Behavior", *Journal of Development Studies* 37 (6): 118-136.

McGillivray, M., and O. Morrissey. 2004. "Fiscal Effects of Aid." In Addison, T., and A. Roe (eds.), *Fiscal Policy for Development: Poverty, Reconstruction, and Growth*. Basingstoke: Palgrave Macmillan in association with UNU-WIDER.

Mecagni, Mario. 1999. "The Causes of Program Interruptions". Chapter 9 in H. Bredenkamp and S. Schadler (eds.), *Economic Adjustment and Reform in Low-income Countries: Studies by the Staff of the International Monetary Fund*. Washington, DC: International Monetary Fund.

Miguel, E., and M. Kremer. 2004. "Worms: Identifying Impacts on Education and Health in the Presence of Treatment Externalities", *Econometrica* 72: 159-217.

Miovic, P. 2004. *Poverty Reduction Support Credits in Uganda: Results of a Stocktaking Study.* Washington, DC: World Bank.

Moore, M. 1998. Death without Taxes: Democracy, State Capacity, and Aid Dependence in the Fourth World. In M. Robinson and G. White (eds.), *The Democratic Developmental State: Political and Institutional Design*. Oxford: Oxford University Press.

Morrissey, O. 2004a. "Conditionality and Aid Effectiveness Reevaluated," *World Economy* 27 (2): 153-71.

Morrissey, O. 2004b. "Making Debt Relief Conditionality Pro-poor". Chapter 12 in T. Addison, H. Hansen, and F. Tarp (eds.), *Debt Relief for Poor Countries*. Basingstoke: Palgrave Macmillan in association with UNU-WIDER.

Morrissey, O. 2005a. "Alternatives to Conditionality in Policy-based Lending". Chapter 25 in S. Koeberle and others (eds.), *Conditionality Revisited: Concepts, Experiences, and Lessons*. Washington, DC: World Bank.

Morrissey, O. 2005b, "Whither Conditionality? Selectivity versus Monitoring". Paper presented at the UNU-WIDER Jubilee Conference, *WIDER. Thinking Ahead: The Future of Development Economics,* Helsinki 17-18 June 2005. www.wider.unu.edu.

Morrissey, Oliver, and Arjan Verschoor. 2002. "Is Ownership A Meaningful Concept in Policy Reform? Policy Learning and the Evolution of Pro-Poor Policies in Uganda". Unpublished paper.

Mosley, Paul, Jane Harrigan, and John Toye. 1995. *Aid and Power: the World Bank and Policy-based Lending*. 2 vols. London: Routledge.

Mosley, Paul, John Hudson, and Arjan Verschoor. 2004. "Aid, Poverty Reduction, and the 'New Conditionality'", *Economic Journal* 114: 217-243.

Mosley, P., and A. Suleiman. 2004. "Aid, Agriculture, and Poverty." Unpublished paper presented at HWWA conference, Hamburg. Forthcoming, *Review of Development Economics*.

Mosley, Paul, and John Hudson. 2005. "Assessing the Volatility of International Aid Flows". Unpublished report for UK Department for International Development.

National Audit Office, UK. 2002. "Department for International Development: A Review of Safeguards against the Misappropriation and Diversion of Aid."

Nellis, John, and Sunita Kikeri. 2002. "Privatization in Competitive Sectors: The Record to Date." World Bank Policy Research Working Paper No. 2860. Washington, DC: World Bank.

Netherlands Ministry of Foreign Affairs. 2003. "Inventory of Program Aid." Policy and Operations Evaluation Department.

Neumayer, Eric. 2003a. *The Pattern of Aid Giving*. London: Routledge.

Neumayer, Eric. 2003b. "The Determinants of Aid Allocation by Regional Multilateral Development Banks and the United Nations Agencies," *International Studies Quarterly* 47: 101-122.

Nilsson, Maria. 2004. *Effects of Budget Support—A Discussion of Early Evidence.* Department for Evaluation and Internal Audit, UTV Working Paper 2004: 4. Stockholm: Sida (Swedish International Development Cooperation Agency). <www.oecd.org/dataoecd/secure/14/24/35031496.pdf>

Nkuzu, Mwanza. 2004. *Financing Uganda's Poverty Reduction Strategy: Is Aid Causing More Pain than Gain?* IMF Working Paper WP/04/170. Washington, DC: International Monetary Fund.

Norwegian Agency for Development Cooperation (Norad). 2004. *From Earmarked Sector Support to General Budget Support: Development Partners' Experience.* http://www.norad.no/default.asp?V_ITEM_ID=2951.

Nyamugasira, Warren, and Rick Rowden. 2002. "New Strategies, Old Loan Conditions: Do the New IMF and World Bank Loans Support Countries' Poverty Reduction Strategies? The Case of Uganda". Kampala: Nongovernmental Organizations Forum, and Washington, DC: RESULTS Educational Fund.

O'Neill, Onora. 2002. *A Question of Trust*, Reith Lectures. London: BBC.

Odén, Bertil, and Tone Tinnes. 2003. "Tanzania: New Aid Modalities and Donor Harmonization." *NORAD Report* 8 (October). Oslo: Norad (Norwegian International Development Cooperation Agency).

Ohno, Izumi. 2002. *Diversifying PRSP – The Vietnamese Model for Growth-oriented Poverty Reduction.* (October.) Tokyo: National Graduate Institute for Policy Studies (GRIPS).

Ohno, Izumi, and Y. Niiya. 2005. *Good Donorship and the Choice of Aid Modalities – Matching Aid with Country Needs and Ownership.* Tokyo: GRIPS Development Forum.

Ojima, Yasuhisa. 2004. "Emerging Issues in Development Finance", *Traffic Engineering* 39, Special Issue, November. Tokyo.

Operations Evaluation Department, World Bank (OED). 2003. "Toward Country-led Development: A Multi-partner Evaluation of the Comprehensive Development Framework." Synthesis Report. Washington, DC: World Bank.

Operations Evaluation Department (OED), World Bank. 2004a. World Bank. *The Poverty Reduction Strategy Initiative: An Independent Evaluation of the World Bank's Support Through 2003.* Washington, DC: World Bank.

Operations Evaluation Department (OED), World Bank. 2004b. *Annual Review of Development Effectiveness 2003: The Effectiveness of Bank Support for Policy Reform.* Washington, DC: World Bank.

Organization for Economic Cooperation and Development (OECD). 1992. *Development Assistance Manual – DAC Principles for Effective Aid.* Paris: OECD.

Organization for Economic Cooperation and Development-Development Assistance Committee (OECD-DAC). 2003. *Harmonizing Donor Practices for Effective Aid Delivery.* DAC Guidelines and Reference Series. Paris: OECD Development Assistance Committee.

Organization for Economic Cooperation and Development-Development Assistance Committee OECD-DAC. 2004a. "Good Practice in Public Finance Management: Increasing the Predictability of Aid Flows." Draft, September. Paris: OECD.

Organization for Economic Cooperation and Development-Development Assistance Committee (OECD-DAC). 2004b. *Managing Aid: Practices of DAC Member Countries.* DCD/DAC (2004) 40, Paris: OECD.

Organization for Economic Cooperation and Development-Development Assistance Committee (OECD-DAC). 2004c. *Survey on Harmonization and Alignment: Measuring Aid Harmonization and Alignment in 14 Countries*. Preliminary Edition. Paris: OECD.

Organization for Economic Cooperation and Development-Development Assistance Committee (OECD-DAC). 2004d. "Good Practice Notes on Capacity Development in Procurement." Roundtable on Procurement. Paris: OECD/DAC.

Organization for Economic Cooperation and Development-Development Assistance Committee (OECD-DAC). 2005a. *Harmonizing Donor Practices for Effective Aid Delivery: Volume 2: Budget Support, Sector-wide Approaches, and Capacity Development in Public Financial Management*. A DAC Reference Document, DAC Guidelines and Reference Series. Paris: OECD. www.oecd.org/dac/harmonisingpractices.

Organization for Economic Cooperation and Development-Development Assistance Committee (OECD-DAC). 2005b. "Draft Good Practice Note on the Provision of Budgetary Support – A Public Financial Management Perspective". (January.) Paris: OECD.

Organization for Economic Cooperation and Development (OECD). 2005c. "Capacity Development in Public Financial Management." Chapter 4 in Volume 2, *Budget Support, Sector-wide Approaches and Capacity Development in Public Financial Management*. Paris: OECD.

Osei, Robert, Oliver Morrissey, and Robert Lensink. 2002. "The Volatility of Capital Inflows: Measures and Trends for Developing Countries," CREDIT Research Paper No. 02/20.

Ostrom, Elinor, Clark Gibson, Sujai Shivakumar, and Krister Andersson. 2002. *Aid, Incentives, and Sustainability: An Institutional Analysis of Development Cooperation*. Studies in Evaluation 02/01. Stockholm: Sida.

Overseas Development Institute (ODI). 2003. *A Review of Experience in Implementing Medium-term Expenditure Frameworks in a PRSP Context: A Synthesis of Eight Country Studies*. London: ODI.

Overseas Development Institute (ODI). 2004. *PRSP Annual Progress Reports and Joint Staff Assessments: A Review of Progress*. London: ODI.

Oxford Policy Management/Overseas Development Institute. 2003. *General Budget Support Evaluability Study*. Evaluation Report EV643, Vol. 1. London: Department for International Development.

Ozeki, Uzuru. 2004. "Program-based Approach Programs and Growth in Vietnam and Ghana – A Note on Comparative Policy Issues". June 12, 2004, compiled with notes for the presentation made by the author at LENPA Forum, June 1-3 in Tokyo, Japan, on "Program-based Approach in Asia – Adapting to Diversity".

Pallage, Stephane, and Michael Robe. 2001. "Foreign Aid and the Business Cycle", *Review of International Economics* 9 (4): 641-672.

Pallage, Stephane, and Michael Robe. 2003a. "Leland and Pyle Meet Foreign Aid? Adverse Selection and the Pro-cyclicality of Financial Aid Flows." CIRPEE Research Paper 03/27.

Pallage, Stephane, and Michael Robe. 2003b. "On the Welfare Cost of Economic Fluctuations in Developing Countries," *International Economic Review* 44 (2): 677-698.

Pallage, Stephane, Michael Robe, and Catherine Bérubé. 2004. "On the Potential of Foreign Aid as Insurance". CIRPEE Research Paper 04/04.

Pavigniani, Enrico. 2001. "Swamped in a SWAp? Experience-Inspired Remarks about Sector-Wide Approaches". Maputo, Mozambique.

Perry, Guillermo. 2003. "Can Fiscal Rules Help Reduce Macroeconomic Volatility in the Latin America and Caribbean Region?" Policy Research Working Paper No. 3080. Washington, DC: World Bank.

Piron, Laure-Hélène, with Alison Evans. 2004. *Politics and the PRSP Approach: Synthesis Paper*, London: Overseas Development Institute, ODI Working Paper 237.

Ravallion, M. 2001. "The Mystery of the Vanishing Benefits: an Introduction to Impact Evaluation", *World Bank Economic Review* 15: 115-140.

Ray, D. 1998. *Development Economics*. Princeton, NJ: Princeton University Press.

Reinikka, R., and J. Svensson. 2004. "Efficiency of Public Spending: New Microeconomic Tools to Assess Service Delivery." In T. Addison, and A. Roe (eds.), *Fiscal Policy for Development: Poverty, Reconstruction, and Growth*. Basingstoke: Palgrave Macmillan in association with UNU-WIDER.

Roberts, John. 2003. *Managing Public Expenditure for Development Results*," ODI Working Paper 203, February.

Rodrik, Dani, ed. 2003. *In Search of Prosperity: Analytic Narratives on Economic Growth*, Princeton, NJ: Princeton University Press.

Rodrik, Dani. 2003. "What Do We Learn from Country Narratives?" In Rodrik, Dani, ed. *In Search of Prosperity: Analytic Narratives on Economic Growth*. Princeton, NJ: Princeton University Press.

Stewart, Frances. 2003. "An Analysis of Poverty Reduction Strategy Papers". Paper presented to conference on the World Bank and IMF, Yale University, April. New Haven, CT: Yale University Press.

Stiglitz, Joseph. 1998. *Towards a New Paradigm for Development*. Prebisch Lecture at UNCTAD, October 19. http://www.unctad.org/en/docs/prebisch9th.en.pdf.

Stiglitz, Joseph. 2003. *Globalization and its Discontents*. London: Penguin.

Strategic Partnership with Africa (SPA) – Budget Support Working Group. 2005. *Survey of the Alignment of Budget Support and Balance of Payments Support with National PRS Processes*. (February.) Brussels and London: SPA.

Svensson, Jakob. 2000. "When is Foreign Aid Policy Credible? Aid Dependence and Conditionality," *Journal of Development Economics* 61: 61-84.

Svensson, Jakob. 2003. "Why Conditional Aid Does Not Work and What Can Be Done about It", *Journal of Development Economics* 70: 381-402.

Uganda Ministry of Finance and Bank of Uganda. 2005. "Export Sector Performance and Exchange rate Appreciation." Joint study by Macroeconomics Department, Ministry of Finance and Research Department, Bank of Uganda.

University of Birmingham. 2005. *Joint Evaluation of General Budget Support 1994–2004. Final Inception Report, 20 May 2005*. International Development Department, School of Public Policy. Birmingham. http://www.oecd.org/dataoecd/secure/.

USAID. 2004a. *USAID Anticorruption Strategy*. Washington, DC: USAID. <http://pdf.dec.org/pdf_docs/PDACA557.pdf>

USAID. 2004b. *US foreign aid: Meeting the Challenges of the Twenty-first Century*. White Paper. Washington, DC: USAID. http://pdf.dec.org/pdf_docs/PDABZ322.pdf.

USAID. 2005a. *The Automated Directives System (ADS)*. www.usaid.gov/policy/ads/.

United States Agency for International Development (USAID). 2005b. *General Budget Support: Key Findings of Five USAID Studies*. PPC Evaluation Paper No. 7.

van de Walle, Nicolas. 2001. *African Economies and the Politics of Permanent Crisis, 1979-1999*. Cambridge: Cambridge University Press.

van de Walle, Nicolas. 2005. *Overcoming Stagnation in Aid-dependent Countries*. Washington, DC: Global Development Center.

van der Willigen, Tessa, Alun H. Thomas, Tubagus Feridhanusetyawan, Uma Ramakrishnan, Steffen Reichold, James P. Walsh, and Juan Zalduendo. 2005. "Review of the 2002 Conditionality Guidelines". Washington, DC: International Monetary Fund.

Varangis, Panayotis, and Donald Larson. 1996. "Dealing with Commodity Price Uncertainty." Policy Research Working Paper No. 1. Washington, DC: World Bank.

Varangis, Panos, Sona Varma, Angelique dePlaa, and Vikram Nehru. 2004. "Exogenous Shocks in Low-income Countries: Economic Policy Issues and the Role of the International Community." Mimeo, Washington, DC: World Bank.

Vaughan, Megan. 1984. *The History of an African Famine: Malawi 1949*. Cambridge: Cambridge University Press.

White, H., and O. Morrissey. 1997. "Conditionality When Donor and Recipient Preferences Vary." *Journal of International Development* 9 (4): 497- 505.

White, Howard. 1999. *Dollars, Dialogue and Development. An Evaluation of Swedish Program aid.* Sida Evaluation 99/17. Stockholm: Sida (Swedish International Development Cooperation Agency). http://sida.org/Sida/articles/4700-4799/4782/pdf/utv99-17.pdf.

Whitely, Paul. 2000. "Economic Growth and Social Capital," *Political Studies* 48: 443-466.

Winters, A., N. McCulloch, and A. McKay. 2004. "Trade Liberalization and Poverty: The Evidence So Far," *Journal of Economic Literature* 42 (1): 72-115.

Wolfensohn, J. D. 1999. "A Proposal for a Comprehensive Development Framework." Speech, Washington, DC: World Bank.

World Bank. 1998. *Assessing Aid: What Works, What Doesn't, and Why.* Washington, DC: World Bank.

World Bank. 2001a. *Adjustment Lending Retrospective,* Report 22723, June 15. Washington, DC: World Bank.

World Bank. 2001b. *World Development Report 2002: Building Institutions for Markets.* New York, NY and Oxford, UK: Oxford University Press for the World Bank.

World Bank. 2002a. *Revised Country Procurement Assessment Report Procedures.* April. Washington, DC: World Bank.

World Bank. 2002b. "Taming Leviathan: Reforming Governance in Bangladesh". Washington, DC: World Bank.

World Bank. 2003a. "Poverty Reduction Strategy Papers: Detailed Analysis of Progress in Implementation." Poverty Reduction and Economic Management Network. Washington, DC: World Bank.

World Bank. 2003b. *Strategic Framework for Assistance to Africa: IDA and the Emerging Partnership Model.* Washington, DC: World Bank.

World Bank. 2003c. "Country Financial Accountability Assessment Guidelines to Staff." Financial Management Sector Board. May 27. Washington, DC: World Bank.

World Bank. 2003d. "Tanzania Public Expenditure Review". Report No. 26807. Washington, DC: World Bank.

World Bank. 2004a. *Programmatic Adjustment Lending Retrospective.* Operations Policy and Country Services. (January). Washington, DC: World Bank.

World Bank. 2004b. "Good Practice Note on the Design of Development Policy Lending." Operations Policy and Country Services. Washington, DC: World Bank.

World Bank. 2004c. "Ethiopia PRSC 2 Program Document." 29772-ET (November). Washington, DC: World Bank.

World Bank. 2004d. "Poverty Reduction Strategy Papers: Progress in Implementation." Poverty Reduction and Economic Management Network. Washington, DC: World Bank.

World Bank. 2004e. "From Adjustment Lending to Development Policy Lending: Update of World Bank Policy." Operations Policy and Country Services. Washington, DC: World Bank.

World Bank. 2004f. "Financial Management Issues in Development Policy Lending." Good Practice Notes for Development Policy Lending No. 3 (October). Operations Policy and Country Services. Washington, DC: World Bank.

World Bank. 2004g. Operations Policy No. 8.60, "Development Policy Lending." Washington, DC: World Bank.

World Bank. 2004h. "Evaluating Financial Management Risk in Country Financial Management Accountability Assessments." Financial Management Anchor. Washington, DC: World Bank.

World Bank. 2004i. "Designing Development Policy Operations". Good Practice Notes for Development Policy Lending No. 1 (October). Operations Policy and Country Services. Washington, DC: World Bank.

World Bank. 2004j. "The Republic of Uganda: Country Integrated Fiduciary Assessment (In Five Volumes)." Volume I. Report No. 29376-UG, June. Washington, DC: World Bank.

World Bank. 2005a. *Review of World Bank Conditionality: The Theory and Practice of Conditionality: A Literature Review.* Development Economics Vice Presidency. Washington, DC: World Bank.

World Bank. 2005b. *Review of World Bank Conditionality: Recent Trends and Practices*, Operations Policy and Country Services. Washington, DC: World Bank.

World Bank. 2005c. *Review of World Bank Conditionality: Modalities of Conditionality*. Operations Policy and Country Services. Washington, DC: World Bank.

World Bank. 2005d. *Review of World Bank Conditionality: Legal Aspects of Conditionality in Policy-based Lending*. Legal Department. Washington, DC: World Bank.

World Bank. 2005e. "Poverty Reduction Support Credits: A Stocktaking." Operations Policy and Country Services. Washington, DC: World Bank.

World Bank. 2005f. *Economic Growth in the 1990s: Learning from a Decade of Reform*. Washington, DC: World Bank.

World Bank. 2005g. *Review of World Bank Conditionality: Content of Conditionality in World Bank Policy-based Operations* (SecM2005-0390/5). Poverty Reduction and Economic Management Network. Washington, DC: World Bank.

World Bank. 2005h. *Review of World Bank Conditionality: 2005 Conditionality Survey.* Washington, DC: World Bank.

World Bank. 2005i. "An Operational Approach to Assessing Country Ownership of Poverty Reduction Strategies." Operations Policy and Country Services. Washington, DC: World Bank.

World Bank. 2005j. *Review of World Bank Conditionality: Summary of External Consultations*, Operations Policy and Country Services. Washington, DC: World Bank.

World Bank. 2005k. "Good Practice Note on Development Policy Lending: Budget Support Groups and Joint Financing Arrangements." Operations Policy and Country Services. Washington, DC: World Bank.

World Bank. 2005l. "Good Practice Note on Development Policy Operations and Program Conditionality in Fragile States." Operations Policy and Country Services. Washington, DC: World Bank.

World Bank. 2005m. "Good Practice Note on Development Policy Lending: Subnational Lending." Operations Policy and Country Services. Washington, DC: World Bank.

World Bank. 2005n. "Results Focus in Country Assistance Strategies: A Stocktaking of Results-based CASs." Operations Policy and Country Services. Washington, DC: World Bank.

World Bank. 2005o. *Review of World Bank Conditionality – Issues Note.* (January.) Washington, DC: World Bank.

World Bank. 2005p. *Review of World Bank Conditionality: Summary Findings.* http://web.worldbank.org

World Bank. 2005q. "Enabling Capacity to Achieve Results – 2005 CDF Progress Report." Operations Policy and Country Services. Washington, DC: World Bank.

World Bank. 2005r. *A Review of Rural Development Aspects of PRSPs and PRSCs, 2000-04.* Agriculture and Rural Development Department. Washington, DC: World Bank.

World Bank. 2005s. "Good Practice Note on Budget Support Groups and Joint Financing Arrangements." Operations Policy and Country Services. Washington, DC: World Bank.

World Bank. 2005t. "Public Financial Management Performance Measurement Framework." June. Public Expenditure and Financial Accountability Program Secretariat. Washington, DC: World Bank.

World Bank. 2005u. *Aid Financing and Aid Effectiveness*, paper prepared for the Development Committee, September 13, 2005, Report No. DC2005-0020. Washington, DC: World Bank.

World Bank. Forthcoming. *Using Budget Support and PRSCs to Scale up Rural Water Supply, Sanitation and Hygiene.* Energy and Water Department. Washington, DC: World Bank.

World Bank and International Monetary Fund (IMF). 2001. *Strengthening IMF-World Bank Collaboration on Country Programs and Conditionality.* Washington, DC: World Bank and IMF.

World Bank and International Monetary Fund (IMF). 2003. *Poverty Reduction Strategy Papers – Progress in Implementation.* Washington, DC: World Bank and IMF.

World Bank and International Monetary Fund (IMF). 2004. *Poverty Reduction Strategy Papers – Progress in Implementation.* Washington, DC: World Bank and IMF.

World Bank and International Monetary Fund (IMF). 2005. *2005 Review of the Poverty Reduction Strategy Approach: Balancing Accountabilities and Scaling Up Results.* Washington, DC: World Bank and IMF.

Zongo, Tertius, Siaka Coulibaly, Gilles Hervio, Javier Nino Perez, and Stefan Emblad. 2000. "Conditionality Reform: The Burkina Faso Pilot Case." Brussels: Strategic Partnership with Africa, Task Team on Contractual Relations and Selectivity.

Index